SOUNDING FORTH
the
TRUMPET

Also by Peter Marshall and David Manuel

The Light and the Glory
The Light and the Glory for Children (with Anna Fishel)
From Sea to Shining Sea
From Sea to Shining Sea for Children (with Anna Fishel)
Sounding Forth the Trumpet for Children (with Anna Fishel)

GOD'S PLAN *for* AMERICA

SOUNDING FORTH

TRUMPET

1837 – 1860

PETER MARSHALL *and*
DAVID MANUEL

Revell

a division of Baker Publishing Group
Grand Rapids, Michigan

Published by Revell
a division of Baker Publishing Group
P.O. Box 6287, Grand Rapids, MI 49516-6287
www.revellbooks.com

Paperback edition published 1999

Fourth printing 2009
ISBN 978-0-8007-3393-3

Printed in the United States of America

ISBN 978-0-8007-3393-3 (pbk)
ISBN 978-0-8007-1944-9 (cloth)

The Library of Congress has cataloged the hardcover edition as follows:
Marshall, Peter, 1940–
    Sounding forth the trumpet / Peter Marshall, David Manuel.
      p. cm.
    Includes bibliographical references and index.
   ISBN 978-0-8007-1746-9 (cloth)
    1. United States—History—1815–1861. 2. United States—Church history—19th century.
  3. History (Theology) 4. Providence and government of God. I. Manuel, David. II. Title.
  E338.M33 1998
    973.6—dc21   97-48640

To
all the men and women
of faith,
laboring tirelessly
and often thanklessly
to be salt
where its savor is needed
and light
where darkness encroaches,
as they bring America
back to God.

Contents

CONTENTS

ACKNOWLEDGMENTS

A project of this magnitude is always the work of many. The authors would particularly like to thank editorial director Bill Petersen, whose patience and understanding are deeply appreciated; consulting editor Lonnie Hull DuPont, who kept them on message and finely tuned; and copy editor Trish Konieczny, who did her best to sort out revisions and keep the final product error free. Above all, they would like to thank Dr. William P. Showalter, a dear friend and gifted counselor, without whose wise and timely help this project would never have reached completion.

With Liberty and Justice
for All

All men are created equal—we say it. We believe it. As the Declaration of Independence declares, it is a truth so obvious that it is self-evident.

It was not always so. There was a time when to many Americans it seemed just as obvious that all men were *not* created equal, much less endowed with certain inalienable rights such as life, liberty, and the pursuit of happiness. This book is about the struggle to establish in people's hearts that truth, which was so foundational to our Republic.

Belief in the equality of all men was there from the beginning, in the hearts of the Pilgrims. And the men who put their signatures to the Declaration knew that God intended such a society for America. They sensed that He had a plan for this country, just as He has a plan for each individual's life, and that He had shown them how to construct a free, representative government that would enable them to preserve and maintain a moral society with liberty and justice for all.

But implementing His plan would require our adhering to Christ's two Great Commandments: To love God with all our heart and mind and soul and being, and to love our neighbors as ourselves. If we would do that, He would bless our endeavors. That was His covenant with us, as the Pilgrims and Puritans understood it.

It was also their understanding that He intended to use America as an

11

example to the rest of the world, "a city set on a hill" was the way John Winthrop had put it—living proof that it *was* possible to live in covenant with Him. But before that part of His plan could become reality, something had to change. Equality among men had to be more than words on paper. It had to become a living reality. This is the story of how that came to pass.

A Northerner traveling in the South soon discovers that the Civil War is called by other names there—the War between the States, or occasionally, the War of Northern Aggression. Until the twentieth century, a Southerner traveling in the North would hear the conflict referred to as the Great Rebellion.

In many places where the Civil War is recalled, it is as if it had been fought half a century ago, not over a century and a half ago. And more than a few seem ready to fight it all over again. The wounds have not healed as they should have, in part because Americans have never come to final agreement on what the war was fought over.

Libraries of books have been written about the Civil War era, yet hardly any have examined its causes from a spiritual perspective. This book will attempt to do that. The war was not fought over economics, though some have claimed that it was. It was not fought just to hold the Union together, though from the North's point of view, that was certainly how it began. Nor was it fought to preserve a way of life, though that was why the South went to war.

It was fought over slavery, the "peculiar institution" that enabled the plantation way of life. As Abraham Lincoln expressed with such luminous clarity in his Second Inaugural Address, it was a national, not a Southern, burden. In the eyes of God, the North was *equally* responsible for the perpetuation of slavery, and for that reason a blood atonement of equal measure would be required.

If this spiritual truth can be accepted, then the healing, so long in process, can be completed.

One thing more: It has been said that if we don't learn from our history, we will be condemned to repeat it. In spirit America in 2009 is so like America in 1858 that the overtones are chilling. To cite just one example, the Supreme Court in that time ruled that a Negro slave was chattel property, no different than a man's horse or his cow, and therefore had no rights. In 1973 the Supreme Court ruled that an unborn child is not fully human and therefore has no rights. But abortion is no more a part of God's plan for America than slavery was, and those who favor it today are as deliberately blind to evil as those who favored slavery were in 1858.

In that year God sent a tremendous revival across our land. Had enough hearts been touched by it, the Civil War could have been avoided. As it was, instead of delivering America from her horrendous ordeal, it prepared her to endure and survive it.

Today, if we turn back to God and seek His face and turn from our wicked ways, we will experience a similar revival. Hopefully it will reverse our downward slide into a new Dark Age. Even if it does not, it will prepare us for what we must go through.

Peter Marshall
David Manuel

1

THE OPENING GUN

O rder! Order!" shouted the Speaker of the House, pounding his gavel on its block as if he were driving a tenpenny nail. "I will have order in this assembly!" But his hammer blows went unheeded in the raging maelstrom.

At its center stood the object of all the tumult and the shouting, a look of benign astonishment on his face—which only served to incite his attackers further. To them there was nothing the least bit innocent about the gentleman from Massachusetts; he was an *agent provocateur* if ever there was one! And every man from the South who considered himself a gentleman ought to be on his feet, denouncing him!

John Quincy Adams, former President of the United States and now Congressman from the district of Plymouth, stood silent before his accusers. He was 69 and bald; the bushy sideburns known as "muttonchops" were a stark white. In contrast to the fine attire of his colleagues, his waistcoat was frayed, and his cream-colored breeches were years out of fashion. The hand that held the offending petition trembled slightly; he did not, however, need spectacles to read it. Neither thin nor tall, he nonetheless possessed a dignity and authority that few in the House equaled and none surpassed.

February 6, 1837, like other alternate Mondays, was traditionally given over to the reading of petitions—documents of appeal whose signatories asked (in many cases, prayed) that Congress give formal consideration to the concerns expressed therein. Dating back to the Magna Carta, the right of petition reflected Christ's encouragement to His followers to approach their Father in heaven, Who was ever ready to hear the pleas of the helpless and needy. Should the Representatives of the people of the United States do less? As each petition was read, members listened politely if not attentively; for all they knew, they might be on their feet two weeks hence, reading a petition from a group of their own constituents. Such petitions occasionally inspired discussion; more often, they elicited a nod or a murmur of concurrence, as they were passed on to the appropriate committees.

At least, that was the way it *used* to be on alternate Mondays, as the House of Representatives began its business. Unlike the Senate, whose members were in those days appointed by the State legislatures and held to represent their entire states, Congressmen were elected by, and therefore directly accountable to, the people in their home districts. Of all the branches of the American government, here was representative democracy in its purest form. And one way the people of a district made their concerns known to their Congressman was by sending him a petition. "We, the undersigned citizens of Barnstable County, do humbly pray that the good members of Congress consider. . . ."

As modern historian William Lee Miller points out in his masterful work *Arguing About Slavery*,[1] the right of petition—along with freedom of speech, freedom of the press, and freedom of assembly—was one of the civil liberties that *defined* the young Republic. The Founding Fathers felt these liberties were so vital that they specifically guaranteed them in the First Amendment to the Constitution.

For years random petitions had come routinely into the Senate and the House, where they were duly read and entered into the record, then referred to committee. Access to one's Congressman was a sacred right, and as such was accorded at least a modicum of respect. But once a petition went to committee, more often than not it would disappear into the ether. Until the 1830s, there had been only one concerted petition drive, part of an effort by reform-minded evangelicals to stop mail delivery on the Sabbath. In that instance, the petitions had been sent to a select committee, which answered them all with a single, cogent, all-purpose response.

But the present situation could not be dealt with so easily. People had begun sending in petitions prayerfully requesting that slavery—or at the very least, the buying and selling of slaves—be abolished within the confines of the nation's capital.

The District of Columbia had not been in existence when the Con-

16

stitution was framed. Created in 1800, it was a Federal city, over which Congress was given overall responsibility. As it had been formed from land ceded by Maryland and Virginia, both slave states, slavery continued within its confines.

From its inception, more than a few Americans had been uncomfortable with slaves being sold on the auction block within sight of the gleaming white marble of the Capitol Building, over which flew the Stars and Stripes—increasingly regarded as the symbol of freedom and liberty by oppressed peoples the world over. Periodically Quakers and other groups had sent petitions respectfully requesting that this anomaly be addressed and redressed. Their petitions had been noted and passed along without comment; no members from the North or South wanted to reopen that still-fresh wound.

During the drafting of the Constitution in 1787, slavery had been the main bone of contention in the nascent United States of America (and had remained so ever since). At that time there had been strong sentiment to abolish it then and there. But the delegates from South Carolina and Georgia (*sovereign* States who did not *have* to agree to anything) pointed out that slavery had been an established institution for 150 years, and threatened to walk out of the convention if any attempt to abolish it were made. A few sanguine pragmatists said, "Let them go; they'll be back soon enough, begging for admission," while farsighted realists were concerned that Great Britain might regard their departure as an opportunity to gain a toehold on the eastern seaboard. But the great majority were confident that, given time, slavery would die out here, as it was dying everywhere else in the civilized Christian world.

In the end, a painful compromise was reached. The only thing that would be abolished was foreign trade in slaves—and that would not go into effect for another 20 years. In the states where slavery already existed, it could not be touched by Congress or any other body. And so the malignant tumor of slavery, too close to the heart of the patient to risk removing, was allowed to remain. And grow.

By the middle of the 18th century there were slaves in all 13 colonies— even in the North, where they made up 14 percent of the population in New York and 10 percent in Rhode Island. But Vermont abolished slavery in its constitution when it entered the Union in 1777, and Massachusetts followed suit in 1781.

In one of its first acts, the Northwest Ordinance of 1787, Congress had abolished slavery north of the Ohio River. And by 1804, the ideals of the Revolution had eradicated slavery in the last Northern State, New Jersey. But with the application of Missouri for admission to statehood in 1820, the issue had erupted again. So great was the storm of controversy over whether she would come in as a slave or free state, that Southern members of the House and Senate had actually expressed the possibility of their states leaving the Union.

That upheaval, revealing how wide the potential rift over slavery could be, had shaken everyone. Thomas Jefferson, chief architect of the Declaration of Independence, was stunned at the depth of the passions unleashed. In a letter to his friend, antislavery crusader John Holmes, he likened it to "a fire-bell in the night which awakened me and filled me with terror. I considered it at once the [death] knell of the Union."

That crisis had a more-or-less happy ending, thanks to the brinksmanship of Henry Clay, known thereafter as the Great Compromiser. His landmark Compromise of 1820 stated that henceforth any state admitted below latitude 36° 30′ (the parallel delineating Missouri's southern border) would be a slave state, and any state coming in above it would be free. Southerners who had been "saber-rattling" now returned their rhetorical blades to their scabbards, and everything calmed down. "It is hushed, indeed, for the moment," concluded Jefferson to Holmes, "but this is a reprieve only. . . . As it is, we have a wolf by the ears, and we can neither hold him, nor safely let him go."[2]

The slavery issue would remain so volatile, in fact, that by tacit gentlemen's agreement it was not mentioned on the floor of either chamber.

Until now.

But now, at the agitation of the abolitionists—antislavery activists who were calling for an immediate end to slavery everywhere—the rate of the petitions to abolish slavery in the District of Columbia was growing. Previously the abolitionists had concentrated on sending vast quantities of antislavery tracts, newspapers, and pamphlets into the South, presumably for distribution to all mail recipients. When the South had violently objected to this use of the Federal mails, President Andrew Jackson had introduced a bill prohibiting the circulation of such materials. The bill had been defeated because the Federal mail was also considered a sacred right, but a blind eye had been turned to postmasters, Northern as well as Southern, who refused to distribute them.

Now the abolitionists, as well as many of the more moderate leaders of the antislavery movement, were calling for a new petition drive to raise the nation's awareness on the whole issue of slavery—which the vast majority of Americans simply preferred to leave alone. Petitions were directed to William Slade of Vermont, the Congressman most sympathetic to the abolitionist cause. Others were receiving them as well, and a few came to the desk of John Quincy Adams. Gradually the trickle became a steady stream. "We, the undersigned ladies of the Congregational Church of . . ."

Women's signatures appeared as often as men's on these documents, and sometimes more often. Though they would not receive the vote for another 84 years, they were the wives and mothers and sweethearts of voters. Few things could be more politically unwise than to dismiss their appeals out of hand.

But in the mind of Senator John C. Calhoun of South Carolina, patriarchal leader of the slaveholders' cause, the question of slavery in the District of Columbia could not even be opened to debate. To do so would be to admit the possibility that Congress *might* have jurisdiction over slavery there. And once *that* was admitted, who knew where it might stop? What if Congress got it in its head to amend the Constitution? No, it was best to bar the meddling at its farthest outpost.

To Calhoun, therefore, it was not enough merely to table such petitions, as was being done in the Senate. Regardless of how meekly the request might be phrased, each petition was, in effect, a calculated insult to the honor of "eleven sovereign States," as he was fond of putting it. As such, it should receive the same treatment as any deliberate affront. If a man came up to you on the street, Calhoun declared, and insulted your honor, the appropriate response was to "knock the scoundrel down."[3] These petitions, inspired by "ignorant fanatics," should receive the legislative equivalent: They should be summarily rejected without even being acknowledged, much less entered into the record.

In the new 24th Congress, under the gavel of James K. Polk of Tennessee, there were any number of gentlemen prepared to press Calhoun's point. On December 18, 1835, Francis Thomas of Maryland likened the "incendiary" pamphleteering of the abolitionists to "madness, worse than madness. . . . These fanatical crusaders . . . pour their poison into the national chalice from which the whole people of the United States have so long quaffed the sweet waters of concord and union."[4]

For four days the Southerners held the floor, taking turns condemning the parade of petitions in favor of abolishing slavery in the capital. John Quincy Adams was growing increasingly restive. In a letter to his son Charles he complained that the debate thus far had been "all on one side. The voice of freedom has not yet been heard, and I am constantly urged to speak her name. She will be trampled underfoot if I do not—and I shall be trampled underfoot if I do."[5]

Finally on December 21, after young Henry Wise of Virginia had denounced "those misguided meddlers," demanding "that the House not receive any further memorials on this subject," and Patton of Virginia had called for "a distinct vote that the House is opposed to such interference," Adams could remain silent no longer.

"If you come to the resolution that this House will not receive any more petitions, sir, you *will* have discussion, a discussion upon the merits of slavery. . . . If discussion is thrust upon us, I might make a speech as incendiary as any pamphlet upon which such torrents of denunciation have been poured!"[6]

Yet there was no question that the gentlemen of the South were pushing the House toward just such a resolution. And becoming more aggressive with each passing day. As outright rejection of the petitions was apparently too extreme for the majority of Congressmen, South Carolina's Henry Laurens Pinckney, publisher of the Charleston *Mercury*, suggested a marginally more palatable proposal: All petitions on slavery would be referred to a select committee, which would be instructed to report that Congress possessed no authority to interfere with slavery in the States and ought not to interfere with it in the District of Columbia. His resolution carried, 174 to 48, and went to committee for refining.

While it was there, debate over it continued. On February 1, 1836, Congressman James Henry Hammond, also of South Carolina, rose to justify it. Clearly tired of the North's attitude of moral superiority, as were all his Southern colleagues, he confronted the whole issue head-on: "Slavery is said to be an evil, that it impoverishes the people and destroys their morals. . . . But it is no evil. On the contrary, I believe it to be the greatest of all the great blessings which a kind Providence has bestowed upon our glorious region."

The time had come to go on the offensive. Hammond stated further: "I do firmly believe that domestic slavery, regulated as ours is, produces the highest toned, the purest, best organization of society that has ever existed on the face of the earth."

As for abolitionists, he gave them a specific warning: Should fate ever deliver one of them into the South's hands, he would suffer a felon's death. "The indignant feelings of an outraged people, to whose hearth-stones he is seeking to carry death and desolation, pronounce his doom; and if we failed to accord it to him, we would be unworthy of the forms we wear, unworthy of the beings whom it is our duty to protect, and we would merit and expect the indignation of an offended heaven."[7]

On May 18, the Pinckney committee was finally ready with its report. There would be three resolutions, of which the first two—that Congress had no power to abolish slavery in any of the States and ought not to interfere with it in the District of Columbia—were of no great concern to Adams. The third, however, was:

> Whereas it is extremely important and desirable that the agitation of this subject should be finally arrested for the purpose of restoring tranquillity to the public mind . . . all petitions, memorials, resolutions, propositions, or papers relating in any way, or to any extent whatsoever, to the subject of slavery, shall, without being either printed or referred, be laid on the table, and no further action whatever shall be had thereon.[8]

In other words, the petitions would be treated as if they had never existed.

Adams leaped to his feet. "Mr. Speaker," he cried, "Mr. Speaker!" But he was shouted down by an organized opposition who had anticipated his response.

Polk deliberately overlooked him and recognized Owens of Georgia, who promptly moved the question.

"Mr. Speaker!" cried Adams, "Am I gagged or not?"

"The motion is not debatable," Polk reminded him, and the first resolution was passed, 182 to 9.

There was an interim for regular business before the second and third resolutions would be voted on, during which John Quincy Adams instructed his colleagues on the one situation in which Congress *would* be empowered to interfere with slavery within a state. And they listened, however grudgingly, for no man alive possessed JQA's* mastery of Constitutional Law.

"Suppose," he postulated, "a civil war. Suppose Congress were called to raise armies, to supply money from the whole Union, to suppress an insurrection, . . . can it for an instant be pretended that Congress, in such a contingency, would have no authority to interfere with the institution in any way?"

He was speaking hypothetically, of course, but he was also showing those who had once rattled the sabers of disunion something that none of them had considered. "From the instant that your slaveholding States become the theater of war—civil, servile, or foreign—from that instant the war powers of Congress extend to interference with the institution of slavery in every way by which it can be interfered with!"[9]

This unprecedented interpretation of the war powers granted by the Constitution caught the slaveholding Representatives by surprise. They had no answer for him. It caught the nation by surprise as well. The *National Intelligencer*, which had printed the speech in full, received so many requests for copies that they brought it out in pamphlet form. Nearly every newspaper in the country carried it, including the one in Springfield, Illinois, where it was studied by a young State legislator who would himself be in Congress in less than a dozen years—Abraham Lincoln.† From that moment on, the press paid close attention to whatever the Congressman from Plymouth had to say, no matter how wearying or obstructionist. But JQA would keep his vow to remain silent on slavery as long as possible. As he viewed it, the tares had been allowed to grow up with the wheat, and both would feel the sickle's blade before the former would be thrown into the fire.

When Pinckney's second resolution came up for a vote, Adams abstained, and it passed without comment. But when the roll call for the third came to Adams, he was anything but silent. At the top of his lungs

---

* To distinguish him from his father, John Adams, and as a sign of affection, John Quincy Adams will be occasionally referred to by his initials JQA, like FDR and JFK.

† Six years later, JQA would go even further: "Under that state of things [i.e., war], so far from it being true that the States where slavery exists have the exclusive management of the subject, not only the President of the United States but the commander of the army has the power to order the universal emancipation of the slaves."

he shouted, "I hold the resolution [summarily tabling all abolition petitions] to be in direct violation of the Constitution of the United States, of the Rules of this House, and of the rights of my constituents!"[10]

The Speaker declared him out of order, and the resolution was passed, 117 to 68.

Adams was exhausted and discouraged; more than half the free States' Representatives had voted with the South. That night he confided to his diary: "This is a cause upon which I am entering at the last stage of my life, and with the certainty that I cannot advance it far. My career must close, leaving the cause at the threshold."[11]

But on Sunday, his spirits revived. His biographer, William Falkner, relates that "over the years he had acquired an almost mystical faith in divine guidance." His church in Washington was the Second Presbyterian, and there in the family pew, he found the specific encouragement he sought in the words of Isaac Watts in the first hymn they sang: "Just in the last distressing hour, the Lord displays delivering power."[12]

After that, his buoyancy returned; he would fight the good fight with all his might, and go down fighting if need be. The battle lines were drawn. The opening gun had been fired. From that point forward, he would challenge the Pinckney Gag Rule with every wile and gambit at his disposal.

John Quincy Adams may have alienated his Northern colleagues—but the abolitionists could not have been more pleased with him. He was one of the very few battling the gag rule, and while he was no abolitionist himself, his parliamentary skills were getting the antislavery cause more national press coverage than anything the abolitionists had ever done. Increasingly they directed their petitions to his desk.

Privately JQA abhorred slavery—the more so, since in the half century from the Constitution's framing, slavery showed no signs of being on the path to ultimate extinction, as his father and the other Founders had expected. In fact, so sure had they been of its imminent demise that they had kept the word "slave" out of their document, so as not to offend future generations.[13] As historian Don Fehrenbacher so aptly put it: "It is as though the Framers were half-consciously trying to frame two Constitutions, one for their own time and the other for the ages, with slavery viewed bifocally—that is, plainly visible at their feet, but disappearing when they lifted their eyes."[14]

From his pulpit in the First Presbyterian Church in New York, N. S. S. Beman would observe: "They would not stain such a fair document with such a foul blot, because they believed and trusted that the whole system with all its adjuncts and appendages would soon be swept away. . . ."

There was just one problem: "They did not reflect that sin never dies a natural death. It may be killed, but it never dies of itself. Had they considered the nature of the evil, when it should be made strong by the love of money and the love of power . . . they would have carried out their own avowed and cherished sentiment by inserting a provision for the final extinction of slavery."[15]

But they had not, and of course no one could have foreseen the invention of the cotton gin, which nine years later would lock slavery in place economically. Short-staple cotton could now be mechanically ginned, which meant cotton growing became profitable across the whole South. The demand for slaves escalated.

With the legitimacy of slavery recognized by the Constitution, JQA considered the floor of the House no place to debate its merits. But the gag rule was another matter. And as his parliamentary skill was unequaled on this side of the Atlantic, on alternate Mondays he was often able to get the gist of his petitions into the Congressional record despite the gag—and into the *Globe* and the *National Intelligencer* and other newspapers that covered the doings of Congress.

The antislavery activists might be delighted with his efforts, but no one else was. His campaign was losing him friends in Congress and gaining him implacable foes; even the other Massachusetts men, members of his own party, were coolly distant.

As for the influential newspapers of the North, most were openly hostile: "Monday is playday for Mr. Adams in the House of Representatives," editorialized the New York *Times*, "and our readers may expect in every report of Monday's proceedings an account of time wasted and business deferred through the waywardness and obstinacy of this strange being. Petulant, irascible, and exhibiting almost childish obstinacy, he makes himself an object of pity and a laughing stock to the House. . . . He boasts that he places all his glory in his independence. If independence is synonymous with obstinacy, he is the most independent statesman living."[16]

On this first Monday in February 1837, Mr. Adams had already presented 28 petitions, each of which had been peremptorily tabled. Now, as he asked the Speaker for permission to present the 29th, the mood among his 242 colleagues from 24 States shifted from restive boredom to resentment and frustration. Members gazed at the ornate columns of the semicircular hall, or counted the folds of the heavy draperies hung between them, or mentally traced the elaborate, repeating-square pattern of the dome above their heads, and wearily hoped that the lamps of the great brass chandelier would not have to be lit for an evening session. Some dozed, others took care of personal correspondence, a few simply stared sullenly at Adams.

"Mr. Speaker," he had said, addressing the Chair but still peering at the paper in his hand, "this petition appears to be genuine—but whether it is or not, I feel it my duty to present it." He paused and looked up. "It is from nine ladies of Fredericksburg, Virginia, and like the others it prays for the abolition of the slave trade in—"

Slam! The man seated next to him brought the palm of his hand down on the surface of his desk with such force that it sounded like a gunshot. In the stunned silence, James Mercer Patton rose to his full height and glared down at Adams. A scion of the FFV (First Families of Virginia), Patton was every inch the aristocrat. As it happened, he himself was from Fredericksburg, and he was outraged that Adams might dare to impugn the character of any of his social circle. "Ladies, sir? Of Virginia?" he exclaimed. "I demand to know the names of these ladies!"

Adams ignored him while the majority quickly voted to table the petition. As he started forward to surrender the document, Patton suddenly made a lunge for it. But Adams was too quick for him; shifting it to his other hand, he placed it on the clerk's table at the foot of the Speaker's dais, where it became the property of Congress.

Returning to his desk, he now faced his fuming colleague: "I will *not* name them, because from the disposition prevailing in the country, I do not know what might happen to them!"[17]

Before Patton could respond to this further slur on his beloved Virginia, Adams turned to the Speaker. Mindless of the tension now crackling about him, he asked permission to submit his final petition of the morning. By coincidence (or careful design), it, too, was from Fredericksburg. Examining it more closely, he frowned and pursed his lips, muttering to himself.

The previous petition may have been genuine, but there was something decidedly questionable about this one. . . .

Looking up apologetically, he said that he really felt he should ask the Chair for a decision on this one which "purported to be from 22 persons declaring themselves to be slaves."

The hall exploded. The Speaker gaveled for order—and was totally ignored. In the midst of mounting chaos, Adams went forward to submit the petition to the Speaker. As he did so, Joab Lawler, a clergyman from Tuscaloosa, Alabama, jumped to his feet and shouted: "I object to it going to the Chair! And I want it noted in the *Journal* that I objected!"

Attempting to restore a semblance of order, the Speaker announced that since the circumstances were so extraordinary, he would take the sense of the House. First to speak was Charles Haynes, a country doctor from Georgia. Not waiting to be recognized, he jumped up and proclaimed that no gentleman worthy of that appellation would act in such a fashion in the company of other gentlemen! Many concurred; the consensus of the members from slaveholding constituencies was that, in so taunting the South by presenting a petition from persons who were clearly not citizens, Mr. Adams had finally committed the procedural error that would open him to retribution. Now at last he would receive the comeuppance he so richly deserved!

Exultantly, Dixon Hall Lewis of Alabama called on the members from the slaveholding states to "come forward and demand the punishment of the gentleman from Massachusetts!" And if the House refused, then let the Southern representatives depart for home at once!

His motion was seconded by Julius Alford of Georgia, who loudly avowed that the moment this petition was presented, "I shall move, as an act of justice to the South, that it be taken from the House and burned!"

"Along with the member who presented it!" cried another.[18]

Waddy Thompson of South Carolina summed up their feelings: A grand jury ought to indict Adams for inciting slaves to rebellion, and his advanced years be d——d! "There is a point at which forbearance ceases to be proper. . . . When the sanctuary [of age] is used to throw poisoned arrows, it ceases to be sacred!"[19]

Members from Alabama and Virginia, from Georgia and the Carolinas—and from New York—were on their feet, bellowing agreement. *"Expel him!"* came the cry from all sides. *"Expel him!"*[20]

The Speaker of the House was on his feet, too, doing his utmost to bring order out of chaos. But when he saw that his admonitions were falling on deaf ears, there was nothing to do but adjourn. Hopefully the respite and a good night's sleep would accomplish what his gavel could not.

As John Quincy Adams left the House of Representatives, his oldest and closest colleagues avoided his eyes. But as this solitary figure descended the broad marble steps that flowed from the Capitol Building like a white waterfall, an observer might have been surprised to note that he was wearing a smile.

2

THE LAST PURITAN

*L*ouisa Adams was surprised to see her husband home so early that afternoon, as he entered the front door of their modest house on 16th Street. At her inquiring glance, he informed her that the House had turned into a hornet's nest, and the Speaker had had no choice but to adjourn. Louisa knew better than to ask who had stirred up the nest. She just settled him into his favorite chair by the fire, tucked a shawl about him, and went to the kitchen to brew him a strong cup of tea.

Staring into the crackling flames, he recalled the events of an hour before—and the smile returned. JQA loved nothing so much as a good parliamentary fight, and now it appeared he was in the battle of his life.

He was also in his seventieth year, at a time when the average male lifespan was considerably shorter than threescore and ten. But if they thought old age had in any way diminished his fighting capacity, they were in for a surprise. Back in Massachusetts, Ralph Waldo Emerson, the Sage of Concord, had read the situation right: "Mr. Adams . . . is no literary old gentleman, but a bruiser, and loves the melee. When they talk about his age and venerableness and nearness to the grave, he knows better. . . . He is an old roué who cannot live on slops, but must have sulfuric acid in his tea."[1]

That Adams' battle was making him the most reviled man in Washington did not trouble him; he had never tempered his remarks to gain approval. When circumstances warranted it, he could be diplomatic, even gracious; on the international front, America had never fielded a more skilled negotiator. But on the floor of the House, when the rightness of his position was challenged, tact and diplomacy were not in his arsenal.

Long ago Adams had set aside any desire for popularity, heeding the counsel of one of the foremost woman thinkers of her age (when women were not expected to be thinkers)—his mother, Abigail Adams. At the outset of his public career, she had advised him not to align himself with any group or special interest, but to consider himself as belonging to the whole nation, as a "guardian of her laws and liberties."[2] He was certainly adhering to that principle, though it had cost him socially as well as politically. Invitations to receptions, balls, and dinners seldom arrived now. Most evenings found him at home with Louisa.

The positive influence of his father, John Adams, second President of the United States, on young John Quincy is well known; less well known is the fact that his mother played an equally important role in shaping his character. He was eight years old in the spring of 1775, when she vividly recounted to him the events of Lexington and Concord that had occurred on April 19. Two months later she had taken him to the top of Penn's Hill near their home in Quincy. From that height they had seen the burning of Charlestown and had heard the guns of the Battle of Bunker Hill. The afternoon had made such an impression on the young boy that 71 years later he would recall in a letter to a Quaker friend: "I saw with my own eyes those fires, and heard Britannia's thunders . . . and witnessed the tears of my mother and mingled them with my own."[3]

Abigail Adams was as fierce a Patriot as her husband John and his cousin Samuel. After John and the others at Philadelphia had signed the Declaration of Independence, her husband had made a copy by hand and brought it home. Abigail read the Declaration aloud to her son and kept it prominently on display in their drawing room.

From his mother he also received his first impression of American slavery, for she had been indignant that the long passage attacking slavery as a "cruel war against human nature" had been stricken from the Declaration, in spite of her husband's protest. Slavery, she had written her husband during the War for Independence, "always seemed a most iniquitous scheme to me—to fight ourselves for what we are daily robbing and plundering from those who have as good a right to freedom as we have."

Later in '76 she gave him her mind on the hypocrisy of slave owners. "I have sometimes been ready to think that the passion for liberty cannot be equally strong in the breasts of those who have accustomed to deprive their fellow creatures of theirs. Of this I am certain, that it is not founded upon that generous and Christian principle of doing to others as we would that others should do unto us."[4]

When it came to public service, Abigail taught John Quincy to regard it as a sacred trust. A public servant was just that: a servant of the people, called by God in the great tradition of William Bradford, John Winthrop, and Thomas Hooker. His father and the other founders of the Republic had followed the example of those illustrious Puritans, and so would he.

And he did. Before becoming President, he was America's most skilled diplomat, concluding the Treaty of Ghent, which ended the War of 1812, and the Transcontinental Treaty, which established America's northern border. As James Monroe's Secretary of State, he also crafted what became known as the Monroe Doctrine, letting the Old World know that America would not meddle in Europe's internal affairs, but neither would she tolerate any further geopolitical adventuring by Europe in the New World.

Whenever Duty called, JQA responded, and Duty was always calling. Indeed, as William Lee Miller has observed, if Duty didn't call, Adams would call *her* and reverse the charges. And now he was back in Washington serving once again—the last living link with the generation of men who had founded the Republic.

If Abigail had been as vehement as an abolitionist on the subject of slavery, so was her son. The public would be unaware of this, though, until the posthumous publication of his diary. For except when lashing back at his attackers, Adams was aloof and reserved, not given to "speechifying" and ill at ease in casual social situations. Only in the privacy of his diary would he let his passions flow.

As early as 1820, during the controversy over Missouri, he would write: "Slavery is the great and foul stain upon the North American Union, and it is a contemplation worthy of the most exalted soul whether its total abolition is or is not practicable. . . . A dissolution, at least temporary, of the Union as now constituted would certainly be necessary. . . . The Union might then be reorganized on the fundamental principle of emancipation. This objective is vast in its compass, awful in its prospects, sublime and beautiful in its issue."[5]

As the Missouri question had flared up, so had Southern feelings, and JQA observed that slaveholders fancy themselves more generous and noble-hearted than the plain freemen who labor for subsistence. They look down upon the simplicity of a Yankee's manners, because he had no habits of overbearing like theirs and cannot treat Negroes like dogs. It is among the evils of slavery that it taints the very sources of moral principle. It establishes false estimates of virtue and vice: for what can be more false and heartless than this doctrine which makes the first and holiest rights of humanity to depend upon the color of the skin?[6]

Louisa now appeared with a small tray containing a steaming cup of tea laced with cinnamon (not sulfur), and two of the sourdough biscuits he liked so much. With a smile she put the tray next to his chair and went back into the kitchen to see how their cook was coming with supper.

Adams gazed after her fondly. She was his best friend, and at the moment his only friend—at least, in this town. Louisa had not wanted to come back here. For her, their four years in the White House had been miserable, an unending "mortification and agony." When it was over she had summed up life in Washington as "a bull bait,"[7] referring to the cruel, low-life entertainment of provoking a powerful, chained animal into a frenzy.

Neither Louisa nor anyone else in his family had been in favor of his reentering that fray by running for Congress. His son Charles had thought it unseemly and demeaning for a former President to return to the political arena at all, let alone in such a diminished capacity. Adams himself was inclined to agree. Besides, after four frustrating years, abruptly ended by a crushing defeat at the hands of Andrew Jackson in 1828, he had been immensely relieved to be back home in the family mansion in Quincy. There, he had looked forward to living out his remaining years in quiet and productive solitude.

Louisa had left the poker within easy reach. He took it and stirred the fire to new life, staring into its flames and recalling their life in Quincy seven years before—before God had sovereignly moved and indicated that despite the stalemated Presidency, He had one more public assignment for him.

What John Quincy Adams considered an idyllic retirement would give a workaholic pause. For him a typical day in Quincy began, as always, two hours before dawn with prayer. Adams was comfortable in the presence of God. In the tradition of his Puritan forebears he held himself accountable daily before Him, recording in his journal those places where he was convicted of falling short of the mark. He has been called the Last Puritan, and he was indeed one of the last of that vanishing breed for whom obedience to God was the sole criterion for a life well lived.

After prayer Adams would continue his communion with his heavenly Father by reading three chapters in the New Testament. Though the family library contained eight thousand leather-bound volumes and was considered the finest private collection in America, the Bible was still the first book he reached for. In addition to the popular King James Version, he had read the Scriptures in the original Greek, in the Latin, in the French Catholic translation, and in Luther's German. Whatever the edition, it always seemed fresh to him as he waited for the Spirit of God to illuminate a passage or give him a new insight.

Next he would spend an hour in the classics (Cicero was a favorite), after which he would write in his diary, sometimes for more than an hour. Then came breakfast with Louisa while the sun streamed into their parlor. The remainder of the morning was spent at his major task: the compilation of his late father's papers. At noon he set aside the files of correspondence and his careful notes and joined Louisa for lunch. Then, after a nap, came his great delight: puttering about in the garden.

In the summer, when the afternoon grew too warm for pruning hook and trowel, he would go down to Quincy Bay for a swim. Inferring from his nagging cough and twinges of rheumatism that his health must have been fragile, historians have portrayed him as sickly. Nothing could have been farther from the truth. Lamenting that he could no longer swim a daily mile in the Potomac as he had done when he was President, JQA still managed to cover half a mile in 16 minutes.* When it grew too cold to swim, he would spend that time on a brisk walk.

Adams' remarkable vitality, coupled with his ability to sustain unbroken concentration, enabled him to accomplish more in a day than most men of any age could in three. At times, however, it played him cruel—leaving him like an old firehorse, yearning to hear the clanging tocsin that signaled action. And so, he may have been not altogether unreceptive when two gentlemen came to call on that September afternoon in 1830.

---

* Impressive time for a modern fitness swimmer half his age!

They turned in at a long, white picket fence that set off a sumptuous, tree-shaded, two-story residence with five gables on the front roof and a widow's walk above. Ivy climbed the four columns flanking the front door, and three chimneys connoted an abundance of hearths within. Finding their man out back of the house pruning his apple and peach trees, the visitors came straight to the point: In the coming election, the National Republicans were in danger of losing the Congressional district of Plymouth, which included the Adams' home. The only man who could secure that seat was John Quincy Adams. For the sake of the party—for the sake of the country—would he consider running again?

Adams was equally direct: "I have not the slightest desire to be elected to Congress, and I cannot consent to be a candidate for election."[8]

Most would consider such a response unequivocal and make polite small talk until they could gracefully leave. But as the sun filtered through the apple boughs above them, Adams' callers discerned that while he made it clear he would not *seek* public office, he seemed to be leaving the door open just a crack. Suppose his neighbors were to implore him to represent them—would he then refuse them?

To Adams such a request seemed exceedingly unlikely. He made friends painfully slowly (though his razor-sharp sarcasm made enemies instantly). He had been an unpopular President, opposing almost everything that his rival, Andrew Jackson, stood for, and that Hero of New Orleans was still ensconced in the White House. It seemed the worst kind of dotage foolishness to think his neighbors on the South Shore of Massachusetts Bay might want him looking after their interests in Washington.

And yet, did he dare believe that despite what he considered his failed Presidency, God might yet have a role for him to play on the national stage?

In this respect, John Quincy Adams was more a product of the 18th century than the 19th. Like his wardrobe, his ideals were old-fashioned—more like his father's and those of the other founders who had felt a profound obligation to serve the common good in whatever capacity God might open to them.

Nor did they regard it as an opportunity to better themselves; many, in fact, suffered reversals of fortune as a result. Public service was a duty to God and country, especially if their families had been blessed and had benefited from a superior education. As children they had been taught the meaning of the Lord's admonition, "For unto whomsoever much is given, of him shall much be required." If the Almighty *did* have one more service for John Quincy Adams to perform, then far be it from him to refuse. And inherent in the situation was the ideal test to see if it *was* God calling: If he allowed his name to be put forward and he was rejected, as he fully anticipated, then so be it. He would rest assured that he had done all God required of him in the service of his country, and with a grateful heart he would spend the remainder of his days compiling and gardening.

But he was *not* rejected. He won in a stunning landslide, gaining more than four times as many votes as his nearest opponent. Outwardly he gave little indication of how much this meant to him, but in the pages of his diary he rejoiced: "I am a member of the twenty-second Congress! . . . No election or appointment conferred on me ever gave me so much pleasure."[9]

Adams prodded the fire and called to Louisa in the kitchen that the leek soup she and the cook were preparing smelled so good, he was not sure he could wait until supper.

The National Republicans were delighted to have one of their own occupying Desk 203. But when they put the 62-year-old freshman Congressman from Plymouth in their column while projecting vote tallies, they were in for a surprise. Recalling his mother's advice, John Quincy Adams held himself accountable to no man or party, save the people back home who had sent him.

It had been an eventful six years. The most pressing national issue continued to be the one that by gentlemen's agreement no one mentioned. Veterans of both Houses would never forget the magma that had spewed forth during the eruption over Missouri; the very Union itself had seemed imperiled. The Compromise of 1820 may have quieted things on the surface, but it had done nothing to relieve the subterranean pressures building up along the fault line.

And now into the still-open fissure from which ominous wisps of smoke wafted, John Quincy Adams had lowered a huge charge of blasting powder and lit the fuse.

He had not sought this battle. But once it was joined, he would never back away from it. He did not care if his Northern colleagues missed his intent. Nor did he care that he had become the focal point of the animosity of the great majority of his countrymen. He *did* care, though, about whether or not his constituents back home understood why he had undertaken this cause. He wrote long, careful letters explaining why he felt that restoring the right of petition was so important that it merited disrupting the business of Congress. These letters were duly published in the Quincy *Patriot*. He dared to hope that his friends and neighbors would approve. They did, loyally returning him for a third term in the midst of his crusade against the gag rule.

Nor were they the only ones who approved. The abolitionists reprinted Adams' *Patriot* letters in every paper they controlled. They were only a handful, but other editors who cared for the freedoms of the Republic also saw to it that the Adams letters were widely reprinted. A small but significant body of support was gathering behind him.

But now it appeared likely that Adams would be censured, after which the only decent thing for a gentleman to do was to resign. And should Adams fail to do that, some were confident that they might be able to have him expelled from the House. When Congress reconvened the following morning, the visitors' gallery overlooking the floor of the House contained a number of reporters.

As Mr. Polk gaveled the session into being, it soon became apparent that a good night's sleep had done little to improve the temper of the assembly. Like hounds scenting the blood of a wounded boar, the slaveholding members were determined to bring down their prey. At last they would be rid of this nasty old tusker; at the very least, they would so humiliate him that his tusks would be pulled for good. And so, while some hammered together a resolution to accomplish this, others took the floor to condemn the old man. Typical was Claiborne of Mississippi, charging that Adams had committed "an outrage that has no parallel in parliamentary history!"[10]

A few Northern hands were raised to speak in his defense, but the slaveholding Speaker overlooked them. For two days the pride of the South held forth, with only Levi Lincoln, the former Governor of Massachusetts, and Caleb Cushing of Newburyport, Massachusetts, rising to Adams' defense.

The resolution, when they could finally agree on its wording, called for Adams to be censured for attempting to introduce into the House a petition from slaves for the abolition of slavery in the District of Columbia. By this act he had committed "an outrage upon the rights and feelings of a large portion of the people of the Union; a flagrant contempt upon the dignity of this House, and by extending to slaves the privilege belonging only to freemen, directly invited the slave population to insurrection."[11]

Curiously, James Patton, champion of the ladies of Fredericksburg, tried to caution his Southern colleagues that the wording of their resolution might be too extreme, that they might, in fact, be assuming too much about the content of the petition (which, after all, Adams had not been permitted to read aloud). But they were circling their prey, closing in for the kill, and paid no attention to Patton.

Adams did. He acknowledged that the "ladies" of Fredericksburg who had signed his previous petition might indeed be freed mulattos, as Patton subsequently attested, and that they might indeed be of dubious reputation, as he inferred. And then, in phrasing that demonstrated to younger journalists why their seniors referred to him as "Old Man Eloquent," John Quincy Adams defended the right of even these to appeal: "The sacred right of petition, of begging for mercy, does not depend on character any more than it does on condition. It is a right that cannot be denied to the humblest, to the most wretched."[12]

The chamber was silent. Up in the gallery, some reporters wrote as fast as they could; others were enthralled.

"Where is your law which says that the mean and low, and the degraded, shall be deprived of the right of petition? . . . Where in the land of the freemen was the right of petition ever placed on the exclusive basis of morality and virtue? Petition is supplication. It is entreaty." He paused. "It is prayer."

There was silence in the hall.

"And where is the degree of vice or immorality which shall deprive the citizen of the right to supplicate for a boon or to pray for mercy?"[13]

He paused again. This was the heart of his cause: If their Republic was to survive, the weak *must* have the freedom to appeal to the powerful. Petition, as he would later amplify, was "a supplication to a superior being; that which we offer up to our God." It was, in fact, the "first and humblest right given from God to every human being. . . . It is the cry of distress, asking for relief."[14]

36

When he finished, there was nothing more to be said. The Speaker adjourned the House for the day.

Adams stayed up that night, long after Louisa went to bed, peering into the flames of his hearth and reflecting on slavery and the future of his country. He recalled the time he had seen a black woman, frantic because she was about to be separated from her family at a slave auction and sold south, break away and run up to the attic of a Washington tavern. As Adams watched in horror, she threw herself out of a window in a suicide attempt. But she did not die; she merely crippled herself so badly that she was no longer of any use to the slave merchant, who left her behind.

Returning to Washington in his present capacity, JQA's private views on slavery crystallized. In the fall of his first year in Congress, at a dinner party, he had met the young French aristocrat with a passion for the new political system in the world's newest Republic, Alexis de Tocqueville. Though only 26, the latter was traveling in America, gathering material for what would soon become his four-volume, world-renowned study, *Democracy in America*. Seated with Adams, de Tocqueville had been delighted to discover that the former President was fluent in "the language of diplomats." They began conversing earnestly and intimately in French. Adams must have been unusually impressed with the perception and sagacity of his young dinner partner, for he unburdened himself to de Tocqueville on the matter of slavery as he had to no other.

"There are two facts which have a great influence on our character," summarized Adams, speaking of the American people: "in the North, the religious and political doctrines of the founders of New England; in the South, slavery."

Did he, then, consider slavery a great evil?

"Unquestionably! It's in slavery that are to be found all the [national] embarrassments of the present and fears of the future."

Were Southerners aware of this?

"Yes, at the bottom of their hearts . . . slavery has modified the whole state of society in the South. There, the whites form a class which has all the ideas, all the passions, all the prejudices of an aristocracy," he frowned. "But don't deceive yourself: nowhere is equality among the white greater than in the South. [In New England] we have a great equality before the law, but it ceases absolutely in the habits of life. . . . Every white man in the

South is a being equally privileged, whose destiny is to make the Negroes work without working himself."

How far the idea that manual labor was dishonorable had permeated the Southern mentality was brought home to him, Adams confided, when he and his wife invited a Southern colleague to dinner. Horrified at seeing a white cook and butler serving them, the guest had exclaimed to Louisa: "I find it a degradation of the human race to use whites for domestics! When one of them comes to change my plate, I am always tempted to offer him my place at table!"

If the white landed gentry did not work in the South, asked the young Frenchman, what *did* they do?

"They devote themselves to bodily exercise, to hunting, to racing; they are vigorously constituted, brave, full of honor"; indeed, smiled Adams ruefully, a *point d'honneur* was "more delicate there than anywhere else. Duels are frequent."

But when de Tocqueville asked how slavery might endanger the Union, Adams remained silent. "He did not answer," concluded the Frenchman, recalling their exchange in his masterwork, "but it was easy to see that on this point, he had no more confidence than I in the future."[15]

That first summer before taking his seat, JQA met one other man who made a memorable impression on him: the Quaker abolitionist and editor, Benjamin Lundy. Encouraged by the progress being made in Great Britain to abolish slavery in her colonies, the abolitionist movement in America was beginning to make its presence felt. Its spokesmen included evangelists like Charles Finney and Theodore Dwight Weld, but by far the loudest was in Boston: William Lloyd Garrison, the strident publisher of the *Liberator*.

As a Quaker, however, Benjamin Lundy preferred a low profile. The Society of Friends (the Quakers' formal name) had been the first to call slavery *sin* and condemn it as such. They had done so quietly, yet Lundy had seen how much could be accomplished by the art of "gentle persuasion." He had only to look to the life of the late John Woolman, whose humble example had done so much to prick the conscience of the New England slave trade.

Woolman's crowning achievement had been to carry the antislavery cause across the Atlantic. Trusting God to open all doors before him, he had gone in blind obedience. And then, through a chain of "coincidences" that only God could have arranged, he had presented his case to Parliament. The impact was incalculable. Another evangelical Christian, Member of Parliament William Wilberforce, made the abolition of slavery his life's work, and in 1833 he would finally succeed: Slavery was abolished in all the colonies of the British Empire.

It was Lundy who had conceived of the petition drive to abolish slavery in the District of Columbia, and while he was unable to gently persuade Adams to endorse their efforts, he did convince him to be the main recipient of the cause's petitions. That was how it had begun, and now in a few hours it might all be ended. In the morning the first business of the House would be to vote on the resolution calling for his censure.

Adams stared at the dying embers in the hearth. More than any public figure alive, he could see clearly the original vision that had inspired the Founding Fathers, nearly all of whom had been personal friends of his parents. He knew what God had intended America to become. And he could see exactly how far she had diverged from that divine course. God's plan for America was in peril, and he knew the reason why. He could also see ahead, farther and more clearly than any man living. But what he saw, he would divulge only to his diary: "If slavery be the destined sword in the hand of the destroying angel which is to sever the ties of this Union, the same sword will cut in sunder the bonds of slavery itself. A dissolution of the Union for the cause of slavery would be followed by a servile war in the slave-holding States, combined with a war between the two severed portions of the Union."

He did not shrink from this consequence. "It seems to me that its result might be the extirpation of slavery from this whole continent; and, calamitous and desolating as this course of events in its progress must be, so glorious would be its final issue, that, as God shall judge me, I dare not say it is not to be desired."[16]

He decided against stirring up the embers and putting the last log on the fire. Though he was not in the least sleepy, he knew that no matter how late he went to bed, his body would awaken him long before sunup.

And it did. One can imagine his thoughts as he lit the taper and washed and prepared for the day, quite possibly his last at Desk 203. Was it for this hour that God had brought him to Washington? To stand alone for his nation, as Esther had? As the eastern sky began to lighten he had to do battle with a foe more subtle than any he had faced on Capitol Hill. All the doubts he had held at bay with his torch of truth and the fire of the rightness of his cause were circling him now, their eyes gleaming in the darkness.

And then, as his torch sputtered, from behind him would come the silken whisper of the tempter: *You need only apologize. Ask their forgiveness, and they will gladly grant it, their sense of honor satisfied. The censure will be lightened to a reprimand, and you will retain your seat. You will retire with dignity at the time of your choosing. And no shame or disgrace will attach itself to your name or blot the Adams family escutcheon. . . .*

But John Quincy Adams was at heart a Puritan, and Puritans knew how to deal with the enemy. Even when they went through the dark night of the soul, as each man and woman inevitably must. And now this old Puritan, putting his hand in the hand of the Shepherd, followed Him into the valley with peace in his heart.

On the morning of the fourth day, the tension that greeted his arrival at the House was enough to turn his stomach. The Senate had suspended its business to attend; the gallery had never been so packed. They were even standing on the stairs, and below, against all the walls. From the looks on their faces, nearly all of them expected to see his downfall. Like witnesses at the hanging of an infamous criminal, they wanted to be able to tell their grandchildren that they had been there the day John Quincy Adams went down.

Adams took his seat. Undoubtedly the tempter was still whispering, *Apologize, apologize. . . . You can avoid the crucifixion with only a few words to the Procurator: "Mr. Speaker, upon sober reflection I find that I have indeed wrongly offended the sensibilities of my Southern colleagues. I would now like to ask their forgiveness. . . ."*

His eyes scanned his surroundings, perhaps hoping to find some island of support, somewhere. And then, up above, in the first row of the right balcony, the one nearest his desk, one can imagine he might have seen something else: the wraiths of his father—and Washington and Hamilton and Madison—waiting to see what he would do.

With a deep breath he drew himself to his full height. He was ready. And he had a surprise for his accusers. He had held back the ace of trumps, to play it now. For there *had* been something amiss in the petition that had precipitated this impending censure. He had suspected that it was a hoax to embarrass him—one to which Patton, if not the instigator, had at least been privy. Now, he would turn the hoax upon the hoaxers.

Before the House voted on the resolution to censure, the gentleman from Plymouth requested permission to address the Chair: "The gentlemen who have such a laudable zeal for the slaveholding part of the confederation charge, first, that I attempted to present a petition from slaves, and, second, that that petition was for their emancipation from slavery."

The hall quieted as he continued. "I did *not* attempt to present the petition. . . . I said I had a paper, which *purported* to be a petition from slaves. . . ."

There was perfect stillness. "If the House should choose to read the petition . . . they would find it . . . the reverse from that which the resolution states it to be. My crime has been for attempting to introduce the petition of slaves that slavery should *not* be abolished!"[17]

Outraged shouts and threats of Southerners (Patton alone not joining in) gradually gave way to the gaveling of the Speaker. Hastily the censure resolution was withdrawn, and a new set of resolves was drawn up, more moderate in tone, almost placating. But Adams would not agree to them, for they made it sound as if he were—apologizing. "I here say that I have not done one single thing that I would not do over again in like circumstances! Not one thing . . . that I have not done under the highest and most solemn sense of duty!"[18]

That having been said, there was nothing to do now but vote.

When the tally of the censure resolution was announced, it was defeated 105 to 21. John Quincy Adams had won a great victory, but he was under no illusion. The battle was still joined; the end was nowhere in sight, and the outcome far from certain. As if by confirmation, the House now voted overwhelmingly that slaves did not have the right to petition Congress.

Not surprisingly, the Southern press condemned him, and the Northern anti-abolitionist press called it yet another example of the Massachusetts Madman's typical mayhem. And from Pittsburgh, he received his first anonymous death threat. But from abolitionists all over, he received warm letters of congratulations for his courage, and more than a few promises of prayer on his behalf.

Meanwhile, others were laboring in this vineyard. If slavery was Satan's master plan to poison the noblest experiment in self-government ever conceived by the mind of man, God had the antidote. But it would take time and patience—and a great many unsung heroes who were prepared to work together and, in the words of the old hymn, trust and obey.

3

THE IMPOSSIBLE DILEMMA

The pale March sun streamed in through the window of the storefront printshop, limning the big wrought-iron wheel of the old hand-powered press. In front of the compositor's desk within easy reach were racks of lead type in tiny pigeonholes, enough to print a small monthly. The layout table near the desk was clear, ready for action. But every other horizontal surface in the room was either stacked with books or strewn with papers.

In 1830 the cutting edge in communications was the newspaper, and anyone with a press and something to say could get in the game. All you needed was enough subscribers to cover the cost of paper, ink, and postage. If you were lucky, there would be enough left over to live on, but you hadn't taken up publishing to make money. You had a point of view, and hopefully there would be people who wanted to hear what you had to say.

There were plenty of readers out there. From earliest Colonial days Americans had put a premium on education. The one-room schoolhouse accounted for the highest literacy rate per capita in the world. European visitors were continually amazed to find that not only could the average citizen read, but he or she was well informed about what was going on in the country and avidly interested in learning more.

The cozy printshop in Baltimore was the headquarters of a thin but significant antislavery sheet, the *Genius of Universal Emancipation*, published and edited by Benjamin Lundy. While its masthead proclaimed it a monthly, actual publication depended on the availability of funds. More often than he wished, Lundy had to rely on the generosity of the audiences at his talks.

His articles and editorials were read by far more people than his modest circulation reached, however, for in those days editors, hard-pressed to fill four, eight, or twelve pages with close-set copy, would use each other's best pieces. To this end, they freely exchanged complimentary copies (Lundy's went to more than a hundred other editors) with the understanding that an editor might reprint anything he cared to, as long as he gave proper credit. As a result, a particularly trenchant editorial, a well-reasoned essay, or a pivotal Senate speech might see print in hundreds of papers across the country and eventually be read by most of the populace.[1]

A number of Lundy's antislavery pieces attained that level. The meekness with which he wrote was unique, as much a part of the message as what he actually said. His Quaker humility impressed readers, softening their hearts to the point where they could hear and accept the truth he was conveying. To Lundy and the other members of the Society of Friends, slavery was more than an unfortunate social evil. It was sin against God. The act of one man holding another in bondage against his will and forcing him to do one's bidding was an affront to God. It had to be dealt with accordingly, but in Christian love. However desirable universal emancipation might be, the end must never be allowed to justify un-Christian means. Lundy and the other moderates would ask themselves: Is this what Jesus would have done?

The spirit of his paper reflected the spirit of the antislavery movement at that time, which was intent on reaching and convicting the hearts of praying slaveholders. If a man was at all concerned about his relationship with God, then it should be possible to touch his heart with a soft-spoken, compelling appeal for him to examine how he truly felt about slavery. In his quiet way, Lundy, then 41, was having a far-reaching effect on many people, not the least of whom, as we have seen, was John Quincy Adams.

The trouble was that he was now dealing with second- and third-generation slaveholders who were far less receptive to the conviction of the Holy Spirit in this matter than their ancestors had been. While they might disapprove of slavery, they regarded it as a dilemma they had inherited to which they could see no viable alternative. For if they did manumit their slaves, no one was going to compensate them for their financial loss.

Whenever the subject was raised, the North's attitude seemed to be that since the Southerners had created this mess, they would have to find their own way out of it. But the South had nowhere near the funds required. And neither did the Federal Government, as James Henry Hammond of South Carolina would soon make abundantly clear from the floor of the House: Suppose the Government *did* want to enact a policy of compensation. If one put a value on each slave of $400 (which was conservative; young, strong slaves were bringing upward of $1,000), then the slave population was worth $900 *million*, and their value was increasing at an annual rate of $24 million. In 1830 the entire revenue of the Federal Government amounted to less than $25 million. Even at 10 cents on the dollar, compensation was out of the question. By sheer economics, emancipation was impossible, and it was ridiculous to even consider it. Those who were not comfortable with slavery, concluded Hammond, would be advised to get used to it; it was here to stay.[2]

In the North, there were other factors fueling anti-abolitionist sentiment. Abolished only two years before, the foreign slave trade had been run by Northern entrepreneurs, shipbuilders, and sea captains. So lucrative was the trade, and so insatiable the desire for more slaves for the new plantations opening in the deep South, that a number of sea captains were willing to risk running slaves as contraband. Constructed in Northern shipyards, the slavers were hideous ships with cargo decks no more than 14 inches apart. The slaves would have to lie flat for the duration of the voyage, crammed in and shackled, often to die of sickness or go mad. Schools of sharks followed these dark ships through the sea, for the dead were thrown overboard daily, and if a slaver was in danger of being caught, all the evidence would be jettisoned over the side.*

The burgeoning cotton crop was being bought and sold to English and American mills by brokers based in New York; the Northern textile industry was, in fact, wholly dependent on Southern cotton. Northern brokers were also handling the other commodities produced by the slave economy, products such as rice, hemp, indigo, and tobacco. And into the slave economy of the South, Northern manufacturers and merchants were selling everything from cotton gins and hand tools to cheap clothing and shoes. The plantation owners might be Southern, but it was Northern businessmen making the slave system economically feasible—and getting rich in the process.

* For a full account of the beginning, spread, and horror of slavery in America, see the authors' second volume, *From Sea to Shining Sea*.

44

Then there was the question of what to do with the slaves, if they were ever emancipated. The antislavery movement took heart from the example of the British, who abolished slavery throughout their empire in 1833. But their slaves were in the West Indies, not the British Isles. It was quite another question to talk of manumitting one-sixth of America's total population *within* America.

What *was* to become of freed slaves? They could not simply be cast adrift with no education, no employment, no tangible means of support, and no one to care for them. That was hardly what God would have wanted.

Whatever *was* done for them, it would have to be done *gradually*, with the full cooperation of the South, since that was where they would be released. But arrangements had to be made. They could not be left to wander the Southern countryside looking for work. In the midst of a slave economy, who would hire them? Would they, desperate to feed their hungry children, resort to stealing? And suppose some of the young freed blacks were embittered and looking for revenge—would they incite other blacks still in captivity to rise up against their masters? A mass slave insurrection, similar to the one that ripped apart the French colony of Saint Domingue (Haiti) less than 40 years before, was the deepest unspoken fear of every slaveholder.

Even if the freed blacks posed no threat of violence, who was to protect them from the violence that might be done to *them*? Unscrupulous landlords and merchants preyed upon trusting freed blacks, tricking them into debt and then holding them in *de facto* slavery. And there were bands of ruthless whites who roamed the cities and byways, making a living by kidnapping freed blacks and selling them back into slavery. It did no good to protest: What white policeman or judge would take a black man's word over a white man's?

And what of the slaveholder himself? What was to become of *his* family and all who depended on him? For many plantation owners, the sum of their wealth was in their slaves and their land, and the latter was unworkable without the former. What, then, would God have the newly converted slaveholder leave for his children? The slaveholder's grandfather had left this plantation to his father, and his father had left it to him. Was he to do less for his own children?

Indeed, the plantation was more than a place; it was a way of life. To the owner it was a gracious, refined way upon which his family had prided themselves for generations. He had raised his children to believe that they would continue in that way of life and would bring up their children in it. Was it right to deny them what had been so generously provided for him? Was it right to suddenly pull their world out from under them for the sake of a spiritual principle that they did not understand, one that he himself had only recently come to grasp?

Emancipation was a many-sided dilemma, infinitely more complex than glib, radical abolitionists acknowledged. The sensitivity of Lundy and the other moderates to these ramifications was what dictated their gradual approach to emancipation and explained why many slaveholders could hear them, whereas they were merely angered by extreme abolitionists quick to threaten them with everlasting damnation if they failed to free their slaves at once.

Eventually the antislavery moderates came up with a plan for how to deal with Negroes once they had been freed. Calling for complete removal, it would transport them beyond the borders of the United States to colonies of other former slaves, where they would be helped to make a new life. One such colony had already been established on the coast of Africa and given the name Liberia (Freedom). Another was being contemplated for Central America. Known as colonization, the plan was warmly embraced as the best solution to the problem.

By today's standards, of course, colonization is the epitome of racism. But in the first half of the nineteenth century, nearly everyone, even the most kindhearted and enlightened, considered blacks to be of an inferior race that could never achieve full equality with whites. Were you to meet any of these people and suggest to them that their plan was racist, they would be hurt and offended, yet it would never occur to them to ask the black individuals or families in question if they *wanted* to be removed.

With regard to slavery, the prevailing attitude in the North seemed to be "let sleeping dogs lie." The rest of Christendom was in the process of abolishing it; in due course the South would also. In the meantime, those few fanatics who were making a nuisance of themselves with their wild accusations ought to shut up or be silenced. And more than a few anti-antislavery men were willing to condone violence against the most outspoken abolitionists.

Thus, for Lundy and the other early laborers in the antislavery vineyard, progress was slow, painfully slow at a time when the plight of the slave was becoming dire.

On a trip to Boston, Lundy met and converted to the cause an outspoken young editor from nearby Newburyport, William Lloyd Garrison. Before hearing Lundy, Garrison had been editor of the *National Philanthropist,* the country's first journal devoted to promoting the cause of absolute abstinence from intoxicating drink.[3] His hatred of alcohol had personal origins: His sea captain father proved to be more fond of rum than family, abandoning his wife and two sons when Garrison was still a boy. His mother, a poor but pious woman of high character, did her best to bring up Lloyd in the fear of God and to ensure that he had a trade with which he could support himself.

But Garrison, quick of mind and impatient of spirit, did not accept training easily from his mother or anyone else. At 10 he tried the trade of cobbler, which did not work out, followed by a brief apprenticeship to a cabinetmaker, from whom he ran away. Finally, at 13, he found his vocation while indentured to the proprietor of the Newburyport *Herald.*[4]

Garrison took to newspapering as if he had printer's ink in his veins. Quickly learning to set type, he became a master compositor. And despite a lack of formal education, he found he had a flare for writing editorials. Expressing his opinions in print soon became his passion, and the moment his seven-year apprenticeship was up, he left to start a new paper, the *Free Press,* whose motto was: "Our country, our whole country, and nothing but our country!"[5] The *Free Press* proved a bit too radical for staid Newburyport and failed.

But Garrison had a trade now, and with news increasingly in demand, he could find work anywhere. He went to Boston and worked as a journeyman printer until the right editorial position opened. In January of 1828, perhaps to strike a blow against the social evil that had taken his father from him, Garrison became editor of the first temperance newspaper. There he labored until the evening he heard Benjamin Lundy, and the abolition of slavery then became his life's work.

Lundy was quite taken with his ardent new convert, just 23 years old. Learning of Garrison's newspaper experience, he invited him to come down to Baltimore to help get out the message in the *Genius of Universal Emancipation.* Honored by the offer, Garrison made plans to join Lundy as soon as possible.

Before his arrival in Baltimore, Garrison had accepted Lundy's firm conviction of the need for a gradual approach in persuading men to free their slaves. But patience was never Garrison's long suit, and soon after joining Lundy in the little printshop, he became convinced that his mentor's methods were far too slow and overly sensitive to the feelings of slaveholders. Garrison was tired of laying the blame for the institution of slavery at the door of previous generations and more tired of putting off the solution to future generations. When it came his turn to compose the editorial page, he began to say so—in no uncertain terms. His terms were so certain, in fact, that the *Genius of Universal Emancipation* became the promulgator of the radical new doctrine of *immediate* emancipation: *All* slaves should be freed *right now, right here!*

Needless to say, young Garrison's editorials were read far and wide. His strident tone might be the opposite of Lundy's, but it surely made his pieces newsworthy. Editors began reprinting his editorials regularly, particularly in the South, where publishers held up his diatribes as typical of the new abolitionist thinking that was beginning to emerge.

Northern publishers were only slightly less offended by Garrison's heated prose, referring to him and presumably all abolitionists as a menace to society. Like a rabid dog, Garrison ought to be put down or at least locked up—which is exactly what happened. In print Garrison had condemned by name the owner of a slave ship in his hometown of Newburyport. The slave trader sued him for libel and won. The fine was $50, a not insignificant sum in 1830 dollars, and more than either Garrison or Lundy could afford. The young firebrand was sent to the Baltimore jail.

During this cooling-off period, Lundy had a chance to reconsider their unevenly yoked partnership, while Garrison continued to publish from his cell. He would write, "The detestation of feeling, the fire of moral indignation, and the agony of soul which I have felt kindling and swelling within me, reach the acme of intensity!"[6]

Not all Northerners disapproved of Garrison. Throughout New England, and especially around Boston, intellectual idealists admired his outspoken courage. For he was saying nay, shouting at the top of his lungs what many of them felt but seldom expressed above a well-modulated aside. Now one of his first admirers came to his rescue. During the brief existence of Garrison's journal of opinion, he had published the first poems of the man who would become the poet laureate of the antislavery movement, John Greenleaf Whittier. Whittier now prevailed upon the Senator from Kentucky, Henry Clay, to pay Garrison's fine. But before Clay could do so, the fine was paid by the New York philanthropist Arthur Tappan, releasing Garrison after seven weeks' incarceration. When Garrison returned to the little office, he and Lundy, their styles now diametrically opposed, agreed to a parting of the ways.

Throughout history, whenever there has been a major outpouring of the Spirit of God, it has invariably been met with two responses. Those who know Him either decide on their own what His purpose is and set out to accomplish it, or they wait upon Him to reveal His plan and their role in it, then pray for the grace to fulfill the task He has set before them.

At the dawn of the 19th century in America, there was just such an outpouring of the Spirit of God, which historians have come to call the Second Great Awakening. As the century unfolded, it seemed manifestly apparent that God had a *dual* purpose: to revive the church and to transform society. As the two melded, they would begin to usher in His kingdom on earth.

Wave after wave of His Spirit swept over the land, and in their wake sprang up all manner of inspired works by new Christians determined to fulfill the Second Great Commandment, as well as the First.* Much of this energy was directed into a wide variety of nondenominational, interchurch efforts led mostly by laymen. Ignoring the differences that had hitherto divided them, the men and women committed to these works were a dynamic, corporate demonstration that the Spirit of God was calling believers to work *together*. Coordinating their efforts, Presbyterians and Baptists, Quakers and Congregationalists sought to bring the power of God to bear on the plight of widows and orphans, on reaching the unsaved with tracts and Bibles, on freeing those caught in the bondage of alcoholic consumption, and on sending missionaries abroad.

The institution of slavery presented the greatest moral challenge of all. And in this field, there were, as usual, two responses, personified in the characters of Lundy and Garrison.

Lundy had a lifetime's experience showing the effectiveness of the low-

---

* The First Great Commandment, to love the Lord God with all one's heart, mind, soul, and strength, was followed by a Second, like unto it; to love one's neighbor as oneself. No other commandments were greater (Mark 12:30–31).

key approach. He might not win many souls to his side, and those who came might not do so in a rush, but in his view the pace was set by God, and the progress was undeniable. Lundy could genuinely sympathize with the slaveholders. He presented them with what he felt was God's perspective and let the Spirit of God do the rest.

Because slavery *was* sin, like Garrison he, too, was for immediate abolition—*gradually* realized. And here they clashed. To Garrison, fresh from a seven-week taste of what it felt like to be confined against one's will and forced to do another's bidding, immediate abolition *immediately* realized was not soon enough.

And as for colonization, that, exclaimed Garrison, was just a sop to make moderates feel better about themselves. It was a "virtuous," feel-good solution for those who could not bear the thought of living side by side with black men and women as *equals*! So saying, Garrison packed his bag and went back to Boston to found his own abolitionist newspaper.

The premier issue of the *Liberator* was dated January 1, 1831. On the front page, William Lloyd Garrison sounded his credo: "Tell a man whose house is on fire, to give a *moderate* alarm; tell him to *moderately* rescue his wife from the hands of the ravisher; tell the mother to *gradually* extricate her babe from the fire into which it has fallen. . . . I am in earnest. I will not equivocate—I will not excuse—I will not retreat a single inch—AND I WILL BE HEARD!"[7]

4

THE WATCHMAKER

*T*he more time one spends poring over history with an eye for God's hand in the affairs of men, the more one is struck by how often the right man or woman shows up in the right place at the right time.

It could be argued that this is mere coincidence, but those who regard the Bible as the premier work of history have learned that God is always standing in the shadows, working His purpose out *through* human decisions. If at a pivotal point in your life (or your country's life) you are presented with a hard choice, and you choose your way over His, His plan may be set back for the moment. But it will not be thwarted; He will find another to do what you would not.

From this perspective, it is fascinating to see God moving key players into position so that they will be ready when they are suddenly, crucially needed. It is as if He has invited us to peer into the back of a vast, gold pocket watch stretching across the night sky. The pocket watch is filled with myriad golden wheels and gears of all shapes and sizes. Some, huge and ponderous, seem motionless. Others are prominent and resolute, making distinct progress in measured increments. Still others are tiny and frantic, whirring at a blurred pace. A balance arm swings and ticks merrily next to another that remains inert. Some gears are obviously turning others, while other gears seem to be turning only themselves.

But "seem" is the operative word here, for only the Watchmaker knows the full role assigned to each wheel, each part. What appears to be an insignificant little cog can be the very part responsible for the chiming of the hour.

On each wheel stands a man or a woman, and as time passes they are carried into or out of the limelight. When two or three key figures converge, all heaven holds its breath to see how they will interact.

John Quincy Adams and Benjamin Lundy, Lundy and Garrison, Garrison and Whittier, the 1830s saw the convergence of an unusual number of significant players, old and young, prominent and unknown. One other among them was Charles Grandison Finney.

The Second Great Awakening never subsided. Thundershower after thundershower passed over the land, each shot through with God's lightning. And of all the new lightning rods, the best known was Finney. This 38-year-old former lawyer was the human agent most responsible for the revival sweeping Oneida County in upstate New York and from there spreading in all directions. Indeed, it seemed that *wherever* he went, divine lightning fell. In the course of a three-day preaching mission, often the whole town came under God's sway. And more often than not, hardened sinners for whom no one held out any hope were marvelously convicted and converted.

There is an old saying that the eyes are the window of the soul. Finney was remarkable for the piercing, even arresting quality of his eyes. Nor is this perception limited to those who actually looked him in the eye. A contemporary observer of his portraits described Finney's eyes as "great staring eyes . . . never was a man whose soul looked out through his face, as his did."[1]

Finney also had supreme confidence. It was not *self*-confidence, for he knew Who was touching the hearts of the people, and that it was His Spirit drawing them to His Son, bringing sinners to repentance, and reconciling their broken relationships. As long as he was meticulously obedient to the leading of the Holy Spirit in thought, word, and deed, God would continue to pour out His grace, as He had for the past nine years. When Finney called sinners by name, fixed them with his gaze, and told them it was time to repent, few did not respond.

Fortunately for Finney (and for the hundreds of thousands who came to Christ under his preaching), his theology was gained from careful study of the Bible. The time he spent in the Word, however, was not like most of ours. He had been a notably successful courtroom lawyer, and the only way you won in that arena was through the most painstaking preparation, with assiduous attention to detail.

To Finney, original sin was "a deep-seated but voluntary . . . self-interest.

All sin consists in selfishness, and all holiness or virtue in disinterested benevolence."[2]

It was simple; it made sense. Jesus was the personification of selfless love. Man, a fallen creature, was by nature the opposite. But if we chose to follow Jesus . . . if we asked Him to forgive us for all our previous sins, known and unknown, and invited Him into our hearts as our Lord and Master, we were saved. If we then cooperated with God's Holy Spirit, as He sought to conform us ever more to the image of His Son, then we could step out of our selfish ways.

By their fruit shall ye know them. . . . Historically, the most significant difference between the fruit of the Oneida Revival and that of preceding revivals was the strong emphasis on democratic freedom and social reform. At the cross of Jesus, *all* were welcome, heathen and Calvinist, highborn and low. And anyone—man or woman, young or old—under the anointing of God, as discerned by Finney and the other elders, could address the assembly.

As for the reformation of society by the Spirit of Christ, Finney felt strongly that the quality of a new convert's faith was borne out by his changed attitude toward his fellow man. As he would remind new converts, there were *two* Great Commandments; unless a person's new love of God was accompanied by spontaneous acts of charity and selflessness, it was not real faith at all.

So Finney encouraged all whose souls had been awakened or revived to ask God how He would have them put their faith to work. They had not been converted to *escape* life, Finney told them, but to begin a new life "in the interests of God's kingdom," where "they should set out with a determination to aim at being useful in the highest degree possible."[3] They did as he bade them. Many received calls to the mission field, and the missionary societies were hard-pressed to process the flood of new volunteers.

Not everyone was pleased with Finney's revival meetings. As with most fresh moves of God's Spirit, there was an old guard looking on with growing disapproval. Old guards were usually comprised of the leaders of the previous move of the Spirit who may have been jealous of the attention and results the newcomers were getting. Finney's case proved no exception. The old guard took strong exception to his "new measures," such as inviting individuals to come forward after a service to inquire about salvation or encouraging women to pray aloud in revival services; they failed to note that God Himself seemed to be using these measures to draw newborn believers into the fold.

Lyman Beecher was the leader of the old guard, and no minister in America was more revered. Beecher had gone to the heart of Unitarian Boston and had single-handedly turned the tide of that heresy, which had threatened to engulf New England. "The most stalwart and eloquent of the defenders of the faith" was how historian Gilbert Barnes described him, noting that a contemporary of Beecher observed that he was the "father of more brains than any man in America."[4]

Beecher and the rest of the old guard were growing increasingly concerned over certain rumors accompanying the glowing reports that made their way back over the mountains from New York State. Oneida County was "completely overthrown by the Holy Ghost . . . in consequence of this display of divine power, the theater has been deserted, the tavern sanctified. . . . Whole customs of society have been changed."[5]

Along with such heart-quickening accounts, however, came whispers of extravagant behavior on the part of Mr. Finney, who in the pulpit was often denunciatory in the extreme. Preaching from such texts as "Ye generation of vipers, how can ye escape the damnation of hell?" (Matt. 23:33), he would pray for sinners by name: "Oh God! Smite that wicked man, that hardened sinner! Oh God! Send trouble, anguish, and affliction into his bed chamber this night! . . . God Almighty, shake him over hell!"[6]

That, plus the matter of women praying aloud, convinced Beecher that Finney had gone too far. "Satan as usual," Beecher declared, "is plotting to dishonor a work which he cannot withstand."[7]

Beecher and Finney were both men of God. They knew what the Bible said: If you had ought against your brother, you must go to him, and in a spirit of charity seek to be reconciled. And so, when someone proposed a meeting between the "new measures" preachers and the old guard, both accepted with alacrity. "Ministers must come together and consult," Beecher declared. "The mask must be torn off from Satan, coming among the sons of God and transforming himself into an angel of light."[8]

They would meet at New Lebanon, New York. Beecher arrived with all the old guard in tow, and Finney with Presbyterian ministers whose churches had experienced revival when he had preached there. As the meeting began, extreme courtesy was the rule, and everything was, of course, soaked in prayer. But eventually the old guard put forward a number of resolutions that the Oneida contingent could not accept, chief among them being that at meetings of men and women for religious worship, women were not to pray. Nor could the old guard agree to Finney's proposal that it was unseemly for workers in one region of the Lord's vineyard to impose their judgments on workers in another.

Finally Beecher lost his temper. "Finney!" he shouted, "I know your plan! And you know I do! You mean to come to Connecticut and carry a streak of fire to Boston." He paused and glared at his young rival. "If you attempt it, as the Lord liveth, I'll meet you at the state line, and call out the artillery and fight you there!"[9] So much for the spirit of charity with a view toward reconciliation.

The two groups sadly parted. Both leaders went back to serving God as they had before, with neither having any idea of the enormous effect their lingering animosity would have on the future of the antislavery movement.

The wheels continued to turn: Lundy and Garrison, Beecher and Finney, and now Finney and Weld.

During the Second Great Awakening, the man most responsible for introducing the antislavery movement as one option available to the reform-minded new convert was Theodore Dwight Weld. Like John Wesley in the previous century, Finney gathered about him a "holy band," a team of zealous young revivalists who traveled with him, helping the spiritually awakened come into the fullness of the Spirit of God. Foremost in this band of holy men was Weld, a former student at Hamilton College near Utica, New York. He had been adamantly opposed to all he had heard of Finney and his new measures, disparaging Finney to his fellow students. Weld being a natural leader, they had all listened, and were subsequently astounded to learn that Weld had met Finney and been won over, quitting college to join his holy band.

Most of Finney's band would wind up in the ministry, but that no longer meant, as it once did, that a man of God might expect to be called to serve a church in one town until he died. In this new evangelical age of revivals, a minister might become an "ambassador of God"[10] who would be expected to go where the evangelical movement, a national movement, most needed him at present.

It was Beecher who had first called for this broadening of a young clergyman's horizon in an ordination sermon in 1814. He exhorted the young minister not to confine his "eye, heart, and ear to the narrow limits of an association [or presbytery or diocese]. . . . The state, the nation, the world demand your prayers and charities and enterprise."[11]

And some men would be called to itinerant evangelism. One of the requisites for being a divine lightning rod seemed to be a zest for "being of the stretch for God," as George Whitefield had put it a century before. As that century had drawn to a close, Francis Asbury had set the example for his legendary Methodist circuit riders. They loved nothing so much as to be in the saddle, leaning forward into the rain on a day not fit for man or beast, carrying the Good News into dark hollows of wilderness that had never known the Light of Christ.

Theodore Dwight Weld was cut from the same bolt of cloth. Possessing immense physical energy and stamina, he was always ready to "shake hands with Toil and call Peril by his middle name."[12] A big man, he paid scant attention to his personal appearance, and one contemporary observed that he perpetually looked like an unmade bed. From portraits it is apparent that his hair had only a nodding acquaintance with a brush or comb, and not even that with a barber. His clothes looked like they had been hastily borrowed from someone else. His expression was invariably serious; "ruminating" was how historian Bertram Wyatt-Brown put it.[13]

Weld's demeanor could, however, change in an instant, the moment he began to concentrate on someone else's problems. Then he was transformed into the soul of compassion, listening carefully and offering gentle counsel or comfort.

In the pulpit he could be strong, even fiery, but usually he was more of a gentle persuader like Lundy than a hammer-and-anvil preacher like Finney. Not that he was any less effective! Indeed, his young converts were so loyal to him that perhaps the best gauge of his personality was that in future years, of all the many activists in the antislavery movement, only he and the poet Whittier were never slandered by their co-workers.

Weld felt he needed more theological training before he could become a full-time preacher, and providentially he had a sponsor: Major Charles Stuart, Royal Army, retired. Converted in the Oneida Revival, this former British officer who had served in India first met Weld when the latter was still a boy and Stuart was principal of the Utica high school. Once Weld had been converted, Stuart recognized his potential. Not only was

Weld a charismatic speaker with a profound influence on his audiences, but he inspired in his colleagues the sort of fierce loyalty that military officers (like Stuart) could only dream of. Urging Weld to "help the help-less, be eyes to the blind, feet to the lame, raise the fallen, bind up the bruised, and guide the wandering," Stuart became his mentor, assuming the cost of his education at the Oneida Institute and shaping his career as a reformer.[14]

Until they met, temperance had been Weld's mission field. To it he brought all the zeal of a young, on-fire evangelist entering spiritual war-fare, ready to do battle with Satan for the souls of men. Society's greatest scourge in the early nineteenth century was drunkenness. In New York State alone 89 million pieces of propaganda were distributed to combat it—in a single year.[15]

On the frontier, a boy's rite of passage was when he became old enough to have a dram of whiskey with his father in the morning, before they set off to work. In every cabin was a jug "for hospitality's sake," and when there wasn't a guest, men drank anyway, for the same reasons they do today.

When a man drank to excess he could become wild, as if possessed; indeed, it sometimes seemed as if a pervasive spirit of intoxication was hell-bent on destroying the fabric of American society. Not for nothing was the Jamaican sugarcane extraction referred to as "Demon Rum."

Weld came against this spirit with the armor and weapons of God Al-mighty, confronting Satan head-on and in most cases winning. He soon became the preeminent speaker of the American Temperance Society, the largest of the New York–based philanthropies, and on more than a few occasions whiskey dealers, after hearing him, went home and emp-tied their barrels.[16] Before long he had a reputation as the most powerful temperance speaker in the West, and was much sought after by everyone, including Finney.

Then Stuart began to talk to him about the antislavery movement.

Weld listened, for the British example in foreign missionary work, Sunday schools, the dissemination of tracts and Bibles, prison reform, and outreach to sailors had inspired the American benevolent societies to go and do likewise. The same was true of the antislavery cause. Thanks to the work of William Wilberforce and his colleagues, Parliament was on the verge of abolishing slavery throughout the British Empire and all its possessions.

As Stuart portrayed the agonizing, hopeless condition of more than two million American slaves, Weld prayerfully made a course correction to his life's voyage and committed himself totally to the antislavery cause. Soon he would write to William Lloyd Garrison of "that great bottom law of human right, that nothing but crime can forfeit liberty."

Moreover, "no condition of birth, no shade of color, no mere misfortune of circumstances, can annul that birth-right charter, which God has bequeathed to every being upon whom He has stamped His own image, by making him a free moral agent." And what of the slaveholder? "He who robs his fellow man of this tramples upon right, subverts justice, outrages humanity, unsettles the foundation of human safety, and sacrilegiously assumes the prerogative of God."[17]

Something else was happening in the wake of the ongoing revival. More and more young evangelicals were viewing slave owning as the Quakers had, as "a sin always, everywhere, and only a sin."[18]

And once it was recognized as such, then the only acceptable atonement was emancipation put in motion immediately, because, claimed the Christian abolitionists, the Bible required sinners to repent and cease wrongdoing *at once*.

Now there were new Christian abolitionists siding with the secular Garrisonites in calling for immediate emancipation, as opposed to the older moderate leaders who still favored gradualism. The new abolitionists had a point: It was one thing to be sympathetic to a sinner's situation, but if the sinner had no intention of giving up his sin, then no amount of gentle persuasion was going to change his heart. Compassion was one thing; condoning the status quo was quite another.

The tension was now affecting all the mainline denominations. Something *had* to be done about slavery; things could not be allowed to continue any longer as they were. Accusing the Presbyterian General Assembly of "moral cowardice" for not calling slave owning a sin, New York lawyer Alvin Stuart emphasized that continued equivocation would place the church on the side of the proslavery forces. For "silence becomes acquiescence, which is soon apology, which is soon defense, which is soon vindication."[19]

What would Jesus have done? He would probably have weighed each case on its own merits. And in more than a few instances, rather than expelling slaves into a hostile environment, it would have been far kinder for a Christian master to continue looking after and caring for them, though now treating them as hired hands.

But there was no question that the grace period for slavery was over. Jesus forgave the adulteress her sins and shamed her accusers into leaving her alone. But He also told her, "Go and sin no more."

As the wheels continued to turn, other figures rotated into prominence: Finney and Weld, Weld and the Tappans . . .

Arthur and Lewis Tappan were silk importers in New York City. They were highly successful and highly unusual. At a time when New York merchants had a reputation for slippery dealing, they were determined to bring Christ's principles to bear in the marketplace. Charging one price to all customers, they kept that price so low that at first they barely made a profit. But as word of their integrity and the honest value of their offer spread, they sold out their inventory as fast as they could restock it. Eventually they became immensely wealthy and used all of their money for the Lord's work.

In 1830 that work in New York City focused on the benevolent societies, "The Great Eight" as they came to be known. They included the American Bible Society (still active today), the American Tract Society, the American Home Missionary Society, the American Education Society, the American Temperance Society, the American Sunday School Union, the American Board of Foreign Missions, and the American Seamen's Friend Society. They even had their own Christian periodical, the *New York Evangelist*, and an abolitionist paper, the *Emancipator*.

In a rare demonstration of harmony, the societies were run by Presbyterian and Congregational ministers and laymen. Many of the men served on more than one board, for example Thomas Smith Grimké, Gerrit Smith, Anson Stokes Phelps, and William Jay. But the names most commonly found on these interlocking directorates were those of Arthur and Lewis Tappan, whose money funded most of the societies' endeavors.

Arthur was the visionary, who could see God's unfolding plan sooner and more clearly than others and who acted on it instantly, putting his money where it was most needed. Lewis, practical, sensible, and steady, had an unusual gift for financial affairs. In 1828 he took over the running of their business to free Arthur to devote himself entirely to the benevolent institutions.

Meanwhile, as these societies were forming in New York City, Finney was bringing the revival wherever God led him. After galvanizing Connecticut, he even carried a streak of fire to Boston, exactly as Lyman Beecher had predicted. The latter was, in fact, forced by his congregation to swallow his words and invite Finney to preach in his church.[20]

In 1830 the Tappans asked Finney to bring the fire to their city, and when he did, he strongly encouraged them to continue their social reforms. They did. "Believing that the accumulation of property for selfish purposes is repugnant to the Gospel; that every person is a steward," the Tappans and the other leaders of the "benevolent empire" entered "into a solemn engagement not to lay up any property we may hereafter acquire . . . but consecrate the whole of it to the Lord, deducting sufficient to supply ourselves and families in a decent manner, as becomes those professing Godliness."[21]

Not long after this covenant, whom should Arthur Tappan meet but Benjamin Lundy, who by coincidence had come north just at that time on a walking tour. Lundy impressed on Tappan the urgent need of the antislavery movement. Of all the latter's Christian endeavors, could any be more crucial than working to free the black man from involuntary servitude? Arthur Tappan agreed, and henceforth the brothers Tappan became prominent figures in that cause, in addition to the others they were already championing.

And so the wheels turned. . . .

Theodore Dwight Weld was attending Oneida Academy preparatory to fulfilling his next goal: to attend seminary. The trouble was, which seminary to attend? The Great Revival had produced dozens of young men like himself, burning to serve God in the ministry. Yet the seminaries back East were staffed by faculty whose own fires had long ago petered out and who were wont to douse crackling fervor with buckets of cold theology.

As it happened, Arthur and Lewis Tappan were acutely aware of the need for a new national seminary where holy fire could be stoked and channeled. Their next project, in fact, was to establish just such a seminary out in the rapidly expanding West, where it was most needed. Unlike other seminaries of the day, this one would be evangelical through and through, chartered by evangelicals, staffed by evangelicals, with a core curriculum designed to bring forth a new generation of evangelical clergy.

They were looking for an appropriate site even as Weld was looking for just the sort of seminary they proposed to found. Lewis Tappan had two sons enrolled at Oneida Academy. He met Weld as a result, and realized their two quests could be fortuitously combined. The Tappans commissioned Weld to find the site for their new seminary with the understanding that he would be among the first students to be enrolled.

Weld's search eventually took him to Cincinnati, where by one of those extraordinary coincidences that reveal God's hand, he discovered a tract of land already given for a seminary by two local merchants named Lane. They had even obtained a charter for such an institution, only to run short of the necessary funds to build it.

One visit to the wooded hill above the city was all Weld needed. He had no trouble convincing Arthur Tappan, who now allocated the capital for construction and began lining up first-rate instructors. The student body would be no problem; the planned seminary was an answer to prayer for many young men converted in the revival. As for the nonexistent facilities, the students themselves would build them. Not surprisingly, the Tappans' first choice to lead their seminary was the leader of the current revival, Charles Finney. When Finney declined, they turned to the dean of active evangelicals, Lyman Beecher.

Finney and the Tappans, the Tappans and Weld, Weld and Beecher; the wheels turned, the gears meshed, all part of the Watchmaker's master plan. But one must bear in mind how many other, less prominent gears were in His watch, how much depended on every single one making the right choice, the hard choice, when it came time to stand up for Him.

Two centuries before, it had not been just Bradford and Winthrop, Hooker and Penn who had set America's spiritual heart beating; it was every Pilgrim and Puritan who had accompanied them as they turned away from the path of least resistance. And it was not just Washington and the Adamses, Franklin and Madison and Jefferson who had laid down the foundation stones of this Republic; it was every Patriot who grabbed his rifle, and every woman who prayed for God's protection over those she loved. Nor was it just Asbury and Cartwright and Dwight who had spiritually reawakened America; it was every circuit rider, every frontier preacher, every man and woman of God who gave themselves selflessly and unsung to His service.

As Lyman Beecher weighed the new position he had been offered and considered the countless thousands of pioneers pouring over the mountains and heading ever farther west, he wrote a letter to his daughter Catharine. "The moral destiny of our nation, and all our institutions and hopes, and the world's hopes, turns on the character of the West, and the competition now is for that preoccupancy in the education of the rising generation. . . . I have thought seriously of going over to Cincinnati . . . to spend the remnant of my days in the great conflict. . . . If we gain the West, all is safe; if we lose it, all is lost."[22]

5

A New Gideon's Army

*P*redawn mist shrouded the river so densely that the only color visible beyond the gunwales was a soft, opaque gray white. A pioneer family, drifting by flatboat down the Ohio River in 1832, would be listening acutely for the sound of the river against either bank and nudging the long handle of the tiller oar to keep in the middle. They would be startled by the blast of a steam packet's whistle, but also relieved: They had finally reached Cincinnati. Grateful for the warmth of the crimson orb rising behind them, if they looked up through the clearing mist they could see a city set on seven hills. . . .

Cincinnati had been named for a society of officers who had served in the Continental Army under Washington and taken their name from Cincinnatus, the Roman farmer who had answered his nation's call in time of war. He had assumed command of her armies and led them to victory, and then, eschewing the high position that might have followed, he had returned to his farm. Likewise, the society's officers had returned to theirs.

Though the traffic heading downriver was heavier, there were northbound packets from New Orleans off-loading cargo and picking up meat that they would carry up to Pittsburgh. Nearly all commercial vessels stopped at Cincinnati, for in addition to being at the confluence of three rivers and several recently improved roadways, a new canal linking it to Dayton had just opened. To add to its meatpacking industry, Cincinnati was also fast becoming a major mercantile center.

There was work in abundance, and the pay was good. In a single year a man willing to lift or tote, haul or pack could easily earn enough to buy a flatboat *and* a team and wagon to take his own family farther west. There was plenty of work for a freed slave, too, and enough other free blacks that he would be among friends. Cincinnati had become a magnet, one of the fastest-growing cities in the West.

But not all of her citizens were happy with the way she was changing. Just as there was a distinct difference between the upper South and the deep South, so there was a difference between the upper North and the lower North. In flavor and outlook Cincinnati was definitely lower North—almost a Southern city on free soil. Except for one thing: Cincinnati was on a main branch of the Underground Railroad, which smuggled escaped slaves to freedom in the North. In the previous decade her overall population doubled, but her black population increased tenfold. She had become a tinderbox. There had already been one race riot four years before, and another might flare up at any time.

In the Old Testament, Gideon was one of God's great commanders. Through him God winnowed out a band of 300 men, with which He routed a vastly superior enemy force. Now, in Cincinnati, He was about to gather a new Gideon's army, and for its commander He had chosen Theodore Dwight Weld.

The charismatic young speaker, of course, had no idea what lay in store for him as he presented the antislavery cause, often in the same Ohio churches where he had spoken on temperance the year before. He toiled tirelessly, seeming to have the heart of a Puritan. As he wrote to his mentor, Finney: "Pride, you know, is one of the chiefest [besetting sins] with me. It makes dreadful havoc in my soul. It would lay me in ruins every day, but for Christ's strengthening."[1]

It is one of God's sweet ironies that the more concerned a man is about his pride, the less of a problem it may actually be. Weld's readiness to have God search the dark corners of his soul was the necessary balance to his passionate intensity. And it was sustained: Ten years after Weld lamented to Finney of his pride, he would write to his fiancée, Angelina Grimké, to warn her of his sinful nature: *Self-indulgence, Downright Indolence. Here I suppose you will almost laugh outright. Well, it is even so. I verily do not know a lazier man than I am.*[2] (Anyone knowing Weld would have laughed; few men of any era were more productive or prolific—that self-incriminating letter ran 6,000 words.)

But other than Angelina, Finney, and a few trusted friends, no one guessed the depth of his inner emotions. He did permit his passion to show in his preaching, where it was a controlled conflagration. Weld was not a shouter; he was a piercer. As biographer Robert Abzug wrote, "Weld's life was a brave one, brave in its common heroism and in its silent inner anguish."[3]

As God does with each of us who accepts His call to a lifetime of service, He tested Weld by giving him modest assignments and seeing how well he carried them out. Weld's faithfulness in little things must have pleased Him, for the assignments quickly grew larger. Barely 28 when he entered Lane Seminary, Theodore Dwight Weld had already become one of the most prominent Christians of his era. And even more unusual, his humility had kept pace with his fame.

Lyman Beecher was 57 in 1832 and painfully aware that the banner of revival was being carried forward by younger men. The Great Revival, Finney's revival, had largely passed him by. Then out of the blue had come the offer of the Presidency of a new seminary to train the most ardent of the revival's converts. Far from being passed by, he would be responsible for producing the next generation's spiritual leaders. Indeed, the first class would include young Weld, who in his temperance meetings had already demonstrated a maturity and organizational ability far beyond his years. In Beecher's estimation Weld was a remarkably saintly and humble young man, altogether an anointed genius.[4] With Weld at his right hand, he would guide the good ship Lane down the uncharted river that lay ahead.

Ominous ripples soon appeared on the river's surface, however: There were rumors that Weld had become an abolitionist. Beecher considered himself firmly in the antislavery camp, but he was of the old school, which held that the way to get rid of slavery was through appealing to the slaveholder's conscience.

Beecher dismissed the rumors. In his last exchange of views with Weld, the latter had agreed that colonization was the only feasible solution to the problem of what to do with the freed slaves. It was, in fact, the solution that Weld himself had put forth, whenever his temperance meetings gave him the opportunity.

In Huntsville, Alabama, Weld had made such an impression on a prominent lawyer named James G. Birney that the latter became the southwest agent of the American Colonization Society. While not a product of the deep South (he had been born and raised in Danville, Kentucky, and educated at the College of New Jersey*), Birney was a *bona fide* slaveholder. As such, he was the society's prize convert, and something of their champion: He wrote a series of articles for their publication, *The African Repository*, rebutting abolitionists who had begun claiming that colonization skirted the moral issue.

Despite the influence of Stuart, his mentor, Weld continued to support colonization, writing to Birney in September of 1832, "If the Colonization Society does not dissipate the horror of darkness which overhangs the Southern country, we are undone. Light breaks in from no other quarter!"[5]

But now light was about to break on Weld from an unexpected source. He was speaking in the little town of Hudson, Ohio, home of Western Reserve College, and this time it was he who was converted. In his audience were Charles Storrs, President of the college; Beriah Green, its Professor of Sacred Literature; and Elizur Wright, Professor of Mathematics. Unbeknownst to him, all three were abolitionists, converted in the revival. Now they felt it incumbent to show Weld the wanton cruelty of the "solution" he was espousing. Yet they did so with compassion, practicing the same patience that Weld himself used.

It would be one thing, they said, if a recently captured slave could be returned to his tribal homeland. But the majority of slaves had been in America all their lives and had begun families of their own here. For better or worse, America was now their country, too. We had brought them here against their will; we must now make room for them to live in our midst.

Was it Christian love, they went on, to uproot someone from his or her circle of friends and ship them over to Africa, where no one knew who they were? Or cared? And what of black families torn asunder on the auction block? As long as they were all in the South, there was a chance, however remote, of their one day being reunited. If one or more were taken away to Africa, that slender hope would be forever dashed.

Weld listened and heard, and that night he became a staunch anti-

* today Princeton University

66

colonization abolitionist. To those who were anti-abolitionist, that put him in Garrison's camp, and from then on wherever he spoke, it took a while for him to overcome the bad taste that Garrison's *Liberator* had put in everyone's mouth. But if they listened, they would see soon enough that in spirit Theodore Dwight Weld could not be farther removed from William Lloyd Garrison.

Throughout the North, the ongoing revival continued to produce hundreds of new converts weekly, young men and women with hearts on fire to enter God's service full time. It was no longer enough to pray together and sing hymns; they wanted to be *doing* something. As Beriah Green exclaimed, not "till we rise to a higher sphere, the sphere of doing," do we come into a true knowledge of God, and "give life to our speculations, substance to our creed, and meaning to our professions."[6]

The question was, doing what? As the new converts prayed to know which work God was calling them to, for many the coincidental arrival of Weld in their town must have seemed an answer to prayer. That impression was confirmed as he related what had happened to him. He had been serving on the mission field of temperance, when suddenly God opened his eyes to the most compelling need on the face of the earth, the battlefield whose outcome could determine the fate of all mankind. Each night in each town he added to the numbers gathering behind the banner of abolition, and as many were drawn by his compassion as by his words. It was not uncommon for entire congregations to be recruited to the cause, and more than a few young men determined to follow him to Lane Seminary as soon as it opened.

Regarding the seminary, one of Weld's first converts to abolition was Arthur Tappan, who rejoiced with him that their seminary would one day be a wellspring of theologically trained laborers in the abolitionist cause. But they would have to proceed with extreme tact, for Lyman Beecher saw no reason why abolition and colonization were mutually exclusive.

Beecher, in fact, saw himself in the role of reconciler, bringing the opposing camps together in harmony. Undeterred by a fruitless attempt to change Garrison's mind about abolition, he now appealed by an open letter to abolition leaders to avoid "the unseemliness of discord among the brethren" and seek grounds for accommodation. "Are colonization and abolition opposed to each other, after all? . . . The good men of both parties have the good of the slave . . . at heart. Now, then, is not union among good men desirable?"[7] Gathering his thoughts into an article for his publication, *The Spirit of the Pilgrims*, he placed it into the hands of his printers and departed for Cincinnati.

Arthur Tappan could foresee major difficulties. He had already come to a private understanding with Weld that Lane Seminary would be not only a center of learning for the West, but also a forum for abolition propaganda. Hoping to avert disaster, Tappan composed an article for Beecher's publication, demonstrating that the differences between the two camps were indeed irreconcilable.

But by then Beecher's position had already been published, and he was not about to change it. To his benefactor he replied: "I am not apprised of the ground of controversy between the Colonizationists and the Abolitionists. I am myself both, without perceiving in myself any inconsistency."[8]

Gerrit Smith also wrote to Beecher, challenging his resistance to the abolitionists' call for immediate action. If a sinner was in the act of committing a sin, and his conscience was being sorely pressed, what could be more counterproductive than to tell him he must stop but "not yet."[9]

Beecher was immovable.

As the first of 40 students arrived at the new seminary in the fall of 1832 and began to erect the buildings that would house them, Weld sensed that God had assembled them for a special purpose. This was no ordinary freshman class. For one thing, they were older men, already well seasoned. Three-quarters of them were over 26 years old. All were college graduates, six were married, and one was a practicing physician. Eleven others had been, like Weld, public speakers of prominence.[10] Three-quarters of them had been converted in the revival and were there in response to a call of God, eager to be molded into His instruments. They fervently believed that in His service they could change America, perhaps even usher in the millennium!

And many of them were there because of Weld. A number had served with him in Finney's holy band, and others had been recruited during his work for abolition. Their loyalty to him was already exceptional; after the summer of 1833, it became extraordinary.

In August a deadly cholera epidemic swept into Cincinnati. It struck the Lane campus, felling the student who lived next to Weld. Without regard for his own health, Weld ministered to him, then to the next to succumb, and the next. *Someone* had to care for them, Weld reasoned, and so he did. Others, inspired by his example, joined him, and Weld organized them into shifts of caregivers. Once again, that which the enemy had intended for evil, God had turned to good.

When at last the scourge subsided, the survivors had been forged into one body, and their head was Theodore Dwight Weld. They had been predisposed to follow wherever he would lead them; now they would lay down their lives for him, if need be. He had done no less for them.

Where he led them was into *immediate* emancipation—a conviction that only a few of them already shared. While all were antislavery, to be sure, not all were ready to embrace immediatism, which they equated with Garrison. Weld talked to them quietly, one on one, showing each by his example the difference between Garrisonism and what he believed.

He started by calling slavery what it was: *sin.* That was the only word for holding another against his will, forcing him to do your bidding, and recompensing him nothing for his labor. Therefore, anyone holding slaves was in sin. If the slaveholder could be brought to see that, if his heart was not hardened against the conviction of the Spirit of God, then he should repent. Weld intended the Biblical meaning of that word: to change one's mind and go in the opposite direction. The slaveholder should commence making plans to release his slaves as soon as possible—not when it was convenient, or if the other family members agreed to it, or if they received compensation for the value of their slaves, or after the cotton crop was harvested, but at once.

Yet their manumission would not be instantaneous, as Garrison was demanding in the *Liberator*. Here, then, was another distinction between Garrisonism and the new evangelical abolition: As Weld and his colleagues clarified and refined it, they realized that immediate emancipation would have to be accomplished gradually, not precipitously.

One of them, William Allen, had been raised in the midst of slavery. He explained their position succinctly: "By immediate emancipation we do not mean that the slaves shall be turned loose on the nation, nor that they shall be instantly vested with . . . political rights and privileges."

Then what *did* "immediate" mean? "Gradual emancipation, immediately begun," which was considerably less alarming.[11]

The concept, which came to be known as *immediate emancipation, gradually accomplished*, was one whose subtlety was unfortunately lost on the majority of Northerners who were unsympathetic to the antislavery cause. Few registered the moderation expressed in the second phrase; all they heard was the first two words. And so they assumed that these ardent new abolitionists were no different than that wild man Garrison up in Boston who was condemning to hell all slaveholders who would not release their slaves instantly. He had, in fact, so tarnished the image of abolition that anyone attempting to speak on its behalf was often mobbed.

Classes at Lane began in the fall of 1833, and whenever school was not actually in session, Weld would take a few classmates with him on the speaking engagements for which he was still in great demand. They would watch him, observing his steadfast meekness and putting it into practice themselves.

Some of the pastors or civic groups who invited Weld may have assumed he would speak on intemperance. If so, the moment he addressed his new great concern, the smiles of ministers and mayors froze. In 1833 the antislavery movement had few advocates among the churchgoing folk of Ohio, and abolitionism had almost none at all. Many had never seen a black person, and it was difficult for them to muster sympathy. When Weld spoke of the freed slaves in Cincinnati and how well they were doing, the good people of Akron and Ashtabula were unmoved. When he described the Negro college Arthur Tappan was planning so that educated blacks could be integrated into white society, the good people of Conneaut and Chillicothe remained stone-faced. Better, they thought, those educated blacks should stay in Cincinnati!

Undaunted, Weld would calmly pursue his theme. Just as no true Christian would enslave another to do his work for him, neither should any true Christian in good conscience condone it. Gradually some of the mayors and some of the ministers—those who came back to hear him the next night—began to see it his way. Which meant they could no longer remain impartial.

Had Weld been content to limit his preaching to revival, he could have filled huge halls and shaken their rafters, rivaling even Finney in popularity. At one point Lewis Tappan had pleaded with Weld to come evangelize New York City, confident that if he did come, revival would sweep the city. But Weld remained true to his calling. Sometimes toiling several days in a town of no more than a few hundred, he would invariably leave behind a small handful of deeply committed Christians prepared to spend the rest of their lives advancing the cause of abolition.

Back on the Lane campus, however, even the most serene passenger was beginning to detect an ominous roar downriver. President Beecher invited his prize student into his office for a friendly chat. In well-modulated tones Beecher explained his eminently reasonable position to Weld: This was a time to be sowing seeds of harmony, not discord. The potential of the West was growing exponentially, and they were uniquely positioned to be key instruments in shaping its spiritual destiny. He smiled and waited, confident that his young protégé would see it his way.

But Weld gave no indication that he was prepared to modify his unconditional support of abolition, and Beecher began to modify his opinion of Weld. He had once been profoundly grateful for Weld's exemplary influence on his classmates; now he was not so sure.

"In the estimate of the class," Beecher would record in his autobiography, "he was President." Weld "took the lead of the whole institution. . . . They thought he was a god."[12]

For his part, Weld never came out from under President Beecher's authority. He remained so respectfully obedient that Beecher later acknowledged that during all the stress of the ensuing months, the two never quarreled.

Matters came to a head in February of 1834, when Weld decided it was time to take a stand. With Beecher's blessing, he organized a public debate on the Lane campus on the question: Should the people in the slaveholding States abolish slavery immediately? The debate would run for 18 evenings, and Weld was determined that it would proceed in the spirit of benevolence.

No one dreamed how pivotal those 18 days would be to the future of America.

The Lane Debate was not really a debate at all; in actuality, it was an abolitionist revival of the sort that Weld had been conducting in his off-campus ministry. He had, in fact, so carefully orchestrated the progression of speakers that he hoped at the conclusion of the debate that most of the audience would be converted to abolitionism.

His opening remarks set the tone. As in his revival missions, the spirit of these meetings was anything but adversarial. Benevolence was the watchword—and that, wrote students Henry B. Stanton and Augustus Wattles to such periodicals as the *Emancipator* and the *Evangelist*, swayed hearts as much as anything that was said. "When the debate commenced," reported Stanton, "I had fears that there might be some unpleasant excitement . . . but the kindest feelings prevailed. There was no . . . denunciation."[13]

Never was the spirit of Christian charity more evident than when Lyman Beecher's daughter Catharine rose to speak. Having changed his mind about participating, President Beecher had asked his daughter to speak for him. Now, as she dutifully presented his plan for assimilating colonizationists and abolitionists, there was no murmuring, no ripple of dissent. Nor did anyone rise to rebut her position when she finished. But neither did anyone rise in support of it.

To the newly converted from whose eyes the scales had fallen, the institution of slavery was manifestly sinful because it exemplified the gratification of self. It turned a person into an object whose sole purpose was to satisfy the desires of another person. If it was money, a master's slaves would earn it for him. If it was the gratification of lust, his slaves would provide that, too. The master held absolute power over his slaves, and power—the ability to force another's will to bend to one's own—has always been the ultimate narcotic. Give someone a little power, and they soon lust for more.

As Satan well knew (and Lord Acton would later articulate), power tended to corrupt, and absolute power corrupted absolutely. If the master abused his slave, the slave had no rights or recourse. Nor was there any mechanism for restraining a master gone bad. Southern gentlemen liked to believe that the threat of social ostracism was sufficient to deter a potentially evil master. But in truth, any master who was maltreating his slaves cared little what his neighbors thought of him.

While there *were* devout Christian slaveholders whose faith held their behavior and appetites in check, the system itself contained no such safeguards. A slave's master might be a model of Christian charity, but that made him no more than a benevolent dictator, and who was to say that his son would be similarly inclined? Or his son's son?

Was slavery the supreme spiritual battlefield in 1834? In terms of commercial profit, it had gained such a powerful hold on America, North and

South, that from the evangelical perspective the Republic was caught in the grip of national sin. In her greed America was becoming the opposite of what God had intended her to be—"a city set on a hill" as a shining example to all mankind. The system of slavery was spreading its dark stain through the entire fabric of society, tainting first the souls of those who aided and abetted the system, then those who profited indirectly from it, and finally those whose spiritual response to it was indifference.

In the audience, feelings ran deep. Many had never seriously considered these aspects of the institution; as they did, a number became abolitionists on the spot. One was a young student named James A. Thome, from a slaveholding family in Kentucky. Later he would recall the moment during the debate when he fully realized slaveholding was sin. "I know of no subject which takes such a strong hold of a man, as does abolition. It seizes the conscience with an authoritative grasp, it runs across the path of the guilty, goads him, haunts him, and rings in his ears the cry of blood! . . . It writes 'thou art the one' upon the heart of every oppressor."[14] But with conviction came repentance, which found Thome "pledged to do [abolition's work]."[15]

From long experience on the mission field, Weld knew how to reach Southern hearts: with former slaves' firsthand accounts of the horrors of slavery. The audience heard of perforated paddles through whose holes spurted blood and flesh, of the use of red-hot tongs as a means of torture. Now these narratives were augmented by the personal recollections of other young men from the South. One student wrote home: "The facts developed in the debate have almost curdled my blood. . . . Facts are great instruments of conviction on this question."[16]

Throughout this revelation (which in shock value must have been akin to the first newsreels from Auschwitz and other Nazi death camps), the mood remained compassionate. Under Weld's leadership, there was no condemnation of slaveholders, only conviction and repentance on the part of those present.

As the debate continued, it attracted national attention. Acting as reporters, young Stanton and Wattles were sending out daily summaries, and more and more Northern newspapers were carrying their running accounts. These were particularly firing the imaginations of other students; on campuses throughout the North abolitionist societies were forming.

Few oratorical moments are as compelling as the testimony of a new convert, and during the debates it became apparent that James Thome had a powerful gift for touching the heart. "When once the great proposition that Negroes are *human beings* . . . is drawn out in the Southern sky, and when underneath it is written the bloody corollary, the suffering of the Negro race, the seared conscience will again sting, and the stony heart will melt!"

To Henry Stanton, Thome was proof that "Southern minds, trained and educated amidst all the prejudices of a slaveholding community, can, with the blessing of God, be reached and influenced by facts and arguments, as easy as any other class of our citizens."[17]

When the debate concluded, the vote for immediate abolition was nearly unanimous. For those newly converted to abolitionism, it now became central to their sense of being called to serve Christ, and evangelizing for immediate emancipation became the primary way they would put the Gospel into action. They were a band far smaller than Gideon's, but God had clearly gathered them; inspired them, and entrusted into their corporate care the responsibility for a key part of the antislavery movement.

Typical was James Birney, who with Weld's encouragement had once become a champion of colonization. Having followed the debate in the press, he now came to Cincinnati to hear of this new doctrine from Weld himself. What he heard convinced him to join the abolitionists, and in his diary he noted of Weld: "I have seen in no man such a rare combination of great intellectual powers with Christian simplicity. . . the most simple-hearted and earnest follower of Christ that I have known."[18]

One student, Huntington Lyman, was from a slaveholding family in Louisiana; his tuition at Lane had come from the proceeds of his slaves' labor. Now he returned home to free his slaves and to find work so that he could support them, while they gained a common-school education. "We have vowed to the Lord," he wrote, "to use our personal exertions and whatever influence we have or may acquire, to raise up the free black population, and to persuade our fellow-men to love them, as they do themselves."[19]

Yet perhaps the most far-reaching impact of all was made on Catharine Beecher's younger sister Harriet. She did not say anything during the debates, nor did she oppose her father in the inevitable post-debate debate at the Beecher dinner table. But she had listened, and what she heard had made a profound impression on her. Years later Harriet Beecher Stowe would credit Theodore Dwight Weld's book, *American Slavery As It Is*, with being the greatest single earthly influence upon her conception of *Uncle Tom's Cabin*.

The Great Revival of 1830, declared Finney, was validated by widespread social reform. So was the abolitionist revival at Lane. Not only were the vast majority of the students converted; they immediately put their faith in action. Augustus Wattles felt called by God to devote his life to elevating the condition of the free blacks in Cincinnati. Tearfully he requested permission to leave the seminary to follow this vocation, and tearfully President Beecher let him go. Wattles founded a school for blacks, and practically all the students on the Lane campus lent him a helping hand. They set up three Sunday schools, an elementary school, and a lending library for the free blacks of the city.

Back in New York, Arthur Tappan was thrilled: It was one thing to preach a new doctrine; it was another to practice it. Without fanfare these young men were rolling up their sleeves and living their new commitment. Tappan sent Weld $1,000, an enormous sum in those days, adding, "Draw on me for whatever is necessary for the schools, teachers, house-hire, books, &c."[20]

Unfortunately, all did not point to a happily-ever-after ending in Cincinnati. In the wake of the 1828 race riot, the town fathers, increasingly alarmed at the rapidly swelling population of free blacks, had called for their wholesale deportation. When this proved unfeasible, frustrated whites grew increasingly resentful that these white students from out of state were deliberately "amalgamating"* with the blacks down in "Little Africa." Only the timely arrival of summer vacation and the dispersal of the students avoided a conflagration.

Beecher dispersed as well, taking the opportunity to travel back East—back home—to attend the anniversary meetings of the New York philanthropies. The last thing he wanted to think about was the recent uproar on the Lane campus. Yet it was the first thing on the lips of fellow college Presidents and old friends as they greeted him. To his consternation he found that the Lane Debate had been front-page news everywhere. The

---

* Amalgamating referred to cohabiting or marrying; the term *miscegenation* would not come into use until much later.

other Presidents expressed concern that the abolitionist societies now sprouting up on their own campuses could create the same turmoil as had occurred at Lane.

They met and resolved that "the times imperiously demanded that all antislavery agitation should be suppressed." Their resolution, to be circulated to all colleges in the country, was unanimous—Beecher had joined them.

When the resolution reached the executive committee of the Board of Trustees of Lane Seminary, they took immediate action, abolishing the student antislavery society, investing in themselves the right to censor all student activity, and summarily dismissing any student who they decided was a disruptive influence. Nor did they equivocate about the intent of their new rules: They were meant to expel Theodore Dwight Weld and put a stop to student involvement with the free blacks of Cincinnati.

When the students returned to the campus in the fall of 1834, President Beecher was still absent, avoiding the imminent conflict by lingering in the East. But the trustees had gravely underestimated Weld's influence on his fellow students. When the cholera epidemic had struck, Weld had ministered to the sick constantly, putting his own health at grave risk. That was what Jesus would have done, and Weld's classmates knew it. So when Weld was left with no choice but to leave, nearly all of them went with him.

In their wake, throughout the North a hailstorm of condemnation drummed down on Beecher and his Board of Trustees. In the months that followed, Beecher brooded on the vacated campus about the shambles of his broken dream and the fact that all of his children save Catharine seemed headed for the abolitionists' camp. Eventually he came to an unshakable conclusion: It was all the evil fruit of the Oneida revival—Finney's revival. Were not most of the students, including Weld, Oneida converts? Was not Weld originally one of Finney's "holy band"? It was Finney and his "new measure" revivals that had wrought this havoc. . . .

While Beecher brooded on the past, Weld was too busy forging the future to spend time in reflection. At last he could devote his full energy to his work as the American Anti-Slavery Society's agent in Ohio. As before, God led him to towns rather than cities, and as always, he first had to overcome the local opposition. Sometimes his welcoming committee was a seething, angry mob.

6

FIRE-STARTER

hale-oil lamps hung on either side of the front entrance, making the First Presbyterian Church the brightest attraction on Main Street on the warm midsummer's night. And people *were* attracted, a few at first, then more and more, walking quickly to be sure of a good seat. The notorious abolitionist Theodore Dwight Weld was coming to town to speak that night.

Weld had spoken there four years before, on behalf of the Temperance Society. In the process of putting the devil and Demon Rum to flight, a number of townspeople had gotten converted. But tonight the subject would be abolition, and not everyone was eager to hear what he had to say. In fact, there had been a town meeting late that afternoon to decide what to do with him when he arrived. The town's banker had reminded everyone that there were already three ex-slave families living on the other side of the tracks, and if Weld had his way, there would soon be more. Did people want a shantytown growing up there? And since ex-slaves were used to working for nothing, what would that do to the few jobs that might become available?

Resolving that no abolitionist would speak in their town, the townspeople adjourned and hurried home to get a bite of supper before gathering in the Presbyterian Church to await Weld.

At the stroke of seven, a tall, broad-shouldered man with dark, piercing eyes strode determinedly up the steps and down the center aisle of the sanctuary. His waistcoat did not match his suit, and his appearance was disheveled, but there was firm purpose in his expression as he stepped to the lectern following a hasty introduction by the local preacher.

Before he could say a word, people began shouting at him, hurling insults and even obscenities, oblivious to the fact that they were in the house of God. There was no letup, and soon they were hurling rotten vegetables along with their insults.

Weld took it all stoically, never flinching, even when an egg broke on his face. His silence only seemed to goad the townspeople further, till there was practically bedlam. But if they thought that verbal and physical garbage would drive him into departing, they were mistaken.

Some of his audience did leave, but Weld was determined to wait out the mob, even if it took hours, his face set like a flint, his demeanor steadfastly calm. That night the tumult and the shouting continued until it was too late for him to speak. Now he thundered back that he would return the next night and the next, if need be, until they allowed him to speak. As one witness described it, he continued "to plead for Constitutional liberty . . . until liberty or he was defunct."[1]

The above scene was repeated with minor variations in town after town. Usually by the second night his verbal assailants would grow lung weary, and seeing that he was determined to outlast them, they would allow him to speak.

With patience and passion he would lay out the cause to which he had devoted his life: to bring an end to the most monstrous, sustained cruelty being perpetrated on the face of the earth. His mission: to persuade these Ohio Yankees that slavery needed to be denounced as *sin*, not simply reformed, with the system left in place. His plea was for immediate emancipation, gradually accomplished, but unlike at the Lane Debates, where he was recruiting predisposed co-workers, he stopped short of relating lurid stories of cruelty done to slaves. As Weld himself noted, "However numerous or authenticated, they would be either scouted as incredible or met with the cry, 'Exception!' "[2]

He did point out that the worst horrors of slavery were "its inflictions on *mind*—its prostration of conscience . . . its destruction of personality—its death-stab into the soul of the slave."[3] And he often called on Southerners who had recently moved to Ohio to confirm the dark side of slavery. In format and fervor his meetings closely resembled revival meetings, the highlights being when slaveholders, visiting friends or relatives in Ohio, would come under conviction and rise to confess their guilt and amend their ways.[4]

Never speaking for less than two hours, he would afterward answer questions and carry on earnest dialogue far into the night. One who heard him reported, "It may seem extravagant, but I have seen crowds of bearded men held spell-bound by his power for hours together and for twenty nights in succession."[5] For unlike some evangelists who flitted from town to town like summer butterflies visiting wildflowers, Weld never made one-night stands.

Having carefully prayed and sought God's will about where he should go, he would not leave a town until God released him. His mission might last a week, two weeks, or even longer. His patience was fathomless, for he knew how long it took to allay the widely held fear that abolition was dangerously irresponsible, and then supplant it with the inner conviction that "immediate abolition, gradually accomplished" was the only possible response for a believing Christian, and a Christian nation.

"In most places," he acknowledged, "I have lectured from six to twelve times, sometimes sixteen, twenty, and twenty-five, and once thirty times."[6]

Traveling alone and staying most often at the home of a local sympathizer,[7] he would remain until the Spirit bade him go. Then he would pray and see where God would have him go next.

Weld's speaking was eloquent and his moral courage unparalleled, but it was the fire of his conviction that his audiences found compelling. "No one," noted one observer, "not even Wendell Phillips, so moved his hearers to the cause." Weld was deemed "one of the most powerful advocates of truth and liberty the world has ever witnessed. . . . Of all the young men in the land [he was] without a compeer."[8]

In most towns the fury of the mob subsided after the initial onslaught, but Weld never knew when it might flare up again. And sometimes they threw harder missiles than eggs and tomatoes. While he was speaking in Circleville, Ohio, a large stone crashed through the window, "so well aimed," he recounted, "that it struck me on the head and for a moment stunned me." He paused for a few moments until the dizziness had ceased, "then went on and completed my lecture." Some of the men in the audience, meanwhile, had hung their cloaks up at the shattered window "so that my head could not be so easily used as a target." Typically, he shrugged the incident off, "though for a few days I had frequent turns of dizziness."[9]

Actually, the most dangerous time was likely to be *after* the meeting, when Weld would often find a mob waiting for him outside. He could usually count on a few young men to act as bodyguards, but sometimes, when the Spirit of God had called him to break ground in a new territory, there would be no one to protect him. Then he would resolutely fold his arms, meet the gaze of the leader or leaders, and start forward, trusting in the God of Moses to part the Red Sea. One time, after walking through a particularly menacing situation, Weld wrote, "The Lord restrained them; not a hair of my head was injured."[10]

In each town the time would come when Weld would ask those who had been converted to abolition to stand. His local supporters would often urge their neighbors to join them, and usually the entire audience would get to its feet. At Steubenville, when he gave the invitation, a young lawyer named Edwin M. Stanton sprang to his feet, turned to the audience, and lifted up his hands; in response they rose as a body. Often, those who had been "foremost in threats and bluster before the commencement of the course, pledged themselves to the principles of immediate abolitionism."[11]

At this point, his work completed, Weld would leave. Never did he tarry to help organize the new abolition society that would inevitably form. Nor did he try to manage it from afar, or tie its converts to himself. For he was not building a kingdom or a denomination or even a constituency. He was simply doing God's work. If God was in the evangelical abolitionist movement as Weld firmly believed, then it was God, not Weld, igniting the fires, and God would raise up local leaders to tend them. Weld's job was to carry the divine spark wherever the wind of the Spirit would blow it next.

Though he freely offered advice and counsel to anyone who wrote to him, Weld seldom knew the direct fruit of his missions. But in Jefferson, Ohio, he did. There, a young lawyer, converted in his meetings, organized a local abolition society that grew to embrace all of Ashtabula County in the Western Reserve. His name would become legendary in the annals of the antislavery movement, and he would work closely with Weld and with John Quincy Adams, when his friends sent him to Congress in 1838. Before he was finished, Joshua R. Giddings would be nicknamed the "Lion of Ashtabula."

Only once did Weld, now called "the most mobbed man in the United States,"[12] come up against a mob over which he could not prevail. In Granville, Ohio, after successive nights of rioting, the town council resolved that Weld should leave their fair city at once. He removed to St. Alban's a few miles away, where he was invited to hold forth in a brick Methodist church. Many of the good citizens of Granville came to St. Alban's by horse and buggy to hear him anyway, and were converted.

One was a lad of 16 named Joseph Tuttle. Years later, having risen to become President of Wabash College, he would recall that evening in St. Alban's: "Never have I seen an audience more excited. . . . There were times when his voice was as tender as a mother's to a dying child, and at others as fierce and loud as a winter storm. There was a quality of passion in his voice which magnetized his hearer. . . . He spoke with indescribable majesty and power—indeed, those two hours and a half that night . . . were the most soul-stirring of my life."[13]

Methodically and prayerfully Weld traveled back and forth across the State of Ohio, sowing his seeds, until by the fall of 1835 there were so many local abolitionist societies clamoring for a State antislavery society that he suggested they have a convention to form one. But where? Why not take the battle to the heart of their adversary, Zanesville, notorious for its anti-abolitionism?

To locate an appropriate site and prepare the way with lectures beforehand, Weld got there three weeks early—only to find the town shut up tight against him. As he wryly noted, he could not find "even a shanty." He removed to the town of Putnam across the Muskingum River, where he did find a hall. But when he began to lecture in it, a mob from Zanesville broke the windows and tore the gate off. When Weld finished and came out, they stoned and clubbed him, and the alarmed custodians of the hall closed it.

At this point even the bravest of men might wonder if he had truly heard God. Weld never doubted. Finding another hall, he suffered similar maltreatment until at last one night the mob listened. The next night he was given a pulpit. Then the good people of Zanesville pleaded with him to come back across the river. Sixteen nights later, hundreds rose to commit themselves to abolition. Zanesville was now the *ideal* site for the convention that founded the Ohio State Anti-Slavery Society!

Weld was not the only laborer in Ohio's abolition vineyard in 1835. Far from being discouraged at their premature departure from seminary, the Lane Rebels, as they came to be known, went forth to do battle with slavery. And it *was* war—a holy crusade, for which these young Soldiers of the Cross prepared the way as Weld had shown them. As troops might hone their blades and clean their weapons before going into combat, they cleansed their souls with daily repentance and encouraged one another.

Relentless in seeking out any darkness that might still be lurking in their own hearts, they were graced with unusual discernment and with mercy, for these men had been through the Refiner's fire: the cholera epidemic and the debate, and the mental and spiritual ordeal following their departure from Lane. They knew how to speak the truth in love, and how to receive it. In reply to a correction from Weld, young J. L. Tracy wrote: "Your kind admonition will not be lost on me. . . . I never expect to find another such friend in this world."[14]

Anyone who has ever attempted to actually *live* in daily repentance knows how hard it is. Yet its fruit of compassion is priceless when it comes to leading another to the light. So difficult to achieve, daily repentance is a practice easily broken, and without its presence as a catalyst golden zeal can transmute imperceptibly into leaden self-righteousness. In the beginning there was so much grace given to these new crusaders that repentance and forgiveness were a natural part of their daily life together, and they had hearts as pure as they fervently hoped for.

These young men were a continuing delight to the brothers Tappan, who were now anxious to provide them with the seminary they had been promised, to replace the one that had fallen so sadly short of the mark. As it happened, they did not have long or far to look.

The Spirit of God is like a flowing river: When His course is impeded (in this case by Beecher's intractable refusal to accept that abolition might be God's plan), He finds another way. In Oberlin, Ohio, the visionary clergyman John Shipherd had gathered a small colony of impoverished New England communitarians who were committed to "a life of simplicity, to special devotion to church and school, and to earnest labor in the missionary cause."[15] Their mission was the Oberlin Collegiate Institute, which Shipherd had established to train ministers and teachers for the West.

Desperately short of funds, he had gone east to seek the aid of Arthur Tappan. In Shipherd and his struggling institute the Tappans saw God's solution to the impasse at Lane. They gave him the money he needed and again approached Finney to provide the necessary spiritual leadership.

This time Finney, recovering from a bout of cholera and looking forward to working again with Weld, was ready to accept the responsibility. And this time the institution would be under the control of the faculty, not a board of trustees. The Tappans would have a say on who was hired; above all, they stipulated, "the broad ground of moral reform, in all its departments, should characterize the instruction in Oberlin."[16]

Oberlin was the first college to admit black students on an equal footing with whites, and the first to admit women on an equal footing with men. The Lane Rebels could not have asked for a more inspiring base of operations.

They needed one. For in addition to evangelizing small towns in the manner of Weld, they were also challenging the mainline denominations to examine their collective consciences regarding their official positions on slavery. And they were getting nowhere. Each denomination had its own reasons for rejecting the antislavery movement. Wanting to avoid division in their ranks, the denominations were more concerned with unity than with truth.

The abolitionists did their best. They reminded each denomination that it professed to follow the example of the early Church, where you went in love to a sinner and confronted him with his sin. But if his heart was hardened against your appeal, if he made it clear that he had no intention of repenting, then you had no choice but to expel him. The gradualism espoused by antislavery moderates had to be discarded; by sanctioning even the temporary continuance of slavery, they were compromising with evil.

Strong medicine, but the abolitionists were well aware that anything less would have no effect. As James G. Birney (who would one day become an antislavery candidate for President) put it: If the churches were to adopt such a method to agitate the slaveholder's conscience, "it would be the largest lever that could be used." And they should seriously consider it, for "nothing short of the fear of hell will make him resign his hold."[17]

Characteristic of the denominational response in 1836 was the statement of Presbyterian Charles Hodge, the influential president of Princeton Theological Seminary. "The assumption that slaveholding is itself a crime, is not only an error, but it is fraught with evil consequence. It not merely brings its advocates into conflict with the Scriptures, but it does much to retard the progress of freedom; it embitters and divides the members of the community, and distracts the Christian Church."[18]

The Dutch Reformed Church stated in its denominational journal: "Sinful as slavery is, it is not more so than a plan of emancipation might be made to be."[19]

As for the Congregational Church, Lyman Beecher had already made his views known. And now in Hartford, Horace Bushnell spoke for many when he said to the South: "This institution is yours, not ours. Take your own way of proceeding."[20]

At their General Conference of 1836, the Methodists declared that they were "decidedly opposed to modern abolitionism, and wholly disclaim any right, wish, or intention, to interfere in the civil and political relation between master and slaves as it exists in the slaveholding States of the Union."[21]

Francis Wayland, president of Brown University, spoke for the Baptists when he accused the abolitionists of fanaticism for no good purpose and stated that they had actually riveted the slaves' bonds tighter.[22]

The Catholics, Lutherans, and Episcopalians were all anti-abolitionist, and, surprisingly, so were the Quakers, who had always been in the forefront of the antislavery movement. By the 1830s the Quakers would not admit any slaveholder into membership. Yet to avoid dissension, they also refused to open their churches to speakers from the ranks of the abolitionists, who had long been impatient with the mildness and slowness of their gentle persuasion.

For the sake of unity, the leadership of the denominations chose to ignore the fact that a growing number of their members now believed that God intended slavery to end as quickly and humanely as possible. By thus putting unity before truth, they eventually brought on themselves the very thing they feared the most: division. Within a dozen years there would be a Southern Presbyterian Church, a Southern Methodist Church, a Southern Baptist Church. . . .

But perhaps most surprising was the response of Charles Finney, who felt that the abolitionists were bringing on the unthinkable. In a letter to Weld, he wrote: "Is it not true, at least, do you not fear it is, that we are in our present course going fast into a civil war? . . . Nothing is more manifest to me than that the present movement will result in this, unless your mode of abolitionizing the country will be greatly modified."[23]

As usual, Finney saw farther into the future than most men. His great hope was to see the revival expand and spread fully nationwide. Immediate emancipation would then be the natural result of enlightened repentance by the Christians of *every* region.

But to Weld and his colleagues, anything *short* of complete national revival would leave slavery in place and intact. Other solutions were now necessary.

The wheels were turning; the Watchmaker had an alternative plan.

The end of 1835 marked the end of Weld's work in Ohio. In all that time he had conducted missions in fewer than forty towns. But in each, the taproot of abolitionism had gone deep. These trees were not the product of a network of shallow feeder roots; they could withstand a whirlwind. And each tree gave seed to others. In another generation, when the whirlwind came, Ohio was a veritable forest of deep-rooted abolitionist buckeyes. And when the whirlwind eventually became a holy crusade to free the slaves, and the call came for men "to die to make men free," more came from Ohio than any other state.

God's Spirit now directed Weld east, first to western Pennsylvania, then to upstate New York. As before, whenever he was invited to major cities, he declined. He knew his mission was to smaller venues, where the people already knew one another and would work together in harmony long after he had gone.

The more effective his ministry became, the more ominous grew the violence that opposed him. His friends began to fear for his safety, even his life. But Weld soldiered on, undaunted, until in June 1836, he went to Troy in upstate New York. There the mayor, enraged at the arrival of this agitator said to favor amalgamating* the races, publicly declared that he regretted not having the power to expel Weld bodily from the city. That gave the signal. On the evening of Weld's first lecture, the town crier rang his bell up and down the streets of Troy: "All ye who are opposed to amalgamation meet in front of the courthouse!"[24]

Hardly had the lecture begun, than a huge mob stormed into the church and up the aisles to attack Weld. But their way was blocked by a band of sturdy young men equally determined that the mob should not reach

---

* Weld favored integration, not miscegenation.

him. There were shouts, blows; a full-scale riot ensued. The attackers were beaten off. Twice more they surged forward and were repulsed.

The mayor, now badly frightened by what he had instigated, called an emergency meeting of the town fathers. Together they escorted Weld from the lecture hall to his lodgings amid a shower of stones. The next day and every day thereafter, whenever Weld went outside the stones began again, and despite his bodyguards many reached their target, inflicting serious wounds.

But Weld would not be driven away. Canceling his other engagements, he let it be known that he would remain in Troy, regardless. And if God required the ultimate sacrifice, then so be it. The forces arrayed against him were only too happy to oblige, and with his imminent demise now likely, the city fathers called a halt. Having no desire to see Troy go down in history as the site of the first martyrdom for the cause of abolition, they gave him an ultimatum: Leave voluntarily or be forcibly removed.

Weld left. The moral victory may have been his, but it was won at a fearful cost. His body was covered with bruises, his health was nearly broken, and his voice would never regain its power and timbre. But in the furnace of this affliction, his spirit had been refined and tempered. And when his strength finally returned, though he could barely speak above a whisper, the power of his message was breathtaking. His last meetings, held in New York State, were the stuff of legend. Thousands were converted to the cause of immediate abolitionism, and of all the States' abolition societies, New York's would become the most powerful.

The enemy had intended to snuff Weld's candle, but God turned his efforts and used them to create a firestorm instead.

Once again the North American continent was witnessing an epic struggle between the forces of light and darkness. This battle was for the souls of men, and the enemy was no more willing to relinquish his hold than he had been two centuries earlier when the first Light of Christ broke on these shores, establishing a beachhead and struggling inland.

Now, as then, no ground would be easily taken, no victory easily gained. The battle would be won street by street, town by town. We have seen what one champion, imbued with steadfast meekness, could accomplish.

Henceforth, fighting shoulder to shoulder with Weld, would be the legendary Lane Rebels.

7

The Flood

hough the overhead lamp did not throw off much light, the green eyeshade was pulled down to the eyebrows of the narrow-shouldered man on the high stool. It was past midnight; all other offices had been dark for hours. But the publisher of the *Liberator* was oblivious to time. Hunched over the compositor's desk, his fingers flying, William Lloyd Garrison was like a man possessed. As he picked the type and packed the leading for his next front-page editorial, his compressed lips slowly formed a smile. He was imagining Southern planters on the verandahs of their big white mansions, choking on their mint juleps as they perused this latest effort.

A year after he had begun publishing, his monthly journal could claim only 53 subscribers; in two more years its subscriber base was still less than 400. Yet so incendiary were his editorials that they were widely reprinted in the North *and* the South, as examples of typical abolitionist thinking. They weren't typical, of course, but try telling that to an editor whose own mind was locked as tight as the racks of clamped type holding his reply.

Sometimes Garrison's reprint rate dropped drastically, as when he directly appealed to slaves to begin their servile insurrection: "Africa, strike for God and vengeance now!"[1] To Northern editors, that attitude was so socially irresponsible that they refused to grant his mad rantings the credibility that might come from publication. The few who ran it, did so to demonstrate the dangerous lunacy of the antislavery radicals known as abolitionists.

To Southern editors, however, Garrison personified the attitude that they suspected was secretly harbored by *all* antislavery activists. They reprinted many of his most vitriolic pieces, with the result that any distinction between Garrison's secular and Weld's evangelical abolitionism was lost on the South.

As each excerpt from the *Liberator* elicited fresh paroxysms of Southern outrage, his notoriety north of the Mason-Dixon line grew. For years no one had paid any attention to him. Now because of the South's visceral reaction to him, he was abolition's best-known spokesman—even though other antislavery leaders felt he was giving the entire movement "a vague and indefinite odium."[2]

By 1837 Theodore Dwight Weld was universally regarded by these same leaders as the spiritual helmsman of the abolitionist movement—even as Garrison gyrated ever farther from its core. The two men were a study in contrasts. From the beginning, Weld had been continually surprised that God would deem him worthy of the responsibility being thrust upon him. Garrison, on the other hand, was never satisfied that he had been given the recognition or place of honor he deserved. Possessing a low flash point, he would explode at the slightest provocation. Anyone disagreeing with him in a speech or editorial, or attempting to counsel him to consider the sensibilities of whomever he happened to be confronting—or daring to suggest that perhaps the end of abolishing slavery might not justify his means—would find himself publicly scourged in the *Liberator* and cast into outer darkness.

Gradually a term had come into use for the adamant spirit of the strident editor and his followers: Garrisonism. Its namesake was flattered by the term, for he considered Garrisonism and abolitionism synonymous; in his eyes, he *was* the movement.

In reality, the soul of the movement now resided in the hearts of Weld and the others who took their guidance from God. And now, at last, their quiet, untiring efforts were bearing fruit. When Weld had lobbied the delegates to the Presbyterian General Assembly of 1835 on behalf of immediate emancipation, he had found to his delight that fully a quarter of them were "decidedly with us on the subject of slavery."

But the converts to abolitionism were exclusively among those ministers whose lives had been touched by the revival. Not surprisingly, at the following year's conference there was a sharp division along North/South lines, with old-school Calvinists blaming abolition on new-school heretics, and Northern adherents of Finney's theology observing that bigotry and slavery went hand in hand.

Into this maelstrom rode Lyman Beecher, supremely confident that he could yet save the day. When both sides coldly ignored his plea for fusion, he departed angry and bitter—and blamed Finney and his revivals. From that moment on, Beecher became the implacable foe of abolitionism—and incredibly, an anti-revivalist.

At the annual Congregational Association, Lyman Beecher, the father of 19th-century evangelists who had once won glorious victories over Unitarianism with his own revivals, publicly recanted: "I wish to confess my sin. I was wrong. . . . The system of evangelism . . . is as if a man should sit down and attempt to eat enough to last a whole year." And once he had declared himself, all his resentment of Finney and of what had happened at Lane bubbled up: "In the church the pastor is the sun, the source of light and center of sweet influence." Disrupt this godly order of things by inviting an evangelist into the pulpit, and "we have . . . the miseries of hell."[3]

With great satisfaction Beecher discovered that at the yearly convocations of Connecticut and Massachusetts Congregational clergy, he was preaching to the converted. Already alarmed at the radical extremes of Garrisonism, his fellow clergy readily responded to his call and voted to ban *all* antislavery preachers and evangelists.[4]

Desperately the abolitionists dispatched Weld and Henry Stanton to save Maine and New Hampshire, before Beecher could close them, too. They succeeded, but great harm had already been done: In Connecticut and Massachusetts, the two States that had been the cornerstones of American constitutional liberty, the majority of clergy now concluded that where the subject was slavery, freedom of speech was too dangerous, too volatile.

Garrison could never accept that while a pastor might be strongly opposed to slavery, he might not appreciate an outsider coming into his church and condemning any parishioners who were not ready, then and there, to rush out and man the ramparts. So when the Congregational clergy of New England closed their doors to Garrisonism, the editor of the *Liberator* called on the abolitionist minorities in their congregations to open their doors and their pulpits *anyway*. If pastor or church expressed their unwillingness to do so, then "the wishes of pastor and church are to be disregarded."[5]

As various denominations failed to live up to Garrison's standards, he consigned them to oblivion. The Methodist Church was "a cage of unclean birds and a synagogue of Satan"; the Presbyterian Church was anathema; the Congregational clergy stood at the head of "the most implacable foes of God and man" toward whom "the most intense abhorrence should fill the breast of every disciple of Christ."[6]

Eventually Garrison decided that *all* clergy were corrupt, including those who made up two-thirds of the delegates to his own New England Anti-Slavery Society in 1835. They were, all of them, "blind leaders of the blind, dumb dogs that cannot bark, spiritual popes that . . . love the fleece better than the flock."[7]

Thus did he remove himself from effective leadership in the antislavery movement, and thus did he alienate many who had been predisposed to become involved in the antislavery crusade. Garrisonism rapidly polarized the undecided, tarring the entire abolitionist movement with its brush, and making the task of Weld and his colleagues immeasurably more difficult.

The antislavery movement was now in crisis. Immediate emancipation gradually accomplished may have eclipsed colonization, but the question of what exactly was meant by *immediate* was dividing the abolitionists. Were the slaves actually going to be set free? Or was it merely "the substitution of one kind of slavery for another"? Were they "gradualists in fact though immediatists in language, liable to all the absurdity of 'immediate emancipation—fifty years hence'"?

To abruptly free one's slaves without regard to the consequences or the mitigating circumstances of each case was "nothing less than insanity." Yet to admit that immediatism was simply "gradualism by another name" was to identify it with the failed previous approach, which had been "in favor of present slavery but opposed to future slavery," of "abolishing slavery by not trying to abolish it," and of "abolition never begun and never finished."[8]

The Lane Rebels' understanding of immediatism—that the process of manumission be begun at once and determinedly carried forward with Christian love, preparation, and compassion for those being freed—was a hard sell. It often took even Weld more than a fortnight to bring a few dozen people—Northern people—into the fold. Certainly it could never be accomplished secondhand, by tract or pamphlet—and until now pamphleteering had been the main outreach of the antislavery societies. Literally millions of tracts had been disseminated all over the country, and especially into the South.

The plan had been to appeal to the consciences of slaveholders, but the general tone of the pamphlets was so accusatory that it generated little conviction and enormous resentment. There are very few recorded instances of conversion by pamphlet among Southern slaveholders, and as the Lane Rebels' insistence that slavery was sin gained acceptance as abolitionist doctrine, hope of persuading the South to voluntary emancipation dwindled.

Indeed, the South, now accused of knowingly persisting in sinful behavior, angrily rallied its own Biblical scholars to prove that the Word of God *condoned* slavery.

Bushels of pamphlets were still being sent south, but without any central control—the pamphleteers were a decidedly mixed bag. Some were writers of compassion like Lundy and Weld, but far more gave vent to their frustration and allowed a tone of self-righteous judgment to creep into their prose. The response they evoked was hardly surprising: When someone who has never met you and knows nothing of your life condemns you as a sinner and sentences you to everlasting damnation, you are hardly likely to nod in agreement as you read his harangue.

When Garrison and his ilk began urging slaves to rise up and slay their masters, the promulgation of such material became a criminal offense in the South—as did teaching slaves to read. In July of 1835, the Charleston post office was broken into, and crates of such pamphlets were taken out and burned, while elsewhere throughout the South postmasters simply ignored the sacks of pamphlets that were arriving—especially after the Postmaster General in Washington had hinted that this one category of printed matter might be treated with less than the customary respect due the Federal mails.

Southern reaction to the pamphlets was extreme. A rally in East Feliciana, Louisiana, pledged a reward of $30,000 to anyone delivering Arthur Tappan to a New Orleans wharf. A Virginia grand jury indicted the entire executive committee of the American Anti-Slavery Society. Southerners boycotted Arthur Tappan's goods on sale in their stores.[9]

The Northern response was only slightly less heated. In Philadelphia, a mob discovered masses of abolitionist literature waiting on a wharf to be shipped south and dumped them into the Delaware River. Likewise, when James Birney fled the South and started publishing *The Philanthropist* in Cincinnati, his press wound up at the bottom of the Ohio. In 1836 Lewis Tappan received a package containing a Negro ear, and Henry Stanton was physically attacked in Newport, Rhode Island. When the English abolitionist George Thompson toured America in 1835, anti-Thompson editorials precipitated riots wherever he went.

In many areas, racism was as virulent in the North as it was in the South. The Attorney General of Massachusetts declared in 1835: "Rather than [the Negro] should mingle with us in the familiar intercourse of domestic life and taint the atmosphere of our homes and firesides, I will brave my share of all responsibility of keeping him in slavery!"[10]

Throughout the North, the abolitionists were seen as radicals and social undesirables. To the anti-abolitionists they were dangerous fanatics who might succeed in nullifying the Federal Union, dislocating Northern society, and instigating rebellion and race war in the South.[11] Governor William Marcy of New York assured Southerners that these "sinister, reckless agitators" were now feeling the full brunt of social reprobation. "The powerful energy of public opinion has been brought to bear directly on this subject and has exerted and is now exerting a benign influence in repressing the fanaticism that has arisen in this section of the Union."[12]

But now, as Southern postmasters began to trash the propaganda arriving through the mails, public opinion in the North began to shift. While it was true that some abolitionists were misguided zealots, it was something else to tamper with the Federal mails. Perhaps, reasoned many Northerners, the South's whole attitude about slavery was a bit intransigent. In the single year between 1835 and 1836, the number of antislavery societies grew from 200 to 527.[13]

In their annual meeting in May of 1836, the Tappans and other leaders of the American Anti-Slavery Society faced reality: The pamphlet campaign was a dismal failure. The one bright light on their cause's entire horizon was the work of Weld and his Lane Rebels, where success was following upon success. Clearly what God was doing was grafting the antislavery movement onto the sturdy revivalist tree. Very well, they would channel all their funds and energies into expanding that effort.

Following the pattern of the original disciples whom Jesus had sent out in pairs, they would handpick 70 men, the best they could find, train them to present immediatism with compassion, and send them out in teams of two.

Accordingly Weld, assisted by Henry Stanton (the most effective abolition evangelist next to Weld himself) and John Greenleaf Whittier, began interviewing young, on-fire seminarians. Before long they had their Seventy—much to the dismay of Finney who, aware of their caliber, complained that they were needed to carry on the work of the revival.

In November of 1836, the Seventy convened in New York City and spent two weeks in the most intensive preparation. Weld lectured day and night. His friends pleaded with him not to; his voice had never fully recovered from Troy, and he was likely to do it permanent damage. Weld paid no heed, and in the end he was barely able to get out a whisper. Yet never had he spoken with greater power.

He did destroy his voice. But he counted it worth the cost, for the fire of the Holy Spirit fell on the Seventy in a way that changed their lives forever. Every one of them sensed that they were being prepared for service that would "result in consequences of the greatest moment to our country, to humanity, and to religion."[14]

Under Weld's direction their effort would be vertical, not horizontal. Instead of fanning out to break new ground, the 35 teams went mostly back to the rural towns and hamlets of Ohio, Pennsylvania, and New York, where Weld had already turned the earth. Instead of feeder roots rapidly going out, the taproot would go deeper. In the storm that was coming, this tree would not go down.

Each pair might convince only a handful. But these few would dedicate the rest of their lives to the cause, forming a local abolition society and convincing others, who would make the same commitment and convince even more. . . .

With public speaking (and therefore missions) now impossible for Weld, he threw himself into the work of the central office in New York. Abolitionists who had feared for his health were moved "to praise God that his usefulness was turned to another channel."[15]

There was much to be done, more than Weld could cope with. But the Watchmaker had foreseen this; meshing gears now brought Stanton and Whittier, Weld's ablest associates, to New York to join him. On his part, Weld refused a salary or even a title, billing the society only for his food and his plain clothes. As always, he led by his example, and no one working closely with him could fail to be moved.

In addition to supporting the Seventy in the field, it was becoming apparent that something would have to be done about the growing number of petitions going to Congress. Local antislavery societies were sending them to Senators and Congressmen totally unsympathetic to their cause, with the result that many were going into the trash without ever being seen, let alone presented. And once again, freelancers with their own axes to grind were drafting petitions that contained the same raging condemnations as the worst pamphlets. This only succeeded in alienating *everyone*, including the small handful of Congressmen willing to help the cause.

Petitions would have to be handled differently. At the annual May convention in 1837, the American Anti-Slavery Society decided that no longer could the petitioning be entrusted to local organizations. There would be a national petition campaign, controlled and coordinated by the head office in New York. The petitions would be composed there, and copies with blank spaces ready for signatures would then be printed and distributed to the local antislavery societies. Thanks largely to the spade work of Weld and the Seventy, there were now more than 1,000 of these societies, with a combined membership of more than 100,000.[16]

This vast army of men and women, going out in pairs after the example of the Seventy, would then canvas every hamlet and township, gathering signatures. Affixed to each petition were Weld's stirring marching orders: "Let petitions be circulated wherever signers can be got. Neglect no one. Follow the farmer to his field, the wood-chopper to the forest. Hail the shop-keeper behind his counter; call the clerk from his desk; stop the wagoner with his team; forget not the matron, ask for her daughter. Let no frown deter, no repulses baffle. Explain, discuss, argue, persuade."[17]

Typical of the tone and tenor of these new petitions was one written by Weld for the female residents of Cuyahoga County in Ohio (or any other county).

Fathers & Rulers of our Country, Suffer us, we pray you, with the sympathies which we are constrained to feel as wives, as mothers, and as daughters, to plead with you on behalf of a long-oppressed and deeply-injured call of native Americans, residing in that portion of our country which is under your exclusive control. [This referred to the District of Columbia, the one place not under the authority of a specific state.]

We should poorly estimate the virtues which ought ever to distinguish your honorable body, could we anticipate any other than a favorable hearing when our appeal is to men, to philanthropists, to patriots, to the legislators and guardians of a Christian people. . . .

We solemnly propose, the grace of God assisting, to importune high Heaven with prayer, and our national Legislature with appeals, until this Christian people abjure forever a traffic in the souls of men. . . . In the name of humanity, justice, equal rights and impartial law, our country's weal, and her cherished hopes we earnestly implore for this our humble petition, your favorable regard. . . .[18]

Though what it was asking for was undoubtedly vexing to slaveholders, the reader would be forced to agree that the attitude of the appeal could hardly be farther from "incendiary."

Thousands of women in Ohio, Pennsylvania, and New York felt they could put their signatures to such a document. And now, for the first time in America's political history, women worked alongside men, carrying equal responsibility, to achieve a common national goal. When the national society's funds ran dry in 1838 (the brothers Tappan were finally tapped out, ruined in the financial crash of 1837), and it could no longer afford to pay the Seventy, the work did not falter. Volunteers took up the burden and actually increased the pace. And the large majority of these were women, just as the majority of petitions received by Congress were sent by groups of women.[19] Among the petition circulators were Susan B. Anthony (just 16 years old at the time), Elizabeth Cady (Henry Stanton's fiancée), Angelina Grimké (Weld's fiancée) and her sister Sarah, Lydia Maria Child, and Lucretia Mott. As they appealed for the free and equal treatment of slaves, their hearts were quickened to the need for another appeal—women's suffrage—that would one day have to be made.

They went everywhere—to church socials and country fairs, to general stores and livery stables, to school picnics and camp meetings.* Never before had door-to-door, face-to-face canvassing been attempted on a national scale, and the results were staggering. When the rate of petitions reached the flood stage, they were arriving by the wagon load at the Capitol, where they were stacked in every available hall, corridor, and antechamber. A conservative estimate has put the number of signatories (each confirmed as an actual resident) at more than a million—in a nation whose entire population numbered only 13 million! Gilbert Barnes has called it "the greatest project in propaganda that had ever been conceived in our history."[20]

But with the success of the petition campaign, the antislavery movement had become politicized. The Great Revival had run its course, and no longer were Northern antislavery activists attempting to bring slaveholders to repentance. The battle was shifting to the seat of Government, and now regrettably the sinner was coming to be hated as much as his sin. Conditions were ripe for a fresh round of violence.

On the night of November 7, 1837, in the little Illinois town of Alton, across the Mississippi River from St. Louis, a liquored-up mob arrived at the offices of *The Observer*, an abolitionist newspaper published and edited by the Reverend Elijah P. Lovejoy. This was not their first visit; indeed, three times before they had destroyed his printing press—or thought they had. But each time Lovejoy had repaired it or brought in new machinery and was able to get a paper out. Four days earlier, he had declared to his fellow townspeople: "I shall not flee from Alton. . . . The deepest of all disgrace would be, at a time like this, to deny my Master by forsaking His cause."[21]

This time the mob made certain there would be no further editions of *The Observer* rising from the ashes. They attacked the building with musketry, forcing their way in. In the ensuing melee, Elijah Lovejoy was shot dead.

It was a shot heard in every village and town in America. And it awakened millions. People who had heretofore been indifferent got off the fence. And many who had rebuffed petitioners now readily signed every document presented to them.

---

* It should be remembered that they were operating without benefit of telephones or automobiles, copying, fax, or mass-mailing machines.

8

DESK 203

The shadowy chamber of the House of Representatives was still and cold. At the request of the solitary figure at Desk 203, the keeper of the House had lit a fire in the stove, but it would be another half-hour before it made the hall comfortable, another hour before the rest of the new Congress assembled.

With the wool scarf Louisa had knitted him wrapped around his neck, John Quincy Adams opened the newspaper that the House keeper had kindly left with him. There was barely enough of the dawn's early light filtering in through the tall windows to read by, but it was sufficient. At his right elbow was the stack of petitions he would attempt to present that morning, for the second Monday in December, 1837, was Petition Day. Another string-wrapped bundle lay at his feet. He would review them all, but first he would see what was happening in the world.

As he read a eulogy for the murdered Elijah Lovejoy, he shook his head. *The first American martyr to the four freedoms,** he thought, and wondered if he might be the next. It was not beyond the realm of possibility. For during the previous recess, something had happened that had changed John Quincy Adams from a silent observer of the antislavery struggle to its outspoken champion. Quite without intending to, he had become personally involved.

He thought back to that pleasant early morning breakfast six weeks before. Congress had adjourned for the fall recess, and he was enjoying the luxury of not having to go to the House by taking breakfast with his

---

* Freedom of speech, of debate, of petition, and of the press—listed in the First Amendment to the Constitution.

brother-in-law, Nathaniel Frye. The nice thing about breakfasting with Nathaniel was that they both preferred reading the paper to carrying on conversation.

As he perused the front page of the *National Intelligencer*, his eye was drawn to a small ad: A slave named Dorcas Allen was up for sale, along with her two daughters. "Apparently," Adams noted aloud, "the woman Dorcas had recently killed two of her other, younger children but had been acquitted by reason of temporary insanity. . . ." He peered at Nathaniel over the paper. "Are you familiar with the case?"

His brother-in-law hesitated. He had lived in Washington for some time, running the family's little grist mill up on Rock Creek, and had become accustomed to the ways of slavery. And he knew JQA, who was quite capable of stirring up a row that could be bad for the mill's business.

"Well?" prompted Adams, sensing he was delaying.

Reluctantly Nathaniel told him the story. Fifteen years before, Dorcas had been granted her freedom by her dying mistress and had married Nathan Allen, a waiter in one of Washington's hotels. They had raised four children and were living a quiet life, when one day while her husband was at work, two white men came and seized her and her children. It seemed that her late mistress had neglected to give her a certificate of manumission, and poor Dorcas had no way of proving that she had been freed. Her late mistress's husband, of course, knew the truth, but he had remarried without bothering to formally emancipate Dorcas and had then died. His widow, in turn, had also remarried, and it was her new husband who had taken advantage of the oversight and sold Dorcas and her children to local slavers.

Thrown into slave prison until they could be resold and facing the prospect of having her children taken from her, Dorcas had gone mad. Somehow she had gotten a knife, intending to kill all of them and then herself. She had dispatched the first two, when the guards discovered what she was doing and stopped her.

"John," concluded Nathaniel, "you mustn't get involved in this. It's one thing to present abolition petitions in Congress; it's quite another for a Northerner to get entangled in a slave's plight down here." He paused. "I'm not thinking of the mill; I'm thinking of your physical safety—and Louisa's. You're not up in Quincy now."

But Adams would not be dissuaded. As he recorded in his journal that evening, "It is a case of conscience with me, whether my duty requires or forbids me to pursue the enquiry in this case—to ascertain the facts and expose them in all their turpitude to the world."

At the same time he remained uncommonly shrewd at assessing the antislavery sentiment of the North. Support for the abolitionists was growing and beginning to coalesce—but it was still far too soon to test that ice. If he acted prematurely, he risked alienating his Massachusetts constituency. "One step further, and I hazard my own standing and influence there . . . and the cause of liberty itself."

And yet that cause drew him irresistibly. Moreover, he saw no one else to advance the banner: "Were there in the House one member capable of taking the lead in this cause of universal emancipation . . . I would withdraw from the contest." He would have preferred to do so, for he could foresee that the contest would "rage with increasing fury as it draws to its crisis," and in light of "my age, my infirmities and my approaching end," he considered himself totally disqualified. Yet—"there is no such man in the House."[1]

After much prayer, and sensing that his involvement in the Allen case would forever alter his stance in the House, Adams decided that God would have him pursue the matter.

He went first to the office of the *National Intelligencer*, where the editor, suspecting the nature of Adams' enquiry and what he might do with whatever information he could obtain, was as reluctant as Nathaniel Frye had been. Nonetheless, Adams ascertained that the district attorney in the case was none other than the author of the national anthem, Francis Scott Key. Calling at Key's office, he was informed that all was perfectly legal. But then Key did offer a ray of hope: Dorcas Allen's husband, Nathan, could buy back his family; in fact, a local retired general was trying to help the waiter raise the necessary funds.

Following up this lead, Adams next consulted with the general, and then to find out exactly how much was likely to be involved, called on the slave auctioneer who had bought Dorcas and her children. The latter, cowed by the intervention of the former President of the United States, agreed to let them go at his cost: $475. The most the general could manage was $330. Adams himself could help very little; he had lost what little he had in the financial panic and collapse that had devastated the country earlier that year. He was reduced to living on his Congressional salary. Even so, by stretching his resources to the limit he was able to pledge $50—more than he made in a week.

They were still nearly $100 short. At the last moment, God stirred other hearts, and the Allen family was joyfully and tearfully reunited.

Adams was deeply satisfied. Yet, however private his action may have been (and few knew of his involvement), he had become an activist.

John Quincy Adams smiled now at the memory. Well, as his British cousins were fond of saying, in for a penny, in for a pound. He was 70 years old now and a bit creaky, but he loved a good political fight, and this was certainly the best he had ever been in.

For more than a year he had been battling the imposition of the Pinckney Gag Rule and was determined to carry on until the gag was repealed, even if it meant dying here at his desk—which would not be such a bad end, come to think of it.

It had been a lonely struggle. The only other member of the House sympathetic to the antislavery movement was William Slade of Vermont. He, too, had attempted to present antislavery petitions, but up in New York, Weld and his associates were now directing the bulk of them to Desk 203.

It would be another year before Joshua Giddings of Ohio would arrive to help; until he did, JQA bore the brunt of the burden alone. Publicly he still refrained from attacking the South's "peculiar institution," condoned as it was by the Constitution. His oft-stated position was that he was merely fighting to reinstate freedom of petition. But privately he saw the two causes becoming inextricably combined. Like it or not, the South would soon be openly and everywhere confronted with the issue of slavery, from which she could never again turn away.

"The conflict between the principle of liberty and the fact of slavery is coming gradually to an issue," he noted in his diary. "Slavery has now the power, and falls into convulsions at the approach of freedom. That the fall of slavery is predetermined in the counsels of Omnipotence I cannot doubt; it is a part of the great moral improvement in the condition of man, attested by all the records of history. But," he concluded ominously, "the conflict will be terrible, and the progress of improvement will retrograde before its final progress to consummation."[2]

It proved to be a hard year. With the decline and ultimate demise of Garrison's antislavery society, active leadership of the movement devolved to the broad shoulders of John Quincy Adams. He had not sought the responsibility, but "with a sacred sense of duty" he accepted it as another assignment that God had set before him.[3] His constituency now stretched far beyond the district of Plymouth; in spirit he represented all antislavery activists throughout the North.

While the abolitionists might have been delighted with him, the same could hardly be said of his colleagues. Never had one Congressman been so loathed by so many others; even his Northern allies were growing weary of his pertinacity. And just as he himself was beginning to weary of the unbroken diet of slander and abuse being heaped upon his plate, William Lloyd Garrison, self-styled national spokesman for abolition, attacked him for refusing to condemn the Constitution, which Garrison now labeled "a covenant with death and an agreement with hell!"[4]

The disapprobation of Adams' Southern colleagues was mild compared to the anonymous death threats now sprinkled among the petitions, threats vowing to slit "your throat from ear to ear," or "cut out your . . . guts," or "shoot you down in the street."[5]

Finally, in January of 1839, JQA decided it was time to declare himself on the subject of the abolition of slavery in the District of Columbia. "I have received a mass of letters threatening to assassinate me for my course. My real position has never been understood by the country. I wish distinctly to aver that, though I have earnestly advocated the right of persons to petition for the abolition of slavery in the District of Columbia, I myself am not prepared to grant their prayer."[6]

What? Was the presumed Congressional leader of the abolitionist movement forsaking the cause? The statement made headlines, North and South. In private, to his friend and fellow Whig Charles Kirkland, Adams explained that while he was wholeheartedly in favor of the eventual emancipation of the Negro and would exert all his influence to bring about the abolition of slave traffic within the District, a motion to immediately abolish slavery there would be outvoted four to one. To attempt it would be the sheerest folly.

Besides, he maintained that the immediate battle was over civil liberty, not slavery, and on that ground the antislavery petitions were invaluable. If they just kept shaking that limb, eventually the whole tree would come down. Slavery *was* vulnerable.

And as if to prove he had not gone soft on slavery, a few days later he demonstrated why he was now referred to as "the genius of the antislavery cause."[7] He proposed a three-part amendment to the Constitution:

1. Henceforth, from July 4, 1842, every child born in the United States or under its jurisdiction, regardless of color or antecedents, shall be born free.
2. Henceforth, with the exception of the territory of Florida, no state whose constitution tolerates slavery shall be admitted to the Union.
3. Henceforth, from July 4, 1845, there shall be neither slavery nor slave trade at the seat of the Government of the United States.

As anticipated, the storm of objections from the slaveholding bloc was instantaneous. As anticipated, the resolutions were never brought to a vote. No matter: From that time on, John Quincy Adams' position on slavery was a matter of public record. And just so there could be no misinterpretation, he amplified his position in two *long* letters* addressed "To the Citizens of the United States, whose petitions, memorials, and remonstrances have been intrusted to me." These were (with a little arm twisting) duly published by the *National Intelligencer* and picked up by the *Niles Register*, which gave them, in effect, national distribution.

In them, Adams explained that the immediate abolition of slavery in the District of Columbia was "utterly impractical. . . . Public opinion throughout the Union is against it." (After a lifetime in public office, he had learned that one did not move in an unpopular direction, unless there was at least some prospect of shifting public opinion.)

Now putting his own stamp on the antislavery movement, he once and for all did away with the confusing doctrine of immediatism, asking its proponents bluntly: "Have you converted many to the true faith of immediate emancipation without indemnity?" Their having made immediatism the test of abolitionist orthodoxy was self-defeating, "a moral and physical impossibility" that only made the abolitionist cause "unpopular and odious, not only in the South, but in all parts of the Union."[8]

His assessment of the abolitionist movement was sobering—and accurate: "The abolitionists are yet a small and, I lament to say, a most unjustly

---

* Letters of 10,500 and 14,000 words respectively, but who's counting.

persecuted party in all the free States. It is their martyr age." Nevertheless, he could foresee the day when slavery would be abolished throughout the country, "either by force, that is by civil war, or the consent of the owners of the slaves."[9]

His remarks heartened antislavery forces everywhere—except at the movement's headquarters, where his refusal to endorse immediatism was met with resentment. But the Garrisonites had lost more than funding; thanks to Adams' letters, they had now lost what was left of their dwindling influence over state and local societies.

At 71, Adams, though not an abolitionist himself, had nonetheless become the *de facto* leader of the antislavery movement in America. As always, he remained a loner, keeping his distance from the abolitionists. Wrote Giddings in his diary: "Adams consults with no one, takes the advice of no one, and holds himself accountable to no one but the nation."[10]

Adams sensed that in time he *would* join their ranks. But that time was not yet. At present, his effectiveness would be greater if he was generally perceived to *not* be an abolitionist. It was difficult. In his journal he observed, "The abolitionists generally are constantly urging me to indiscreet movements which would ruin me and weaken and not strengthen their cause. . . . I walk on the edge of the precipice in every step that I take."[11]

In the meantime, he sought to shift the antislavery movement's focus from conversion of recalcitrant slaveholders to halting the spread of slavery. No further slaveholding Territories should be admitted to the Union, he insisted, and the Republic of Texas, which he was convinced would be immediately carved into five or more slave States, should not be annexed.

With remarkable prescience he foresaw that slavery's repeated violations of America's civil liberties would be the next great battleground, that slavery could be constitutionally ended under the War Powers Act, and that one day there *would* be an amendment to the Constitution terminating slavery with the Union intact.

And then, in the summer of 1839, a gripping drama unfolded that arrested the attention of the nation, stoked the fire under the cauldron of slavery, and firmly ensconced John Quincy Adams as *the* hero of the antislavery movement.

9

SOUNDING FORTH THE TRUMPET

A low moon ghosted behind thin clouds as the black-hulled schooner weighed anchor and slipped out of Havana's harbor under cover of darkness. Harbor officials had been bribed to look the other way, for in her hold was a cargo of contraband: 53 Mendi tribesmen, freshly taken from Africa's Sierra Leone. The international slave trade had been outlawed for a generation, but so great was the need for slaves on Cuba's vast sugar plantations that planters were willing to make it worth a slave runner's while to take any risk.

In this instance, there was one risk they hadn't counted on, for the men chained below were not the usual captives whose spirits were easily broken. These 53 happened to be fierce warriors, prepared to die to regain their freedom. While the captain of the *Amistad* and the two Spanish planters who had hired him were congratulating themselves on how smoothly their departure had gone, one warrior below managed to get free and release his comrades. The tribesmen took over the ship, killing all the whites save the two Spanish planters. Using sign language they would force these two to take them back to Sierra Leone.

The Mendi knew nothing of navigation, but they knew their home lay to the east. As long as the sun was up the Spaniards steered the *Amistad* (whose name meant "Friendship") in that direction. But as soon as it got dark, or whenever it was overcast or foggy, the Spaniards gradually reversed course. For two months they zigzagged back and forth across the North Atlantic. Eventually in Long Island Sound they were challenged by an American coastal survey brig. The Spaniards, who could speak English, explained what had happened, and the *Amistad* was taken captive.

The case became an instant *cause celebre*: Were the Mendi the property of those who had bought them and therefore murderers? Or were they, since there were no laws governing slave "property" on the high seas, free men who had killed in self-defense as they struggled to regain their freedom?

The Van Buren administration was prepared to extradite them to Havana for trial as mutineers if so requested, but William Jay* argued that they should be regarded as heroes, not criminals, and should be defended.

The case attracted worldwide attention. It also attracted the attention of John Quincy Adams, then enjoying Congress's summer recess. He had promised Louisa that he would do nothing but rest and regain his strength for the fall session, but as in the case of Dorcas Allen, JQA could not resist becoming increasingly involved. Inevitably, he wound up masterminding the Mendi's defense.

After a year of appeals, the *Amistad* case went up to the Supreme Court. But who should speak for the Mendi before that august bench? The best courtroom lawyer in the country was Daniel Webster. But he was also the most expensive, and Lewis Tappan no longer had the wherewithal to help in that department. All eyes turned to Adams. He was too old, he told his friends, too inefficient. He had not done trial work in 30 years, and he had an election coming up in two weeks.

His friends merely reminded him that the lives of 53 men literally hung in the balance.

Abruptly, to everyone's surprise (including perhaps his own), Adams heard himself saying, "If, by the blessing of God, my health and strength shall permit, I will argue the case before the Supreme Court."[1]

Privately he was worried. What if, in the heat of debate, he were to lose his temper, as seemed to be happening with increasing frequency? "I implore the mercy of God," he wrote in his diary, "so to control my temper, to enlighten my soul, and to give me utterance, that I may prove myself in every respect equal to the task."[2]

When his day in court came, Adams was brilliant, once again "Old Man Eloquent." He began by telling the eight men gazing down on him that he derived "consolation from the thought that *this* is a court of *justice*." And

---

* Son of the first Chief Justice, John Jay, William had helped to found the American Bible Society.

then, without meaning to be sarcastic, for he truly did not want to prick the slaveholding interests on the bench above him, he reminded them of the definition of justice: "the constant and perpetual will to secure to everyone his own right."[3]

Taking more than four hours, he laid out the Mendi's case in careful, logical progression. Then he ranged far beyond, into the ramifications of the decision that the justices would render. "I know of no other law that reaches the case of my clients," he concluded, "except that law"—he pointed to a copy of the Declaration of Independence displayed in the courtroom—"the law of Nature and of Nature's God, on which our fathers placed our own national existence."[4]

"Extraordinary!" exclaimed Justice Joseph Story in a letter to his wife that evening. "Extraordinary, I say, for its power and its bitter sarcasm. . . ."[5]

Adams won. The Mendi were freed. The abolitionist press went delirious.

But at Desk 203, grim reality soon reasserted itself. On January 28, 1840, William Cost Johnson of Maryland requested an amendment making the gag permanent, *a standing rule of the House*, rather than a resolution that had to be annually renewed. Moreover, it would be tightened: No petition or memorial praying for abolition "shall be *received* by the House, or entertained in any way whatever."[6]

The Johnson amendment passed, but by a narrower margin than ever before—a mere six votes. When the gag had first been imposed in the spring of 1836, the number of Free-State Congressmen voting for it had been 64. When it was renewed the following year, that number had fallen to 51. The next year it was 49, and the next, 28.[7]

Clearly the momentum was shifting. More and more people were recognizing Adams' fight for what it was, a struggle to regain a Constitutionally guaranteed freedom. The abolitionist caucus was determined to catch the turning tide. In addition to Adams, Slade, and Giddings, their number now included Weld convert Seth Gates of New York, Sherlock Andrews of Ohio, and Francis James of Pennsylvania. With the exception of Adams, they all resided at Mrs. Spriggs' boarding house ("Abolition House," as it came to be known) and were all loyal Whigs. But their party was in trouble, struggling for relevance, and its leaders, fearing a North/South split that would shatter the party, had insisted that economic measures, *not* slavery, should be their main concern. Reluctantly the abolitionist Whigs had conformed to the party line.

But the time for conforming was over. They decided that from now on, instead of reacting to each new move of the proslavery forces, they would go over onto the offensive. They announced that "they were determined to carry the war in upon the enemy—to shift the plan of campaign, and attack slavery at every point."[8]

In December of 1841, a new boarder arrived: Theodore Dwight Weld. He had come because these Congressmen, whose speeches were reprinted by newspapers throughout the North, were "in a position to do for the [antislavery] cause by a single speech more than our best lecturers can do in a year."[9]

When he was introduced to Adams, the latter asked, "Are you Mr. Theodore D. Weld?" When Weld nodded, Adams warmly shook his hand. "I know you well, sir, by your writings."[10]

He invited Weld to a dinner party that he and Louisa were giving for his antislavery colleagues. "It was a true abolition gathering," wrote Weld enthusiastically to the Grimké sisters, "and the old patriarch talked with as much energy and zeal as a Methodist at a camp meeting. Remarkable man!"[11] And clearly no longer the lone eagle.

Weld soon became invaluable to Adams, researching all day in the Library of Congress for the points Adams needed for the following day, and in the evenings helping him plan his attack. Weld thought so much like Adams that he could anticipate his needs even before the elder statesman expressed them. Weld's comments on the gag rule, for example, sounded like those of Adams himself: "The right of petition [has been] ravished and trampled by its Constitutional guardians, and insult and defiance hurled in the face of the sovereign people."[12]

The two became quite close. In all his life, Adams had never had a trusted friend he could rely on, and as for the younger Weld, he idolized his mentor, as his letters to his wife, Angelina, made clear.

With his own forces coalescing, and his enemies now including members of his own party, Adams thrust forward into the salient. The perfect opening soon came in the form of a petition sent to him from Georgia, requesting the removal of John Quincy Adams as chairman of the Foreign Relations Committee because of his monomania where race was concerned. In all likelihood it was a hoax, meant to irritate him. But Adams had a penchant for turning hoaxes to advantage. He introduced the petition, then requested the opportunity to defend himself. The Speaker of the House granted it.

In his defense Adams attacked every conceivable aspect of slavery—to the teeth-clenching consternation of Southern members. He had done it again! He had adroitly maneuvered around the Pinckney Gag Rule.

Weld was present and described the scene in a letter to his wife. "Old Nestor lifted up his voice like a trumpet, till slaveholding, slave trading, and slave breeding absolutely quailed and howled under the dissecting knife."[13]

Pandemonium raged until the gentleman from Massachusetts was gaveled down for being out of order. But the points had been made; as Weld so aptly put it, John Quincy Adams had sounded forth the trumpet that would never call retreat. It was the first blast of many, and before Adams lowered his trumpet, it would be joined by others. Their combined fanfare would herald the last act in the tragedy of the Slavocracy in America.

The Whig leadership was furious. Adams had once again ignored their directive and put his battle against the gag rule ahead of the party's legislative agenda. This time, they decided, they would discipline him themselves. All they needed was the right opportunity, ideally one having nothing to do with slavery.

Adams gave it to them with his very next petition, from 46 citizens of Haverhill, Massachusetts, who prayed that the members of Congress would "immediately adopt measures peaceably to dissolve the Union of these States."[14]

Uproar! Henry Wise of Virginia asked the Speaker if a move to censure was in order. Thomas Gilmer of Virginia immediately made such a motion. Adams demanded the opportunity to defend himself before the vote for censure be taken. The Speaker adjourned the House.

That night both camps rallied around their leaders. The Whig leadership, North and South, planned their strategy for the following day, while at Abolition House it was decided that Weld and the journalist Joshua Leavitt should go to Adams and offer assistance in the preparation of his defense. According to Giddings, "the aged statesman listened attentively, but for a time was unable to reply, laboring under great apparent feeling. At length he stated that the voice of friendship was so unusual in his ears, that he could not express his gratitude."[15]

When the proceedings resumed the following day, the lodgers at Abolition House voted to lay the censure motion on the table, as did other cooler heads who felt it unworthy of serious consideration. But JQA voted on the *other* side, along with Wise and Gilmer and Marshall, and the Southern "fire-eaters."* For this was a contest much to his liking—an opportunity, even better than before, to fully air the case against slavery—and he would not be denied his day in court. And so, the motion carried. The routine business of the House was suspended, and the "trial" of John Quincy Adams began.

From the outset, the Whigs handled the prosecution, as it were, while the Democrats remained silent, content to let them deal with their insurgent. A new Whig member, young Thomas Marshall of Kentucky, nephew of the great Chief Justice John Marshall and heretofore not associated with the slaveholding faction, would be their point man. Professing shock that a patriot with such a distinguished service record should submit such a petition, he requested that the grievance warranting censure should be raised to high treason. Adams "might well be held to merit expulsion," Marshall concluded, "but in grace and mercy they only inflict upon him their severest censure for conduct so utterly unworthy of his past relations to the state. . . . For the rest, they turn him over to his own conscience and the indignation of all true American citizens."† 16

When Adams rose to make his opening remarks and define what would be the nature of his defense, a hush fell over the hall. Announcing that he would need at least a week, he requested that the clerk of the House read the Declaration of Independence, which would be the foundation of his defense. After all, it was the law of the land, he pointed out, every bit as much as the Constitution; in fact, until the Constitution was drafted, it *was* their Constitution.

The clerk read through "Whenever any form of government becomes destructive of these ends, it is the right of the people to alter or abolish it. . . . When a long train of abuses and usurpations . . . evinces a design

---

* These "fire-eaters" were so ravenous for a fight that they were reminiscent of carnival performers who appeared to eat fire.

† It was faintly ludicrous to infer that the son of John and Abigail Adams was somehow less than a true American.

to reduce them under absolute despotism, it is their right, it is their duty, to throw off such government."

Adams slammed his hand down on his desk. "Right and duty to alter and abolish it!" he repeated. "If there is a principle sacred on earth, and established by the instrument just read, it is the right of the people to alter, to change, to destroy the government if it becomes oppressive to them. There would be no such right existing, if the people had not the power, in pursuance of that right, to petition for it."[17]

That would be the essence of his defense: The Haverhill petitioners, of whose proposal he categorically disapproved, had the same right as their forefathers to petition for the redress of grievances!

The battle was joined. Henry Wise set its tone: "Words cannot express the personal loathing, dread, and contempt I feel for . . . this fiend, the inspirer and leader of all abolition." He shook his head in sorrow. "That one should so have outlived his fame . . . the last link that bound this age to the Revolutionary Fathers! . . . I thank God that the gentleman, great as he was, neither has, nor is likely to have, sufficient influence to excite a spirit of disunion throughout the land. . . . The gentleman is politically dead! Dead as Burr! Dead as Arnold!"[18]

But Adams was not quite as politically dead as Wise hoped; the whole nation was following each day's events with avid interest. Every paper in the country was covering the story, many bringing out special editions devoted to the latest-breaking developments. And once again, Adams was more attuned to the Northern mood and temperament than the other members of the House. Nearly all the Northern papers were portraying him as the doughty old underdog, the champion of the disenfranchised, the lone eagle battling to restore a lost freedom, fighting for the rights of free men everywhere.

Petitions of a different nature began arriving at the desks of Northern members—petitions demanding that they cease at once their persecution of this righteous man!

Adams made clear that *none* of the Founding Fathers, all of whom were known personally to him, had been in favor of slavery. He had been appointed to high office by a succession of Presidents and had worked closely with Washington, Jefferson, Madison, and Monroe. To a man, they abhorred slavery and shared the firm conviction that it was on its way to extinction. Until that time, it would be tolerated. If a state agreed it was legal, so be it, but it should go no further. In other words, freedom, not slavery, was the founding principle of America, the common-law right of man, and the natural, self-evident truth of God. Freedom was national; slavery was local.[19]

As *that* word went around the country, Southern members began to wish that they had never opened this Pandora's box!

With the trial continuing into its second week, the change in the Northern attitude could be tracked in the reactions of New York's former Whig mayor, diarist Philip Hone. At the outset he noted that the "former President's insane movement . . . disgusts his friends." A week later, as pro-Adams petitions poured into Washington, he revised his opinion of "that indomitable, pugnacious, wonderful man of knowledge." A few days later he was calling him "the old hero," while the New York *American*, hailing him as the torchbearer of independence, reported that he was now being called "Old '76."[20]

Soon everyone could see that the tide had turned, and incredibly Adams seemed to be growing stronger with each passing day. "The energy with which Mr. A speaks is astonishing," wrote Weld to Angelina. "Though seventy-five years old, his voice is one of the clearest and loudest in the House, and his gestures . . . are most vigorous and commanding. . . . Wonderful man!"[21]

The first crack in the Southern edifice appeared on February 5th, when a Southerner objected that Adams was discussing the forbidden subject of slavery. The Speaker ruled against the objection. Another member appealed to the House to rule on his ruling. There was a vote. The Speaker's ruling was sustained, 97 to 25. It was the first time in the history of the House of Representatives that the Slave Power, as Adams increasingly referred to it, had been defeated. That night Adams wrote in his journal: "I saw my cause was gained. . . . I came home barely able to crawl up to my chamber but with the sound of *Io triumphe* ringing in my ears."[22]

Two days later, the triumph was complete. After two weeks of non-stop proceedings, JQA said he would need at least another week to complete his defense (groans). But if the members preferred to table the motion to censure (murmurs of relieved assent), he would be satisfied. They immediately called the roll. The motion to table carried 106 to 93. He had won!

"Right is vindicated and victorious!" trumpeted the New York *American*.

"The House of Representatives have done justice to themselves at last, to the 'Old Man Eloquent', and to the Constitution!"[23]

In those days there was nothing quite so lethal as a gentleman of the South who felt his honor had been maligned. And with the Northern press jubilant at Adams' victory, there was no question that in the eyes of the Southern gentlemen of the House, they had been held up to national ridicule.

Maligned honor demanded satisfaction. But since Adams was now acclaimed as a hero, they would take their revenge on someone of less stature, whose teeth and parliamentary skills were less sharp. Someone like Giddings of Ohio . . .

Six weeks after Adams' vindication, Giddings more than obliged them when the *Creole* case came before the House. In November of the previous year, a cargo of slaves, transshipped from Newport News to New Orleans aboard the coastal vessel *Creole*, got free. As on the *Amistad*, they took over the ship, killed one of the owners, and forced the crew to take them to Nassau. There, however, the outcome was somewhat different. The British authorities tried and hanged the murderers, and set free those who were not involved. The owner whose slaves had been freed demanded compensation for them, demanded, in fact, that the United States should go to war with Great Britain, if necessary, to attain it.

Led by Weld, Abolition House had been carefully developing the doctrine which Adams had articulated: that the laws governing slavery as property applied *only* in those States that had legalized the institution. And since the South kept insisting that slavery was strictly a State, not a Federal, matter, Giddings rose and applied their own States' Rights argument to the *Creole* affair.

"Slavery, being an abridgement of the natural rights of man, can exist only by force of municipal law, and is necessarily confined to the territorial jurisdiction of the power creating it." So far, so good. But slaveholding members were apoplectic at what came next. "[When] a ship belonging to the citizens of any State of this Union leaves the waters and territory of such State and enters upon the high seas, the persons on board cease to be subject to the laws of such State. . . ."[24]

In other words, the moment the *Creole* left Virginia's territorial waters, the slaves aboard her ceased to be slaves. By the doctrine that Giddings had introduced, slaves were only "property" within the boundaries of the slave states. They could not be taken into a free state, or onto the high seas, or into the Territories. And, Giddings maintained, once a fugitive slave crossed the Ohio River, he or she could not be returned.

Slaveholding members, Whig and Democrat, were so appalled that their initial response, when they found their voices, was to scream for Giddings' immediate expulsion. His resolutions were voted down, with many Northern Whigs abstaining. Then, from his Whig colleagues, came the motion not for expulsion, but for censure. It passed, again with abstentions among his erstwhile friends. In keeping with custom, Giddings promptly resigned. As he left the floor presumably for good, he shook hands goodbye with his friends, including one who had voted against him.

There was nothing sweet in the sorrow of this parting. A bereft Adams wrote in his journal that night, "I can find no language to express my feelings at the consummation of this act."[25]

But Joshua Giddings had accomplished his purpose. The full proceedings of his censure were published nationally, and in the North people read them with new interest, awakened and piqued by the Adams affair, of which this seemed a coda. There was a gathering resentment toward the South's bullying tactics in Congress and a growing repugnance to the whole concept of the Slave Power. And among Northern Whigs there was increasing disgust with their leadership's pandering to the Southern Whigs.

There is a happy postscript to this episode. When the election was held to fill Giddings' unexpired term, his friends in the Western Reserve insisted that they wanted *him* to represent their interests in Washington, no one else. The Whig party most emphatically did not want Giddings and put up an alternate candidate, campaigning heavily for him. But the politicians had no comprehension of how deeply Weld and the other Lane Rebels had tilled this soil. These people were *proud* that their Congressman was an outspoken abolitionist! And throughout the North many fair-minded people who did not think of themselves as abolitionists, nonetheless felt that Giddings had been wrongly dealt with. William Cullen Bryant, the renowned poet and editor of the New York *Evening Post*, spoke for many when he wrote that he wished that he lived in the Western Reserve, so that he could vote to return Giddings.

Returned by the largest majority ever achieved in Congress, the Lion of Ashtabula gave immediate evidence that he had not been subdued. In his first speech back, he argued powerfully for the new doctrine of local or "municipal" jurisdiction for slaveholding law and for the right of free discussion in the House. The Whig leadership could only glower; he had proven immune to their discipline.

For the rest of 1842 and well into 1843, Weld and Adams continued to work together, the former providing the latter with case precedents every time Adams rose to make a speech.

Though the gag rule was still in effect, slavery was now being openly debated on the floor, something that had never happened before. And support for the gag itself was growing weaker; the last time Adams tested it, it was sustained by four votes. He was encouraged, but he was also deeply tired. He wondered if he would live to see the day it would be repealed. He promised Louisa that during the recess for the summer of 1843, he would spend the entire time resting. And he meant it; in his diary he wrote that he expected "to see the sunrise and to visit and study my seedling plants and listen to the matinal minstrelsy of the bobolink, the spring bird and the robin, with the chirp of the sparrow and the new whistle of the quail . . . all the aerial music of the time and place."[26]

But the town of Quincy had changed. No longer a rural retreat on a quiet road, the Adams home was now surrounded by a growing, bustling community. And Adams himself had changed—or at least the public perception of him had. For he was a hero now, the champion of the antislavery movement in America. And as public awareness of the evil of slavery and the urgent need to do something about it heightened, so did the luster of his image.

As soon as he got home, Adams was besieged with speaking invitations—to the point where he was relieved to be able to join his daughter-in-law, her father, and a few family friends on a July excursion to Niagara Falls. With the improvement of various modes of transportation in the 19th century, viewing the world's natural wonders had become a fashionable leisure-time pursuit, and Niagara Falls was one of the greatest natural wonders in North America.

The trip started off pleasantly, with Adams enthralled at the view unfolding as their train chuffed through western Massachusetts. It was haying time, and families were working in the fields, the farmers swinging long-handled scythes while their wives and children gathered the hay into little stacks—"the face of the country like the Garden of Eden," he wrote in his journal. Beyond Springfield (their first overnight), the country became "a wild region of dark forests and stupendous rocks."[27] Wilderness was not far from home in those days.

At Pittsfield they alighted and took a carriage for ten miles over a "heavy mountainous road" to Lebanon Springs, where they enjoyed the therapeutic spring-fed baths. As usual, Adams was up the next morning at four, watching the sun come up from the second-floor balcony. He noted the arrival of a horseman, who was ushered into his presence. "Sir, my name is Spellman," the horseman said, doffing his hat. "I come from Pittsfield. I heard you were here, and I came to ask if I could shake your hand."[28] They shook hands, and without another word, the man left and rode back to Pittsfield. Adams was astounded: The man had ridden 20 miles just to shake his hand! But it was only a harbinger of things to come.

They went by lake steamer to Buffalo, where "we were received by shouting multitudes at the landing."[29] A guest of the city, he was praised in a warm speech by Congressman Millard Fillmore, who was frequently interrupted with thunderous applause. The evening was topped off by a torchlight procession, and Adams went to bed thoroughly dazed. In Batavia, where their train stopped to take on wood and water, a crowd had gathered, so large that the station's platform collapsed. (Fortunately no one was seriously hurt.) They had come just to catch a glimpse of him and give him a cheer. He was nonplussed; not even his father had been the object of *cheering*.

At Rochester they were met by "an immense crowd of people shouting," a twenty-one-gun salute, and the pealing of church bells. At Canandaigua they were met by a military parade, a band, and a procession of carriages a mile long, which escorted him to the park. There, the retired postmaster, after a cannon salute and the ringing of church bells, delivered a glowing welcome which, Adams noted, "left me in amazement to enquire of myself what all this was for."[30]

None of the tour was preplanned. When a town heard that JQA was coming, they simply did everything they could, as quickly as possible, to show him how grateful they were for his long fight for right. Adams' diary reflects how completely unnerved he was by all of this. He had no problem with people hating him; that went with the territory when you were doing your duty and speaking the truths no one wanted to hear. But to be the object of public love and affection—most unsettling! More than once he was moved to tears and then embarrassed by it.

In Auburn, where all in his party were the guests of Governor William H. Seward, there was a torchlight parade of volunteer firemen. At Utica, a delegation of blacks detached themselves from the cheering crowd, and their spokesman thanked him "for your efforts in protecting the right of petition and promoting the abolition of slavery."[31] Again tears came to his eyes.

The celebrations were repeated in Herkimer, Little Falls, Schenectady, Albany—their quiet pleasure trip had turned into a triumphal tour, covered by the national press every step of the way. Suddenly, to his utter astonishment, he had become the most popular man in America! What a change from having been the most reviled! (And how God must have smiled.)

JQA arrived home exhausted but exhilarated. And when he went back to Washington to resume the good fight, he was strengthened by the prayers of thousands of friends he had never known he had.

He returned to find that under Weld's guidance and organization Abolition House had become a smoothly functioning instrument for the furtherance of God's plan. This time, when he tested the gag rule he came within three votes of overturning it. He continued to battle for the cause of abolition. Though physically weaker (in July, he had turned 77), he actually found the fight a bit easier. Many of his arch foes had departed the House, either shifting to the Senate or the Governor's mansion, retiring, or accepting ambassadorships. Gone were W. C. Johnson, Henry Laurens Pinckney, Thomas Marshall, James Henry Hammond (now Governor of South Carolina), Waddy Thompson (Minister to Mexico), and Henry Wise (Minister to Brazil).

The newcomers who had taken their desks were not as anxious to cross swords with Old Man Eloquent, and all members, North and South, were acutely aware of the enormous public support he now had behind him. Plus, the two parties were increasingly dividing along regional lines. Northern Whigs and Democrats, reflecting the mood of their constituents—and the nation—were no longer as ready to back their Southern colleagues' interests merely for the sake of maintaining party unity.

On December 3, 1844, John Quincy Adams introduced a resolution to rescind the Pinckney Gag Rule, and it carried, 108 to 80. Of the votes to repeal, 55 were cast by Northern members of the opposing Democrats.

He had won.

The battle he had waged for eight long years was over. The right of petition was restored. And for the first time in the history of Congress, a major defeat had been handed to the Slave Power in the United States.

That night in his diary he simply wrote: "Blessed, forever blessed, be the name of God."[32]

10

THE EAGLE HAS DEPARTED

Outside the tall south window, dew glistened under the first rays of sun. From the limb of an old evergreen, an oriole, down from Baltimore, saluted the dawn in his black dress uniform emblazoned with gold chevrons. In the distance a brindle cow ventured onto the Mall.

The arrival of the old milker brought a wry smile to the lone figure gazing out the window of the Oval Office, hands clasped behind him. How badly the good ladies of Washington society wanted their "city" to appear refined to foreign dignitaries from Paris and London! But with the exception of the Capitol Building and this Executive Mansion, nothing here could match the grand capitals of Europe.

They might as well face it, he thought: Washington was a raw and gritty new town of scarcely 30,000 inhabitants. Its scattering of rude-framed boarding houses, one-story dwellings, and nondescript Government buildings lined broad but unpaved avenues. On them foraged pigs and chickens, and through them meandered a foul-smelling sewage stream wryly nicknamed the Tiber. A disdainful English gentleman recently likened their pride and joy, the white stone, triple-domed structure on Capitol Hill, to a general without an army, surrounded only by "a parcel of ragged, dirty boys."[1]

For that matter, America was a raw and gritty new nation—but she was fast coming of age. And one day, sooner than her Old World aunts and uncles might imagine, her capital would fulfill the vision of its planner, Pierre L'Enfant, the gifted young French engineer who had served with Washington. In the meantime, the society doyennes would lament the day in 1783 that the capital was removed from Philadelphia's elm-shaded streets and courtly brick facades and would go on chiding the town's few constables for allowing Washington's streets to resemble a barnyard.

As the figure at the window turned to his desk, his smile vanished. On this fourth Monday in June, 1845, his usually squared-back shoulders were bent, his chest sagged. He seemed of only average height now, a spare man whose cold gray eyes and stern mouth warded off casual contact.[2] This morning the sharp, angular features were etched in sorrow.

On the gleaming desk before him lay two folders—one so full that its binding ribbon could barely contain it; the other so flat it appeared to be empty. It was the contents of the former that caused his grief. Three weeks ago, the long-suffering Andrew Jackson, bedridden at the Hermitage, his home outside Nashville, Tennessee, had gone to be with the Lord. Ten days later an express rider had arrived in Washington with the news and a long, handwritten account of the funeral on foolscap by someone who knew the President would appreciate it. It was soon followed by editorials, long-ready eulogies, and letters of condolence.

In time there would be several folders, which could not begin to contain the nation's sense of loss. With the passing of "Old Hickory," America had lost her greatest living hero, the most popular President since George Washington. Andrew Jackson had been a populist, a leader who forever saw himself as the champion of the common man, defending him against a powerful impersonal Government, against the Eastern banking establishment, against any power mongers who would take advantage of him. Somehow the people knew the first "people's President" was the genuine article, as they put it, and they trusted him.

And now the eagle had departed. The flags of Washington were already at half-mast, and on Friday the 27th, the President had called for a mile-long funeral cortege to process in solemn commemoration up Pennsylvania Avenue to the Capitol.

With a sigh, James K. Polk slowly shook his head. It was hard for him to believe the old man was gone. During the campaign, some of Polk's supporters had dubbed him "Young Hickory," and in an era when simple slogans had enormous impact, it had been a perfect fit. Not only was he at 49 the youngest President ever elected, he bore an uncanny resemblance to his mentor. Further, he espoused the General's principles to the core, and his character was a similar mix of single-minded determination and flinty integrity.

But there the likeness ended. Polk was a calculating, intensely private person, humorless and uninspiring. He was not one to order an advance, then step out in front, confident that every man who could still shoulder a rifle would fall in behind him. Nor had he the gracious, courtly charm that Jackson could summon up on intimate social occasions. Yet while he saw eye to eye with the General on practically every issue, James K. Polk was his own man—a quality not lost on the men of his district in Tennessee. They sent him to Congress for seven consecutive terms, after which the State elected him Governor.

How he came to be standing where Jackson himself had last stood eight years before was something of a fluke. For Polk was not the man whom the General had originally picked to succeed him; his Secretary of State, Martin Van Buren, was. And when the time came in 1836, the American people decided that Van Buren, nicknamed "Old Kinderhook" for his tiny hometown in upstate New York, was indeed O.K. But when it came time to reelect Van Buren in 1840, the nation was dragging through its first economic depression. Wanting a fresh face in the White House, the people turned to the Whigs' 1812 war hero, "Old Tippecanoe," William Henry Harrison, who died a month after assuming office.

Van Buren was far from finished, however, and four years later he was the odds-on favorite to win the Democratic party nomination. But he had lost his number-one supporter. Andrew Jackson, now a frail 77 and wracked with pain, was still the kingmaker of the party he had created; indeed, he *was* the Democratic Party. He soured on Van Buren when he learned that he had committed himself in print as being opposed to the annexation of Texas. Worse, Van Buren had apparently made a pact with Jackson's archrival, Whig candidate Henry Clay, not to bring up Texas during the coming campaign.

Old Hickory decided that Old Kinderhook was no longer electable. To block him, he had his people move immediately to have the party's candidate elected by a two-thirds majority, knowing that the Southern delegates would never support Van Buren. And once again he was right: Van Buren had no trouble achieving a simple majority, but a two-thirds majority was beyond his grasp. After eight ballots, the convention was deadlocked—and ready for Jackson's new man: James K. Polk, who did favor annexation (and everything else the old eagle espoused). Suddenly this "dark horse"* burst from the pack, and Young Hickory was on his way to the White House.

---

* This was the first time this expression had ever been used in politics.

Polk made his own decisions, the most difficult of which was on the single sheet of paper in the other folder on his desk. And how he would have appreciated the advice of the aptly nicknamed Sage of the Hermitage! Not that he wasn't well acquainted with the General's views on Texas. From the beginning of his military career, Jackson's primary concern had been for the nation's defense—even if the best defense was sometimes to take the offensive, as in his conquest of Spanish Florida. But now—with Britannia maneuvering to gain control of Oregon, sending agents to California, insinuating her influence in the affairs of Mexico (which still dreamed of regaining Texas), and sending feelers to the Lone Star Republic itself—Jackson saw a British noose being tightened around the neck of Western America.

The War of 1812 had been fought in large measure to discourage further British hegemony in North America, and to convince her to leave America alone. Yet it had scarcely given the British pause; only after their resounding defeat at the hands of Andrew Jackson in the Battle of New Orleans would they concede that control of the Mississippi was no longer attainable.

Now, 30 years later, they were again adventuring into the New World. In Canada, the Hudson Bay Company had made a fortune trading with Indians and *voyageurs* and was looking to make another in Oregon—and perhaps a third in California. Jackson's assessment of British aims proved astute: As long as there was unsecured territory to be had, Britannia's dreams of empire would remain undiminished.

So when Texas had applied for statehood, Jackson had written Polk: "The safety of the republic being the supreme law, and Texas having offered us the key to the safety of our country from all foreign intrigues and diplomacy, I say accept the key . . . and bolt the door at once!"[3]

The alternative was unthinkable. Were Great Britain to ally herself with the Republic of Texas (and friends in Texas confirmed that overtures *were* being made), then she could move "an army from Canada, along our western frontier," march through Arkansas and Louisiana, retake New Orleans, "excite the Negroes to insurrection . . . arouse the Indians on our west to war . . . and throw our whole west into flames that would cost oceans of blood and hundreds of millions of money to quench and reclaim."

Jackson's inescapable conclusion: "Texas must be ours; our safety requires it."

To his friend Major William Lewis, the General was even more explicit: "We must regain Texas—peaceably if we can, forcibly if we must!"

But not even Andrew Jackson could force annexation through the Senate. In April of '44 they rejected it, 35 to 16. Even so, the mood of the country was shifting; the old eagle could sense it. It was only a matter of time. He knew he was dying, but he had to hang on—a little longer.

James K. Polk was the first Presidential candidate to stand on a so-called "platform," the planks of which were the Jacksonian positions on all major issues, including the "re-occupation of Oregon and the re-annexation of Texas* at the earliest practicable period."[4]

Polk was elected by the narrowest of majorities, less than 2 percent of the popular vote; indeed, had the abolitionists not put forth James Birney as a third-party candidate, Henry Clay would have won. While the election could hardly be construed as a mandate for annexation, it nonetheless left Jackson greatly relieved. With Polk in the White House, "the Republic is safe!"[5] But the election left Jackson exhausted. Though bedridden, he had done everything in his limited power to help, writing letters on Polk's behalf every day.

Jackson's iron will was all that was keeping him alive. He could not let go of life, not until he was sure that Texas, too, was safe.

At the beginning of 1845, Polk had paid a call at the Hermitage on his way to assume the Presidency. As always, the General had excellent advice, and Polk took it, forming a new Cabinet and requiring each member to foreswear any future Presidential aspirations they might harbor. But when it came to picking the Cabinet, Polk did that on his own, confiding to a friend, "I intend to be myself President of the U.S."[6] The General was singularly unimpressed with his selections, observing that the new Secretary of State, James Buchanan (who had been decidedly ambiguous in renouncing Presidential ambitions), was a moral lightweight.[7]

It was in foreign affairs that the old eagle's advice proved invaluable. When Polk had declared that the future of Oregon lay with the United

* Jackson never lost an opportunity to underscore that those territories had once belonged to the United States under the Louisiana Purchase—hence the prefix *re*.

States, the British response had been a thinly veiled threat of war. Jackson calmly counseled the new President to stick to his guns: "This is the rattling of British drums to alarm us."

"Rest easy," Polk had written back, the "blustering manners and tone of defiance" were probably meant "to test our nerves." We wanted peace, he added, but we were prepared to maintain our rights "at any hazard."[8]

At that, Old Hickory did rest easy; the new hand on the helm of the ship of state was firm and steady. He could let go.

As the end drew near, the General, looking back wistfully over his life, asked his visiting friend John Edgar: "Doctor, what do you think will be my fame with posterity? I mean, what will posterity blame me for most?"

Seven years before, Dr. Edgar, a Presbyterian minister, had led the General to forgive his enemies—all his enemies, even the ones Jackson thought didn't deserve it. Now Edgar thought for a moment, then suggested that perhaps the attack on the Bank of the United States was excessive. The General shook his head and allowed as how the facts would not support such a complaint.

Adroitly Edgar shifted the focus, asking Jackson what he would have done with Calhoun and the other South Carolina nullifiers, had they persisted in their resistance to federal authority.*

"Hung them, sir!" he shot back, "as high as Haman! They should have been a terror to traitors of all time, and posterity would have pronounced it the best act of my life."[9]

Though facing the possibility that each morning might be his last, Jackson nonetheless spent more time looking forward than back. When another friend asked what the future might hold, he mustered all his strength and gasped his response: "Sir, I am in the hands of a merciful God. I have full confidence in His goodness and mercy. . . . The Bible is true. I have tried to conform to its spirit as near as possible. Upon that sacred volume I rest my hope for eternal salvation, through the merits and blood of our blessed Lord and Savior, Jesus Christ."[10]

Jackson's pain was relentless, yet he spoke of it only once: "When I

---

* In 1828, to protect Northern manufacturers from European competition, Congress passed a round of tariff hikes, which South Carolina dubbed "the Tariff of Abominations." Calhoun held that any state had the right to declare null and void any federal law it considered unconstitutional. When President Jackson made it clear he would collect the tariffs by force if necessary, South Carolina had backed down.

have suffered sufficiently, the Lord will take me to Himself. . . . But what are all my sufferings, compared to those of the blessed Savior, who died on that cursed tree for me? Mine are nothing."[11]

On his dying day the slaves of the Hermitage sensed he was about to leave them. Without being summoned, they began to gather on the porch outside his bedroom window, the little ones sniffling because their parents were so sad and silent. The old hands who knew him best were invited into the bedroom, joining his children and grandchildren. Seeing them all, he rallied briefly—long enough to urge them to "keep holy the Sabbath day and read the New Testament." Those whose salvation was not assured, he beseeched to "look to Christ as their only Savior."

Then he addressed the blacks, telling them that as much was expected of them as of whites. He had been their friend and protector, too, but could no longer fill that role. To his daughter and the rest he said: "God will take care of you for me. I am my God's. I belong to him, I go but a short time before you, and I want to meet you all in heaven, both white and black." Tears came to all, in the room and without. When some broke into sobs, it surprised him. "Oh, do not cry—be good children, and we will meet in heaven."[12]

Those were his last words. Just before sundown, Andrew Jackson went to be with the Maker to Whom he had drawn so close.

The funeral was held on a warm, still Tuesday morning. Though there had been scant notice, more than 200 carriages arrived at the Hermitage, and saddle horses were tethered everywhere, for some 3,000 friends and acquaintances had gathered to pay their respects. At the graveside, all wept openly; the old hero was much loved. There is a story that someone, presumably a reporter, asked one of the grieving slaves if he thought the General had gone to heaven. The slave frowned and then smiled. "If General Jackson wants to go to Heaven, who's to stop him?"[13]

As the grave was closed, three ranks of Nashville Blues took one pace forward. The first rank fired a crisp volley, followed by the second, then the third. Silence fell—broken only by the mournful tolling of a church bell down in the valley, while on a distant hill, a battery of cannon fired at one-minute intervals.

11

Proceed without Delay

*T*he 11th President, still mourning the passing of the 7th, now sat down at the mahogany desk and drew the slender folder to him. Opening it, he withdrew a carefully penned dispatch from the Commander in Chief to Brigadier General Zachary Taylor, Commander, United States Army Detachment, Fort Jessup, Louisiana. General Taylor was to proceed without delay across the Sabine River into Texas and take up position at Corpus Christi on the Nueces River. Upon receiving notification that the Republic of Texas had accepted annexation, Taylor was to move at once to the Rio Grande, and take all measures necessary to ensure the safety and well-being of American citizens dwelling there.

About to reach for the pen in the silver penholder, he paused—his signature on this order might well instigate war between the United States and Mexico. One last time he reviewed the events that had culminated in this dispatch.

In 1821, Mexico, having successfully waged her own war for independence, had thrown off the yoke of Spain. Her most urgent problem was the situation in the vast territory that stretched from the Rio Grande north and east to the Sabine River (the western border of Louisiana). Known as Texas, it was plagued by bands of Comanche marauders sweeping down from the north and terrorizing the peasant farmers trying to scratch a living out of the hard, dry soil. The cost of garrisoning enough troops up there to ensure their safety was simply more than the fledgling nation could afford.

Her new Federalist Government hit upon a novel solution: The American Stephen Austin had approached them with a request to start an American colony there—why not open the territory to *all* Americans? Invite them to come down and settle. Offer them self-rule, duty-free imports, and land so cheap they could not refuse. Even allow those from the South to bring their slaves, although Mexico herself had abolished slavery. Promise them the same rights as Mexican citizens, as guaranteed under the new Constitution of 1824, including the right to defend themselves (and their Mexican neighbors in the process).

The offer was made and accepted by hundreds, then thousands of American settlers—fully 30,000 by 1836.[1] The new Texans worked hard, farming and raising cattle. They got along with their neighbors and with the Federalist Government down in Mexico City, 1,000 miles away. The latter left them alone, free to govern and police themselves as they saw fit.

The only people they didn't get along with were the Comanche raiders, and that was only at first. When the Comanches tested the newcomers, they received a shock: The Anglo-Texans, or *Tejanos* as the Mexicans called them, were not afraid of the Comanches. On the contrary, they all seemed to be expert marksmen, and their rifles had a great reach.

Some of the newcomers who had experience with hostile Indians made a treaty with the Comanche leaders and got them to agree to stay out of Texas. Later, when some renegade braves decided it was easier to take another man's harvest or stock than grow their own, the Texans raised a force, tracked them down, and dealt with them. Thereafter, the Indians left the tall *Tejanos* alone, along with their *Mexicano* neighbors.

Down in Mexico City, the Government was pleased. Their policy of opening Texas to Anglo settlement had worked beautifully; their citizens were now safe, at no cost to the Government. Peace reigned—for seven years.

But then the Government changed. From the beginning there had been two diametrically opposed factions in Mexico vying for ascendancy. The first to gain it were the Centralists—the established aristocracy, the moneyed interests, and the landowners. These favored a strong centralized government in Mexico City, the way things had been when Spain was running the country. In 1823 they had been overthrown by the Federalists—peasant farmers and idealists who wanted an elected government like that of the United States. It was the Federalists' democratic Constitution of 1824 (closely modeled on the United States'), and their relaxed rule that had attracted the *Tejanos* in the first place.

But in 1830 a series of revolutions and counterrevolutions had begun, which ultimately saw the Centralists, led by Antonio López de Santa Anna, regain power. Instantly the climate changed. Discarding the Constitution of 1824, the Centralists determined to bring the independent *Tejanos* to heel; if necessary, they would send an army north to subdue them by force.

Pride was the culprit here—and it mattered not whether it wore a sombrero or a beaver-skinned Stetson. Just as up in Washington President Jackson reflected the spirit of an awakening America, down in Mexico City Santa Anna reflected the spirit of an aroused Mexico. Neither side, Texans or Mexicans, could understand the motivation of the other—nor had the least interest in doing so. And so the outcome would be decided by force of arms—first at the Alamo, then at San Jacinto.*

The Texans had won their independence the hard way, but Mexico still dreamed of retaking the immense expanse to the north. While Mexico was willing to let the Lone Star flag fly (for now), she was decidedly unwilling to ever see that star join twenty-seven others in a field of blue. For the *norteamericanos* would not be satisfied with Texas; soon they would want California, too, and probably even Mexico herself.

After his ignoble defeat at the hands of a Texas army (inferior in numbers but unmatched in their resolve to avenge the Alamo), Santa Anna went into exile at his country estate in the province of Jalapa. But in 1838, when the French fleet bombarded Vera Cruz, he mounted his white horse and galloped off to war. Officer comrades rallied round him, and soon the self-styled "Napoleon of the West" was again in command of the Mexican army.

While the French bombardment was minor, it was not all comic-opera: A cannonball so injured his left leg that it had to be amputated. As always, the enterprising Santa Anna saw an opportunity to turn adversity to advantage. At the head of his column, he rode into Mexico City—a grievously wounded but victorious war hero. Once again his popularity and charisma, fanned by his ever-loyal *Santanistas*, so captivated his countrymen that they jubilantly made him their leader for the *fifth* time. And once again he turned the Presidency into a dictatorship.

* For an account of the birth of Texas, see the authors' previous volume *From Sea to Shining Sea.*

In Santa Anna's case, the absolute corruption of absolute power affected his mind: He had his severed leg disinterred and brought to Mexico City, where with great ceremony it was reinterred atop a magnificent cenotaph erected for it in the cemetery of Santa Paula.[2]

North of the Sabine, the fate of the new Republic of Texas was very much on people's minds. In President Jackson's assessment, slavery was not an issue in the annexation question; he dismissed the abolitionists as rebellious radicals, noisy but inconsequential. Yet here, and perhaps only here, he was several years out of touch. True, William Lloyd Garrison railed with typical thunder and brimstone: "All who would sympathize with that pseudo-republic hate liberty and would dethrone God!"[3] But Jackson was unaware of the quiet, deep work of Theodore Dwight Weld and the other Christian abolitionists, nor could he appreciate the groundswell of support now piling petitions on the desk of Congressman John Quincy Adams.

The nation was beginning to polarize on the topic of slavery; before long it would be the core issue of every major dispute. With the tide of immigration rising, and most of the newcomers heading north, it was only a matter of time before the South, even with the three-fifths rule in effect,* lost control of the House. Only in the Senate could they maintain parity, as long as there were as many slave states as free. But with so many antislavery immigrants settling in the North, that delicate balance was in jeopardy. Were California to come into the Union, it would likely come in free, and Oregon most certainly would. If, on the other hand, Texas came in as a slave state—or maybe as five, since America surely could not absorb a single state larger than all of New England and New York . . .

When Great Britain, birthplace of the abolitionist movement, recognized the Republic of Texas (where the great majority of the settlers had come without slaves), she entered into an agreement with her to suppress the slave trade. The Slave Power became alarmed; if left to herself, Texas might soon abolish slavery altogether! General Lamar, a former President of the Republic, expressed this concern in a letter to slaveholding friends in Georgia in 1842: Unless annexation came quickly, "the antislavery party

---

* For the purpose of determining Congressional representation—and only for that purpose—five slaves counted as three whites.

in Texas will acquire the ascendancy, and . . . there is every probability that slavery will be abandoned."[4]

The Slave Power stepped up efforts to achieve immediate annexation—for if Texas came in free, slavery itself, blocked from further westward expansion, might wither and die. As it happened, their specific concern coincided with the growing national concern of visionaries young and old, who were convinced that God intended the Stars and Stripes to fly from sea to shining sea.* Clearly, Texas was part of that plan.

If so, then it was equally clear that Mexico was impeding that plan. And here the end subtly began to justify the means—any means to dislodge the impediment. Mexican pride had already become an affront to American pride. El Presidente Santa Anna, reflecting (and appealing to) the machismo of his countrymen, and personally chafing at the humiliation he had suffered at the hands of the Texans, had dispatched a raiding party across the Rio Grande to attack San Antonio. When the Texans retaliated with an expedition to Santa Fe, he captured the lot of them, treating them cruelly until the aging Jackson personally interceded on their behalf.

Throughout history dictators have fomented wars to rally national spirit and get their countrymen's minds off their resentment toward the oppression under which they lived. No one knew this better than Santa Anna. By 1842 he had incited a full-scale border war with the Republic of Texas. Ironically, nothing could have affected Mexico's cause more adversely. The war news, including atrocities vividly reported from the Texan perspective, was hardening American hearts against Mexico—hearts that had been previously sympathetic. Acting privately, Americans began sending munitions and supplies to their beleaguered Texas cousins, and more than a few, spoiling for a fight, drifted south with their long rifles on their shoulders.

On May 12, 1842, Mexican Minister of Relations Bocanegra lodged a formal protest against these acts of American aid with Secretary of State Daniel Webster. He declared that while Mexico was not seeking war with the United States, she would certainly do all that was "imperatively required for her honor and dignity." A continuance of said aid to the Texans would be regarded as "a positive act of hostility."[5]

Webster replied that the American Government rejected all such

---

* Though how far north and south varied from vision to vision.

charges brought against it, that it had maintained and would continue to maintain strict neutrality, and that President Tyler found Bocanegra's language "highly offensive."

In both countries, the press played to the emotions of the people, helping to bring both sides "closer to the tented field," as historian Justin Smith put it. And just when matters could hardly be more precarious, Commodore Catesby Jones of the U.S. Pacific Squadron belatedly heard this news. Assuming that war had undoubtedly broken out by now, he occupied the Mexican port of Monterey. Learning that he was premature, he lowered his flag, saluted the Mexican Governor, and sailed away. When news of his escapade reached Mexico City, the Government was apoplectic.

Capitalizing on the surging anti-American feeling, Santa Anna decreed in June 1843 that all foreigners (i.e., norteamericanos) taken in action on Texas soil would be executed. A month later he ordered the Governors of California and three other northern territories to expel all citizens of the United States residing therein, and to permit no more to enter.

Two months later Bocanegra spelled out exactly how Mexico would regard annexation: "The Mexican Government will consider equivalent to a declaration of war against the Mexican Republic the passage of an act [by the American Congress] for the incorporation of Texas with the territory of the United States; the certainty of the fact being sufficient for the immediate proclamation of war."[6]

In 1844 fresh British overtures toward Texas turned up the heat. It was rumored that antislavery philanthropists in England were prepared to compensate any Texans who would free their slaves. Alarmed, Southern slaveholders prevailed upon their champion, John C. Calhoun, to do something—and as it happened, he was in a position to do so, having just been appointed Secretary of State by President Tyler.

Apprised of what was afoot, Great Britain disavowed any of the machinations of which rumor accused her. In a letter dated April 8, 1844, her Ambassador officially informed the Government of the United States that while it was well known throughout the world that she desired the abolition of slavery wherever it existed, she would not unduly interfere to accomplish it. She aimed at no dominant influence in Texas, and in striving to achieve liberty for those in bondage, her government would neither "openly nor secretly resort to any measures which can tend to disturb the tranquillity, or thereby affect the prosperity of the American Union."[7] Her disavowal was sincere, as later attested by none other than Sam Houston, who from his new desk in the Senate stated: "England never proposed the subject of slavery or of abolition to Texas."[8]

But Calhoun chose not to interpret the British assurance as it was intended. On the same day he shot back a response, informing their Ambassador that the President viewed with deep concern Britain's avowed desire for the abolition of slavery. In his opinion, Texas, standing alone, could not withstand a compliance with this desire. Therefore, "It is the imperative duty of the Federal Government . . . to adopt in self-defense the most effectual means to resist it." And so, in obedience to this obligation, a treaty of annexation had been concluded.[9]

The moment word got out that the United States meant to annex Texas in order to protect American slavery from the "reprehensible" British effort to interfere there and from her effort to bring about universal abolition,[10] the argument over annexation in both House and Senate became an argument over the expansion of slavery.

John Quincy Adams was livid. But as he attempted to organize Northern opposition in the House, he came to the hard realization that most Americans, especially those in the West, did not see Texas annexation as a slavery issue. They tended to view slavery as their President did, primarily an economic problem whose morality could be sorted out later. Right now, the mood of the country was strongly in favor of westward expansion, and further resistance to annexation was likely to prove futile. Even Northern newspapers that had attacked annexation now editorialized that it was inevitable and should be accomplished with as much grace as possible.[11] Texas would be admitted into the Union and would come in as a slave state—but if JQA had anything to say about it, it would remain only one state, not five. As his last official act, President Tyler sent a dispatch to Texas, offering the Republic the opportunity to become the 28th state in the Union. And as he had threatened to, the Mexican minister, General Juan Almonte, immediately left the capital, thus severing diplomatic relations between Mexico and the United States. A state of war did not yet formally exist between the two nations, but it was drawing perilously close.

James K. Polk did not want a war, either with Britain over America's exclusive claim to the lower part of the jointly occupied Oregon Territory, or with Mexico. And most emphatically he wanted to avoid every nation's nightmare: war on two fronts. He did want to add new territory to the Western frontier, but he was confident this could be accomplished through diplomatic channels. One of the campaign slogans of his supporters had been "Fifty-four Forty or Fight!" It referred to a line of latitude so far above the 49th parallel (which currently separates the Western United States from Canada) that it would have included Edmonton, Calgary, and Saskatoon.

Privately Polk was prepared to compromise with the British. To achieve a mutually acceptable, permanent border, he was prepared to agree to a substantially lower line. Yet it could not be too low; 5,000 pioneer families had trekked over the Oregon Trail and settled along the Columbia River and in the Willamette Valley. Lower Oregon would have to become part of the United States. He made that clear in his Inaugural Address, and even clearer that same night with his new Secretary of the Navy, George Bancroft.

Years later, Bancroft* would recall their conversation that evening, as the two sat by a fire. Waxing rarely expansive, Polk outlined what he hoped to accomplish in office: "There are four great measures which are to be the measures of my administration: one, a reduction of the tariff; another, the independent treasury; a third, the settlement of the Oregon boundary question; and lastly, the acquisition of California."[12]

California—it was a name to conjure with. In the minds of most Americans (including their President) that spring of 1845, it was more a mythic land of promise than a firm reality. The mountain men/explorers had found ways through the massive high wall of the Rocky Mountains, and the first settlers to arrive in California sent back extravagant reports of green fertile valleys and magnificent seacoast vistas. It all sounded like the sort of fabled islands once rumored to be in the Western ocean, far beyond the Mediterranean Sea.

Technically California belonged to Mexico. But it was twice as far from Mexico City as Texas was, and even more difficult to administrate. Though

---

* Bancroft would become the dean of America's 19th-century historians.

Mexico maintained a Governor and a garrison there, California's Anglo citizens were openly discussing annexation with the United States, as if it were imminent. It was obvious to them that where California wound up depended on which country wanted her. France was showing more than passing interest, and Great Britain was definitely nosing about, anxious to keep her from falling into the hands of the burgeoning American behemoth. But Britannia was at the moment preoccupied. At war with both the Chinese and the Afghans, she could hardly give her undivided attention to developments in the western reaches of the Western Hemisphere.

What were the intentions of the United States? In the previous year, John C. Frémont, a lieutenant in the Army's Topographical Corps (and Missouri Senator Thomas Hart Benton's son-in-law), had surveyed, mapped, and blazed the Oregon Trail to the Pacific—and had then impetuously headed south into California. There, at what is now Sacramento, he met a short, round, blue-eyed Swiss entrepreneur named John Sutter, who was sitting rather comfortably on a 50,000-acre Mexican grant.

Frémont fell in love with California and went back to Washington, D.C., extolling its virtues and rallying support for a return expedition. Benton and his son-in-law called on the new President in the White House and confirmed that Polk desired to gain both Oregon *and* California. In the spring of 1845, Frémont prepared a new expedition. He would go back to California, accompanied by 60 hardened adventurers—mountain men, topographical engineers, Delaware Indian scouts. There were only 800 or so Americans out there, mostly sailors who had left their ships to become beachcombers, but they were a nucleus. In the meantime, in the event that Mexico declared war on the United States . . .[13]

Once set in motion, developments between Mexico and the United States seemed to be taking on a life and momentum of their own. Under other circumstances, the Republic of Texas, given half a chance, might have been able to make it on her own; indeed, there were adventurers among her citizens who envisioned their new Republic expanding west across Arizona and New Mexico to absorb California.

But the continuing Mexican raids over her southwestern border brought reality into sharp focus. In the event of a concerted Mexican thrust, Texas could not raise and sustain an army sufficient to guarantee the safety of her citizenry. She was going to need a champion. She was also going to need a trading partner to provide manufactured goods in exchange for the cotton that she was beginning to grow. The British indicated they were ready to assume that role, but the logical life partner for Texas was the one whence most Texans had originated. An offer of annexation from America would in all likelihood be unanimously received.

In Washington, the abolitionists were accusing the pro-annexation forces of trying to whip up war with Mexico, to secure not only Texas but all the other territory west of the Rio Grande up to and including California—all for a vast new slave empire. To buttress their case, the abolitionists drafted a documented chronology of deliberate U.S. provocations. Most modern historians tend to agree that the Harrison/Tyler administration, with its proslavery ministers and Cabinet members, *did* want to see slavery expand in a southwesterly direction.

Yet it was hardly a case of a schoolyard bully (the United States) intimidating a smaller, defenseless child (Mexico), as modern textbooks would have us believe. The New England abolitionists may have published their chronology of American provocations, but a number of respected historians from earlier in the twentieth century (and closer in time to the actual events) listed their own *casus belli* (just causes for war). Chief among these was Justin Smith, professor of history at Dartmouth, who in 1919 summarized their case in one (very long) sentence:

Mexico, our next neighbor, on no grounds that could be recognized by the United States, repudiated her treaties with us, ended official relations, aimed to prevent commercial intercourse, planned to deprive us of all influence on certain issues vitally connected with our declared foreign policy, seemed likely to sell California to some European rival of ours, made it impossible for us to urge long-standing claims or watch over [American] citizens dwelling within her borders, refused to pay even her admitted debts to us, claimed the privilege of applying to our government publicly the most opprobrious epithets in the vocabulary of nations, designed to keep our people in a constant state of uncertainty and alarm, intended to cause us the expense of maintaining for defensive purposes a large army and a large navy, planned to destroy our commerce by commissioning privateers, claimed the right to harry Texas, a part of the Union, at will, threatened and prepared for war, and proposed to assume such an attitude that, whenever encouraged by foreign support or any other circumstances, she could fire upon us without even giving notice.[14]

Two modern historians, Odie B. Faulk and Joseph A. Stout Jr., decided to investigate the recent abrupt shift in the academic perception of the Mexican War, which today characterizes it as

> the most disgraceful episode in American history . . . with the United States deliberately provoking a war to acquire the territory now known as the American Southwest—a clear case of imperialism, pure and simple. As a result, despite the many excellent books which have been written about the Mexican War proving that neither side was exclusively to blame for the conflict, most textbooks used in college survey courses of American history specifically charge the United States with starting the war for territorial aggrandizement.[15]

What had caused them to write their own book, challenging this contemporary interpretation? At random they had opened a history instructor's manual and found this multiple-choice question: "President James K. Polk deliberately provoked war with Mexico in order to acquire a) New Mexico, b) California, c) the entire Southwest." There was no asking *if* Polk had started the war; the only question was how much territory he intended to acquire.

Further evidence of the recent skewing of perspective was provided by historian Seymour V. Connor in the April 1972 edition of *Journal of the West*. In a comprehensive survey of 766 works about the war published between 1846 and 1970, he found that "statistically there is no basis for the flagellation of Americans of the 1840's for the war with Mexico."

His summation: "Overall, most writers on the Mexican War appear to have taken a fairly moderate and objective position on national culpability." It was all the more curious, therefore, that "in so many survey texts on American history, the United States emerges as some sort of vicious and greedy imperialist. And it is even more curious that when Robert Kennedy said publicly that the Mexican War was a disgrace to the national honor, only a handful of American historians, Allan Nevins prominent among them, challenged his statement."[16]

Then, as now, the mortar that held the global society together was national morality. A nation's word was its bond, and if it did not keep its word, then it forfeited its right to be treated as a member in good standing. Mexico was notorious for breaking her word. Under the guidelines of international arbitration, she would admit that she owed certain funds to other nations, and she would agree to a reasonable schedule of repayment. Then she would renege on her agreements.

In those days national honor was taken more seriously than today. When Mexico ignored her repayment agreement with France, the latter bombarded Vera Cruz. When she did the same to America, it did not precipitate the war, but it did add one more item to the growing *casus belli* list.

Another point upon which the facts were way out of line with the current academic assessment was that the impending war would prove to be a tragically unequal contest. In the assessment of military historian John Eisenhower,* America at that time had never truly proven herself in a war. The War for Independence ended because Britain wearied of expending further money and men for a military victory. The War of 1812 ended because both sides grew too weary to continue. In the eyes of Europe's top military commanders, the French-trained Mexican Army was every bit the equivalent of a well-disciplined European force, especially skilled in the sophisticated military sciences of artillery and engineering (as American generals would later attest). "There are no better troops in the world, nor better drilled and armed than the Mexicans," declared Calderón de la Barca, the Spanish Minister in Washington.[17] In the opinion of Europe's seasoned generals, the Mexican Army would make quick hash of any American force foolish enough to oppose them.

Moreover, if pride was the backbone of any fighting unit, then the Mexicans had their full share. The *gringos* might think they could grab Mexico's Northern lands—but they would never keep them. The *Santanistas'* leader, Santa Anna, had pledged it, and he spoke for every one of them.

Reluctantly James K. Polk picked up the pen. He was not seeking war with Mexico. But there was no question that Mexico, driven by the Centralists, who needed a popular war to retain control over the people, was seeking one with America. Indeed, they themselves had already declared it. Polk had made no secret of his desire to acquire Texas, California,

---

* son of President Dwight Eisenhower

and Oregon, nor of his willingness to fight for them, if it came to that. Where Mexico herself was concerned, however, he was still confident that diplomacy—and a generous offer of remuneration—might avoid armed conflict. A former small-town lawyer, Polk knew that it was almost always in his client's best interest to cut a deal and avoid going to court.

An entry in Polk's diary suggests that in dispatching Taylor to the Rio Grande he was engaging in brinksmanship, not provocation. It was hard to believe, he wrote, "that Mexico will be mad enough to declare war."[18] Going to the edge of war over Oregon had worked with the British; surely it would work with the Mexicans as well.

But here he made a crucial error in judgment, for he was not dealing now with a mature, pragmatic nation well grounded in reality. He was dealing with a young, emotional, wildly irrational nation whose leadership was in a perpetual state of flux. With Mexico, there was only one constant: enormous pride.

In the last analysis, the inexorable march of events had taken the decision out of his hands. Now that the Texans had been offered U.S. citizenship, America had to be prepared to defend her newest citizens. Like it or not, she had inherited the Republic's controversy with her neighbor to the south.

With a sigh, Polk dipped the pen and signed the order.

12

"Hostilities Have Begun!"

he dispatch was on its way; in a matter of days Taylor would be headed for the southern border of the Republic of Texas. Believing that he was dealing with a rational adversary, Polk was convinced that this show of force would bring Mexico to the bargaining table.

"The appearance of our land and naval forces on the borders of Mexico and in the Gulf," he wrote in his diary, "would probably deter and prevent Mexico from either declaring war or invading Texas."[1]

How far he had misjudged the Mexican character would soon become all too apparent.

In the meantime, one more peace card remained to be played. Mexico's latest President to succeed Santa Anna (now in ignominious exile in Cuba), was José Joaquín de Herrera, a "temperate, honest man who actually seemed to desire peace."[2] Though not a Federalist, Herrera was nonetheless a moderate, and Polk had received private assurances that Mexico would welcome a commissioner to negotiate the two countries' differences.

Accordingly, in November 1845, he sent John Slidell, a New Orleans lawyer fluent in Spanish, to act as his "Minister Extraordinary and Plenipotentiary"—despite warnings that Mexico would never accept an envoy with as high a rank as "minister." Slidell's mission: to get agreement on a permanent boundary between the United States and Mexico, ideally the Rio Grande, from its mouth to El Paso. If Mexico agreed, then the United States would assume payment of all outstanding claims by American citizens against the Government of Mexico, amounting to some $2 million.*

Should the climate prove propitious, Slidell was empowered to go farther: If the boundary was then extended from El Paso due west to the Pacific, with "Mexico ceding to the United States all the country east and north of these lines"[3] (i.e., Texas, New Mexico, Arizona, and California), Polk thought a fair price would be $15 million to $20 million. But he was prepared to go as high as $40 million (in 1845 dollars that was a staggering sum). Polk was confident it would be an offer Mexico could not refuse.

But neither Polk nor Slidell had any idea how far relations between the two countries had deteriorated, or how virulent the anti-American sentiment had become.

When he arrived in Vera Cruz, Slidell was shocked: The newspapers, there and in the capital, were whipping the people into a war frenzy. And he knew that newspapers in Mexico were like those at home—unless they accurately reflected the mood of the people, no one bothered to read them. To make matters worse, the nature of his mission had leaked to the American press—and had been picked up in Mexico.

Moreover, during the brief period between Slidell's departure and his arrival, Herrera's position had become exceedingly tenuous. One prominent editor denounced "the vile government" of Herrera, convinced that it was about to secretly enter into "an ignominious treaty on the basis of the surrender of Texas, and we know not what other part of the Republic. This is as certain as the existence of God in heaven!"[4]

Under Santa Anna, such an editorial would have had its author before a firing squad by sundown, but Herrera's ministers knew that the editor was speaking for the people. They begged Slidell not to come to Mexico City. For him to do so would invite the hard-line Centralist, General Mariano Paredes y Arrillaga, waiting in the wings with 7,000 troops, to step in and depose Herrera.

---

* As directed by the King of Prussia, acting as an impartial adjudicator, Mexico had begun payment, but after a few installments had defaulted.

As it turned out, Paredes needed no invitation. He, too, could read the papers. Assessing that the timing would never be more propitious for him to assume supreme leadership, he did—for the sake of his country, of course. As his first act in office, he declared his intent to defend Texas as Mexican Territory all the way to the Sabine River.[5] So much for the internationally recognized Republic of Texas! So much for the Texans' overwhelming acceptance of U.S. annexation! So much for peace.

Meanwhile, back in Washington on December 2, 1845, Polk made his first State of the Union address to both houses of Congress. In it he further defined the Monroe Doctrine of 1832: The United States would no longer tolerate any foreign interference on this side of the ocean, north of the equator. "It should be distinctly announced to the world as our settled policy that no future European colony or dominion shall with our consent be planted or established on any part of the North American continent."[6] While it was obvious that he had primarily Oregon in mind, foreign ministers rightly inferred that the doctrine applied to California and Mexico as well.

In 1845 the only telegraph wire stretched from Washington to Baltimore. Telegraph poles would soon be erected alongside every mainline railroad, but until they were, the news was carried to major cities by rail, express rider, or ship. Philadelphia's newspapers were a day behind Washington's; New York's were two days behind; and Boston's were three.

For a speech as important as the State of the Union address, in the Washington railyard locomotives would already have steam up, waiting to speed Polk's words on their way. The speech would be read publicly in cities and towns to large crowds who, in this case, frequently interrupted with cheers. "Jackson is alive again!" cried one New York gathering in the grip of patriotic fervor.[7]

At the same time, the President sent personal, secret instructions to his commodores to take care that their fleets not provoke hostilities. And to Mexico herself, he determined that the peace overture should still be made, despite the likelihood that it would be rebuffed. As instructed, Slidell presented his credentials to the new Paredes government. They were refused, and Slidell was summarily sent home—the ultimate affront to America's national honor. The last hope for peace vanished.

The Mexican newspapers were jubilant. "We have more than enough strength to make war," cried *La Voz del Pueblo (The Voice of the People)*. "Let us make it then, and victory will perch upon our banners!"[8]

In reaction to this final affront, the American press (with the exception of the abolitionist and New England Whig papers) reflected an identical sentiment: "We have borne and forborne long enough," inveighed the *Missouri Reporter*, "and a resolute stand should be taken at once."[9] And the New Orleans *Commercial Bulletin* declared: "The United States have borne more insult, abuse, insolence and injury from Mexico, than one nation ever before endured from another."[10]

When Slidell returned to Washington, he reported to the President that all Mexico was mad to go to war, and nothing short of war would satisfy her. Reluctantly Polk accepted the reality of the situation. He ordered Commodore Connor to bring his Home Squadron in the Gulf of Mexico close in to the Mexican coast; the moment hostilities broke out, Connor was to subdue Vera Cruz, Mexico's main trading port on the Gulf of Mexico. And Taylor, proceeding south to the Rio Grande with more than half the Regular Army, could be counted on to respond vigorously to any attack in his vicinity.

In a January 13th order to Taylor, Polk was particularly careful in his wording: "It is not designed, in our present relations with Mexico, that you should treat her as an enemy; but should she assume that character by a declaration of war, or any open hostility toward us, you will not act merely on the defensive, if your relative means enable you to act otherwise."[11]

America would not fire the first shot. But if fired upon, she would return fire, and (if able) would hotly pursue her attackers—even, apparently, across the Rio Grande.

Desert travel was slow going for an army on the march. All they could do was 10 miles a day—for 20 of the most grueling days most of the infantry had ever put in. The sun poured down on them like "liquid fire," and at one point they were 36 hours without water. The wind blew a dry, caking dust, and occasionally they encountered bushes with thousands of tiny needles—the deadly chaparral.

It was definitely a new experience for 1,490 of the 3,550 men under Taylor's command. These were the foreign-born troops—Irish mostly, but also German, with a scattering of English and Scots. Perhaps the fact that America was not their native land, and this was unquestionably the harshest corner of America, accounted for the desertion rate of one in seven. But for the most part they were professional soldiers, and they bore such hardship with stoic humor.

So did their commanding officer, who shared their lot, right down to the food they ate. Among his men, with whom he was extremely popular, Zachary Taylor's nickname was "Old Rough and Ready." It fit. He was rawboned and heavyset, broad of shoulder and short of leg, gray-eyed and stubborn as a mule. Taylor did not have much use for the spit-and-polish, by-the-book product West Point was turning out these days—a distaste he did not hide from the young gentlemen officers who had received orders to join his corps. Around camp, his preferred attire was an old, stained linen duster, and on one occasion a junior lieutenant from one of the First Families of Virginia, just arriving, offered the old fellow a dollar to polish his sword.

But Taylor had a double measure of common horse sense and was a shrewd judge of character. He cared for his men, and they knew it—and so they followed him into an inferno like southern Texas with a resilient humor. In addition, Taylor had combat experience, first as a junior officer in the Black Hawk War during the War of 1812, then as commander of the U.S. forces in the Seminole War. Under fire he was remarkably cool and intrepid, with a deep belief in himself, and he was a shrewd judge of his opposite number's likely response. His officers, who had at close hand experienced (or soon would) his cool wit and courage under fire, idolized him. For many, he became the role model of what a true combat general should be, and more than a few under him would one day command divisions of their own: Sam Grant, George Meade, Kirby Smith, O. O. Howard, and Robert E. Lee.

When Taylor and his column finally reached the mud-brown river that now marked the southwestern border of the United States, he set up camp across the Rio Grande from the Mexican town of Matamoros. With its sparkling white houses and tropical gardens, it looked "like a fairy vision" to American eyes. It was a garrison town now, occupied by a force approximately the same size as the Americans'. Under a white flag, Taylor sent an emissary to the Mexican commandant, General Francisco Mejia, to assure him of his peacefulness. But Mejia refused to meet with him; in his country's eyes, Taylor's arrival constituted an "invasion."

So they settled down to a period of watching and waiting—with the Mexicans watching the *norteamericanos* dig. The American engineers now put their men to work excavating and erecting a five-sided star fort whose earthwork walls were 9 feet high and 15 feet thick.

The waiting ended April 11. From Mexico City arrived a young general from Cuba, Pedro de Ampudia, at the head of a column of some 3,000 men. The Mexicans now outnumbered the Americans two to one. General Ampudia immediately sent General Taylor an ultimatum: Unless he decamped and withdrew back to the Nueces River (whence he had come) within 24 hours, there would be war.

Taylor graciously regretted that he was unable to comply with this request, and the two sides went back to what they had been doing before, with the Mexicans watching the Americans dig.

Three days later General Ampudia was busy making plans to carry out his threat, when a courier arrived to inform him that President Paredes was dispatching General Mariano Arista north to take command. Ampudia was being relieved for getting ahead of Paredes's timetable.

Arista's orders, dated April 4, commanded him to cross the Rio Grande and attack the Americans. But under no circumstances was the action to take place until April 23. On that day in Mexico City, Paredes would declare the commencement of a "defensive" war against the United States of America.[12]

But in the rapidly changing kaleidoscope of Mexican politics, Paredes's own situation was becoming precarious. There were still many moderates of Herrera's persuasion; if war did not happen soon . . .

On April 18, Paredes sent Arista an urgent letter: "It is indispensable that hostilities begin, yourself taking the initiative."[13]

Promptly on the morning of April 23, Arista sent his general of cavalry, Anastasio Torrejón, across the Rio Grande with 1,600 horsemen upriver of the U.S. encampment. Sensing enemy movement and not knowing its strength, Taylor sent a patrol of 63 mounted dragoons under Captain Seth Thornton up his side of the river to reconnoiter. The recon patrol had little trouble locating the enemy about 20 miles north of camp—but soon found themselves in a great deal of trouble. Surrounded and hugely outnumbered, they attempted to fight their way out. But the odds were hopeless, and they lost 16 killed or wounded before the rest were taken captive.

"Hostilities have begun!" reported an exultant General Arista to his President.

"Hostilities may now be considered as commenced," wrote General Taylor in a dispatch to his President—which would take two weeks to reach him. Then, as previously authorized, he sent an urgent request to the Governors of Texas and Louisiana for 5,000 three-month volunteers.

Shortly before sunset on Saturday, May 9, the Adjutant General arrived at the White House with Taylor's dispatch. Polk called his Cabinet into emergency session, even as the Washington *Union* rushed to press with a late edition whose headline screamed: "American Blood Shed on American Soil!"[14]

When the President went before Congress Monday to announce that a state of war existed, war fever was already running high—so high, in fact, that the Speakers of both houses refused to allow any negative debate. With dissent thus stifled, the House approved his war message, 173 to 14, and the Senate, 40 to 2.

America was at war. But the dissenters would not remain silent for long.

13

FLYING ARTILLERY

*C*aptain Sam Walker was a tall drink of water—lean as a rail, with steel blue eyes and the long hair and long-handled mustache favored by most of the Texas Rangers. He had led a column of them into General Taylor's camp, 77 in all, the first men to respond to the General's call for volunteers. The Rangers were organized in 1835 when the Republic of Texas was fighting for her life. Their duties—"maintaining the law, restoring order, and promoting peace"—took them ranging over vast prairies and high chaparral country.

Most of them had on linen dusters like the General's, and they wore their broad-brimmed hats down low over their eyes, to create a few inches of shade in that sun-blasted terrain. Riding slowly to expend as little energy as possible in the enervating heat, their bearing was about as unmilitary as it was possible to be; even their horses seemed to be slouching.

In the camp the youthful products of West Point gathered to observe this colorful parade. None had ever seen combat, yet with the certainty of well-schooled but untested youth, these future generals considered themselves without equal when it came to assessing combat capability.* They quickly decided that these bizarre, tobacco-chewing ruffians passing by, clearly without discipline and so rebellious they would only confuse an engagement, would be a detriment to any detachment to which they were assigned. Each bore two revolvers with strange curving handles and ramrods under the barrels—where did they ever get such sidearms?

What these highly self-esteemed leaders of men did not know was that

---

* Fifteen years later more than 200 officers who served in Mexico would become generals in the Union or Confederate armies.

the Rangers' Captain had designed these six-shooters. The U.S. Army had no use for the Colt revolver (then), but Texas and her Rangers did. So Sam Walker had gone up north to obtain 1,000 from his friend Samuel Colt. He had some unique specifications for the gunmaker: For rough use on the frontier the new weapon would have to be much more rugged than existing models. The butt should be curved to fit the hand, the cylinder should be longer to hold bigger charges, and the trigger should have a guard to prevent accidental discharge. Most important of all, it had to be reloadable at full gallop; a Ranger being pursued by a band of Comanches could hardly stop and dismount to reload his piece.

The resulting firearm was the legendary Walker Colt, and the Rangers were crack shots with them. Here, where it counted most, they were disciplined.* In the heat of a gunfight, the Ranger took an extra split second to confirm his aim. As a result, he usually killed his opponents, rather than just winging them or missing them entirely. In this fashion he also conserved ammunition; it was just plain stupid to wind up in a scrape with four rounds left and seven plug-uglies coming at you.

When the Rangers asked where to water their horses, the old sergeant major of cavalry formed a different opinion than the junior lieutenants. He was looking not at their costumes, but at their mounts. A good judge of horseflesh, he saw that beneath the trail dust were the finest horses he had ever seen. And he noted with approval the care each Ranger showed as he rubbed down his mount, not letting his animal drink too quickly or too much.

General Taylor himself would soon reach a similar conclusion. While acknowledging their appalling behavior and their refusal to subordinate themselves to any but their own captains, he would come to value the Rangers above all his other volunteers. "On the day of battle," he said, "I am glad to have Texas soldiers with me, for they are brave and gallant; but I never want to see them before or after."[1]

His first appreciation of them would come at Fort Polk, his base of operations in Point Isabel at the mouth of the Rio Grande. After the shooting war had begun, he had repaired there with the main body of his troops, leaving behind a garrison of 700 men under Major Jacob Brown

---

* The opposite of the hip-shooting, hammer-fanning frontier lawmen soon to be popularized in dime novels.

146

at the earthwork revetment opposite Matamoros. Now, that earthwork encampment, nicknamed "Fort Texas," had come under fire. Being some 20 miles away as the crow flies (or nearly 30, as the river meandered), Taylor and his troops could hear the distant *crump* of Mexican artillery.

The natural thing would have been to lead a forced march back there at once—which General Taylor suspected was exactly what General Arista was counting on. In addition to letting Major Brown know that help was on its way, he needed to find out two things: how long the garrison could hold out, and the disposition of the enemy's forces. Since the Texans knew this territory better than anyone, he asked for a volunteer from the ranks of the new arrivals.

Rank having its privileges, Sam Walker decided that he would go himself, with four handpicked companions. That night they went on foot, slipping through the enemy lines surrounding the earthworks and into the moat at its base. Walker identified himself to the Army sentries on the walls, and they helped him up and inside.

The engineers had done their work well: The broad earthworks of Fort Texas were holding up well under the bombardment; indeed, only one man and a few animals had been killed. On the plus side of the ledger, Major Brown's two heavy 18-pounders had succeeded in knocking out two of the Mexican cannon. The only reason they weren't continuing to return fire was to save powder, which might be needed to repel an infantry assault.

The next night Walker and his partners went back over the wall and worked their way back to Fort Polk. When Walker informed General Taylor of how well Fort Texas was doing and that the enemy was straddling the road to Matamoros at a place called Palo Alto, the General decided that he could afford the two additional days necessary to complete the fortification of his home base.

On the morning of May 7, Zachary Taylor issued the following marching orders: "The army will march today at 3 o'clock. . . . It is known that the enemy has recently occupied the route in force. . . . The Commanding General has every confidence in his officers and men. If his orders and instructions are carried out, he has no doubt of the result, let the enemy meet him in what numbers they may. He wishes to enjoin the battalions of Infantry, that their main dependence must be in the bayonet."[2]

Well, there it was: There was going to be hand-to-hand combat. The infantry was apprehensive, but also relieved: Their 1822 flintlocks were none too accurate when it came to line-abreast volleys. Certainly they were far inferior to the rifles of the Rangers, which could drill an ace of spades at a hundred paces. But fix a bayonet on those old muskets, and you couldn't ask for a better close-in weapon.

Promptly at 3:00 they moved out—cavalry, infantry, and artillery—2,000 men in all, encumbered by a lumbering, creaking supply train of some 200 wagons, and further slowed by two enormous 18-pounders. In Europe, field artillery had gradually evolved to the point where it was so cumbersome that not even Napoleon, who had first mastered its use, had much call for it now. These two American guns required teams of 20 oxen each, but the American "brass choir" had other voices besides these *basso profundos*. Major Samuel Ringgold, commander of artillery, had developed a radical innovation—a dozen first and second tenors and a couple of baritones—all much lighter bronze guns. Slung low on caissons between oversized wheels, these short-barreled cannon were only 6-pounders, but they had a maximum effective range of nearly a mile. Drawn by teams of six horses, they were pulled behind two-wheeled containers called limbers, which carried shot, shell, canister, powder bags, matches, and rams. Their crews were so highly trained that they could fire and reload in ten seconds.

Did the General need a battery to shore up his left flank? He had only to call for "Ringgold's Flying Artillery," and the batteries would arrive at full gallop, unlimber, and be ready for action in a matter of minutes.*

After traveling 11 miles, the army encamped for the night, sleeping within reach of their weapons. The enemy also slept—but only after General Ampudia, with his Fort Texas besiegers, had been sent for and had joined General Arista's main force, giving it a better than two-to-one numerical advantage over the Americans. As the morning of the 8th dawned, General Arista had some 5,000 troops drawn up on a spacious grassy plain in a double line almost a mile long, waiting for the *norteamericanos*. On the road in the center were his artillery pieces, a dozen in

---

* The concept had never been tested in battle, but artillery was about to undergo the same paradigm shift that occurred in 1915 when First Lord of the Admiralty, Winston Churchill, perfected the idea of a landship, which he code-named a "tank."

all, the heaviest being two 8-pounders. On his left flank was his prize weapon, the 1,500 Mounted Lancers of General Torrejón.

At high noon the blazing sun was glinting off a long line of fixed bayonets, when the Americans came into view. The Mexican bands started to play *"Vive La Republica"* and other martial airs, as banners unfurled and General Arista rode slowly up and down the entire length of his corps, encouraging his men. It was a gala, breathtaking sight—and a little unnerving to the young West Pointers who suddenly realized that their manuals and textbooks were about to become reality.

Old Rough and Ready, sitting on his favorite horse, Old Whitey, was unimpressed. Laconically he deployed his own troops—Captain Ephraim Kirby Smith with his Fifth Infantry on his left flank, then Sam Ringgold and his flying artillery, then the Third Infantry, then the two 18-pounders in the center, then the Fourth Infantry under Sam Grant, then James Duncan's artillery battery, then the Eighth Infantry on the right flank. The mounted dragoons would be in reserve, guarding the supply train in the rear.

Ringgold's men, moving in practiced rhythm with their horses, had their guns unlimbered and ready to fire in less than a minute. But the two bassos at the center took much longer, with great shouts of "Haw, Buck!" and "Whoa, Brandy!" as the oxen dragged them in a great semicircle, until their mouths were facing the enemy.

Lieutenant Sam French, waiting impatiently for their duet to begin, recorded of his men (and himself) in his journal: "Hearts beat, pulses kept time, and knees would not be still." As more time passed and nothing happened, his impatience shifted toward the Mexican commander: "Arista must have thought he had performed his whole duty when he barred the road with his troops. . . . He had been in line of battle all morning awaiting our coming, yet he permitted us to deploy undisturbed."[3]

But General Taylor was in no hurry either. He gave orders for each company to send every other man to visit a nearby freshwater pond, have a good drink, and fill his canteen, and then the other half should do the same. This would take an enormous amount of time, but he didn't mind; it would give the men the opportunity to recover from their march. And for the bayonet charge he anticipated, they would need every bit of energy they possessed. In this intense heat, the sudden, maximum exertion in their dark blue wool uniforms would exhaust them in 15 or 20 minutes, unless they had plenty of water in them.

When it came down to the swing and club and thrust of hand-to-hand combat, as you did your utmost to kill and not be killed, there were no time-outs, no chance to wipe the blood and sweat from your eyes or catch your breath, much less take a drink. With your mind numb, your lungs on fire, and your arms like lead, you stayed locked in that mortal *pas de deux* until the other side broke off. It could go on for an hour or longer.

If the men's impatience matched that of their officers, well and good; Taylor wanted them fairly pawing the ground before he finally loosed them. He had all the time in the world—let the enemy stand out there at rigid attention in parade formation, broiling. Also, it gave the men coming to the pond a chance to see him lounging with a leg thrown over the pommel of his saddle on Old Whitey, casually chewing tobacco, and to go back and discuss it with their mates. If the General was that relaxed, maybe there wasn't so much to worry about after all. Zachary Taylor was a wise leader; on this day he had won half the battle before it even began.

Finally, a full two and a half hours after the Americans had arrived at Palo Alto, the General was informed that all canteens had been filled. He gave the order to advance, with no talking and no shouting. Forward the line went, through the prickly palm grass, shoulder high in places, around the Spanish Bayonet plants with their sharp, pointed stalks, avoiding the chaparral, maintaining an eerie silence.

The Mexicans watched them coming—steady, straight lined, with no drums, no trumpets, no sound at all. Just coming. And as they watched, they began to remember the stories they had heard of *Los diablos Tejanos* who had defended the Alamo; on the ground around each was a circle of the men he had slain. Now their cousins were approaching—1,000 yards away, 900, 800 . . .

When the front rank of Americans was about 700 yards distant, Arista gave his artillery the command to open fire. But his guns' range was decidedly less than 700 yards. So the cannonballs came to earth and bounded through the tall grass toward the American line. As they came near, the Americans opened ranks and let them pass through. There were a few sarcastic comments, until the sergeants restored silence.

Major Ringgold and Captain Duncan brought their eight 6-pounders forward about 20 paces in front of the infantry, and held fire as the enemy also began to advance. When they were certain that the Mexicans were well within range, they opened fire, raining shot and shell. Behind them the infantry, well out of musket range, halted and observed the unfolding artillery duel with interest, being careful to sidestep the Mexican balls as they bounded through.

During the long months waiting at the Nueces, Taylor's gunners had drilled and practiced until their fire was now deadly. And now the bassos joined the chorus. The huge 18-pounders at the center of the line fired at the concentrations of troops where the enemy lines were the thickest. Loaded with exploding shells, they were devastating. Lieutenant Sam Grant, waiting in front of his Fourth Infantry, noted their effect: They did "a great deal of execution," clearing "a perfect road" through the enemy ranks.[4] But the Mexicans, he also noted, were uncommonly brave; they kept closing ranks and standing firm—without firing. Their flintlock muskets, however, were woefully short ranged; observed Grant: "At the distance of a few hundred yards, a man might fire at you all day without you finding it out."[5]

For the next hour the effect that light, highly mobile artillery in the hands of expert gunners could have on massed infantry made a profound impression on him, one that he would never forget.

The quickest way to put a stop to the unequal contest, reasoned General Arista, was to turn the Americans' attention behind them. Accordingly, he now dispatched General Torrejón and his Lancers with two cannon around the Americans' right flank, to get at their supply wagons in the rear. Seeing what they were about, Taylor sent Ephraim Kirby Smith and the Fifth Regiment to intercept them. Captain Smith took his men on a rapid right oblique maneuver, which put them squarely in the Lancers' path.

As the Mexican buglers sounded the charge, the dashing Lancers swung into a line abreast. Lowering their lances to the horizontal, they spurred their horses to the gallop, pennants flying, bugles shrilling, lance points shining in the late afternoon sun.

"Here they come!" cried one American, stating what everyone could plainly see—and what they could now feel, as the pounding hooves of 800 horses shook the ground in front of them.

None of the Americans had ever faced a full cavalry charge, and there must have been a powerful temptation to bolt. But where would you go? Off into the desert? Besides, you couldn't leave, not with your mates standing firm on either side. If only one of the other boys would hightail it first . . .

Thanks to his West Point training, Captain Smith knew exactly what to do—what Wellington had done so effectively when facing the charge of Marshall Ney's cavalry at Waterloo. He formed his men into a hollow square, standing shoulder to shoulder, ready to fire a volley on command. Forty yards away, the Mexican Infantry now opened fire as they advanced. A few Americans were wounded, but the square stayed firm. Then, as the Lancers swept past them on either side, they fired a volley into their midst with staggering effect.

And then, out of nowhere, to the right of Kirby Smith's square, appeared Sam Walker and 20 Texas Rangers on foot. Calmly they poured a second volley into the surprised attackers. Kirby Smith was astonished—and grateful, as Torrejón, his charge broken, now determined to destroy the square with his artillery. But before his gunners could bring their pieces to bear, Lieutenants Sam French and Randolph Ridgeley swung two of Ringgold's light guns into position, unlimbered them, and loaded them with grapeshot* and canister.† They managed to get off a withering round that cut down the enemy gun crews before they could fire a shot.

Taylor now sent the dragoons in pursuit of the retreating Mexicans. But while the enemy's left flank bent farther and farther, it did not break, and despite the murderous cannonade, the center held. The battle raged on for more than an hour, until a burning bit of wadding from one of Captain Duncan's guns started a grass fire. Soon a conflagration engulfed the plain between the two forces, and wind carried the smoke into the enemy's eyes.

When the air finally cleared, Captain Duncan found that the enemy opposite him, instead of retreating under the cover of smoke, had *advanced*. Furiously his batteries, gun barrels lowered as far as they could go, fired into them. Never had his crews loaded and reloaded so rapidly; they were getting off an incredible eight rounds a minute!

The enemy fell back, and with dusk approaching rallied to attempt one more charge. That charge, too, was beaten off, and both sides retired from

---

* bags of small lead balls the size of grapes or golf balls
† cans filled with nails and other small metal objects

the field exhausted, withdrawing to lick their wounds. General Taylor had lost 50 men to the enemy's 500, but among his casualties was one he could ill afford to lose: Major Sam Ringgold. The daring innovator of the flying artillery that had saved the day for the Americans was himself torn apart by a cannonball.

It was not a quiet night. Carrying torches, parties of American stretcher bearers searched the charred battlefield, listening for the cries and groans of the wounded. And since there did not seem to be any Mexican stretcher bearers doing the same, they brought in all the wounded they could find, regardless of uniform. All night long the screams from the surgeons' tents were loud and piteous, and in the morning, burial details went out to finish the work.

The pride of the Mexican Army had been dealt a crippling blow. Their officers had convinced their men (and themselves) that the Americans, outnumbered and poorly disciplined, would break and run. The opposite had proven to be the case. The Mexican generals concluded that while their men had fought with great courage, "skill and valor [alone] could never bring victory." The night sky, illuminated by the still-raging grass fire, seemed to "portend a sinister splendor."[6]

Dawn brought a revelation: The entire Mexican Army had decamped! Throughout the night, reconnaissance patrols had reported enemy movement in the direction of Matamoros, but no one realized the extent of it. Calling a council of war to consider their next move, General Taylor asked his senior officers for their recommendations. Seven out of ten advised him to stay put; they were still vastly outnumbered, and in a few days he could expect reinforcement from the volunteers he had called for at the outbreak of hostilities.

Typically, Old Rough and Ready sided with the handful who were ready for more action. "Gentlemen, you will prepare your commands to move forward."[7] Immediately he sent small detachments in opposite directions: his wounded and the Mexican prisoners with a small escort back to Point Isabel, and Sam Walker and his Rangers ahead to locate the enemy.

The main body marched stoically forward, sweating in the relentless sun—one mile, two, three. . . . Fort Texas lay only seven more miles away. Perhaps the Mexicans had crossed the Rio Grande for Matamoros, and they would not have to fight again. But around 2:30, the sound of small-arms fire ahead put that dream to flight.

Once again the Mexican Army had dug in across the road. But this time, they were out of sight—and out of the line of fire from the artillery that had wrought such destruction in their ranks. They were hidden in a resaca—an old, dry riverbed of the Rio Grande—and had been reinforced by fresh troops from Matamoros, more than the number of casualties they had suffered the day before. They now outnumbered the Americans by *three* to one. Their artillery was not hidden: Their biggest gun was squarely in the middle of the road, and other cannon were up on the front edge of the resaca, trained on the Americans' approach.

The past 24 hours had done wonders for Taylor's attitude about artillery, especially his own. He now called on Lieutenants French and Ridgeley to get their flying artillery up to the front of the column to put the enemy's pieces out of action. In no time, Ridgeley's caissons were rolling over hill and over dale, while the rest of the army scrambled to the side of the road to get out of their way. When they arrived at the head of the column, Sam Walker led the two lieutenants and their batteries forward until they came under Mexican artillery fire.

Now they wheeled their guns and went into action. This time, they were well within the enemy's range. Grapeshot slashed through the dense and thorny underbrush around them, while pounding up the road at them was the cavalry, lances at the level. But the American guns were ready now, and they poured canister into them, stopping the charge in its tracks.

The Americans were nonetheless having a bad time of it. The enemy infantry, firing from concealment in the resaca, were taking their toll of the gunners, while the American foot soldiers desperately sought an opening through the chaparral thickets to come to the aid of the batteries.

Just as Kirby Smith found a way and led the Fifth through it, Taylor sent the dragoons forward at the gallop—a stirring sight, which brought cheers from those in blue. While the clouds of dust from their charge still hung in the air, Taylor, sensing the shift in momentum and capitalizing on it, now sent the Fifth forward in a charge.

The dragoons, meanwhile, were discovering that mounted troops were worse than useless against dug-in infantry. Taking heavy casualties, they wheeled and headed for the safety of their lines. Their foray was not entirely for naught; not only had the tide of battle turned, but they had captured the Mexican field commander, General Romolo Dias de la Vega.

So certain had General Arista been that Taylor would not attack a second day in a row, that he had turned the command over to one of his staff officers. Now seeing that disaster was imminent, Arista spurred forward and himself led a vainglorious cavalry charge at the American line. But the line held, and Arista was turned back.

The Fifth was locked in vicious hand-to-hand work along the edge of the resaca before the Mexican line finally broke. Their retreat soon deteriorated into a rout, with every Mexican fleeing for his life. Eight cannon were abandoned, along with 1,500 muskets; General Arista himself left behind all his papers and personal belongings. Those on foot ran for the safety of Matamoros. But first they would have to cross the river without boats, and in their panic as many as 300 drowned. All told, their losses numbered around 1,500 that day, while the Americans mourned 120 killed in action.

That evening, the young future generals had a different attitude about combat now that they had had a taste of it. Lieutenant Sam French could still find some glory in it, recording in his journal: "The conduct of our troops was . . . courageous in the extreme. Banners were captured by gallant old officers from the hands of the enemy and were held aloft in the front during the conflict."

Captain Kirby Smith was relieved, thanking "a kind God who yet spares me." And Lieutenant Sam Grant, whose company had hardly needed him to tell them to hit the dirt to avoid the enemy's heavy fire, wryly allowed as how "the battle . . . would have been won just as it was, if I had not been there."[8]

14

"A New Spirit Abroad in the Land"

As the last bundle of the extra edition went into the waiting wagon, the apprentice printer peeled off the top copy and nailed it to the front door, for people were sure to come to their offices, demanding a paper. Even in the flickering light of the gas streetlamp, the headline, which took up the entire top half of the front page, could be easily read several paces away:

WAR!

In city after city the scene was repeated, as editors and pressmen labored to turn out still later editions, garnered from just-arrived reports. They, too, would be sold out in minutes, for the entire nation was caught up in what was happening down at the Rio Grande and also in the capital.

From Washington came news that Congress had just approved President Polk's War Measures Bill, granting him permission to raise 50,000 volunteers to serve a one-year enlistment or until the cessation of hostilities with Mexico, whichever came first. Moreover, an expenditure of $10 million had been authorized to prosecute the war—a breathtaking sum in 1846, but no more than fitting: The Stars and Stripes had been fired upon, and America, the Home of the Brave, was going to war!

As usual, the newspapers mirrored the mood of their readership, and not all of them were cheering. In the New York *Tribune*, Whig editor Horace Greeley lamented: "People of the United States! Your rulers are precipitating you into a fathomless abyss of crime and calamity!"

But the prevailing attitude was expressed by poet Walt Whitman, then editor of the Brooklyn *Eagle*: "Let our arms now be carried with a spirit which shall teach the world that, while we are not forward for a quarrel, America knows how to crush, as well as how to expand."[1]

With the exception of deeply antislavery regions, including States like Massachusetts and Ohio, the country was ready for war. Among her young men, north, south, east, and west, was a great restiveness. They had been farming or clerking or digging or loading for what seemed like years. Peace and stability were all well and good, but they were also—boring. The young were ready for some adventure.

Each generation, it seems, must learn the true horrors of war all over again, and more than a generation had passed since Old Hickory stood atop the earthworks and directed Yankee fire into a mass of charging Redcoats. True, there had been the Black Hawk War and the Seminole War, but they had been Indian uprisings, put down by the professionals. There had not been a war for everyone, and young men who had grown up singing "The Battle of New Orleans" wondered if there would ever be a war for them, which others would one day sing about.

The New Orleans papers were closest to the action and the first to publish popular accounts of what had happened. Their coverage was reprinted in other cities as soon as the first edition arrived. Some of the major dailies had sent war correspondents to travel with Taylor, and often their accounts from the front would travel north on the same packet as the military dispatches. As a result, much of the nation knew what was happening before Washington did. And as other papers republished what the majors carried, many could not resist embellishing it and weighing in with editorials calling on all red-blooded Americans to respond to the dire predicament of our vastly outnumbered expeditionary force. Were they going to permit a repetition of the Alamo? Of Goliad? Never!

All over America, young men responded to the President's call—so many, in fact, that each state's quota of enlistments was over-subscribed, and volunteers had to be turned away. In Illinois, which was asked for four regiments, enough men volunteered to fill 14. In Tennessee 30,000 came forward to fill a quota of 3,000; when none would go home, the selection was made by lot, and men complained that you couldn't even *purchase* a place in the ranks! North Carolina offered three times her quota, and in the Gulf States there was concern that so many men were leaving there was no one left to look after their slaves. In Kentucky, it took a proclamation by the Governor to put a stop to the volunteering. Within two weeks of the call, even abolitionist Ohio had sent 3,000 off to the rendezvous.

It has been said that the war sense of the United States seems to be in inverse ratio to its war spirit,[2] and in the days following the opening of hostilities, America was truly caught in the grip of war fever. On Capitol Hill, opponents of the war, fearing for their political futures, dared not speak against it. One of the two Senators who did vote against it, however, was the leader of the Whig opposition, Henry Clay, who would soon exclaim: "All the nations, I apprehend, look upon us in the prosecution of this present war, as being actuated by a spirit of rapacity and an inordinate desire for territorial aggrandizement."[3]

There was no question that the war bill had been railroaded through; indeed, as Thomas Hart Benton, himself an expansionist, observed, "Without that event* it would have been difficult—perhaps impossible—to have got Congress to vote it; with it, the vote was almost unanimous."[4]

Of all the western States so quick to respond to the President's call to arms, none was quicker than Missouri. Many Missourians had kin or friends who had died fighting for Texas's independence. From firsthand accounts they knew the ruthlessness of General Ampudia (now the Mexican Army's Supreme Commander, in the wake of Arista's disgrace), how he had cut off the head of a rival general and boiled it in oil. This was the devil who now held Captain Thornton and his dragoons captive. Clay County, as soon as it heard the call, sent a full company of 120 men up the Missouri River to the rendezvous at Fort Leavenworth. Most of them, mindful of the extra 40 cents per diem that went to each soldier who outfitted himself, brought their own horses, wet-weather gear, and bedrolls. When they arrived, they were informed that they would be Company C of a regiment known as the First Missouri Mounted Volunteers.

Company C had two members who would stand out in any group. One was John T. Hughes, a pensive, articulate schoolteacher who decided to keep a journal of his war experiences. In it he wrote his own summation of why he joined up, and though he was writing for himself and perhaps his children, he was speaking for most of the men who rode or marched

---

* The "event" being the attack on Thornton's patrol on the Texas side of the Rio Grande.

beside him. He listed the indiscriminate murder of Texans who fell into Mexican hands, the repeated acts of cruelty and injustice perpetrated on American citizens residing in the northern provinces of Mexico, the detention of American citizens in prison, and the Mexican army's crossing of the Rio Grande in force, with hostile intent. "Or should we have forborne," he concluded, "until the catalogue of offenses was still deeper dyed with infamous crimes, and until the blood of our brothers, friends, and consanguinity, like that of murdered Abel, should cry out to us from the ground?"[5]

The other standout in Company C stood literally half a foot above the rest. Alexander William Doniphan was 6'5" tall—a prominent lawyer who had gained military experience leading the 1838 campaign against the Mormons. In those days, volunteer units elected their officers from among their ranks, and Private Doniphan was soon elected Colonel Doniphan, the regimental commander. He, in turn, would report to the commander of the newly forming Army of the West: General Stephen Watts Kearny, commander of Fort Leavenworth's First Dragoons, the one Regular Army regiment amongst all the volunteers.

In their first meeting, Kearny gave Doniphan his formidable assignment: As soon as his men were fully outfitted and provisioned, he was to take the First Mounted Missouri Volunteers south, to connect with the Santa Fe Trail. They were then to head west. Their mission: to take Santa Fe—the seat of government for the province of New Mexico.

Another force, half the size of Doniphan's but every bit as intrepid, was about to be galvanized into action by the news from Texas. Out in California, John C. Frémont and his expedition had received no communication from Washington more recent than the orders in his saddlebags, dated a year before. Ostensibly he and his "topographical engineers" were there to make accurate maps of California and Oregon. But there were 62 of them, far more than necessary for a peaceful surveying party; indeed, in that sparsely populated country they amounted to a small army.

Moreover, each was worth several ordinary men, for they were all hardened adventurers, wearing Bowie knives and balancing long rifles across the pommels of their saddles. Frémont's chief scout was none other than Kit Carson, and their ranks included 12 Delaware Indians, plus such legendary mountain men as Tom "Broken Hand" Fitzpatrick, Joseph Walker, and Alexis Godey.

In the back of all of their minds was the likelihood that Mexico and the United States would soon be at war. In that eventuality Frémont had also received secret verbal orders from President Polk: The moment he received official confirmation that hostilities had commenced, he was to take as much of California as he could, acting in concert with the Pacific Squadron under Commodore Sloat.

Frémont's great drawback was his impetuosity. Two months earlier, he had ignored the ultimatum of the Mexican commander, General José Castro, headquartered on the coast at Monterrey, to leave California at once. Instead, Frémont had his men erect a log fort atop a hill, above which he had raised the Stars and Stripes.

Only when a large Mexican force accompanied by cannon appeared did he begin to think the better of what he had done: he had been told to *await* word of hostilities between the two nations, not *precipitate* them. That night under cover of darkness he and his men abandoned their fort and left California—though they stopped just over the Oregon border.

On May 9, the same day that Taylor won his victory at Resaca de la Palma, Lieutenant Gillespie of the Marine Corps reached Frémont with new secret orders (only eight months old), plus letters from his wife and his father-in-law, Senator Benton. There was also an instruction to Thomas Larkin, the U.S. Consul at Monterrey, to assist native Californians, should they desire, as Texas had, to break away from Mexico and join the great North American Union. In his letter, Benton encouraged Frémont to uncover any British initiative in California, and, as he would recall in his memoirs, "so far as it was in my power, to counteract them."[6]

That night, as he read and reread the letters from home by the light of the campfire with the night wind whispering through the tall pines, Frémont dreamed of the glory that at last might soon be his. Had Gillespie not informed him that the Pacific Squadron was momentarily expecting word of hostilities? In his reverie he neglected to set a watch and was soon fast asleep, perhaps dreaming of leading his corps, joined by eager volunteers, in an assault on General Castro's headquarters.

His dream was rudely shattered. "Indians! Indians!" cried Kit Carson, sounding the alarm. Grabbing rifles and Bowie knives, his men fought off the sneak attack by warriors of a local tribe, killing their chief—but not before three of their own had been murdered in their bedrolls. Thereafter, whenever they were in camp, Frémont made certain a double watch was posted.

Back in early fall of '45, when Senator Benton had written his free-booting son-in-law of his grave concern about British "intermeddling" in California, he was expressing the fears of a great many Americans. The British, and for that matter the French and any other European power capable of projecting force halfway around the globe, posed a real threat to the emerging North American Republic. God had not brought the Pilgrims and Puritans, the Catholics and Moravians, the Anglicans and Baptists—and the Jews—over the ocean to this wild continent, only to see them revert back into Old World darkness. As they themselves knew and recorded in their diaries and letters, in this wilderness He had set before them a banquet table, anointed them, and filled their cup to overflowing. He had intended them to be an example to the rest of the world that, by embracing Biblical principles, it *was* possible to live together in harmony, humility, and compassion.

Their fathers and grandfathers had fought and died for the right to become one nation under Him, with liberty and justice for all. *For freedom Christ has set us free; stand fast therefore, and do not submit again to a yoke of slavery* (Galatians 5:1) was one of the verses with which preachers had encouraged their forefathers to march off to war. God had given them the victory, and His new Republic was to be a wellspring of Freedom, to which all who thirsted might come and drink deeply.

Before God, then, they had an obligation to keep the portion of North America that He intended them to have free from foreign entanglements. It was a sacred obligation, not only for the sake of their descendants, but also for the hundreds of thousands of immigrants who would come thirsting for freedom in perhaps the only land left on earth where true freedom could be found.

It was hardly a new idea. As the Reverend Samuel West had said in Boston at the beginning of the War for Independence, "I cannot help hoping, and even believing, that Providence has designed this continent for to be the asylum of liberty and true religion."[7] By 1846 the idea had become part of the spiritual fabric of American society. Down in Mississippi, Governor A. G. Brown speculated that "in the order of Providence, America might become the last asylum of liberty to the human family."[8]

This awareness that God might have a plan for America found its way into print under the pen of a young visionary named John L. O'Sullivan. Trained to be a lawyer, O'Sullivan's first love was the written word. In 1837 he started a literary journal called the *Democratic Review,* which published some of the earliest work of Nathaniel Hawthorne, Edgar Allen Poe, and John Greenleaf Whittier.

A year later, he first shared his vision:

> The far-reaching, the boundless future will be the era of American greatness. In its magnificent domain of space and time, the nation of many nations is destined to manifest to mankind the excellence of divine principles; to establish on earth the noblest temple ever dedicated to the worship of the Most High . . . its congregation a Union of many Republics, comprising hundreds of happy millions, calling, owning, no man master. But governed by God's natural and moral law of equality, the law of brotherhood—of "peace and goodwill amongst men."[9]

Destined to manifest—it was a theme to which O'Sullivan would frequently return. After the annexation of Texas he rejoiced in "the inevitable fulfillment of the general law which is rolling our population westward— the connection of which with that ratio of growth in population . . . is too evident to leave us in doubt of the manifest design of Providence in regard to the occupation of this continent."[10]

And during the debate over the future of the jointly occupied Oregon Territory, O'Sullivan (who was also editor of the New York *Morning News*) opined: "And yet after all, unanswerable as is the demonstration of our legal title to Oregon . . . that claim is by the right of our manifest destiny to overspread and to possess the whole continent which Providence has given us for the development of the great experiment of liberty and federated self-government entrusted to us."[11]

The first person to refer to the concept of Manifest Destiny on Capitol Hill was Robert Winthrop of Massachusetts. On January 3, 1846, he called into question "the right of our manifest destiny to spread over this whole continent," concluding with a request to see in Adam's "will" where he bequeathed this exclusive title by manifest destiny.[12]

Delighted with the term, the expansionists took it as their own. Congressman Edward D. Baker addressed himself "to a point which had excited some sneers; namely to the doctrine that it was our manifest destiny to come into the ultimate possession of this territory of Oregon." He insisted that there *was* such a thing as the manifest destiny of a nation, a providential end, foreshadowed by history.[13]

It fell to the redoubtable John Quincy Adams to provide chapter and verse. On February 9, 1846, he was, as usual, being given a hard time by Southern members, and as usual, he was giving as good as he got. He had just finished replying to Robert Barnwell Rhett of South Carolina, when Thomas Butler King of Georgia asked him to defend his assertion that America's right to Oregon was "clear and unquestionable."

Adams rose and turned to the new Speaker of the House, John W. Davis. Pointing to "the little book you have on your table, which you employ to administer a solemn oath," he asked that the Bible be passed to the clerk, and that the clerk read aloud Genesis 1:26–28.

When the clerk read, "and God said unto them, Be fruitful, and multiply, and replenish the earth, and subdue it: and have dominion," JQA broke in.

"There, sir," he exclaimed, "in my judgment is the foundation, not only of our title to Oregon but the foundation of all human title to all human possessions."[14]

Then he asked for the eighth verse of the Second Psalm: "Ask of me, and I shall give thee the heathen for thine inheritance, and the uttermost parts of the earth for thy possession."

His colleagues nodded approvingly. No one objected or raised a point of order on "separation of Church and State."* Nor did anyone offer a countertext, for none of them knew the Bible as well as Adams.

In conclusion he maintained that Americans were called to continue carrying out God's plan, as they had been doing in their steady expansion westward. They were to continue farming the land, building churches and schools, rendering the vast, untamed wild a veritable garden for the flourishing of freedom and liberty. "We claim that country—for what? To

---

* In those days almost all accepted (or purported to accept) the authority of God's Word.

make the wilderness blossom as the rose, to establish laws, to increase, multiply, and subdue the earth, which we are commanded to do by the first behest of God Almighty. . . . She [Britain] claims to keep it open for navigation, for her hunters to hunt wild beasts. . . . There is the difference between our claims!"[15]

The motion to terminate the joint occupation treaty with Britain carried, 163 to 54.

In comparing the foreigners' intent and their own, Adams struck a resonant chord in many breasts. To them, it was a sin to let arable soil, provided by God, go untilled! As the New York *Morning News* put it: "It has been laid down and acted upon, that the solitudes of America are the property of the immigrant children of Europe and their offspring. Not only has this been said and reiterated, but it is actually . . . the basis of public law in America. Public sentiment with us repudiates possession without use, and this sentiment is gradually acquiring the force of established public law."[16]*

While many feared a third war with Britannia, especially after her bellicose response to Polk's Inaugural Address, some felt strongly enough about the principle of Manifest Destiny to say: If it's war they want, let it begin there.

When it came to hawkish sentiments, the newspapers were, as usual, in the forefront. Noted the *United States Journal* in Washington: "There is a new spirit abroad in the land—young, restless, vigorous and omnipotent. . . . [the Republic] will plant its right foot upon the northern verge of Oregon, and its left upon the Atlantic crag, and waving the Stars and Stripes in the face of the once-proud Mistress of the Ocean, bid her, if she dare, 'Cry havoc, and let slip the dogs of war!' "[17]

While widespread, fear of war over Oregon was not well-founded. Already embroiled in two other far-flung wars, Great Britain had no taste for commencing a third. She instructed her minister in Washington to offer a compromise along the 49th parallel, which the Americans had originally suggested.

It took time, of course, for that word to reach Washington; even with the advent of the lofty clipper ships, an Atlantic crossing still took more

---

* Eventually it did. The law said, in effect: Go ahead and stake your claim, sodbuster, but you'd better work that claim within a year, or it will revert to the status of unclaimed land.

than two weeks. The British proposal was in midocean when Polk met in emergency session with his Cabinet over what to do about Oregon. With half his regular army already engaged in a war on his southern border, he obviously preferred a peaceful solution. But he was prepared to go to war, should the British force the issue.

All the President's men agreed, save for his Secretary of State. James Buchanan had lost his nerve. He urged Polk to send Great Britain *and* France pledges that America's reasons for going to war with Mexico had nothing to do with territorial aggrandizement. His obsequious, pandering proposal infuriated Polk, who recorded in his diary: "I told him that before I would make the pledge he proposed, I would meet the war which either England or France or all the powers of Christendom might wage, and that I would fight until the last man among us fell in the conflict!"

The President was only gathering steam; he went on to tell Buchanan that "neither as a citizen nor as President would I permit or tolerate any intermeddling of any European powers on this continent!" He reiterated that "sooner than give the pledge he proposed . . . I would let the war he apprehended with England come and would take the whole responsibility."[18]

When the dove from England arrived on June 6 with an olive branch in its beak, the Cabinet met again. Polk was inclined to accept the proposed 49th parallel—and was amazed to hear Buchanan now reverse his position and insist that they not settle for less than their original demand of 54° 40'! There could be only one explanation for such a bizarre reversal: His Secretary of State was doing a bit of early campaigning for his own run at the Presidency. He was making sure he could claim to Western voters that he had opposed the compromise. Disgusted with him, Polk decided to let the Senate settle the question. That body endorsed the 49th parallel boundary, 38 to 12, and on June 15 the Oregon Treaty was signed.

Oregon, the newest addition to the vast continental tapestry, now raised the question, just how far *was* the country going to expand? And how far *should* it expand?

Men of prayer like John Quincy Adams were supremely confident that God was with them every westward step of the way. But how far *did* He intend them to go on multiplying and subduing? Once men thought of the Mississippi as God's natural boundary. Then they thought of the Rockies. Now it was clearly the Pacific Ocean. But what about north and south? It would seem that He intended the United States of America to include Texas and Oregon, but what of the land north of the 49th parallel, known as British North America (now the Northwest Territories)? And what of the territory west of Texas? For that matter, what of Mexico itself? And even beyond?

Had you voiced such speculation ten years before, your neighbors may have thought your compass had lost its north. Now, some would call you a man of vision. Men were dreaming of extending railroads across the continent. Within the next generation people would be able to travel from coast to coast in a matter of days and send messages in minutes. Was it so far-fetched to think of one nation under God, stretching from sea to shining sea?

In Congress, young Stephen A. Douglas of Illinois "would blot out the lines on the map which now marked our national boundaries on this continent and make the area of liberty as broad as the continent itself." But according to the record of the House proceedings, "he did not wish to go beyond the great ocean—beyond those boundaries which the God of nature had marked out."[19]

Soon other editors were referring to America's Manifest Destiny, elevating the concept to a self-evident Truth. Even the Mexican War's most vehement detractors grudgingly acknowledged the likelihood of God's hand in the resulting westward expansion. Wrote a Boston literary society in its newsletter: "There can be no doubt of the design being entertained by the leaders and instigators of this infamous business, to extend the 'area of freedom' to the shores of California. . . . [The war] is to be viewed as monstrously iniquitous, but after all it seems to be completing a more universal design of Providence."[20]

In any contemplation of the possibility of a manifest destiny, the great pitfall was (and is) pride: If God intends this for us, who is to say we shouldn't have it? But such spiritual arrogance invariably wound up with the end justifying the means. The means should have been in the forefront of the national conscience, instead of being barely an afterthought. For implied—indeed, embedded—in this corporate call of God to span the continent was an obligation to care for all those who would be displaced, to treat them with consummate compassion.

In a sense, we were to be missionaries to the tribes and peoples we found as we moved west, showing them by our example why it was a good thing to follow the principles of Christ. In addition to our religion, we were expected to introduce them to the advantages of our civilization—medicine, education, and republican government.

At least, that was the vision. But that was not how it played out.

First, not all who came to the Land of the Free were free. Hundreds of thousands had been taken forcibly from their native land, from homes and families and society, and held in perpetual bondage. Was *that* God's will?

It was precisely on this point that John Quincy Adams' ardor for westward expansion began to chill. Oregon was one thing, but Texas? California? New Mexico? And now possibly Mexico herself? Adams and the anti-expansionists began to see the whole movement as a gigantic, subtle scheme of the Slave Power to retain their political dominance. What could be more hypocritical than expanding "the area of freedom by enlarging the boundary of slavery"?[21]

Here Adams was wrong (it was one of the few places). Expansionism was a *national,* not a regional concern of Southern slaveholders, and the majority of Americans firmly believed that it was their collective mission to extend the light of freedom clear to the Pacific. Indeed, the enterprising, courageous pioneer, once an offshoot of society, now seemed the very essence of what it meant to be an American.

And there was genuine altruism in the westward movement. The pioneer family may have been focused primarily on the new homestead that awaited them, but statesmen behind them had a broader vision. Proclaimed Congressman James E. Belser of Alabama: "Long may our country prove itself the asylum of the oppressed. . . . When the waters of despotism shall have inundated other portions of the globe, and the votary of liberty be compelled to take himself to his ark, let this government be the Ararat on which it shall rest!"[22]

But what of the native Americans, on whose lands the pioneers were homesteading? The western Indian tribes had roamed the plains and prairies with complete freedom—until the white man claimed ownership of land that had always belonged to all, and started building fences to keep others off what he now insisted was his. Did God want the Indians pushed off their hunting grounds and herded into reservations?

These were not easy questions to answer, and only an arrogant fool would claim to be sure of knowing God's complete plan and intent. This much was obvious: God intended all men, black or white, red or yellow, to follow the example of His Son in their dealings with one another.

Many Christian pioneers did get along well with their Indian neighbors. They had come in peace and lived in peace. But among any people, even among those who consider themselves Christian, there will be some who are cruel and insensitive. Given free rein with minimal accountability, they can soon overcloud the sunniest of days.

In his natural state, man is instinctively selfish; it takes supernatural inspiration for him to live selflessly. A system of laws must be erected to protect the rights of all—which is the great strength of a republic. In America the system was not yet working for the black man, and it was not working for the red man, either. But one day it would; God was on His throne. It might take far longer than it should have and far longer than some would like, but one day His will would prevail.

In the meantime, the Indians would be disenfranchised, uprooted, and given land that no one could imagine white men ever wanting (until they decided they did want it). The Indians were given Federal treaties, solemn promises from the Great White Father in Washington and all his elders: This will be your land from now on, in perpetuity; never again will we take your land from you. And then they took it—again.

It should not have been that way. At the very least, the Government of the United States should have honored its word and its obligations—obligations under treaties it imposed on tribes who could do nothing but accept them. Together with slavery, our treatment of the Native Americans is the other dark chapter in our history.

But in the 1840s, hardly anyone was thinking that way. An 1844 editorial in the Boston *Times* summed up what it called the spirit of Young America: "[It] will not be satisfied with what has been attained, but plumes its young wings for a higher and more glorious flight. The hopes of America, the hopes of humanity, must rest on this spirit. . . . The steam is up, the young overpowering spirit of the country will press onward. It would be as easy to stay the swelling of the ocean with a grain of sand upon its shore, as to stop the advancement of this truly democratic and omnipotent spirit of the age."[23]

And out in California, the western destination of that spirit, the setting sun was rendering everything in burnished gold. . . .

15

IDYLL IN PARADISE

aradise—the word appeared often in the glowing reports of California sent back East in 1846. And no wonder: Any Yankee pioneer accustomed to the harsh climate and thin soil of New England would be astounded when an absolutely perfect day—warm, balmy, with a gentle rain in midafternoon, which cleared by sunset—would be followed by another. And another. And another—until he or she bemusedly wondered if they had been transported to the Garden of Eden.

Everything grew here! Hardy Northern grains, juicy Southern fruits, even exotic tropical varieties—and practically year round; the growing season just never seemed to quit. All you had to do was poke a seed into the rich, black soil, and God would do the rest.

Naval Lieutenant Joseph Warren Revere,* serving aboard the *USS Portsmouth* in the Pacific Squadron, spent enough time ashore to become thoroughly besotted with this land of perfect days and perfect crops. "The soil is of incredible fertility, the yield of wheat being as high as a hundred-fold, while corn and vegetables of all kinds, including the finest potatoes I ever saw, flourish most luxuriantly. The fruits of the temperate zone thrive here side by side with those of the tropics. Peaches, pears, apples, melons, of all kinds, and rich luscious grapes may be seen growing in the same garden with sugar cane, dates, figs, and bananas. . . ."

No wonder Mexico was so reluctant to relinquish California, and the English Bulldog could not keep from nosing about.

"There is reason to believe," Revere concluded, "that California will be

---

* grandson of Paul Revere

dependent on no other country for the necessaries of life. . . . Indeed, it is difficult to name any product of the earth whether it be to eat, drink, or wear, which California cannot yield, while her mineral wealth excites the astonishment of the world."[1]

Perhaps the most surprising thing about California in 1846 was the paucity of Anglo settlers who had found their way there. True, it had been only a few years since the mountain men had opened the first passes through the seemingly impenetrable snowcapped Rockies. And true, it took months to get here by wagon, and it was a journey fraught with peril—yet would you not risk all for Paradise?

In 1846 the population density in California was one person per 26 square miles—and these settlers were so far from Mexico City that they were for the most part self-ruling. If a settlement was large enough to be a town, it might have an *alcade*, or mayor, and possibly a garrison with a handful of soldiers. But for the most part the settlers were on their own, much as the settlers in Texas had been. All told, there were only 25,000 people in California, and of these approximately 10,000 were "savage Indians" and 5,000 "semi-civilized Indians." Of the remainder, the vast majority were *Californios*—Mexicans who had come up to farm or raise cattle or horses, in a land so generous that less work was required there than practically anywhere.

Less than a thousand inhabitants were Anglos from the United States. Word of paradise on earth was increasing the trickle of transcontinental pioneers, but by no more than 400 a year.

It takes a bit of doing today to look down from the hills above Los Angeles, San Diego, San Francisco, or any of the cities that have grown up around the tiny mission settlements that once dotted the coast of California and imagine what it must have been like a century and a half ago. Rolling green hills and sparkling streams and clear, pure air—it was almost too beautiful to be real. Indeed, if you were making a movie, it would be like shooting all the scenes in the last half hour before sunset, when everything takes on a magical, rosy golden hue. Golden was the color that befitted California.

What happened there during the Mexican War was more like a movie than reality—like one of the romantic sort Hollywood used to make in the 1930s. The story line was so preposterous, so full of derring-do and bizarre coincidences and grandiose envisioning that it would never get past a modern script editor. But back then, movie-goers were more in-nocent and more willing to suspend disbelief. And so, up on the silver screen one man with boundless dreams could persuade others to believe too, and a handful of men could become an army. Incredibly brave, amaz-ingly bold, they could accomplish—anything.

And like its 1930s Hollywood counterparts, the unfolding of California was a movie with a small budget and a tight schedule: Few of the action scenes ever involved more than a hundred extras. Frémont and his 60-odd "topographical engineers" constituted the largest quasi-military force in all of California. And basically, it was a feel-good movie: In their unkempt hair and greasy buckskins, Frémont's men were a wonderfully scruffy lot, with the occasional posturing Mexican official providing comic relief.

The teaser before credits rolled was the arrival of Lieutenant Archibald Gillespie with "fresh" news from Washington. The movie opened with Frémont and his men passing the time at New Helvetia, the idyllic ranch of the Swiss entrepreneur, John Sutter, on the Sacramento River, awaiting word that the war with Mexico had begun. There were rumors aplenty. According to one rumor, Pio Pico, the self-styled Governor of Southern California, had invited the British to take over the province. Another had it that Mexican General José Maria Castro, who regarded Northern California as his personal fiefdom, was about to enlist the Indians in a war on the American settlers. But there was no official word of any sort.

Finally Frémont could wait no longer. He dispatched some 30 American settlers under Ezekiel "Stuttering" Merritt to Sonoma, the nearest town, where a retired *Comandante General*, Mariano Vallejo, had a modest hacienda. At daybreak on June 14, Vallejo was awakened by a commotion outside his house. To his surprise he found it surrounded by ruffians whose leader now entered his living room and informed him that the revolution had begun. What revolution? The American settlers were throwing off the oppressive California Government and establishing a republic! Where? Here! Sonoma was the first town to be liberated, and the Vallejo family were their prisoners.

The former General was far from dismayed. He, too, had long been disgusted with the regional government and had looked forward to the day when California would become part of the United States. Now he excused himself and went back into his bedroom. When he returned, he was wearing his dress sword, which with great solemnity he proffered to his captors. When they were not interested, he took the sword back into his bedroom. Next he brought them something they *were* interested in: *aguardiente* (sugarcane brandy).

One bottle led to another, and before long his guests were drunk—not gracefully inebriated, as at the General's former elegant dinner parties, but roaring drunk in true frontier fashion. They started quarreling, and rounded up all the *Californios* in the town (15) and marched them off to Sutter's "Fort" to turn them over to Frémont.

Merritt left 20 men behind in Sonoma, and one of them, young William Todd,* designed a flag to commemorate their newly won independence. It had a star and a stripe and the words "California Republic." Then someone suggested it ought to have a symbol of the territory, and someone else suggested it ought to be a grizzly bear. Todd did his best, though according to some of his comrades, his best looked more like a pig than a bear.

William Ide, the man left in charge of the new Bear Flag Republic, now made a proclamation: They would provide peace and security for all law-abiding individuals, but their intent was nothing less than the overthrow of the Province of California's Government, which he now denounced as selfish and incompetent, as well as oppressive.[2]

Over in Monterey, the head of that Government, General Castro, was enraged when he heard what had happened at Sonoma. Vowing to retake the town as soon as he could raise an army, he recruited 50 *Californios* and marched north. The Bear Flaggers (as they were now called), numbering about 40, marched south. Outside San Rafael, the two "armies" met. A brief but hot skirmish ensued. When two of the *Californios* were killed, the rest decided that perhaps discretion *was* the better part of valor. They and their general opted for a strategic withdrawal and headed for home, with General Castro vowing enmity and revenge.

About this time back in Washington there occurred an episode so bizarre that no good screenplay writer would have touched it, not even to include in a golden hued comic opera.

* Todd's Aunt Mary, back in Springfield, Illinois, had recently wed a country lawyer named Lincoln.

Santa Anna, the Mexican *Presidente* who had barely escaped with his life the year before, was impatiently waiting for destiny to deliver him from exile in Havana. Hardly anyone who has tasted absolute power can long bear to be deprived of it, and Santa Anna was miserable. But he had a plan. . . .

To the White House in February of 1846 came a shadowy figure on a confidential assignment: Colonel Alejandro José Atocha. Refusing to divulge the nature of his visit to anyone but the President himself, Atocha was eventually granted a private audience. He told Polk that Santa Anna expected momentarily to return to power; indeed, he hinted, the Paredes coup had actually been a front for the charismatic general. When the time was right, he would once again return, to the cheers of his countrymen, just as he had before.

Colonel Atocha came to the heart of his message: For a private payment of $30 million, Santa Anna, as *Presidente*, was prepared to accept the boundary of the Rio Grande to the Colorado River in the West, thence through the Bay of San Francisco to the Pacific, relinquishing all of present New Mexico and northern California. But, cautioned Santa Anna through Atocha, the terms must appear to be forced on Mexico; no ruler could publicly endorse such terms and survive. Atocha concluded by quoting his general: "When you see the President, tell him to take strong measures; such a treaty can be made, and I will sustain it."[3]

After Atocha departed, Polk was skeptical in the extreme. Still—if there was the remotest possibility that he was telling the truth, Polk would welcome any opportunity to save American lives, even if it meant indulging in high-level bribery . . .

Polk told Navy Secretary Bancroft to send a confidential message to Commodore Connor, who was commanding the Home Squadron blockading Mexico's east coast: "If Santa Anna endeavors to enter the Mexican ports, you will allow him to pass freely."[4] And to Santa Anna he sent Commander Mackenzie of the Navy as a secret emissary. His message: President Polk wanted him back in Mexico *now*.

Unwittingly Polk had just opened the door to the return of the most dangerous foe America could possibly face—the one man who could unite a fractured and dispirited Mexico and galvanize her into total war with the United States.

Fade to California—

On hearing that in their first test of arms the Bear Flaggers had prevailed, Frémont now proceeded with all deliberate haste to Sonoma. There, by popular demand, he assumed leadership of the Bear Flag Republic. There he celebrated the Fourth of July—and may have overcelebrated: He publicly announced his intention to conquer all of California.

After the euphoria (and *aguardiente*) had worn off, and contemplating the fact that war between the United States and Mexico was (as far as he knew) still undeclared, he sent his father-in-law a letter resigning his commission, to be used should ensuing events prove embarrassing to the United States Government.

On July 9 Lieutenant Revere arrived at Sonoma and summoned the newly formed California Battalion to the public square. Formally congratulating them, he confirmed that a state of war *did* exist between the United States and Mexico. Thunderous cheers went up, and a fusillade of pistol and rifle shots was fired into the air. When calm returned to the plaza, Lieutenant Revere solemnly claimed California for the United States. The Bear Flag, after flying for 25 days, was lowered, and the Stars and Stripes was raised.

Up and down the California coast cruised the Pacific Squadron under Commodore Sloat. About to retire, he was hoping his replacement would arrive before he was forced to take action. He had been aware of the events at the Rio Grande for several weeks, yet he hesitated—for he was also aware of the disgrace that his predecessor, Catesby Jones, had brought on himself four years before at Monterey. In the wake of that national embarrassment, Sloat's orders were quite specific: Until hostilities had actually commenced, he was "to be assiduously careful to avoid any act which could be construed as aggression."[5] Hostilities *had* commenced, but he had yet to receive confirmation from Washington.

His indecision vanished in June, when it was rumored that British Admiral Sir John Seymour was about to take Monterey himself. The Pacific Squadron crowded on sail and entered Monterey's harbor on July 2. Upon being informed of the new Bear Flag Republic, and assuming that Frémont had acted under orders from Washington, Sloat promptly demanded the surrender of Monterey and received it from the heavily outgunned General Castro.

When Sloat finally met Frémont, he was shocked to learn that he had acted on his own initiative. Naturally, Sloat was immensely relieved when his replacement, Commodore Robert Stockton, arrived. Stockton, a younger and more vigorous commander, devised a plan with Frémont for a two-pronged assault on Los Angeles, where General Castro and Governor Pico were preparing a serious defense of the city and the provincial government. Stockton would lead a landing force of some 360, while Frémont's California Battalion, having been transported down to San Diego by the Pacific Squadron, would ride north.

For once, the best-laid plan did not go astray; it worked perfectly. The threat of the combined force proved too much for Los Angeles, which capitulated on August 12 without a shot being fired. . . .

Cut to Kearny's force from Fort Leavenworth arriving in Santa Fe, much the worse for wear. He had driven them hard. They had averaged an incredible 20 miles a day over a hot, barren wasteland, sometimes forced to drink water so bad that their horses refused it. There were a superior number of Mexican soldiers in New Mexico's capital, but their commanding officer had no stomach for a fight; the city—and New Mexico—were surrendered peacefully.

On being informed that California was now completely occupied, Kearny sent two-thirds of his force back to Kansas. But his news had been two months old. Unbeknownst to him, the *Californios* had returned to Los Angeles in force and retaken the city. When Frémont refused Stockton's request to come down from the Sacramento Valley by ship to help him get the city back, the commodore decided to do the job himself with a landing force of 225 men and what garrisons he could gather, about 400 men all told.

Augmented by Kearny's dragoons, Stockton's bell-bottomed infantry requited itself well. On January 8 the fate of the City of the Angels was decided in the "battle" of San Gabriel. American losses: 1 man killed, 13 wounded. California was at last firmly in American hands.

But now the golden sunset movie turned sour. In the orders General Kearny brought with him, President Polk stipulated that once Kearny had brought California under control, he was to be Governor of the occupied territory. But Stockton had already brought California under control and appointed Frémont Governor. Refusing to acknowledge Kearny's orders, Stockton insisted that *he* was the Senior Officer Present. At this point Frémont, perhaps enjoying being the first Governor of California, made a career-destroying error in judgment. Instead of staying completely out of it and letting the two senior officers settle it, he backed Stockton. Since the two of them commanded nearly all the men under arms, that left Kearny little choice but to submit and bide his time.

Enter a young lieutenant in the Regular Army, William Tecumseh Sherman, arriving with some comrades, having just rounded the Cape of Good Hope. Disgusted with the state of affairs, Sherman recorded what many were asking: "Who the devil *is* the Governor of California?"[6]

The matter was settled with the arrival of Stockton's successor, Commodore Branford Shubrick, who immediately recognized Kearny's authority. Soon thereafter, a Regular Army colonel, Richard Mason of the First Dragoons, arrived with more recent orders from the President—appointing *him* Governor, as soon as General Kearny should determine that the territory was "pacified."[7]

Frémont was furious. When Colonel Mason attempted to "regularize" his California Battalion, he threatened a revolt and challenged Mason to a duel. But he held no more high cards, and he knew it. The California Battalion, its job done, melted away, and the sunset movie faded to black.

Sometimes such movies have a trailer, letting the audience know what happened to the heroes. Kearny had Frémont court-martialed for insubordination. The latter was stripped of his commission and dismissed from the service. President Polk, though approving the court's finding, was appealed to by Senator Benton and his daughter, and restored Frémont's commission—which the latter then angrily resigned.

But John C. Frémont would not go quietly into that dark night; he would have significant roles in sequels still to come.

Roll credits and turn now to the real war.

16

"A LITTLE MORE GRAPE, MR. BRAGG"

*I*f the California chapter was shot in perpetual sunset, the rest of the Mexican War was filmed at high noon, under a sweltering sun that wore out men and horses alike.

Zachary Taylor's precarious situation, followed by spectacular victories at Palo Alto and Resaca de la Palma, had given the nation much to cheer about. They had also resolved a thorny problem President Polk privately faced: the burgeoning political ambition of Major General Winfield Scott, for whom he had developed an intense personal dislike.

At the beginning of a war, all soldiers are heroes, and none was more in the public eye than the Commander in Chief of the army. Scott was a thorough professional who had served with valor in the War of 1812, becoming at 28 its youngest Brigadier General. But he was as arrogant and overbearing as he was tall, and at 6′5″ he was the tallest man in Washington. When he met with the diminutive President, it soon became apparent in what low regard he held the opinions of the little man in the White House.

Like all the Regular Army's generals, Scott was a Whig, one that Polk considered "in full chase of the presidency."[1] And now Polk would have to offer Scott command of the Mexican campaign, despite misgivings that he was not "in all respects suited to such an important command,"[2] and knowing that its success would make him the likely Whig candidate and possibly the next President.

Yet Scott had the seniority; bowing to the dictates of military protocol, Polk made the offer, and Scott immediately accepted.

Scott's departure, however, was far from immediate; he took the next four months making preparations. Renowned for the thorough planning to which he credited much of his military success, Scott had earned the nickname "Old Fuss and Feathers." To the soldiers under him, it was a term of endearment; to his Commander in Chief, it was something else.

Scott had one great flaw: He could not bridle his tongue, not even when it came to committing his perceptions to paper. He had not learned the wisdom of never putting in writing anything that one would not want to be read aloud in court. In a letter he had offered the opinion that western Democrats would never give an eastern Whig a commission in a western regiment. The letter came to Polk's attention on the same day as another Scott epistle came into the hands of Secretary of War William Marcy. In it, the author explained his reason for delaying his departure: He was "too old a soldier" not to "feel the infinite importance" of avoiding that "most perilous of all positions: a fire upon my rear, from Washington, and a fire in front, from the Mexicans."[3]

How fortuitous, then, was the arrival of the splendid news from the Rio Grande! Polk could go to Congress and ask them to make Taylor a major general. His request would be greeted with unanimous acclaim. He could then leave Taylor in command down there and keep Scott in Washington for the present, well out of the limelight. There was just one problem with this scheme—the newspapers were now falling all over themselves to get out more stories about "Old Rough and Ready." And Taylor was also a Whig. . . .

After his victories Zachary Taylor occupied Matamoros, where he had to wait six weeks for long-sought supplies to arrive. He was seething at the inactivity, which was literally doing more damage than combat. In the two previous battles he had suffered approximately 400 casualties; he was losing more than that now to amoebic dysentery and yellow fever. In those days no one had made the connection between sanitary living conditions and the absence of disease. As a result, in the Mexican War more than six times as many men would die of disease as of wounds.[4]

It was the same everywhere. In Camp Belknap at the mouth of the Rio Grande, the mustering place for the First Ohio Volunteers, a quarter of the camp was sick by June. Nor did the situation improve when Taylor finally broke camp on August 4 and got under way. His objective: the largest city in northern Mexico, Monterrey.* To get there he would travel up the Rio Grande before striking south across an uninhabited, sun-blasted barrens. At Camargo, his summer camp on the Rio Grande, nearly a third of his 12,000 men were soon bedridden; he would bury 1,500 victims of disease.

At least when they were moving, he reasoned, the soldiers had something to think about other than the rapidly expanding burial ground. Taylor drove them hard and found, as Kearny had discovered in New Mexico, that hundred-degree heat and high humidity did not mix well with woolen uniforms. The graves by the side of the trail were shallow and hastily dug. The dead horses were left to the vultures.

For this march, Taylor had decided not to wait for the extra wagons he would need. Instead, he hired 1,900 Mexican mules and mule skinners. But who would oversee this braying battalion? A young lieutenant in the Quartermaster's Corps had a reputation as a horseman—and that was how Lieutenant Sam Grant received his new command.

"It took several hours to get ready to start each morning," he would later recall, and by the time the last mules were loaded, the first ones had gotten fed up with standing around and started pitching their loads off or rolling on them. "I am not aware of ever having used a profane expletive in my life," Grant added wryly, "but I would have the charity to excuse those who may have done so, if they were in charge of a train of Mexican pack mules at the time."[5]

They came in sight of Monterrey on September 19. Taylor's force of 6,640 men faced 7,300 well-trained and well-motivated soldiers in heavily fortified defenses. Their commander was none other than General Pedro de Ampudia, who had first faced Taylor at Matamoros, before being relieved by General Arista. When the unwashed, undisciplined, uncivilized *gringos* had beaten Mexico's finest in a fair fight, the only possible explanation had been incompetence at the highest level. President Paredes's suspicions were confirmed when Ampudia informed him of Arista's decision to leave the field command to one of his staff. Paredes

---

* This should not be confused with Monterey up on the California coast.

had summarily relieved Arista and appointed Ampudia the new Commander of the Army of the North.

Taylor studied the defenses through his field glass. At West Point they taught that you needed at least three times as many troops to dislodge a well-defended adversary. They also taught that if you were outnumbered, you *never* divided your force. But Taylor was never one for going by the book. He sent Brigadier General William Worth with 2,000 men around behind the city to take the two hills that commanded its western approach. With him went a detachment of Texas Rangers under Jack Hays.

Riding well ahead of the main column of infantry, as was their custom, the Texans suddenly encountered a great mass of waiting Lancers. Drawing his saber, Hays shouted a challenge in perfect Spanish to the Mexican commander: Let the two of them meet on the field of honor. The Mexican commander agreed, threw down his lance, and spurred his horse to the gallop. So did all his Lancers behind him. Hays steadied his mount and waited. Calmly he sheathed his saber and drew his Colt. Taking careful aim, he shot the officer dead, then wheeled and galloped back to his men. "Dismount," he shouted, "and get behind your horses! Here they come, boys; give 'em h——l!"[6]

The Texans opened a devastating fire on the Lancers, but they were badly outnumbered and about to be overrun. Suddenly a distant bugle sounded behind them; the infantry was coming! They arrived on the double, accompanied by two batteries of flying artillery. Three times the Lancers, now themselves outgunned, rallied and charged. Recalling their bravery that day, one Ranger would later write: "I have never called a Mexican a coward since."[7]

On the other side of the city, Taylor's attack on the northeast sector was not going well. Every street leading to the main plaza was covered by cannon, and soldiers were firing from the flat roofs and from loopholes cut into the soft adobe walls. When the First and Third Regiments attempted to enter the city, they were met with a hail of bullets and canister rattling and ricocheting down the streets at them. One captain described it as if "bushels of hickory nuts were hurled at us." Sustaining severe losses, the attacking force shuddered and fell back.

Now the old Fourth Infantry got ready to charge, and accompanying them was the young lieutenant from the Quartermaster's Corps who had been with them at Resaca de la Palma. Hearing the distant gunfire, Sam

Grant could not bear to be out of the action. Disobeying orders to remain in the rear in charge of supplies, he borrowed a horse and galloped forward, joining the Fourth just as the command was given to charge. They fared no better than the First or Third. Within minutes they had lost a third of their number and were reeling back. Seeing that the regimental adjutant was exhausted, Grant gave him his horse. Moments later the adjutant was shot out of the saddle and killed.

At this point another general might have withdrawn to reconsider the situation. But Taylor was bulldog tenacious. Next he sent in the First Tennessee, and then as they were falling back, the First Ohio. Only darkness and a sudden torrential rain brought a merciful end to the first day's fighting. Taylor had lost 394 men killed or wounded, fully a tenth of those engaged,[8] and the defenses of Monterrey were barely scratched.

The next day went better, at least on General Worth's side of the city. His men assaulted the fortified ruin known as the Bishop's Palace, atop Independence Hill. By the grace of God, it was still raining, and visibility was poor as the blue-uniformed troops climbed up hand over hand on all sides of the mountain. A skirmish line of Mexicans awaited them, and from far below and away, Lieutenant Sam French, attached to Braxton Bragg's battery, viewed the scene.

Without a field glass, all he could see were two wreaths of muzzle smoke, encircling the hill and moving slowly upward—the upper wreath from the Mexican muskets shooting downward, the lower wreath from the Americans shooting upward. The lower one was gradually closing on the upper. Near the top, the two became one, and a 12-pounder, disassembled and carried up on the backs of its gunners, was reassembled and started blasting the palace ruin. The defenders broke and ran down the hill, and Sam French and his men flung their caps in the air.

Day three: With the high ground outside the city now in American hands, General Ampudia withdrew all his forces to Monterrey's central plaza for a final stand. Slowly the U.S. Infantry worked its way into the city. When Grant's unit (once again, gunfire had held more attraction for Grant than tending mules) started running low on ammunition, the regimental commander asked for a volunteer to get the word to Taylor. Grant volunteered. He would go by horse, but to get there he would have to cross those long streets with their withering fire.

Grant was renowned as a horseman, and what he did next would become a favorite stunt in early western movies a century later: Holding onto the cantle of the saddle with one foot and hanging an arm around the neck of his mount, he hid behind his horse as they raced across intersection after intersection, drawing a burst of fire at each. By the skin of his teeth he made it—and became something of a legend in his own right.

The fighting was door to door now, and General Taylor himself stood in the streets directing the action, as axemen broke down doors and squads of troopers rushed in to clean house. It was hardly the first time the commanding General had been seen to be cool under fire, nor would it be the last. Once, exposed to a particularly heavy artillery barrage, a colonel suggested that they might move back a few hundred yards, for safety's sake. "Let us ride nearer," Taylor replied, "and the balls will fall behind us."[9]

Late in the afternoon, with the Americans closing in on the plaza from all sides and the outcome inevitable, a white flag appeared. It was a welcome sight to Taylor; he had already lost too many good men.

When General Ampudia surrendered his sword, he assured Taylor that the war would soon be over: The Government in Mexico City had already invited the Government in Washington to send commissioners to negotiate a peace and had appointed the Mexican commissioners who would meet with them. It was this development, concluded Ampudia, that had absolved him of his obligation to defend Monterrey to the death.[10]

Magnanimous in victory and believing that the last battle of the war had just been fought and won, Taylor agreed to a truce. He allowed Ampudia and his men to leave with their horses and sidearms, and gave his word that he would not advance beyond that point for eight weeks.

Some of his officers, particularly among the Texans, thought he should have demanded unconditional surrender. Not all were critical, however. Grant approved, and so did another lieutenant in the Regular Army, George Meade: "It was no military necessity that induced General Taylor to grant such liberal terms, but a higher and nobler motive."[11]

Thanks to the war correspondents traveling with the army, news of the victory at Monterrey spread like wildfire, and Zachary Taylor's popularity shot up like a roman candle. Not since Old Hickory had America had such a hero! Everyone was thrilled—everyone, that is, except the leaders of the Democratic Party. They were convinced that the Whigs would now move heaven and earth to get Taylor on their ticket two years hence. They were right: The Whig leaders were sending each glowing report to America's Hero, urging him to run for the sake of his country. Taylor read each clipping—and began to believe.

In the White House, James K. Polk was beside himself: He had created this monster. He remonstrated with Taylor for having accepted a truce and allowing the enemy to depart intact, instead of pursuing him and finishing the war then and there. Now he would have to try another tactic. . . . For Polk, like other Presidents who found it easier to delegate responsibility than authority, had gathered the reins of the war wagon into his own hands. Commander in Chief now in fact as well as figurehead, he was managing the war himself and formulating its strategy. "Mr. Polk's war," his opponents had derisively labeled it; well, now it was.

But what to do next? Taylor had once suggested opening a second front with an invasion at Tampico or Vera Cruz. Very well, that would be the next, and in all likelihood, the final phase. But whom to choose as its leader? Senator Benton had put forth his own name, and the idea of this aggressive western Democrat as a military commander, in place of those two Whig Presidential hopefuls, had a certain appeal. He would ask Congress to create a new rank, Lieutenant General, which would make Benton senior to Scott *and* Taylor. But Congress would not hear of it. Secretary of War Marcy then suggested to Polk that, after all, Scott *was* the best qualified, and in the end, despite his personal aversion to the man, Polk agreed.

Actually, appointing Scott might prove a shrewd political move: Let some other general besides Taylor receive the public's adulation for a change, maybe even credit for ending the war. Old Fuss and Feathers would never attain the stature that Old Rough and Ready had achieved overnight. But what to do about Taylor? Issue him new orders: Hold firm at Monterrey. No more action. (No more headlines.) And to make certain he stays put, with no further opportunities for glory, take away his army. Instead of issuing another call for volunteers, which in the wake of the latest war news would be instantly oversubscribed (every red-blooded American and his brother now yearned to march through the halls of Montezuma), instruct Scott to commandeer 9,000 of Taylor's best troops for the invasion of Vera Cruz. With Taylor thus stripped to the barest minimum, he couldn't go anywhere—even if he wanted to.

Shortly before Taylor received Scott's orders, his Texas Rangers brought him reliable intelligence: The Mexican Army at San Luis Potosi, revitalized and reinforced, had begun moving northward, presumably to retake Monterrey. Nonetheless, Taylor complied with his new orders, dispatching more than half his force east to the coast, where the Home Squadron would pick them up. In all, he sent some 4,600 men, including nearly all his regulars—all he could spare, in view of the impending threat. Convinced that Polk's motive was more political than strategic, Taylor's mood was black and bitter.

But if the Mexicans really *were* coming, he had to deny them the town of Saltillo—the only place they could get food and water before attacking him, after crossing 300 miles of desert. Moving out to invest Saltillo, a day's march to the south, would mean disobeying the President's "stay put" order. But Polk was two weeks and 2,000 miles away; by the time Taylor could apprise him of the change in his situation, the Mexicans would be upon him. So he made a field decision: He moved what was left of his army south. If the Mexicans wanted a fight, it was going to be on his terms: They would have to fight him exhausted, starved, and half-mad with thirst. That would help level their three-to-one numerical advantage.

And what of the Mexicans? After surrendering Monterrey, Ampudia had led his bedraggled army south to San Luis Potosi, where they waited— for a miracle. It was not long in coming, though whether from the hand of God, *quién sabe?*

Earlier in the year, the garrison at Vera Cruz, fed up with the fumbling, bankrupt Paredes administration, had revolted—and had demanded the return of Santa Anna, the Savior of Mexico, who had first come to power there.

Power is the greatest narcotic known to man, and politics, in its most corrupt state, is the art of acquiring power through popular appeal. In the mid-19th century there was no more adept demagogue than Santa Anna. He could persuade a populace who would have gladly executed him two years before to forgive him, accept him, and even exalt him. The phrase "politics makes strange bedfellows"[12] would not be coined for another 24 years, but it applies perfectly to the strange match of Santa Anna and Alonzo Gomez Farias, leader of the long out of power

Federalistas. It was they who had first raised Santa Anna to power, and they whom he had betrayed the moment he became *Presidente*, banning their Constitution of 1824 that had made Mexico a democratic republic, and allying himself with the hated Centralists. Now the Federalists cautioned Farias that Santa Anna was not to be trusted, but their leader had convinced himself that the magnetic general had reformed.

Santa Anna sensed the time for his return had arrived. Were his people (at least the garrison in Vera Cruz) not calling for him? How could he not respond? Thanks to the discreet intervention of President Polk, he was allowed to pass quietly through the naval blockade. When he landed at Vera Cruz, he was greeted with a show of support, staged by Farias. But Santa Anna was shrewd enough to note how few people stood behind the cheering flag wavers. So instead of going straight to Mexico City, he went to his hacienda for a month, to give the water level in the well of his popularity a chance to rise. He was confident that it would—as soon as word spread that he was back on native soil.

The fall of Monterrey hastened the rising. The nation needed a savior now, and only one man could fill that bill. When disgust with Paredes was deep enough and the clamor for Santa Anna loud enough, with breathtaking humility he bowed to the will of the people and entered the capital city. Farias had staged another reception; cheering throngs (though not multitudes) lined the streets. A few Federalists were not cheering; with bitter irony they noted that the banner attached to his carriage was the one for the Constitution of 1824—the same banner the defenders of the Alamo had been flying when Santa Anna had crushed them ten years before.

When it came to politics, Mexicans (like Americans) had short memories. Santa Anna was their *aguardiente*—and they were so addicted to him, they forgot what horrible hangovers he had always given them. Now, as he vowed to rally the army and carry the banner forward to expel the *norteamericanos* who defiled their motherland, they drank deeply—and believed.

And so did Santa Anna, for that was his charisma: He passionately *believed* whatever he was saying. Some historians have questioned whether he had ever intended to honor his secret understanding with Polk, regarding it as just a gambit to get through the blockade. But Santa Anna ultimately convinced Polk precisely because he *did* believe that a peaceful settlement was the best thing for Mexico—then.

Now he believed with equal fervor that a holy, cleansing war was the only possibility.*

But not all the people were demanding that he become their *Presidente* again; many Centralists, as well as Federalists, were still skeptical. Sensing it, Santa Anna refused to take the oath of office until he had first gone north to rid their soil of Taylor and his *gringos*. That won over the doubters, and once again he had all Mexico behind him. There was just one problem: Armies were expensive. A new one would need new uniforms, weapons, munitions, and provisions—and the Government was, as usual, broke. Except for a few landowners (like Santa Anna) and the Church, no one in Mexico had any money. Very well, he privately told Farias, his new Vice President: Get the money from the Church. Pass a law, if necessary, but get it.

Calling on all true sons of Mexico to join him, he raised a new army at San Luis Potosi and re-instilled pride in the old one. Before long, he had 20,000 men ready to follow him north to retake Monterrey. There was just one problem: The Church balked at being coerced into supporting the army. When it threatened to excommunicate any official who tried to force it to pay, there was rioting in the streets.

Santa Anna was in a momentary quandary: It was *his* policy that had caused this. But wait a minute: What was it the people in the streets were shouting? They were on the *Church's* side! All right, then! Santa Anna publicly condemned Farias: How could his Vice President attempt to levy funds from holy Mother Church!

With great fanfare, cheering crowds, and señoritas flinging flowers, he led his army out of San Luis Potosi. The Mexican newspapers heralded his departure; their savior would soon be their deliverer! With an army four times the size of the *gringo* expedition, how could he possibly fail?

The news was soon picked up by other papers, and before long all America was holding its breath. Surely this immense force would soon overwhelm poor Taylor and his troops! General John E. Wool and his 2,400 volunteers were hurrying down to help them, but would they get there in time? And even if they did, would they really make any difference? Were they about to see another Alamo, on a much more horrendous

---

* Just because a President has no principles does not mean that his sincerity is unconvincing.

scale? For this was no unknown general coming at them; this was Santa Anna, the best the Mexicans had! All else was forgotten as, half-dreading the news, the nation prayed and awaited the outcome.

Santa Anna was in a hurry, driving his men unmercifully over the 300 miles. For an American dispatch had fallen into his hands, one revealing that Taylor had sent more than half his force, including most of his veterans, to Scott on the coast. He now had the opportunity to destroy Taylor's much-reduced army, before turning south to face the threat at Vera Cruz.

But the fierce desert sun burned Mexican flesh as readily as it had American—and as Taylor had anticipated, they arrived in bad shape; indeed, more than 4,000 had fallen out of ranks from exhaustion or desertion.

Chance, on the other hand, seemed to be favoring Taylor. General Wool arrived with his volunteers. With the exception of a detachment of regulars under a young captain named Robert E. Lee, they were mostly inexperienced. But they brought Taylor's combined strength up to 6,000, and he reckoned he would need every man. Ben McCulloch, the intrepid commander of the Texas Ranger detachment, had just returned from slipping inside the enemy's vast encampment 60 miles to the south. They were three times Taylor's strength and moving fast. McCulloch estimated they would arrive in another three days.

As it turned out, it was more like two: Santa Anna had compelled his army to cover 50 miles in the final 24 hours, not stopping for water, and eating the last of their food. On the night before the main battle, instead of a meal he gave them something to look forward to: Tomorrow they would feast on the captured supplies of the Americans.

Buena Vista was a hacienda about four hours' ride south of Saltillo. Approaching it, the road from San Luis Potosi to Monterrey had to pass through a narrow defile. It was here that General Wool proposed they place the American defenses. They had left their supplies back in Saltillo with a detachment, effectively lowering Taylor's battle line to 4,500—nearly all volunteers, of whom eight out of nine had never seen combat.

Santa Anna arrived on the morning of February 22. It was a date that meant nothing to the Mexicans but quite a bit to the men they faced, being the birthday of America's first Commander in Chief.

Under a white flag, Santa Anna sent an emissary forward with a demand that Taylor surrender or risk annihilation. Remembering the Alamo and

Goliad and all the other locales of Santa Anna's perfidy, Zachary Taylor's instruction to his adjutant, Major William Bliss, was, according to Lieutenant French (who was within earshot): "Tell Santa Anna to go to h——l!" But not for nothing was his adjutant's nickname "Perfect" Bliss. For the history books, he rendered Taylor's response: "Sir, in reply to your note of this date, summoning me to surrender my force at discretion, I beg leave to say that I decline acceding to your request."[13]

The Mexican Army spent the next several hours deploying into position. Finally at 3:00 they were ready, and a few light skirmishes and sporadic artillery and small-arms fire ensued. Clearly the main attack would come the next day. Sensing that their supplies might be a prime target of acquisition and having received reports that Mexican cavalry had been sighted in the vicinity of Saltillo, Taylor rode back that night to check on the city's defenses. He took with him the First Mississippi Rifles, under their colonel, Jefferson Davis. Had Davis and his Mississippians not requited themselves well at Monterrey, it might have been an awkward situation.

As a young officer fresh out of West Point, Jeff Davis had served in the Black Hawk War under then Colonel Taylor, and had fallen in love with his commanding officer's daughter Sarah. He had started courting her, but Taylor, not wanting his daughter to marry into the army, had forbidden the marriage. Putting love before career, Davis had resigned his commission, and the two were wed. Seven weeks later, Sarah had died of malaria, and now Taylor's former son-in-law was back in army blue and riding beside him.

The following morning they got up before dawn to arrive back at Buena Vista by 9:00, confident that the Mexicans would not attack before then. But Taylor had underestimated his enemy. Santa Anna was more eager than Arista, more resolute than Ampudia. He had attacked at first light, attempting to turn the American left flank. And he was succeeding: Two of his best divisions had hit the Second Indiana, which had broken and fallen back, abandoning Lieutenant John Paul Jones O'Brien and his battery of three guns and taking the Mounted Arkansas Rifles with them.

Panic and confusion reigned among all the volunteers. The Indiana boys ran back through the ranks of the Second Illinois, which now also began to pull back, albeit more slowly and in order. Only the massed firepower of Major John Washington's artillery had kept it from becoming a rout.

But the flank had been turned, and the Mexican Lancers under General Torrejón were sweeping around their left and heading for Saltillo.

This was the situation when Taylor arrived. "General," a dejected Wool greeted him, "we are whipped!"

"That is for me to determine!"[14] snapped Taylor, spurring Old Whitey forward and ordering Davis and the First Mississippi Rifles to rally the fleeing Second Indiana. Wool then released the Third Indiana to reinforce Davis, and Taylor committed the last of his reserves. The line held. And now, in the nick of time, the flying artillery arrived. Under the withering canister of the American guns, the Mexican divisions shuddered, stopped, and stubbornly withdrew.

Now the Third Indiana, on one side of a ravine, and the First Mississippi Rifles, on the other, awaited the next Mexican charge. The Rifle regiment made a colorful sight in their slouch hats, red shirts, and white trousers. But these were more than Sunday afternoon parade-ground soldiers; their breech-loading 1841 rifles were the most modern weapons in any army, and their reputation as "the finest marksmen in the world" was well earned.

The Mexican buglers blew their fanfare, and the charge came—straight into the open mouth of the V the Americans had formed and on up the ravine. The Americans waited in silence. The Mexican horsemen, perplexed by the complete absence of defending fire, hesitated and came to a halt. Then, from a distance of less than a hundred yards, the Americans did open fire in a single tremendous volley, raining down a sheet of flame on their stationary targets from both sides of the ravine. The enemy attack was shattered—at what would be the turning point of the Battle of Buena Vista.

There was one more test, as once again the Mexicans charged in a different sector. This time Captains Braxton Bragg and Thomas Sherman were barely able to get their flying artillery over in front of them. Taylor rode over to them as they unlimbered their guns and began to fire. "What are you using, Captain," he asked Bragg, "grape or canister?"

"Canister, General."

"Single or double?" Taylor asked, referring to the bags of metal scraps being loaded into the muzzles.

"Single."

"Well, double-shot your guns, and give 'em h——l, Bragg."

Bragg did as ordered, and the first salvo of slashing metal staggered the Mexicans. The second salvo stopped them, and the third turned them around. The battle was over. The resulting newspaper account embellished the episode only slightly. Taylor was quoted as saying: "A little more grape, Mr. Bragg"[15]—and the phrase would soon enter American folklore.

It had been a terrible day. The Americans had suffered 746 casualties, including 290 killed or missing.* Forced to commit every last cook and mule skinner, Taylor had barely held the field. Low on ammunition and supplies, his men exhausted, he did not look forward to the coming day.

Neither did Santa Anna. Meeting with his general staff in the eerie, fog-shrouded moonlight, one by one he asked his senior officers for an appraisal of their troops. One by one they reported sadly but realistically that these men, who had been more than brave throughout the long day, were starved now and freezing, with no more fight left in them. Santa Anna slowly nodded. They would leave now, after building up their fires so that the *yanquis* would not know they had decamped. And so, under a spectral moon a silent column of bent, bedraggled silhouettes began the long, slow march south.

When they would eventually come in sight of San Luis Potosi, the welcoming shouts of the townspeople would die away into shocked silence. Could these shambling scarecrows be their proud soldiers? And *Madre de Dios, where were the rest?*

Less than half had returned.

---

* Among the dead was a gallant young officer named Henry Clay Jr., son of the Senator from Kentucky who had been so opposed to the war. When young Clay's unit got trapped in a gully, he was mortally wounded. His last words were for his men to leave him and save themselves.

17

SIX THOUSAND MILES

"Heave!" A hundred backs bent with the effort; knuckles whitened as 100 pairs of hands clenched around the dragropes. The heavy supply wagon moved another two feet up the slope of the bluff. "Heave!" Backs arched, ropes tautened, and the wagon rose a little higher. If anyone recalled their gala departure from Fort Leavenworth a few days before, on June 26, 1846, it was with bitter irony. Pennants had been flying then, children cheering, ladies in bonnets waving—the regimental band was playing "The Girl I Left Behind Me." It was as glorious a send-off as any young farm boy/soldier could ask for, and the First Missouri Mounted Volunteers, finest outfit in any man's army, marched off on the road to glory, ready to lick the Mexicans all by themselves.

Only there was no road. Once they reached the Great American Desert, there wasn't even a track. And they were no longer mounted; they were down on the ground, hauling. Because the sun was too hot, the mules were too weak from lack of water, and the bluffs were too steep.

And then there were the blasted rattlers everywhere; you had to watch out, reaching behind a shrub to gather buffalo chips for a cookfire; you hear that rattle, you get yourself out of their way! And talk about bold; they'd even slither into your bedroll with you!

But the worst thing by far was the flies and mosquitoes. They had been waiting, famished, ever since they were born for their one big meal—which had finally arrived. Many men's eyes were swollen shut from the bites. But the poor animals had it worse; their flanks were streaming with blood from open sores, and the flies would just sit on them and feast, ignoring the pathetic swish of their tails.

When the volunteers finally intersected the Santa Fe trail, things got better. The ground was fairly level and packed hard from twenty years of traders' wagons. General Kearny was able to move the Army of the West at a faster pace. Normally, a good day on the prairie was 15 miles. But there was a war on; Kearny now made 20, 25, even 28 miles.

The heat from the midsummer sun was like the open door of a blast furnace. And sudden windstorms would lift the loose sand and drive it at them like thousands of needles, filling their eyes and ears. With water holes ever fewer and farther between, the horses began to die, and gradually the Missouri Mounted Volunteers became the Missouri Walking Volunteers. The trouble was, their boots weren't made for infantry duty, and after a week or so you could track the army's progress by the bloody footprints in the sand.[1]

Doniphan's March, as it came to be known, did not stop at Santa Fe. When the capital of New Mexico was taken without a shot, Kearny headed on to California with his First Dragoons. But before he left, he gave Colonel Doniphan new orders: He and his volunteers were to strike south into Mexican territory via El Paso. His ultimate destination was the city of Chihuahua, capital of the province of that name. It was an overwhelming assignment for such a small force, but Kearny assured Doniphan he would not be undertaking it alone: General Wool with 2,400 men would be coming down from the northeast and should actually be at Chihuahua well ahead of him.

And so, reprovisioned and remounted, the Missouri Mounted Volunteers resumed their long trek south. It was mid-December now, and at an altitude of 7,000 feet the men would have welcomed a pause in front of an open blast furnace door. The worst part was the raw wasteland, which, their guides helpfully informed them, was known as the *Jornada del Muerto*, the Journey of Death. No wood, no water, just desolation—for 90 miles.

Doniphan decided that since there was no decent place to stop, they would just keep going—and they did, marching or riding into the darkness. For a moment of warmth, just to remind their bodies what it felt like not to be cold to the bone, the soldiers would set fire to bunches of tinder-dry sagebrush and prairie grass. These would flare up and die away so quickly that their bodies, as they clustered round, could scarcely register the fleeting warmth. And when the cold returned, it seemed even worse than before. Logic dictated that they would be better off not tantalizing themselves, but after another quarter hour they would light off another bunch.

Men and animals began to straggle, till their line of march stretched out for several miles. But though the night was pitch black, there was no getting lost; their way was illuminated by the sudden distant flares farther up the line.

At midnight Doniphan called a halt, and the men collapsed on the desert stones, many falling immediately into exhausted slumber. For those still awake, there was no supper; there was no fuel to cook it with. Nor was there any breakfast when the bugles sounded reveille at dawn. Just get up and get moving. But they completed the *Jornada* without losing a man.

Reaching the hamlet of Doña Anna on December 22, they rested. Three days later they arrived at another hamlet, Brazito, about 15 miles north of El Paso. It being Christmas, and to give the more than 300 stragglers a chance to catch up, Doniphan declared a shorter march than usual. In the afternoon the main body relaxed and tried not to think of home. Doniphan and some of his officers were playing a game of cards, when one of the pickets came racing in: A large force of Mexicans was approaching!

Carefully Doniphan laid the hand he had just been dealt face down on the table. "I'm afraid we'll have to stop the game long enough to whip the greasers," he allowed, rising to his full 6'5", "but just bear in mind that I'm ahead in the score. We'll play it out, after the scrap is over."[2]

The Mexican force under General Ponce de Leon was comprised of some 1,300 men, of which 500 were the renowned Vera Cruz Lancers. They now formed a line of battle athwart the road to El Paso, against which Doniphan had approximately 500 men, whom he now ordered into an opposing line. When the distance between the two advancing lines had narrowed almost to musket range, a Mexican officer galloped forward under a flag—not the customary white flag, signaling a conference of leaders, but a black flag with two skulls. The Texans among the scouts knew its meaning: It was the flag of no quarter. No prisoners would be taken—as at the Alamo, this would be a battle to the death.

Doniphan and his interpreter, a lean, buckskinned plainsman with his wide-brimmed hat down low over his eyes, rode out to meet him.

The Mexican officer announced that General Ponce de Leon demanded the American commander present himself to him immediately.

"If your general is so all-fired anxious to see Colonel Doniphan," the plainsman laconically replied, "let him come over here. We won't run away from him."

"We'll come and take him then!"

"Come right ahead, young feller," the plainsman smiled. "You'll find us right here, waiting for you."[3]

"Then prepare for a charge!"

"Charge and be d——d!" Doniphan retorted, when his interpreter informed him of this last.[4]

No sooner had the officer delivered this message than the Mexican trumpets began to sound. On the left flank the Vera Cruz Lancers deployed into a line abreast, trotting forward, lances high. They made a magnificent battlefield vista—green tunics trimmed with scarlet, blue pantaloons, brass-plated helmets plumed with black horsetails. . . . The trumpets sounded again, and the lances came down, as the riders spurred to the gallop, crying, *"Viva Mexico!"*

If fear surged through the hearts of the dismounted and waiting farm boy/soldiers, none budged. The wave of cavalry came closer and closer, yet still they held their fire. Then, at 150 yards, the command was given: "All right, boys, let 'em have it!"

A torrent of lead tore into the wave, shocking it to a halt. Riders toppled to the ground; others reeled in their saddles, crimson splotches spreading across their green tunics. Mexican officers rode frantically up and down the line, urging it to re-form for another charge.

At this moment, with the battle on the left flank in the balance, Captain Reed ordered his company forward in a bayonet charge. On they ran, with such furious determination that though they were fewer than 100, they caused the Vera Cruz Lancers to wheel and ride away.

Over on the right flank, the Chihuahua infantry, moving forward under cover of high chaparral, now advanced in a line, firing as they came. They were aiming high, Doniphan noted; he ordered his men to hit the dirt and hold their fire.

Never having seen such a maneuver before, the Mexicans assumed their foes had fallen under their fire and rushed forward to complete their work.

Suddenly the whole right flank rose up as one and administered a paralyzing volley. "Now, boys, go in and finish them!" roared Doniphan. The Missourians charged, bayonets extended, uttering the piercing, high-pitched war cry that would one day become known as the Rebel Yell.

The Battle of Brazito was over. The Mexicans departed the field in haste, leaving their dead and wounded, and not stopping at El Paso, but continuing all the way down to Chihuahua. As the regimental commanders gave their situation reports, there was immense relief at the casualty count: none killed and only eight wounded.

Doniphan waited in El Paso for more than a month, until the artillery he had requested could catch up with him. It finally arrived—a battery of six guns, manned by 100 men under the command of Lieutenant Meriwether Lewis Clark.* The guns were small—four 6-pounders and two 12-pound howitzers—but they would have to be enough. As they approached, they fired off a salute.

Doniphan's men, overjoyed to be finally resuming their march to Chihuahua, scrambled to answer with an ancient Mexican cannon they had located. In their haste, one soldier used his socks as wadding, and when the salute was returned, the socks flew into the face of an onlooking soldier. Everyone convulsed with laughter, save the stricken soldier who, removing them from his visage, allowed as how he would rather have been struck with a cannonball than a pair of socks that had marched from Fort Leavenworth.

A few days after leaving El Paso, Doniphan received ominous news: With Santa Anna moving north toward Taylor, Wool had been diverted to Saltillo to reinforce the badly outnumbered General. Chihuahua had meanwhile become the rallying point for Mexicans not marching with Santa Anna; if Doniphan proceeded, he would face a force several times his number, without the aid of Wool. And the enemy would be ready and waiting for him.

To go farther seemed suicidal. They were deep in enemy territory as it was, with no line of reinforcement or resupply. They were already living on whatever they could hunt, purchase, or capture, and ahead lay another desert to cross. Plus, their one-year enlistments were nearly up, and most potentially demoralizing of all, they had received no new orders, despite

---

* Son of famed explorer William Clark, who named him for his expedition partner.

Wool's being redirected. It was as if their country had forgotten them. Clearly the wise thing to do was to pack it in and head for home.

And yet—they had come so far, overcome so much! They may have been green as grass when they left, but they were not green anymore. Shared adversity had bonded them as tightly as any group of fighting men had ever grown, and they had fought with discipline and immense valor. . . . In the end, Doniphan left it up to his men: What did they want to do?

To a man, they chose to go forward.

The last desert would be worse than anything they had yet faced. The sand was so fine that the wind lifted and gathered it in drifts, like snow. Often the wagons sank into it up to their hubs, and the mules were too weak from lack of water to extricate them; once again the men were forced to toil alongside their beasts. By the second day the canteens were empty, and more horses began to die. By the third day the men were so crazed with thirst that many were delirious. The column staggered to a halt. As an act of mercy, the men unyoked the mules and oxen and let the poor animals go.

As it happened, less than ten miles away was Gyagas Springs, but they were finished. They lay down on the burning sand, no longer caring whether they lived or died. Some scrawled notes to loved ones; others prayed. The buzzards that had been following them, feeding on the carcasses of their dead animals, began to circle overhead. It appeared that the end of Doniphan's March would be marked by a strange memorial: a thousand skeletons picked clean, bleaching in the sun.

And then, above the distant mountains to their right, a cloud appeared—and another and another. It began to rain up there—so torrentially that before long water was rushing down the dry arroyos and spilling out onto the plain where they were. Soon there were gullies and puddles everywhere, enough for every man and beast to drink his fill. Isaac George of Company B likened it to the fountain that God had caused to leap from the rock to quench the thirst of the Israelite army in the desert, and more than a few volunteers gratefully renewed their relationship with the Almighty that day.[5]

Refreshed, the expedition carried on to the springs, where they laid up and recovered. Then it was on to Chihuahua, where they arrived on February 28—three days after the Battle of Buena Vista some 675 miles away, though word of that engagement would not reach them for another week.

Knowing that they were coming, the Mexicans had prepared to meet them eight miles in front of the capital. They had constructed a series of massive, connected redoubts and entrenchments between the Sacramento River and a dry arroyo. To man them, they had some 3,000 soldiers and 1,000 *rancheros,* against which Doniphan was coming with just over 900 soldiers and 150 teamsters. The Mexicans, dug in and well-nigh impregnable, were so confident of victory that they had brought a vast quantity of shackles with which they intended to march their prisoners back to Mexico City.

Had Doniphan followed the textbook and ordered a frontal assault, in all likelihood those chains would have been put to the use intended. But Doniphan was an innovator. Forming his force into a hollow square, he suddenly moved the entire body laterally across the dry arroyo and up onto the plateau beside the Mexican position. Now the enemy would have to leave their fortifications and come out to fight—and the odds would be only four to one.

Once again the Mexican cavalry, 1,200 strong, made the first move. To bugles and kettledrums they swept down from the heights in an earth-shaking charge. But this time Doniphan didn't have to wait until they were within musket range. This time he had artillery—not much, but enough. The six field guns, squarely in the center of the American line, now went into action. Loaded with grapeshot, they began rapid firing at an astonishing twelve seconds per round. Before the charge reached the American lines, it was broken.

The better part of an hour now passed in an indecisive artillery duel, while the U.S. officers readied the now mounted volunteers for a charge of their own. When the moment came, in a perfectly dressed line they raced across the open ground and up the hill to the Mexican fortifications. Without pausing at the summit, they fired a volley into the ranks of the defenders. The pivotal moment came when two scouts on horseback, seeing a Mexican cannon wreaking havoc on the advancing Missourians, went after it, jumping trenches as in a steeplechase. So astounded were the gunners that they turned and ran. The scouts, now joined by others on foot, turned the cannon around and began using it on their foes. The retreat crumbled into a rout.

The next day, as Colonel Doniphan rode into Chihuahua at the head of the First Missouri Mounted Volunteers, whose casualties had been one killed and eleven wounded, the regimental band played "Yankee Doodle." But now Doniphan laid down the law: They could celebrate, but there would be no outlaw behavior, no molesting of civilians, let alone burning, raping, or pillaging. And in the two months that they occupied the capital, law and order were strictly maintained, the streets were kept clean and policed, and the rights of the citizenry were respected.

When at last they received orders to evacuate the city and join General Taylor at Saltillo, they left it in better condition than they had found it.

Warmly congratulating them, General Taylor arranged for them to go home in relative comfort, transported by ship the last leg from the mouth of the Rio Grande to St. Louis. But before they left, they would be formally reviewed by their commanding General.

As Old Rough and Ready rode past them, the First Missouri Mounted Volunteers sat at attention on an assortment of mounts that included Indian mustangs, mules, and donkeys. Halfway down the line, a giant soldier sat astride a donkey. His legs were so long, and the donkey was so small, that the man was practically standing on the ground. Taylor quickly put a handkerchief to his mouth to hide his smile.

The veteran hollered at him: "Well, old man, what do you think of this crowd?"

General Taylor burst out laughing. Finally, he collected himself. "You look as though you'd seen hard times."

"You bet!" the volunteer replied, failing to see what everyone was laughing at.[6]

By the time they reached home on July 1, 1847, more than a year after they had left, Doniphan's men had covered 6,000 miles and conquered an area larger than the United States. Their uniforms were in tatters, but they were heroes whose feats had never been equaled. Thomas Hart Benton traveled out to greet them personally and to thank them on behalf of a grateful nation. And William Cullen Bryant, editor of the New York *Post*, likened their exploits to Xenophon's legendary retreat with 10,000 Greek legionaries across the plains of Asia Minor, four centuries before Christ. Doniphan and Xenophon, he declared, were "two military commanders who have made the most extraordinary marches known in the annals of warfare of their times."[7]

A historian writing 80 years ago lamented that Doniphan's home town of Liberty had erected no statue to him, nor was there one anywhere else. But he was truly renowned in his day. Years later, when he was introduced to President Lincoln, the latter looked him in the eye and said, "Colonel, you are the only man I have ever met whose appearance came up to my previous expectations."[8]

18

VERA CRUZ

*W*infield Scott was arrogant, foolish, stuffy, and ego driven. But when it came to military preparedness, he was brilliant. And now his gift was needed. This war, like most wars, was taking too long—even for its ardent proponents. When President Polk saw that General Taylor's capture of Monterrey had not persuaded the Mexicans to sue for peace, he finally realized that nothing short of ultimate victory was going to end the war. That meant the taking of Mexico City, and as soon as possible. The national elections were around the corner, and if the war dragged on much longer, it would sink the Democratic party. As John C. Calhoun observed, "The administration and the country are already tired of the Mexican War, and are in as great haste to get out of it, as they were to get into it."[1]

But they would have to make haste slowly; the Mexicans were demonstrating a remarkable ability to rally. Just when you thought you finally had them beaten and they could never rise and fight again, you found a whole new army waiting around the next bend. So, however frustratingly methodical Winfield Scott might be, he was the right man for the job.

That was doubly true when it came to the coming invasion of Vera Cruz, the largest amphibious landing ever attempted. Nearly 12,000 troops, transported by 100 vessels, were to be put ashore in a single day. When it came to logistics and coordinating the movement of men and matériel, no one in America and perhaps the world was Scott's equal. Yet still, months after his urgent request, the number of surfboats needed to carry the men ashore was woefully inadequate. Scott would have liked to wait for the remainder to arrive, but he had a relentless goad driving him, far more significant than the impatience of his Commander in Chief in the White House.

Spring was coming. And with it, warmer weather. Which brought *el vomito*—"the black vomit," or yellow fever, as the Americans came to call it. In 1847 no one realized that it was borne by mosquitoes; all they knew was that once it started to get muggy and fetid along the Mexican coast, the higher, drier, cooler ground inland was much safer. Scott estimated that if they lingered beyond the end of April, he would lose more men to *el vomito* than to 1,000 Mexican cannon loaded with grapeshot. Four out of 10 was his grim estimate.

They were fast approaching the absolute last date they could land: On March 9, ready or not, they would have to go. Fortunately he was blessed with the presence of Commodore David Connor, new commander of the Home Squadron, which was blockading the Gulf Coast and transporting Scott's men. Connor, an old navy man, offered much advice, which at first Scott's pride made him reluctant to accept. But Connor had been on station in the Gulf far longer than Scott, and when he recommended the Collado Beach as the ideal landing site, the latter listened. Scott was also receptive to Connor's suggestion that Vera Cruz, with its 15-foot-high walls and its two-centuries-old island fortress of San Juan de Ulúa, might fall more easily to a siege than to a frontal assault.

Though General Worth and others were all for taking the city by storm, Scott had learned to count the cost. In his journal he assessed the "probable loss of some two thousand, perhaps three thousand, of our best men in the assault. . . . How could we then hope to penetrate the interior?"[2] Scott hated to waste anything, especially the lives of his men. If the coming engagement took the life of one man beyond a hundred, "I shall regard myself as his murderer."[3]

Three days before the landing, Scott took his staff officers aboard the small steamer *Petrita* to survey at close hand the beach Connor had recommended. With him were Generals Worth, Twiggs, Patterson, and Persifor Smith with their staffs, and Colonels Ethan Allen Hitchcock and Joseph Totten, the commander of artillery. Having seen the beach, Scott ordered the little steamer to inspect the walls of the city, and in so doing they drifted in range of the guns of Fort Ulúa. Totten, examining the fort through a field glass, noted: "They are manning their batteries." Smith, taking the glass, concurred: "We shall have a shot presently." Scott ordered the *Petrita* to stop making headway, to give them a fair target.

In gunnery, the first objective in gun laying is to align the gun with the target; the second is to correct for range—first by firing beyond the target, then firing short. Once the target is bracketed, the gunner, with incremental over-and-under adjustments, ladders his shots into the target.

A puff of smoke from the fort indicated that a shell had been fired, and momentarily a large plume of water erupted 100 yards to their right. The second was in a direct line with them, but a hundred yards beyond; the third was a hundred yards short. They were now bracketed—and still Scott did not give the command to get under way. Only when the eighth shell exploded so close to them that fragments from it landed on the deck, did Scott give permission for the *Petrita* to get up steam and pull out of range.

Colonel Hitchcock was incensed at this ridiculous display of bravado; a direct hit could have ended or drastically altered the campaign.* Shortly after dawn on the ninth, the invasion began with a line of seven shallow-draft gunboats paralleling the beach and raking the dune beyond with canister and shell. Two hundred to 300 cavalry had been seen in that vicinity, and there were rumors of heavy batteries hidden behind the dunes, just waiting for the surfboats full of helpless infantry to start rowing ashore. At 11:00, 65 surfboats, filled with 50 to 80 men apiece and manned by six or eight navy oarsmen, slipped through the line of gunboats, formed a first wave, and rowed swiftly for the beach.

Back on the big ships the bands were playing "The Star-Spangled Banner," but in the boats it was deadly quiet. "Not a word was said," noted Lieutenant George McClellan in one of the boats. "Everyone expected to hear and feel [the hidden] batteries open every instant. Still we pulled on and on."[4]

A few skirmishers did fire at them, but the preceding naval bombardment had done its work: There was no cavalry, and the rumors of heavy artillery were, as war rumors so often are, phantoms of overactive imaginations. The landing went unopposed. By midnight, in an uninter-

---

* The death of the junior officers would have had far greater consequence to the outcome of a future war: On board were Lieutenants George Gordon Meade, P.G.T. Beauregard, Joseph E. Johnston—and Captain Robert E. Lee.

rupted symphony of well-orchestrated efficiency, the entire army was safely ashore. It was to this point Scott's finest achievement.

Quickly the city was encircled, and the cordon drawn tight; there would be no relief for Vera Cruz. Were time not a factor, Scott and his men could have just waited until Vera Cruz got hungry enough to surrender. But time *was* a factor; the yellow-fever season was almost upon them. They would have to help Vera Cruz make up its mind.

On March 22, General Scott issued General Juan Morales an ultimatum: Surrender Vera Cruz and the fort, or Scott would be forced to bring them under his heaviest guns. But Morales and the city fathers were confident that their own gunners could go round for round with the enemy and his fleet. Besides, they were convinced that they would soon be relieved—had Santa Anna not sent them word of his wonderful victory at Buena Vista? Since he had just returned from humiliating the *gringos* there, surely he would do the same to them here.

Well, replied Scott, if that was their decision, so be it. Would they at least send out the women and children? No. They were perfectly capable of protecting their families. And so, there was nothing else to do but set the guns to their dreadful work. On March 23, the bombardment began.

Seeing that Scott's 24-pounders were having scant effect on the walls of the city, let alone the ancient fortress, Commodore Connor offered the use of six of his heaviest guns, including three 32-pounders, themselves weighing three tons each, and three Paixhans, which could fire a 64-pound exploding shell. No wall could withstand those monsters, and they had the extra blessing of being highly accurate.

Once again Scott was reluctant to accept the Navy's offer. But once again wisdom prevailed over pride, and soon the almost impossible task of getting those guns ashore was begun. Colonel Totten picked the sites himself and had enough wisdom to accept the modifications to his plan urged by a bright young lieutenant of artillery named Beauregard.

The biggest guns would require the construction of special wooden platforms simulating the gun deck of a ship, and this assignment fell to the captain of engineers, who was fast becoming General Scott's right-hand man. At 40, Robert Edward Lee was a little older than the other junior officers at Vera Cruz. In the War for Independence his father had been a cavalry commander and a hero, much praised by General Washington. Known to his men as "Light-Horse Harry," in civilian life the senior Lee had served three terms as Governor of Virginia. But it was not to please his father that young Lee had gone to the Military Academy; the two could hardly have been farther apart in personality. Robert was more like his mother—thoughtful, self-disciplined, compassionate, and mentally very quick.

To say he did well at the Academy would be an understatement: He graduated second in his class. As a cadet he accumulated another record that has astounded West Pointers ever since: He never received a single demerit. Upon graduation he joined the Corps of Engineers, where he served well but without recognition, languishing in grade as all peacetime officers did in those days. Prior to Vera Cruz, he had remained a captain for eight years. He never complained, but committed himself to doing the best job he possibly could at whatever the assignment, and leaving the rest to God.[5]

Robert E. Lee's bearing was erect, which made him seem taller than his 5'11" frame. Clean-shaven, with deep brown eyes, he had a commanding presence, and at social occasions he was always gracious, even courtly. Men liked him; women found him irresistible. The one who captured his heart was Mary Custis, daughter of George Washington's adopted son, and soon after his mother died, he wed Mary in the Custis mansion in Arlington, Virginia, overlooking the Potomac and the nation's capital.

When the Mexican War broke out, Lee did not approve of it—not just because he was a Whig and felt it could have been avoided—he was opposed to all war on principle. Civilization could not advance, he believed, until reason and compassion prevailed in settling disputes. But he was a professional soldier and would do his duty, whatever it might be. And now that the war was a reality, in truth he yearned for action. So he was delighted when new orders finally arrived, direct from the office of the Chief of Engineers: He was assigned to join General Wool in San Antonio.

Another officer, receiving orders to a distant theater of war, might have lingered in taking leave of his wife and seven children. Not Lee. He made out his will, settled his family in the Arlington mansion, and got down to San Antonio as quickly as possible, reporting for duty 33 days after receiving his orders.

He was with Wool near Saltillo when the latter summoned him to his headquarters. He had just received a communiqué from General Scott requesting that Lee (and only Lee) report immediately to his command. That was how the quiet captain from Virginia happened to be in Vera Cruz, working on the gun positions.

Late on the evening of May 19, after completing their work for the day, Lee and Beauregard were returning to camp when a sentry challenged them: "Who goes there?"

"Friends," answered Lee.

"Officers!" added Beauregard.

The nervous young sentry, fearing they were Mexicans, pointed his pistol at Lee and fired. The ball passed between his arm and his side, so close that it singed his tunic. When Scott heard about the incident, he was furious and insisted on punishing the soldier, despite Lee's interceding on his behalf. The story quickly circulated through the officer corps, among whom was a young lieutenant whose life would be tragically taken by just such an accident 16 years later: Thomas J. Jackson.

On March 24, the second day of the bombardment, Lee had the position ready—and who should arrive to command the 64-pounders but Navy Lieutenant Sidney Smith Lee—his brother! By 10:00 A.M. the huge guns added their deep voices to the others. The difference they made was instantly apparent: These shells would soon open a breech in the city's walls. And when fired over the walls—they could not see the devastation, but they could hear it. "The shells thrown from our battery were constant and regular discharges, so beautiful in their flight and so destructive in their fall," observed Captain Lee. "It was awful! My heart bled for the inhabitants. The soldiers I did not so much care for, but it was terrible to think of the women and children."[6] (Later testimony of survivors would confirm his misgivings: The streets were filled with women and children crying and running this way and that, because *nowhere* was safe.)

Other American officers were similarly shocked. Captain Ephraim Kirby Smith wrote home: "We hear the distress of the city has been dreadful, some hundreds of women and children having been killed by our shells. This is horrible!" That was also the adjective chosen by Colonel Hitchcock, who wrote in his journal: "I shall never forget the horrible fire of our mortars. . . . going with dreadful certainty and bursting with sepulchral tones often in the center of private dwellings—it was awful. I shudder to think of it."[7]

On the 26th, two days after the naval guns had joined the bombardment, the white flag appeared. Firing ceased. Like Taylor's at Monterrey, Scott's terms for surrender were generous: He agreed to parole the defending soldiers, allowing them to leave the city and the fort on their word that they would not fight again. The rights of the Mexican civilians were guaranteed.

Three days later a formal surrender ceremony took place on a plain outside the city's south wall. Scott, so gifted at planning, knew exactly how this ceremony should proceed. There would be two long files of U.S. soldiers and sailors, representing each of the units that had fought. These files, leading out of the city, would be facing each other at attention in parade dress. Between them would march the defeated foe, bearing their small arms. At the end of the file, their rifles would be neatly stacked, and they would depart. Then the U.S. troops would march into the city.

Above all, insisted Scott, an atmosphere of absolute dignity and respect would be maintained throughout the surrender. There would be no cheering or exulting, no mocking of the enemy or disorderly conduct, no sign of disrespect, not even in facial expression. And he impressed on his junior officers that he would hold them personally responsible for the least infraction among their men.

The surrender went exactly as planned. Even the weather cooperated: It was a clear, sunny day as the Mexican defenders marched out of the city to fife and drum. Some turned and sadly waved to those remaining behind; others were accompanied by their wives and children. If the watching Texans remembered the Alamo, and how the victorious Mexicans had mutilated the bodies of those defenders, they bridled their tongues.

A perfect stillness was maintained. It made a profound impression on a young lieutenant standing at attention in those files. Eighteen years later, at a rural courthouse in Virginia, Sam Grant would accord the same respect to the troops of Robert E. Lee.

19

MR. WILMOT'S PROVISO

*B*y the late summer of 1846, enthusiasm for the Mexican War was definitely ebbing away. The entire nation's attention was still fixed on the theater of battle; little else ever made the front page, and extra editions were needed after such stunning victories as Palo Alto and Monterrey. But a few pages back appeared something that had never been published before: the death rolls. Long columns listed the names of those who had fallen in combat, and even longer columns were needed for the names of those who had succumbed to fever and other camp illnesses.

No one had expected the war to last this long or cost so many lives. Everyone in Government was feeling the strain, none more than the President. Increasingly people were speaking out against "Mr. Polk's War," and his health had so deteriorated that he was now forced to use a cane.

Most of the opposition was centered in Massachusetts, where Henry David Thoreau was jailed for refusing to pay taxes to a United States that "condoned slavery and war."[1] From his Boston pulpit, Unitarian minister Theodore Parker thundered: "War is an utter violation of Christianity. If war be right, then Christianity is wrong. . . . We can refuse to take part in it, and we can encourage others to do the same."[2] And the abolitionists never relented in their drumbeat insistence that the war was being fought to expand the territory of the Slave Power.

Their persistence was finally having an effect. Gradually, thoughtful, temperate men and women in the North were being persuaded that slavery really *was* something they should be personally concerned about—*now*. America was at war. She appeared to be winning that war. In all probability a great deal of new territory would soon accrue to her. Though these thoughtful, temperate souls would take umbrage at being classed with those wildly radical abolitionists, they nonetheless began to subscribe to the opinion that slavery really ought to be prevented from spreading any farther.

The northern Whigs, either anti-expansionist in general or anti-expansionist where slavery was concerned, had been against the war from the beginning. But now antislavery feelings were beginning to surface and create factions in the Democratic party as well. David Wilmot, the portly young freshman Congressman from Pennsylvania, had dutifully voted for the war and for every other Democratic initiative. But in August of 1846, when his party's leader, President Polk, went to Congress for a $2 million appropriation to be used for "extraordinary expenses" in negotiating the eventual peace treaty, this party-line loyalist balked. He asked to know exactly what these special funds would be used for.

Privately (and Polk was a very private person), the President intended to use them as "earnest money," a down payment toward the $15 million (or more) he was prepared to pay for the Territories of New Mexico and California. Quite privately, he thought it might be a sufficient bribe to induce Santa Anna to agree to peace in exchange for ceding the Territories—it might even, in fact, enable him to pay the army that was keeping him in power. For that matter, it could shore up whichever administration happened to be in power down there long enough to get a peace treaty out of them. (In Mexico City, political longevity was never in great supply, particularly if an administration was seen to be treating with the enemy, an act of high treason.) But the secretive Polk had no intention of sharing these reasons beyond his Cabinet.[3]

In a rare Saturday evening session on August 8, as Polk's request was brought before the House, David Wilmot felt compelled to rise. When he had voted for the war, he informed his colleagues, he had not considered it a war of conquest, nor did he now. But why did the President want this extra money? Not to pay for land (Texas) that we already claimed to be ours, but presumably to acquire more territory—of which Wilmot also approved. But he did *not* approve of extending slavery into that territory, where it had been abolished by the Mexicans.

He therefore proposed that the following provision be added to the appropriation: "that, as an express and fundamental condition to the acquisition of any territory from the Republic of Mexico by the United

States . . . neither slavery nor involuntary servitude shall ever exist in any part of said territory."[4] If the wording of this provision sounded faintly familiar, it was meant to: It deliberately echoed the Ordinance of 1787, forbidding slavery in the Territories that were rapidly drawing settlers across the Appalachian Mountains. The Wilmot Proviso, as it came to be known, was passed in the House but filibustered in the Senate by Southern Senators until adjournment.

Polk was furious. Dismissing the proviso as "a mischievous, foolish amendment," he wrote in his diary: "What connection slavery had with making peace with Mexico, it is difficult to conceive."[5]

At that point in time, he was still speaking for the majority of his party, North and South—but barely. A vast sea change was under way, to which he was oblivious.

It would be a few days before the earthquake of the Wilmot Proviso would register around the country. But with the exception of the Pinckney Gag Rule petitions and the agitation of a few abolitionists, it marked the first time that slavery had been openly questioned from the floor of either house. By gentlemen's agreement the subject had been left unspoken for the 26 years since the Missouri Compromise—the gentlemen on both sides of the aisle being well aware of the issue's potential for wrecking the Union. Now the Wilmot Proviso had broken that tacit understanding, and from this time forth slavery would be the final, pivotal issue in any debate on any national question. David Wilmot had just rung the "firebell in the night" that Thomas Jefferson had so dreaded.

The abolitionists stepped up their rhetoric, and the Whigs, scenting blood in the water, circled for the kill. To attack the war itself was still politically unwise, but there was no such restraint on ridiculing the man who owned it. People began to mock Polk as a little man of little means. Tom Thumb was a tiny midget in P. T. Barnum's caravansary; wags now began referring to Polk as "Tom Thumb's cousin Jim," and to his Cabinet as "the little fellows."[6]

By December, Polk had become defensive to the point of paranoia. In his second State of the Union Address, he reiterated the administration's position: "The war has not been waged with a view to conquest, but, having been commenced by Mexico, it has been carried into the enemy's country and will be vigorously prosecuted there with a view to obtain an honorable peace." Then he lashed back at those who were using terms like "unjust, unnecessary, and aggression"; they were doing so "to encourage the enemy and to protract the war."[7]

But he was no longer speaking for the whole Democratic party; indeed, he now represented a minority. Four years before, Andrew Jackson's "Party of the People" had been the dominant political force in the nation; now in the wake of the Wilmot Proviso the party was beginning to split asunder. There were antiwar Democrats, anti-expansion Democrats, high-tariff Democrats, Old South Democrats, New South Democrats, pan-South Democrats, antislavery Democrats—and a number of ex-Democrats who had abandoned their party altogether and become Whigs.[8]

Polk was further enraged to hear that even John C. Calhoun favored the election of Zachary Taylor as his successor. The rumor proved false, but it evoked Polk's true feelings: "I cannot express," he confided to his diary, "the contempt I feel for Mr. Calhoun for such profligate political inconsistency."[9]

Time after time the Wilmot Proviso would be passed by the House, only to be defeated in the Senate. Yet it was only a symptom, not the cause, of the shift in the mood of the country, and had Wilmot not proposed it, someone else soon would have.

It was a shift that Polk had missed: "The slavery question is assuming a fearful . . . aspect," he wrote in early 1847. There would be "terrible consequences to the country, and [it] cannot fail to destroy the Democratic party, if it does not threaten the Union itself." So far, he was correct, but then he added: "Slavery was one of the questions adjusted in the compromises of the Constitution. It has . . . no legitimate connection with the war with Mexico, or the terms of a peace which may be concluded with that country."[10] That telltale word "adjusted" reveals how far Polk was out of touch with the slavery crisis. To think that such a profoundly moral issue could simply be adjusted out of existence was the height of self-delusion.

Like a bolt of lightning down the wire from old Ben Franklin's kite, the proviso galvanized the nation. The legislatures of 10 Northern states passed resolutions endorsing it; the legislatures of Virginia, Kentucky, Tennessee, and Missouri passed resolutions denouncing it.[11]

In April of 1847, Massachusetts resolved: "That the present war with Mexico . . . was unconstitutionally commenced by the order of the President to General Taylor, to take military possession of territory in dispute between the United States and Mexico . . . for the dismemberment of Mexico . . . with the . . . object of extending slavery."

Virginia spoke for the South, holding that slavery was a matter for each state to resolve, and over which the United States Government had no control, either "directly or indirectly."[12]

And the feelings were hard. Southerners regarded the proviso as an attempt to exclude their system from the new Territories on the grounds that it was—i.e., they were—morally inferior to the North's system. The South, asserted Calhoun, would secede rather than submit, and this time he *was* speaking for more than just South Carolina. As Governor Brown of Mississippi wrote to Governor Smith of Virginia, if all friendly means to resolve the issue failed, then the South would not hesitate "to become enemies and defend our rights with those means which God and nature have placed in our hands."[13]

The embattled President, who was in favor of simply extending the Missouri Compromise line to the Pacific, was as put out with Calhoun as with Wilmot, writing in his diary that he intended to set his face equally "against Southern agitators and Northern fanatics."[14]

But the great compromise of 1820 was rapidly becoming a thing of the past. At the next Democratic party convention, William Yancey would lead his state's delegates to draft the "Alabama Resolutions," repudiating the Missouri Compromise, declaring that slavery could not be touched in the Territories, and threatening secession if the Wilmot Proviso became law. (It never did; when the Senate reconvened, it was narrowly defeated.)

Resistance to "Mr. Polk's War" was now coming from all directions. None was as rabid as William Lloyd Garrison, who declared in the *Liberator* that "every lover of Freedom and humanity throughout the world must wish [the Mexican army] the most triumphant success." But Horace Greeley summed up the war for the majority in the New York *Tribune*: "We are in the predicament of a man who has a wolf by the ears; it is dangerous to hold on, and it may be fatal to let go."[15]

Everyone, it seemed to Polk, was mad at him about something. Senator Benton was mad that he (and Congress) would not make him a Lieutenant General and give him command of the Mexican War. Even Polk's old friend Sam Houston, now a Democratic Senator from Texas, was mad that he had not been given an army command, or that his own Presidential aspirations had not been considered.

A few politicians, out of sheer old-fashioned patriotism, continued to take the high ground: Wartime was no time to debate whether your country should have gotten into a war. They supported each request for war appropriations and kept their misgivings to themselves. One of these was a tall, angular freshman Congressman from Illinois named Abe Lincoln.* Elected too late to cast a vote on whether America should go to war, Lincoln was convinced that "good citizens and patriots" should "remain silent" on whether it was justified, "at least till the war should be ended."[16]

But as the President persisted in assuming that every silent vote to send more supplies as needed was an endorsement of his policies, Lincoln grew increasingly resentful. Finally he could stand it no longer. Challenging Polk to prove that the war had begun on American soil, to show him the spot, the young country lawyer declared, "Let him answer with facts and not with arguments. . . . But if he cannot or will not do this . . . then I shall be fully convinced of what I more than half suspect already: that he is deeply conscious of being in the wrong. . . . How like the half-insane mumblings of a fever dream is the whole war part of his message!" Lincoln angrily concluded, "Mr. Polk knows not where he is. He is a bewildered, confounded, miserably perplexed man. God grant that he may be able to show there is not something about his conscience more painful than his mental perplexity!"[17†]

Polk developed a siege mentality, practically barricading himself in the White House, conferring only with his Cabinet, and confiding only to his diary. In it, Taylor was his scapegoat: For his success he was "indebted not to his own good generalship, but to the indomitable and intrepid bravery of the officers and men under his command. . . . General Taylor is a hard fighter, but has none of the other qualities of a great general. From the beginning of the existing war he has been constantly blundering into difficulties and fighting his way out of them, but with very severe loss."[18]

The first of April brought the first welcome war news: official confir-

---

* Another was Sam Grant. Until his memoirs were published in 1885, the public had no inkling that he regarded the Mexican War as "one of the most unjust ever waged by a stronger against a weaker nation."

† While not as harsh as other condemnations in the House, Lincoln's Whig constituents regarded his attack on the policies of the Commander in Chief as tantamount to treason. Reviling him as "the Benedict Arnold of our district," they refused to renominate him.

mation of the tremendous victory at Buena Vista. The nation had held its breath at the perilous position of Taylor and his courageous but outnumbered troops. Now it breathed a huge sigh of relief, followed by a triumphant shout of joy: Far from being wiped out, Taylor had miraculously prevailed! And there was more good news: Scott's landing at Vera Cruz had gone unopposed! Ten days later came even more joyous headlines: Vera Cruz had fallen! Scott was safely up in the high country, just ahead of the yellow-fever season!

Polk was in a classic Presidential dilemma: He needed these war victories to keep the Whigs from proving that the war was a disaster and sweeping the Democrats from office next year. Yet either Scott or Taylor would in all likelihood be the Whig's Presidential candidate, and each victory was making them more politically attractive.

In the end, James K. Polk was more a statesman than a politician. Much buoyed by the good news from the front, he sent the chief clerk of the State Department, Nicholas Trist,* to join Scott and be prepared to negotiate a "just and honorable peace" at the first indication of the enemy's desire to do so. The details of Trist's mission were top secret: Polk had authorized him to offer the Mexicans $15 million, to be paid in three annual installments of $5 million, for ceding Upper and Lower California and New Mexico to the United States. Naturally, since this was going to be a great story, a few war correspondents booked passage on the same packet as Trist.

Five days after Trist sailed, Polk was plunged back into consternation. The New York *Herald* published the exact details of his highly confidential mission. "I have not been more vexed or excited since I have been President," fumed Polk in his diary. "The success of Mr. Trist's mission I knew in the beginning must depend on keeping it a secret from that portion of the . . . press and leading men in the country who, since the commencement of the war with Mexico, have been giving 'aid and comfort' to the enemy. . . ." Polk knew that what the *Herald* printed today, the world would print tomorrow. "I do not doubt that Mexico has been and will be discouraged from making peace, in the hope that their friends in the United States will come to power at the next Presidential election."[19]

---

* Trist was actually third in command of that diminutive department, after the Secretary and Assistant Secretary.

20

"My Duty Is to Sacrifice Myself"

$\mathcal{A}$s Santa Anna returned to Mexico City, the capital was in precisely the condition he thrived in—caught in the throes of another revolt. The people were fed up with acting *Presidente* Gomez Farias because of his attack on the Church. Neither did they care much for the man who wanted to replace him, General Peña y Barragan. Chaos and shooting in the streets were the results.

But in the outlying town of Guadalupe Hidalgo just to the north, where Santa Anna paused before entering Mexico City, there was joy. A crowd gathered round his coach, smiling and calling to their friends. Standing to address them, he once again began to weave his spell. He showed them the captured battle flags and cannon of the vanquished Americans, told them how bravely their countrymen had fought in their great victory at Buena Vista. Dark rumors to the contrary had filtered down from up north, but as the people gazed up at him they laughed and nodded, believing—because they so badly wanted to.

Not all believed, however; some prominent citizens still remembered their last *aguardiente* hangover. Sensing their reserve, with a great show of humility Santa Anna declined to enter the capital city until all violence had ceased. His reluctance to reassume the reins of power once more won over the doubters, and made the rest love him all the more. A delegation came out from the city to plead with him to lead the country again, and he, humble servant that he was, bowed to the will of the people. As his coach proceeded into the capital, where a day before the streets had echoed with gunfire, now there was only cheering: *Viva el Presidente-general!* The Savior of Mexico had returned!

The Mexican Congress gave Santa Anna almost unlimited power. A truly gifted organizer, he quickly reestablished a functioning Government and refinanced the treasury with the aid of the Church. Next, he set about raising yet another army, for the *gringos* were now threatening to pierce the very heart of the motherland. Before leaving to meet them, he issued this ringing proclamation to the people of Mexico: "My duty is to sacrifice myself, and I will now fulfill it! Perhaps the American hosts may proudly tread the imperial capital of the Aztecs. I will never witness such opprobrium, for I am decided first to die fighting!" Now he addressed each father, each husband: "Mexicans! You have a religion—protect it! You have honor—then free yourselves from infamy! You love your wives, your children—then liberate them from American brutality!" Finally he appealed to their honor: "Mexicans! Your fate is the fate of the nation! Not the Americans but *you* will decide her destiny! Vera Cruz calls for vengeance—follow me, and wipe out the stain of her dishonor!"[1]

What red-blooded man or boy could resist such a stirring call to arms? Hundreds instantly responded, and Santa Anna added them to the nucleus of several thousand combat-hardened regulars who were still with him after Buena Vista. To each new arrival he gave a copy of his proclamation, that they might be re-inspired.

His headquarters would be at his hacienda, El Encero, 4,000 feet above sea level, from which the distant Gulf of Mexico was visible. Here he gathered his army. Just as he had at San Luis Potosi, he rallied and recruited many of the Vera Cruz parolees who were happy to break their noncombatant promise to Scott. With the pesos he had coerced from the Church, he bought supplies and uniforms for them all, and he slaughtered his own cattle to feed them. As before, there was no time to drill or train; the conquerors of Vera Cruz were on the move and would soon be on the doorstep.

Santa Anna decided to mount his defense at a nearby strategic height known as *Cerro Gordo*, "Fat Mountain," where the National Road from the coast to Mexico City climbed up from sea level through a series of mountain passes. Scott would have to come this way, the same way Cortez had come on his march toward the halls of Montezuma. Though Santa Anna would enjoy only a slight numerical superiority, this time it would be *he* who was dug in and waiting. And this time he had all the artillery he could ask for—more than 40 guns, which he placed on the high ground overlooking the road. His right flank extended to the edge of the steep cliff above the Rio del Plan, and his left flank to terrain so rough, steep, and choked with chaparral that he deemed it impassable; not even a rabbit could get through there. When his best engineer, Manuel Robles, had the temerity to challenge this assumption, Santa Anna dismissed him with withering contempt: "Cowards never felt safe anyway."[2]

When Scott sent General David Twiggs ahead with 2,600 infantry, Twiggs sent the new commander of engineers ahead to reconnoiter the territory. Following up an earlier reconnaissance by Lieutenant Beauregard that indicated that the enemy's left flank might be passable, Robert E. Lee picked his way through the dense underbrush. With great difficulty he managed to find and plot a torturous, circuitous route by which a rabbit— and a narrow file of infantry—might indeed get around the enemy's flank and cut off his retreat.

Lee almost didn't live to tell about it. He was at a spring when an enemy patrol suddenly appeared. He barely had time to hide under a fallen tree, on which the enemy soldiers now sat. Others joined them in this pleasant glade and had a picnic, spending most of the day there, while Lee lay motionless, unable to brush off ants and spiders, which were having a picnic of their own. It was nightfall before the last soldier left and he could arise and get back to the American lines with his plan. They would have to dismantle and carry any light artillery they wanted to take with them, he informed Scott, and cut their way through with axes. But it could be done.

The work was begun at night, under cover of darkness, and when Worth's division arrived, Lee's handiwork was admired by Lieutenant Sam Grant.* "Under supervision of the engineers, roadways had been opened over chasms . . . where the walls were so steep that men could barely climb them. Animals [mules] could not. . . . Artillery was let down the steep slopes by hand. . . . In like manner the guns were drawn by hand up the opposite slopes."[3]

The following morning, when one of Santa Anna's pickets reported hearing the sound of chopping off to their left, the Napoleon of the West

* Grant himself had done such a commendable job as conditional regimental quartermaster (mule tender and wagon boss) that the assignment was made permanent.

smiled and explained it was impossible. When a second messenger came with the same message, he threatened to discipline him for spreading falsehoods.

And so, when the attack came, Santa Anna was undone. The Americans made a strong feint at his front—too strong: They suffered 431 casualties going up against the grape-shot-spewing Mexican cannon. But their main thrust was at Santa Anna's unprotected left, and enough of them got around behind him that he felt compelled to take leave of his men before the battle was half over. There was no time to retrieve his personal belongings; the Americans captured his money chest with 50,000 pesos and his formal-attire false leg.* Indeed, he and a few attending staff officers were now riding for their lives, with General Worth's dragoons in hot pursuit.

Santa Anna hoped to take refuge at El Encero, but his pursuers were too close, and he had to keep going. If in his flight he recalled his pledge to the people that he would stand and die for them, it undoubtedly also occurred to him that they would have even greater need of him now than before. To share the fate of his soldiers—that would have been a selfish if valorous death. It would have meant abandoning his countrymen at their time of greatest peril. Only a coward would do such a thing!

When the battle was over, amongst the Mexican fallen were little pieces of paper. They were everywhere, like butterflies in a summer field, fluttering here and there when stirred by a gentle breeze. An American soldier picked one up, but it was in Spanish. He called to a Texan who could read it: "My duty is to sacrifice myself, and I will now fulfill it! Perhaps the American hosts may proudly tread the imperial capital of the Aztecs. I will never witness such opprobrium, for I am decided first to die fighting! . . ."

General Scott had a new problem: what to do with 3,000 prisoners. Once again, having no way to feed or keep them, he paroled them. It was a wise move; the parolees would remember the Americans' leniency and spread word of it. If they or their friends ever stood and faced the Americans again, they might be all the quicker to surrender. But for the moment, no one stood between Scott and Mexico City, 180 miles inland.

---

* For many years afterward the leg was on display in the Illinois State Capitol.

All through the night Santa Anna and his companions rode for their lives. He paused at a church and asked to exchange his exhausted horse, but the curate took one look at *el Presidente-general*, the Savior of Mexico, and refused. Finally, in the town of Orizapa, the cloud of despair under which he had been riding lifted. A Mexican detachment was there, and they were still loyal, still ready to savor the *aguardiente* one more time. He addressed them, and they cheered, and others rallied to him. By the time he returned to Mexico City, it was with an escort of 4,000 men!

En route, at Puebla, the last city before the capital, he had tried to organize another defense. But distrust of Santa Anna now ran higher than desire to repel the Yankee invader. He did organize bands of guerrillas, commissioning them to wreak havoc on the American line of supply. Scott's communications with the coast (and hence Washington) were often cut for days at a time, and supply trains required almost a full regiment to escort them the 240 miles from Vera Cruz.

On May 22, Santa Anna reclaimed the active Presidency, proclaiming that the capital would never be surrendered; he would die first. And he *believed* it. So did the people. But they sipped the *aguardiente* a little more slowly this time. While the Mexican Congress gave him the power he requested, they made a point of forbidding any communication between him and the enemy and condemning to death *anyone* attempting to treat with the invader.

With his customary verve and charisma, Santa Anna set about raising an army and preparing the defenses of the city. And once more he performed miracles: Before long, he had 30,000 men under arms. There was no shortage of officers: In 1840, the official rolls of the Regular Army carried 20,000 regular soldiers—and 2,400 officers. As a career in the army was more for social and political advancement than for military service, there were many generals and many more who aspired to the gold braid. But there were comparatively few professional noncommissioned officers, who were (and are) the backbone of the U.S. Army.

Against Santa Anna was coming Winfield Scott—with about 4,000 able-bodied troops left. Having sent home 3,000 volunteers whose one-year enlistments were about to expire, Scott's ranks were now so thin that he had to wait a month in Jalapa for enough reinforcements to go forward. When they finally arrived, however, they had been severely diminished by yellow fever and other illness. By the time Scott reached Puebla, 75 miles from Mexico City, his effective fighting strength was down to 5,820 men. So precarious was his situation that he decided on a drastic measure: He would call up all the garrisons he had left behind, who were holding open the road to Vera Cruz. This meant there would be no more supplies. From now on, he and his men would have to live off the land.*

When word of Scott's decision reached England, where his progress was being closely followed by his old acquaintance, the Duke of Wellington, the latter's assessment was grim: "Scott is lost! He has been carried away by successes. He can't take the city, and he can't fall back on his bases."[4]

On top of everything else, Scott was outraged by the arrival of Trist. This State Department clerk, who had done nothing more worthy of note than marrying Thomas Jefferson's granddaughter, had apparently been given the authority to call a halt to military operations whenever he felt it propitious to achieving a peace treaty. Making matters worse, Trist was struck down with illness in Vera Cruz and had to communicate with Scott by correspondence. Their ensuing clash of egos was breathtaking: When the two finally met, they would not speak to each other. The British envoy in Mexico City had to act as their go-between, while Scott and Trist each fired off angry letters to Washington denouncing the other.

It was a patently ridiculous situation that could have ended in disaster; instead, it was resolved by a simple act of kindness. When Trist was again struck low by illness, Scott sent a jar of guava jelly for his "sick companion." Trist sent him a grateful reply, and the two soon became fast friends, each writing to Washington to commend the other and to ask that all previous correspondence be disregarded.

The grace of God was also evident elsewhere. Inspired one evening to pen an appeal to the Mexican people, Colonel Hitchcock pointed out that his countrymen had not come as robbers or rapists. In every city they had taken, law and order had been preserved and the rights of the Mexican citizens respected. "We have not a particle of ill-will towards you—we treat you with civility—we are not, in fact, your enemies; we do not plunder

---

* Three centuries before, Hernando Cortez had reached a similar decision: He had burned his ships at the coast so his little army would have only two alternatives—conquer or die.

your people or insult your women or your religion. . . . We are here for no earthly purpose except the hope of obtaining peace."[5] Thousands of copies of this appeal were circulated, and a number of Mexicans later indicated that they had been swayed by it.

With the Americans about to advance on the capital itself, Santa Anna redoubled his efforts. But now for the first time he encountered serious resistance, even mockery. He responded with a barrage of proclamations and began arresting political foes. Neither approach worked. So on May 28, he fell back on the one tactic that had never failed: He resigned the Presidency: "I this day terminate forever my public career."

He expected the people to flock to him as before, begging him to return and not abandon them in their hour of supreme need. Then he, of course, ever submissive to their will and born only to serve them, would humble himself and wearily reassume the heavy burden of responsibility they had placed on him. He would forgive them their trespasses, and they would once again adore him.

Only this time it didn't play out that way. One day passed, and another— where were the pleading throngs? Where was the delegation from Congress, sombreros in hand? On the contrary, the Mexican Congress seemed entirely disposed to accept his offer. Very well, they were probably in shock; he would give them one more day for the enormity of his resignation and its likely aftermath to sink in.

On the fourth day, he summarily withdrew his resignation and assumed dictatorial authority.

Through the auspices of the British envoy, Santa Anna now opened a back-channel dialogue with Trist and Scott, who were waiting in Puebla for more reinforcements. The latter, with many moral misgivings, offered him a bribe of $1 million if he would agree to peace, reasoning that the lives it would save would be worth the price. As an earnest, they sent him $10,000 for "expenses."

But as time passed, and Santa Anna's power base grew more secure, he once more identified with his people, exhorting them to "War without pity unto death!" To Scott and Trist he sent word that his Congress had forbidden foreign entanglements under pain of death. (He neglected to return the $10,000.)

In the American camp, waiting and inaction were as hard on the men as always. Captain Ephraim Kirby Smith, under an unshakable premonition, wrote his wife: "How sick and tired I am of a war to which I can see no probable termination. . . . How sad and dreary the hours pass. . . . I hardly think you will ever see these pages, or the hand which guides the pen may be cold in death before they reach you. . . . I almost despair when I reflect on the destitute situation in which you will be left, with three children dependent upon you."[6]

The largest block of fresh soldiers to reach Scott was 2,500 recruits under the command of Brigadier General Franklin Pierce. Scott had been highly skeptical of the blatantly political appointment of this former Democratic Senator from New Hampshire, but Pierce turned out to be a capable and effective general.

After two months Scott was forced to face the fact that he had received all the reinforcements he was going to get. With a little over 10,000 able-bodied men, he would be going up against a force three times that number—typical of the odds the Americans faced in all the major battles of this war. Well, there was no point in further delay. It was time to advance.

21

To the Halls of Montezuma

*I*n the distance Mexico City was breathtaking, its white domes and towers rising like a shimmering mirage from the valley floor. Surrounded by lakes sparkling in the sun and accessible only by raised causeways, it was a beautiful illustration out of a book of fanciful tales.

The hard reality, however, was that it was going to be an extraordinarily difficult assault. Any attacking force would have to go down one or two of those narrow, confining approaches, with no shelter and no opportunity to alleviate pressure by sending out flanking movements.

As was then customary, Captain Lee and the Corps of Engineers were dispatched to make a preliminary reconnaissance. Lee reported that Santa Anna had prepared defenses in the three outlying towns into which the causeways fed, and that the most direct route passed by a conical hill about 300 feet high, called *el Peñón*, where Santa Anna was waiting with 7,000 men and 30 cannon. But thanks to the intelligence Lee had gathered, Scott did not approach that way. Instead, he swung the army southwest along a route that skirted Lake Chalco.

By August 18, having encountered only light skirmishing, he had reached the outlying town of San Augustin and sent out more recon patrols. They discovered that the little town of San Antonio, heavily fortified and unflankable, was now effectively blocking the road. To the right of the road were impenetrable marshes, and to the left (south) was a vast lava field five miles across called the *pedregal*. It was a nightmarish, jagged terrain resembling a black, storm-tossed sea that had been suddenly frozen. Santa Anna must have considered it impassable, for there were no defenses beyond it, until one turned north toward the capital. Was there any way across it? Lee and a small detachment of infantry and dragoons under Lieutenant Richard Ewell* went to investigate. After negotiating three miles of sharp inclines and deep chasms, they came under fire from a Mexican patrol, which quickly fled. Obviously the *pedregal* was passable on foot, possibly even by artillery, if enough men could be put to smoothing and widening the worst places.

As Lee made his report to Scott, a staff officer observed that Lee "examined, counseled, and advised with a judgment, tact, and discretion worthy of all praise. His talent for topography was peculiar; he seemed to receive impressions intuitively, which it cost other men much labor to acquire."[1]

As usual, Scott took Lee's advice—and thus avoided the heavily defended outer towns and causeways. But the Mexicans could see what he was doing, and it took them far less time inside the defense perimeter to redeploy their forces where they would be most needed. Santa Anna ordered General Gabriel Valencia, who had been in charge of defending the town of Guadalupe Hidalgo north of the capital, to bring his Army of the North south, to occupy a fortified hill at the hamlet of Padierna beyond the *pedregal*. By the time Twiggs' division crossed the lava field, Valencia was already there.

But Twiggs' lead elements, though pinned down by enemy fire, had located a ravine that would enable them to get around behind Valencia's position and attack from the rear. They would need a major diversion at Valencia's front—which only Scott could authorize. A volunteer would have to go back over the *pedregal*—at night, in a driving rainstorm—to get word to Scott. Lee went.

Scott approved the plan but could spare no men. The diversion would have to come from forces already in place out there. And since Lee was the only one who knew the way back, he spent his second sleepless night making the return trip to confirm Scott's approval, guided by flashes of lightning that silhouetted the hills in the distance.

Valencia, aware of the buildup in front of him, had pleaded with Santa Anna to come to his aid, but instead the Commanding General ordered him to give up his position and withdraw into the city. Valencia refused, and Santa Anna, put out with his ambitious rival, shrugged and left him

---

* Years later Ewell would again serve under Lee, this time as a corps commander.

to his fate. Had he instead ordered a combined attack on the exposed force caught between them, he might well have ended the American campaign then and there.

Once again, the element of surprise proved a major factor. Concentrating on the cannon fire and maneuvering going on at his front, Valencia never saw the detachment at his rear until they burst from the woods with their high-pitched wailing yells. Panic swept the Mexican ranks. Before their gunners could swing their cannon around, they were overwhelmed. Begun with artillery, the battle now ended with the bayonet. The Mexican line collapsed, and the Americans now turned the captured cannon on the fleeing enemy, wreaking terrible devastation. In 17 minutes approximately 1,500 Mexican soldiers were killed, wounded, or captured. American losses numbered 60 killed or wounded.

The bridge over the Churubusco River proved a tougher nut to crack. A quarter mile to the southwest stood the fortified convent of San Mateo, with thick adobe walls 12 feet high. For once American determination and perseverance were matched by Mexican determination and perseverance. For three long, desperate hours the battle raged around the bridge and the convent, with neither side gaining the upper hand. Finally Scott himself took direct field command and flung his entire army at the defenders. The Fifth and Eighth Infantry charged directly into the mouths of the Mexican cannon guarding the bridge, absorbing their last rounds of grapeshot. But their comrades swarmed over the parapets with bayonets fixed, and the enemy was forced back from the bridge and into the city.

The cost to Santa Anna had been fearful—4,000 casualties and 3,000 prisoners—a fourth of his entire army. But Scott's casualties were also great, including one man he could ill afford to lose: Colonel Pierce Butler, brave commander of South Carolina's famed Palmetto Regiment. All told, he had lost another 1,000 men to effective service, leaving him with fewer than 8,000—hardly enough to take and hold this city of 200,000 hostile citizens. . . .

He might not have to take it! The next day, the Mexican Government formally requested an armistice and peace negotiations—perhaps they would all be going home soon, after all!

Despite grumbling in the ranks that they ought to just go on and get the job done, Scott decided to trust Santa Anna. He granted the armistice, giving his word that he would not use the interval to improve his military position. Santa Anna gave the same guarantee and agreed to sell food and supplies to the American forces.

During the lull, Scott took the opportunity to draft an official report of the engagement thus far. In it, he praised the performance of his chief engineer, R. E. Lee.* Scott called Lee's journeys across the *pedregal* "the greatest feat of physical and moral courage performed by any individual, in my knowledge in the pending campaign." Moreover, according to his generals' reports, it seemed that every one of them had been singularly impressed with Captain Lee's gallantry.

Five days later Scott awarded him a double promotion, to Lieutenant Colonel. True, it was a *brevet* or battlefield promotion,† but it was an indication of how highly he was regarded. And not only by the brass; young Sam Grant noted that "the work of the engineer officers who made the reconnaissances and led the different commands to their destinations was so perfect that the chief was able to give his orders to his various subordinates with all the precision he could use on an ordinary march." And as it happened, in Lee's own report he made a point of singling out the performance of "Lieutenant Grant, regimental quartermaster, who was usefully employed in his appropriate duties."[2]

Less encouraging was the progress in the negotiations—there was none. And when the tone of the Mexican commissioners became openly antagonistic, it soon became apparent that Santa Anna had merely been stalling for time. True to his word, Scott had ordered a cessation of recon patrols; reliable sources nonetheless confirmed that Santa Anna was busily fortifying his defenses, especially the two main strongpoints beyond the walls: a former foundry called Molino del Rey and the castle of Chapultepec on a hill, both guarding the two main causeways to the city. Not only had he tricked Scott, he was also said to be re-forming his army; indeed, through his charismatic appeals he had apparently been able to muster some 18,000 men under arms!

Colonel Hitchcock, now one of Scott's staff officers, was frustrated but not surprised. He had come to know the mind of the Mexican much better than most, as witnessed by the success of his appeal. Now he observed:

* In those days, to be "mentioned in dispatches" was a great boon to a military career.
† A brevet meant that, unless the promotion was confirmed by Congress, Lee could later be reduced back to his regular rank. In Lee's case this happened.

"I never was in favor of this war, and have hoped within a few days that the end of it was near. I have not relied much on it, though. The pride of this people is very great, and that pride has been wounded: this will probably go further to continue the war than any injustice of which they complain."[3]

Hitchcock would probably have agreed with those who had come to the conclusion that the war, right or wrong, could not be settled until the Mexicans were defeated—completely. Anything short of that, and they would soon convince themselves that they had not been defeated at all.

"Fatal credulity!" lamented Captain Kirby Smith. "How awful are its consequences to us. . . . And now, alas, we have all our fighting to do over again."[4]

On September 8, it fell to Scott to convince the Mexicans, once and for all, that they were beaten. It was rumored that the enemy was taking church bells into the former foundry to melt down and cast into cannon. And now Scott committed a military blunder to match his diplomatic one: He inexplicably failed to send out his engineers to ascertain the veracity of these third- and fourth-hand accounts. For the Molino del Rey, which could have been easily bypassed, was not being used to make cannon. It *was* being used to hide cannon, however, along with several thousand waiting defenders.

Scott picked Worth's division to conduct the dawn attack against the foundry. The first wave would consist of 500 hand-picked men, the best from all his units. After an adequate artillery barrage had softened up the foundry's resistance, the first wave—or "the forlorn hope," as they wryly called themselves—would lead the charge.

In the silver gray half-light before dawn, the barrage began. And then, far from adequate, it abruptly stopped. Worth was too anxious to get on with it. And so the forlorn hope became just that—horribly cut down by grapeshot and massed musketry. The second wave, led by Captain Ephraim Kirby Smith, fared no better, faltering when their dauntless leader received a fatal musket ball in the face, sadly fulfilling his dread premonition. The third wave did manage to clear the foundry, and Lieutenant Grant, once again preferring action to mule tending, led a band of skirmishers to the roof, which they also cleared.

By the end of the day, the Mexicans had lost 3,000, including prisoners, and Worth had lost one man in four. Molino del Rey was in American hands, but the enemy still retained the redoubtable Chapultepec Castle. Formerly the summer residence of Spanish viceroys, since Mexican independence it had served as the Republic's military academy. Its broad parade-ground terrace made an excellent gun platform.

Scott's army was now reduced to barely 7,000 effectives. If he lost many more in the assault on that terrace, he would not have enough left to carry the city. Needless to say, the next day's preliminary bombardment was long and thorough; indeed, it lasted the entire day, with the Mexican guns answering. It did have one salutary effect: Many of the soldiers defending the heights began to slip away, until the castle's commander, General Nicolás Bravo, had only 1,000 men left, including 50 teenage cadets who had refused to be evacuated.

The general sent an appeal to Santa Anna for reinforcements, and the latter personally hastened to his aid with a force of reserves. But when Santa Anna surveyed the situation, he decided that his presence was more vitally needed back inside the city's walls preparing her defenses, and so were his reserves. He withdrew his force, leaving Bravo and his men and boys to go it alone.

The following morning, August 13, the guns commenced their barrage at 6:00. Captain Thomas J. Jackson was on the left, in a predicament: A Mexican fieldpiece, protected by a breastwork directly in front of them, was raking the approach with cannon fire. Jackson's men dived for cover. Not Jackson; he strode up and down the road, oblivious to the heavy fire, exhorting his men to get up and come with him to storm the breastwork. It was a miracle he wasn't hit; at one point a cannonball even bounded between his legs.

Jackson's courage under fire was already becoming the stuff of legend. William Gardner, one of his classmates at the Academy (where he was affectionately known as "Old Jack"), was standing near him when they earlier came under fire. He noted that Jackson was "as calm in the midst of a hurricane of bullets, as though he were on dress parade at West Point."[5]

But all his courage was not enough to move his men, so he decided to take out the Mexican gun by himself, with one of his own fieldpieces. To do so, he would have to get it over the deep ditch that cut across the approach. He started pulling it, but no one would come out and help him. He managed to get it down in the ditch, but the gun was too heavy to haul up alone. Just then a sergeant ran up to help, and the two of them succeeded in positioning the piece. Jackson and the sergeant started firing and loading their gun in a muzzle-to-muzzle duel.[6]

At that moment, Captain of Artillery John P. Magruder arrived and started pulling a second gun into position. And at the sight of that, Jackson's men rallied to help. The Mexican gun was knocked out, and Jackson's troops stormed the breastwork.*

An hour later the artillery barrage lifted—the ominous silence signaling that it was the time of the infantry. Under shot and shell, the Americans ran up the shallow slope. Hitchcock watched in the distance as Lieutenant Lewis A. Armistead led the charge and was immediately wounded. Right behind him came the colors, borne by Lieutenant James Longstreet. Running beside him was Lieutenant George E. Pickett.† Longstreet was hit and went down, but even as he fell, the Stars and Stripes was snatched in midair by Pickett and carried forward up to the castle.[7]‡

Scaling ladders were needed to storm the walls of the castle. The first men up were killed, and their ladders repelled. But soon there were 50 men mounting ladders simultaneously, more than could be pushed off. Once they had gained a foothold, they cleared the walls and held them, while their comrades joined them. The castle was falling. One of the cadets, rather than let their flag be taken, hauled it down and ran across the roof of the castle toward a stairway. Shot before he could reach it, he plunged to his death on the rocks below, still clutching his flag. Today the site is marked with a memorial to *Los Niños Heroicos*—the six heroic youths who gave their lives there.

Watching from the city walls, an officer standing next to Santa Anna was heard to mutter: "God is a Yankee."[8]

The surviving defenders were taken prisoner, and Scott now had 500 fewer men with which to assault the city. This time when the Stars and Stripes was raised over the castle, he did not halt his troops or even hesitate, but sent them on down the causeways to the city—and into it as soon as possible.

---

* For this action and two others, Jackson would be breveted three times—more than any other officer in the war.

† As historian John Waugh notes, Pickett was last in his class at West Point but first at Chapultepec.

‡ Longstreet would be double breveted for valor, and both he and Pickett would be in gray at another pivotal charge 16 years later.

General John A. Quitman took his division onto the causeway leading to the heavily fortified Belén Gate. Down the middle of the causeway ran an elevated aqueduct. Sprinting from one of its stone arches to the next, a courageous infantry company was able to reach the gate and gain access to the city. But now a fierce counterattack drove them back outside, where they were pinned down and barely able to hold their position.

Scott accompanied Worth's division down the Verónica causeway, which was also split by an aqueduct whose arches offered minimal protection from the metal whizzing at them. Where it intersected the Tacuba causeway, which they would take to the also heavily fortified San Cosmé Gate, Worth thought he saw a safer route: a line of stucco buildings along the causeway's north side. Using a tactic developed at Monterrey, they blew a hole in the sidewall between the houses, went through it, cleared the roof, then blew a hole in the next wall. Their progress was considerably slower than Quitman's, but they were protected on all sides and overhead.

Lieutenant Sam Grant, still AWOL* from his mules, was in the first party to reach the Belén Gate. Seeing the gate well defended, he led a recon party south, where he located a church whose belfry would give them an excellent vantage point above and behind the gate. Imagining what might be accomplished from there with a little mountain howitzer, Grant scouted up a lieutenant in charge of such a gun and told him his plan. The latter caught Grant's vision, and soon a few men were disassembling the gun and carrying its parts and ammunition to the front door of the little church.

Grant knocked. A priest came to the door but declined to admit them. With the little Spanish at his command, Lieutenant Grant explained the tremendous property damage to the church that could be avoided by admitting them. "He began to see his duty in the same light I did," Grant later recalled, "and opened the door."[9]

Once they were in the belfry, Grant realized that they were no more than 300 yards from the rear of the Belén Gate. Working as quickly but quietly as they could, desperately hoping no one would see them, they reassembled the howitzer. Minutes stretched like hours, until at last it was ready. There was no time for gunlaying or bracketing. The first shot would have to be on the mark; if it wasn't, they would be in for it. With their best guess at windage and elevation, they fired.

* absent without leave

Their first shell caught the gate's defenders totally by surprise, causing enormous confusion. Before the Mexicans could focus on where the shell had come from, the two lieutenants got off a second round and then a third. The defenders, convinced now that the enemy had somehow gotten behind and above them with artillery, hastened into the city. The Belén Gate fell, and the city was penetrated.

General Worth, observing the daring initiative, yet not knowing who was in command, sent another officer, Lieutenant John Pemberton, to present whoever was in charge with his profound congratulations.* Another young officer favorably mentioned in that day's dispatches and later cited for the "highest qualities of a soldier—devotion, industry, talent and gallantry" was the artillery captain who had remained rock steady as he personally outdueled a Mexican battery north of Chapultepec: Thomas J. Jackson.[10]

The city's defenses were breached, but while others were jubilant, Scott remained concerned. He had lost still more troops on the causeways and now had to occupy the city and pacify the countryside. Plus, Santa Anna still had approximately four times as many men under arms as he did.

As it happened, Santa Anna solved his problems for him. In a rage he confronted the general who had been in charge of the Belén Gate, slapping his face, tearing off his insignia, and placing him under arrest. Then at midnight, under cover of darkness, he left the city, moving the seat of Government north to Guadalupe Hidalgo and taking his remaining soldiers with him. There, he tried one last time to rally the people. But no one had a taste for his *aguardiente* anymore; there were too many dead compatriots in his wake. Also, the people had gotten wind of his secret dealings with Scott and Trist and the money he had received, even as he had been urging them to prepare to give their lives in defense of their capital.

A delegation from the city surrendered to Scott, who, on the following morning, September 14, rode in full-dress procession down the main Avenida Francisco I. Madero to receive their formal surrender. As he approached the plaza in front of the National Palace, the waiting regimental bands struck up, but their music was drowned out by the cheers of 6,000 battle-scarred veterans at the sight of their commander. It was over.

* Fifteen years later these two would meet again over a matter of artillery, with Grant besieging Vicksburg and Pemberton commanding her defenses.

Two days later Santa Anna resigned the Presidency, naming Manuel de Peña y Peña to take his place. But the old fox had one more card to play. Taking the remnant of his army to Puebla, he planned an assault on the American garrison there. If he could break Scott's line of supply and communications to the coast, the conqueror would soon be the conquered, and Antonio López de Santa Anna would again be a hero, restored to a place of honor instead of disgrace.

The unauthorized attack was a disaster, and on October 16 he received a dispatch from Peña y Peña relieving him of all military command and informing him that his entire conduct of the war was now under investigation. Santa Anna was still free to go where he wished in the country, but when he tried to go to Oaxaca on his way to Guatemala, Governor Benito Juarez, his old political rival, refused him passage.

Meanwhile, Nicholas Trist was having difficulty securing a peace. Nothing seemed to satisfy the Mexican peace commissioners, and continuing guerrilla activity plagued the route to Vera Cruz. Washington was growing increasingly impatient, and when Polk learned that at one point Trist had mentioned the possibility of accepting the Nueces River as the southern border of Texas, his frustration boiled over. He summarily recalled Trist in a dispatch that reached Mexico City on November 16. Hearing this, and realizing that the next American commissioner might be more inclined to dictate than negotiate, the Mexican commissioners pleaded with Trist to stay.

Trist now faced a difficult decision: If he did stay, he would be in direct insubordination, acting only as a private citizen and against the express wishes of the U.S. Government. But—he knew exactly what Polk wanted, and he seemed to be in a unique position to obtain it. The window of opportunity would not remain open long. . . . Both Scott and the British consul urged him to stay—and he did.

The Republic of Mexico agreed to cede California and New Mexico*— more than half of all her territory—to the United States of America. The border between the countries would run from the Gulf of Mexico up the

---

* Territory that today includes New Mexico, Arizona, California, Nevada, Utah, and significant parts of Wyoming and Colorado.

Rio Grande to New Mexico, thence west along the 32nd parallel to the Pacific, one marine league (three miles) below San Diego. In exchange, Mexico would receive the sum of $15 million, and the United States would assume responsibility for the $3.25 million in outstanding claims of American citizens against Mexico. On February 2, 1848, the Treaty of Guadalupe Hidalgo was signed.

Shortly before the signing, a final scene would unfold between Santa Anna and his oldest adversaries, the Texas Rangers. Other than the slowness of the peace negotiations, Scott's biggest headache was the guerrilla bands who continued to roam the countryside, preying on the helpless and terrorizing any who dared oppose them. Ignoring the peace and the repeated orders from their Government to cease and desist, they were nothing but outlaws now—ruthless and cunning, as dangerous as rattlesnakes. As there was no Mexican army or *guardistas*, dealing with them became the responsibility of the commander of the occupying forces. Scott had precious few soldiers to spare for "deinfestation" duties, but he called on the outfit that was more than a match for the outlaws: the Texas Rangers. Indeed, the only thing *los bandidos* feared was *los diablos Tejanos*.

The Rangers did their work with their customary efficiency, but there was one bit of business that remained unfinished: locating and destroying the king of the rattlers, Santa Anna. He had gone to ground somewhere, and they owed him—not just for the Alamo and Goliad and all the other atrocities he had perpetrated during his campaign against the Republic of Texas, but for what had happened the month before in Huamantla. The village was 25 miles from Puebla, whose garrison had been under siege for a month by Santa Anna in a classic Mexican standoff: The garrison was too strong for Santa Anna to take, and Santa Anna's 1,000 soldiers and bandits were too many for those in the garrison to break through.

Finally Scott was able to send a relief column of some 3,000 under General Joseph Lane, augmented by the Rangers. Riding in advance of the column was their former leader, Sam Walker, who had been made a captain in the Regular Army and was now leading a company of mounted rifles. As always, Walker's detachment was well out front. When they reached Huamantla, they were suddenly jumped by Santa Anna and several hundred men.

Sam Walker called for a charge and went straight at them, both Colts blazing. His detachment followed, but they were heavily outnumbered and badly mauled. Hearing the gunfire, the column pressed forward on the double, the Rangers in the lead. But when they reached the village, they found Sam Walker lying in the dirt, fatally wounded in the head and chest. Looking down at their fallen leader, the Rangers said nothing. But more than a few had tears in their eyes.

The Rangers buried a number of good men that day, and now they had a personal score to settle with Santa Anna. So when they heard that he was hiding out in Tehuacán, southeast of Puebla, they rode all night to catch him, arriving two hours before dawn—only to find that someone had tipped off their quarry moments before. The terrified Napoleon of the West had fled in such haste that he abandoned 17 packed trunks. A freshly lit candle and an inkwell revealed how tantalizingly close they had come to catching him. The inkwell had been knocked over across a white satin writing pad. The spilled ink was still wet.

Santa Anna managed to elude his pursuers until his Government concluded its investigation of his war conduct and banished him from the country. Knowing he would never get out of Mexico alive without an escort, he requested a guarantee of safe passage from the American authorities. On December 8, his carriage, accompanied by a Mexican guard of honor, started down the road to the coast. There he would board a ship bound for Jamaica, his place of exile.

The Rangers were in Jalapa. When they learned that Santa Anna would soon be coming their way, they immediately laid plans to kill him, and were only dissuaded by their regimental adjutant, John S. "Rip" Ford, who pointed out the shame such an act would bring upon Texas. The rest of the world would regard them as assassins.

"Well, just let us talk to him, then," they pleaded, but Ford knew where "talking" would lead. It was agreed that they could line each side of the road down which his carriage would pass, provided that no one said or did anything that would dishonor Texas. It was the sternest test of self-discipline the Rangers would ever face.[11]

On a gray, chill December afternoon, a rider galloped into Jalapa. "He's coming!" Immediately the Rangers formed a long, shoulder-to-shoulder double file, through which Santa Anna's carriage would pass. In their long dusters with their broad-brimmed Stetsons down low over their eyes, the Rangers awaited the man who had been responsible for the deaths of so many of their comrades and family members, and also their beloved captain. No one knew if they would hold ranks or succumb to the temptation to exact a little Texan justice. No one knew if they would give voice to what lay so heavily on their hearts.

The gilt-trimmed carriage came into view. In it was Santa Anna in a full-dress uniform, and a young woman next to him, presumably his wife. Seeing the Texans, his eyes widened, and the color drained from his face. He straightened, sitting ramrod erect, ready to accept a soldier's death. His wife, oblivious to the significance of this strange guard of honor, smiled and waved at them. But the hard-faced men just kept staring at her husband with their cold eyes.

No one moved. No one spoke. The honor of Texas—and the United States—remained intact. When the carriage was out of sight,* the Rangers broke ranks and returned to camp.

---

* Incredibly, this was not the last Mexico would see of Santa Anna. Six years later the Centralists engineered yet another revolution and returned him to power. Nothing had changed: To raise money for an expanded army, he sold off another piece of Mexico to the United States for $10 million, the territory south of the Gila River known as the Gadsden Purchase. Two years later when the Reformists, led by Benito Juarez, came to power, Santa Anna again went into exile, but he never stopped scheming to return. When at last he did, it was as a blind and broken old man of 80 who was allowed to live the last two years of his life in poverty in Mexico City until his death in 1876.

22

TRANSITIONS

*A*t the tall window where he had stood so often the past three years, the lone figure with his hands clasped behind him stared out at the chill February night. The only illumination in the Oval Office came from the fire in the hearth and the pale glow of the new gaslight fixtures on the walls—barely enough light for him to tackle the paperwork still on his desk.

When he had come here, his stature had been erect; now it was stooped, the shoulders bent. The pressures of the Presidency took their toll on any man, but they had aged James K. Polk more than any of his predecessors (and many of his successors). The raven dark hair had gone white; deep furrows had been etched into his face. The dark eyes were sunken now and had lost the fire they once had. Never had the President felt so alone.

Having only a few close friends when he came into office, he had managed to alienate every one, while making none to replace them. Thomas Hart Benton, one of the great stalwarts of the Democratic party, whom Polk saw every Sunday at church and with whom he had once had a warm relationship, now refused to speak to him when they passed.[1] Other leaders of the party, whose nominal Chief he still was, were openly critical of him both in the press and on Capitol Hill. Outside of his Cabinet there was hardly any person of influence in America who still supported his handling of the Mexican War. And even within the Cabinet there were those who were undercutting him and feathering their own nests. Secretary of State James Buchanan could be counted on to voice a contrary opinion (even when he *agreed* with his Chief), so that in his own bid for the Presidency he could claim that he had opposed Polk.

Unlike John Quincy Adams, whose diary reveals how often during his tenure in the White House he turned to God, Polk's diary reveals that he had only himself to turn to. And invariably convinced that he was doing the right thing, when anyone turned against him he put it down to vindictiveness or political jealousy. Increasingly seeing himself as the victim of fate and circumstance, he resolved to work harder—and no one in Washington, not even JQA, could match the long hours he put in at his desk.

But they were thankless hours—what expression of appreciation did he receive from anyone? The leaders of the Democratic party seemed embarrassed by his continuing presence in their midst. Well, it would not be for much longer. One more year—then he could leave this city and retire to the lovely home awaiting him in Tennessee.*

There was a knock at the door: A courier had just delivered an urgent communication from Nicholas Trist in Mexico City. Trist! Another insubordinate acting on his own authority, against the express wishes and ignoring the explicit recall of his Commander in Chief, apparently bent on bringing further humiliation to the United States and its President. Polk would have gladly consigned the large envelope and its contents to the hearth fire, but he decided to see what was inside.

It was the Treaty of Guadalupe Hidalgo. The President called an emergency session of the Cabinet the following day (Sunday) and was gratified when their initial response mirrored his own: Throw it away! Trist had no authority! He was a private citizen! Send a proper ambassador down there, one who would *impose* surrender terms, not negotiate them!

But second thoughts prevailed. After all, Trist *had* secured every point that Polk had wanted. And through hard experience they had all learned how mercurial Mexican governments could be: If peace was postponed, who was to say that the Mexicans might not convince themselves that the war had not truly been lost? That they had been betrayed by Santa Anna? At the very least, long, drawn-out warfare with bands of outlaws still hiding in the mountains would take more American lives—at a time when the overwhelming desire of the nation was to bring the boys home. In the end Polk and his Cabinet decided to pass the responsibility for approving or rejecting the treaty's terms on to the Senate.

There it quickly stirred up a storm! Pro- and anti-expansionist sentiments were extreme in both parties and all regions. They had, in fact, been

---

* Sadly, he would live only three months after yielding the Presidency to his successor.

debating that very issue, when the Guadalupe Hidalgo Treaty interrupted their proceedings. The timing of its arrival was providential, some felt, for it looked like the all-of-Mexico-down-to-Mexico-City crowd were about to have their way.

Daniel Webster, the great lion of the upper house, roared once again his belief that this unjust war should never have been fought, and that its victors should accrue no spoils beyond the State of Texas. Others claimed that it was part of America's Manifest Destiny to regenerate Mexico. As for the generosity of the terms, brash young William Tecumseh Sherman of Ohio was appalled: Who had lost the war, he demanded, Mexico or the United States?

But thanks to the Wilmot Proviso, which had repeatedly been sent up to the Senate by the House (Congressman Lincoln recalled voting for it at least 40 times), slavery, specifically its status in the new Territories, was now *the* underlying issue—and would remain so in both houses for the next dozen years. The abolitionists were insistent that slavery not be introduced into territory where it had already been prohibited by Mexican law. And the ever dwindling voices of moderation were adamant that at least the slave/free dividing line along the 36th parallel, agreed upon in the Missouri Compromise of 1820, should be extended to the Pacific.

The proslavery forces, however, now vehemently resented the implication that their system was in any way morally inferior. They demanded that *all* new territory be open to slavery, even though they privately acknowledged that the cold climate to the north and the desert to the southwest made this economically unfeasible. Acrimonious to begin with, the debate deteriorated to the point where the treaty was on the verge of being rejected out of hand—simply because no one wanted anyone else to benefit from it.

And then God intervened.

That February of 1848, John Quincy Adams had seemed in good health. At 82, he was by far the oldest member of either house, and though he spoke infrequently now, his wry wit had lost none of its edge. What *had* changed was his colleagues' attitude toward him. Ever since his long, lonely, and ultimately triumphant struggle to overturn the gag rule, the House regarded him in a different light. The entire nation, in fact, had come to appreciate what a remarkable gift he was. Even his former antagonists had developed a fondness for him.

On the morning of the 21st, he seemed frail but steady. Only a few days before, he had hosted a large reception for his friend (and once bitter rival) Henry Clay. But now, just as he was rising to make a point, he clutched his heart and collapsed over the arm of his chair. "Stop, stop!" cried someone. "Look to Mr. Adams!"

Some senior members carried him to a sofa, while the rest looked on in shocked silence. Among them was the newest boarder at Abolition House, Abe Lincoln of Illinois. Five members of the House were physicians, who now prescribed fresh air. Quickly the sofa was carried outdoors—and even more quickly brought back in; it was well below freezing out there!

Still on the sofa, he was carried to the Speaker's Room. There he lay dying, and all knew it. He had prayed once that he might "die upon the breach," and God was answering that prayer. Calm and serene, John Quincy Adams' last words before slipping into a coma were: "This is the last of earth—I am content."[2]

All through the night his wife and daughter kept a bedside vigil, as did towering Joshua Giddings of Ohio, who never left his side. Nor had he ever left it during Adams' long battle as the champion of the antislavery cause. Giddings would now inherit that mantle. A giant of a man, his courage matched his size. Two years before, in the midst of a heated debate, Black of Georgia, who was armed with pistol and sword cane, had threatened to chastise Giddings. "Come on!" bellowed Giddings, "The people of Ohio don't send cowards here!"[3]

He was subdued now, as he sat beside the prostrate form of "the greatest statesman of the age, slowly sinking into the arms of death," as he recorded it.[4]

Their vigil continued on the 22nd, Washington's Birthday, normally a festive occasion. Out of deference to Adams, all celebrations were canceled. Throughout the day knots of colleagues from both houses gathered at the doorway. Henry Clay came and left, overwhelmed with grief. Here lay the last great link to the generation that had founded the Republic, and for many the curtain of that noble era was now descending. More than a few reflected on God's timing: The sixth President lay dying on the birthday of the first, much as his father, the second President, and Thomas Jefferson, the third, had both died on the Fourth of July, 1826—50 years to the day after the signing of the Declaration of Independence.

John Quincy Adams stopped breathing on the 23rd, and in Washington and Massachusetts the outpouring of grief—with tolling bells, cannon salutes, solemn ceremonies, and long lines of mourners—assumed proportions that foreshadowed the death of future great Presidents. Moving eulogies were preached and printed everywhere.

Even in Charleston, the seat of his most vehement adversaries, the *Courier* draped its columns in black, noting that America had abundant cause for pride in his versatile brilliance and statesmanship.[5]

But no one said it better than Edmund Dwight of Springfield, Massachusetts, who observed: "His character seemed an embodiment of the heroic past," and he anticipated "the ideas by which the world is to be carried along in its future progress. . . . He led the van in the contest of liberty against slavery; the future history of this country is to be influenced, molded, formed, shaped, more by his spirit than by that of any other man of the age."[6]

Even in his death, John Quincy Adams served both God and country. His passing reminded the nation's elected representatives of their heritage and inspired them to live up to it. When the Senate reconvened, it was with a more sober appreciation of the great responsibility entrusted to them. Daniel Webster, to be sure, complained that if they annexed all that new territory, they would soon have six new Senators representing less than 300,000 people, while New York, Pennsylvania, and Ohio had that number of Senators for 4 or 5 million.[7] But the nobler spirit was sustained; they dispensed with further debate and ratified the Treaty of Guadalupe Hidalgo, 38 to 14.

The Mexican War was the costliest war young America had ever been engaged in. It was fought brilliantly by Scott, and while many today think of the victory as a forgone conclusion, it was far from it. Some modern historians regard it as the turning point in our history, the point at which the Civil War truly began. In the sense that it forced the issue of slavery to the forefront of national consciousness, and that slavery was *the* issue over which the Civil War would be fought, that was certainly true.

On the distant Mall, the grass was turning green with the hope and promise of spring. It did not reflect—or lift—the mood of the President's heart. The political parties were gearing up for their national conventions to pick their Presidential candidates, and Polk had created a monster—a war hero likely to put his Democratic party out of office.

In all fairness, the honors for the successful conclusion of the Mexican War should have fallen to Winfield Scott. But Scott had proven intemperate when it came to keeping his mouth shut in public, and at the moment he was embroiled in a degrading, all-too-public controversy with his subordinate generals over who deserved credit for what in the final chapter of the war. Having become an embarrassment to the administration, he had been summarily relieved of command—"turned out," Robert E. Lee sadly observed, "as an old horse to die."[8] Zachary Taylor, on the other hand, reacted stoically to being passed over for the vacated top command. Keeping his resentment to himself, he returned to his private affairs involving his plantation in Mississippi and his residence in Louisiana, to begin life as a civilian.

Taylor also refused to be drawn into the unseemly fracas going on in Washington—and the less he said, the more statesmanlike he appeared. All across America, young Whigs began calling for Old Rough and Ready to be their candidate—though they were not even sure he was a Whig. They need not have concerned themselves on that account; after his treatment by the present administration, the one thing Taylor was certain of was that he was no Democrat. But on the burning national issue of the free or slave status for the new Territories, he wisely said nothing. His silence enabled moderates to think of him as a moderate—which he actually was, despite the Mississippi plantation, which made him one of only 1,800 Americans who owned more than 100 slaves.

When the Democratic convention met in May 1848, the party was a shambles. Sectional interests now prevailed over any attempt to pull the party together as a national force. Southern Democrats, adamant that the extension of slavery should be in no way restricted, distrusted any Northern or Eastern or Western Democrat who had ever seemed at all receptive to the prospect of free soil in the new Territories. Northwestern Democrats, distrustful of anyone east or south of them, again put forth their favorite candidate, Senator Lewis Cass of Michigan, as the ideal compromise candidate.

When asked the litmus-test question of where he stood on the status of the new Territories, Cass embraced the doctrine of popular sovereignty, which was rapidly gaining adherents amongst moderates everywhere, especially in the Northwest. The chairman of the new Senate Committee on the Territories, Stephen A. Douglas, was one of its eloquent champions: Let every settler heading West do as his conscience dictated. Then, when the time for statehood was at hand, each Territory's population could decide for themselves whether they would come in slave or free. This doctrine, which Senator John C. Calhoun of South Carolina derisively dubbed "squatter sovereignty," would become a plank in the Democratic platform.

To the intense resentment of the Southern delegates, Cass was nominated on the fourth ballot. He had voted for the hated Wilmot Proviso, and in Calhoun's eyes his scheme of popular sovereignty was even more dangerous: It might close the door to slavery in *all* the Territories.[9] The Free-Soilers were even more resentful, reading it the other way: Cass would *open* the territorial door to slavery.

As it happened, there was similar division at the Whig convention that summer. But they at least had two eminently worthy candidates: Henry Clay and Daniel Webster. Together, the Great Compromiser and the Great Orator had epitomized the Whig Party in its finest hour. Though neither would ever step aside for the other, either one could have restored the party to its former glory. And each was more than deserving of the candidacy.

But Clay and Webster were giants of an earlier era. Their appeal was largely to older men—and it was the young Whigs who were formulating party strategy now. In their eyes both men had been on the stage too long. Plus, they were too regionally oriented: After 30 years Clay was still "Harry of the West,"* and Webster, the finest speaker on this side of the Atlantic, was definitely from the East, the preferred candidate of the Whig *cognoscenti* and rumored to be in the pocket of the industrial interests.

What was needed, thought the bright young Whigs, was a candidate of truly national appeal—and the hero of Buena Vista was the obvious choice. Zachary Taylor's views were unknown (and therefore no liability), and his personal courage and character were unquestioned. By rights the nomination should go to Clay. But once before his party had set him aside to nominate a war hero, Old Tippecanoe. Poor old William Henry Harrison had barely survived the campaign trail and had died a month after taking office. Still, he had lived long enough to take the Whigs to the White House, and now Old Rough and Ready would do the same.

---

* nicknamed after Shakespeare's portrait of young Henry V

Webster had seen the General's political star in ascendancy sooner than most. Scarcely had the news of Buena Vista been received, than he ruefully predicted that Taylor would be the next President.[10] So did New York editor Horace Greeley, the most influential voice of the antislavery Conscience Whigs (as opposed to the mercantile Cotton Whigs). Greeley deplored Taylor's "no-party utterances, his well-understood hostility to the Wilmot Proviso, his unqualified devotion to slavery," adding "If we nominate Taylor, we elect him, but we destroy the Whig Party."[11]

In June Henry Clay sailed into the Whig convention in Philadelphia, assuming he was the clear front-runner. He was stunned when the first ballot went to Taylor with 111 votes (followed by Clay 97, Scott 43, and Webster 22). At that moment, had Clay and his supporters acted quickly, they might have forged a Clay-Scott ticket and won the day. But they were too dazed. When they finally recovered, and the overtures went out, it was too late. Webster's followers announced that they had thrown in with Taylor. Why not with Clay? Because Taylor seemed certain to win and was far more likely to give Webster a role in the future administration.[12]

Taylor won on the fourth ballot, and to balance the ticket Millard Fillmore, a steadfast antislavery man from New York, was named Vice-Presidential candidate. The platform contained no position on slavery in the Territories. Like the Democrats, the Whigs had decided that the only safe course was to avoid the subject wherever possible. As a result, so many were so disgusted with both parties that for the first time in America's history a major third party was launched.

If the two main parties seemed devoid of principle, the new Free Soil Party most emphatically was not. Under its wings gathered abolitionists, antislavery Democrats, Conscience Whigs, and Liberty Party men (who had supported James G. Birney in '40 and '44)—anyone opposed to the spread of slavery. Some bright stars joined this new firmament—Joshua Giddings, Salmon Chase, Charles Sumner, Charles Francis Adams, Richard Henry Dana, and William Cullen Bryant. Convening in August, the Free-Soilers nominated Van Buren for President, and by acclamation Charles Francis Adams as his running mate.

Thirty years later, looking back at all the conventions he had attended, JQA's son singled this one out: "For plain downright honesty of purpose, to effect high ends without a whisper of bargain or sale, I doubt whether any similar one had been its superior, before or since."[13] Certainly their platform was unequivocal: "Free soil, free speech, free labor, and free men!" There would be no new slave States, no new slave Territory, no compromise with slavery anywhere. But for all their magnificent crusading spirit, they did not materially affect the outcome of the election.

It was not much of a campaign; indeed, the apathy was so pervasive that old Frank Blair, who had been Andrew Jackson's editor of choice, observed: "The people have fallen into such a state of indifference to the Presidency, that they care very little who holds it."[14]

In Charleston, the *Courier* backed Taylor: "It is of vital importance that the South—the whole South—shall march to this question with an unbroken front, and give decisive answer. By birth, education, sentiment, feeling, association, and interest, General Taylor is one of us."[15]

But not all Charleston's sons were ready to march in lockstep. John C. Calhoun, for two decades the champion and guiding light of Southern independence, anticipated (correctly) that Taylor, after a career in the military, would prove far more Northern and nationalist in outlook than the *Courier* might like to believe. His solution: The South should form its own political party. Though here he anticipated what would eventually come to pass, at the time the thought of abandoning the Democratic party, let alone going into competition with it, was a little too radical for his fellow South Carolinians. They followed the State's other leader, Barnwell Rhett, into the Cass camp.

Meanwhile, the Free Soil Party, with no real hope of winning, nonetheless fought the good fight. But they were unable to overcome the baggage of Van Buren's reputation for political craftiness; too many remembered that John Quincy Adams had denounced him for "fawning servility" and "profound dissimulation and duplicity."[16]

A light turnout on election day gave Taylor a surprisingly low 53 percent of the 2.87 million popular vote. At first the Free-Soilers were disappointed at having received only 291,000 votes—until they realized that in any close vote in the House, their nine new seats could make the difference. And they sent their first Senator to Washington: Ohio's Salmon P. Chase.

After the election race was over, the nation seemed to relax. Though sectional feelings were as intense and bitter as ever, for now, everyone rested on their oars. . . .

While out in the golden-hued far West, the curtain was about to go up on America's final adventure before her great ordeal began.

23

Gold in California!

*E*ighteen months after the Bear Flag had been lowered over John Sutter's New Helvetia, the vast 100,000-acre ranch remained as idyllic as ever. Crops flourished in the fertile Sacramento Valley. Twelve thousand head of cattle grazed the verdant pastureland, 2,000 horses roamed the hills, more than 700 people enjoyed an Edenic existence there. The vineyards received just the right balance of sun and rain to produce luscious grapes, and when trampled these yielded rich, full-bodied vintages.

The number of arriving settlers increased dramatically once California became a U.S. Territory. Gaunt and haggard from their trek over the Rocky Mountains, they could scarcely believe their eyes. The reports were not exaggerated: California *was* the proverbial land of milk and honey!

John Sutter was prospering. His gristmill, his tannery, his big general store—everything he touched seemed to turn to gold. Seeing how badly the new settlers needed lumber to build homes, he decided to put up a sawmill on the American River, a tributary of the Sacramento, some forty miles away. In charge of this project was his most reliable foreman, John Marshall, under whose experienced hand Sutter's Mill soon began to take shape.

One bright, chilly morning in January 1848, Marshall was supervising the completion of the millrace to bring water to the mill's wheel, when he happened to notice something metallic glinting under the shallow water. Curious, he fished it out. It was a nugget about the size of a pea, and as he held it up, turning it in his fingers, the early morning sun flashed off its many facets. Looking back down in the millrace, he noticed another tiny sample. And another. Gathering them up, he laughed, "Boys, I believe I've found a gold mine!"[1]

But after applying every known test for gold, he was no longer laughing. Without a word he quickly saddled his horse and rode hard to New Helvetia. Nor was there any laughter from Captain Sutter when he heard the report. Instead, he pledged Marshall to secrecy and sent the samples into San Francisco to be professionally assayed.

His agent there was, alas, not so reliable. If the samples proved genuine, Charles Bennett was to go directly to Colonel R. B. Mason, the U.S. Government's man in California, to confirm Sutter's claim to the block of land formerly granted him by the Mexican Alcalde. But to keep big news quiet requires almost superhuman self-discipline, and Charlie Bennett proved all too human. The word got out: Gold had been found on the American River!

So many tall tales had already floated down the Sacramento to San Francisco that this one created little stir—at first. Some poor sodbuster must have found iron pyrites or mica or suphuret of copper. Most people just smiled and turned back to their work. The local *California Star* denounced the story as a "sham, as superb a take-in as ever was got up to guzzle the gullible."[2]

Up at the mill, Sutter, Marshall, and the handful of men busily prospecting were, of course, delighted to have it so lightly dismissed. But then Sam Brannan, a rival storekeeper, got wind of the secret. To drum up business for his store (and perhaps out of jealousy over Sutter's unbroken string of successes), he rode into San Francisco one morning and began shouting up and down the streets: "Gold! Gold on the American River!" He, too, might have been ignored. A burgeoning seaport of 900 souls, San Francisco was a pretty wild town; it was not unusual for a few of the boys to get liquored up early. Except for one thing: Brannan had hard evidence with him. In his hand was a glass bottle full of nuggets.

The gold rush was on. It was localized at first, confined to friends of friends who had friends who had actually come back with nuggets or pouches of gold dust, but the ripple effect expanded rapidly. Overnight, tent cities sprang up along the American and other nearby rivers where gold was found. At the news of each new strike, a fresh wave of men would come from San Francisco, joined by others frustrated at coming up empty at sites they were already working.

Whether you were working your own claim or working for someone else till you could accumulate a grubstake, there was plenty of work for everyone. In the gold fields, the average pay for a day's work was an ounce of gold, worth sixteen dollars in 1848—which was an indication of how sky-high everything had gotten: Back East, a day laborer was earning around a dollar a day.*

To go prospecting you needed a shovel, a pickaxe, a crowbar, a dishpan or fry pan suitable for panning gold, a bedroll, a tent, and enough grub to stay out for three or four weeks. You also needed a mule to carry it all. And if you could afford one, a horse to carry you. You also needed a strong back, a healthy constitution, a stout heart, a heap of patience, and more than a little faith. If a Bible wasn't in your kit, then perhaps a bottle of whiskey would be, to get you through that dark night when you'd be ready to quit.

The prices of these things had soared. That bottle of whiskey cost an ounce of gold, a pick or shovel half an ounce, a barrel of flour, twenty ounces. And good luck finding a large dishpan; they weren't to be had for love or money.[3]

Life in the camps was rough-and-tumble, and their names reflected it: Whiskey Bar, Humbug Creek, Devil's Retreat, Jackass Gulch, Hell's Half Acre, Flapjack Canyon, Murderer's Bar, Shirt Tail Canyon, You Bet, Gouge Eye, and Gomorrah. All day long men dug for gold, panned for gold, washed for gold. The camps attracted some low-life hard cases, but there were enough men of Christian principles present to offset them. Eventually, if the gold held out or if a big mining consortium settled in, the miners would send for their families, and churches and schools would go up among the saloons and gambling halls, with the former usually prevailing over the latter.

In the meantime, each camp developed its own rough justice: Vigilance committees were formed to deal with wrongdoers, and if the crime warranted it, a noose was thrown over the limb of a tree. Without established law and order, these overnight communities fell back on the fundamental social principles of self-government, much as the Pilgrims had with their Mayflower Compact, but without the Pilgrims' godly motivation. If the

* As nearly as the authors can calculate, an 1848 dollar was worth about fourteen 1998 dollars.

camps survived, eventually there would be a sheriff. But more often than not, the camps emptied as quickly as they had filled, with their inhabitants rushing on to the next new site.

Back in San Francisco, except for the saloons and the dry good stores, which could charge pretty much what they pleased for supplies, doubling and then redoubling the price of tools and pans, most of the city's establishments had to close; the clerks had simply disappeared. Before long, San Francisco was practically a ghost town, her harbor a forest of masts—of vessels whose crews had jumped ship to go prospecting.

Even United States soldiers and sailors deserted. As one AWOL private put it: "The struggle between *right* and $6 a month and *wrong* and $75 a day is a rather severe one."[4] Curiously, for the remainder of 1848 the gold rush remained largely a California phenomenon. Perhaps so much wild enthusiasm about this fabulous land had already filtered back across the mountains that these new stories of gold fields were discounted along with all the rest. The reports aroused little interest, although outgoing President Polk did manage to kindle some when he mentioned the gold discoveries in his December 5 address to Congress.

All that changed abruptly two days later, with the arrival in Washington of Colonel Mason's agent, Lieutenant Edward Beale, USN. Not only did Lieutenant Beale bear official confirmation of the findings, he brought some samples in a tea caddy. There was no doubting the word of a career naval officer, and talk about hard evidence: That little tea caddy contained 230 ounces of assayed gold!

That afternoon may have marked the first time an editor ever shouted "Stop the presses!" The Washington papers headlined the news, GOLD IN CALIFORNIA! and the telegraph wires hummed. Papers around the country picked up on the story, and the entire nation woke up to the incredible bonanza that was taking place out in California.

Suddenly gold was all anyone was talking about. Typical was Prentice Mulford's account of what happened in the whaling village of Sag Harbor on New York's Long Island, when Captain Eben Latham returned in June of 1848. According to Mulford, who was a lad at the time, "the first gossip he unloaded was that 'them stories about finding gold in Californy was all true.' The report slumbered during the summer in our village, but in the fall it commenced kindling, and by winter it was ablaze. . . . The gold fever raged all winter."[5]

It seemed that every village in America had men who had "seen the elephant," the term used to describe the obsessive lure of the gold fields. And the best thing about it was, it was a truly *democratic* bonanza: *Anybody* could be a prospector. It did not matter who you were, or where you came from, or how well educated you were. Prospecting did not require a degree in geology or a large fortune (though a small one came in handy if you wanted to get there in a hurry—and everyone did). Once there, to become a player in the biggest bonanza in American history, all you needed to know could be learned in 10 minutes.

And in the beginning, you didn't even need to own the land on which you found gold. All you had to do was stake a claim, register it, and start working it. After that, it was "finders, keepers"—whatever gold you found was yours, and there were numerous reliable accounts of instant millionaires. Who was to say that you would not be the next?

Thus began what historian Page Smith calls the greatest movement of people in modern history. New York financier George Templeton Strong became alarmed when three of his good friends suddenly joined the throng. "It seems as if the Atlantic Coast is to be depopulated, such swarms of people are leaving for the new El Dorado. It is the most remarkable emigration in the history of man since the days of the Crusades!"[6]

In Philadelphia, Sidney George Fisher echoed his concern: "The accounts of gold in California . . . at first were not believed. But subsequent information from many and respectable sources confirms them, and the excitement produced is unparalleled. . . . Thousands are leaving every day."[7]

Strong and Fisher were not exaggerating: In January 1849, no less than 61 California-bound vessels embarked from eastern seaports in a single day![8]

All across America, young men and old were downing tools and simply walking off the job to go find gold. Men with steady jobs saw opportunities to make their fortunes, and those in debt or poverty saw a chance to finally provide financial security for their families. The end of the rainbow *did* have a pot of gold at it, and it ended in northern California!

Gold fever wrought incalculable damage to the fabric of American society. It wrenched families apart and decimated neighborhoods.

At the dawn of the 19th century, the island of Nantucket off the coast of Massachusetts had been a thriving whaling community. But with the

British blockade during the War of 1812 and the center of whaling shifting to New Bedford, Nantucket had fallen on hard times. The discovery of gold fired the imaginations of desperate Nantucketers, and in 1849 alone, 705 men, more than a tenth of the island's entire population,* left to seek their fortunes in California.

In Marietta, Ohio, Elisha Douglas Perkins left his pregnant wife and their drugstore to find gold. Another husband, William Pierce, wrote his wife, Georgianna, of the pain he felt in leaving her and their son, "my best friend on earth and that darling blue-eyed boy." But then he articulated the dream and compelling motivation of thousands of gold seekers. His success would, he assured her, place them "where we will be slaves to none, independent of want, able to go through life with plenty and cultivate social feeling, virtue and peace without being compelled to struggle for daily bread."[9]

Nearly all the ministers of America were preaching against gold fever, trying to persuade husbands and fathers to resist the temptation and stay at home where they had God-given obligations and responsibilities. The Reverend James Davis of Woonsocket, Rhode Island, spoke for all clergy when he denounced the craze as "the emblem of human depravity." In the great scheme of things, "the New England Primer is worth more than all the gold mines of California, and would weigh more in the balance of the Almighty than all the gold-diggers on the banks of the Sacramento!"[10]

But it was no use; those bitten by the gold bug were determined to go.

So the ministers did the next best thing: They solemnized the leave-taking with services in their churches, exhorting those departing to be missionaries of Christian virtue in the land of gold. In Boston's Tremont Temple at the end of January 1849, a service was held for the soon-departing New England & California Training & Mining Association. Dr. Edward Beecher[†] challenged them: "An object, therefore, arises before you, higher than the attainment of wealth; it is the work of affecting, for evil or for good, the character of future generations of California. . . . Never forget that it is in your power to have the eternal honor of carrying from New England to California, that which is of infinitely more value than

---

* which, according to the census of 1860, was 6,094

† Edward was one of Lyman Beecher's two sons who followed him into the ministry, the other being Henry Ward Beecher.

anything California is now able to send back in return. She can send gold and silver, but you can carry the examples and principles and virtues of your Pilgrim Fathers."[11]

Prentice Mulford recalled being in a similar service in Sag Harbor, watching the young men about to leave. "How patiently and resignedly they listened to the sad discourse of the minister, knowing it would be the very last they would hear for many months. How eager the glances they cast up to the church choir, where sat the girls they were to marry on their return. How few returned. How few married the girl of that period's choice."[12]

But once you were set on going, nothing, not even a beautiful soprano, would deter you from your date with destiny. Getting there, of course, was the hard part. No matter how you did it, it wasn't cheap, and the faster you wanted to go, the more it was going to cost you. For men of means, this was not a great problem, but most would-be prospectors had to use their life savings or borrow from family or friends.

There were three ways to get there, each with its advantages and drawbacks, all hotly debated by those itching to go. The surest was also the most expensive: joining a company of Argonauts* who would hire or purchase a clipper to take them from the East Coast around Cape Horn and up the Pacific Coast to San Francisco. That could take as little as two months, but it was extremely expensive: $500 to $1000, depending on how much was being put up by the armchair adventurers who would stay home—and take a share in any future profits, usually half.[13]

But rounding the Horn was perilous business: You could spend literally weeks stuck down there fighting gale-force winds, and a number of vessels were never heard from again.

The next fastest way, of course, was to get down to New Orleans and catch a packet down to Chagres on the east coast of Panama, then join a stagecoach or pack train across the Isthmus to the Pacific, and wait in Panama City to catch a ride on the next northbound steamer. Conceivably the trip could be made in under three months. But this was by far the riskiest way; unscrupulous ticket agencies were blithely selling "through tickets," presumably booking passage ahead on riverboat, packet, stage-

---

* Named for the heroes of Greek legend who accompanied Jason in the ship *Argo* to fetch the Golden Fleece.

coach, and steamer, and presenting the purchaser with long, official-looking tickets. But horror stories were already making their way back to the States, that once one left the U.S., reserved seats and berths and hotel accommodations were nothing more than figments of the ticket agency's vivid imagination.

The slowest way was overland, along the wagon trails opened and now guided by such mountain men as Jim Bridger and Broken-Hand Fitzpatrick. But they were open only in the summer, which meant that depending on when you left home, it could take as long as a year. At $300, it was certainly the cheapest way,[14] if you joined a wagon train already making the journey. Normally it was also the safest, if your train had a seasoned guide and a strong wagon master. But in the summer of 1849, an outbreak of Asiatic cholera swept through train after train, and not even Kit Carson could ensure a safe journey. For 5,000 gold bugs crossing the prairies that summer, the wages of greed were death.

Safety, of course, was the last thing on the mind of a '49er, as these modern-day Argonauts came to be called. Most were heavily armed in the event of an encounter with hostile Indians, though few had any experience with small arms. As a result, there were far more casualties along the trail from accidental, self-inflicted wounds than ever would have been suffered in a major Indian action.

The one thing common to all of them was impatience. Gold fever was as contagious as typhus and as addictive as any narcotic known to man. Caught in its grip, a man could do crazy, terrible things—risking his life, the lives of his family, maybe even taking another man's life.

Above all else, the gold bugs were in a desperate hurry—so much so that by the fall of '49 there were more than 800 Americans stranded in the dusty, squalid old town of Panama City, watching their money run out as ship after overloaded ship refused them passage. Hundreds more men had been lost in the treacherous seas around Cape Horn. And thousands died on the trails and up in the high mountain passes, either because their wagon trains were moving too slowly to suit them, or they ignored the dire warnings of early snows and thirty-foot drifts.

There were stories of '49ers overworking their teams and watching them die off one by one, of lightening loads till even the wagons themselves had to be left behind, of loners on foot being stalked by circling carrion birds overhead. But such stories seldom got much play around the campfires or in the saloons. What did get told and retold was the news of each new strike. When gold was found at the mountain named for Zebulon Pike, many a wagon hurried West with "Pike's Peak or Bust!" painted on its canvas. And more than a few came sadly back bearing a different slogan: "Busted, by God!"

Still there was no discouraging them, as they gave new lyrics to Stephen Foster's famous plantation ballad: "Oh Susannah, now don't you cry for me; I'm going to California with a wash pan on my knee!"

When all the tallies were in, 1849 alone accounted for more than 10 million ounces mined, and production for 1852, the peak year, exceeded 80 million ounces.

Life in the all-male club of the mining camps was anything but idyllic. Even the breathtaking beauty of the Sierra Mountains could not alleviate the perpetual dog-tired weariness of day after day spent standing in bone-numbing cold mountain streams, shoveling and hauling gravel and dirt, sifting and washing, and watching for those few tiny flakes that seldom amounted to more than an ounce by sundown. Mining was rough and dangerous work—crushed hands, sprained knees and ankles, and constant backaches seemed to go with the territory. Crowded conditions in the camps, plus poor sanitation and no fruit or vegetables, added dysentery, smallpox, and scurvy to the list of woes.[15]

And after awhile, not being of Anglo-Saxon extraction could be un-healthy, too, as antiforeign sentiment mounted swiftly among the miners, until they had finally succeeded in purging the diggings of foreigners.[16]

Not all the Argonauts wound up toiling in the gold fields. A number of new arrivals quickly concluded that significant money could be made in the booming local economy that supported the miners. The selling of lodging, food, clothes, boots, tools, tents, horses, and mules often produced a 50 percent profit for merchants. An arriving dentist soon found that he could make more money drilling teeth than drilling for gold. On a good Sunday a dentist could make three ounces of gold filling teeth![17]

And one lawyer, William Daingerfield, wrote his parents that he had made $3,300 in his first 10 days of practice![18]

On Sunday the miners took a day of rest. Some went to services held by missionaries to the camps, but more yielded to the temptations of whiskey and cards. The enforced idleness of winter, when the ground was hard-frozen and covered with snow, proved the ruin of many miners.

Faced with a month of Sundays, then another and another and another, they would greet spring having drunk and gambled away all their hard-won earnings.

There were other ways of losing one's earnings, like investing in elaborate damming or sluiceway schemes, only to see them washed away in minutes by a flash flood. Overall, the life of a '49er really was a giant crapshoot. As Louise "Dame Shirley" Clapp, one of the very few women Argonauts, wrote from Rich Bar, California, "Gold mining is Nature's great lottery scheme. A man may work in a claim for many months, and be poorer at the end of the time than when he commenced; or he may take out thousands in a few hours."[19]

As tens of thousands of new hands arrived,* the price of a day's labor began to drop. In two years it had dropped from $16 to $10, and by 1852 it was down to $6.[20]

And the gold was getting harder to find. Miners found themselves digging deeper and deeper, on smaller and smaller claims. All the likely streams were so overprospected that a man working alone could no longer count on finding enough pay dirt to wash through his pan to make it "pan out." Many miners were sinking ever deeper into debt.

Finally it got to be almost impossible to make it alone. Men now teamed up with partners to dig together, or formed companies to erect dams and sluiceways to wash more ore. But the writing was on the wall; eventually only the biggest companies could afford the heavy equipment it took to make processing low-grade ore pay.

By the end of 1853, the fields were pretty well played out, and the '49ers returned home. But not all; out of shame or pride or hope that they might yet strike it rich, many stayed, while back home their parents tried to adjust to never seeing them again, their girlfriends got tired of waiting and married someone else, or their abandoned wives tried to pick up the pieces of their lives.

And some fell in love with California, with her golden sun, magnificent vistas, and rich soil. They decided to try farming there, and either sent for their families or went back and got them.

All told, more than 300,000 men eventually joined this great thrust westward. Fewer than 1,000 struck it rich, but nearly all who went would

---

* By 1852 an estimated 100,000 active miners were in the fields.

agree that they were immeasurably richer from the experience. California gained, too: The '49ers who came and stayed were an imaginative, resourceful, independent lot, exactly the sort of men and women with whom you would want to populate a new wilderness state. The United States of America benefited, as well: In the eight years from 1848 to 1856, half a billion dollars' worth of gold was taken out of the ground, more than doubling the world's supply.[21]

Enough wound up in the Federal coffers to make a serious difference in the ordeal that was coming soon.

When one considers the discovery of gold in California in terms of God's timetable for America, one is struck once again by His incredible timing. Had the discovery come three years earlier, when California was still the property of Mexico and there was no war to indicate the situation might ever change, it would have drawn a preponderance of Mexicans north, rather than Americans west. It would have also fueled (and financed) Mexico's determination to wrest Texas back from those who had taken it, and the map of the United States might well have looked radically different than it does today.

Had the discovery come three years later, with the Compromise of 1850 in place, California would have become embroiled in the slavery whirlpool and might not have become a state as quickly as it did. As it was, the Territory's permanent population went from under 20,000 in 1848 to more than 220,000 four years later. But there were few slaves among the Argonauts—when it did join the Union, it came in free.

Perhaps the greatest contribution of the California Gold Rush was an intangible concept that took root in the mind of most Americans: With California suddenly populated, America was geographically complete now. And much greater than the popular imagination had ever dreamed she would be. Whether or not you believed it was God's Manifest Destiny for her, it did seem right that she now stretched from sea to sea. And most Americans were convinced that she should remain undivided. What God hath joined together, let no man put asunder.

In any event, by 1853 the days of the solitary '49er were pretty much over. But for years afterward, farsighted wagon-train guides would occasionally catch glimpses of lone prospectors high up in the Sierras. Late in the afternoon, when the last rays of the sun fired the snowcapped peaks a rosy gold, a flash of light would reflect off a big washpan hanging from the pack of an old prospector's mule. The guide could just make him out, leaning on a staff as he led his old friend over a path made by mountain goats. They were still looking for the outcropping that would lead to the vein that would take them to the mother lode that had eluded them all these years. But it didn't really matter whether they found it; they were doing what they loved to do—their quest had become their gold.

24

THE GO-AHEAD AGE

ear the whistle blow"—the refrain from an old railroad song conjures up twin ribbons of steel gleaming in the moonlight, stretching away through dark woodlands and across a slender trestle with the silver thread of a river far below. Over it roars Old #9, her big drivers pounding, her headlamp piercing the darkness, the rest of the train a dark silhouette behind her. With her throttle nearly wide open, the white trail of smoke lies flat along her back, as her mournful wail echoes down the rocky chasm.

A century and a half ago, the railroads were just coming into their ascendancy. Prior to them, for Americans heading out West, wagons were the prime movers. People and goods traveled over traces that gradually became roadways and eventually turnpikes. They also went by water: A barge was slower than a wagon, but it could carry many times the load. To ship cargo west by water from the northeast industrial centers, however, meant going either far north to the St. Lawrence and the Great Lakes, or down the Ohio and the Mississippi.

Necessity gave birth to the Erie Canal in 1825, a waterway 363 miles long, with 82 locks. Now the Hudson River was linked to Lake Ontario, making it possible to ship goods by water directly from New York to Cleveland, Detroit, and Chicago. When farsighted Senators and Congressmen called for major Federal expenditures for internal improvements in the 1830s, canals and waterways were as important as turnpikes.

But the railroads would soon eclipse all other modes of transportation, and it happened as quickly as the ascendancy of the automobile or the airplane in the next century. In 1830 the Baltimore & Ohio was the first railroad to be chartered as a common carrier of freight and passengers.

The B&O bore its initial revenue traffic down its 14 miles of track—pulled by a steam engine named the *Tom Thumb*, which could cover that distance in just under an hour.

The race was on! A year later, behind an engine named the *DeWitt Clinton*, the new Mohawk & Hudson Railroad pulled three cars at twice that speed.[1] Other railroads were rapidly coming into being, also named for the population centers they joined: the New York, New Haven & Hartford, the Boston & Maine, the Chesapeake & Ohio, and the Pennsylvania Rail Road (between Philadelphia and Pittsburgh). In the South, the cities of Charleston and Hamburg were linked by the South Carolina Canal and Rail Road Company, precursor of the Southern Railway system, and the Portsmouth & Roanoke was the first segment of what would be known as the Seaboard Line.

In this new "Go-Ahead Age," nothing was going ahead faster than the railroads. In a single decade, 14 miles became 2,800, and in another decade that amount would triple. When the Chicago & North Western Railway made its initial run in 1848, the city that had begun as a trading outpost at the foot of Lake Michigan named Fort Dearborn was on its way to becoming the largest rail center in the country. Soon it was possible to travel from New York to Chicago in 36 hours, a trip that took more than a week by stagecoach. Before long, Chicago, the natural trade distribution point for the burgeoning Northwest, would be the terminus for 12 trunk lines.

In the middle of the 19th century, if you were to take a map of the 30 United States and draw a line from any major city to the nearest city of equivalent size, if a railroad did not already connect them, you could be sure that a team of surveyors was out planning its route and would soon be followed by a track-laying crew. A flood tide of immigrants was disembarking at the eastern seaports of this fabled "land of opportunity," but there was more than enough work for all of them if they were willing to swing a pick or drive a spike.

The steam locomotive, prime symbol of this era of breathtaking progress, had itself undergone a rapid metamorphosis. In 1825 the first steam locomotive in regular service ran in England, a cute but fragile, hissing little creature with a tall smokestack to keep cinders out of its passengers' eyes. England's Industrial Revolution may have begat America's age of technology, but the daughter soon surpassed the mother. By 1850 the

American steam engine had become sleek and glamorous—and recognizably close to her final form. She was also vastly more powerful, capable of pulling trains many times her length for ever greater distances at ever increasing speeds.

Yankee ingenuity was more than just a saying: Bright young men born in that cold and rocky, hard-scrabble region had a penchant for figuring out better ways to do things. Just because a tool had been used by one's father and his father's father didn't mean it couldn't be improved.

An ingenious Connecticut Yankee named Eli Whitney figured out a mechanical way to remove the seeds from cotton, which hitherto could be done only by hand. The new steam-driven mills up north and in England were waiting for just such an innovation. In no time cotton became the largest cash crop in America.

The first plows to come to this country, heavy and wooden just as they had been for centuries, kept breaking on the hard roots and hidden boulders of New England. Someone got the bright idea of making them out of cast iron, and that helped. But it was not until a Vermont blacksmith named John Deere* made a steel plow in 1837 that a farmer's most back-breaking task was suddenly made easier. Now, using a plow light enough that a big farmer could carry it on his shoulder, a man walking upright behind a four-horse team could turn two acres in a single day!

A farmer's next most arduous task came at the other end of the growing season. From Biblical times, wheat, rye, and barley were harvested with a scythe. But just because it had always been done that way. . . . A Virginia farm lad named Cyrus McCormick developed a mechanical reaper with moving blades. On its first test it harvested six acres in a day, where a man swinging a scythe might cut one acre. For the site of the new factory that would produce the McCormick Reaper, he picked the location that could reach the most markets the quickest: Chicago.

And what of the farmer's wife? What could be done to lessen the time *she* spent at hard labor? Elias Howe, a Massachusetts machinist's apprentice, got the idea of creating a machine to sew cloth. In 1846 he patented his invention, which was improved on by another Yankee inventor, Isaac Singer. Working the foot peddle of a Singer Sewing Machine, the first

---

* Deere was following an old, unpublished design by an inventive gentleman farmer named Thomas Jefferson.

labor-saving household appliance, a housewife could accomplish in an hour what used to take all day.

But perhaps nothing compressed time more than the invention conceived by the son of Jedidiah Morse, the fiery old-guard preacher whose impatience with the vague maps and vaguer descriptions led him to become "the father of American geography."[2] Like his father, Samuel F. B. Morse went to Yale, after which he studied painting in England. Sharing his father's scientific inclination, he became intrigued with Ben Franklin's observation that "electricity passes instantly over any known length of wire."[3] What if *information* could be somehow passed over that wire?

The idea would not leave him, and sailing back to America after studying portraiture in England, he worked it out. Others had been experimenting with sending electricity alternately through 26 different wires, one for each letter of the alphabet. Yet suppose a single wire were to carry a sequence of electrical impulses? But 26 impulses for the letter Z were too cumbersome. What if there were *two* impulses, one short and one long, in 26 different combinations? By the time he reached America, he had devised the dot-dash code that would bear his name.

Samuel F. B. Morse had no money, but he had his father's gift of persuasion. In 1844 he prevailed upon Congress for a grant to erect a telegraph line from Washington to Baltimore. At the public demonstration of the electromagnetic telegraph, the first message sent was: "What hath God wrought!"[4]

The nation was dumbfounded. Even professional commentators were (almost) speechless. Editor Richard Henry Dana gasped: "This is incredible! . . . I see the result . . . but I have no faith of the understanding of it." Alexander Mackay, visiting reporter for the London *Morning Chronicle*, wrote: "The effect which this invention, as thus developed, has produced, and that which it is still likely to produce on many of the operations of society are almost beyond comprehension." Leave it to the Methodists' *Ladies Repository* to embrace its full potential: This "noble invention" would be "the means of extending civilization, republicanism and Christianity over the earth. . . . Then will wrong and injustice be forever banished. Every yoke will be broken, and the oppressed go free. Wars will cease . . . for each man shall feel that every other man is his neighbor—his brother."[5]

Alongside each new railroad trackbed, linemen strung copper wire between tarred pine poles. Each train depot soon functioned as a telegraph station as well, but unlike trains, the wires didn't need tunnels to cross mountains, or bridges to span valleys. The first impact of this new mode of communication was on the newspapers. If a boiler exploded on a side-wheeler in New Orleans, killing eight passengers, you could "read all about it" in New York the following morning. When a transatlantic steamer arrived in Boston with diplomatic dispatches from London and Paris, their contents were known in Washington within the hour. And that afternoon their news would be on the front page of the *National Intelligencer.*

Because the first comers to the New World, especially the Pilgrims and Puritans, put such a high premium on education—the sooner a boy or girl could take their own instruction from the printed Word of God, the better—most Americans could read before they reached their teens. And because *all* freemen had a vote, and therefore a say in how the Government ran the country, Americans developed a powerful thirst for newsprint from the nation's earliest days. Foreign visitors were astonished to find farmers and day-laborers not only literate but well-informed on the issues of the day and ready to debate points of the utmost complexity.

The telegraph further whetted our appetite, till we became a nation of news-aholics. What were the latest developments in Europe, on the western frontier? What new wonder would spring from the soaring imaginations of the young inventors, in this most breathtaking of all ages? As diarist Philip Hone noted: "Newspapers have become the most agreeable of all reading. . . . The nations think simultaneously, and everything that occurs of the slightest public importance is almost instantly known throughout the civilized world. We have every morning news from all parts of the Union up to the previous evening!"[6]

Throughout the country newspapers were avidly read. In 1854 there were some 400 dailies in America and more than 2,200 weeklies. In New York, James Gordon Bennett's *Herald* was the best source of hard news, especially if that news had a dash of shock value. Daily circulation: 60,000 (many copies being shared). But the *Herald* was anti-abolitionist, and if you were not, then you would probably prefer reformer Horace Greeley's *Tribune,* the most influential purveyor of thoughtful opinion. Its daily circulation was 150,000. Other cities had fine newspapers—the Boston *Atlas,* the Richmond *Examiner,* the Cleveland *Plain Dealer,* the Chicago *Tribune,* the Charleston *Mercury,* the Louisville *Courier,* the New Orleans

Item—with none more highly regarded than the *National Intelligencer* out of Washington. But it was the weekly or monthly magazines that reached the farthest. Often illustrated with engravings, such publications as *Harper's Monthly*, the *Methodist Quarterly*, and for women, *Godey's Lady's Book*, had a combined circulation in the millions.

As the editors of that day were outspoken men with scant concern for tact or opprobrium, physical courage was a requisite for the job. Where the benign influence of the revival had not yet extended, tempers were hot and fuses short, especially in the South and on the western frontier. Not infrequently a sharp-tongued editor was required to put his life where his mouth was, and more than a few lost their lives on the field of honor. Frequently, outspoken papers took to adding a "fighting editor" to their staff—a crack shot, hired to deal with insulted gentlemen storming into the office to demand satisfaction.[7]

The dailies, weeklies, monthlies, and quarterlies reflected the vibrant optimism of the age, which percolated through all aspects of Northern life. Some have credited this exuberant, unquenchable buoyancy to the heady combination of technological progress, prowess at arms, and unlimited expansion. Not once, but *twice* Americans had beaten the greatest military power on Earth. And now they had defeated the only other military force on this side of the world. Their dominion now extended over more land than they could develop in a dozen generations. As for technological innovation, where they had once looked to Europe for leadership, now Europe was benefiting from *their* inventions and improvements.

There was another, major factor in the prevailing go-ahead spirit, one that could be traced back to the Second Great Awakening. A true revival is measured by two things: its endurance and the reforms that follow in its wake. Charles Finney gave the hoop of that turn-of-the-century revival a tremendous whack in the 1830s, and it just kept rolling. Now it had produced a new generation of high-profile evangelists—with Lyman Beecher's son Henry Ward Beecher being the brightest star in the firmament. A touring minister from Scotland, David Macrae, said of him: "In America, Beecher is an independent power. Wherever he lectures or preaches, people crowd to hear him; his sermons are printed in newspapers as far west as California; democrats abhor him; grog-sellers dread him; Princeton theologians shake their heads over his theology; but everywhere, liked or disliked, the name of Henry Ward Beecher is known and his power recognized."[8] If you wanted to hear young Beecher take on New York's corrupt judges, "Just take the ferry to Brooklyn," went the saying, "and follow the crowd."[9]

The Second Great Awakening also produced a new generation of young men and women on fire to serve God on the mission field. America had already begun to match Great Britain in sending missionaries abroad; now they responded to the need at home. In 1855 the Home Mission Society was supporting more than 1,000 missionaries in 27 States and Territories. As for the American Tract Society, it had 659 representatives, each of whom would call on nearly 1,000 families a year.

The continuing waves of revival in the 1830s did much to shape the character of the age. For those who had become newly acquainted with Him, Jesus' encouragement in the Gospel of Mark became their watchword: "If thou canst believe, all things are possible to him that believeth" (Mark 9:23). Heaven only knows how many frustrated young inventors turned to the Source of all inspiration for help. Or how many pioneer families recited those words as they headed West. Or how many outnumbered and outgunned commanders used them to keep from giving up.

With God all things are possible, young entrepreneurs reminded themselves, as they sought venture capital to support their latest enterprises. To be sure, many ill-conceived or undercapitalized schemes went belly up. But many more succeeded, for success seemed to be in the very air. If you believed—and had the grit and were willing to work from sunup to sundown—there was nothing you could not accomplish!

God was drawing many others to this land of opportunity, mostly from England, Ireland, and Germany. In 1842 a terrible potato famine ravaged Ireland, sending some 50,000 fleeing to these shores. Eight years later, at the peak of Irish immigration, more than 221,000 came to these shores. Increasing numbers of Germans were coming as well; in 1854 more than half of the 425,000 newcomers were German.

For the first generation, the Irish stayed mostly in the eastern seaports, while the Germans headed for the Mississippi Valley, or what is now known as the Midwest. The majority of immigrants of all nationalities arrived "tearful, pallid, dirty and squalid . . . ill . . . and penniless,"[10] and many died of cholera and other epidemics soon after coming. Yet they were inspired to believe they could make it in their adopted land, and their collective determination became an integral part of the spirit of American optimism.

Reform was the second mark of true revival: A powerful, dynamic Christianity *wanted* to become involved in implementing God's plan in the world! Mindful of Christ's second Great Commandment, a man of God could not turn a blind eye to the misery of his fellow man; to do so was to break that second Commandment and imperil his soul.

"I can do all things in Christ"—to no one's surprise, the reform movement in the middle of the last century was bent on reforming *everything*— all of society, from bottom to top. And now for the first time, women were playing prominent roles in all areas of reform. No longer did they meekly accept the male judgment that "a woman's place is in the home." Half a century ago, historian Alan Nevins shrewdly observed that 19th-century women "were victims not of conscious repression, but of a male chivalry which masked subconscious conservatism and selfishness. They were treated as 'superior' beings, because men did not want the trouble of treating them as equals."[11]

Prison reform was now a major concern, and Eliza Farnham, the courageous and compassionate superintendent of the women's prison at Sing Sing, New York, did her best to keep it that way. The eloquent and outspoken Angelina Grimké fell in love with Theodore Dwight Weld, and was a true partner and helpmate in his life's work of abolishing slavery. The brilliant young poet Julia Ward hoped for such a pairing when she fell in love with Samuel Gridley Howe, whom historian Page Smith called "the beau ideal of the romantic reformer." As director of the Perkins Institute for the Blind, Howe developed the use of Braille and made his institution the most enlightened in the country. But in private he proved far less "emancipated" than his young wife had imagined, and it was not until they joined the abolitionist cause that they were able to work together in harmony.

Attending lectures was one of the public's favorite pastimes in this golden age of oratory, and the lecture circuit often boasted as many women as men, particularly when the topic was women's suffrage. Lucy Stone, Elizabeth Cady Stanton, and Susan B. Anthony were familiar figures on the platform. The Quaker preacher Lucretia Mott and ordained minister

Antoinette Brown could often be found in the pulpit as well. And two black women who had been slaves, Harriet Tubman and Sojourner Truth, made striking speakers.*

Of all the reform movements apart from antislavery, none was stronger than the temperance movement. Today liquor stores, bars, and serving restaurants must all be licensed and are often severely restricted by local law and custom. In 1852 there were few if any restrictions on the sale and consumption of alcohol. New York City had issued licenses to *6,000* grog shops—and 1,000 more were operating without a license. That year the police chief issued a telling report: Of the 180,000 arrests made in the city during the previous six and a half years, 140,000 involved the use of liquor.[12]

Amelia Bloomer was one of the most prominent temperance evangelists, and in her crusade she was joined by Lyman Beecher's daughter Harriet. Temperance lectures, which often had the spirit of a camp-meeting revival, struck a responsive chord. In 1851 the State of Maine enacted prohibition. Other states soon passed their own version of the Maine Law, and by 1856 all the Northern states save Illinois had followed suit. The South would have none of it, however, dubbing it another "Yankee-ism." And in truth, many Northern municipalities simply ignored the ban.

Perhaps the most remarkable personal crusade of the 19th century was launched by Dorothea Dix. As a bright and precocious child of 14, she began teaching school. But at 33, after a health sabbatical, she branched into an entirely different field. At the insane asylum in Danvers, Massachusetts, she had seen a young woman caged in a narrow cell, naked and filthy, confined under conditions so horrific that if an animal was kept that way, its owner would be arrested. Shocked, she dedicated the rest of her life to achieving reform in America's mental institutions. Wherever she went, she made careful notes of the deplorable conditions she observed in a given facility, then recruited strong and earnest young people to staff and reform it.

In eight years she traveled more than 10,000 miles, visiting practically every state in the Union. By 1852, 11 states had built mental hospitals as a direct result of her crusade.

* See chapter 32.

One time in Michigan, the stagecoach in which she was traveling was held up. When the bandits relieved the passengers of their wallets, purses, and other valuables, she roundly upbraided them. The bandits' leader exclaimed: "I know that voice!" In jail in Philadelphia he had heard her speak on prison reform. The passengers' belongings were returned forthwith.[13]

The most revealing assessment of a community, or a country, often comes from without. Europeans visiting midcentury America were continually astonished. A generation before (with the notable exception of de Tocqueville) they had been largely scornful of the crude towns and rude people they had encountered in their travels. They had noted with patronizing bemusement the hogs on New York's main thoroughfare, and the cows grazing on Washington's Mall.

But now the letters and journals of foreign visitors brimmed with praise. The scientist Charles Lyell, arriving in stately, aristocratic Boston, was surprised to find the harbor and the city beautiful. He was then delighted to discover that "one flourishing town after another, such as Utica, Syracuse, and Auburn," had risen from the wilderness. Indeed, throughout his travels in the North he was pleased to see no beggars or signs of want, "but everywhere the most unequivocal proofs of prosperity and rapid progress in agriculture, commerce, and public works."[14] The British consul, T. C. Grattan, at the end of his six-year tour of duty, concurred, declaring that the United States was "better adapted than any country on earth for securing the greatest good to the greatest number of mankind."[15]

Travelers from England found New York bright and sunshiny, with its high buildings and free use of white marble, and were taken by the rough-and-ready cheerfulness of the people. The Scottish minister David Macrae summed up America's largest city: "In New York, all that is best and all that is worst in America is represented. Fling together Tyre and Sidon, the new Jerusalem, Sodom and Gomorrah, a little of heaven, and more of hell, and you have a faint picture."[16]

To the English visitor, Philadelphia was the most attractive of the eastern cities; compared to its handsome squares, broad tree-shaded streets, neat red-brick houses, and scoured white-stone doorsteps, Manchester or Lyons seemed cramped, dingy, and poor.[17] Bostonian Charles Francis Adams was similarly taken with Philadelphia, finding "something solid and comfortable about it, something which shows *permanency.*" Lamenting his own city's "unbending rigidity," he nonetheless considered Boston far above her sisters when it came to patronage of the arts—"for public spirit Boston is incomparably beyond all cities."[18]

Whatever similarities Boston, New York, and Philadelphia might have had, they were not at all like Washington. The nation's capital was a Southern town in mood and appearance; her atmosphere was more relaxed, and as most of her foreign and domestic citizenry were transient, there was a sense of impermanence about her. She had no proper sewage system or water system, and did not receive gas lighting until 1847.

But when Congress was in session, she was transformed! Now journalists and visitors crammed the Capitol Building to hear some of the greatest orators in the world holding forth in the House or the Senate. At night the windows of the finest houses glowed with hundreds of candles for formal dinners or gala receptions. When the Government was in high gear, Washington society was at the height of its season, and there was no more exciting city in which to be!

Traveling west, Pittsburgh, with its burgeoning iron foundries and rolling mills operating around the clock, filled the night sky with an eerie glow—truly she was "the Birmingham of America." On the Ohio River, Cincinnati reigned as "the Queen of the West." Although nicknamed "Porkopolis" for the half-million hogs annually shipped from her and the more than 20,000 tons of ham and bacon processed there, Cincinnati was nonetheless a city of light and beauty where cultivated people enjoyed one another's company.

But with the opening of the Erie Canal linking the Atlantic States to the Great Lakes, the main thrust of westward movement shifted north, away from the Ohio River. Chicago, the new western terminus, began outstripping Cincinnati. Before long it would have its own blast furnaces, processing iron ore from the upper Michigan ranges, and would receive 120 trains a day![19] Chicago had become the fastest growing city in North America.

In the South, two cities took a backseat to none: New Orleans and Charleston. At the mouth of the Mississippi, the city originally known as *La Nouvelle Orleans* was still very French in its flavor. Visitors approaching by steamer were invariably impressed by its broad, open amphitheater waterfront, with three miles of warehouses and offices lining the levee. With its willow trees and wrought-iron balconies, and the plethora of gaily

266

colored riverboats and oceangoing clippers in her harbor, New Orleans was a stunning combination of bygone elegance and modern commerce.

Charleston was the jewel of the South. The owners of the great plantations built houses in the city, where the gentlemen could reside while they conducted their business, while their ladies entertained during the season. With their double verandahs and streets lined with palmetto trees, their town houses were as gracious as their magnificent, white-columned plantation homes.

Whenever a foreign visitor traveled in the South, he or she was invariably taken with the leisure, courtliness, and pride of the plantation hosts. But if, venturing beyond the plantation, they took a close look at their surroundings, they were shocked to find poverty in the extreme—unlike anything they had seen elsewhere in America.

Many came to the same conclusion: The only explanation was that the Southern economic system was built on slavery.

25

THE WAGES OF FEAR

ear. If it were possible to run all aspects of slavery through a giant computer, the key word that would surface most often, regardless of perspective, would be fear. Most obvious was the slave's fear of physical punishment, which was invariably swift, inexorable, and severe. Fear of inflicted pain (possibly unto death) was the driving force that fueled the engine of slavery.

Other fears, less immediate though equally tormenting, made the slave's existence at best uncertain and at worst a matter of perpetual anxiety. There was the fear of your family being broken up or being sold south to one of the new factory plantations, where a field hand was a tiny cog in a vast piece of agricultural machinery, with an abbreviated life expectancy. You might live longer, had you risen to be a steward or housekeeper or body servant—but even there, your circumstances could change in the twinkling of an eye. And the worst part was, there was nothing you could do to prepare for it.

No aspect of slavery was more wrenching than the breaking up of one's family. Mary Chesnut was the wife of Senator James Chesnut of South Carolina and mistress of one of their State's largest plantations. She hated slavery. But she kept her thoughts to her diary and remained loyal to the South, right through the coming Civil War. In the company of a visiting Englishwoman, she passed a slave auction, where black families, despite the wails and pleading of all concerned, were being torn apart and sold to the highest bidder. "If you can stand that," Mary Chesnut said bitterly, "no other Southern thing need choke you."[1]

Nor could the slaves breathe any easier if they were fortunate enough to belong to a God-fearing, benevolent owner. Some owners were indeed compassionate, though these were not nearly as prevalent as proslavery apologists would have had their critics believe. Observed one Southerner to another: "Men of the right stamp to manage Negroes are like angels' visits—few and far between."[2] An epidemic like cholera or smallpox could take a kind owner in the prime of life, or his misjudgment of the next shift in the highly volatile cotton market might ruin him overnight.

Or it might simply be the arrival of a new overseer who took a personal dislike to certain slaves—and determined to make their lives a living hell. And there would be nothing they could do about it. If an overseer was excessively cruel, word did eventually filter back to the master. Then he had to decide whether the bottom-line profit (which, more often than not, the new overseer had been hired to improve) was worth the added misery of his slaves. "I have this day discharged my overseer, Mr. Brewer," wrote one plantation owner in Alabama. "I found so much dissatisfaction amongst the Negroes that . . . I could not feel satisfied to continue him in my employment."[3]

Sometimes the bottom line won out, even with a good-hearted plantation owner. Mississippi planter Gustavus Henry wrote to his wife: "I do not know whether I will keep Harris another year or not. He is a first-rate manager, except that he is too cruel. I had my feelings greatly shocked at some of his conduct." But his overseer made big crops, and the planter was reluctant "to break it all up by getting a new manager." In the end he decided to keep Harris, though he made him promise to be less harsh.[4]

Running a large plantation was much like running a factory, and the planter had as many myriad details to look after, personality problems to sort out, and decisions to make as a factory manager. To run a plantation well required a great deal of attention, and if the planter preferred to spend his days riding and hunting and his nights drinking and gambling, someone else had to look after the details. In a surprising number of cases it was his wife. And the true unnoticed heroes of the antebellum South were the plantation wives who managed the finances, made most of the key decisions, and were still able to be ever gracious hostesses.

More often, it was the overseer who actually ran the daily operation. The *South Carolinian*, a publication for gentlemen, addressed the matter this way:

Planters may be divided into two classes, viz., those who attend to their business and those who do not. And this creates corresponding classes of overseers. The planter who does not manage his own business must, of course, surrender everything into the hands of his overseer. Such a planter usually rates the merits of the overseer exactly in proportion to the number of bags of cotton he makes, and of course the overseer cares for nothing but to make a large crop. To him it is of no consequence that the old hands are worked down, or the young ones over-strained, that the breeding women miscarry and the sucklers lose their children, that the mules are broken down, the plantation tools destroyed, the stock neglected, and the lands ruined: so that he has the requisite number of cotton bags, all is overlooked. He is re-employed at an advanced salary, and his reputation is increased. . . . It seems scarcely credible that any man owning a plantation will so abandon it and his people on it entirely to a hireling, no matter what his confidence in him is, yet there are numbers who do it habitually.[5]

Another journal of the time, the *Southern Agriculturist*, expressed a remarkably similar opinion of overseers: "No wonder, then that the overseer desires to have entire control of the plantation. No wonder he . . . drives [the sick] out again at the first moment and forces sucklers and breeders to the utmost. He has no other interest than to make a big cotton crop. And if that does not please you and induce you to increase his wages, he knows men it will please."[6]

One can discern quite a bit from a careful reading of the agricultural journals of the day—not just how plantations were run, but how their owners thought, especially when they passed along advice to other planters: "The master and overseer should always pull on the same end of the rope," wrote one. "Negroes soon discover any little jarring between the master and the overseer, and are sure to take advantage of it."[7] Indeed, since better treatment depended on their success in convincing the master (or occasionally the overseer) to take their side against the other, the slaves were as divisive as they could be.

They also sought to improve their lot by subtly playing to the paternalistic inclinations of their masters, who liked to see themselves as their slaves' protectors. And some were far more clever than their masters supposed, using every wile, including flattery. One planter quoted an old Negro man on his plantation: "These young overseers ain't worth noth-

ing. One man like Mas' Dick is worth more 'n all of 'em put together!'"
Not surprisingly, Master Richard approved of his old slave's assessment,
"which struck me as sensible."[8]

This paternal spirit of a master extended beyond the black/white relationship; the owner of a large plantation regarded himself as the benefactor of all the poor whites in his domain—much like the Scottish lairds
of Sir Walter Scott's novels. And the poor whites who depended on his
benevolence and largesse deferred to him accordingly. Writing at the
end of the 19th century, the son of an aristocratic South Carolina planter
sadly recalled:

> An unconquerable pride grew up in the hearts of this class—the pride of
> unchallenged domination, of irresponsible control of others, of unques-
> tioned power, of uncriticized conduct. Each man became a lord within
> his own domain. He was the source of law among his slaves, and his self
> interest and good or ill will was the rule of his actions; the laws of the State
> did not readily reach him, and public opinion of his own class naturally
> coincided with his views. There thus resulted an absolute indifference to
> the opinions of others.[9]

W. E. B. Du Bois, the black scholar and educator who cofounded the
National Association for the Advancement of Colored People in 1909,
offered a more acerbic view of the Southern planter:

> The psychological effect of slavery upon him was fatal. The mere fact
> that a man could be, under the law, the actual master of the mind and
> body of human beings had to have disastrous effects. . . . Their "honor"
> became a vast and awful thing, requiring wide and insistent deference.
> Such of them as were inherently weak and inefficient were all the more
> easily angered, jealous and resentful; while the few who were superior
> physically or mentally conceived no bounds to their power and personal
> prestige.[10]

The only check that these planters faced came from their peers, and it
was mild. "Harmony among neighbors is very important in the successful management of slaves," observed one agricultural correspondent, for
it did no good to enforce discipline on your plantation if your neighbor

did not. Those who tended to be lax were urged to stiffen discipline, and those who tended to be harsh were called on to exercise restraint.[11]

There were laws against maltreatment of slaves, but they were seldom invoked, and since no black man or woman could give testimony against a white, their chief function was apparently to assuage the collective conscience of the slave owners. The Chivalry, as the gentlemen of the South had taken to calling themselves, in Walter Scott fashion, liked to think that no proper gentleman would ever abuse his slaves. Yet unless they themselves were blessed with saintly self-control, they would never rebuke a neighbor for losing his temper. Occasionally, irate planters did bring charges against a particularly brutal slave owner, but this usually took an act so atrocious that it could not be overlooked.

To be sure, magazines like *Southern Agriculturist* and *The Southern Planter* ran frequent appeals for better treatment for slaves. Obviously seeking to deflect the accusations of the abolitionists, Chancellor Harper wrote:

> It is wise, too, in relation to the world around us, to avoid giving occasion to the odium which is so industriously excited against ourselves and our institutions. For this reason, public opinion should, if possible, bear more strongly and indignantly than it does at present, on masters who practice any wanton cruelty on their slaves. The miscreant who is guilty of this not only violates the law of God and humanity, but . . . endangers the institutions of his country and the safety of his countrymen.[12]

Such remonstrations did little to alter the general treatment of slaves. In time, however, treatment *did* improve—but not through a change of heart on the part of the planters. With the foreign slave trade remaining firmly closed despite slaveholding efforts to reopen it, Virginia could not provide enough new slaves to replace those who were being systematically worked to death. Conservation—better treatment of a valuable resource—became a matter of commonsense wisdom.

Eventually slaves were fed enough to do the work that was required of them, which extended from sunup to sundown. In the summer most masters gave their field hands a two-hour break at noonday, so that their total work time did not exceed twelve hours.[13] As for living conditions, slaves were somewhat better clothed now and more protected from the elements—it made no economic sense to lose a thousand-dollar asset because a damp, drafty cabin turned a cold into pneumonia. In truth, by 1850 most slave quarters were nearly the equivalent of those of poor whites living nearby.

Historians have concluded that of the many testimonies of ex-slaves, the most trustworthy are those taken directly after the subjects gained their freedom.* In their previous book, the authors have cited numerous accounts; in this one, the words of Elizabeth Keckley will suffice. After 30 years of servitude, she was able to buy her freedom with her "pin money"—saved from what she had been able to earn on the side as a seamstress. She moved to Washington and secured a position in the White House, while Abraham Lincoln was President. In her childhood she had learned to read and write, and with Mary Todd Lincoln's encouragement she wrote her autobiography, which was published in 1868.

She had been owned by a Colonel A. Burwell of Dinwiddie Courthouse, Virginia. Her mother Agnes also belonged to Mr. Burwell, but her father, George Hobbs, belonged to another man and was allowed to visit his wife and "Little Lizzie" only twice a year, at Easter and Christmas. To reward her mother's long and faithful service, Mr. Burwell made an arrangement with the owner of Lizzie's father, so that the family could be reunited. Lizzie was overjoyed; her mother even more so. "The old weary look faded from her face, and she worked as if her heart were in every task."

These were the happiest days of young Lizzie's life. One morning "my father called me to him and kissed me, then held me out at arm's length. . . . 'She's growing into a large, fine girl,' he remarked to my mother. 'I don't know which I like best, you or Lizzie, as both are so dear to me.'"

At that moment, as they were speaking warmly of the future, Mr. Burwell entered the cabin with a letter in his hand. The man who owned Lizzie's father was moving to Tennessee and intended to take his slave with him. The news struck the little family like a thunderclap. "I can remember the scene as if it were but yesterday," wrote Lizzie, "how my father cried out against the cruel separation; his last kiss; his wild straining of my mother to his bosom; the solemn prayer to Heaven; the tears and sobs; the fearful anguish of broken hearts . . . the parting was eternal." This

---

* Old slaves interviewed in the 1920s and 30s were inclined to tell their Southern white interviewers what they assumed they wanted to hear. And since the ex-slaves were then quite old and quite poor, their accounts tended to focus on the happier memories of childhood.

cloud "had no silver lining, but I trust it will be all silver in Heaven. . . . At the grave, at least, we should be permitted to lay our burdens down, that a new world, a world of brightness, may be open to us."

Lizzie's mother was beside herself, and her grieving got on Mrs. Burwell's nerves. "My old mistress said to her: 'Stop your nonsense; there is no necessity for you putting on airs. Your husband is not the only slave who has been sold from his family, and you are not the only one that has had to part. There are plenty more men about here, and if you want a husband so badly, stop your crying and go find another.'" Her father and mother kept in touch by letters, always hoping that somehow in the future they would be reunited—but "my mother and father never met again in this world."

When one of Lizzie's uncles lost a pair of plow lines, Mr. Burwell replaced them without giving him a flogging, but he warned him that if anything happened to the new set, the consequences would be severe. A few weeks later, the new plow lines were stolen. "My mother went to the spring in the morning for a pail of water, and on looking up into the willow tree which shaded the bubbling crystal stream, she discovered the lifeless form of her brother suspended beneath one of the strong branches. Rather than be punished the way Colonel Burwell punished his servants, he took his own life."

When Elizabeth grew older, Mr. Burwell gave her to his nephew, an impoverished Presbyterian minister. His wife grew jealous of her and determined to break her spirit, but her husband refused to whip Elizabeth for no reason. So Mrs. Burwell got the schoolmaster, Mr. Bingham, to do it. He took her in his study and told her to take down her dress to receive a flogging. Elizabeth refused, saying that she would not submit to anyone flogging her save her master. Bingham subdued her by force, tied her up, and whipped her with rawhide until she bled. But she did not give him the satisfaction of uttering so much as a groan.

When she was released, she went home and demanded of her master to know why she had been flogged. Instead of answering, he told her to go away. When she persisted, he seized a chair and struck her with it, knocking her to the floor.

As Bingham had pledged himself to Mrs. Burwell to subdue what he called Elizabeth's "stubborn pride," there would be two more episodes, with her battling him each time. Finally, shaking and exhausted, he burst into tears, asked her forgiveness, and never raised his hand to another servant again. But Elizabeth's ordeal was not over; now Mrs. Burwell demanded that her husband beat Elizabeth himself. "One morning he went to the wood-pile, took an oak broom, cut the handle off, and with this heavy handle attempted to conquer me. I fought him, but he proved the strongest. At the sight of my bleeding form, his wife fell upon her knees and begged him to desist." He did, and Elizabeth was so sorely wounded, she was unable to get out of bed for five days.

This was still not the end of it. The Reverend Mr. Burwell, "who preached the love of Heaven, who glorified the precepts and examples of Christ, who expounded the Holy scriptures Sabbath after Sabbath from the pulpit . . . resolved to make another attempt to subdue my proud, rebellious spirit—made the attempt and again failed. Then he told me with an air of penitence that he should never strike me another blow, and faithfully he kept his word."[14]

As shocking as Elizabeth's story may seem to anyone new to the testimonies of ex-slaves, it is not at all unusual. What *is* unusual is that she eventually won a measure of triumph. Under another master whose heart was closed to the conviction of the Holy Spirit, she would almost certainly have been killed for her defiance.

Being so totally out of control of their circumstances, and so utterly helpless to alter them, slaves were dogged by fear. And there was another fear. . . .

If you didn't like the way the master's son was beginning to eye your wife or your young daughter, all you could do was hope that you were wrong. If you weren't, and worse came to worst, there was *still* nothing you could do. If you tried anything, you would only make matters infinitely worse. In other words, you did not dare be the father or protector whom God had created you to be—and that crushed a male slave's spirit like nothing else.

Antebellum novelists could write all the happy endings they cared to; on the plantation, real-life endings were almost always measured in degrees of tragedy.

While fear may have been the predominant element in the slave quarters, surely it was not also the uninvited guest at the candlelit, silvergleaming dining table in the Big House? Yet it *was* there—an unseen, shrouded specter in the corner shadows. Later, as the master and his wife tried to fall asleep, or later still, in their uneasy dreams, it would loom larger. . . .

Iniquity has been defined as "sin, knowingly persisted in." If you are continuing in some behavior that you know is displeasing God, and if you have no intention of reforming, there are only two ways for you to cope with the burden of guilt. One way is to harden your heart against the pricks of conscience, and it *is* possible to so deaden the conscience that it ceases to be an inhibitor. (There is, of course, a price: total loss of sensitivity in all realms of the spirit.)

The other way is to convince yourself that wrong is right.* Some men are adept at compartmentalizing—at dividing their lives into separate compartments, each secured by a watertight door. They are capable of staying focused only on the present situation, without concern for what it might mean to the future, or the debt owed to the past.

A plantation owner might have been having an affair with one of his slave girls, slipping out as often as possible to carry on late-night assignations. Yet at the head of his dinner table, he would be the soul of decorum. With a fine sense of honor he would take umbrage at the least slight to a lady of the South, especially to his dear wife. He loved to hear himself wax eloquent in praise of Southern womanhood, and bask in the beaming approval of guests and family. Were anyone to challenge his sentiments, he would be insulted and possibly enraged—perhaps because he so fervently wanted to believe the words he spoke. But when the conversation shifted elsewhere, and he and his lofty sentiments were no longer center stage, his mind would drift back to the dark clearing by the brook under the willows, and he would wonder if Delilah would be waiting.

For Southern women, the burden was especially difficult. The Chivalry had placed them on such a high pedestal, they dared not descend—or the whole facade would collapse. Nor could they find much sympathy from their mothers, who had been trained by *their* mothers to accept this role.

So a wife would beam as she was expected to, while her husband extolled her virtues, and later she would will herself not to wonder where he might be going as, unable to sleep, he eased out of their bed. Why, he was probably just going down to the verandah to have a cigar. . . . And when the slave girl Delilah's child was born with red hair, the mistress of

---

* Chapter 28 will deal with the lengths to which the Slave Power went to convince itself and the world that God approved of slavery.

the house would steadfastly refuse to consider that the only red-headed man in the county was the one at the head of her dinner table.

In their hearts most Southern women *knew* slavery was wrong. Some, like Mary Chesnut, confided as much to their diaries; a few, like the Grimké sisters, spoke their minds publicly—and were ostracized from polite society. The majority simply played the game, as locked into the system as their husbands were. In the North, women were increasingly outspoken, crusading for all manner of causes; in the South, such women were looked on as social aberrations. As a result, Southern women of conscience were often plagued by fears they dared not acknowledge even to themselves, while their men seemed comparatively untroubled.

Iniquity can sometimes be indulged in with seeming impunity for an extended season. Indeed, at times it seems that accountability might be postponed indefinitely, as one plunges into living in the present with all the style and élan one can muster.

But anyone who knows God, knows that one day He *will* require an accounting. The dark prince of this planet may appear to be the master of the dance, but God has not abdicated His throne, and the day of reckoning, the day the music stops, will come—as it does to all men.

In their previous volume, the authors presented a few of the numerous accounts of masters on their deathbeds gathering their slaves around them and tearfully begging their forgiveness. With the possibility of eternal damnation suddenly looming large, they were in a panic to avoid, or at least alleviate, what they belatedly realized must certainly be their fate.*

Other than fear of where one might spend eternity, the deepest low-level anxiety, seldom expressed but pervasive throughout the South, was of a massed slave uprising. It *had* happened, just a few years before, in Haiti. Of all France's colonies, Saint Domingue, as it was known in the 18th century, was the most prosperous; two-thirds of all her foreign investments went into its vast slave plantations, which produced sugar, coffee, cocoa, and cotton, filling the holds of more than 700 vessels a year.[15]

But news of the French Revolution had inspired a slave named Toussaint L'Ouverture to lead a servile insurrection. The slaves swept the western end of the island, overthrowing their masters, abolishing slavery, and

---

* There were even recorded instances of horrified slaveholders peering into the infernal abyss that yawned before them, and screaming as they died.

declaring themselves independent. To quell this uprising, Napoleon dispatched his brother-in-law with 25,000 seasoned troops, but even they could not prevail. In 1803 France gave up trying and recognized Haiti as an independent nation.

Clearly, what had taken place a few hundred miles from Florida could happen in America. A generation later, it almost did. In 1831, in the Virginia Tidewater Country, a slave named Nat Turner instigated a rebellion. He and seven others murdered their masters in their beds, confident that slaves throughout the South would rise up and join them as soon as they heard what was happening. More than a few did; in two days time, Turner's band had swollen to 10 times their original number. And so had the count of their victims: They had slain 55 whites—men, women, and children.

But most of the slaves they encountered were too fearful to join them, and soon companies of State militia tracked the rebels down and defeated them. For two months Turner himself eluded capture, while rumors of fresh Turner-led rebellions tormented the South. When he was finally taken, he was swiftly tried and hanged. How badly frightened the entire South was became evident in what happened next: To prevent any part of his body being spirited away by his followers and revered as a martyr's relic, his bodily remains were boiled down into grease.

Declared Southern author Edwin Clifford Holland: "Let it never be forgotten that our Negroes are freely the Jacobins of the country, that they are the anarchists and the domestic enemy, the common enemy of civilized society, and the barbarians who would if they could, become the destroyers of our race."

An Alabama farmer put it to journalist Frederick Law Olmsted more simply: "Folks was dreadful frightened about the niggers [rising]. I remember they built pens in the woods where they could hide. . . . I remember the same thing where we was in South Carolina. . . . We had all our things put up in bags, so we could tote them, if we heard they were coming our way."[16]

A number of the slave owners were believing Christians, and from the beginning they faced a terrible dilemma. In order to live with the fact that they were holding fellow human beings in bondage against their will, they had to convince themselves that their slaves were not human beings at all—that, in fact, their two-footed "property" was no different than their four-footed livestock. Or that if slaves *were* human, they were a race so inferior that they were suited only to serving whites, for which purpose God had clearly created them.

But regardless of the mind games Christian slaveholders played, in their hearts they knew better. And any heart that had not become impervious to conviction was guilt-ridden. For even those who were treating their slaves as well as they possibly could were not doing unto others what they would want done unto them. As much as they might gainsay it, their consciences did not rest easy, and in on that guilt rode fear.

Rarely articulated, the fear was evident in the laws that sprang up in the wake of Turner's Rebellion. Because of tracts inciting slaves to rise up against their masters, and Garrisonite editorials saying much the same thing, it became a crime to teach a Negro to read. It also became a crime to teach him to write; escaped slaves like Frederick Douglass were writing too many antislavery tracts as it was.

It was now against the law for Negroes to walk together in the road. No Negro was allowed to leave his plantation without a pass, and there were patrols of white men constantly afoot to make sure these laws were strictly obeyed, since in areas of the Deep South the blacks vastly outnumbered the whites. Negroes were not allowed to gather together or have meetings; even their worship was strictly controlled.

Slaves would attend the owner's mandatory worship services and listen to one white preacher after another emphasize the Eighth Commandment, Thou shalt not steal. Or Paul's admonition to the Colossians: "Slaves, obey in everything those who are your earthly masters, not with eyeservice, as men-pleasers, but in singleness of heart, fearing the Lord." Or Peter's even more direct exhortation: "Servants, be submissive to your masters with all respect, not only to the kind and gentle but also to the overbearing."*

Slaves who were strong Christians themselves would listen to anyone with polite attentiveness and even compassion, as long as he was preaching from his heart. But when one earnest young white minister began his sermon with: "Primarily, we must postulate the existence of a deity," an old Negro nodded and murmured, "Yes, Lord, dat's so. Bless de Lord!"[17]

---

* Colossians 3:22 (RSV); 1 Peter 2:18 (RSV)

Occasionally slaves were allowed to hear an itinerant black preacher (as long as a white man was present)—but only one who came recommended and could be counted on to stick to the prescribed Scriptures. Not surprisingly the slaves grew weary of the same lesson over and over. Confided Hannah Scott of Arkansas, "All he say is 'bedience to de white folks, and we hears 'nough of dat without him tellin' us!"[18]

The slaves were more resourceful than their masters supposed.* Late at night the slaves would have their own secret meetings, where one of their own would lead them. There, they would worship the Lord Jesus as they saw fit. There, the texts ran more often along the lines of Malachi's appeal: "Have we not all one father? hath not one God created us?"† In their hearts the slaves knew that all human beings were equal at the foot of the Cross and in heaven.

One of the best-known black preachers, John Jasper, loved to proclaim: "Ev'body got to rise to meet King Jesus in the morning, the high and the low, the rich and the po', the bond and the free, as well as me."[19]

Most slaves were devout Christians, and their faith sustained them, giving them a sense of worth before God and man. Because they *knew* Christ had died for *them*, they found inner strength to resist the humiliations many slaveholders sought to impose on them. The underground church has always thrived under persecution, and the black slave church was no exception; its members numbered some of the strongest believers in the history of Christendom. The faith of the slaves was the perfect antidote to the dripping poison of despair. Their faith *did* set them free; with it, they could endure anything, because they knew God loved them. And because their faith strengthened their love for one another as well, they were able to build a sense of community as brothers and sisters in Christ.

Along with the rest of the believing Christians, the slaves accepted the Biblical judgment of their sinfulness. But rather than focus on their personal deliverance from sin as whites did, they concentrated more on the delivering aspect of the Gospel—where it concerned deliverance from slavery, in the Promised Land of the life to come, when all their burdens would be lifted.

---

* As a form of resistance, they often played dumb and lazy—so convincingly that many Southern whites came to regard them as shiftless, almost useless.

† Malachi 2:10

Some owners acknowledged their slaves' spiritual equality. George Hooper of Alabama referred to the death of a slave as not only the loss of a friend but of a "brother in Christ." To his wife he wrote, "I verily believe that God has a high place prepared."[20]

Even if plantation owners did not spend much time thinking about heaven, let alone sharing it with their blacks, they could not help but be powerfully affected by the spirituals that came out of the slave worship—"Go Down, Moses"—"Didn't My Lord Deliver Daniel"—"Swing Low, Sweet Chariot." These songs of sorrow summed up the ache in 4 million hearts, and their message was always the same: God will deliver us, if we will have faith in Him. And so they sang of Daniel and Jonah and Moses—especially Moses, who delivered his people out of bondage in Egypt. He became the figure of redemption and promised freedom to them. One of their favorite spirituals was, "Go down, Moses, way down to Egypt Land. Tell old Pharaoh, 'Let my people go!'"

On a moonlit night, with the ground mist gathering under the willows, you could hear the songs coming up out of the slave quarters. One deep voice would start it, then others, hearing it, would blend their voices until the singing seemed to come from everywhere.

"The river of Jordan is muddy and cold . . ." As the haunting melody wafts up the hill to the house with the white columns, the host and hostess invite their guests out on the verandah to enjoy the molasses-smooth harmonies.

"It chills the body, but not the soul . . ." Though the night is warm, one young lady shivers, drawing her shawl close. Her escort gallantly puts his dinner jacket around her shoulders, but it doesn't help. "All my trials, Lord, will soon be over . . ."

On the neighboring plantation, where the lament has been picked up, the master is sipping a julep, reading the paper; his wife is fidgeting with a sampler. "I've got a little book with pages three . . ." Hearing the plaintive strain, the mistress commands their steward to shut the windows against it, despite her husband's protest about the humidity. It is fainter now, but she can still hear it: "and on each page's spelled Liberty . . ."

Angrily she storms up to her room. Shutting the French doors to the balcony, she draws the heavy velvet draperies closed. But she can still hear it; the song is inside her head now, and tonight it will haunt her dreams. "All my trials, Lord, will soon be over . . ."

26

THE PECULIAR INSTITUTION

*S*unday afternoons might find her on the stoop of her shack, telling a circle of children the stories that her mother had told her when she was their age. The rest of the week, Mammy was in the Big House organizing the meals, seeing to the cleaning, making sure the laundry was done right, settling disputes between the house servants, and in general making sure the manor continued to project the tranquility and gracious hospitality for which it was renowned.

Among the black believers, some of the strongest were these matriarchs. Even-tempered and firm-willed, they were a source of strength for the entire black community on the plantation. When they were in the Big House, they were often in charge of everything. Noted Annie Laurie Broidrick of Mississippi: "Consequential, important, and next in authority to the owners were the old 'black mammies' who raised and superintended the care of the children. As they grew old, they were exempt from hard work and ruled white and black with equal severity. Our old 'Mammy Harriet' raised two or three generations of children. We had the greatest love for her, but it was tempered with fear, for she never overlooked a fault. . . ."

But, if Mammy Harriet punished, she also forgave and consoled. If a child was spanked by her mother, Mammy would wipe away her tears: "But, honey, why does you make your ma so mad, actin' like such poor white trash?"[1]

Mammy usually functioned as the mistress's executive officer, and was looked up to by all the blacks on the plantation as the keeper of the keys. She was in charge of all the children, black and white, and was often so wise and moral that her rectitude set an example not only for the black population but for the white as well. Even overseers treated her with respect, for a displeased mammy could turn a plantation upside down. "When Mammy ain't happy, ain't *nobody* happy!" White mothers entrusted the upbringing of their little children to these black "governesses"—and the attachments thus formed were deep and lasting. It was not unusual for a white child to love his black mammy as much as his real mother—and vice versa.

Ironically, the more capable any house servant became, the more the master and mistress relied on him or her, and a very real dependence could build up. The servants knew all the master's and mistress's faults, all their shortcomings. If there was Christian love in the equation, it covered a multitude of sins. Body servants could rescue drunken masters from ruinous card games and even life-threatening situations. Personal maids could become young mistresses' confidants, and often prevented them from making decisions of the heart they would later rue. But where love was lacking, jealousy often sprang up. House slaves could suddenly find themselves working in the fields, where overseers were only too happy to help them find new humility.

When the relationship between master and servant was bad, for the slave it became a living hell, from which there was no escape save death. But when it was good, it could be very good indeed; many plantation owners insisted that they thought of their house servants as family.

Often, when there had been a long and good relationship, owners would want to give their older slaves their freedom—until the slaveholding states passed laws forbidding manumission. Otherwise, in one more generation there might be hundreds of thousands of freed slaves on the loose, with no visible means of support.

To the slaveholders, having free blacks around the countryside was extremely undesirable. Not only did it put the wrong ideas into the heads of neighboring slaves, it raised the shadow of amalgamation—one of the planters' deepest unspoken fears.

To Southerners, slavery seemed the only way to maintain tight control over the black race, and though many did not care for it, there seemed to be no other solution. As one Missourian would write to the New York *Tribune*: "If slavery could be voted out of the State of Missouri without having the Negroes set free among us, a majority of our people would be found at any time favorable to such a measure."[2] And according to Frederick Law Olmsted, this was the prevailing opinion of nonslaveholders *throughout* the South.

What to do with the freed blacks was one of the greatest obstacles to emancipation, and the harshest critics up North had no answer. "Free them *now*," demanded the Garrisonites, "and let God sort it out."

Slavery *was* a moral evil, conceded Governor Collier of Alabama, yet the South was not required to abolish it, if doing so brought greater evils. "I have never heard of a plan for immediate abolishment of slavery in the Southern States that was at all practicable, or which would not introduce grievances incalculably more prejudicial to society than slavery itself."[3]

Keeping the blacks "in their place" was a major preoccupation of slaveholders, and it was usually done with the whip. Even gentle masters considered whipping indispensable to the maintenance of discipline, though hopefully the mere threat of the lash would be sufficient to keep a slave obedient. "Were fidelity the only security we enjoyed," wrote one planter in the *Southern Patriot*, "deplorable indeed would be our situation. The fear of punishment is the principle to which we must and do appeal, to keep them in awe and order."[4]

For slaves, their first whipping was a shattering experience. Andy Anderson of Texas described it: "After dat whippin', I doesn't have de heart to work for de massa. If I seed de cattle in de cornfield, I turns de back, 'stead of chasin' 'em out."[5] A slave from Texas recalled a whipping inflicted by a new master: "I just about half died. I lay in the bunk two days getting over that whipping, getting over it in the body but not the heart. No sir, I have that in the heart till this day."[6]

Inflicting pain on another person did not come naturally to children, and so plantation owners had to train their children to whip their slaves, particularly if they had grown up playing together. What this did to the blacks is obvious—but it also wrought pernicious havoc in the souls of the whites. After two or three generations of presumed superiority (with the whip ever at hand to enforce it), whites had grown accustomed to thinking of themselves as a race intended to be masters. To be sure, many smaller farmers with only a handful of slaves toiled in the fields alongside them. But so ingrained was the master-race mentality in some that they would often expend more energy hunting up the slave who was supposed to have fixed the fence and making him do it right than they would have simply fixing it themselves.

When an owner caught a slave stealing from him, especially a slave whom he suspected of subtly flaunting his authority, he was more than likely to lose his temper. The Reverend Charles Pettigrew of North Carolina warned his sons of this when he willed them his estate: "To manage Negroes without the exercise of too much passion is next to an impossibility. . . . I would therefore put you on your guard, lest their provocations should on some occasions transport you beyond the limits of decency and Christian morality."[7]

A generation earlier, Thomas Jefferson, who freed his slaves in his will, recognized the inevitable bottom line in most master/slave relationships: "The whole commerce between master and slave is a perpetual exercise of the most boisterous passions, the most unremitting despotism on the one part, and degrading submission on the other."[8]

In his autobiography, Mark Twain recalled how he himself, as a young boy, had lost his temper at a slave boy named Sandy whom his family had hired in Hannibal, Missouri. He went raging to his mother, "Sandy had been singing for an hour without a single break, and I couldn't stand it, and wouldn't she please shut him up!"

Mark Twain's mother was an exceptional woman. The first thing that came to her mind was that Sandy had been sold away from his family in Maryland when he was barely old enough to know what was happening. With tears in her eyes she replied, "Poor thing, when he sings, it shows he is not remembering, and that comforts me. But when he is still, I am afraid he is thinking, and I cannot bear it. He will never see his mother again; if he can sing, I must not hinder it, but be thankful for it. If you were older, you would understand me; then that friendless child's noise would make you glad."[9]

Probably the most egregious abuse of absolute power came in the treatment of female slaves. If their daughters turned out to be plain, slave mothers were consoled by the thought that the girls were less likely to be sexually abused. For the beautiful ones, there was only going to be trouble down the road. A white master not constrained by a strong faith might begin to notice a young girl filling out, might begin to think about the fact that he might woo her or simply take her, and no one would know, because he could threaten to kill her if she told.

One white Southern woman did tell—and journalist Frederick Law Olmsted quoted her letter: "It is one great evil hanging over Southern slave States. It is summed up in the single word: *amalgamation.* . . . White mothers and daughters have suffered under it for years—have seen their dearest affections trampled upon . . . their future lives embittered, even to agony," Mrs. Douglass of Virginia concluded. "I cannot use too strong language in reference to this subject, for I know it will meet with a heartfelt response from every Southern woman."[10]

Who was this journalist Frederick Law Olmsted, to whom so many felt they could confide so much? In 1852, at the request of the New York *Times,* Olmsted began a three-year tour of the South, which would take him to every region and locale. At Yale he had been a student of science and engineering, and he would later design New York's Central Park and the campus of Stanford University. Olmsted was as neutral an observer as could be found; as he himself said, "Few men could have been so little inclined to establish previously formed opinions." A believer in democracy, he could not approve of human bondage, but he recognized the Southern States' "clear constitutional right to continue their peculiar institution, as it is, and where it is." To him, slavery was "an unfortunate circumstance for which the people of the South were in no wise to blame," and he regarded abolition as no more immediately practicable than the abolition of penitentiaries or hospitals.[11]

Southern gentlemen might take vehement exception to the abolitionists' blanket portrayal of them as brutal slave abusers, but none denied the ubiquity of amalgamation, to use Mrs. Douglass's term. There were a number of instances of planters or their sons falling in love with slave women and taking them North, where they could live together in honesty, as man and wife. One large planter in Louisiana confided to Olmsted that he was sending his young sons North to be educated, as there was no possibility of their being brought up in decency at home. He confirmed that the practice of amalgamation "was not occasional or general, it was universal. 'There is not,' he said, 'a likely-looking black girl in this State who is not the concubine of a white man. There is not an old plantation in which the grandchildren of the owner are not whipped in the field by his overseer.'"[12]

But perhaps the most ringing condemnation was pronounced by Mary Chesnut in her diary, which was not published until 19 years after her death. "God forgive us, but ours is a monstrous system, a wrong and an iniquity! Like the patriarchs of old, our men live all in one house with their wives and their concubines, and the mulattos one sees in every family partly resemble the white children. Any lady is ready to tell you who is the father of all the mulatto children in everybody's household but her own. Those, she seems to think, dropped from the clouds."[13]

While Southern gentlemen would never mention their ladies' distress over amalgamation, one fear *was* freely discussed: fear of the future. Imminently that translated into fear of the next downturn in the economy. By 1850, cotton was not only king but tyrant. It was America's greatest export, and the South's overall agricultural production accounted for 60 percent of all that the country shipped abroad.[14] In the boom years, plantation owners had committed every available piece of land to growing cotton and had reaped a fortune—and spent it buying more land to grow more cotton and more slaves to pick it. But then the age-old law of supply and demand had kicked in. The price of cotton on the world market plummeted, and now the planters were stuck with all their capital tied up in slaves, and so little profit at the end of the year that a Northern farmer, grossing perhaps a hundredth of what a large plantation cleared, actually enjoyed a better standard of living. The Northern farmer's equipment all worked, his barn was tight, his livestock was healthy, his house didn't leak, and his sons could go away to college.

How many Southerners were actually affected by this boom-and-bust cycle? According to the census of 1850, less than a third of the more than six million whites in the South were members of slaveholding families. Among the 300,000 slaveholders, the majority owned no more than five slaves; indeed, the plethora of vast plantations conjured up by abolitionists was largely a myth. Fewer than 8,000 men owned 50 slaves or more. Only 254 owned more than 200 slaves, and of these only 11 owned more than 500.[15] This comparative handful of men and their families constituted less than 1 percent of the white population in the South. Yet they were regarded as the aristocracy, and the decisions they made would affect the whole South.

Using the census of 1850 (which also included the size of the cotton crop) and the then-current price of cotton (seven cents a pound), Olmsted calculated that fully half of all the slave owners were clearing no more than $125–$150 a year—about the wages of the lowest-paid member of the New York City police force! It was a startling conclusion, yet confirmed by countless visits to slaveholders throughout the South. Nor was the cotton market likely to improve; the vast new plantations in Mississippi, Louisiana, and Texas seemed certain to keep the market depressed for the foreseeable future.

The great irony was, North and South had started off equal. To be sure, the summer climate was hotter and more humid in the South, but it was not so intolerable that only those of African descent could stand to work in it—as slaveholders claimed. Olmsted observed that white settlers in Texas, white workmen in New Orleans, and countless thousands of white farmers "testify that the climate is no preventive of persevering toil." The planters' widespread aversion to manual labor Olmsted credited to generations of conditioning to regard such work as unfit for white men. "It is this habit of considering themselves a privileged class, and of disdaining something which they think beneath them, that is deemed to be the chief blessing of slavery. It is termed 'high tone' and 'high spirit', and is supposed to give great military advantages to those who possess it."[16]

Under the broiling sun of harvest time, small farmers would gladly have hired part-time help, but in a slave economy there were hardly any day laborers to hire. As slavery took root in the South, it had driven away free-market labor—and that, not the oppressive heat and humidity, was what had curtailed industrial growth. A few Southern entrepreneurs had attempted to build factories and run them with slave labor. Yet, where anything above the most rudimentary skills was required, slaves proved unsuitable—not because they couldn't master the more complex procedures, but because they didn't care enough to learn them. A Northern worker did care, because higher skills meant higher wages. A slave never got any wages in the first place, and so had no incentive to improve.

As a result, the South eventually found itself dependent on Northern or European manufacturers for everything from plows and pumps to shoes and harnesses. We have seen the fruits of progress in the North; Olmsted was profoundly saddened by their lack in the South. "Let a man be absent from almost any part of the North twenty years, and he is struck on his return by what we call the 'improvements' which have been made. Better buildings, churches, school-houses, mills, railroads, etc. In New York City alone, for instance, at least $200 million has been re-invested merely in improved housing of the people." He went on to cite the new waterworks, gasworks, and labor-saving machinery, and noted that equivalent improvements could be found in the rural countryside laced with roads, canals, and railroads, as well as with new houses, barns, and fences.

"But where will the returning traveler see the accumulated cotton profits of twenty years in Mississippi? Ask the cotton planter for them, and he will point in reply, not to dwellings, libraries, churches, school-houses, mills, railroads, or anything of the kind; he will point to his Negroes," proud that slaves that once cost $500 a head were now worth $1,000. Even in Virginia, the state that profited most from supplying slaves to others, "the total increase in wealth of the population during the last twenty years shows for almost nothing. One year's improvements of a free State exceed it all."[17]

Were a Southern planter to come into $10,000, he would spend it on 10 able-bodied field hands. With an equivalent amount, the Northern farmer would buy several hundred acres, build a comfortable house, add to his livestock, and repair his fences.[18] In what we know as the Midwest, the average value of land in 1850 was $11.39 an acre, while in the South it was $5.34. In the eight Northern states around New York City, there was a mile of transportation by railroad or canal for every 11 square miles. In the five cotton states, there was a mile of railroad or canal for every 80 square miles.[19]

Olmsted could see what his Southern friends could not: Slavery was literally impoverishing the South.

Nor were his Southern friends interested in revising their uninformed assessment of life in the North. In his travels Olmsted found that south of Virginia, everyone assumed that the free laborers in the North were living and working in conditions worse than those of Southern slaves. This view was maintained by planters, "most of whose neighbors lived in a manner which would make them an object of compassion to the majority of our Northern day-laborers."[20]

The contrast between the two regions was forcibly brought home to Senator W. C. Preston of South Carolina, whose observations while traveling on the Erie Canal were published in the Columbia *Telescope*:

No Southern man can journey, as I have lately done, through the Northern States and witness the prosperity, the industry, the public spirit which they exhibit . . . without feelings of deep sadness and shame, as he remembers his own neglected and desolate home.

[In the North] no dwelling is to be seen abandoned, no farm uncultivated. . . . The whole land is covered with fertile fields, with manufactories, and canals, and railroads, and edifices, and towns, and cities. Along the route of the great New York canal . . . a canal, a railroad, and a turnpike are to be seen in the width of perhaps a hundred yards, each of them crowded with travel, or overflowing with commerce. . . . Passing along [the canal], you see no space of three miles without a town or village, and you are never out of the sound of a church bell. . . .

How different the condition of these things in the South! Here, the face of the country wears the aspect of premature old age and decay. No improvement is seen going on—nothing is done for prosperity—no man thinks of anything beyond the present moment. Our lands are yearly tasked to their utmost capacity of production, and when exhausted, are abandoned for the youthful West.[21]

Had anyone from the North written such an assessment (and Olmsted did write in a similar vein, though not as poignantly), the South might be expected to shrug it off. But this was one of their own—a Senator who clearly loved the South. Even so, the Preston report received scant attention and changed few preconceptions.

On the other hand, it should be borne in mind that while the North was increasingly deploring slavery, it was also buying most of the cotton being produced by the slave economy. Not *all* Northerners were calling for abolition; the cotton brokers in New York and Boston (who were often making more than the planters they represented) and the mill owners throughout New England were the strongest Northern opponents to the antislavery movement.

But the tide was turning up North; more and more people were shifting from neutrality on slavery to active opposition to its expansion. And this became the slave owners' ultimate fear of the future: that the North with its steadily increasing immigrant population would soon have enough political leverage to prohibit slavery from expanding. Northerners— *moderate* Northerners—were already calling for the containment of slavery, confident that it would then gradually die out, as it already had everywhere else in the civilized world.

Fear of slavery's enforced demise now fueled the Southerners' drive to revise their basic thinking about the institution. It was now imperative that Southerners come to see that slavery was good, not evil.

But privately, as one Mississippi planter confessed to Olmsted (not knowing he was from the North), many still hated it. "I know slavery is wrong, and God'll put an end to it. It's bound to come to an end, and when the end does come, there'll be woe in the land."[22]

27

"A Great Good!"

*T*he Speaker lays down the gavel and smiles. "Sorry to interrupt, gentlemen, but it's past my supper-time. I know not what awaits you at your place of abode, but I *do* know what awaits me: Mrs. Thompson. And Mrs. Thompson does not appreciate *any* of her lodgers arriving half an hour after they are expected at table." There are appreciative chuckles from a number of members. "Her wrath makes that of the gentleman from Savannah and the gentleman from Toledo seem like teacup-tempests!" Laughter. "I, therefore, declare this House adjourned until ten o'clock Monday morning!" And with the gavel he strikes a final blow.

You are relieved. As a freshman Congressman, just bloodied in your first verbal combat, you are ready to leave; you are ready, in fact, to go a lot farther than your boardinghouse. When your neighbors in Beaufort decided to send you up to Washington as their Representative, you were flattered; your father had served here with distinction. But the people of the county had made it clear that they had picked you on your own merit. When you had confided to your wife that you doubted you could live up to his standards, she had reminded you that March Wind plantation had been in your family for four generations, and no one, not even your father, had run it better than you.

Your first glimpse of the Capitol's gleaming white marble was exhilarating; you were awed at the thought that for the next two years (and maybe longer) you would actually be working here! As a lad, you had listened to your father tell your uncle about the inner workings of one of the two most exclusive men's clubs in the country (the other being the Senate), where gentlemen from every state in the Union gathered to conduct the affairs of state and make the Republic's laws. You had dreamed of serving here yourself one day, but had never really thought it would happen. And now you were here.

But the division between North and South had not been so vitriolic in your father's day; his closest friend had been the Congressman from Lowell who had taken lodgings in the same boardinghouse. Then, as now, most of the boardinghouses catered to gentlemen from the same state or region. And their boarders preferred it that way; at the table or in the drawing room afterward, they could discuss business and strategy with the confidence that they were among friends.

But a few houses attracted a more heterogeneous clientele and stipulated a no-politics rule to encourage it. Mrs. Perkins' was such an establishment, and your father, confiding that he saw entirely enough of his Southern colleagues at home, had chosen to lodge there. So had you. Mrs. Perkins was much older now, but she remembered your father fondly, and had made you feel welcome. Coming home to a pitcher of her iced buttermilk was the high point of your day. And there, you, like your father, had befriended a Massachusetts man—Josiah Tucker from New Bedford. A good deal older than you, he had been kind enough to show you the ropes.

But today you need more than a glass of cold buttermilk to revive your spirits. Today had been a nightmare! No one had warned you that you were about to enter a bear pit! Gone was any semblance of gentlemanly comportment. With the gag rule long ago rescinded, the topic of slavery was open for discussion, and it seemed that no one cared to discuss anything else. No matter what the issue, or how much merit a new proposal might have, sooner or later the discussion would circle around to its bearing on slavery. And invariably that would stir deep feelings and provoke a rising tide of personal invective.

It was a rule of the House that no man could be sued for libel or slander for what he said from the floor, and dueling was outlawed. But that did not stop gentlemen from seeking redress on the field of honor. Outraged sensibilities demanded satisfaction and issued challenges—which were routinely ignored.

Older Congressmen despaired. In the previous flare-ups over slavery, as in 1820 over Missouri's application for entry into the Union, when civil war had been threatened cooler heads had prevailed. Henry Clay had presented his magnificent compromise, and the fires of sectionalism had been banked. There had been other storms, each a little more acrimonious than before, but there had also been subsidences. This time, however, when the old guard had tried to calm the young hotheads on both sides, their admonitions were straws in a windstorm.

Until this afternoon you had kept silent. But finally you'd had a bellyful of these self-righteous abolitionists who consigned every slaveholder to eternal hellfire. So you had risen and given, as your maiden speech, your word of testimony. You felt God was pleased with your treatment of your slaves, almost as if He had entrusted them to your care, a flock for you to look after. On Sundays your people worship with you; in fact, you regard them not as slaves but as family. And you honestly believe that if you were to suddenly offer them their freedom, they would look at you as if you had taken leave of your senses. Where on earth would you have them go? What had they done to offend you, that you would send them away from their beloved March Wind?

There were murmurs of approval from some of your younger Southern colleagues, and then the Speaker recognized the "gentleman" from Erie, who rose in reply. Looking at you, Asa Worthy asked if your father, who was fondly remembered in these halls, had supported the Declaration of Independence.

"Of course!" you retorted.

"Then he believed that all men were created equal? And entitled to life, liberty, and the pursuit of happiness?"

Seeing where he was going, you sat in stony silence.

"Consider your 'flock' for a moment: They are free to pursue happiness, as long as their pursuit of it does not interfere with your own happiness—which of course depends on their doing exactly what you want, when and how you want it done. Now with which of these black members of your family would you be willing to trade places?"

You started to reply, furious at being made to feel as if you were on trial.

But he wasn't finished. "And another thing, my young friend: If you are so confident of God's approval of your beneficence toward your slaves, and by extension the institution of slavery itself, how do you square that with Exodus 21:16?"

You glared at him.

"Ah, I see that you who purport to be on intimate terms with the Almighty are not a student of His Word. In *my* Bible, Exodus 21:16 reads: "And he that stealeth a man, and selleth him, or if he be found in his hand, he shall surely be put to death." He paused and looked around the assembly. "Can the gentleman from Beaufort honestly say that the God who caused those words to be written in His book *approved* of slavery?"

With a chuckle he turned to the most senior of the South Carolina delegation: "Harry, perhaps you'd better take your young knight to Sunday school, before you set him back up on his charger!"

The House roared with laughter; even the elder Southern Congressmen could not help smiling.

It had been the most humiliating moment of your life! At that moment, you who had always disapproved of dueling would gladly have sent Asa Worthy your card.

Now, with Congress in recess for the weekend, you head for Mrs. Perkins' without much appetite. But supper will give you something to do, until you can retire to your room and write your wife. How you wish you could just mail yourself home in the envelope!

At supper, Josiah Tucker takes a seat across the long table from you, although there are places set at the other end that he could have taken.

"That was pretty rough play this afternoon," Josiah says, helping himself to a yam and passing them to you.

"It didn't feel much like play," you acknowledge, managing a smile.

Josiah laughs. "You'll get used to it." Reaching down the table for the platter of ham, he helps himself to a slice and passes the platter to you. "Worthy's not such a bad fellow, once you get to know him. But he's passionate on the subject of slavery. He's one of Finney's converts. Then he joined up with Weld at Lane." He takes a biscuit, offers the basket to you. "I gather from your expression," he smiles, "you're not familiar with our abolitionist movement."

"Are *you* an abolitionist?" you ask, startled.

"No," he replies with a chuckle. "Least ways, not yet."

"Then you could become one?"

He sighs and pours each of you some buttermilk from the big white pitcher. "The way things are going, I may not have much choice."

"What do you mean?"

"Well, your fire-eating colleagues seem determined to drive all us Yankees into that camp."

You put your fork down sharply. "Seems to me, it's *your* colleagues who are doing the driving!"

"All right, young fella, cool down; I'm your friend, remember?"

You nod. "Sorry. No point in bringing that dogfight in here."

He smiles. "The truth is, the problem's not with the drivers on either side. It's the institution itself." He pauses and looks out the window. "Sooner or later, we are *all* going to have to deal with it. We can't just keep putting it off, hoping it'll go away."

When he turns back, the smile is gone, replaced by a look of deep sorrow. "Frankly, I don't see how we're going to settle this thing amicably. Each week there are fewer and fewer reasonable men who have not been driven to one pole or the other. The drivers, of course, don't want it settled; they would prefer to see the Union divided."

"After today," you mutter, "I wonder if that would be such a bad thing."

Josiah puts down the biscuit and gives you a sharp look. "Don't say that; don't even think it! If you believe in God, and from what you said this afternoon you do, then you cannot deny that He intends *all* of us, the entire Union, to be part of a noble experiment in self-government. You spoke of family up there—well, *we* are a family. A national family. And we'd better learn how to get along!"

At the far end of the table, Mrs. Perkins gently clinks her glass with the edge of her spoon and frowns at Josiah. "*Mister* Tucker," she declares, "I should not have to remind you that this is *my* house, not yours. When you are in *your* House up on the Hill, you may carry on any way you please. But *here* you will abide by *my* rules. And as you well know, one of them is: No politics at the table!"

"Sorry, Ma'am," Josiah replies sheepishly.

In spite of yourself, you smile; your friend's expression looks like that of a truant pupil who has just been reprimanded.

"All right, *Mister* Tucker," you say with a smile, keeping your voice low, "where do we begin?"

"Begin what?" he asks, also lowering his voice to a conspiratorial whisper.

"To find this common ground, where we can be in one accord."

"I think, my young friend, it is going to have to begin with you admitting that you are on the horns of a terrible dilemma."

Mrs. Perkins is watching them, one eyebrow raised. She suspects they have gone back to politics, but she can't be sure.

"What dilemma?" you quietly demand.

"You will have to decide whether your slaves are chattel or family; you cannot have it both ways."

"What do you mean?"

Before replying, he politely indicates to the gentleman next to him the dish of cherry cobbler residing just out of reach. Taking a portion, he holds the dish out to you. You shake your head, and he returns it to the table.

"I mean," he resumes, "that when the census taker is counting heads to see how many of your colleagues will be coming to Congress, your slaves become people—or at least 60 percent people; five of them equal three of you. But when one of them runs away and comes up North, you want him returned as if he were a runaway horse. Now he has become your property, and the laws of property require that he be returned to his rightful owner. If *he* breaks the law, on the other hand, he becomes a person again, accountable for his misdeeds. To get around this, some of your colleagues claim that he is an inferior person of an inferior race that God created to be your servants."

Seeing you scowl, he smiles and adds, "But you claim to have encouraged him to become a believer in Christ, which would make him not just a person, but your equal at the foot of the Cross. And if he can be thus spiritually and morally elevated, can he not also be educated and prepared for emancipation? Is this, in fact, not what you have led him to hope for?"

You open your mouth to speak, but no words come.

The others have left the table, and Mrs. Perkins glances in your direction. Josiah concludes: "Suppose, God forbid, misfortune visits your plantation, and you are forced to sell off your assets to save it, including your new brother in Christ. Once again, he becomes chattel, to be sold for the best price you can get."

He sighs, rolls his napkin, and inserts it into the silver ring bearing his initials. Rising to his feet, he smiles, "You indeed have a terrible dilemma, my young friend; all of your colleagues do. And it will only get worse." He puts in his chair and places his rolled napkin with the row of others on the side table. You do the same.

"You have my complete sympathy, by the way," he murmurs, as you follow him out. "I know you have a good heart and are of good character. But," he sadly shakes his head, "I cannot see how your dilemma—*our* dilemma—is going to be resolved, other than tragically."

How could things have come to such a pass? If God did have a plan for America, if He had brought the First Comers here and set before them a table in the wilderness, if He had lifted them up as a "city on a hill" for the whole world to see—how had the weed of slavery become so deep-rooted?

The first slaves to arrive on these shores were pirate booty, raided from a Spanish slave ship and off-loaded at the Colony of Jamestown in 1619. In the 17th century, the triangular trade between Great Britain, her American Colonies, and her West Indies was flourishing. Slaves provided the labor on Britain's vast sugar plantations in the Caribbean; it was inevitable that some would find their way to the New World's shores.

At first the colonists of Virginia regarded them as indentured servants, no different than the white laborers who had agreed to work for seven years in exchange for passage to America. But the Africans were not worldly-wise; they did not know what a contract was, let alone how to read one, and it was an easy thing to simply keep extending the term of their indenture, until it finally became "indefinite."

By the 18th century, all pretense of indenture had been dropped; the black servants had become, in effect, slaves. Most were put to work at unskilled but labor-intensive agricultural operations.

What was the reaction of Christian people in the South? Did they not object? Of course. From the beginning, the Society of Friends made opposition to slavery one of the basic tenets of their faith. One of their leaders, John Woolman, traveled far and wide, usually on foot, praying and speaking quietly against the institution of slavery.

Francis Asbury, the founding spirit behind the legendary Methodist circuit riders, was profoundly impressed by Woolman's example, as was the founder of Methodism, John Wesley, who condemned slaveholding as "villainy" that violated "all the laws of Justice, Mercy, and Truth." In 1780, at a conference of Methodist preachers, any circuit rider owning slaves was ordered to free them at once, and all other Methodists were strongly advised to follow their example. The reason: Slavery was against "the laws of God, man, and nature, and hurtful to society, contrary to the dictates of conscience and pure religion."[1]

Other evangelical denominations followed suit, until there was scarcely a preacher worth his salt who had not inveighed against the evils of slave-holding (except perhaps those who owned slaves themselves). But the Methodists were in the vanguard, and four years later they went further, attempting to do in a single bold stroke what had taken the Quakers more than a generation: The Methodist leadership decided any Method-ist not divesting himself of his slaves within the next two years would be excommunicated. The Presbyterians were not far behind; in 1787 they prayed for the "final abolition" of slavery. And two years later, the Baptists declared slavery to be "a violent deprivation of the rights of nature and inconsistent with a republican government."[2]

To be sure, some slaveholders, having prayed about what their leaders were preaching, did manumit their slaves. But most did not. For beneath the surface, resistance ran far deeper than anyone had supposed. Many Methodist slaveholders, faced with divesting themselves of their property or being excommunicated, decided that they would divest themselves of Methodism. Suddenly the young denomination was in crisis, and rather than destroy it, Asbury and his cohorts backed down and rescinded their order.

The next opportunity to do away with slavery came during the Con-stitutional Convention of 1787. There had been vigorous debate over slavery, but the delegations from Georgia and South Carolina declared that if slavery were in any way deplored or prohibited by the Constitution, there would be only 11 new States, instead of 13.

The antislavery movement in the South did not subside with the ratify-ing of the Constitution; indeed, before 1820 there were more antislavery societies below the Mason-Dixon line than above it. The high-water mark came in 1831, when the fundamental merits of slavery were weighed in formal debate in Virginia's House of Delegates. Speaking in favor of eman-cipating and deporting slaves to Africa were some of the most promising and articulate young men of the First Families of Virginia, including Thomas Jefferson's favorite grandson, Chief Justice John Marshall's eldest son, Governor Floyd's nephew, and Patrick Henry's grandson.*

---

* There was no question of emancipating the slaves *without* deporting them; very few planters would hire them, and as mentioned, the prospect of loosing thousands of unemployed blacks in the Virginia countryside was unthinkable.

298

But there were problems with the emancipationists' proposition: The fee for shipping a slave to Africa was $80. To deport all the slaves in Virginia would cost $100 million—more than could be raised by selling every home and estate in the Old Dominion![3] And then, who was going to compensate the slave's owner for the fair market value of his property?

In the end the proposition was defeated, and was never again seriously debated in the South.

Nonetheless, Southern editors continued to rhapsodize about American liberty. To them, the Fourth of July sent a ray of light "far, far into the dark spots of oppressed distant lands." And a leading Charleston newspaper proclaimed that Americans were "the peculiar people, chosen of the Lord, to keep the vestal flame of liberty, as a light unto the feet and a lamp unto the path of the benighted nations who yet slumber or groan under the bondage of tyranny."[4]

Two other events in 1831 combined to produce a major shift in the Southern attitude toward slavery: William Lloyd Garrison started publishing the *Liberator*, and Nat Turner waged his bloody rebellion.

Nothing riled a Southern man of honor so much as having that honor impugned and then having no recourse to attain satisfaction. Now, as Garrison's strident attacks were widely reprinted throughout the South, frustrated outrage was building. The Southerners needed an inspired leader around whom they could rally, a farsighted general who could conceive of a battle plan—an overarching strategy that would effectively defend their beloved Southern culture.

And they had such a man. The strongest intellect the South had produced was the senior Senator from South Carolina, John C. Calhoun. Tall and erect, with a mane of gray hair and deep-set dark eyes, he was the spectral éminence grise from Charleston. Born of Scots-Irish parents pioneering in the Carolina Piedmont, Calhoun had completed his education at Yale and entered the practice of law in Charleston. Within a year he had fallen in love and married—and moved to the plantation of his in-laws. As Vice President with John Quincy Adams and Andrew Jackson, he became in time a champion for the cause of States' Rights and the chief spokesman for the Southern establishment.

In formulating political theory, Calhoun would begin with his desired conclusion and reason it back to its premises. Intensely serious, it was said that his logical mind would never permit him to write a love poem (though according to historian Merrill Peterson, he often tried), because every line began with "whereas."[5]

He maintained that since the states had voluntarily relinquished a certain measure of their autonomous authority to form the Federal Government, whenever that Government passed an act that conflicted with a state's sense of what was constitutional, that state had a right to nullify it. When South Carolina, following Calhoun's reasoning, had proposed to nullify a new round of Federal tariffs, President Jackson had intimidated its residents by threatening to use Federal troops to quell their insurrection.

But the cause of States' Rights had refused to die, and John C. Calhoun was its preeminent spokesman. He made a profound impression on everyone he met. After making his acquaintance in 1835, English reformer Harriet Martineau described him as "a cast-iron man, who looks as if he had never been born and never could be extinguished."[6]

His Southern countrymen were in awe of him—for he seemed able to discern future events better than most men.

What he saw gave him grave concern. The South had lost its majority in the House, and was barely maintaining parity in the Senate. Immigrants (many fleeing oppressive regimes and wage slavery in Europe) were flooding into America. But they weren't coming to the South (where wage earners could not compete with slaves). They were going North to build the railroads and industrial centers, or West to settle the virgin farmland.

The Territories were rapidly filling with such people, and if Senators Dickinson and Cass had their way, the Free-Soil settlers would banish slavery, and those Territories would come into the Union as free states. The slaveholding states would be completely surrounded, and slavery, denied any possibility of expansion, would wither.

Meanwhile, present immigration trends would continue, and Southerners would increasingly find themselves the objects of scorn. Eventually the time would come when the North had the three-quarters majority necessary to pass an amendment abolishing slavery. It was inevitable. It was humiliating. And it was intolerable!

What could the South do? The first thing she could do, Calhoun concluded, was to stop apologizing for slavery. It was time to do away with misgivings and ambivalence, time to stand up for the institution that had made possible the way of life they all cherished. Slavery was not evil! It was, he thundered from the floor of the Senate in 1835, "a good! A great good!"[7]

He condemned the abolitionist assault as "a war of religious and political fanaticism, mingled, on the part of the leaders, with ambition and love of notoriety." Its object was "to humiliate and debase us in our own estimation, and that of the world in general; to blast our reputation while they overthrow our domestic institutions."[8]

Once John C. Calhoun had declared to the world that slavery was a positive thing, Southern politicians and academicians, planters and farmers, editors and ministers fell in behind him.

In December 1835, the *United States Telegraph*, Calhoun's national news-organ of choice, gave the marching orders: "We must satisfy the consciences, we must allay the fears of our own people. We must satisfy them that slavery is of itself right—that it is not a sin against God—that it is not evil, moral or political. . . . In this way, and this way only, can we prepare our own people to defend their institutions."[9]

A few of the South's old guard continued to speak out against slavery. Calhoun's colleague in the Senate, William Rives of Virginia, resoundingly denounced the new thinking: Slavery was "a misfortune and an evil in all circumstances!" Never would he "deny, as has been done by this new school, the natural freedom and equality of man, to contend that slavery was a positive good."[10]

But if Calhoun and his followers were emphatically claiming that Negroes were inferior to whites, what did that do to the Declaration of Independence—the creedal statement of the Republic's beliefs?

It declared that all men were created equal and endowed by their Creator with certain inalienable rights: life, liberty, and the pursuit of happiness. Obviously, slaves were denied liberty all of the time, the pursuit of happiness most of the time, and at times, even life itself.

Two Southern signers of the Declaration, both from Maryland, would have been stunned at this rejection of the noblest document America had produced. Avowed Luther Martin in 1788: The retention of slavery was "a solemn mockery of, and insult to, that God whose protection we had then implored, and could not fail to hold us up to detestation and render us contemptible to every true friend of liberty in the world."[11]

And William Pinkney had challenged his constituents: Was not their beloved Maryland "at once the fair temple of freedom and the abominable nursery of slaves? The school for patriots and the foster-mother of petty despots? The asserter of human rights, and the patron of wanton oppression? It will not do thus to talk like philosophers and act like unrelenting tyrants; to be perpetually sermonizing with liberty for our text and actual oppression for our commentary!"[12]

But that, said the new school of Southern philosophers, was just the point: All men were manifestly *not* created equal. God clearly intended some men to rule, and others to be ruled. Declared Mississippi Senator (and former Governor) Albert G. Brown: "In the South, all men are equal. I mean, of course, white men: Negroes are not men, within the meaning of the Declaration."[13]

The Declaration of Independence had to be discredited, even if it meant that the South's other great intellect, Thomas Jefferson, must have been misguided when he penned it. In his *Disquisition on Government*, Calhoun sowed the seeds for a new doctrine of inequality: Liberty was *not* the right of every man equally. Instead of being born free and equal, men were "born subject not only to parental authority, but to the laws and institutions of the country where born, and under whose protection they draw first breath."[14]

Seeing where Calhoun was heading, Dr. Thomas Cooper, a chemist, observed: "We talk a great deal of nonsense about the rights of man. We say that man is born free, and equal to every other man. Nothing can be more untrue: no human ever was, now is, or ever will be born free!"[15] And George Fitzhugh took up the banner. "For thirty years the South has been a field on which abolitionists, foreign and domestic, have carried on offensive warfare. Let us now, in turn, act on the offensive, transfer the seat of war, and invade the enemy's territory!"[16]

Southerners had always cherished liberty and been champions of equality. Many had fought with valor and even given their lives in the War for Independence, and their descendants treasured these values. Stated Thomas R. Dew, professor of political law at the College of William and Mary: "No white man feels such inferiority of rank as to be unworthy of association with those around him. Color alone is here the badge of distinction, the true mark of aristocracy, and all who are white are equal, in spite of the variety of occupations."

J. B. D. De Bow, founder and publisher of *De Bow's Review*, would eventually insist that no whites in the South opposed slavery. The non-slaveholder, even the poorest sharecropper or tenant farmer, preserved the status of the white man. "No white man [in] the South serves another as a body servant, to clean his boots, wait on his table, and perform the menial services of his household. His blood revolts against this. . . . He is a companion and an equal."[17]

Southern Biblical scholars now set about erecting a Christian defense of slavery. It would prove to be a tall order.

28

THE NEXT BEST THING

*I*n the 18th century, evangelical Baptists, Methodists, Quakers, Presbyterians, and others across the South had been labeled "dissenters," because they had stood against the power structures of society in the fight for religious freedom. But the climate had changed. By the time Calhoun had proclaimed his new doctrine of slavery as a positive good, it had become clear that evangelical Christians were not going to be able to rid the South of slavery. Had they enjoyed a broader base of support in society, perhaps they might have prevailed. But they had none. In every state, the pillars of society—the professional men, the farmers, the merchants, and even the clergy,* as well as the planters—were slaveholders.[1]

Moreover, it should be borne in mind that throughout the South, owning slaves was not only socially acceptable, it was a measure of one's status. A poor white farmer aspired to the day when he could afford a field hand or two. A white housewife in town looked forward to the time when her husband could give her one or two black servants. Slavery was so ingrained in society and so protected by civil law that eradicating it was viewed as hopeless.

The older preachers who had condemned slavery had given way to a new generation of men who refused to do so. As if to presage this, the Presbyterian General Assembly of 1818 had gone on record as downgrading the "inherited condition" of slavery from a "social evil" to a "moral dilemma." And they began officially discouraging emancipationists, whose

---

* By 1844, 200 Methodist itinerant evangelists owned a total of 1,600 slaves, and 1,000 local preachers owned 10,000 slaves.

304

conduct was labeled "socially disruptive."[2] When Presbyterian ministers James Gilleland and George Bourne spoke out against slavery from their pulpits, they were disciplined by their presbyteries.[3]

The Methodist Church had similarly modified its once unequivocal condemnation of slavery: "Under the present existing circumstances . . . little can be done to abolish a practice so contrary to the principles of moral justice." Slavery was "past remedy," because the South's civil statutes made emancipation "impracticable," and "it was not in the power of the General Conference to change them."[4]

Many Southern Quakers, realizing that no amount of gentle persuasion was going to change the situation, sadly moved away to Northern states, leaving homes and farms that had been in their families for generations. Other Southerners of conscience followed (though the great majority of Southern evangelicals remained).

By the 1830s there were only a handful of the old antislavery preachers still holding forth in the South. They had either left, like the legendary circuit rider Peter Cartwright, or fallen silent on the issue. And some had become slaveholders themselves.[5] Men in a unique position to influence future ministers, like John Holt Rice, head of Union Theological Seminary, and Robert Hall Morrison, president of Davidson College, though privately opposed to slavery, refrained from passing on their views to their young students.[6]

A few of the younger preachers might have still spoken out against the institution, but if so, they had to do it very carefully. Any preacher truly calling for emancipation would soon find himself without a pulpit.

In 1835, when radical abolition pamphlets flooded the South, the virulent reaction further intimidated ministers. At an anti-abolitionist meeting in Clinton, Mississippi, which declared that slavery was "a blessing both to master and slave," it was resolved that "the clergy of the State of Mississippi be hereby recommended at once to take a stand upon this subject," or "be subject to serious censure."[7]

Southern clergy began defending themselves. Andrew Broaddus wrote to the Richmond *Whig* that he had been sent three abolitionist newspapers and had returned them to the publisher with a letter stating that although he was "in principle, opposed to slavery . . . he was utterly opposed to your scheme of Abolition and Amalgamation." And presbyteries, associations, and conferences issued pronouncements claiming that the Bible supported slavery and rejecting the meddling of "mistaken philanthropists, and deluded and mischievous fanatics."[8]

To Southerners, plantation life was the epitome of their culture, and their way of life was in every way superior to the Yankee way of doing things. The gentlemen of the plantation prized honor, breeding, and good manners. They were as adept on the dance floor as French courtiers, yet they could also ride as hard and shoot as straight as any frontiersman. The ladies of the plantation possessed such social graces as the finest finishing schools could produce, and their gracious hospitality, polished by mothers and aunts, knew no equal.

But plantation life depended on slavery. And most nonplantation Southerners—merchants and farmers, tradesmen and professionals—were tied to the great plantations, many depending on them for their livelihood. The poor white farmers ginned their cotton there, repaired their tools there, and were usually in debt to the plantation owner.

Slavery was thus integral to the entire Southern culture. To give up slavery would be to give up—everything.

But Southern evangelicals were now giving up the Church's historic prophetic role and submitting to the standards of their culture. Getting involved in social reform, they felt, was outside the Church's jurisdiction.

Southern physicians and men of science lent their credibility to "scientific" efforts to demonstrate that Negroes were physiologically inferior, while others claimed their inferiority was self-evident through their behavior. Dr. S. C. Cartwright of the University of Louisiana argued that because of the Negro's inferiority, republican institutions and freedom were not only unsuited to him but would be harmful to his well-being and happiness.[9]

There was another consideration: Everyone agreed that the lopsided ratio of blacks to whites, especially in the Deep South, made the racial situation latently volatile. Even evangelicals admitted that slavery, with all its faults, was the only safe way white Southerners had found to govern Africans.

Freeing one's slaves had never been regarded in the South as a proof of conversion. And now, they reasoned, since God condoned slavery in the Old Testament and did not explicitly condemn it in the New, if they could demonstrate that His grace was active in their lives, how could anyone say they weren't good Christians?

How could so many Christians become so deceived?

On Cape Cod, familiar to the authors, it can be a perfect summer day—clear and sunny with a light breeze keeping the humidity down. Then, unnoticed, a fog begins to slide in. Shadows on the ground lose their edges, and one shivers. It is still a nice summer day—but the temperature has dropped 10 degrees. Like a Cape Cod fog, a spiritual malaise gradually crept over the South.

Southern Methodist minister James McNeilly later explained:

> The majority of earnest, sincere, upright Southerners who studied the subject believed that the relation of master and slave was not in itself sinful, but that it was . . . sanctioned by the Word of God . . . and could be so administered as to foster and develop some of the noblest traits of character, such as protecting care and wise direction of the weaker race in the master, such as devoted loyalty and honest service in the slaves.[10]

McNeilly was speaking for most of the evangelical ministers in the South, who were coming to the conclusion that since it seemed humanly impossible for Christians to eradicate slavery from Southern society, they would do the next best thing—they would attempt to resolve the moral dilemma *within* the system. They would do their utmost to Christianize the institution by converting both masters and slaves to Christ.

Thus was the Mission to the Slaves begun—an outreach to the blacks (and their owners), to bring Christ into the daily life of the plantation to the fullest extent possible. Not only was it a vast mission field begging for laborers, it should also have a strong pragmatic appeal to the masters, who were ever complaining that their slaves were lazy and shiftless creatures who lied and stole at every opportunity. Well, let the Mission make Christ a reality in their slaves' lives, and with the slaves now accountable to God, just watch the change in their habits! Honesty and diligence would replace thievery and sloth, lasciviousness would be curtailed, and violence would be a thing of the past.

Foremost among the clergy who led the Mission movement were William Capers of South Carolina, editor of the *Southern Christian*

Advocate and later a leading bishop of the Southern Methodists, and Charles Colcock Jones, a Presbyterian minister from Liberty County, Georgia. Born into a plantation family, Jones had seen how slavery brutalized both slave and slaveholder alike. When he had been a seminary student up North at Andover and Princeton, he had hated slavery. But after returning home and beginning to care for his plantation's slaves, his views changed. "Our whole country groans under the sin of the neglect of the salvation of these people!"[11]

Bishop Capers, also a slaveholder, even prepared a catechism for the Methodist Missionary Society. Slaves under his instruction memorized such Scriptures as: "Servants, be obedient to them that are your masters," and "Let as many servants as are under the yoke count their own masters worthy of all honour."*

Jones and Capers were joined by other Southern evangelicals who had never thought much about slavery until Garrison began his vicious attacks on it. Their primary motive was their desire to defend the South against abolitionist accusations, so they turned to the Mission to prove the South's benevolence toward its slaves.

As for the masters, for the most part they were distrustful. A prosperous Louisiana planter named John McDonogh wrote Jones to make him "aware of the state of apathy, not to say irreligion, in which our white population is plunged." The French Louisianans gave religion mere lip service, while "the Americans settled amongst them forget it, if they ever had any." Of the planters he knew, and he was acquainted with practically everyone in the delta, he ventured that "ninety-nine out of a hundred, and I fear even the hundredth, are diametrically opposed to the introduction of religion among their slaves—they cannot even speak of it with calmness. Having no religion themselves, they are naturally opposed to the introduction of it among their slaves."[12]

Planters throughout the South did not take to any outsider tampering with their slaves. They were afraid that Sunday services would disturb the slaves' day off, interfere with their growing their own food, and could prevent the master from using them on Sunday if he wished.[13]

They were even more fearful that the Gospel would awaken in them a longing to be free, and might even encourage them to revolt. The planters

* Ephesians 6:5; 1 Timothy 6:1

also suspected that allowing missionaries to come to the plantation would open the door to abolitionist ideas. The missionaries were, after all, still linked to their Northern denominational brethren who were known to be sympathetic to abolitionism.[14]

Not all masters resisted the Mission to the Slaves. Some hoped that Christianity would make their slaves more docile and easier to control. Former slave Harriet Jacobs explained: "After the alarm caused by Nat Turner's insurrection had subsided, the slaveholders came to the conclusion that it would be well to give the slaves enough of religious instruction to keep them from murdering their masters."[15] Those who allowed missionaries to come and preach to their slaves did see a number of the changes that the preachers had predicted.

But there was a catch, as each master discovered, listening to his minister guest at the dinner table: Something would also be required of *him*. If the master wanted his slaves to live contentedly under his authority, then he, in turn, had a responsibility before God. He was like a patriarch of the Old Testament—the head of a large family, responsible for the well-being of *all* his tribe, bond servants and laborers as well as kith and kin. God required the chief of the tribe (the planter) to be the protector and the responsible father, as well as the magistrate.

Northern abolitionists regarded the entire Mission movement as a vast plot to improve the institution of slavery (which it was). Far removed from democratic America, it sounded like a reversion to medieval feudalism— the lord of the castle surrounded by his loyal serfs.

But to Southern ears it sounded like the days of Abraham! They termed it "Bible slavery,"[16] and its acceptance was almost universal. In Alabama, the widow of a planter recalled: "We regarded slavery in a patriarchal sense. We were all one family, and as master and mistress, heads of this family, we were responsible to the God we worshipped for these creatures to a great extent, and we felt our responsibility and cared for their bodies."[17]

It was now the master's *duty* to provide religious instruction to those whom God had entrusted in his care. Indeed, here in the patriarchal South, where slaveholding was now regarded as a Christian's moral obligation, allegiance to the Bible's revealed truth was being preserved. In their minds, that made their faith superior to that of their Northern brethren, whose academic institutions were being corrupted by the new "higher criticism" from Germany that questioned the authenticity of Biblical texts.

In letting their slaves be evangelized, the masters were, of course, undermining the old chattel argument, that Negroes were not men, but property. Invoked most often in legal disputes, this viewpoint still had its adherents. But due largely to the actions of smaller slaveholders, it had lost much of its credibility. The great majority of masters owned no more than a handful of slaves, and the fewer a slaveholder owned, the more likely he was to work alongside of them and eventually regard them as fellow human beings. Besides, if a slave could accept Jesus Christ as Savior and Lord, then that slave was obviously a person, with a soul.

The master who opened his plantation to missionaries was often in for a lot more than he had bargained for. But it was worth it, he was assured. C. C. Jones encouraged the slaveholder that "one grand means of elevating his own moral and religious character will be an attempt to improve that of his servants."[18] To which Leonidas Polk, the Episcopal Bishop of Louisiana, added: "You may not save [your slave], but you will save yourself."[19]

Plantation Christianity was definitely intended to apply as much to masters as to slaves. In 1851 the Reverend Robert L. Dabney* remarked that in order "to enjoy the advantages of this Bible argument in our favor, slaveholders have to provide for the spiritual needs of their bondsmen."[20] And *The Soil of the South* concluded: "Experience proves that when taught the precepts of the Christian faith, the slave is happier in his destiny and more faithful to fulfill it."[21]

Being a master, then, was a sacred trust. As James Furman (founder of Furman University) remonstrated with a master suspected of abusing a slave: "We who hold slaves, honor God's law in the exercise of our authority."[22] And Virginia churchwoman Lucy Kenny amplified this widespread conviction: "It is in the interest of the master to observe to his slave that kind of love which makes [the slave rejoice] to serve and obey his master, not with eye-service," she exclaimed, but with heartfelt Christian "willingness."[23] On the floor of Congress, young Jefferson Davis put it more pragmatically: "The man must be wanting in common sense who does not perceive that the owner of slaves will desire them to understand the great maxims of rectitude" contained in the Bible. Oral instruction of his slaves was "in his interest, if he had no higher motive to prompt him."[24]

---

* who would later serve with Robert E. Lee as one of his chaplains

In sum, the master was now expected to show the compassion of Christ when it came to caring for his slaves.

Some did.

Most did not.

When a group of people wants badly enough to believe that something is true, they will affirm and reaffirm it to one another, until it begins to take on a "truth" of its own. Such groupthink was what Southern proslavery writers and philosophers were now practicing, as they assured each other that their slaves truly loved being in bondage. They even began to believe that, given a choice between freedom and slavery, the slave would choose to remain a slave. In the words of James H. Hammond, the slave enjoyed the best of all worlds: "Peace, plenty, security, and the proper indulgence of his social propensities—freed from all care for the present, or anxiety for the future with regard either to himself or to his family."[25] William Gilmore Simms of South Carolina concurred: "There are few people so very well satisfied with their condition as the Negroes—so happy of mood, so jocund, and so generally healthy and cheerful."

From the pages of the *Southern Quarterly Review*: "There are few slaves, we believe, in the Southern country who would change their present condition, which is one of dependence, for all the advantages freedom would bring." A later issue waxed rhapsodic over how "many a poor fugitive to the land of freedom . . . has wept to return to the indulgent master and the well-filled corn-crib."[26] And Maunsel White declared: "We view our slaves almost in the same light as we do our children."[27]

There was, of course, only one trouble with that light: If the slaveholder saw himself as the father of an extended household, with a father's absolute authority, then there was nothing but his good Christian conscience to restrain him, should one of his children defy him. And if it happened to be one of his *black* children. . . .

Groupthink had also persuaded the South that the industrial North was thriving on the back of wage slaves who were worse off than the most harshly treated Southern slaves. Reality seldom broke in, but when it did, as we have seen from Senator Preston's account of his excursion on the Erie Canal, it came as a shock. Similarly, when Congressman Holmes, also of

South Carolina, accompanied the funeral cortege of John Quincy Adams to Massachusetts, he was stunned by his visit to the mills of Lowell. Block after block of the well-dressed workers' houses were neat and tidy, as were their schools and numerous churches. Shaken, he told the Charleston *Courier* that what he observed in no way coincided with what he had been led to expect, namely, that Yankee wealth had been "wrung from the bone and sinew of these laborers by oppression and exaction."[28]

Half a century ago, historian Allan Nevins observed: "The most significant fact about the Southern myth of the social and moral superiority of slavery was its fantastic character, its divorce from reality; and it was divorced from reality because the realities were too grim to be frankly faced."[29]

On the rare plantation where both master and slaves *were* simultaneously converted, one might find conditions as nearly ideal as was possible under the slavery system. Such plantations were scarcer than hen's teeth, as the saying went, yet they made great propaganda when it came to dealing with the increasingly virulent stream of criticism coming down from the North. They were also a great encouragement to doubting Southerners; in planters' circles, their stories would be told and retold, as masters (and their wives) reassured one another that the ideal *was* attainable. In agricultural journals and quarterly magazines, prizes were offered for the best accounts of wise Christian dealing with slaves.

Southern Biblical scholars now busied themselves demonstrating that God approved of (or at least condoned) slavery. They pointed to the Tenth Commandment, which said "Thou shalt not covet thy neighbor's manservant or his maidservant." Since slavery clearly existed in Moses' time, and since nowhere were believers encouraged to overthrow the existing system—did Paul not send Onesimus back to Philemon?—surely that proved that God accepted it.

Jesus was a spiritual, not a political, revolutionary, they insisted. As He kept reminding His followers, His kingdom was not of this world. In *this* world, one rendered unto Caesar what was Caesar's. Slavery was already an established fact of life when Moses came into the world. It was still part of the social fabric when Jesus was born.

But, while Jesus never called His followers to the violent overthrow of existing governments, neither was He a friend of tyranny or slavery. And once slaves were free, He intended them to remain that way. As noted,

Galatians 5:1 was the chief verse that American Patriot preachers had used to rally their flocks in support of the movement for Independence: "For freedom Christ has set us free; stand fast therefore, and do not submit again to a yoke of slavery" (RSV).

And if one was going to summon the Ten Commandments as one's authority, then what of the Eighth? "Thou shalt not steal." Surely a man's most prized possession, after life itself, was his liberty. As Jonathan Edwards Jr. put it in 1791: "To steal a man or to rob him of his liberty is a greater sin, than to steal his property, or take it by violence. And to hold a man in a state of slavery, who has a right to his liberty, is to be every day guilty of robbing him of his liberty, or of manstealing."[30]

And what of all the Scriptures that said a laborer was worthy of his hire? The whole tenor of New Testament Christianity was love and compassion, mercy and justice. Slavery ran directly counter to it.

Nor was the Biblical case for slavery convincing to all Southerners. As late as 1849, a proslavery professor at the University of Alabama complained to Calhoun that as yet no one had published a satisfactory *New Testament* defense of it, and he warned the Southern leader that the "many religious people [of] the South who have strong misgivings on this head" constituted a greater threat to slavery than the Northern abolitionists.[31]

The Biblical defenders of slavery may have sensed they were on shaky ground, yet once they had set foot on the path of demonstrating God's approval of it, they could not leave it—though their logic soon outstripped any reasonable acceptance. Not only did God approve of slavery, they claimed, but He was pleased at the use to which it was being put. It was, in fact, the highest form of evolved civilization—"the greatest of all the great blessings which a kind Providence has bestowed!" exclaimed Hammond.[32]

A number of ministers *were* swayed by their argument. One from Virginia confessed that after having been a "quasi-abolitionist" all his life, with a conscience that had been "more or less offended by slavery," he was now greatly relieved. The Scriptural defense of slavery had convinced him that he had been "in error."[33]

Publicly "the whole Southern mind with an unparalleled unanimity regards the institution of slavery as righteous and just, ordained of God, and to be perpetuated by man," proclaimed the *Southern Literary Messenger*.[34]

But privately many Southern evangelicals remained gravely ill at ease. The Reverend Basil Manley Jr. was one slaveholder who could never come to peace. In a letter to his father he confided that he longed for the "cessation of slavery for the South and Negroes and for ourselves," and he hoped that God would soon provide "a way to escape from it."[35]

And North Carolina Congressman David Outlaw wrote his wife these words (meant for her eyes only): "To expect men to agree that slavery is a blessing, social, moral, and political, when many . . . have all their lives been accustomed to . . . believe exactly the reverse, is absurd!"[36]

A few slaveholders continued to come under divine conviction that slavery was wrong. Wrote one Methodist farmer, Daniel Grant: "When I consider that these people of their forefathers were born as free as myself and that they are held in bondage by compulsion only . . . when I consider that they are human creatures indeed, with immortal souls capable of everlasting happiness or liable to everlasting misery as well as ourselves . . . it fills my mind with horror and detestation."[37]

And Benjamin Mosby Smith, who longed to be freed from the "sore evil" of slaveholding, lamented: "I am more and more perplexed about my negroes. I cannot just take them up and sell them, though that would be clearly the best I could do for myself. I cannot free them. I cannot keep them with comfort. . . . Oh, that I could know just what is right."[38]

Despite the fact it was now illegal, slaveholders on their deathbeds continued to release their slaves. As one North Carolina master put it: "I wish to die with a clear conscience, that I may not be ashamed to appear before my Master in a future world."[39]

Proslavery spokesmen were infuriated by these spontaneous manumissions, as each one was a condemnation of the entire system. They railed against the "superstitious weakness of dying men [which] induces them in their last moments to emancipate their slaves." One Charleston editor complained: "Let our women and old men, and persons of weak and infirm minds, be disabused of the false . . . notion that slavery is sinful, and that they will peril their souls if they do not disinherit their offspring by emancipating their slaves!"[40]

Some of the staunchest proslavery spokesmen, nevertheless, had private qualms. "I assure you, sir," confessed George Fitzhugh in a confidential letter, "I see great evils in slavery, but in a controversial work I ought not to admit them."[41] William J. Grayson made a similar private confession:

"I am perfectly aware that slavery is repugnant to the natural emotions of men, [but] I take the stand on the position that our natural feelings are unsafe guides for us to follow in the social relations."[42]

So much for the pangs of conscience.

But for many, the pangs would simply not go away. In North Carolina, a planter told his son that he could not discipline his slaves properly, believing them to be "as much entitled to liberty as myself." Such pangs could be found even in the rich Mississippi Delta, home of some of the largest of the new factory-style plantations. One planter confessed that he was "always an abolitionist at heart [but] did not know how to set them free without wretchedness to them and utter ruin to myself."[43]

Only rarely did such misgivings find their way into print.

After the Turner Rebellion, the outspoken Richmond *Enquirer* had quoted a South Carolinian: "We may shut our eyes and avert our faces if we please, but there it is, the dark and growing evil at our doors. . . . What is to be done? Oh, my God, I do not know, but something must be done!"[44]

Tension increased, as more and more moderate Northerners began speaking out against slavery. No longer could Southern fire-eaters lump all Northern abolitionists in the Garrison bag; too many well-respected men of character and principle were joining their ranks. In the 1840s the national antislavery banner was carried by James G. Birney, himself a former slaveholder in Alabama. He had rejected slavery for the same reason it troubled so many other Southerners: It was "inconsistent with the great truth that all men are created equal."[45]

When one is confronted with a sin he has vehemently denied (to himself, as well as everyone else)—but of which, deep down, he suspects he may be guilty—he will often explode, his anger far disproportionate to the tenor of the confrontation. The moment slavery was mentioned in less than a laudatory context, Southerners invariably exploded, withering their perceived adversary with their fury.

Matters were coming to a head. Stung by the lash of two generations of Northern disapproval, Southerners had truly had a bellyful. Ultimately Southern evangelicals demanded that their Northern brothers agree that slavery was an amoral situation in which moral decisions by a converted master could transform the institution.

But their Northern brethren would not agree. And when Southern evangelicals finally claimed that God *approved* of slavery, the tension within the denominations became unbearable. The Methodists split in 1844, and the Southern Baptists decided to have their own Convention in 1845. The Presbyterians were already divided in spirit, though the formal schism would not come until later.

Ironically, once these splits had become reality, plantation masters were more amenable to having missionaries come preach to their blacks. Rejoiced a correspondent to the *Southern Christian Advocate*: "The late separation of Methodists and Baptists in the South, from those of the North, has had a most happy effect in dispelling the just suspicions of the slaveholders, and opening the cabin doors of the Negroes everywhere throughout the South to the blessed influence of the Gospel."[46]

A *Southern* Methodist or Baptist could now be trusted; his commitment to the South and its way of life had caused him to break with his Northern abolitionist-influenced brethren. He would preach an acceptable Gospel. The one positive result of this was that, as the masters came to trust the ministers and the Mission to the Slaves, some of their own hearts were touched. And overall, the physical conditions of the slaves actually began to improve. Some Southern States even went so far as to amend the slave codes to establish minimum standards for the treatment of slaves.[47]

A few modern historians have claimed the improvement occurred because owners finally woke up to the fact that it simply made good economic sense to take care of one's property. But the authors believe that God was indeed touching the hearts that were open to Him, and that more planters' hearts were opened in the final thrust of the Mission movement.

As an attempt to Christianize the institution of slavery, the Mission to the Slaves failed, because hardly any masters attempted to turn their plantations into Christian communities. C. C. Jones had hopefully claimed in 1845: "There is a turning of the minds of men to this work and duty all over our country!"[48] But the final word on the Mission's actual effectiveness must fall to his wife, Mary. Seven years later she wrote to their son that his father's labors "were but poorly appreciated at the time by the owners themselves. The reward of the good man must ever come from above."[49]

As historian Charles Grier Sellers Jr. put it: "The American experience knows no greater tragedy than the Old South's twistings and turnings on the rack of slavery." Obviously the blacks in bondage endured by far the greatest suffering. Yet it was the white men of the Old South who "drove toward catastrophe by doing conscious violence to their truest selves." As for those historians who would cast the Civil War as a conflict between "two civilizations," "no analysis that misses the inner turmoil of the antebellum Southerner can do justice to the central tragedy of the Southern experience."[50]

As the crisis deepened, one New Orleans editor wrote: "The South has been moved to resistance chiefly . . . by the popular dogma in the free States that slavery is a crime in the sight of God. The South, in the eyes of the North, is degraded and unworthy, because of the institution of servitude."[51]

But in the sight of God, slavery had never been part of His plan for America. It could not stay indefinitely, and now events began their inexorable march toward the only other means of abolishing it.

A few farsighted patriots could see the inevitable end, and it greatly saddened them. At times they must have felt as if they were caught in a Greek tragedy, where everyone knew the outcome, yet kept desperately striving to avert it. Something desperate did seem to be on the verge of happening—but it was not the end that the Southern fire-eaters were hoping for. America had not lost her noble spirit. She still had a few great statesmen, and now they would play one last scene before exiting the stage.

29

THE GRAND OLD GUARD

*F*or 13 days at the end of 1849, the machinery of Government stood paralyzed while the 229 members of the House of Representatives wrangled over who would be their next Speaker. With 112 seats, the Democrats had only seven more than the Whigs, and neither party was about to let the 12 Free-Soilers play kingmaker. But the two major parties were themselves split along regional lines, and with each passing day the rift widened. Physically and emotionally spent, they fumed and fulminated through ten ballots . . . twenty . . . thirty. . . .

Not that they were that anxious to get on with the nation's business—tempers were at the boiling point from long and fruitless debate over California's application for statehood. President Taylor proposed to bring her in as a free state, according to her Territorial constitution. Southerners argued that would be *de facto* acceptance of the detested Wilmot Proviso, banning the further extension of slavery. Congressman Clingman of North Carolina exclaimed that any men of the South who would "consent to be thus degraded and enslaved, ought to be whipped through their fields by their own Negroes."[1]

Southerners were once again alluding to leaving the Union by force, if not allowed to leave peacefully. Alexander Stephens of Georgia, though at heart a Unionist, nonetheless called on his fellow Southerners to resist "the dictation of Northern hordes of Goths and Vandals" and suggested that Southern states should be "making the necessary preparations of men and money, arms and munitions . . . to meet the emergency."[2]

Particularly galling to Southerners was their growing perception that the South was being deliberately "degraded into inequality," as John Lamar of Georgia put it. That the North no longer regarded them as moral equals was apparent, and it cut their pride to the quick. John C. Calhoun had spoken for all of them when he declared: "I would rather meet any extremity on earth than give up one inch of our equality. . . . What, acknowledge inferiority? The surrender of life is nothing to sinking down into acknowledged inferiority!"[3]

Calhoun had called for a Southern convention and a Southern ultimatum. Mississippi, whose population of 600,000 was more than half black, had picked up on that, proposing such a convention be held in Nashville the following June. Though unstated, its purpose would be obvious: to discuss the South's secession from the United States of America.

Meanwhile, the wrangling and the balloting continued, through forty ballots . . . fifty. . . .

On the evening of December 13, Ohio's Joshua Giddings penned a letter to his son recapping some of the day's exchanges. Mead of Virginia made an excited speech favoring disunion. He was promptly ridiculed by Root of Ohio. Other disunionist speeches followed, with the tempers of all members steadily rising. When Duer of New York accused Mead of being a disunionist, the latter hotly denied the charge. Duer immediately called him a liar, whereupon shouts of "Shoot him! Shoot him!" and "Where is your Bowie knife?" were heard.[4]

Finally, on the sixtieth ballot the Speaker's gavel passed to Howell Cobb of Georgia.

Watching from the entry, Henry Clay, back in Washington as one of Kentucky's two Senators, was alarmed. To be sure, Southerners had always talked of leaving the Union. Thirty years ago, the fathers and grandfathers of these gentlemen of the South had threatened to fight their way out, if necessary. Back then, he had been able to craft a compromise and avert disaster. Men had called it a stroke of genius and had credited him with saving the Union. But his Missouri Compromise had not resolved the contest over slavery; he had only put it to sleep for a while.

Henry Clay, perhaps more than any political leader in America (with the exception of Calhoun), had wanted to be President. He was perennially one of the most popular figures in America, but unfortunately he belonged to a party intoxicated with war heroes, first Old Tippecanoe and now Old Rough and Ready.

Had he been a lesser man, he might have sequestered himself on his beloved estate, Ashland, and spent the sunset chapter of his life fighting old battles and ruminating on the injustices life had dealt him. But Henry Clay came from a nobler breed. And like his onetime adversary and finally dear friend John Quincy Adams, he would give his country his greatest service at the end of his life. His ardor for the Union was certainly undiminished; if anything, it burned purer and brighter. And now, watching these Congressmen physically threaten one another, he had never felt such a grave concern for the future of the Republic.

Until this last return to Washington, he had discounted the imprecations of both the Southern fire-eaters and the Northern abolitionists. But he sensed a mean-spiritedness and vindictiveness here that had not been present before. These men regarded each other as sworn enemies. They would not greet one another or exchange cordial pleasantries in the Capitol cloakrooms, much less raise a glass to one another at a party or a reception. In fact, hostesses had to exercise extreme care as they prepared their guest lists; more than one dinner had been ruined by two men flaring up and continuing a scalding dispute that in earlier years would have been left on the Hill.

While they still referred to one another as gentlemen, they were gracious only among those whose opinions they shared. That saddened Clay, for he was of an era whose champions on opposite sides of issues never lost their respect for one another, and were sometimes even friends.

What concerned Clay most was that the voices of moderation had fallen silent. Where were the men of reason and compromise? Where were the patriots? Where were the older and wiser heads who could still put the national interest ahead of selfish interests and still hold the vision that the founding generation had unfurled?

These moderates had grown weary of being insolently rebuffed and shouted down. Many now despaired of ever restoring tolerance or consideration of others' views. And the truth was, Clay realized, that the moderates on both sides—the influential editors and opinion makers, as well as these politicians—did not fully appreciate how determined were the extremists on the other side. Northern moderates had not grasped how many influential Southerners really *did* want the South to secede, and the sooner the better. Calhoun was not bluffing; come summer, he wanted every Southern state to send delegates to the Nashville convention.

And Southern moderates who were still pro-Union did not realize how many abolitionists would be just as happy to see the South leave; in fact, the sooner the better. Newspaper editor Francis Blair wrote of a "Free Democracy standing aloof," while the Cleveland *Plain Dealer* insisted that "rather than see slavery extended one inch beyond its present limits, we would see this Union rent asunder!"[5] Edward Everett, former Governor of Massachusetts and current President of Harvard, considered the parting inevitable and hoped it could be peaceful. He pleaded that it be brought about in a friendly spirit, "like reasonable men."[6]

The brawl over the Wilmot Proviso revealed how far the chasm had widened. If the Proviso ever got through the Senate, "then indeed the day of compromise will have passed," said the Governor of Virginia, "and the dissolution of our great and glorious Union will become necessary and inevitable."[7] The Sumter (South Carolina) *Banner* went further; if the Proviso passed, it called for the "secession of the slaveholding states in a body from the Union and their formation into a separate republic."[8]

In the North, jaws were similarly hardening. Salmon Chase of Ohio, speaking for his antislavery colleagues, declared that "no menace of disunion . . . no intimations of the probability of disunion in any form, will move us from the path which in our judgment it is due to ourselves and the people whom we represent to pursue."[9]

As depressing as such declarations were to Henry Clay, they caused John C. Calhoun to rejoice that "the alienation between the two sections [had] . . . already gone too far to save the Union."[10] Assessing the mood of the House, he wrote: "The Southern members are more determined and bold than ever I saw them. Many avow themselves to be disunionists, and a still greater number admit that there is little hope of any remedy short of it."[11]

But not every Southerner facing the likelihood of secession was rejoicing. Many, like Robert Toombs of Georgia, viewed it with deep sorrow and reluctance: He addressed the Speaker,

> Sir, I have as much attachment to the Union of these States under the Constitution of our fathers, as any freeman ought to have. I am ready to concede and sacrifice for it whatever a just and honorable man ought to sacrifice . . . [but] I do not . . . hesitate to avow before this House and the country and in the presence of the living God, that if by your legislation you seek to drive us from the territories of California and New Mexico . . . and to abolish slavery in this District [of Columbia], thereby attempting

to fix a national degradation upon half the States of this Confederacy, *I am for disunion*; and if my physical courage be equal to the maintenance of my convictions of right and duty, I will devote all I am and all I have on earth to its consummation.[12]

It fell to Clay to see perhaps more clearly than anyone just how close the South was to actual secession—and it deeply troubled him. Once before, with his rare gift for appealing to reason and men's better natures, with his candor and disarming sense of humor, he had rescued the Republic. Could he do so again? Would Congress even listen?

His discernment of the heart of the country told him that despite the incendiary rhetoric, many more Americans wanted to stay together than to separate. He was old now, almost 73, and bone weary. Yet he might have one great effort left.

He would have to surpass himself. He would have to arouse the moderates from their somnolence. And he would have to act quickly; a few more sessions like today's, and there would not be enough moderates left to achieve a consensus.

But first, he would have to secure the support of the one man whose influence was as great as his own—the man who had been his rival for party leadership for more than a quarter of a century. He knew that Daniel Webster did not care for him personally, though the senior Senator from Massachusetts had been magnanimous enough to support him, even taking the stump on his behalf, when he was running against Polk in '44.[13] Now he had to go to Webster in humility and for the sake of the Union, to ask for his help.

And so, despite a serious cough, Henry Clay went out in a snowstorm on the night of January 21, to call on Daniel Webster. Webster welcomed him warmly and soon recognized that while neither of them could do it alone, by working together they might be able to save the Union.

The two men conferred for more than an hour as Clay outlined his plan: In eight days he would go before the Senate and propose a bill that would address *all* the major issues then in contention, from California's status as she entered the Union to the need for a new fugitive slave law. On that occasion he would merely present his proposal, keeping his remarks brief and giving Congress a week to mull it over. Then he would return to defend the resolutions, asking from each side a little more than they were prepared to give—a little more, in fact, than they might be comfortable in giving. On balance, he would ask a little more from the North than from the South, so that the South could never claim that he preferred the North.

Such an "omnibus" of a bill had never been attempted before; it might be just big enough to shake the Senate—and the country—out of its rut, at least long enough to give its contents fresh consideration.

Webster concurred. But what of their friend from Charleston? Surely Calhoun would not let such a bill go unchallenged.

Clay estimated that it would take Calhoun three or four weeks to prepare a rebuttal. And when he delivered it, hearts that had softened would soon reharden.

But there was an antidote: Suppose Webster were to have a major speech in support of Clay's bill ready and waiting, with printed copies available for distribution to the newspapers. . . . Then shortly but not immediately after Calhoun's speech—say, three days, to avoid the appearance of collusion—Webster would stand and deliver. With his speech following so soon after Calhoun's, it would more than offset whatever impact the former might have.

Webster agreed, and Clay promised to give him a draft of his resolutions as soon as he had them ready. The two shook hands on it.

The Senate in 1850 was basically a small if ornate room, with lush red carpeting and purple hangings. In a word, it was *dignified*—a proper setting for the 60 Senators who occupied it. Dressed in black long-coats and never seen outside without their tall, black silk hats, they peered through eyeglasses suspended on long black ribbons and frequently consulted gold pocket watches kept in waistcoat pockets, from which extended watch fobs on gold chains. For writing notes or signing documents, they used quill pens, carefully sanding their ink and blotting it. They were, in sum, as dignified as their surroundings—not like that rowdy bunch over in the House of Representatives.

On Tuesday, January 29, the visitors' gallery and all the anterooms were packed. Word was out that Henry Clay was about to make a major speech—one that just might have a solution for the nation's woes. Anyone who had any influence with anyone who could find them a seat in the gallery, used it. The heat from so many bodies packed into that chamber sent the mercury climbing—clear up to 100 degrees.[14]

When Clay got to his feet, "not a sound above a breath could be heard."[15] Like the others, he was dressed in black, with a starched white shirtfront and black bow tie with trailing ends. He was still tall, still bright eyed as he looked around the room. But he was tired, his cheeks were gaunt, and there was no extra flesh on his frame.

As he began to speak, people relaxed and smiled: His voice was still dipped in silver. "I hold in my hand a series of resolutions which I desire to submit to the consideration of this body. Taken together in combination, they propose an amicable arrangement of all questions in controversy between the free and slave states, growing out of the subject of slavery."[16]

He then held up another object: a fragment that someone had given him from the coffin of George Washington. "The venerated Father of his Country" was warning Congress from Mount Vernon to "pause and reflect" before destroying the Union he had done so much to create. "I now ask every Senator . . . in fairness and candor . . . to examine the plan of accommodation which this series of resolutions proposes, and not to pronounce against them until convinced after a thorough examination."[17]

Henry Clay was the soul of moderation and fairness as he proceeded to enumerate the resolutions: California would be admitted as a state without Congressional action on the matter of slavery. In other words, the constitution of that Territory's inhabitants, which declared California to be free soil, would be allowed to stand. It was a little irregular, but—

Jefferson Davis of Mississippi interrupted to protest that he, for one, would never accept the exclusion of slavery anywhere below the line of 36°30', which the Missouri Compromise stipulated. There were murmurs of concurrence among the Southern Senators, but Clay refused to be drawn into debate.

Concerning the remaining Territories acquired from Mexico, he went on, as slavery was unlikely to be introduced in them anyway, Territorial governments would be set up without provision either for its inclusion or exclusion. While some Southern Senators were on principle displeased that slavery should be restricted anywhere, others acknowledged that the land was unsuited for the labor-intensive agriculture that required slavery.

The extravagant western boundary claims of the State of Texas, some of which encompassed half the New Mexico Territory, would be reined in. But the Federal Government would assume the former Lone Star Republic's outstanding debts.

He came now to the question of slavery in the District of Columbia. Abolitionists and fire-eaters leaned forward; there had been threats of secession if it were abolished. Clay did not go that far. There would henceforth be no more trading in slaves, which meant no more slaveblock auctions, no more slave pens, and no more chained coffles driven past the steps of the Capitol. But slavery itself would continue to be allowed there, as long as it was in the adjacent State of Maryland, or until the people of Washington and Maryland should accept compensation for their slaves. In other words, slaves could be brought into the District, but not for the purpose of resale.

Clay had saved the most volatile issue for last: the need for a new fugitive slave law. The old one was a travesty, honored more in the breech than in the execution. A number of Northern states had even passed their own laws saying that it was illegal for former slaves to be forcibly returned to their masters. A new and more effective fugitive slave law would be passed, and the principle that Congress had no jurisdiction over the interstate slave trade would be formally recognized. At this there were smiles of satisfaction on Southern faces, and looks of consternation on Northern ones. But a number of discerning members from the North saw that if they could swallow this last, there might actually be a chance for compromise.

Those sentiments were reflected in the nation, as the resolutions were disseminated far and wide. Clay had done a masterful job. As Webster commented to a friend: "I never listened to him with so much admiration and wonder, as on that occasion. He is a very great man, there is no mistake about that; he is a wonderful man!"[18]

As Clay had anticipated, the hotheads responded instantly and predictably. But among the moderates, he could feel a consensus building.

A week later, when the Senate's doors opened in the morning, newspaper reporters were waiting to get inside, and with them some of society's most elegant ladies. Great oratory was the premier attraction for spectators of refinement, and Henry Clay was one of the greatest. Today, as he spoke on behalf of his resolutions, they would be present at an occasion that they would one day recall for their grandchildren.

An hour before he was due to speak, a large crowd had assembled outside the chamber, sensing perhaps that what might well be Clay's last endeavor might also be his finest.

Doubts about his health were confirmed when he appeared, assisted by the Chaplain of the Senate. Slowly he climbed the Capitol steps, pausing frequently to cough and catch his breath. Friends had offered to call for adjournment, but nothing would sway him from his course.[19]

When at last he was in his seat and then arose to address the Senate, he was greeted by applause from all present—and a great, muffled roar from the crowd outside.

Appealing to down-to-earth common sense, he went over each point, warning them in conclusion of the civil cataclysm that would surely be brought on by secession if no compromise was reached. "I conjure gentlemen . . . solemnly to pause . . . at the edge of the precipice, before the fearful and disastrous leap is taken into the yawning abyss below," and he raised his eyes heavenward, and asked that if dissolution should indeed occur, he should not survive to behold it.[20]

When he finished, for the first time in months men inside the Senate—and then beyond it, as the nation devoured his words—actually began to hope that the crisis might yet be averted.

He was attacked, as he knew he would be, by hip shooters on both sides. But he was also supported, and from quarters he had not expected. Sam Houston, Senator from Texas, was one. Thomas Ritchie, editor of the Washington *Union,* was another. He called on Clay at the old National Hotel, and when he got Clay to agree that the people in the remaining Territories should be allowed to decide for themselves about slavery, the *Union* came out in favor of the Compromise, and thereafter fought for it.

One quarter from which he had *not* expected to be attacked was the White House. Clay was doing all he could to save the Union, and the President was known to be a staunch Unionist. But Taylor was jealous of Clay, especially now that the latter seemed to be providing genuine leadership, and the American people seemed to be responding. So Taylor became an obstructionist. And his attitude was stiffening resistance in others, even as Clay's was softening it.

Regardless of who said what, as America absorbed what Clay had proposed, his Omnibus Bill seemed to take on a life of its own. Like grass turning green after rain had broken a long drought, hope was reemerging, where there had been only despair.

All eyes now turned to Calhoun. A few weeks shy of 68, he was the same age as Webster, a little younger than Clay. But the years had not been kind to him. His health was failing rapidly; three times during the previous session he had fainted in the Senate lobby. It was obvious to him, as it was to everyone else, that he had little time left. Yet his resolve was still firm, his self-control still absolute, and his intellect still acute. When he spoke, every word was heard from the Atlantic to the Rio Grande.

His admired and admiring colleague, Daniel Webster, when asked who was the greatest among them, said without hesitation: "John C. Calhoun . . . a man of extraordinary power! Much the ablest man in the Senate."[21] As long as Calhoun was able, the South would have no other speak for her. He had worn her colors and been her champion for all these years; now she would ask him to rise one more time to defend her honor.

Four weeks after Henry Clay defended his proposals, John C. Calhoun was ready to respond. On Monday, March 4, he entered the chamber slowly, supported by Senator James Mason of Virginia and his old friend John Hamilton. At his entrance, some of the women gasped, for Calhoun, tall and brooding, was a spectral presence. His cheeks were hollow and the eye sockets sunken, almost cadaverous, but in them the eyes still glinted, still had the power to hold any on whose gaze they fell in their thrall.

All were hushed, sensing a moment historians would write about in future generations. Calhoun was too weak to deliver the speech himself; gently his friends lowered him into his seat, and he listened for the next hour and a half, as Mason read the points he had so laboriously drafted.

When Clay had spoken here a month before, the mood he evoked had been genial, even conciliatory. Harry of the West had appealed to the nobility of spirit in all men, granting the South more than any Northerner would have, and prevailing on the North to see the situation from the Southern point of view. In the face of such evenhandedness, men had been inclined to be charitable. Even traces of the old cordial collegiality reappeared, as reasonable men began to believe they might yet find a way out of this quagmire.

But now, as Mason read the cold, diamond-hard words of the South's great intellect, the mood changed. For Calhoun was not really responding to Clay's proposals, nor was he appealing to moderate sensibilities. He was, instead, rehearsing all the South's old grievances. And the tone of his message was violent and extreme. Expressions became solemn. In the heavy quiet, one could almost hear the crackle of ice forming.

Calhoun began by claiming that the Federal Government was "as absolute as that of the autocrat of Russia, and as despotic in its tendency as any absolute government that ever existed." The North, which received more than its share of customs duties, was investing them in industry that was creating more capital, which was attracting more immigrants, which was leading to more Northern representation in Congress and eventually to more Northern states. The South was being overpowered.

Secondly, the Union was being endangered by the North because of the North's incessant attacks on slavery and its efforts to abolish it. One had only to look at the splitting of the national religious denominations to see what lay in store for America.

Next, the rights of the states had been swept aside. This was a battle he had been waging ever since Andrew Jackson had faced him down, 19 years before. Now he was calling for redress—and more, much more.

He had saved his most explosive point for last. He now proposed nothing less than an amendment to the Constitution, calling for two Presidents and granting the South a concurrent majority by giving each state the right to veto any national legislation with which it disagreed.

The chamber sat in stunned silence.

To Calhoun it must have seemed right and reasonable. But what he was calling for would create nothing but utter chaos. Charles A. Dana of the New York *Tribune*, who was in the gallery, saw it that way, too: Calhoun was threatening to break up the Union if 6 million Southerners were not granted equal power with 14 million Northerners. Dana, who had never taken his eyes off Calhoun, noted: "Not a change passed over his face, not a movement betrayed any sense of the interest with which every Senator listened to his words. But with his eyes partly closed and head never wavering from its erect posture, he waited till the last word before he exchanged a glance with the friends around."[22]

When the speech was over, Southern moderates were of one mind: Calhoun had gone too far—way too far. The violence of his tone antagonized all of them. And his call for a Constitutional amendment was, well, ridiculous. Even the fire-eaters were beginning to feel that perhaps the Compromise with its new, tough fugitive slave law was going to benefit them more than Calhoun realized. And so they deserted him. Not one Southern Senator seconded his motion.

The reaction of the general population was of a similar vein. Wrote the New York diarist Philip Hone:

> The leader of the disunionists, the slaveholders' oracle, the daring repudiator, has made his speech. The gaping gossipers have "supped deep" on oratorical horrors. . . . If this manifesto is to be taken as the textbook of the South, all attempts at conciliation will be fruitless. It is a calm, dispassionate avowal that nothing short of absolute submission to the slaveholding States will be accepted.[23]

But by his very extremism, Calhoun had shown how important it was for reasonable men to reach a reasonable accord, before it was too late. His speech, intended to derail the Compromise, had done just the opposite—it had greatly improved its chances of passing.

30

"PEACE IN OUR TIME"

*G*od is no respecter of persons. And yet—He often seems to have a special final assignment for those who have given a lifetime of meritorious service to His work. We have seen the magnitude of the task He gave John Quincy Adams, at an age when most men would have long since retired. We saw the triumphal tour that so surprised JQA—God's way of saying *Well done, good and faithful servant.*

We have just seen Henry Clay and John C. Calhoun enjoy their final defining moments in the arena where they fought the most significant battles of their lives. Now, three days after Calhoun's time, the wheels of God's pocket watch turned farther and brought the last of the grand old guard into that special light of prominence.

Daniel Webster was America's finest speaker, admired not only for his delivery but for the close and careful reasoning of his mind. In the Webster/Hayne debate of 1830, Webster's defense of the Federal Union was regarded by connoisseurs of oratory as the finest speech ever given in the Senate, perhaps in America. Now, in anticipation of his assessment of the Omnibus Bill, all of Washington was trying to get into the gallery, or at least within earshot. They even crowded the halls and vestibules, waiting to hear what those with better access would pass on. The rest of America waited to read his response.

Inside the Senate Chamber, standing room went to Representatives and diplomats, while ladies in fine silks and bombazines occupied the first row of the gallery. Outdoors, the March weather might have been crisp, but there was no need for a fire in the Senate stove; body heat had made it sweltering.

Like Clay and Calhoun, Webster, too, was deeply tired. He had been seriously ill for some time, yet his mind, like theirs, could not rest. Plagued by insomnia, he had gotten even less sleep than usual since Clay's nocturnal visit. As he rose to his feet to speak, he mopped his brow; he was sweating profusely—not so much from the heat as from the effects of his lingering fever.

Like Clay and Calhoun, his glory days were behind him, but they were not forgotten—not by his friends, and not by the nation. No description of him surpassed Henry Hilliard's of Alabama:

> He recalled to me the idea of classic grandeur; there was in him a blended dignity and power. . . . It seemed as if the whole weight of the government might rest squarely on his broad shoulders. His large, dark eyes were full of expression, even in repose; the cheeks were square and strong; his dark hair and swarthy complexion heightened the impression of strength. . . . There was in his appearance something leonine.[1]

Webster had even impressed the renowned Scottish historian Thomas Carlyle, who wrote to Ralph Waldo Emerson: "Not many days ago I saw at breakfast the notablest of all your notables, Daniel Webster. He is a magnificent specimen. . . . The tanned complexion, that amorphous crag-like face, the dull black eyes under the precipice of brows like dull anthracite furnaces needing only to be blown, the mastiff mouth, accurately closed . . ."[2]

The dark hair was mostly gone, but the eyes still burned with a fierce intensity. He was ready now, and universally regarded as the only man qualified to follow Calhoun. If this was to be his last major speech, he was determined that it would also be his best.

"Mr. President, I wish to speak today, not as a Massachusetts man, not as a Northern man, but as an American. . . . I speak today for the preservation of the Union. 'Hear me for my cause.'"[3]

There was a rustle, and all eyes turned to the entrance to the Senate Chamber. There, a tall, gaunt form in a long black cloak and flowing white hair appeared and was helped to his desk, where he sank into his seat. It was John C. Calhoun, come to hear the Senator whom he admired and respected more than any other. It took all of Calhoun's indomitable strength of will, but he would be nowhere else.

Webster had earlier visited him and invited him to hear the reply. Calhoun was touched, he said, but feared he was on his deathbed. Yet he had made this supreme effort and was here. (In 11 more days he would once more be in this chamber—lying in state.)

Webster did not see him at first, and even lamented the absence of "the distinguished and venerable Senator from South Carolina."[4] Then Calhoun made his presence known, and Webster nodded to him, touched by how much it had cost Calhoun.

The old orator's voice grew stronger as he spoke, and he was able to carry on for more than three hours, never once looking at his notes. First, he dealt with the history of slavery, deliberately doing so from a narrow, economic perspective, knowing that the moment he diverged into the morality of it, all willingness on the part of his listeners to suspend personal feelings would be lost.

He pointed out that at the beginning of this century, the South had been more critical of slavery than the North. Then the North, finding it unprofitable, began to denounce it, while the South, profiting from it, began to defend it and demand its extension. But the status of every foot of the continent had already been determined. All land north of 36°30′ was free; all land south of it was slave. That had already been established by the Missouri Compromise. All land ceded by Texas was slave, and all land taken from Mexico was, by its very nature, free—so why "re-enact the will of God?"

To Southern Senators, he repeated the North's objection that "instead of slavery being regarded as an evil, as it was [in the days of their fathers]— an evil which would be extinguished gradually—it is now regarded as an institution to be cherished, and preserved, and extended."[5]

Then he turned to his Northern colleagues, specifically to those who had been urging adoption of the Wilmot Proviso: Why wound the pride of Southerners by a wanton denial of equal privileges, "derogatory to their character and their rights?"[6]

Clay, in the content and tenor of his speech, had extended an olive branch to the South; now Webster, continuing in this frank and candid mode, did the same. He agreed that the South had just complaint about the North's having hindered compliance with the existing fugitive slave law, and that counterlegislation of certain Northern states (his own among them) had made the passage of a new law imperative. Furthermore, he felt the South was justified in its resentment of "infernal fanatics and abolitionists."[7]

But the North also had cause for complaint: The Southern attempt to introduce slavery into the Territories was unwise, unwarranted, and a rejection of the long-term understanding that it would be restricted to where it already existed. And the North was justified in its resentment of Southern claims that the North was exercising wage slavery, and that Northern laborers were worse off than Southern slaves.

As Webster demonstrated impartial sympathy to both sides on each point in the Omnibus Bill, it became clear to many that there were *two* messages being delivered. One was directed to the minds of the listeners; the other was to their hearts. For here was the heart of a man who loved his country, appealing to other hearts to follow its example.

Webster began his conclusion with a passionate plea for the Union. *Peaceful* secession? Impossible! Too many social, economic, cultural, and domestic ties bound the two sections together; civil war could be the only result. "Sir," he exclaimed, referring to the new Southern concept of peaceful secession, "your eyes and mine are never destined to see that miracle—the dismemberment of this vast country without convulsion! The breaking up of the fountains of the great deep without ruffling the surface! Who is so foolish . . . as to expect any such thing?"

He ended with this challenge: "Never did there devolve, on any generation of men, higher trusts than now devolve upon us for the preservation of this Constitution, and the harmony and peace of all who are destined to live under it. Let us make our generation one of the strongest, and the brightest link in that golden chain which is destined, I fully believe, to grapple the people of all the States to this Constitution for ages to come!"[8]

He sat down—and received an ovation that seemed to go on forever. And as it did, it gradually became apparent to all that the applause was expressing hope for America's future.

The extremists on both sides, of course, could see it only their way. And so, Webster's constituents in Massachusetts, because he indicated that he would favor a new fugitive slave law, attacked their own senior Senator. Much of the New England intelligentsia, including poets and essayists Emerson, Thoreau, Longfellow, Garrison, and Whittier, condemned him as a turncoat. One called him Benedict Arnold; another likened him to

"Lucifer descending from heaven."[9] Nor had Horace Greeley, editor of the New York *Tribune,* any use for him.

Webster had anticipated this; it was a price he was prepared to pay for the sake of the Union. But it still hurt.

Elsewhere, however, men of reason who had long remained silent now expressed their gratitude. The *National Intelligencer* came out in support of him, as did Edward Everett of Harvard, and a surprising number of Northern clergy.

In the South, what most men of influence responded to was his tone of conciliation. Said Calhoun appreciatively: Mr. Webster "shows a yielding on the part of the North," and the Charleston *Mercury* went so far as to say that "with a spirit such as Mr. Webster has shown, it no longer seems impossible to bring this sectional contest to a close."[10]

As for the ordinary people, Clay and Webster had correctly discerned the tenor of the nation: The overwhelming response was one of relief. At last someone had said what needed to be said without name-calling or mudslinging, and had put things into perspective; now maybe those men in Washington could start acting like grown-ups and get something done! In this new spirit of cooperation, that was exactly what was beginning to transpire.

Allan Nevins put Webster's appeal into historical perspective: "No speech more patriotic or evincing a higher degree of moral courage had ever been made in Congress." Webster had risen to the highest level of statesmanship, with but one motive: love of the Union, fear for the Union, ambition to save the Union.[11]

By the end of March, more than 120,000 copies of his speech had been circulated, and in Nevins' estimation "beyond question, the Seventh of March Speech marked the great turning-point in the history of the compromise."[12]

In its wake, disunion sentiment subsided. Clay had shown the way out of the impasse, but it was Webster who had reminded the people that they were Americans first. More than any other man, Daniel Webster had been responsible for the perpetuation of the Founding Fathers' original vision: that the Union was a sacred trust. More than any other, he had implanted in the minds of Americans that that trust must remain inviolate.

The speech over, an equally daunting challenge now faced Webster. He must, as it were, put his money where his mouth was. He must *support* the new fugitive slave law. If he did, he would lose many lifelong friends. If he did not, any hope of compromise would be lost. For without his prestige behind it, the North would never support such a law. And if the Compromise was lost, so was the Union.

Personally Webster believed that slavery was both a moral and a political evil. He felt it was destined for extinction in America, as everywhere else, and had only been granted a temporary reprieve because of cotton. For the sake of the Union, then,* he was willing to make *temporary* concessions. His decision guaranteed eventual passage of the resolutions in the Omnibus Bill.

Four days after Webster's speech, another Senator rose to speak on the bill, William Seward of New York. Because he was known to be an avowed abolitionist, almost no one, including the Senate's members, was present to hear him. Nonetheless, he spoke for the "conscience Whigs" of his party—and for the conscience of America.

Compromises, he proclaimed, meant the surrender of the exercise of judgment and conscience. Stating that each of Clay's resolutions should be considered on its own merit, he attacked Calhoun's proposals: Sections had no unique standing in the Government of the United States, and no rights or favors should be granted to any one section. He said that slavery was out-and-out sin, and Americans could not claim to be freemen, if they gave in to it.

Then he came to the heart of his message, and the reason why this speech would be remembered: Every just human law was a reenactment of the law of God. A new fugitive slave bill would be "unjust, unconstitutional, and immoral." And if the Constitution recognized men as property, then there was a higher law than the Constitution. Human law "must be brought to the standard of the law of God . . . and must stand or fall by it."[13] Similarly, the Territories, entrusted to men by their Creator, were meant to be regulated in accordance with that higher law.[14]

Seward's doctrine of the higher law infuriated practically everyone who read it. The South was apoplectic. "Monstrous and diabolical" cried the Columbia, South Carolina, *Telescope*.

"I will not be on good terms with those who wish to cut my throat!" exclaimed Calhoun.

Even the President, whose close advisor Seward had been until the

---

* the same reason that had motivated the framers of the Constitution in 1787

335

speech, moved quickly to distance himself. "The speech must be disclaimed at once, authoritatively and decisively," Taylor sputtered to the editor of the *Republic*. And so it was. Seward was ridiculed as one who proclaimed that he held his credential from Almighty God, authorizing him to reject all human enactment.[15]

But the concept that God's higher law must take precedence did not fade away. Abolitionists embraced it and reprinted Seward's speech, and gradually the concept took on quiet but growing force.

On March 31, John C. Calhoun died. His passing was universally mourned in the South, though there were many Southerners who were privately relieved. For the old leader had lost touch with the times. The South he loved was the South of a generation before, and the South had changed since then. Yet he alone had the stature and commanded the respect to unite and rally the splintered factions of the South. And perhaps for that reason, the timing of his departure was providential; for the immediate future, at least, there would be no single strong voice urging secession, no towering giant around which to rally.

Clay's Omnibus Bill was referred to committee for further study, where it languished for several weeks. But time was working in its favor; with Calhoun dead, Southern newspapers, which had been crying for secession a year before, now came out in favor of the Compromise. The groundswell was building: Without Calhoun to beat the drum for it, the June Nashville convention fizzled.

Now, of all people, the chief opponent of the Compromise was the President! Like Webster, Taylor was a Unionist, but his jealousy of Clay had clouded his vision. Plus, there was an ominous new wrinkle on the horizon: Texas was now claiming so much of New Mexico that Albuquerque, Santa Fe, and Las Vegas would all be within her borders.

Concerning the New Mexico Territory, Taylor had urged the people of that Territory to follow California's lead: They should form a constitution and apply for statehood. Accordingly, Colonel John Munroe, Territorial Governor and commander of the U.S. forces there, called a constitutional convention. Sitting in May, it voted, among other things, to exclude slavery, and within a month the people in the Territory had ratified it.

Taylor's idea was to get New Mexico into the Union; once it was as state, the boundary issue could be sorted out by the Supreme Court. New Mexico in the meantime was to include the district of Santa Fe.

But that was not the way the Texans saw it. Forthwith, they sent a commissioner with full powers to take over Santa Fe. The only problem was, the people of Santa Fe did not *want* to be amalgamated into the great State of Texas. With Colonel Munroe's quiet approval, they sent the commissioner back.

Texas responded in typical fashion, calling for volunteers to settle the matter with their Walker Colts. And since many preferred fighting to farming, as soon as the word went out, half the men of Texas were ready to do battle. And when the word went farther, so were half the men of the Deep South.

To make it official, the militant Governor of Texas, Peter H. Bell, asked his legislature to authorize sending a force to Santa Fe large enough to implement Texas laws, saying that if a collision did take place with Colonel Munroe's troops, it would be the fault of the United States. Mississippi's Governor, John A. Quitman, promised Governor Bell that in the event of a clash of arms, he would send 5,000 picked men.[16] And the hero of San Jacinto, Texas Senator Sam Houston, got ready to leave the capital and hurry home as quickly as horse could carry him, to lead the Texas troops into battle.

On the other side, Colonel Munroe, a seasoned professional with distinguished service in Mexico and on the western frontier, was armed with the expressed intent of his Commander in Chief. Though he might be vastly outnumbered, he would never back down.

Taylor was furious. He told Congress what Texas was planning, and of his own conviction that the Federal Government should remain in control of the Territory until the boundary question could be adjudicated. He sent an order to Colonel Munroe to resist by force any attempt of Texas to exercise jurisdiction over Santa Fe. And if that were not enough, a dispatch arrived from St. Louis on June 25 to ratchet up the tension several notches more: New Mexico's newly ratified constitution was on its way to Washington.

Southern Whigs were horrified at their President's recalcitrance. On July 3, Georgia Congressmen Robert Toombs and Alexander Stephens paid a call on Taylor to advise him how strongly his party disapproved of his present course. Enraged, Taylor refused to budge an inch. California must come into the Union at once, he told them, and the moment New Mexico's constitution reached him, he would insist on her admission as well! And if that meant he had to sacrifice one wing of the Whigs for the other, then he would not give up the 84 members from the North for the 29 members from the South!

Enraged, Toombs and Stephens rode away from the White House, and later that day Stephens would write to the *National Intelligencer*: "The first Federal gun that shall be fired against the people of Texas, without the authority of law, will be the signal for the freemen from the Delaware to the Rio Grande to rally to the rescue!"

Stephens was still seething when he and Toombs encountered Secretary of the Navy William Preston. "If troops are ordered to Santa Fe," he exploded, "the President will be impeached!"

"Who will impeach him?" asked Preston.

"I will," shouted Stephens, "if no one else does!"[17]

But his wrath was no greater than that of the President himself. When Thurlow Weed, editor of the Albany *Journal* and influential Whig leader, arrived at the Oval Office soon after Toombs and Stephens had exited, Taylor shouted: "Did you meet those traitors?"

He then proceeded to fill Weed in on what just transpired. When he had told them that, regarding New Mexico, he would approve any constitutional bill that Congress might pass, they had threatened a dissolution of the Union. "I told them," thundered Taylor, "that if it becomes necessary, I will take command of the army myself to enforce the laws! And I said that if you men are taken in rebellion against the Union, I will hang you with less reluctance than I hanged spies and deserters in Mexico!"[18] (No wonder Toombs and Stephens were agitated!)

The next morning, the Fourth of July, Taylor began drafting an angry message to Congress, declaring that New Mexico had every right to U.S. protection from Texas, and vowing his personal determination to furnish it to the last extremity.

He had not quite finished when he was called away to a ceremonial function at the base of the new, as yet unfinished Washington Monument. He resented the interruption, but duty called; it was only appropriate that the twelfth President, a former general himself, should pay homage to the first.

It was a hot day, and though he already had a fever, he was required to stand in the broiling sun for an hour and a half. When the ceremonies were finally concluded, he went home, drank a vast quantity of ice water and milk, ate some cherries—and succumbed to an acute attack of gastroenteritis. Typhoid fever soon made the situation critical, and five days later the old soldier died.

Zachary Taylor had made a surprisingly competent President. Though he lacked Jackson's political skill or Polk's deftness at maneuvering, he had nonetheless brought to the office high moral character, and the American people appreciated his integrity, honesty, and courage—intangibles that added significant weight to the highest office in the land.

Since the authors believe that God did—and does—have a plan for America, it is not inappropriate to speculate what might have happened, had Zachary Taylor not died when he did. Had he lived one more day, he would have set in motion something that perhaps no one could have stopped. His belligerent message would have gone to Congress, where it would have had the effect of instantly hardening hearts along the regional divide. He would have pursued his quarrel with Toombs and Stephens, splitting the Whigs, and would have exacerbated the national split by insisting on bringing in New Mexico as a free state.

But it was the dispute with Texas that, more than anything else, would have caused the pot to boil over. In all likelihood, there would have been armed conflict in the southwest, which almost certainly would have drawn thousands of Southern volunteers into the fight on the side of Texas. And Taylor, perceiving the fate of the Union to be at stake, would not have backed down. As Daniel Webster observed to his friend Hilliard: "If General Taylor had lived, we should have had civil war."[19]

Had the Civil War begun then, the South would have won, and not just because they had a preponderance of the best generals (which they did). They would have won for the very reason that nations usually win wars: They would have possessed the greater resolve.

America won its War for Independence, first because it was God's will, and the Patriots' key leadership was seeking His will. But they also won it because they had the greater resolve. Against formidable odds, they hung on—long enough that Great Britain, preoccupied with containing Napoleon, finally lost her taste for continuing the war. When that war had begun, George III and his nobles were determined to hold on to their American Colonies and bring the rebels to heel at all costs. But after eight years, the cost had become more than they were prepared to keep on paying. America's resolve had finally won the day.

In 1850 the South's resolve would have coalesced and hardened to the point where the North would simply not have been prepared to pay the enormous price of keeping her in the Union. After two or three years of total warfare, the North would finally have let her leave and take her slaves with her.

A divided country was *not* God's plan for America. He knew that the North would need another 10 years before her resolve would be a match for the South's. Even then, the price for preserving the Union would come perilously close to being more than the North was willing to pay.

As Allan Nevins observed: "The clash of two civilizations was postponed until the North was relatively much stronger, and a far wiser leader sat in the White House."[20]

The President's funeral had a calming effect on the nation. From the moment Vice President Millard Fillmore was sworn in as President, he relied heavily on the counsel of Webster and Clay. Webster he named his Secretary of State, and Clay became the administration's chief spokesman. And when Clay made it apparent to the country that the new President favored the Compromise, hope for its passage revived.

But the Senate was still dragging its feet, with some Southern extremists threatening military resistance to any Northern measures forced down their throat. Finally, on August 1, Henry Clay vented his frustration with his learned and esteemed colleagues. "If any one State, or a portion of the people of any State, choose to place themselves in military array against the Government of the Union, I am for trying the strength of the Government!" It was time, he said, to find out "whether we have got a Government or not!"

And now he shouted at them: "Even if my own State, lawlessly, contrary to her duty, should raise the standard of disunion against the residue of the Union, I would go against her! I would go against Kentucky herself in that contingency, much as I love her!"[21]

Mentally, physically, and emotionally exhausted, fearing that his Compromise was doomed, Henry Clay left Washington and went to Newport, Rhode Island, to recover his health.

But the Compromise was not doomed. And a Democrat, not a Whig, would be its redeemer. Illinois Senator Stephen A. Douglas saw the way to make it happen: break the Omnibus Bill out into separate bills and then concentrate on getting each of them passed. This he did, and it worked.

A native Vermonter, Douglas had been active in the Democratic Party since moving to Illinois at the age of 20 in 1833. Ten years later he was elected to Congress as one of the youngest members in the history of the House of Representatives. A hard worker and a gifted orator, he was elected to the Senate three years later.

A contemporary provided this physical description: "Broad-shouldered and big-chested," with "a stout, strong neck . . . a square jaw and a broad chin . . . quick, piercing eyes . . . [long, dark hair] which, when in excitement, he shook and tossed about defiantly like a lion's mane . . . [he was] the very incarnation of forceful combativeness."[22] All of that was on a frame that measured only 5'4"—no wonder men called him "the Little Giant"!

Though Douglas' motivation was more political than patriotic, he got the job done. On August 9, the Texas boundary bill was passed. With the subsequent, not surprising approval of the Texas legislature, it fixed the borders of the Lone Star State where they are today (which granted Texas 33,333 square miles *more* than the Omnibus Bill had).

Four days later, California was granted statehood. It added two more Free-State members to the Senate, but ironically wound up benefiting the South more. The majority of Californians joined the Democratic party and were sympathetic to the South.

The next day, the New Mexico Bill was passed. Though New Mexico would not become a state until 1912, the bill decreed that the slave or free status of the New Mexico and Utah Territories would be decided by their inhabitants—a major popular sovereignty victory for Douglas.

It took another four weeks to pass the bill prohibiting the importation of slaves into the District of Columbia for resale. The bill did not abolish slavery there, but it did pave the way for the new fugitive slave law—the price the North would have to pay if they wanted to achieve the Compromise.

For many moderate Northerners, it was an exorbitant price, in that it seemed to legitimatize the South's claim that their slaves were property. And it would soon force many moderates off the fence; in fact, the new fugitive slave law would prove to be a moral watershed; after its passage, it would be impossible to remain neutral on the subject of slavery.

The new law was harsher than the old, and like it or not, it *was* constitutional. When the vote for it came, most Whigs abstained, and the Fugitive Slave Act was passed. The last of the resolutions (which collectively came to be known as the Compromise of 1850) was law.

Celebration broke out across America! Bonfires, parades, speeches, suppers, multigun salutes were everywhere, and exhilarated crowds shouted, "The Union is Saved!" It was no exaggeration. Looking back on that time from the vantage point of many years, Thurlow Weed would comment: "The country had every appearance of being on the eve of a revolution."[23]

But now the nation could breathe a sigh of relief; contrary to what so many had feared, there *would* be "peace in our time."* J. M. Foltz described the scene in the capital to James Buchanan: "Every face I meet is happy. All look upon the question as settled. . . . The successful are rejoicing, the neutrals have all joined the winning side, and the defeated are silent."[24]

Webster noted much the same thing: "The face of everything seems changed. You would suppose nobody had ever thought of disunion. All say they always meant to stand by the Union to the last."[25] And now at last he could get some rest. "I can now sleep of nights," he wrote to a friend. "We have now gone through the most important crisis that has occurred since the foundation of this government."[26]

After months of being caught in an ever mounting storm at sea, the calm was so welcome that everyone wanted to believe it was permanent. Fervently they assured one another that the Compromise of 1850 had resolved the slavery issue once and for all time.

But in reality, nothing had been resolved. As one Southern editor, Richard Harrison Shryock, would later observe: It was "the calm of preparation, and not of peace."[27]

For the South had accepted the Compromise with a codicil: "for now." Everything depended on whether the North would honor the new Fugitive Slave Act. The South adopted a "wait-and-see" attitude.

They did not have long to wait.

---

* As British Prime Minister Neville Chamberlain assured his greatly relieved nation upon returning from a conference with Hitler in 1938.

31

REACTIONS

*B*oston's Beacon Street boasted some of the most elegant town houses in America. Looking in from the sidewalk (if their drawing-room draperies were not closed), one might catch a glimpse of detailed molding, rich paneling, and fine portraiture. Almost every evening one or another would be ablaze with light as hostesses welcomed guests to an elegant dinner party or reception.

On one particular evening in the fall of 1850, however, one can imagine a gathering far from social. The arriving carriages gleaming in the street's gas lamps looked no different than on other evenings. But as their polished doors swung open, only men emerged. And judging from the solemn expressions they wore, they were looking forward to something other than gracious conversation and delectable food.

Had a seasoned newspaper reporter, familiar with who was who in Boston, happened to be strolling home along Beacon from quaffing a pint or two with friends after work, he might have been surprised at who was arriving. Had he lingered, he would have been astonished at how many subjects of front-page stories were entering at that door. Had he the brass to inquire as to the nature of their gathering, he would have been rebuffed—which would have intrigued him all the more.

For here might have come Charles Francis Adams, the former Vice-Presidential candidate of the Free-Soil Party two years before and the son of John Quincy Adams. And Theodore Parker, the most popular preacher in the city. And Charles Sumner, whom the Conscience Whigs wanted to see in the Senate. And Ralph Waldo Emerson, the famous essayist. And Wendell Phillips, the renowned antislavery spokesman. And Samuel Gridley Howe, founder of the Perkins School for the Blind. And

Richard Henry Dana, the outspoken attorney and journalist who had written *Two Years Before the Mast*.

The reason none would divulge the purpose of this evening was that they had come to discuss ways and means of violating Federal authority. This night they would, among other things, form a Vigilance Committee whose sole purpose was to thwart the new Fugitive Slave Act. Each member would be on the alert for any slaveholder or his agents arriving in Boston for the purpose of capturing free or escaped blacks and hauling them back into the hell of slavery. The moment they saw the same, they would immediately inform the others in the group, who would then do everything in their power to obstruct the slave hunters, while raising the alarm and gathering as sizable a crowd as possible.

For the first time in nearly a century, a group of Americans was espousing civil disobedience. Each man present could conceivably go to prison for what they were contemplating. Yet they saw it as the only honorable response to a dishonorable policy. In this very city their Patriot forefathers, calling themselves "Sons of Liberty" and having determined that resistance to tyranny was obedience to God, staged a "tea party" that encouraged similar acts by Patriots in the other Colonies. So great was their passion that in the subsequent War for Independence, Boston became known as the "cradle of freedom." Now its sons were living up to that heritage.

Increasingly they were being urged on in this course by their clergy. As Gilbert Haven preached in a sermon that was widely reprinted,

> When any human law is opposed to the evident decisions of divine law, those edicts are to be disobeyed, both in what they command us to do, and in what they command us to refrain from doing. . . . With God as our guide and inspirer, we should not hesitate to advance in the way that He marks out against such a stronghold of Satan. . . . We must suffer, if need be, the penalty of disobedience, rejoicing that we are counted worthy to endure such contradictions of sinners, and that Christ gives us strength sufficient for the high resolve.[1]

Other Northern ministers began to speak out in a similar vein, openly encouraging their flocks to disobey the law, and calling on them to heed the Lord's commandment in Deuteronomy: "Thou shalt not deliver unto his master the servant which is escaped from his master unto thee" (Deuteronomy 23:15). The struggle against slavery was beginning to take on the air of a holy crusade.

Gilbert Haven certainly cast it in those terms, and once a nonslaveholding Christian heard him, it was hard to see it otherwise. "God and Satan can have no pact or compromise. If you wish for the cause of God to prevail, you must enroll yourself among the active opponents of every institution and effort designed to support or extend the cause of sin, and labor earnestly and persistently for the righteous victory."

He challenged those who would passively observe or actively cooperate with the implementation of the new fugitive slave law: "If a human soul beats in your bosom, can you place the manacles on those bleeding hands? Can you allow him—through your vigilance in assisting in his arrest, or your negligence in affording him the means to escape—to be dragged back in chains to the lash, the block, the more than death, from which God and his strong will have rescued him?"[2]

In cities throughout the North, meetings were held to discuss specific ways that citizens could disobey the new law. After such a meeting in Syracuse, one abolitionist observed: "It would be almost certain death to a slaveholder to appear on his infernal mission in our streets."[3] In Chicago the City Council declared that the Fugitive Slave Act violated the Constitution and the higher laws of God, that Northern members of Congress who acquiesced in it should be ranked with Judas Iscariot and Benedict Arnold, and that citizens, police, and all other public officials should refuse to aid in its enforcement.[4]

Such meetings, however, often provoked strong counterfeelings; the great majority of the Northern clergy were for compliance with all civil law, including the Fugitive Slave Act. (Garrison supporter Samuel May estimated that of the 30,000 ministers of all denominations, fewer than 1 percent spoke out against the act.)[5] And at another mass meeting in Illinois, Senator Douglas condemned the Chicago council and called for the faithful execution of Federal law.[6]

Of course, things looked considerably rosier on Capitol Hill (then, as now, the politicians there were not always in the vanguard of where the people were heading). In Washington, the long-termers had already lived through years of soul-grinding contention over slavery and were completely wrung out by it. The city wanted so badly to believe that the Compromise would put an end to the sectional strife that they began to believe that its passage actually had. In his first State of the Union address (in the preparation of which he was ably assisted by Daniel Webster), Millard Fillmore expressed confidence that the overwhelming majority of Americans would embrace the Compromise as "a final settlement."

He struck a responsive chord, and his comforting and encouraging phrase became an oft-repeated refrain. Just before the Christmas recess, Stephen A. Douglas, who deserved credit for bringing to closure what Henry Clay had initiated, announced to his Senate colleagues: "I have determined never to make another speech on the slavery question." Then he appealed to them: "Let us cease agitating, stop the debate, and drop the subject. If we do this, the Compromise *will* be recognized as a final settlement."[7]

Newspaper editors were not immune to the euphoria. With the exception of those in the Deep South, most were still Unionists, and they, too, wanted to believe. The Boston *Evening Traveler* hailed the Texas boundary bill as snuffing out "disunion and treason in Congress and the country." The Philadelphia *Pennsylvanian* felt confident that "peace and tranquillity" would soon be secured. The *Illinois State Journal* called for "national jubilation."

Many Southern editors agreed. The Nashville *Republican* urged friends of free government to congratulate each other. The New Orleans *Picayune* stated, "We hope that the question is now definitely settled," and predicted that "contentions and bickering will cease, and harmony be again restored."[8]

And so, despite the efforts of the abolitionists, the subject of slavery faded out of the newspapers, and people stopped talking about disunion.

Douglas was pleased. The Democratic Party that Andrew Jackson had joined together was not about to be torn asunder by conflict over slavery. And with the Whig Party in disarray, a truly national Democratic Party might now elect as President whomever it chose to nominate—which soon might be none other than Stephen A. Douglas.

But slavery was not a political problem; it was a profoundly moral one—one which no purely political solution was going to resolve for long.

By the fall of 1851, response to the Compromise had jelled, and it was mostly favorable. The one bright note for the abolitionists was the election of Charles Sumner to the Senate, yet it remained to be seen how much of an asset he would be. At 6'4" he was an imposing figure with a gift of eloquence. But there was a dark side to him. One Boston society matron observed that he was "a specimen of prolonged and morbid juvenility."[9] It was a discerning assessment; when his will was crossed, Sumner exhibited the bad temper and illogical crudity of a spoiled child.

Before he discovered his public voice, Sumner had failed to gain a coveted professorship at Harvard and had then failed to attain the reportership of the Supreme Court. But now he was Senator Sumner, the darling of the Conscience Whigs, and he was determined to speak out against the Fugitive Slave Act the moment he reached Washington. Yet such a loose cannon was he, that even his friends shuddered at the thought. Robert C. Winthrop, whose seat he would be filling, said he would be glad to yield to either Charles Francis Adams or Horace Mann, "but spare me from Sumner, or rather, spare the Commonwealth, spare the country, from him!"[10]

In the North, the moderate majority supported the Compromise. In the South, there were three different reactions to it: The ultra-secessionists, led by Rhett, Yancey, Quitman, et al., were still demanding immediate secession. The ultra-Unionists, including Senators Clay and Foote and the conservative Whigs, were as adamant on the other end. The moderates, who believed in both the Union *and* States' Rights, hoped the two could somehow be reconciled. These moderates, at the moment still in the majority, did feel that the burden for maintaining the Union now rested with the North.

The Governor of Georgia called for a state convention to respond to the Compromise. When the delegates met on December 10, the convention issued the "Georgia Platform," which would become famous. A basically pro-Unionist statement, it nonetheless delivered this ultimatum: "The State of Georgia . . . will and ought to resist . . . to the disruption of every tie that binds her to the Union, any future act of Congress abolishing slavery in the District of Columbia . . . or any act prohibiting the introduction of slaves into the Territories of Utah and New Mexico; or any act . . . modifying the laws now in force for the recovery of fugitive slaves."[11]

In Mississippi, a similar convention resolved "that it is our deliberate opinion, that upon faithful execution of the Fugitive Slave Act, by the proper authorities, depends the preservation of our much-loved Union."[12]

The South had chosen to remain a part of the United States of America. But everything would depend on how sincerely the North intended to enforce the new law. The Southerners knew that the law's harsh measures would be repugnant to many up North, yet if the Yankees did not honor their word, then the South was prepared to leave. Disunion, once so unthinkable that no one spoke of it, was now a matter of public referendum: In the elections of 1851, 42 percent of the voters in South Carolina, Georgia, Mississippi, and Alabama went on record that they favored it.

The North, meanwhile, was having its own reactions to the new law, ranging from moderate disapproval to seething fury. Under it, the slaveholder himself no longer needed to be present to take his escaped slave before a civil magistrate; he could authorize an agent to do this for him. If a magistrate could not be found, all the agent need do was go to one of the newly appointed Federal commissioners authorized to remand a fugitive to slavery without any stay or appeal. The commissioner's fee was 10 dollars* for each fugitive he returned to slavery, but only 5 dollars if he ordered the slave's release.

Up to that point, the new measures might be said to be definitely slanted, but not necessarily excessive. But there was more. The extra five-dollar incentive was accompanied by a very big stick: Any marshal or deputy refusing to carry out the arrest of a fugitive was liable to a fine of a thousand (1850) dollars. That was also the fine for anyone caught aiding, shielding, or hiding a fugitive slave, *plus* another thousand dollars in civil damages for each slave they helped—*plus* six months in jail!

The group on which the law was having the greatest impact was the moderates. It was hard to remain impartial when a gang of slave hunters grabbed a black family in the middle of your town, beat them into submission, manacled them, and started driving them south. It was harder still when an acquaintance of yours was arrested and fined a thousand dollars for having offered the fugitives a ride in his wagon. It became impossible when someone reported *you* to the authorities as an accomplice—because you knew what your friend had done and had not reported him yourself.

* 1 percent of the value of the average Carolina slave

It was one thing not to object to an institution that had been in place for more than a century before America had become a Republic and that was condoned by the framers of the Constitution. It was quite another to be required to offer assistance to a slaveholder's agents. And now there were well-publicized instances of *free* blacks being seized. In Pennsylvania, Euphemia Williams was claimed by a Maryland slaveholder, who said she had run away from him 22 years before. Euphemia insisted that she had lived all her life in that state and had raised her six children there—all of whom were also claimed by the Marylander, as his property's children. In a hearing, a local judge decided that Euphemia was the one telling the truth.

In Poughkeepsie, New York, a tailor named Boulding was suddenly taken from his family and dragged down to South Carolina. His friends were able to raise the $1,750 required to buy him back.[13]

Even Northerners, once as convinced of white superiority as any slaveholder, found themselves modifying their convictions as they witnessed or read about such events—which were taking place in virtually every State in the Union.

In the opinion of historian Page Smith, "The Fugitive Slave Law was undoubtedly the most misconceived piece of legislation ever promoted by Southern members of Congress. It stirred up more hostility against slavery than any event in the history of sectional conflict, because it brought with it the enactment of dozens of excruciating dramas of fugitives pursued, recaptured, and returned to slavery. Or, increasingly, of slave captors being thwarted by lovers of freedom."[14]

Ironically, all the furor was over a comparative handful of slaves. In the decade after the new law was enacted, only 332 slaves were ever recaptured—at huge expense, often far more than the fugitive slave's dollar value. In light of the depth and extent of the rancor the law provoked, the South economically would have been far better off simply absorbing the annual loss of their escaped "property." Yet it was never a question of money or the number of runaways recovered. It was the principle involved. And there, neither side would give an inch.

Increasingly the Christian journals were now being heard from: The New York *Evangelist* said that no human law could bind the conscience of the people to such revolting work as helping recapture slaves. The Boston *Christian Register* was for treating the Constitution, as far as the fugitive slave law was concerned, as a dead letter. Antislavery spokesmen lent their voices to the cause, with renowned orator Edward Everett declaring that he would never obey the law. "I admit the right of the South to an efficient extradition law; but it is a right that cannot be enforced!"[15]

Ralph Waldo Emerson called it a "filthy law," and Joshua Giddings of Ohio declared: "Let the President drench our land of freedom in blood, but he will never make us obey that law."[16] In New York, Greeley's *Tribune* declared that the law was unconstitutional, in direct violation of the Fifth and Seventh Amendments.* It was, therefore, of no moral binding force, and readers should "help slaves escape all the more zealously."[17]

Before the new law had been on the books a month, runaway slaves had been arrested in Detroit, Harrisburg, and Philadelphia. Each incident evoked a response heard around the country. In major Northern cities, vigilance committees like the one in Boston sprang up. They had their work cut out for them: Not only were there cases of mistaken identity, but a growing number of free blacks were being deliberately kidnapped for sale to slavers. It became apparent that border state ne'er-do-wells had discovered that retrieving (or kidnapping) blacks was a lucrative pastime.

The new vigilance committees proved remarkably effective: In several cities, so great were their numbers and so vehement their protest that Federal troops had to be called out to quell the ensuing riot. Eventually blood was shed. A Maryland plantation owner named Edward Gorsuch led a party of six, including his son, a nephew, a cousin, and a Federal marshal, into Pennsylvania on the trail of four of his slaves who had escaped and had joined a community of blacks living in the little town of Christiana near Lancaster.

But this would not be a replay of the sad drama so often seen. For in Christiana lived a prominent black man, William Parker, who had been inspired by former slave and now abolitionist speaker Frederick Douglass to form a band of blacks pledged to their mutual self-defense against slave hunters and kidnappers. One abolitionist admiringly described Parker as "bold as a lion, the kindest of men, and the most steadfast of friends."[18]

When the posse arrived, the pursuers started firing into the house of William Parker, where the blacks had barricaded themselves. But this

---

* No one shall be deprived of life, liberty, or property without due process of law; everyone has the right to a fair trial by a jury of his peers.

time, to the astonishment of the attackers, the blacks started firing back. And when the posse paused to reload, the defenders swarmed out and fell upon them, beating and clubbing them until Gorsuch lay dead, his son was severely wounded, and the rest of the party ran for their lives.

Media reaction was predictably split. Southern papers said that if the blacks responsible were not quickly and severely punished, the South should at once secede from the Union. Some Northern papers blamed the affair on abolitionists who had encouraged "their innocent dupes, the colored mob" to offer resistance. A local paper ran the headline:

"CIVIL WAR—THE FIRST BLOW STRUCK!"

The *Christian Register* declared: "All the natural rights and claims and apologies are on the fugitive's side. He only did what any white man would have been applauded for doing." Greeley's *Tribune* agreed, adding: "No act of Congress can make it *right* for one man to convert another into his personal property."[19]

The nation's attention soon shifted to Boston, which now demonstrated what a well-funded and well-connected vigilance committee could accomplish. Two agents from Georgia arrived to reclaim the fugitive slave couple William and Ellen Craft, whose daring escape would become one of the most celebrated of fugitive slave narratives.

Capitalizing on the fact that Ellen was so light-skinned that she could pass for white, William and Ellen had devised a bold and courageous plan to escape from their Macon plantation. For a long time they had been saving bits of money that came their way, as they would soon need it. Ellen would disguise herself as "William Johnson," an invalid gentleman of infirm gait who was therefore accompanied by his body servant (the real William). And unable to either read or write, she would have her right arm in a sling so she would not be expected to sign a register.

On the night of December 21, 1848, when it came time for them to slip away, recorded William, "we blew out the lights, knelt down, and prayed to our Heavenly Father to assist us, as He did His people of old, to escape from cruel bondage."

Taking separate compartments on the train to Savannah, William's heart sank when he recognized the cabinetmaker for whom he worked. The cabinetmaker had come to the station looking for him and was searching each car. He looked into Ellen's compartment but did not recognize her. In another moment he would be at William's compartment. But just then the bell rang, alerting nonpassengers that the train was about to leave.

The cabinetmaker got off, but now it was Ellen's turn to be terrified. For who should William's wife be sitting next to but Mr. Cray, an old friend of her master who had dined with her master's family the day before. He had known Ellen since childhood, and now he turned to her and tried to engage her in conversation.

Numb with fear, all she could think to do was feign deafness. It worked; Mr. Cray turned to a neighboring passenger and spent the rest of the trip to Savannah talking about slaves, cotton, and the abolitionists.

In Savannah William and Ellen booked passage on a steam packet bound for Charleston up the coast. It was the best kind of trip: uneventful, save for one unpleasant encounter when a crude and persistent slave trader tried to convince Ellen to sell him her body servant. Fortunately a young army officer, with whom Ellen had briefly exchanged pleasantries a few hours earlier, now interceded, and the trader left.

In Charleston, Ellen tried to buy tickets for them on another steamer through to Philadelphia, only to learn that in wintertime the service did not continue farther up the coast than Wilmington, North Carolina. Very well, Wilmington would have to do. When the steamer's officer asked her to sign the ledger, she asked him if he would mind doing it for her, since her arm was incapacitated. To her surprise, the officer refused; it was against regulations. And then the ship's captain came over to see what the trouble was.

At that moment, the army officer whom she had befriended came up and vouched for her. The captain's demeanor instantly changed; he personally registered Ellen and her servant. Later, en route to Wilmington, he said to her, "It was rather sharp shooting this morning, Mr. Johnson. It was not meant out of any disrespect to you, sir, but they make it a rule to be very strict at Charleston." He shook his head. "If they were not very careful, any d——n abolitionist might take off a lot of valuable niggers."

"I suppose so," Ellen replied, thanking him for his help.

The next morning they arrived in Wilmington, took a train to Fredericksburg, and then another steamer to Washington. From there they bought a train ticket to Philadelphia, their final destination. There was just one more hurdle; they had to change trains in Baltimore. It shouldn't be a problem. . . .

Except that it was. They were on the platform, about to board the train to Philadelphia, when one of the railroad's junior officers came up to them. Would they please accompany him to the stationmaster's office? Why? Because Ellen could not take a slave out of Baltimore without his permission. They had no choice but to follow the young man into the office.

The stationmaster looked up from his desk and asked Ellen to produce proof of ownership of William, which she did not have. Doing her best to bluff, she showed him their through ticket to Philadelphia, and with all the gentlemanly indignation she could muster, she told him that he had no right to detain them on a technicality.

The man behind the desk bristled. His power might be limited, but it was absolute; not even President Polk could get on that train, unless he said so.

"Right or no right," he retorted testily, "we shan't let you go!"

William later recounted that at that moment "we felt as though we had come into deep waters and were about to be overwhelmed." In their hearts they cried out "to Him who is ever ready and able to save."

The bell rang, signaling the train's imminent departure. The stationmaster glared at them—then in great agitation he ran his fingers through his hair and said to the other officer, "I really don't know what to do." He paused. "I calculate it's all right." He stood up and turned to his subordinate. "Run and tell the conductor to let this gentleman and his slave pass. As he's not well, it's a pity to stop him here. We will let him go."

Ellen thanked him and remembered to hobble, as William helped her out the door. The train was starting to move. With William assisting her, the invalid "gentleman" hurried down the platform as best he could. Finally, as William put it, "I tumbled him unceremoniously into one of the best carriages, and hopped into mine, just as the train was gliding off." They had made it!

On the train, a free black fell into conversation with William. He told him that if he wanted to leave his master when they reached Philadelphia, there was a boardinghouse run by an abolitionist, where he would be safe. He gave William the address. So when they reached the City of Brotherly Love, they took a carriage, and Ellen gave the driver that address.

At last they were truly safe! When the realization hit Ellen that it was over, and she could just be herself, she collapsed sobbing into William's arms. "Thank God, William, we are safe!"

When they reached their lodgings and took a room, they realized it was Christmas Day. They knelt down and "poured out our heartfelt gratitude to God, for His goodness in enabling us to overcome so many difficulties in escaping out of the jaws of the wicked."[20]

William and Ellen Craft made their way to Boston, where they joined Theodore Parker's church. Everyone knew they were escaped slaves, yet for almost two years they led upstanding lives, William working as a cabinetmaker and Ellen sewing. They also made a number of friends, who now rallied round them when the Vigilance Committee spread the alarm that two slave-hunting agents from Georgia had just arrived and were looking for them.

Unable to find a commissioner willing to serve the warrants they had brought with them, yet not about to forfeit the bounty they had been promised, the agents did not give up. But now they themselves were served with warrants—drawn by magistrate Ellis Gray Loring, alleging slander for having accused the Crafts of stealing, and asking damages of $10,000!

These agents were tough customers, however, and were not easily intimidated. So the Vigilance Committee posted flyers vehemently denouncing them, and Parker himself led a committee of vigilantes to the agents' hotel room, where he confronted them and demanded that they leave town.[21] They refused, and were subsequently arrested and rearrested on charges ranging from slander to attempted kidnapping, carrying concealed weapons, smoking on the streets, and (not surprisingly) "profane cursing and swearing."

Finally the agents ran out of funds and left. But they vowed to return, and so the Crafts' friends sent them to Canada and thence to England, where other abolitionists, among them the reformer Harriet Martineau, took them under wing.[22]

32

FREEDOM ROAD

*D*espite the tumult and the shouting stirred up by each recapture incident, things had pretty much quieted down by the spring of 1852. The economy was doing well, and business interests, North and South, were anxious to keep it that way. That meant keeping the troublemakers (i.e., the abolitionists) damped down. The Boston *Courier* had even proposed a systematic boycott of all storekeepers, physicians, lawyers, and clergymen who resisted the Fugitive Slave Act. So great was the economic pressure, in fact, that antislavery radicals began to complain that the money powers were curbing the national discussion on slavery.

Ultimately the House passed a resolution declaring the Compromise to be a finality, and both parties, Whigs and Democrats, made that resolution a firm plank in their platforms for the Presidential elections in the fall. Twice before, the Whigs had won the Presidency by nominating a war hero (though both Old Tippecanoe and Old Rough and Ready had died in office); now they tried the gambit one more time with Old Fuss and Feathers. But Winfield Scott was perceived to be in Seward's pocket, and Seward, ever since his "higher law" speech, was perceived to be an antislavery extremist. The country went for the more moderate Franklin Pierce.

Slaves were still escaping, still trying to find their way to the "Promised Land"—anywhere they could live in peace without fear of recapture. For many, that meant Canada, beyond the reach of the U.S. fugitive slave law. Escaping was not the hard part; there were no walls or barbed wire holding them on the plantation. But evading recapture *was* hard. For their pursuers were mounted professionals who knew far more about the terrain than most slaves did, and they used tracking dogs. The majority of runaways were quickly apprehended, and to crush their spirit and set an example to any who might be similarly tempted, their punishment was extreme.

Still, the pull of freedom was strong, and was often exacerbated by anger at having received a harsh whipping, or by fear of a threatened one. Other motives for running included a desire to find family or kin, or the fear that one's family was about to be broken up for sale.

Once a slave got far enough away that he or she could no longer hear the baying of the hounds, the next biggest problem was knowing where to go. One observer reported that numerous slaves confided to him that they would try to escape, if they only had a compass. The lucky ones knew how to find the North Star and follow it. But most would never have made it to freedom without the help of a sympathetic white person.

Even more would give the main credit to God. A slave from Mississippi told of working her way through the swamps and canebreaks, and whenever she heard the hounds closing in on her, she would head for running water and wade through it to throw them off the scent. One time, she heard them when there was no water handy. She knelt down, pleading with God to protect her, then arose and calmly awaited the dogs. As they ran up to her, she reached in her pocket, took out the last piece of cornbread she had been saving, and held it out to them. Instead of jumping *on* her, they playfully jumped *around* her, taking the morsels she offered, licking the crumbs off her hand, and then running off into the woods.

Eventually she arrived in Detroit, where a ferry took her across to Canada. When she got there a black minister noted that she fell on her knees thanking the Lord for His mercy, then "jumped up and down for half an hour, shouting praises to God."[1]

The runaways had one thing in their favor: a band of courageous men and women, white and black, who were willing to risk their lives to hide and protect the runaways in their homes; feed, clothe, and care for them; and pass them along to other safe houses. It was perilous work; if caught, these helpers could be fined and sent to prison. But many felt God had called them to do no less, and so their homes became "depots" on what came to be known as the "Underground Railroad."*

---

* In 1831, a Kentucky slave named Tice Davids escaped by swimming the Ohio River. When his master came after him, Tice had vanished without a trace. Mystified, his master said

One of the most colorful characters ever associated with the Underground Railroad was Harriet Tubman, who escaped from slavery in Maryland in 1849, after learning she was about to be sold south. She ran away to the house of a white woman who had once offered to help her. True to her word, the woman did help, passing Harriet on up the Underground Railroad until she reached Pennsylvania. When she crossed the state line, Harriet said, "I looked at my hands, to see if I was the same person, now I was free. There was such a glory over everything, as the sun came up like gold through the trees and over the fields, I felt like I was in heaven."[2]

Going to work in Philadelphia, she immediately began saving money to slip back down into Maryland to rescue her sister and her two children in 1850. Then a few months later she went back down and got her brother and two others. All told, she would make 19 such trips, rescuing more than 300 slaves.

Her code name was Moses, because she led so many of her fellow blacks out of the Egypt of their bondage. Before heading south on one of her missions, she would alert prospective runaways with a message like: "Tell my brothers to be always watching unto prayer, and when the good old ship of Zion comes along, be ready to step on board."

The escape would begin on a Saturday night, so that the runaways' master could not start advertising for them until Monday morning. Sometimes she would hire a free Negro to follow the master's agent, tearing down the posters that the former tacked up. And if their pursuers ever got too close, Harriet would take her fugitives aboard a train heading *south,* knowing that their pursuers would never think to look for them heading in that direction.

On a mission, she required strict obedience from her charges. If a fugitive began to get cold feet and wanted to get off Freedom Road and go back and give up, she could not risk him betraying the rest of their party to the authorities. So she would shore up his courage with her Colt. Pointing her long-barreled revolver at him, she would say, "Dead niggers tell no tales; you go, or you die."[3] She never had to kill any of them, but they never doubted that she would.

A Christian of deep faith, she was utterly fearless, listening carefully in

---

he must have gone off on an "underground road." With the retelling of the story, the phrase became popular, eventually expanding to Underground Railroad.

her heart and going only where she felt God was leading her. One time in November of '56, she was leading four slaves along a road when suddenly she sensed imminent danger in the road up ahead. She quickly got them off the road and plunged down an embankment until they came to a fast, cold river. The others were afraid of the icy water, so Harriet went first, showing them it was possible to wade across. When they were safely across, they hid for the night. In the morning, when it was safe, they went back up to the road and continued on their way. Around the next bend they found evidence that a slave-catching patrol had been waiting for them there the day before.

Harriet gave all the credit for such escapes to God. "Just so long as He wanted to use me, He would take care of me," she said. "I always told Him: 'I'm going to hold on steady to You, and You've got to see me through.'" Said Quaker Thomas Garrett: "I never met any person of any color who had more confidence in the voice of God."[4]

As word of her exploits spread, antislavery leaders sought her out between missions and invited her to speak. Said New York Governor William Seward, "I have known Harriet long, and a nobler, higher spirit or a truer, seldom dwells in human form." And Frederick Douglass told her, "I know of no one who has willingly encountered more perils and hardships to serve our enslaved people than you have."[5]

There was another female ex-slave with a prominent place in the annals of Freedom Road. Given the slave name Isabella when she was born, and freed in 1827, this tall, "spare but solid" itinerant evangelist came to be known all over America as Sojourner Truth. She spoke at camp meetings and revivals, and became a favorite on the emerging women's lecture circuit. Possessing tremendous inner strength and a deep, hauntingly resonant voice, whenever she spoke, she also sang—and those who heard her would speak of it years afterward.[6]

She said exactly what was on her heart, and though it sometimes took people's breath away, they could not deny the truth of it. At a women's rights convention in Akron in 1851, she declared:

> I *am* a women's rights. I have as much muscle as any man, and can do as much work as any man. I have plowed and reaped and husked and chopped and mowed. . . . I can't read, but I can hear, and I have heard the Bible and

358

have learned that Eve caused man to sin. Well, if woman upset the world, give her a chance to set it right side up again![7]

Her friend Harriet Beecher Stowe recalled Wendell Phillips's account of an antislavery meeting at Faneuil Hall in Boston. Frederick Douglass, having lost faith that blacks would ever receive justice at the hands of white Americans, had just finished a fiery speech, claiming that blacks must seize their freedom by force of arms. "It must come to blood!" he concluded. "They must fight for themselves, or it would never be done."

He sat down, and there was silence in the hall. It was broken by Sojourner Truth, sitting in the front row. "Frederick," she inquired in her deep, majestic voice, *"is God dead?"*[8]

Becoming a symbol of what any woman of Christian faith could accomplish, even if she was a former slave and illiterate, Sojourner Truth had a 30-year impact on the antislavery movement.

Just as some of the greatest heroes of the last century were the men and women who risked their lives hiding or smuggling Jews out of Nazi-held Europe, so some of the greatest heroes of the nineteenth century were those who became slave-smuggling "conductors" on the Underground Railroad. One would be dubbed "president of the Underground Railroad"—a Quaker schoolteacher named Levi Coffin.

Born and raised in North Carolina, Levi was seven years old when he witnessed a slave coffle being driven by a man on horseback. The sight of that string of slaves, bound together by a neck chain, had a profound effect on him, being "the first awakening of that sympathy with the oppressed which, together with a strong hatred of oppression and injustice in every form, were the motives that influenced my whole after-life."[9]

The Quakers had been the first of God's people to regard antislavery work as part of their call, and now Levi began to follow in the footsteps of the legendary John Woolman. While still a boy, with his father's blessing Levi used to sneak food to runaway slaves hiding in the woods near their farm. He loved to listen to their stories as they spoke "of the glorious hope of freedom which animated their spirits in the darkest hours and sustained them under the sting of the lash."[10]

But "slavery and Quakerism could not prosper together,"[11] and so North Carolina Quakers began to leave the state. In 1825 his parents sold their farm and moved to Newport,* Indiana. A year later, directly after his marriage, Levi, now age 37, followed them. He opened a small mercantile business, which the Lord prospered, and 10 years later built a mill for the manufacture of linseed oil.

But his primary concern continued to be the UGRR, as he obliquely referred to it, which had become his life's work after an incident in Lambertville, North Carolina, in 1828. There Levi, observing a slave auction, had watched a young mother with a year-old child in her arms step up on the block. The auctioneer recommended her as a good cook, house servant, and field hand. She was even a Christian, he exclaimed, obviously an unusually valuable piece of property!

When she was bought, she begged her new master to also buy her child, but he ignored her pleading. The child was sold to another man, but when he came to take the child from her, she would not let go. Her new master now tore the child from her arms, and she was dragged away, sobbing and crying out.

Levi could not stand to remain, but as he left, "I heard the voice of the slave mother, as she screamed: 'My child! My child!' I rode away as fast as I could, to get beyond the sound of her cries. But that night I could not sleep; her screams rang in my ears and haunted me for weeks afterward."[12]

He committed the rest of his life to the UGRR.

Finding that other Quakers in his Indiana neighborhood were reluctant to become involved,

I told them that I read in the Bible when I was a boy that it was right to take in the stranger and administer to those in distress, and that I thought it was always safe to do right. The Bible, in bidding us to feed the hungry and clothe the naked, said nothing about color, and I should try to follow out the teachings of that good book. I was willing to receive and aid as many fugitives as were disposed to come to my house.

A great many did; the Coffin home soon became the junction of three main lines from the South. And now his example began to touch the hearts

* now Fountain City

360

of his Quaker friends. Some "who had formerly stood aloof from the work, fearful of the penalty of the law, were encouraged to engage in it."

Like Harriet Tubman, Levi did not know the meaning of fear. "As to my safety, my life was in the hands of my Divine Master, and I felt that I had His approval. I had no fear of the danger that seemed to threaten my life or my business. If I was faithful to duty, and honest and industrious, I felt that I would be preserved."[13]

In 1847 Levi and his family moved to Cincinnati, where his work grew larger. He had an unusual gift for discernment and would need every bit of it there, as slave hunters tried to catch him by bribing free blacks in his employ to betray him and the railroad, or by introducing fake runaways into the system.

Typical of those he helped was a wise old mammy named Aunt Betsy who drove her vegetable cart onto one of the ferries that went back and forth across the Ohio River. Hidden inside the cart was her entire family. When she reached the Ohio side, Levi took them under his wing and hid them in his house. Then, so that they would not be traced by her former owner, he dispatched one of his black helpers to hire a German who could speak a little English to take the vegetable wagon back over the river and leave it on the Kentucky side. Next he asked the ladies of the Antislavery Sewing Society to create costumes suitable for disguising the family as black gentry, which enabled them to ride out of town in a carriage at high noon, when people would be indoors having dinner.[14]

One slave he helped was a young mother from Kentucky named Eliza Harris. Two of her children had died; she had only one left, a bright little two-year-old boy. On a wintry day Eliza learned that her master, beset with pecuniary difficulties, planned to sell her boy. That night she determined to run away, and grabbing up her child she headed for the Ohio River. Normally at that time of year it was frozen solid, and the road to freedom led straight across it. But this winter had been unusually mild, and when she reached the river, its ice cover had broken into large cakes.

With her pursuers and their hounds now close behind her, Eliza, her little boy clutched in her arms, had jumped onto the nearest ice floe, then from one to the next. "She became wet to the waist with ice water," Levi reported, "and her hands were benumbed with cold. But as she made her way from one cake of ice to another, she felt that surely the Lord was preserving and upholding her, and that nothing could harm her."

A man who had been standing on the Ohio side of the river, watching her desperate progress, helped her out of the river and directed her to a nearby safe house. She and her little boy were passed from house to house, until she wound up at Levi Coffin's home, where she stayed several days and told Levi her story.[15]*

So many slaves passed through the Coffin home that Levi lost count of them all. But one statistic he never forgot: "Not one, so far as I ever knew, was captured and taken back to slavery. Providence seemed to favor our efforts for the poor slaves, and to crown them with success."[16]

Before taking leave of the president of the UGRR, one final episode is worthy of note. It occurred aboard a Mississippi steamboat on which Levi was traveling on business in 1858. The deckhands were slaves, and one was about to be whipped for disobeying the mate. As the gentlemen passengers gathered to witness the punishment, a Baptist minister among them invited Levi to see "the fun." Levi refused and went to his cabin, the only man aboard who would not watch. But he could not avoid hearing the slave's agony:

> The cries of the poor slave pierced my ears. . . . In my agitation, I walked the room, thinking, "How long, O Lord, will such cruelty be permitted on the earth?" . . . I had often been in the South, but never before had been so sensible of the Egyptian darkness that overhung the land. I was deeply impressed with the belief that the day was not far distant when the fetters of slavery would be broken.[17]

---

* Her desperate escape captured the imagination of Harriet Beecher Stowe, who would soon immortalize it.

33

THE LITTLE LADY

A sadness came over the nation in 1852, as first Henry Clay, then Daniel Webster, died. With this passing of the guard, America sensed that a great era had drawn to a close. Diarist George Templeton Strong spoke for his countrymen when he observed: "From the old heroic race to which Webster and Clay and Calhoun belonged, down to the rising race of Sewards and Douglases and Fishes, is a dismal descent."[1]

The long battle for the Compromise and the subsequent need to continually defend it had broken Henry Clay's health. The previous December, he had resigned his seat in the Senate. A bad cold had worsened into tuberculosis, and he had repaired to his old quarters in the National Hotel to await death. It came on June 29, with his wife and his son at his bedside. He caught and held his son's hand for some minutes, then gradually his grasp relaxed, and he ceased to breathe.

At the funeral services held in the Senate Chamber two days later, Whigs and Democrats were united in their grief. If Webster was renowned for his oratory and his ability to project authority, Clay was loved for his charm and irresistible smile. No one could take the arm of an adversary and whisper a few ingratiating cajoleries more successfully than Harry of the West. And if Clay could get a man to smile, more often than not he could get him to agree. It has been said that American politics is the art of compromise; if so, there was no greater master than Henry Clay.

An observer at his funeral was surprised at the bereavement of Daniel Webster, "the saddest I saw at the ceremonies,"[2] since Clay and Webster had been lifelong rivals. But he must have been unaware of how close the two had grown as they worked together on the Compromise.

Also, Daniel Webster knew that his own end was nigh. It did not shake him; all autumn he noted his own deterioration with equanimity. On Sunday evening, October 10, he asked a friend "to read to him the passage in the ninth chapter of St. Mark's Gospel, where the man brings his child to Jesus to be cured, and the Savior tells him, 'If thou canst believe, all things are possible to him that believeth.' And strongly the father of the child cried out, with tears, 'Lord, I believe; help thou mine unbelief' [Mark 9:23–24]."[3] When the friend did as bidden, Webster decided that that would be the theme of his epitaph, which he then composed. It was published two weeks later, on the occasion of his death.

Simplicity and lucidity highlighted Webster's great arguments before the highest bench in the land. Now, as he presented himself before the Supreme Court of the Universe, his simple words were luminous:

LORD I BELIEVE; HELP THOU MINE UNBELIEF.

Philosophical
argument, especially
that drawn from the vastness of
the Universe, in comparison with the
apparent insignificance of the globe, has sometimes shaken my reason for the faith which is in me;
but my heart has always assured and reassured me that the
Gospel of Jesus Christ must be a Divine Reality. The
Sermon on the Mount cannot be merely human production. This belief enters
into the very depths of my conscience. The whole history
of man proves it.

—Daniel Webster

No one had done more to establish the concept of the Union in the basic thinking of his countrymen. Historian Page Smith summed up his contribution: "Where all the natural tendencies were toward provincialism, regionalism, and sectionalism, Webster had tied the States together in what were to prove indissoluble bonds by the power of his rhetoric."[4]

After Webster's funeral, Richard Henry Dana expressed the feelings of thousands:

> No death since that of Washington has excited so general a grief. . . . With all his greatness and smallness, with all the praise and blame, gratitude, admiration, censure and distrust with which we look upon his life, there is something so majestical, so large of mind and heart about him, that an emotion of pride and tears swells at the very thought of him.[5]

For all the agitation of the abolitionists and the quiet, frontline service of heroes like Levi Coffin, the post-Compromise mood of the country was settling back into complacency. With the rancorous debate over slavery now absent from the chambers of the House and Senate, many in Congress convinced themselves that they had truly reached the final settlement.

And then in a family living room in Brunswick, Maine, the Spirit of God lit a small but significant spiritual bonfire.

While Harriet Beecher's father, Lyman, had been president of Lane Seminary, their home had been on a bluff overlooking the Ohio River. Hattie, as her family called her, had attended the abolition debates, where Theodore Dwight Weld and his classmates had made a profound impression on her. When they left in 1834, Hattie remained with her family, and two years later at the age of 25 married one of the seminary's faculty members, the Reverend Calvin Stowe.

Those were turbulent times, and Cincinnati was the focus of much abolitionist and anti-abolitionist activity. Soon after her marriage, Hattie witnessed a mob in Cincinnati wrecking the press of James Birney, publisher of the antislavery newspaper *The Philanthropist*. Three years later, Calvin and her brother Henry Ward would rescue her free black maid from kidnappers bent on selling her back into slavery. Then in 1840, a white mob turned on the black community with torches, guns, and even cannon. Murdering and raping, they used the ensuing chaos as a cover to steal black children, whom they sold into slavery.

From her home Hattie could see the fires and hear the cries of the desolate mothers. The sounds and images of that horrific night were seared into her memory. They galvanized her into action, and she began writing pieces for various antislavery publications.

When Calvin Stowe was invited in 1850 to join the faculty of his *alma mater*, Bowdoin College in Maine, he accepted. While passing through Boston to their new home, Hattie stopped to visit her brother Edward and his wife, Isabella. The new fugitive slave law had just been enacted, and the first instances of free blacks being kidnapped had outraged the city's intelligentsia, including Edward and Isabella. Hattie shared their determination to do something about it.

Her son Charles later described what happened when she received a letter from Isabella. "Hattie," it said, "if I could use a pen as you can, I could write something which would make this whole nation feel what an accursed thing slavery is."

She rose up from her chair, crushed the letter in her hand, and with an expression on her face that stamped itself on the mind of her son, vowed: "I *will* write something! I will, if I live."[6]

And she did, though it was a little while in coming. As He has done with Christian writers through the ages, God inspired Hattie by giving her scenes in her mind's eye. The first came during church on February 1, 1851. She was waiting her turn to take Communion, not thinking about anything, her mind just drifting . . . when in her imagination she began to see a white-haired old black slave. He was on the ground, but he had his arm up, trying to protect himself. He was being whipped by two other younger slaves, who were being urged on by a cruel white master. The master was demanding to know the whereabouts of other slaves who had run away. But the old slave would not betray them. His lips were moving—what was he saying? Hattie was shocked: He was praying for those who were flogging him.

It was all Hattie could do to keep from leaving church, then and there. As soon as she got home, she wrote down the scene exactly as it had come to her. And then she put it away. A month later Calvin came upon it, read it, and with tears streaming down his face, asked her what it was. When she told him, he said, "Hattie, you must go on with it. You must make up a story with this for the climax. The Lord intends it so."[7]

At his urging, she wrote down some more episodes and sent them to Gamaliel Bailey, editor of the eight-page antislavery publication *The National Era*, to which she had been an occasional contributor. Deeply impressed, he sent her $300 for what he thought would be a series of sketches. With that encouragement she set to work. More scenes began to come to her, and she dutifully wrote them down, until it began to appear she might have the makings of a novel.

Today, with so many entertainment diversions—myriad-channel television, malls, movies, cars, radio, music, theater, and now the Internet—competing for our leisure-time attention, few people sit down and read anymore. A century and a half ago, there was little else to do on a cold winter's evening or a warm summer's night. For light reading, the men had their newspapers, the women their illustrated weeklies. For more serious reading, there was history, biography, translations of the ancient classics, and above all, the Bible.

And for pure enjoyment, there were novels. Men and women alike enjoyed James Fenimore Cooper's adventures like *The Pathfinder, The Deerslayer,* and *The Last of the Mohicans.* Washington Irving's sketches like *Rip Van Winkle* and *The Legend of Sleepy Hollow* delighted schoolchildren and their parents, and the 1850s had their own Stephen King in the inventor of the classic horror novel, Edgar Allen Poe. *The Fall of the House of Usher* and *The Murders in the Rue Morgue* had given people nightmares from coast to coast.

The works of foreign novelists were also finding their way to our shores. Bowdlerized versions of Daniel Defoe's *Robinson Crusoe* and Johann Wyss's *Swiss Family Robinson* had been read aloud at countless family hearths.* Most young ladies of society had read all of Jane Austen's novels from *Pride and Prejudice* to *Emma* and *Sense and Sensibility.* And those with a taste for the dark side thrilled to Mary Shelley's *Frankenstein.* The entire South was besotted with (and significantly transformed by) the romantic adventures of Sir Walter Scott. (He was popular in the North, too; young Hattie Beecher reread *Ivanhoe* seven times one summer.) If you had the time and the inclination, there was no end of good novels to read.

And so, Harriet Beecher Stowe began to try her hand at knitting her scenes and sketches into a book-length story. . . . She had a name for

---

* In the early 19th century, Thomas Bowdler, an English doctor and man of letters, produced *The Family Shakespeare* and other classic works, with inappropriate language modified to render them suitable for reading aloud to the family.

the saintly old slave; he would be Tom. There would be a cruel overseer named Simon Legree, a lighthearted, childlike, rebellious slave named Topsy, and a young slave mother named Eliza who, rather than have her baby boy taken from her and sold, fled with him in the night. To escape the hounds, she crossed the ice floes of the Ohio River. . . .

By the time Hattie finished, she also had a name for her work: *Uncle Tom's Cabin*. Ten months before the novel came out, installments started running in Bailey's *National Era*, so there was a ready market for the 5,000 hardcover copies of the first printing in March of 1852. It sold out in two days. The next printing sold out as quickly. And the next, and the next. Soon three presses were running 24 hours a day—and still could not keep up with the demand.

Diarist Sidney George Fisher called it:

The great book of the year. . . . No book had ever had such sudden and universal success. It is read by everybody with interest and delight. It is bought as fast as it can be printed. It is advertised in every paper in America and England and the Continent. It is sold in hotels and railroads and read by all classes in cottages and palaces, by the wayside and the fireside. . . . Altogether, the work displays genius—creative, imaginative, fruitful, and original.[8]

Before long, there were 30 road companies touring the country with stage presentations. By the end of the year, 300,000 copies had been sold, and the presses were still at it. Today, that would make it a top-of-the-list bestseller; a century and a half ago, it was an unheard-of publishing phenomenon. Nor was it solely an American event; when it was introduced in Great Britain, it sold 1.2 million copies in the first year. All told, it was translated into 25 foreign languages.

In Russia, there were reports of Russians so moved by it that they freed their serfs. And Leo Tolstoy, soon to write *War and Peace*, would rank it with *Les Miserables* and *A Tale of Two Cities* as high moral art.

The famous German poet Heinrich Heine, ill in Paris, said it led him back to the Bible and faith. The Swedish novelist Fredrika Bremer had two years before lamented to her sister, "I cannot understand why, in particular, noble-minded . . . American mothers who have hearts and genius do not take up the subject [of slavery] and treat it with a power which should pierce through bone and marrow. . . . I am convinced that the earth, the spiritual earth of the United States, must quake thereby and overthrow slavery!" Now she wrote Hattie: "It was the work I had long wished for, that I long anticipated, that I wished while in America to be able to write. . . . and God be praised, it has come!"[9]

Back home, the critical response was equally encouraging. Henry Wadsworth Longfellow, one of America's great poets and men of letters, wrote in his diary: "At one step she has reached the top of the staircase up which the rest of us climb on our knees year after year."[10]

Hattie particularly connected with women readers. She had lost a young son to cholera in the summer of '49, and she drew on the agony of that time to portray the plight of a young slave mother. As she wrote to a friend,

> I learned what a poor slave mother may feel when her child is torn away from her. In those depths of sorrow which seemed to me immeasurable, it was my prayer to God that such anguish might not be suffered in vain. There were circumstances about his death of such peculiar bitterness, of what seemed almost cruel suffering, that I felt I could never be consoled for it, unless this crushing of my own heart might enable me to work out some great good to others.[11]

In America, it swept the country—*all* the country, for Southern women were reading it as avidly as their Northern counterparts—until the proslavery spokesmen realized what a powerful piece of antislavery propaganda it was. True, the author treated Southern owners with sympathy, but she was dramatizing the woeful plight of the slave, at a time when they were declaring the institution to be the kindest thing that the white race could do to the black race.

A modern reader might be bemused at her melodramatic style, and in truth Hattie *was* wont to dip her pen in heliotrope ink. But that was the literary fashion of her age. On the other side of the balance, Hattie was a born storyteller with an instinctive sense of pace and suspense. Once you got into her story, you were quickly caught up in it and compelled to keep reading. You became involved with her characters and stayed involved with them, caring a great deal about what happened to them. You were sad to see the remaining pages dwindling, and when you finished, you could never again regard slavery with indifference.

It was said that with one book Harriet Beecher Stowe had created two million abolitionists. Historian Charles Foster noted: "After *Uncle Tom's Cabin*, objective analysis of the slavery issue was almost impossible." Abraham Lincoln was not far from the truth when he greeted Hattie as "the little lady who started the great war."[12]

And historian Allan Nevins, not given to superlatives, was impressed that it was *not* condemnatory or strident in tone, but had a warm, intensely human compassion. "It is the feeling of John Woolman, not that of Garrison. . . . It attuned itself no less to the essential spirit of Christianity—the spirit of Him who died for all who were weary and heavy-laden."[13]

After Hattie finished writing the story, she felt compelled to add a few "Concluding Remarks." In them she credited the Fugitive Slave Act of 1850 as providing her main motivation, and made a personal appeal to the mothers of America: "By the sacred love you bear your child . . . by the prayers you breathe for his sacred good, I beseech you: pity the mother who has all your affections and not one legal right to protect, guide, or educate the child of her bosom! . . . Is this a thing to be defended, sympathized with, passed over in silence?"

She closed her appeal with a solemn warning. "O Church of Christ, read the signs of the times! . . . A day of grace is yet held out to us. Both North and South have been guilty before God; and the Christian Church has a heavy account to answer." The only hope lay in "repentance, justice, and mercy, for not surer is the eternal law by which the millstone sinks in the ocean than that stronger law by which injustice and cruelty shall bring on nations the wrath of Almighty God."[14]

34

Kansas-Nebraska

Clink—clink, clink—clink . . . a pair of men, one on either side of the rail, swung carefully timed sledgehammer blows on the brace of spikes holding the steel rail exactly in place on the cross-tie. They drove their spikes in concert, keeping the rail tight against the steel spacer bar between their rail and the parallel one, exactly 56″ away.

The spikemen were the elite among the workers at the end of tracks. Others cleared the way ahead, dug out the track bed with pick and shovel, filled it with stone ballast, set the cross-ties, tamped in more ballast to keep them from shifting, laid the next rails, and set out the spikes. There might be a hundred men in the camp—Irish immigrants fleeing the potato famine, black freemen, busted prospectors back from California. Only the young and strong needed to apply, for as the song went, "all the livelong day" ran from first light to last. The wake-up whistle blew while it was still dark, and Dinah blew her breakfast horn soon behind it.

The moment a new line was finished it was put in use, for the backers were looking for a speedy return on their investment. The engine drivers were always wary of the last miles laid. If a new line's construction had fallen behind schedule and run short of funds, then instead of going around a mountain or tunneling through it, they would simply go over it. A grade was never supposed to be too steep to stop on, or include a sharp bend. But if the company had been staving off bankruptcy at the end, it happened.

And so, when a sudden cold snap froze the rain on the rails, and a train, running late and hauling too many cars, came over the summit a little too quickly. . . . Once she hit ice, no locomotive on earth had the brakes to haul her down. The steepest grades had emergency shunts running back up the mountain, with switchmen on duty to divert a runaway. But too often the train would have gathered too much momentum. Whistle screaming, sparks flying from her locked drivers, the engine would chew right through the thrown switch and keep on going until the first bend. If her crew were lucky, they might be able to jump free before she left the rails. Then there would be a fiery cataclysm of bursting steam boilers, and before long a railroader would pull out his banjo and compose a mournful lament to the wreck of the next "Old 97."

Dangerous or not, railroads were rapidly stitching America together in 1854. A 20-car train could haul more freight than a hundred wagons, and passenger trains were not only faster than stagecoaches, they could run all night; in fact, the only time they needed to stop was to let off and take on passengers, wood, and water.

As noted earlier, by 1840 nearly 3,000 miles of track had been laid. In the next decade that figure would triple, and by 1860 it would triple again.[1] Most of the track was being laid north of the Ohio River, since most of the South's capital was tied up in land and slaves.

The South was not unaware of the disparity; indeed, farsighted Southerners were pleading with their brethren to consider at least minimal diversification and agricultural reform. Addressing the agricultural society of South Carolina in 1857, the Honorable J. Foster Marshall summed up their situation:

> Our present system is to cut down our forest and run it into cotton as long as it will pay for the labor expended. Then cut down more forest, plant in cotton, plow it uphill and downhill, and when it fails to give a support ... sell the carcass for what you can realize and migrate to the Southwest in quest of another victim. This ruinous system has entailed upon us an exhausted soil, and a dependence upon Kentucky and Tennessee for our mules, horses, and hogs, and upon the Northern States for all our necessaries from the clothing and shoeing of our Negroes down to our wheelbarrows, corn-brooms and ax-handles.[2]

Now that several rail lines had reached the Mississippi and continued west on the other side, a transcontinental line became a topic of urgency in both the press and Congress. The main issue was where it would go. In the Senate, Jefferson Davis of Mississippi and Sam Houston of Texas were making a serious case for a Southern route. But with Chicago now the major rail hub of the Midwest, Illinois' Senator Stephen A. Douglas was pushing hard for the Northern route. (He also had personal reasons: He was heavily invested in railroads and western real estate.)[3]

Only one thing stood in the path of a Northern route: It would have to go through the vast expanse of land from the Canadian border down to Texas and out to the Rockies, loosely known as "Nebraska country." It was a wild land, largely uninhabited except for nomadic tribes that followed the great buffalo herds across the Great Plains. But it was also a fertile land, especially the wooded prairies to the east. It might be broiling hot in the summer and numbingly cold in the winter, but the rainfall was reliable. In short, it was an excellent climate for all grains—wheat, rye, oats, barley, and of course, corn.

The prairies were already attracting settlers, and even the plains farther west, which were good for grazing, were drawing a few hardy pioneers. Without a tree on the horizon, these "sod-busters," as they were called, would build houses made from squares of thick turf cut from the ground. Then they would write their friends and families back home, and soon other covered wagons were leaving the wagon trains far short of the Rockies.

But unless the region was quickly organized into formal Territories prior to admission to the Union, and unless their governments could soon guarantee stability and order, the transcontinental rail line was certain to go south.

Stephen A. Douglas, an unsurpassed master of political maneuver, rolled up his sleeves and got to work. Two years before, though the leader of the Northern Democrats, he had been denied his party's nomination. The Democratic party was simply too divided. With the next Presidential election now only two years away, he was determined to prevent that from reoccurring. And nothing would unite Northern and Southern Democrats faster than to give them a common cause: ushering in the next new States. As chairman of the powerful Committee on Territories, he bargained closely with the Southern members of his committee and then forged the "Nebraska Bill," which would establish two Territories, Nebraska to the north and Kansas to the south.

What would be their status regarding slavery? That, proclaimed Douglas, ever the champion of popular sovereignty in the Territories, would be decided by the settlers themselves in a referendum. There was just one problem: Both of these new Territories were north of latitude 36°30'—the line established by the Missouri Compromise in 1820, above which slavery would never be allowed. Declaring popular sovereignty in the Kansas and Nebraska Territories would be tantamount to repudiating the Missouri Compromise, which many regarded as the sacred last word on the future of slavery. For while the majority of Northerners were willing to allow slavery to continue where it had already been established and was recognized by the Constitution, the same majority was most emphatically against allowing it to expand into virgin territory north of 36°30'.

Contrarily the South insisted that the proposed bill contain a formal repeal of the Missouri Compromise, and after some soul-searching, Douglas agreed. After all, California, whose lower regions extended below that line, had come in as a free state, and the status of the New Mexico and Utah Territories had already been decided by popular sovereignty. Besides, in Douglas's view the comparatively cold climates of the Kansas-Nebraska Territories made them wholly inhospitable to slavery. He did not believe slavery could be made to work in either Territory, and so, as Daniel Webster once commented, "Why re-enact the will of God?"[4] He was so sure of this, in fact, that he assumed everyone else felt the same as he did. "I do not believe there is a man in Congress who thinks it could permanently be a slaveholding country."[5]

But quite a few did. Parts of Kansas were no less suitable to slavery than Delaware, Maryland, or Kentucky. Cotton might not grow in Kansas, but tobacco would, and parts of Kansas were ideal for the South's newest cash crop, hemp. Hemp fibers were essential in cordage—for twine, yarn, rope, and string, and the oil from its seed was used in varnishes and soaps. In less than two years the price of a bale of hemp had risen from $75 to $130. Hemp growers in Kentucky had moved to the counties along Missouri's western border, and Missouri, with a thousand planters and a hundred thousand slaves, was now producing more hemp than Kentucky.[6] Both states considered slave labor indispensable to hemp production, and those planters in the border counties of Missouri were now eyeing all the unclaimed land across the border in Kansas.

The Free-Soilers were well aware of what might happen if popular sovereignty became the law in those Territories, but it never occurred to Douglas that so many moderate Northerners could be so immoderately opposed to the expansion of slavery. Since he himself had never found slavery morally repugnant, he could not comprehend that other reasonable men might. "The civilized world," he said, "has always held that when any race of men have shown themselves to be so degraded by ignorance, superstition, cruelty, and barbarism as to be utterly incapable of governing themselves, they must, in the nature of things, be governed by others, by such laws as deemed applicable to their condition."[7] Wherever he assessed slavery, it was on strictly economic terms: Where it paid, it was good; where it didn't, it was bad.

As for popular sovereignty, what could be more American than letting the people choose for themselves what sort of Territory they would live in? But the pro-choice argument breaks down when one choice involves doing extreme harm to one of the parties involved, for the sake of the other's convenience. This is not democratic choice; it is immorality and sin.

Douglas remarked with wry amusement that his new bill would undoubtedly create a major "storm."[8] He had no idea just how fierce would be the whirlwind he would reap.

Suddenly it seemed that all the newspapers in the North were in agreement, something that had never happened before where slavery was concerned. They agreed that a sacred principle of trust was about to be broken. For more than 30 years the Missouri Compromise's restriction on the northern expansion of slavery had been honored by both sides. Now it was about to be consigned to the dustbin of history. Allegations appeared that Southern leaders had secret plans to invade Cuba privately and wrest it from Spain (which was true), and that James Gadsden, U.S. minister to Mexico, had been empowered to procure far more than the railroad right-of-way, which eventually became known as the Gadsden Purchase. Once again Northern editors were speculating on a Slave Power conspiracy to add a vast panoply of slave states to the Union. Only this time the speculation was coming from all over the North, and this time there was something to it.[9]

Even hitherto Democratic dailies broke with the party line. The Chicago *Democrat* joined the Cleveland *Plain Dealer*, the Detroit *Free Press*, the Cincinnati *Gazette*, and the Indianapolis *Morning Journal*, as well as all the New York dailies, except the *Herald*. The power of their concerted wrath had never been seen before, and these were formerly *moderate* voices, not Garrisonites and other extreme abolitionists.

How did the Southern newspapers regard the tumult and the shouting? They acknowledged that the truce over slavery was broken; the much-heralded "final settlement" had lasted all of three years. The North seemed more riled up than at any time previous.

Yet the South was not unduly concerned. Said the Charleston *Mercury*, "We find society convulsed, all the slumbering elements of sectional bitterness aroused, and the slavery agitation awake again. . . . Never before has the Northern sky portended such a storm. Never before have the Northern press approached so near to unanimity in the cause of Abolition." And yet in the South, "all is calm and easy indifference. The thunders which come rolling from the North die away before they reach our latitude, or if heard at all are scarcely heeded."[10]

In the House, Richard Yates of Springfield, Illinois, summed up the moderate objection:

> If slaveholders are permitted to take their slaves into Nebraska and Kansas, the inequality and injury are to the free white men of the North and South who go there without slaves. . . . The effect of slave labor is always to cheapen, degrade, and exclude free labor. . . . The introduction of slavery will retard the prosperity of the State. Slave labor converts the richest soil into barrenness; free labor causes fertility and vegetation to spring from the very rock.[11]

All across the North, urgent meetings were held to discuss the pending bill, and the opinion was well-nigh unanimous: It must not pass. In New Haven, aged Yale Professor Benjamin Silliman, founder of the influential *American Journal of Science*, made the first political speech of his life. He had been born during the War for Independence, he told the crowd, and had observed every major event of American history since then; for the first time he was filled with fear for the future of the country. In Boston, merchants met in Faneuil Hall to declare their opposition, as did businessmen in Chicago, Cleveland, and other centers of industry.

Had the politicians in Washington been listening, they would have noted that until now the commercial interests had always been opposed to the antislavery movement, which was deemed to be disruptive to the smooth flow of commerce. But no longer was "business as usual" the watchword of the day; the Kansas-Nebraska Act had touched a deeper chord.

That was the trouble: The politicians in Washington were *not* listening—at least, none of Douglas's supporters were. When even the usually timid clergy, who were still divided over the Fugitive Slave Law, spoke with a common voice, Douglas greeted their protests with scorn. On March 14, a petition from 3,050 New England ministers was laid before the Senate, solemnly protesting the proposed bill "in the name of Almighty God."

Douglas was an oratorical brawler, whose customary debating style was to heap personal abuse on his opponent. The German-born journalist and antislavery activist Carl Schurz had never seen a "more formidable parliamentary pugilist," whose attacks were "so exasperatingly offensive that it was all the antislavery Senators could do, to keep from retaliating."[12] Now Douglas assailed the churches for trying to coerce Congress, sneering at clergy who posed as spokesmen for the Almighty. And just as Garrison had when he condemned the Bible, Douglas succeeded in alienating himself from most Northern evangelicals—they felt that speaking for the Almighty was precisely what their ministers *ought* to be doing. As for the separation of Church and State, whenever the State proposed extending a moral wrong, it was the duty and even the obligation of the Church to express her opposition by every means at her disposal.

If the Northern churches and clergy were opposed, and the commercial interests were opposed, and the majority of moderates were opposed, who up North was in favor of the bill? Not enough to get it passed, it would seem. But Douglas and President Pierce made it painfully clear to regular Democrats that how a Senator or Congressman voted on this bill would be considered a test of his loyalty to the party.

Some of the party faithful refused to fall in line; a few like Sam Houston chose to sacrifice party ties rather than sacrifice principle. Just before the Senate vote was taken at dawn on March 4, after an all-night session, Senator Houston gave what he considered the best speech of his career. In it, he observed that a hurricane was raging throughout the North; since, as some said, the bill was not likely to result in another slave state, why not jettison it for the sake of national harmony? "Maintain the Missouri Compromise! Stir not up agitation! Give us peace!"[13]

By the time the roll was called, some members had already gone home exhausted. The bill passed, 37 to 14.

Confided Douglas to his brother-in-law afterward, "I passed the Kansas-Nebraska Act myself. I had the authority and power of a dictator throughout the whole controversy in both houses. The speeches were nothing. It was the marshaling and directing of men and guarding from attacks, and with a ceaseless vigilance preventing surprise."[14]

But the bill still had to pass the House, and before it came up, something happened in Boston to make its passage far from sure.

An escaped slave named Anthony Burns was working as a clerk in a clothing store, when he did a foolish thing: He wrote a letter to his brother in Virginia. His former master intercepted the letter and through it traced Burns to Boston, where, with the aid of a Federal marshal, he had him arrested.

The Vigilance Committee sprang into action. When Burns was brought before Commissioner Ellis Gray Loring, Richard Henry Dana volunteered to act as his counsel, though at this point Burns feared that any legal resistance would only result in more severe punishment when he was returned to his master. He was, observed Dana, "a piteous object . . . completely cowed and dispirited."[15]

Succeeding in winning a delay of Burns' hearing, Dana found his client to be both literate and intelligent—so much so, that since the age of seven his master had hired him out. Burns had only run away when he became convinced his master was about to sell him south.

Down in Washington, meanwhile, Douglas and his cohorts relentlessly pressed for passage of the Nebraska Bill in the House, where the vote would be much closer. Perhaps the most stirring speech against it was delivered by none other than Thomas Hart Benton of Missouri. Benton's outspoken opposition to the extension of slavery into the Territories—when the majority of Missourians were all for it—had finally cost him his Senate seat of 30 years. Now returned as a Congressman, his scathing condemnation had lost none of its edge. "What is the excuse for all this turmoil and mischief? We are told it is to keep the question of slavery out of Congress! . . . It was out of Congress completely, entirely, and forever out of Congress, unless Congress dragged it in by breaking down the sacred laws which settled it!"[16]

Despite Benton's speech, the House passed the bill by a vote of 113 to 100. One of the most volatile pieces of legislation in American history had just become law.

Back in Boston, two nights before Anthony Burns' hearing, a mass meeting was held in Faneuil Hall. Richard Henry Dana was surprised at the presence of many prominent Whigs who had been proponents of the Compromise of 1850 with its Fugitive Slave Act. "Men who would not speak to me in 1850 and 51," he recorded, "stop me in the streets and talk treason. This all owing to the Nebraska bill."

Dana's biggest surprise came when Amos Lawrence, the cotton tycoon who had long opposed any measures that might alienate the South, informed him that he and his colleagues were prepared to pay the legal expenses incurred in the defense of Burns. Why? Because they were determined that it "be known that it was not the Free-Soilers only who were in favor of the liberation of the slaves, but the conservative Compromise men."[17]

All this had come as a result of the just-concluded debate over the Kansas-Nebraska Act. Indeed, it was already being said that in two months Douglas had converted more Northerners to intransigent Free-Soil doctrine than Garrison and Wendell Phillips had converted to abolitionism in 20 years.

That night at Faneuil Hall, first Theodore Parker, then Wendell Phillips brought the crowd shouting to its feet. "I want that man set free in the streets of Boston!" thundered Phillips. "If that man leaves the city of Boston, then Massachusetts is a conquered State!"[18]

The crowd roared out of the hall and stormed the Federal courthouse where Burns was being held. But the Federal marshals and their deputies were waiting for them, and they had guns. In the ensuing melee a deputy was killed, and nine assailants were jailed. At that moment it looked as if all Boston might soon be up in arms, so two artillery companies were called out, then a company of regular army troops, and then a company of Marines.

Under this heavy guard, with the court building cordoned off, the hearing proceeded. It lasted four days and reached the only determination possible under the new fugitive slave law: Burns would have to be returned. As the army contingent escorted Burns to a Virginia-bound ship, the soldiers were roundly condemned by the throngs of onlookers, while the flags of Boston flew at half-mast, and the city's church bells tolled a mournful dirge. "When it was all over," wrote Boston attorney

George Hillard, "and I was left alone in my office, I put my face in my hands and wept."

Over telegraph wires flashed the news, and countless Northerners were similarly moved. "We went to bed one night old-fashioned, conservative, Compromise Union Whigs," noted one, "and waked up stark mad abolitionists."[19]*

From that moment, the North became convinced that the South had broken the spirit of the Compromise of 1850, and was hell-bent on extending slavery in every direction, as far as she possibly could. And from that moment, throughout most of the North the Fugitive Slave Law was worthless.

With the passage of the Kansas-Nebraska Act, Douglas thought he had achieved the political solution that would unite not only his party but his country. He could not have been more wrong. For now the fate of Kansas would be decided by how many Free-Soil pioneer families settled in that Territory versus how many proslavery families came.

Seward had seen it coming. As dawn was approaching at the end of the debate in the Senate, he declared, "Come on, then, gentlemen of the Slave States! Since there is no escaping your challenge, I accept it in behalf of the cause of freedom. We will engage in competition for the virgin soil of Kansas, and God give the victory to the side that is stronger in numbers as it is in right!"

Douglas jumped to his feet. "I accept your challenge! Raise your black flag; call up your forces; preach your war on the Constitution, as you have threatened it here. We will be ready to meet your allied forces!"[20]

The competition, never friendly to begin with, would soon devolve into the bloodiest confrontation on American soil since the War of 1812. "Before Kansas-Nebraska," observed prominent historian Bruce Catton, "the country's chances of avoiding a civil war were problematical, but fair; after Kansas-Nebraska they were virtually nonexistent."[21]

The South had long been spoiling for a fight. Now the North was ready for one, too. And now the editors, *all* the editors, were leading the charge, with Horace Greeley in their van. "We of the North have not sought this struggle, but if it is forced upon us, why, we are ready!"[22]

---

* Burns' freedom was purchased by two Massachusetts ministers, who brought him to Boston. He died in Canada in 1862.

Even George Templeton Strong, hitherto opposed to the abolitionists' goal of what he dubbed "Niggerocracy," was surprised at how deeply the new Fugitive Slave Act and the return of Anthony Burns had affected him. "I'm resisting awful temptations to avow myself a Free-Soiler. . . . Every indication of Northern sentiment points to a vigorous reaction against the Nebraska bill and the formation of a strong antislavery party at the North."[23]

The new party would soon be forthcoming, and the Kansas-Nebraska Act brought it into being. Indeed, so strong was anti-Nebraska sentiment throughout the North that hundreds of meetings sprang up across the country to protest the new law. To them came antislavery Democrats, conscience Whigs, abolitionists, Free-Soilers, and many who simply felt that slavery should not be allowed to spread. Long-term political enemies now found themselves shoulder to shoulder in a common cause: The Missouri Compromise should not have been repealed, and slavery should not be allowed to expand. These meetings inspired other larger meetings, at which the resolution of those present grew steadily deeper. They began to call themselves Republicans, and in the summer of 1854 the Republican Party was born.

Into it streamed many Whigs whose own party was dying from dissension and irrelevance. Founded to oppose Jacksonionism, under the leadership of Clay and Webster the Whig party had been a major political force in America. But slavery had divided it, and there were no great leaders left to reunite it. To the Republicans also came thousands of disenfranchised Northern Democrats whose party, in uniting behind the Nebraska Bill, had cast itself as pro-choice where slavery was concerned.*

Along with giving rise to the Republican party, the Kansas-Nebraska Act also had one unnoticed but far-reaching effect: It drew Abraham Lincoln back into politics.

---

* Two other parties deserve a footnote. The Free-Soilers also ran in the 1852 election, but received only 5 percent of the popular vote—half what they had four years before. And the Know-Nothing party, refuge for those vehemently opposed to the flood of immigrants to America, was enjoying its brief zenith.

35

RAIL-SPLITTER

*T*he long, lanky figure tilted back in his desk chair so that his feet could find a resting place on the broad, paper-strewn desk. His white shirtsleeves had the cuffs turned back to keep them clean, should unexpected formality require him to don the black coat that hung on a peg on the back of the door. There was a tarnished brass spittoon beside the desk, for the benefit of clients who chewed. On the shelf behind him was a set of books of Illinois case law, out of alphabetical order because he kept the ones he used most often closest to hand.

He wasn't using them now. His hands were clasped behind his head, and he was gazing out the window at the pattern the noonday sun made on the old sycamore tree. Anyone glancing in the open door might have thought the gaunt country lawyer was daydreaming. But he wasn't. He was thinking. And when Abe Lincoln put his mind to a thing, he was at work.

When the Whigs chose not to renominate him for Congress because of his opposition to the Mexican War, Lincoln had been perfectly content to resume his private practice in Springfield, Illinois. While in politics, he had certainly had his share of ambition, but once politics was done with him, he was done with it. He shrugged and went back to practicing law on behalf of the local farmers and small businessmen. He was disappointed, but not bitter. Not one to demand attention or assume that he deserved preferential treatment, he never forgot his humble origins and never thought himself better than another man—which meant that just about everyone who met him liked him.

Abraham Lincoln was born on a small farm in Kentucky in 1809. His was a pioneer family, and they moved with the frontier—first to Indiana, then to Illinois. His father, Thomas, was a good farmer and "straight as a string," as the saying went. His mother, Nancy, was a devout woman who often read the Bible to him and his sister, until she died when he was nine.

In the distant future, tales of his hardscrabble childhood would waft around the 6'4" Lincoln, with seemingly little more substance than the smoke of a prairie campfire. But in his case they were true. He *did* read voraciously by the light from the hearth fire, devouring *Robinson Crusoe*, *Pilgrim's Progress*, and the plays of William Shakespeare, for which he had sufficient regard to commit long passages to memory. He also studied the Bible and could quote Scripture at length and at ease. He *did* walk miles to borrow a book or return a dime, and he *did* split countless rails for countless fences.

He was good with an axe and good with a team of oxen. But he was also good with his mind, and by the time he was 21 he had determined that he was not going to be a farmer. He worked as a storekeeper, a postmaster, a flatboatman down the Mississippi, and the elected captain of his company of volunteers in the Black Hawk War. He liked daily contact with people and was considering a career as a blacksmith, when he took up law instead.

What accounted for the abrupt and unlikely transition? Lincoln, who always loved to tell a story, told it this way:

One day, a man who was migrating to the West, drove up in front of my store with a wagon which contained his family and household [goods]. He asked me if I would buy an old barrel for which he had no room in his wagon, and which he said contained nothing of special value. I did not want it, but to oblige him I bought it and paid him, I think, half a dollar for it. Without further examination, I put it away in the store and forgot all about it. Sometime after, in overhauling things, I came upon the barrel and emptying it out upon the floor to see what it contained, I found at the bottom of the rubbish, a complete edition of *Blackstone's Commentaries*. I began to read those famous works [on the law], and I had plenty of time; during the long summer days, when the farmers were busy with their crops, my customers were few and far between. The more I read, the more intensely interested I became. Never in my whole life was my mind so thoroughly absorbed. I read until I devoured them.[1]

A powerful analytical mind, yoked with an immense strength of will, is a wondrous team to behold. Abraham Lincoln had such a mind and such a will. His great passion was to understand an idea so deeply that he could see where it would lead, how it would affect different people, and what must be done to achieve the greatest good. When casual acquaintances referred to him as being "lost in thought," in reality his concentration was as acute as that of a chess master whose entire world had narrowed down to 64 squares. This extraordinary acuity enabled him to reduce a complex concept to its fundamental elements, so that anyone could understand it. Until he had gotten an idea that simplified, so that an ordinary man of the fields could readily grasp it, he would keep on thinking.

As it had been when he was preparing cases for trial, simplicity continued to be his watchword—which made him an anomaly in the golden age of oratory. At a time when America's favorite spectator sport was watching a great speaker cast a spell with finely wrought phrases, lofty sentiments, and burnished grandiloquence, Lincoln refused to play the game. He could quote Shakespeare or the classics with the best of them, but he preferred to deal in homespun logic and common sense, presenting a succession of simple truths that generated a power of their own. It was the power of understanding. Once you opened your mind even halfway to what Lincoln was saying, it was awfully hard to see it any other way.

Lincoln had two other things going for him as he embarked on his career as a prairie lawyer, and later as a politician: integrity and honesty. Never, under any circumstances, would he try to win more for his client than he felt the client in justice deserved. If you wanted him to represent you, you first had to convince him that your cause was just. Moreover, if it ever turned out that you had deceived him, he would simply quit the case.

His associate and secretary, Ward Hill Lamon, recalled one closely contested civil suit in which Lincoln's client was "a very slippery fellow," though Lincoln did not know it at the time. After Lincoln had presented his client's side, the opposing attorney produced a receipt that proved Lincoln's client had been lying. By the time the attorney had finished, Lincoln was missing. The court sent for him at the hotel at which he was staying. "Tell the Judge," said he, "that I can't come; my hands are dirty, and I came over to clean them."[2]

There were many such stories, and out of them came the nickname that would stick with him throughout his legal and political career: "Honest Abe."

Compassion was the other thing that drew country people to Abraham Lincoln's shingle. Had he gone into the ministry, he would have been said to possess that rare commodity, a true pastor's heart. He genuinely *cared*—and the people whom he represented knew it. If they were strapped for cash, he would reduce his fee, or even waive it altogether. His clients never forgot that. It was a philosophy that Lincoln was wont to pass on to young lawyers just starting out: "Discourage litigation. Persuade your neighbors to compromise whenever you can. Point out to them how the nominal winner is often a real loser, in fees, in expenses, and waste of time. As a peacemaker, the lawyer has a superior opportunity [to be] a good man. There will be business enough."[3]

For Lincoln there certainly was. By the time he went to Congress in '47, he had earned a reputation as being one of the most distinguished and successful lawyers in the West, perhaps even in the country. So when he returned to private practice, in addition to the disadvantaged, his client list included the Illinois Central Railroad and various banks and corporations. He was soon making $1,500 a year. (The Governor of Illinois was paid only $1,200 a year.)

All his life, Lincoln's footsteps were dogged by melancholy, which may explain why he so dearly enjoyed a good story. In those days of few diversions, storytelling was an art. Most men tried their hand at it, but few were gifted. Lincoln was one of the best. Not only was he an astute judge of character who knew exactly what would delight his listener, he was also a master raconteur, with perfect timing and the confidence to let the scene build in his listener's imagination. It came in handy in the courtroom, and even more so after a gracious dinner or standing at a tavern bar.

Such opportunities to make use of his talent arose in his practice, as the attorneys and judges often traveled together when the circuit court made its rounds. Judge Davis later remembered that Lincoln "never complained of the food, bed, or lodgings. If every other fellow grumbled at the bill of fare which greeted us at many of the dingy taverns, Lincoln said nothing."[4]

Though out of politics, Lincoln never lost his national perspective. Indeed, he had spent the five years prior to the passage of the Kansas-Nebraska Act wrapping his mind around slavery, examining the institution from every conceivable angle. As he did so, his own position gradually matured: While still no abolitionist, he was now adamantly and unalterably opposed to its spread. More than that, he was fully prepared to fight to keep it from spreading. So when Kansas-Nebraska passed, he felt impelled to take action. What could one man do? Abraham Lincoln was going to find out. He reentered the political arena.

He did so as a Whig. He had been one for 20 years, and Illinois was one of the few states left where the Whigs' party structure was still strong. In the fall of 1854, he was elected to the State Legislature. In running for that office (and aware that a U.S. Senate seat would be open the following spring), he gave his first major anti-Nebraska speech. The culmination of all his careful thinking, it would set the tone for the speeches that followed.

The annual Illinois State Fair was under way in Springfield, and it seemed as if every Illinois farmer and his family were there. Senator Douglas was there, too, back on his home turf to drum up support for the Kansas-Nebraska Act—and indirectly for himself, since the next Presidential election was barely two years away.

Why was it necessary to stump the state for a bill that was already law? Because Douglas was belatedly discovering how wildly unpopular was the act that he had rammed through Congress. As he himself wryly observed, he could have traveled from Boston to Chicago by the light of the fires burning him in effigy. The A in Stephen A. Douglas stood for Arnold, and anti-Nebraska men wondered in print if his first name should have been Benedict. One group even sent him 30 pieces of silver.

But in Chicago he planned to set all of that aright. Chicago, the fastest-growing, most industrialized metropolis of the West, was where he was confident he would turn the tide. He would give a major address that he was certain would put Chicago solidly behind Kansas-Nebraska (and behind its author for President in '56). The rest of Illinois would follow suit, and with his home state firmly behind him, he would begin his march east toward the White House.

There was just one problem: Three-quarters of Chicago seemed to be anti-Nebraska. In fact, the animosity was so deep-seated that Douglas's friends in Chicago urged him to stay away. But Douglas was a scrapper, and this was just the sort of challenge he thrived on. The speech would go on.

Douglas supporters did their utmost to ensure a favorable outcome. They chose North Market Hall in the heart of his Irish constituency, and let it be known that any hecklers would be roughly dealt with by a large, well-armed bodyguard of Irishmen. Sales of revolvers were brisk.

On the evening of September 1, the entire city held its breath. Showing their disapproval, ships in the harbor lowered their flags to half-mast, and church bells in town commenced a solemn tolling. But the people that began to arrive (of the highest classes of society, said the newspapers) were in a surprisingly affable mood.

Douglas opened by saying that he wished to elucidate the Kansas-Nebraska Act, since he doubted anyone in the audience understood it properly. (The audience emitted three hearty groans, the papers reported parenthetically.) After all, said Douglas, the bill had never been published in the city's papers. (Laughter and groans.) Amid such frequent punctuation, he did his best to make the case for Kansas-Nebraska, but to the ears of his listeners every sentence seemed tinged with proslavery sentiment. When he declared that he had only been carrying out the wishes of the electorate, he was interrupted with cries of "No!"

As the temperature in the hall rose, tempers on both sides of the footlights rose with it. Thoroughly exasperated, Douglas bellowed that they were behaving like a mob, and he would silence the mob or they would stay there till morning. (Members of the audience burst into song: "We won't go home until morning, we won't go home until morning!")

At that, Douglas lost what remained of his composure and shouted at them that in that case he *would* go home. (Cries of "Good! Good!") Jamming his hat on his head, he shook his fist at them and shouted, "It is now Sunday morning; I'll go to church, and you may go to h——l!"[5]

But Douglas did not quit. He *was* a fighter, and a powerful and persuasive speaker. He swung south, and southern Illinois was more receptive to what he had to say. The audiences grew larger, the responses more positive. Everywhere he went, he had the floor to himself; there was no one speaking against the Kansas-Nebraska Act. And he began to prevail; the public mood began to shift. Those who had been lukewarm became positive, and those who had been negative became neutral. It began to look like, with the exception of Chicago, Illinois might be his after all.

Then he came to the Springfield State Fair. On October 3, he spoke in the packed-out House Chamber of the State Capital. It was the same speech he had made elsewhere, and it was as warmly received. But this time it would not go unopposed.

On the very next night, announced flyers and handbills, Abe Lincoln would also speak in the House on the Kansas-Nebraska Act.

Now 45 years old and still rail thin, Lincoln appeared in his shirtsleeves without a tie, sweating in the humidity like everyone else. He had personally invited Douglas to attend, and there in the front row sat the Senator, glowering up at him. But this was not the same awkward and gangly adversary whom Douglas had known five years before.

At first Lincoln's voice was shrill with nervousness, but it soon settled down, as with simple, commonsense logic he proceeded to dismember Douglas's case point by point.*

The need for organizing the new Territories in no way called for the repeal of the Missouri Compromise. A bill without it had already passed the House and would have passed the Senate, had Douglas not injected the slavery issue. As for the Territories' geography precluding slavery, one had only to look across the border in Missouri: What was now flourishing there could hardly be expected to wither and die a few miles away on the Kansas side.

Why did he oppose the Kansas-Nebraska Act? Slavery. The bill's declared indifference to slavery's spread would actually encourage it.

> I hate it because of the monstrous injustice of slavery itself. I hate it because it deprives our republican example of its influence in the world, enables the enemies of free institutions with plausibility to taunt us as hypocrites, causes the real friends of freedom to doubt our sincerity. And especially because it forces so many good men among ourselves into an open war with the very fundamental principles of civil liberty, criticizing the Declaration of Independence, and insisting that there is no right principle of action but self-interest.[6]

* As this speech represented the distillation of Lincoln's thinking on slavery for the previous five years, and the essence of his position for the next six, it will be examined in detail.

He next turned to the issue of popular sovereignty, the best-liked aspect of the bill. *Was* it right for the settlers of a Territory to decide its status for themselves? The Territory *was* national domain, and therefore what occurred in it was the concern of every citizen of the United States, not just those who settled there. Moreover, the Compromise of 1850 *in no way* negated the Missouri Compromise; it was merely a specific bargain at a specific time and place.

Then he looked at the mechanics the new bill failed to address: When exactly would the new settlers decide? When there was a thousand of them? Ten thousand? Fifty thousand? And if it was decided early, what if all those who came later did not agree? Would there be another referendum? In the absence of any procedural legislation, there was no guarantee that popular sovereignty would be decided peaceably at the ballot box.

Quite the contrary, exclaimed Lincoln: Some Yankee organizations were already sending emigrants to Nebraska to exclude slavery from it. But the Missourians were hardly asleep.

> They resolve that slavery already exists in the territory; that more shall go there; that they, remaining in Missouri, shall protect it; and that abolitionists should be hung or driven away. Through all this, bowie-knives and six-shooters are seen plainly enough, but never a glimpse of the ballot box. . . . Is it not probable that the contest will come to blows and bloodshed? Could there be a more apt invention to bring about collision and violence on the slavery question, than the Nebraska project is?

They saw it. Many for the first time.

Mounting waves of applause were now interrupting him, and he responded. "If this fight should begin, is it likely to take a very peaceful, Union-saving turn? Will not the first drop of blood so shed, be the real knell of the Union?" He looked from one open, hardworking face to the next. "Let no one be deceived: the Spirit of Seventy-Six and the spirit of Nebraska are utter antagonisms, and the former is being rapidly displaced by the latter."

Like anyone who had done much thinking about the Declaration of Independence, it was for Lincoln the bedrock on which the nation was founded. The Founding Fathers, he said, knew that slavery was evil, and recognized that it was too entrenched to be uprooted in a single stroke.

But as it was fundamentally opposed to the spirit of the Declaration, they had deliberately confined it to "the narrowest limits of necessity," hoping thereby that they were dooming it to extinction.

What he meant by the "Spirit of Seventy-Six" was, quite simply, government by the consent of the governed. Slavery was a "total violation" of that principle, but now the proponents of Kansas-Nebraska were claiming the right to take their "property" there—and by extension "to every other part of the wide world, where man can be found inclined to take it."

In other words, the spirit of Nebraska was proclaiming "that there can be a *moral right* in the enslaving of one man by another . . . sad evidence that, feeling prosperity, we forget *right*—that liberty, as a principle, we have ceased to revere."

Lincoln stated flat out what the nation had for decades been avoiding: A man was a man, no matter what the color of his skin. He was not, Lincoln made clear, advocating full social and political equality.* Nor was he advocating abolition. He was making common cause with the Founding Fathers: He knew a necessary evil when he saw one, yet he did not know what to do about it. Of one thing he was certain: It was a *national,* not a Southern, responsibility. And he reminded his Northern brethren that Southerners "are just what we would be, in their situation."

He acknowledged the *Constitutional* right of Southerners to hold slaves and admitted the legitimacy of the Fugitive Slave Law. *But*—"it should not in its stringency be more likely to carry a free man into slavery than our ordinary criminal laws are to hang an innocent one."[7]

Above all, the black man was a human being. God had most certainly created him equal, as the Bible made clear and the Declaration affirmed. And because the nation had tacitly agreed with this, she would have to make a choice: either the Spirit of the Declaration, or the spirit of Nebraska. And as she made up her mind, the whole world was watching. America had raised the banner of freedom and given downtrodden multitudes all over the globe cause for hope. Now that banner was faltering.

In conclusion, Lincoln called for a repudiation of the Kansas-Nebraska Act and a restoration of the Missouri Compromise. "Let us turn slavery from its claims of 'moral right' back upon its existing legal rights. . . . Let

---

* In 1854 white Americans, including most of those who opposed slavery, were not yet ready to accept that concept.

us re-adopt the Declaration of Independence. . . . If we do this, we shall not only have saved the Union, but we shall have so saved it, as to make and to keep it *forever worthy of the saving!*"[8]

The hall was on its feet cheering, including the newspaper reporters who had become so enthralled that they had forgotten to take notes.

But they remembered to do so twelve days later, when Lincoln gave essentially the same speech in Peoria. Soon what Lincoln had stated was reported all across the country:

> Judge Douglas, frequently, with bitter irony and sarcasm, paraphrases our argument by saying: "The white people of Nebraska are good enough to govern themselves, but they are not good enough to govern a few miserable Negroes!"
>
> Well! I doubt not that the people of Nebraska are, and will continue to be, as good as the average of people elsewhere. I do not say the contrary. What I do say is that no man is good enough to govern another man without that other's consent. I say this is the leading principle, the sheet-anchor of American republicanism.[9]

Abraham Lincoln had found his national voice—and his calling.

With fairness and compassion he had spoken the truth. And anyone with ears to hear it and a heart to accept it knew that it *was* the truth—plain, unvarnished, and eternal.

Lincoln had sown seeds in prairie soil that would soon grow into an overwhelming harvest.

36

BLEEDING KANSAS

*T*he faces reflecting the glow of the campfire were cheerful, but also sad. Though they were only three days out of Independence, three of the circled wagons would be leaving in the morning. The rest of the train would continue west over the plains for the next two months and would take another month to get over the Rockies. But these three families would drop off here and head southwest, to find homesteads along the Dragon River. The farmland would be good, perhaps not as fertile as the Eden that awaited the others in California, but these three families had not come just to farm.

After much prayer, they had decided to start new homes in the Territory of Kansas, to be part of the peaceable light of freedom that was being kindled there. Their preacher had encouraged them, telling them that they would be part of God's plan to see that Kansas came into the Union free, not slave. But they had also done their own praying and gotten their own guidance. And they did feel that He would have them go, together.

Even before the Nebraska Bill became law, pioneers had been trickling into the Territories. That flow now became a steady stream. And as a result of the doctrine of popular sovereignty, it was a contest clearly drawn and in desperate earnest: Whichever side had the most settlers at the time the constitution was drawn up would decide how Kansas entered the Union.

Back East, nearly all the antislavery activists were too tied down or had too many important commitments to actually come themselves. But there were hundreds of immigrant families just waiting for the opportunity to emigrate west. The trouble was, carving out a homestead—building a cabin and a barn, purchasing equipment and a team, then clearing, fencing, plowing, planting, and harvesting fields—took money.

For an emigrant family to make it through the first year to the point that they could bring produce to market generally took between four and five thousand (1855) dollars. Most would-be pioneers did not have a tenth of that. So those who could help them organized societies to raise the necessary funds. Eli Thayer of Worcester, Massachusetts, incorporated the first such organization, later known as the New England Emigrant Aid Society. If you had some available discretionary income and detested slavery, if you wanted to see Kansas come in free but were not in a position to go yourself, the next best thing was to enable a family who was ready and willing to go. In its first year, Thayer's society sent 1,240 people to Kansas. It was not a great number, but other organizations were also doing the same thing.

The slaveholders in Missouri's western border counties, who stood to be the most affected if Kansas wound up free, sent out their own urgent appeals throughout the South. Proslavery societies sprang up to help anyone with slaves who was prepared to move to Kansas. Some Southern ladies even sold their jewelry for the cause.

But there were not as many takers in the South. Anyone with slaves would think twice about taking all his "capital" into such an unstable situation, especially when there was the distinct possibility that Kansas might become a free state. For all its recruiting efforts, the South was falling farther and farther behind. By anyone's count, more Free-Soilers were moving into Kansas and making their headquarters in the frontier town of Lawrence.

The proslavery men along Missouri's western border, now convinced that their very way of life was imperiled, took matters into their own hands. They organized societies of a different kind: gangs of heavily armed irregulars whose sole mission was to intercept Kansas-bound Free-State homesteaders and dissuade them from continuing, or to uproot those already settled in the Territory. Comprised of men who would rather fight than farm anyway, they took to their new assignment with great gusto.

By 1855 the telegraph was well established, and nothing could happen out in Kansas that wasn't talked about the next day back in Massachusetts. If rough was the way the "Border Ruffians," as they came to be called, wanted to play, then rough was the way it would be. From now on, each homesteading family sent west would be equipped with one of the new breech-loading Sharps rifles. They cost $25 apiece, but, said the fund-raising abolitionists, they were worth every penny. As Henry Ward Beecher proclaimed from the pulpit, "One Sharps rifle will have more moral influence upon slaveholders than a hundred Bibles!"[1] Accordingly, from his congregation he raised enough money to send 25 Sharps rifles to Lawrence. In the accompanying letter, he wrote: "There are times when self-defense is a religious duty. If that duty was ever imperative, it is now, and in Kansas."[2]

From then on, shipments of rifles, sent to Lawrence in boxes variously labeled "Books," "Revised Statutes," and even "Bibles," bore the wry nickname "Beecher's Bibles."

Out in Kansas, chaos reigned. It was about to become bloody chaos. Confided Missouri Senator David Atchison to Mississippi Senator Jefferson Davis: "We will be compelled to shoot, burn, and hang, but the thing will soon be over."[3]

The proslavery press was hardly confidential; it put its appeal right out there for all to read. The *Kansas Pioneer* called on Southern men to come with rifle, knife, and revolver to get rid of the abolitionists: "Send the scoundrels back to wherever they came from, or send them to hell, it matters not which."

On May 8, Atchison's *Squatter Sovereign* was even more explicit. Recounting one incident, it cried, "Blood for blood! But for each drop spilled, we shall require one hundredfold! Let us purge ourselves of all abolition emissaries . . . and give distinct notice that all who do not leave immediately for the east, will leave for eternity!"[4]

Moving to stave off further bloodshed, Territorial Governor Andrew Reeder called for the immediate election of a Territorial legislature. The election was scheduled for March. By rights it should have been an undisputed victory for the Free-Staters, who now clearly outnumbered the proslavery homesteaders. But it did not turn out that way.

Every able-bodied border-county Missourian who could ride a horse or a buckboard was urged to cross over into Kansas and vote—as many times as possible. Some slashed a blaze on a tree to indicate that they intended one day to raise a farm there; most did not even bother. They came not only to vote but to discourage Free-Staters from the advisability of going to the polls, and this they did their liquored-up best to do. According to a census taken just before the election, only 2,905 eligible voters resided in the Territory. Nonetheless, the final tally read: Free-Soil votes, 791; proslavery votes, 5,427. In the tiny settlement of Douglas with some 30 residents, 226 ballots were cast.[5]

It was clear to Governor Reeder (and everyone else) that a massive fraud had been perpetrated. But the Border Ruffians were everywhere and intimidating; Governor Reeder allowed the results to stand. Instantly petitions were sent to President Pierce, who declared the election results legal, despite the mounting evidence of fraud.

The situation rapidly deteriorated. The proslavery majority in the newly elected legislature now banded together and expelled the few elected Free-Staters in their midst. Then with a free hand they made it the law of the Territory that anyone heard expressing doubts about slavery could find themselves in jail, and anyone caught harboring a fugitive slave would be hanged.[6]

Things went from bad to worse during the remainder of 1855. Governor Reeder, attempting to preserve some semblance of justice, dissolved the legislature. But for that action, President Pierce removed him from office and replaced him with a reliable proslavery Governor, Wilson Shannon. The Free-Staters, now finding conditions in the Territory intolerable and appeals to the President futile, elected their own Governor and legislators, and declared that they, not the proslavery administration headquartered in Leavenworth, were the rightful representatives of the Territory's citizens. At a convention in Topeka, they drew up a Free-State constitution and applied to Washington for statehood.

At this point, with two rival governments each claiming legitimacy and the danger of hostilities escalating into all-out civil war, a strong President would have done three things: Send in enough Federal troops to secure and maintain order in the Territory; launch a thorough, impartial investigation into all charges and countercharges; and hold a new, rigorously scrutinized election in which only bona fide residents could vote. But Pierce was neither strong nor impartial. Giving the full support of the U.S. Government to the proslavery government in Leavenworth, he denounced the Topeka convention and branded the Free-Staters as rebels, warning them that if their movement led to organized resistance by force, it would be considered "treasonable insurrection."[7]

The effect of this was to further encourage the Border Ruffians, who now formed companies with such colorful names as the Atchison Guards, the Doniphan Tigers, and the Kickapoo Rangers. Throughout the South, men were recruited to join their ranks and rescue Kansas from the abolitionists. Major Jefferson Buford of Alabama raised a company of 300 irregulars, sold 40 of his slaves to finance their expedition, and led them to Kansas, where Governor Shannon welcomed them and designated them the "Kansas Militia."[8] With 500 other irregulars they marched on Lawrence, arriving on May 21, 1856, and demanded that all arms in the town be surrendered.

Vastly outnumbered, the townspeople elected to eschew resistance and made no attempt to defend themselves. They turned over a howitzer, four small cannon, and a score of rifles. But their peaceable attitude only infuriated their adversaries the more. The invaders now became an unruly mob, ignoring their leaders. They got drunk and took over the town, destroying its two presses and burning down its main building, the Free State Hotel.

News of the raid elicited a storm of indignation throughout the North. Subscriptions were taken up to replace the presses, more boxes of Beecher's Bibles were shipped west, and out in the Territory some hard men determined to take revenge. One was a bearded fanatic and self-styled prophet named John Brown.

Back East, the situation was scarcely quieter. In March, Congressman Preston Brooks of South Carolina, who had served with the Palmetto Regiment during the Mexican War, published a letter that summed up the Southern mindset: "The admission of Kansas into the Union as a slave State is now a point of honor with the South. . . . It is my deliberate conviction that the fate of the South is to be decided with the Kansas issue."[9]

Men on Capitol Hill were again talking openly of civil war. As far as Andrew Butler, the elderly and highly esteemed Senator from South Carolina, was concerned, the Union *was* dissolved. "Really, it is broken already; for the spirit which cherished it has been extinguished, and the very altars upon which we ought to worship have been profaned by false fires."[10]

The North had its own grating men, and none more strident than Senator Charles Sumner of Massachusetts. Regarding himself as an unerring exponent of moral law, Sumner had declared war on slavery: "All that I am or may be, I offer to this cause."

In his eyes, that was a substantial contribution, for he considered himself perhaps the most erudite and gifted member of either house. Nor was he considered any less by New England abolitionists, who were proud to have him in Washington.

But Charles Sumner was also insufferably haughty and arrogant, a man utterly devoid of humor, who could tolerate no opinion that deviated from his own. He also had a cruel streak in him and took pernicious delight in his skill at using words as a duelist would a rapier, from the safety of the parliamentary protocol that under no circumstances should a member of Congress ever fear physical reprisal for what was said in either house.

That protocol was based on the presumption that the members of both houses were gentlemen, and no gentleman would address another in terms unbecoming or inappropriate to their high office. Charles Sumner considered himself above such constraints; as a result, his attacks on the personal character of his opponents made him the most detested member of the Senate, a man to whom many affronted Southern Senators simply refused to speak. In the South, only Garrison was more loathed.

The day before the Lawrence raid, Sumner rose in the Senate and delivered a speech that he had printed out in advance, so that it might be telegraphed to abolitionist editors who could be counted on to reprint it. To Theodore Parker he had boasted that it would be "the most thorough philippic" ever heard in a legislative body, and for several evenings he practiced its delivery in his boarding establishment, which caused boarders in neighboring rooms to leave the house. Sumner was supremely confident that this speech would earn him his deserved place in history. But when he showed the finished draft to his colleague, William Seward, the latter, instead of encouraging him, recoiled and urged him to tone it down. He didn't.

Sumner opened by condemning the crime against Kansas as "the rape of a virgin territory, compelling it to the hateful embrace of slavery!" As far as new information or a fresh perspective was concerned, the speech had nothing to offer. It was, in fact, no more than an occasion for personal invective, and he reserved his most vitriolic remarks for his colleague from South Carolina, at that moment absent from the forum. Mocking

Andrew Butler's manner of speaking, he scornfully derided him for having "chosen a mistress to whom he has made his vows, and who, though ugly to others, is always lovely to him; though polluted in the sight of the world, is chaste in his sight—I mean the harlot, Slavery."[11]

At which point Stephen A. Douglas, shaking his head, was heard to mutter, "That d——n fool will get himself killed by some other d——n fool!"[12]

Sumner's disdainful ridicule, coupled with its *double entendre* reference to an extramarital relationship so singularly out of place regarding Butler, managed to offend everyone, even Sumner's abolitionist colleagues. Lewis Cass condemned the speech as "the most un-American and unpatriotic that ever grated on the ears of the members of this high body."[13] And Douglas, whom Sumner had contemptuously dismissed as playing Sancho Panza to Butler's Don Quixote, deplored the attack on the "venerable, courteous, and distinguished Senator from South Carolina," calling the speech "a Yankee bedquilt . . . of classic allusions, each one distinguished for its lasciviousness and obscenity . . . unfit for decent young men to read."[14]

To which Sumner retorted: "The noisome, squat, and nameless animal, to which I now refer, is not a proper model for an American Senator—will the Senator from Illinois take notice?"[15]

One man decided that the time had finally come for more than name-calling. As it happened, Butler had a cousin over in the House, none other than Palmetto Regiment hero Preston Brooks, who now chose to disregard the time-honored Congressional code of behavior. That code was for gentlemen. And Sumner, in his vile and cowardly attack, slurring the honor of a senior member of Brooks's family who was not even present, had clearly forfeited his right to be treated as a gentleman. Sumner had behaved as a cur and needed to be disciplined as such.

On May 22 (the day after the Lawrence raid), Brooks did just that. Taking his heavy gutta-percha walking stick, he strode into the Senate Chamber after that body had adjourned and went to Sumner, who was at his desk franking copies of his speech. Announcing that he had read Sumner's speech twice and found it libelous, Brooks proceeded to rain down blows on Sumner's head and shoulders, continuing even as the stout cane broke into smaller and smaller pieces. Sumner was beaten senseless to the floor.

Northern outrage was instantaneous. Spontaneous mass meetings sprang up; nothing in years had so deeply incensed so many. "A ruthless attack upon the liberty of speech, an outrage of the decencies of civilized life, and an indignity to the Commonwealth of Massachusetts!" cried that commonwealth's legislature. "We regard every blow inflicted upon our Senator as a blow aimed at us!"[16]

Robert Winthrop, whose seat in the Senate Sumner had assumed, wrote from Boston: "You can have little idea of the depth and intensity of the feeling which has been excited in New England. The concurrence of the Kansas horrors has wrought up the masses to a state of fearful desperation."

Even George Templeton Strong was moved to observe: "I hold the antislavery agitators wrong in principle and mischievous in policy. But the reckless, insolent brutality of our Southern aristocrats may drive me into abolitionism yet."[17]

The House of Representatives could not muster the necessary two-thirds majority to expel Brooks, but it did censure him. He forthwith resigned, only to be immediately and nearly unanimously reelected by an approving constituency. For the Southern reaction to the incident was that Sumner had it coming to him. And from a number of slaveholding gentlemen, Brooks received gifts of elegant walking sticks to replace the one he had broken in caning Sumner.

It would take Sumner more than three years to fully recover from the blows. In the meantime, his vacant seat in the Senate bore mute testimony to just how far collegial goodwill had deteriorated.

Eight months later, there was a startling postscript to the episode: Preston Brooks, ill with a fever and a sore throat, suddenly and inexplicably died of a respiratory seizure, which his doctor said was brought on by croup. While South Carolina eulogized its fallen young champion, Charles Francis Adams privately wrote what many others were thinking: It seemed "like a providential visitation."[18]

Perhaps the most accurate summation of the prevailing situation— certainly the most ominous—was recorded by William Cullen Bryant of the New York *Evening Post*: "Violence reigns in the streets of Washington. . . . Violence has now found its way into the Senate chamber. Violence lies in wait on all the navigable rivers and all the railways of Missouri, to obstruct those who pass from the Free States into Kansas. Violence overhangs the frontiers of that Territory like a stormcloud charged with hail and lightning."[19]

News traveled two ways on the telegraph wires that stretched to Kansas. And now, as news of the caning of Sumner reached the frontier, it set off a lightning storm of violence that made all that had gone before it pale in comparison.

37

CAPTAIN BROWN

*T*hey rode in silence through the night, seven forms emerging from the shadows and returning to them. Even the horses' hooves seemed muffled. When the creek they were following left the woods and came out into the open, the faint light of a quarter moon glinted off the shafts of steel attached to the men's belts—government-issue broadswords, forged to protect gun crews in the event that they were overrun by cavalry. They were long, straight, and two-edged, and for this night's work the edges had been honed razor sharp.

When the man at the head of the column turned to check on the others, the moonlight reflected off his white beard and close-cropped hair. It caught his steely bright eyes, sunken deep above the gaunt cheekbones. Limned in the pale light, he looked like an avenging angel—which was exactly what he thought he was.

For this was John Brown, and on this night he would at last fulfill the two verses of Scripture that he had quoted over the years with such fondness. From Job: "And I brake the jaws of the wicked, and plucked the spoil out of his teeth." And from Hebrews: "And almost all things are by the law purged with blood; and without shedding of blood is no remission."*

When he was young, John Brown had thought God was calling him to the ministry, but he had been forced to drop out of the preparatory schooling due to lack of funds. He was called; he knew that. But God had not yet revealed the nature of his calling. Until He did, everything Brown turned his hand to failed—farming, tanning, sheep growing, wool brokering, land speculation.

* Job 29:17; Hebrews 9:22

He had been caught passing bad checks and embezzling, and though freed upon his promise to repay every cent, by the time he left Ohio he had been involved in no fewer than 21 lawsuits. The endless cycle of repeated failure had begun to grind on him to the point where, even were there not a strong history of insanity in his family,* the failures by themselves might have been enough to drive him mad.

In 1837, at a memorial service for the slain abolitionist editor Elijah Lovejoy, John Brown finally found his calling. No sooner had Elijah's brother Owen finished his eulogy, than Brown, standing at the back of the church, raised his right hand as if taking an oath and solemnly swore: "Here, before God, in the presence of these witnesses, I consecrate my life to the destruction of slavery."[1]

And so he did. Yet even here, failure dogged him. Incensed at the Fugitive Slave Act, he had attempted to raise a company of free blacks and escaped slaves, which he would arm and teach how to resist anyone coming North looking for slaves. He even had a name for them, the League of Gideonites. But no black man in his right mind would follow this Gideon (who might not be in *his* right mind) down the bloody path where he proposed to go.

These were not normal times in America, however; they were mad times. The radical abolitionists were beside themselves with impotent rage, frustrated beyond belief by proslavery's unbroken succession of political victories. So, what others might regard as a dangerously unbalanced, even pathological fanaticism, some of the more extreme abolitionists applauded as exactly the sort of resolute, charismatic leadership that the times called for.

And so the abolitionists of Boston society adopted John Brown, much as they had such former slaves as Frederick Douglass, Harriet Tubman, and Sojourner Truth. Julia Ward Howe, who with her husband, Samuel, would become one of his supporters, found him "a Puritan of the Puritans, forceful, concentrated, and self-contained,"[2] while Douglass assessed him as "lean, strong, and sinewy, of the best New England mold, built for times of trouble . . . a figure straight and symmetrical as a mountain pine."[3] Indeed, said Douglass, "whenever he spoke, his words commanded

---

* His mother and grandmother died insane, and three uncles from that side of the family were similarly afflicted.

earnest attention. His arguments seemed to convince all, and his will impressed all."[4]

But Boston businessman John Murray Forbes discerned something that had escaped the others: a "little touch of insanity about his glittering gray-blue eyes."[5] And of his eyes, Sumner himself would note that he had never met a man whose eyes more resembled cold steel.

To the Boston abolitionists, John Brown became a hero in the making. They might hold their large rallies and their clandestine meetings, might write impassioned letters to the newspapers, but John Brown was actually going to Kansas, was actually going to use those Sharps rifles with which they were happy to supply him! Outfitting him completely, they sent him off with their prayers and good wishes, and all the money he would need.

For the first time in his life, John Brown was a success. Accompanied by a son and son-in-law, he was going to Kansas, where five of his other sons and their families had sought a new life.* Now he joined their little settlement on Osawatomie Creek and soon formed an armed company to repel any Border Ruffians that might come their way. It was a small company, not more than 10 men in all, and most of them his sons. But he proudly named them the Osawatomie Rifles and installed himself as their commander. Henceforth, he would be addressed as *Captain* Brown.

It did not take long for Old Brown (which is what nonfamily called him behind his back) to run afoul of the law, such as it was on the frontier. Up on nearby Pottawatomie Creek, a German saloon keeper named Henry Sherman also owned and operated a farm with the help of his brothers, William and Peter. He had accused Brown and one of his sons of stealing 24 cows and two horses. Also, Brown's eldest son, John Jr., following his father's example, had recently been found in contempt of court for challenging the legitimacy of the new proslavery edicts. Young Brown would soon be going on trial to face these charges.

But all of that was set on the back burner by the raid on Lawrence. A frantic call for help had gone out, but by the time the Osawatomie Rifles arrived, the hotel and the Governor's house were in smoldering ruins. "Something must be done to show these barbarians!" exclaimed Captain Brown, and it was evident that he intended to be the instrument.[6]

---

* Brown had no trouble fathering children: He had 7 by his first wife, 13 by his second.

Two days later, the telegrapher's key clicked with the news of the attack on Senator Sumner, and Brown reacted as if he himself had received the blows. One of his sons reported that the Old Man "went crazy—*crazy!*"[7]

He soon calmed down and informed his men that tomorrow night, May 24, would be payback time. So far, by Brown's count, five Free-Staters had perished at the hands of Border Ruffians. Very well, tomorrow night the score would be evened. The proslavers lived by the sword; tomorrow night five of their number would die by the sword.

And so the avenging angel of Osawatomie rode out at the head of a column comprised of four of his sons and two others.

Their first destination was the home of James Doyle, the second was Allen Wilkinson's, and the third was "Dutch Henry" Sherman's. None of them owned slaves, but all were known to be proslavery sympathizers. There was method in Brown's madness—these were not random selections. Doyle and Wilkinson were the two witnesses who could give testimony against his son in the contempt citation, and Dutch Henry had sworn out an affidavit against Brown for rustling.

As they approached Doyle's cabin, the latter's two dogs started barking—and were quickly silenced. A soft knock brought Doyle to the door, whereupon he was commanded to surrender to the "Army of the North."[8] They dragged him outside, then went in after his three sons. His wife, Mahala, sensing the worst, begged them to spare her youngest, and they did.

Out under the prairie moon they hacked Doyle and his two sons to death, splitting open their skulls like melons. Once the blood started flying, the murderers lost control and began slashing at the bodies until one of the arms was completely severed.

As they passed by the cabin on their way on up the creek, Mahala Doyle screamed at Brown, demanding to know: How could he do such a thing? Brown replied that if a man stood between him and what he thought was right, he would take that man's life as coolly as he would eat his breakfast.[9] Then they departed, the wails of Mahala Doyle ringing in their ears.

Less than a mile up the creek they came to the sod house of Wilkinson, who, despite the screams and pleading of his wife, was dragged outside and executed with the same cold-blooded butchery as the Doyles had been. Then John Brown went marching on, for he had one more call to pay.

At Dutch Henry's Crossing, it turned out that Dutch Henry was out on the prairie that night searching for missing cattle. But his brother Dutch Bill was home, and he would do as well. They slaughtered him as they had the others, again hacking away at the remains until one of his hands was cut off.

In the morning, as word of the Pottawatomie Massacre spread, one of Brown's sons who had not gone on the raid asked him: "Did you have anything to do with that bloody affair on the Pottawatomie?"

"I approved of it."

"Whoever did it, the act was uncalled for and wicked."

"God is my judge," Brown calmly replied. "The people of Kansas will yet justify my course."[10]

The people of Kansas had no difficulty reaching judgment about who had done it; it was almost as if the murderers had left eyewitness survivors on purpose. Brown led his band out onto the prairie to lie low till things died down, and help came from back East. It was not long in coming, and incredibly it came in the form of adulation.

Though journalism had no such thing as medicine's Hippocratic Oath, by which doctors solemnly swore to do their utmost to save and heal their patients, there was supposed to be a code of objectivity. When reporting the news, it was understood that newspapers would only deal with the facts: the who-what-where-when-and-how. Opinions and emotions would be reserved for the editorial page. But when feelings ran as high as they did over Kansas in 1856, the temptation to present the truth in a certain light was overwhelming. And what might appear to be perfectly objective to the staff of one paper might strike the staff of another as egregiously slanted.

"WAR! WAR!" screamed the front page of the Westport, Missouri, *Border Times*. And while it was true that Brown's action touched off a fresh round of reprisals and counteractions, these seldom involved more than a score of men on each side.* But to read the lurid descriptions of these actions in the Southern press, one envisioned brigades and battalions

---

* One of the most opportunistic raiders was William Quantrill, who started off as a Free-State farmer leading raids into Missouri, then switched sides and started leading raids into Kansas. Ultimately he would become the prize villain of Kansas history, sacking Lawrence as a Confederate captain.

wheeling and marching—as if the civil war that many had been dreading (or eagerly anticipating) had already begun.

On the other hand, the antislavery press, which now included nearly all the Northern newspapers, took so much liberty with what actually happened at Pottawatomie Creek that even Brown was astonished. At first they said that he and his band had been set upon by a vastly superior force and were only trying to defend themselves. But as each editor or magazine writer added his own embellishments, the account grew progressively more grand. The final version had it that a band of Border Ruffians had fallen upon a poor Free-Stater and were about to hang him, when Captain Brown and his troops (still vastly outnumbered), arrived in the nick of time. They put up such a heroic defense that they were able to save him and drive the Ruffians off.

Of those more familiar with the evidence, none thought it curious that the men who died at Pottawatomie had been unarmed and slain in their nightshirts in front of their homes. When their widows offered to give testimony, they were ignored. When they submitted sworn depositions, the documents were suppressed. Thus was the legend of John Brown born, and it proved so dear to the abolitionists that they were able to keep the truth of Pottawatomie from coming out for 22 years.

The only thing competing with the border war for front-page newsprint that fall of '56 was the next Presidential election. In a belated effort to improve his image in the hope that his party would renominate him, President Pierce had finally appointed a new, strong Governor to the Territories, John W. Geary. Arriving with sufficient troops to impose immediate law and order, and treating proslavers and Free-Staters with an even hand, Geary brought things under control. At last, tensions out in Kansas began to subside.

When Brown returned East a year later, he was lionized as the first *bona fide* war hero of the abolitionist cause. He basked in the praise—and began laying plans for a *real* coup, a raid so bold and daring that it would ignite the North-South holocaust he longed for. And he would be the spark.

He did not talk about it with anyone, not at first. But in his eyes, there was a new gleam.

38

1857

As far as the Democratic party was concerned, what President Pierce had belatedly done to restore order in Kansas was too little and too late. Meeting in Cincinnati on June 2, 1856, to determine whom they would put forth as their Presidential candidate in the fall election, the majority of delegates felt that the country would not put up with four more years of Pierce's indecision and pandering to Southern sensibilities.

Clearly the best choice was Stephen A. Douglas. But the Kansas-Nebraska Act, for which he had claimed all the credit and was now harvesting the lion's share of the blame, had produced high negatives. These had been exacerbated by the caning of Sumner, his outspoken adversary.

Consummate politician that he was, Douglas well knew that in four years' time, with Kansas peaceably absorbed into the Union as a free state, both the North and South factions of the party would be looking to the new Harry of the West for leadership. Deciding to wait until 1860, Douglas withdrew his candidacy.

That left James Buchanan. A handsome and successful lawyer and life-long bachelor, Buchanan was the ideal compromise candidate. His record of public service was decidedly undistinguished—James K. Polk, whom Buchanan served as Secretary of State, despised his craven opportunism, as he "takes on small matters and magnifies them into great and undeserved importance."[1] But it was also unmarred. He had no skeletons in the closet. And though from Pennsylvania, he was something of a "doughface" (a Northerner with Southern principles). He had never expressed any moral repugnance for slavery, believing that the South should simply be left alone. He loathed abolitionists and Free-Soil Republicans alike, and frankly could not distinguish between them. Nor did he care to, though others went to great lengths to differentiate them. To keep Northern Democrats from bolting the party, he had to stress the right of the Kansans to decide for themselves about slavery. But being a thoroughly political animal, he was aware that the party's center of gravity had shifted South; two-thirds of the delegates who voted for him were slaveholders.

Buchanan was, therefore, adamantly opposed to the Wilmot Proviso. And there was something else that recommended him to the slaveholders: As Minister to Great Britain, at a meeting in Belgium he had played a large part in drafting a secret dispatch calling for the United States to wrest Cuba from Spain, to prevent the sort of servile insurrection there that had overswept Haiti half a century before. (Cuba would then, of course, be added to the slaveholding states.) It was the high-water mark of the Slave Power's adventuring in the Caribbean, and when the contents of the dispatch were leaked to the press, the outcry over the "Ostend Manifesto" was so great that the administration was forced to disown it. But the slaveholders had not forgotten who authored it. Adding further to the ticket's appeal to the South was the choice of Buchanan's running mate: Congressman John C. Breckinridge of Kentucky.

But this was not the most significant political gathering of 1856. That distinction belonged to the meeting that had taken place four days before, in Bloomington, Illinois. Billed as an anti-Nebraska convention, it attracted more Republicans than anything else. But there were also a great many men who were not yet ready to call themselves Republicans, as the emerging party was still equated with abolitionism. There were bolting Democrats, a scattering of Know-Nothings, and a number of old-line Whigs, including the delegate from Springfield, Abraham Lincoln.

Feelings were running high. Scarcely a week had passed since the "sack of Lawrence" and the caning of Sumner, so it was not surprising that the opening oratory was ranting and extreme. Then a cry went up for Lincoln to speak. As he stood up and prepared to do so, men shouted, "The platform! The platform!" They wanted him up in front of them, the better to see and hear him. Many had heard about his speech in Peoria and were anxious to hear what he had to say.

Lincoln was solemn as he began. Looking to Kansas, he called for calmness and moderation, and they listened, for that evening he seemed able to see beyond the horizon.

Unless the violence unleashed in Kansas was soon halted, he exclaimed, "Blood will flow . . . brother's hand will be raised against brother." As he gazed on this grim vision, his face took on an expression that was "earnest, impressive, if not, indeed, tragic . . . as to make a cold chill creep" over his audience.

He then went on to demand the restoration of the Missouri Compromise, but asserted that the South was entitled to a "reasonable and efficient" fugitive slave law.

"No!" cried someone in the audience.

"I say *yes!*" replied Lincoln. "It was part of the bargain! . . . but I will go no further!" (Thunderous applause.)

He spoke then with great love of the Union, of its sacredness and the necessity of preserving it, no matter what the sacrifice. This was his greatest and deepest concern, and as he concluded, he rose up on his toes (so that, noted one observer, he "looked seven feet tall") and threw down the gauntlet to the enemies of the Union: "We will say to the Southern disunionists: We won't go out of the Union, *and you shan't!*"[2]

Tumultuous cheering greeted this proclamation, which would go down in history as one of the great declarations of principle, alongside Andrew Jackson's toast rebutting Calhoun: "The Federal Union, it must be preserved!" and Daniel Webster's "Union and liberty, now and forever, one and inseparable!"

Abraham Lincoln had stated his credo—and the credo of the Republican party, which that night he had done much to clearly define.

But outside Illinois, Lincoln was practically unknown; for every man who knew of him, a thousand knew of Douglas. So when the Republicans held their national convention in Philadelphia a fortnight later, Lincoln's name was not on anyone's short list of potential Presidential candidates.

There was tremendous enthusiasm at that convention; observers likened it to the fervor of a revival meeting. All the seasoned Whig leaders were there—William Seward, Thaddeus Stevens, Charles Francis Adams, Horace Greeley, as well as such antislavery champions as Joshua Giddings and Henry Wilson. David Wilmot, despised in the South but a hero here, brought in a platform that called for no extension of slavery into free territory and the prompt admission of Kansas into the Union as a free state.

Seward was the most prominent Republican, but after his "Higher

Law" speech, he was perceived as being too radical to stand a chance of winning. There being no war heroes left, they chose the next best thing, an intrepid frontier adventurer—John Charles Frémont. Capitalizing on his widely published (and enhanced) exploits, they nicknamed him "the Pathfinder." Lincoln received 110 delegate votes as Vice President and was inwardly relieved when he was not chosen. As historian Albert Beveridge has pointed out: "Frémont's strongest characteristics were those which Lincoln did not trust—impulsiveness, insubordination, overgallantry, and dash."[3]

Be that as it may, the Republicans had their ticket and their slogan: "Free Speech, Free Soil, and Frémont!"

As the campaign got under way, Kansas became the key issue. To Southerners, the new Republican party was abolitionist to the core. Henceforth, most would never refer to it simply as the Republican party, but as the "Black Republican party," signifying how overly enamored of the Negro race they felt the Republicans were. A number of Southern states threatened to secede if the Republican candidate won. A meeting of Southern Governors went further, declaring that if the Black Republican won, it was not just a threat; their states *would* secede.[4]

It was a hard-fought, bitter campaign, causing diarist George Templeton Strong to comment after attending a Frémont rally: "Frémont won't be President, my dear, deceived, short-sighted brothers. . . . Ten years hence there will be some Frémont who can make it worth one's while to hurrah for him, but *you,* my unknown vociferous friends and fellow-citizens, are premature!"

His entry on the opening of the Democratic convention was more sobering: "Can civil war between North and South be postponed twenty years longer? I fear we, or our children, have got to pass through a ruinous revolutionary period of conflict between two social systems before the policy of the U.S. is finally settled. The struggle will be fearful, when it comes."[5]

When the election came, to no one's surprise the Democrats won. But to everyone's surprise, the Republicans, who were not even on the ticket in the South, made it a much closer race than expected. They won most of the North and came within a whisker of winning in Buchanan's native Pennsylvania. To win in 1860, all they would have to do would be to hold on to the states they had just won and pick up Pennsylvania and one other Northern state—Illinois, Indiana, or New Jersey.

As it happened, there was a third candidate in the race—old Millard Fillmore, backed by an uneasy coalition of Whigs and Southern Know-Nothings, who siphoned off enough Northern votes to make Buchanan a minority President, having gained only 45 percent of the popular vote.

At Buchanan's inauguration on March 4, 1857, the President-elect was seen in long private conversation with the Supreme Court's Chief Justice, Roger Taney. Speculation as to the nature of their discussion, in light of the decision soon forthcoming from the Court, would fuel the fires of Northern paranoia.

But on that balmy day as Buchanan raised his right hand, he had no comprehension of the magnitude of the Kansas problem and the enormity of the slavery issue that loomed behind it. In his Inaugural Address, he declared that the goal of his administration would be to restore peace between the sections of the country, so that the public's attention could shift from slavery to what he deemed were matters of "more pressing and practical importance."[6]

In 1834, when Andrew Jackson appointed Attorney General Roger Taney to be Chief Justice of the Supreme Court, he had every reason to believe he was the best possible man for the job. Shortly after Taney had married Francis Scott Key's sister and begun his legal career in Baltimore, he had represented a Methodist minister indicted for preaching an anti-slavery sermon. In defending him, Taney had forcefully exclaimed that slavery was "a blot on our national character, and every lover of freedom confidentially hopes that it will be effectually wiped away. And until that time shall come when we can point without a blush to the language held in the Declaration of Independence, every friend of humanity will seek to lighten the galling chains of slavery!" Nor were these ringing phrases mere courtroom rhetoric; Taney forthwith manumitted his own slaves.[7]

But in the 23 years since then, much had happened in Maryland and the United States. Taney was now most definitely of the Southern mindset, as were four of the other justices who were slaveholders. So when the Dred Scott case came before them, Taney's interpretation of the Declaration was somewhat different than it had been in his youth.

Dred Scott was an elderly black slave whose owner had been an Army surgeon named Emerson, stationed in Missouri. When Dr. Emerson was transferred to Illinois in 1834, he took his slave with him, though slavery was outlawed in that state. Two years later he was posted to the Wisconsin Territory, where slavery was also outlawed. Eventually he and Scott returned to Missouri, where Emerson died in 1843.

Three years later, with the help of local antislavery lawyers, Scott sued to gain his freedom, on the grounds that the years he spent in Illinois and Wisconsin made him a free man. He lost his case, then won on appeal in 1850, only to have the State Supreme Court reverse the appeal. In 1854 the case was tried again in the Federal courts, and finally it was heard by the U.S. Supreme Court.

There were two prickly questions posed by the case: First, was Scott, a slave, also a citizen, since only citizens had the right to sue in the Federal courts? Second, was the Missouri Compromise's prohibition of slavery constitutional?

The Constitution defined a slave as *property*, and the Fifth Amendment guaranteed that no one should "be deprived of life, liberty or property without due process of law."

The Supreme Court's decision came down on March 6, two days after Buchanan's Inauguration. It was a split decision, 5 to 4, and Chief Justice Taney wrote the opinion for the majority: Dred Scott had no right to sue. At the time the Constitution was written, blacks "had for more than a century been regarded as beings of an inferior order . . . so far inferior that they had no rights which the white man was bound to respect."[8] Therefore, slaves and freed descendants of slaves were *not* citizens.

As for Scott's freedom, Taney decreed that Scott had none of that either. Slaves were property, and slaveholders had an absolute right to take their property with them into the Territories. Moreover, decided Taney, going far beyond the parameters of the case before the bench, any law such as the Missouri Compromise that abridged the constitutionally protected right of property, was in itself a violation of due process. Not only was the Missouri Compromise thus declared unconstitutional, but by Taney's interpretation Congress had no authority to prevent slavery in any Territory. In fact, no Northern state could refuse to admit a slaveholder bringing in his slaves!

The reaction to such blatant judicial social engineering was immediate and intense. The New York *Tribune* declared that "Chief Justice Taney's opinion was . . . based on gross historical falsehoods and bold assumptions that went the whole length of the Southern doctrine," and the headline in the New York *Independent* announced that "The Decision of the Supreme Court is the Moral Assassination of a Race and Cannot be Obeyed."[9] On Capitol Hill, Congressman John Potter of Wisconsin spoke for many of his colleagues when he condemned the decision as "sheer blasphemy . . . an infamous libel on our government . . . a lasting disgrace to the court from which it issued, and deeply humiliating to every American citizen."[10]

Taney may have meant well, hoping that he had thus laid the slavery question to rest, once and for all. Instead, he had stirred up the worst hornet's nest anyone had ever seen. The Missouri Compromise had been observed for 36 years, and in many Northern minds it had taken on a sacred character. "If epithets and denunciations could sink a judicial body, the Supreme Court of the United States would never be heard from again," commented one observer.[11]

As Kenneth Stampp points out in one of his books,* slavery was a local institution, whereas freedom was a national birthright. The Taney decision had abruptly reversed that: Slavery was now national and freedom local. Said William Cullen Bryant in the New York *Post*, the Court's decision had transformed what had once been the South's "peculiar institution" into "a Federal institution, the common patrimony and shame of all the States. . . . Wherever our flag floats, it is the flag of slavery. If so, that flag should have the light of the stars and the streaks of morning red erased from it; it should be dyed black, and its device should be the whip and the fetter."[12]

The Slave Power had gained yet another victory—but it was a Pyrrhic one: When the dust from the Dred Scott decision settled, many formerly moderate Northerners were now convinced that there was indeed a malevolent "slavocracy" conspiracy at work behind the scenes, controlling the Executive branch, the Senate, and now the Supreme Court as well. While Northerners hardly had a corner on paranoid speculation, in truth there were very few who were still neutral on the subject of slavery.

There was one more hand to be dealt and played before 1857 drew to a close. Shortly before Buchanan became President, the territorial legislature of Kansas began a drive for statehood. Buchanan encouraged them, looking forward to a new Democratic State, and called for a census to be

---

* *America in 1857: A Nation at the Brink*

taken, so that districts could be laid out and delegates sent to a constitutional convention in the territorial capital of Lecompton.

The Free-Staters assumed the election of delegates would be fraudulent, as before, and they were not disappointed. The proslavers so gerrymandered the districts that there was no way a constitution could be passed that prohibited slavery.* The Free-Staters boycotted the election, with the result that the Lecompton convention was made up entirely of proslavery delegates. Not surprisingly, they passed a constitution with slavery.

Would it be accepted? President Buchanan now made the greatest blunder of his career. Under immense pressure from both sides and paralyzed by his own indecision, he went first one way, then the other. (If ever a case was to be made for the importance of character in selecting a President, it was here.) Northern Democrats warned him that if he failed to declare the Lecompton constitution invalid, he would be trampling on the very soul of popular sovereignty.

But Buchanan was already under the sway of his closest Southern advisors, who were pointing out to him the advantages of accepting it as it stood: He would appease the Southern fire-eaters in his party, and could then force the Northern Democrats to stay in line. In this way, he could get both Kansas and himself out of the national limelight.[†]

It became increasingly apparent that Buchanan was about to reverse himself on the principle he had formerly espoused, that the people of Kansas should have a full, free, and fair opportunity to approve or disapprove their constitution.

At this crucial moment, Stephen A. Douglas, popular sovereignty's champion and the *de facto* leader of the Northern Democrats, came to Washington for the climactic confrontation of his career to date. Arriving on December 2, he was greeted by cheering crowds and bonfires, and urged on by supporters who were convinced that he alone could save the situation—and the Democratic party.

---

* When Elbridge Gerry was Governor of Massachusetts in 1812, his party redrew the boundaries of the State's districts to give their members the maximum number of counties, while confining their opponents to the minimum. On the map of these new districts, Essex County was so distorted that it had the fanciful appearance of a salamander. It was promptly dubbed a Gerrymander.

† It was the worst possible advice. Buchanan (and the South) would have benefited far more by letting Kansas come in free, as at that time the vast majority of her voters were popular-sovereignty Democrats. They would have greatly strengthened the party (which was still sympathetic to the South), instead of precipitating its schism.

The following day he paid a visit to the White House. Speaking as a friend, the Senator advised the President not to recommend acceptance of the Lecompton constitution. But Buchanan, whose message to Congress lay in a drawer already written, declared that he would urge acceptance.

"If you do," Douglas replied, "I will denounce it the moment your message is read."

The President stood up and terminated the interview, glaring down at the Senator. "Mr. Douglas, I desire you to remember that no Democrat ever yet differed from an Administration of his own choice without being crushed!" Then he added, referring to two Democrats who had dared to oppose Andrew Jackson, "Beware the fate of Tallmadge and Rives!"

Douglas glared back and angrily tossed his great mane of black hair. "Mr. President, I wish *you* to remember that General Jackson is dead!"[13]

The Democratic party was broken. The President urged Congress to accept the Lecompton constitution and therefore receive Kansas as a slave state, and true to his word Douglas rose in opposition. Calling the President on going back on his word, Douglas stated: "If this constitution is to be forced down our throats, in violation of the fundamental principles of free government, under a mode of submission that is a mockery and insult, I will resist it to the last!"[14]

He gave the most honest and therefore most moving speech of his life, and when they read it, most Northern Democrats agreed that he had done the honorable thing. He received letters from adversaries complimenting him on his forthrightness, and even from some Southern Democrats who had no more stomach for the fraud.

One Republican Senator, James Dixon of Connecticut, expressed his admiration in a letter to Gideon Welles:

> I see more and more what a struggle it cost him to sever all personal and political ties, and take his stand on the foundation of eternal truth and justice. . . . He could have had the assurance of fifteen States in the next Presidential election, with a good prospect of Illinois, Pennsylvania, and perhaps others. But he was decided and resolute. . . . The South never made a greater mistake than in provoking his opposition. He will prove a terrible foe.[15]

But Douglas was unable to sway enough of his colleagues in the Senate away from the Administration's position; the issue would be decided in the House.

Northern Democrats now appealed to Buchanan to modify his message. If the party stayed split, the Republicans were certain to win four years hence, for there would be no political entity to stop them. But by now Buchanan was beyond compromise: The bill would be presented "naked," without any softening language.

Out in Kansas the regularly scheduled elections for a new legislature had taken place. As Free-Staters now outnumbered proslavery settlers by almost two to one, the new legislature was strongly antislavery. It pushed through a bill putting the Lecompton constitution to a popular vote on January 4, 1858, 14 days after it had been passed. Seeing that they were certain to lose, the proslavery settlers boycotted the vote, and the Lecompton constitution was overwhelmingly rejected.

Back in Washington, on April 1, 1858, the U.S. House also refused to accept the Lecompton constitution. But a compromise of sorts *was* worked out. Congress sent the Lecompton constitution back to the voters of Kansas with a thinly veiled threat: If they did not accept it as it was and come in as a slave state, then they would not be eligible to reapply for admission until their population reached 90,000, which would take several years.

Again the voters of Kansas overwhelmingly rejected it.*

Thus 1857 saw the destruction of the last truly national political party, the only remaining instrument holding North and South in common purpose. With the Democratic party hopelessly split, men began to wonder what would now become of the Union itself.

There was a tragic irony in the reality of what was at stake: Scarcely 100 slaves were actually living in Kansas, among more than 30,000 whites. The climate *was* as inhospitable as Douglas claimed, and soon enough this smattering would have evaporated.

But not the principle; the principle was enormous. As Allan Nevins put it: "Ghostly armies fought in the clouds above Kansas, while legions with flaming swords stood in her red sunrises and purple sunsets."[16]

By now, millions of men and women in the North and South were caught in the grip of their emotions, further inflamed by memories of old affronts. But the overriding emotion was fear.

The North, looking at the South's near stranglehold on the Federal

---

* Kansas would wait four more years for statehood.

Government,* was just waiting for the South to carve Texas into five slave states, to say nothing of rumored Southern schemes to add the northern provinces of Mexico and Nicaragua, and perhaps other Central American countries as well, to their slave empire.

The South, equally paranoid, saw the inevitability of Oregon and Montana, as well as Kansas and Nebraska, coming in as free states, plus a burgeoning immigrant population and a huge industrial economy that would soon overwhelm them.

Historian Kenneth Stampp makes a strong case that 1857 was the pivotal year, "when the North and South reached the political point of no return—when it became well-nigh impossible to head off a violent resolution of the differences between them."[17]

The authors do not agree. There was no one point or one year that could be singled out as the watershed after which a peaceful solution was no longer possible. With God nothing was impossible, not even the situation in 1857.

More than a few men and women of God in America could see the writing on the wall, and shuddered at what they saw—horrendous judgment coming on both North and South if America, *all* of her citizens, did not face up to the slavery dilemma, accept responsibility for it, and determine to resolve it.

And now, God Himself was about to give America one last opportunity to avoid His judgment. But would she listen?

---

* They controlled the Supreme Court, the Executive branch, half the Legislative branch, and the chairmanships of the key committees in both houses of Congress.

39

REVIVAL!

*T*he tall man knelt on the floor, listening to the silence. Far below, he could hear the muffled sounds of the city, but here in the third-floor meeting room there was only the slow *tick . . . tock . . .* of the wall clock. Its hands stood at 12:14. In a shaft of noonday sun through the south window, a mote of dust hung suspended.

Jeremiah Lanphier watched it, for at that moment the tiny particle defined him—moving neither up nor down, entirely at the mercy of any shift of air. But there was no movement, no change, visible or invisible.

Jeremiah reflected on what had brought him to this place at this time, kneeling in this empty, still room. He had been born 49 years before, in a little town on the Hudson River called Coxsackie, about 20 miles south of Albany. For all his growing-up years, he had watched the steamships and barges passing by on the river, until it seemed that the whole world—and life—were passing him by.

When he was 31 years old he could stand it no longer and decided to seek his fortune downriver—in New York City, the largest metropolis on this side of the world. He entered the mercantile business, and in 1842 an extraordinary thing happened to him. At age 33, Jeremiah Lanphier discovered that Christ was real, and that He had died on the Cross, in order that all Jeremiah's sins might be forgiven.

This astonishing realization was followed by action: Jeremiah gave his life to Christ, and started to live "under new management," as a business-man might put it. Looking for a "going" church to join in downtown New York, he eventually settled into the Brick Presbyterian Church. Under its auspices he spent more and more of his free time working as a lay evangelist—passing out tracts, inviting people to church, and telling anyone who would listen about the marvelous Savior he had encountered. One observer later described him as having "a pleasant face, an affectionate manner, and indomitable energy and perseverance . . . a welcome guest in any house, shrewd and endowed with much tact and common sense."[1]

New York in 1857 was changing as rapidly as the rest of America. As the downtown districts became more and more industrialized, most of its citizenry who could afford to move did so, relocating farther uptown, where the cross streets were numbered in the 50s and 60s. Increasingly their former dwellings were taken by newly arrived immigrants who could not yet speak English and could get only the most menial jobs. The business offices, of course, remained downtown where the business was, and so New York produced the first commuters, men who would walk or ride horse-drawn trolleys to and from work each day.

As the membership of the downtown churches dwindled, a number of them, including the Brick Presbyterian Church, followed their congregations uptown. But one, the old North Dutch (Reformed) Church on Fulton Street, did not. The board of that church decided to see if they could draw a new congregation from among the immigrants now living around their church. To reach them, they hired as a full-time lay evangelist that tall, energetic fellow from Brick Presbyterian, Jeremiah Lanphier.

His chief assignment was to personally call on everyone who lived within walking distance and was not already attending a church. To each he would give a pamphlet describing the church and its services, a Bible if they did not possess one, and an invitation to join them the next Sunday. It was a daunting task, but it was just the sort of work Jeremiah loved, and commencing on July 1, he was even going to be paid for it!

As the weeks of summer passed and few responded to his invitations, he must have been tempted to become disheartened. But Jeremiah was a man of prayer. He *knew* God was with him in this venture, and he prayed for the grace to persevere. He did miss having a chance to pray with others and have his spiritual energy recharged in the midst of a busy day, and he wondered if the businessmen hurrying here and there ever wished they could have a quiet moment with their Creator.

"One day as I was walking along the streets," he recorded in his journal, "the idea was suggested to my mind that an hour of prayer, from twelve to one o'clock, would be beneficial to businessmen, who usually, in great numbers, take that hour for rest and refreshment."

The more Jeremiah thought about it, the more enthusiastic he became: "The idea was to have singing, prayer, exhortation, relation of religious experience, as the case might be; that none should be required to stay the whole hour; that all should come and go as their engagements should allow or require, or their inclinations dictate."[2]

A *weekly prayer service*—the meeting would be for businessmen, but workmen of all trades would be welcome. And because businessmen's lives ran on tight schedules, if they could drop in for only 5 or 10 minutes, fine. People could pray aloud if they felt so led; they could request the prayers of others for a personal concern, or they could share a word of testimony.

He printed up and passed out handbills, telling where and when the first businessmen's prayer meeting would take place: at noon, September 23, to run one hour in the North Dutch Church's third-floor meeting room on Fulton Street. "This meeting," the handbills said, "is intended to give merchants, mechanics, clerks, strangers and businessmen generally an opportunity to stop and call on God amid the perplexities incident to their respective avocations."[3]

But now, as the wall clock struck the half hour, it looked as if no one was coming. The mote of dust was at the edge of the sunbeam now, but that was because the sun had moved, not the air.

Anyone who has ever started a new project and wondered if anyone else would be interested knows the doubts that must have assailed Jeremiah as he knelt there in the stillness. But he did not get up, brush off his trousers, and with a sigh go to lunch. God had called him to do this. And so he stayed in communion with his Maker, trusting and obeying. And waiting.

The mote of dust lifted. Downstairs, someone had opened a door. There was a creak on the stairs. A man came into the room, saw Jeremiah, and without a word knelt beside him.

Another came, and another. By one o'clock there were six.

The following week there were 20.

The week after that there were 40—and these asked if they could start meeting every day; a week was too long to go without that blessed communion.

By October 8, there were so many men that they had to move down to the larger meeting room on the second floor. Jeremiah rejoiced. "There was a spirit of reconsecration to the service of Christ," he wrote, "and a manifest desire to live near His Cross."

By the fourth Wednesday there were "over a hundred present, many of them not professors of religion, but under conviction of sin and seeking an interest in Christ; inquiring what they shall do to be saved."[4]

As men were blessed, they encouraged friends and acquaintances to accompany them. And as Jeremiah had anticipated, the meetings drew men from all classes of society and all trades. Draymen would tie up their teams, slip in for a few minutes, then come out and go about their business. Shop foremen would mention the meetings to their workers; hotels would recommend them to their guests.

The "Fulton Street Meetings," as they came to be known, drew more and more men, and now a few women as well, until all three of the church's meeting rooms were full, and the John Street Methodist Church around the corner opened to handle the overflow. Other churches began to follow suit, many opening at the noon hour, with others opening before work. Soon there was such a need for places to pray that police and fire stations opened their doors for prayer.[5]

A traveler in New York on business, invited to attend such a meeting, might be surprised at what he found. At one meeting, speaking to some 3,000 New Yorkers in Burton's Theater on Chambers Street, Henry Ward Beecher related this recent incident:

> A merchant came here from Albany and called on one of our New York merchants to buy some goods. At twelve o'clock the New York merchant looked at his watch and asked to be excused for an hour. The other objected, as he was in haste to get through with his business.
>
> He replied that he must go to the prayer-meeting; it was of more importance than to sell his whole stock of goods. The gentleman from Albany inquired if he could not pray enough at morning and night without leaving his business at noon? The merchant said he could not; and by persuasion and gentle force he induced his friend to go to the prayer meeting with him. That man went to the meeting, became interested, and came out a converted man. He went home to Albany, and immediately started those prayer meetings there which have been so blessed of God.[6]

Beecher's words had the desired effect. When the meeting's leader offered two minutes of silent prayer for any present who had special needs, quite a number in various parts of the large hall rose and stood with heads bowed. After which another man offered to pray especially for those who wanted to come to the Savior. But before he could pray, another young man up in the balcony added in a quiet but audible voice: "If you are seeking Christ, do not be ashamed of it. It is the design of the devil to make you ashamed to allow your wants to be made known. Heed him not, but come to the Savior without delay."[7]

For many, the most refreshing aspect of these prayer meetings was that they were unstructured; their sole purpose was prayer. There was no liturgy, no preaching, no song leader announcing preselected hymns. Jeremiah Lanphier's original rules and directions were set down on paper and became the guide for all new prayer groups that would pattern themselves after the Fulton Street Meetings.

The most important direction was that the meeting commence precisely at twelve o'clock, and that the leader take no more than 10 minutes in opening it. There would be one hymn of not more than five verses nor less than three. There would be a prayer for the meeting and a portion of Scripture. Then the meeting would be open for prayer, with the attention of all drawn to the rules, posted in a prominent place: "Brethren are earnestly requested to adhere to the Five-Minute Rule. Prayers and Exhortations are not to exceed five minutes to give all an opportunity. Not more than two consecutive prayers or exhortations. No controversial points discussed."[8] A breach of the rules would be curtailed by the ringing of a bell.

Written prayer requests could be sent forward to the leader, who was directed to read only one or two at a time, with prayer to follow. In the event of anyone making a suggestion or a proposition, the leader was to remind all that this was simply a prayer meeting and that the speaker was out of order, and he was to call on another brother to pray. At five minutes to one o'clock, the leader was to announce the closing hymn and request a benediction from a clergyman, if one be present.

The punctuality and the strict adherence to the rules in these meetings became their hallmark. No exceptions were ever made, except to permit a member to finish his prayer. Individuals with a propensity to speak or pray beyond their allotted time might resent the bell, but businessmen under pressure were grateful for it.

Many commented on the powerful presence of the Spirit of God, and many men were moved to tears. Sometimes someone would start a well-known hymn, but it was always spontaneous, not forced or programmed.

Nor was any particular denomination featured in any way. If a preacher did stand up and give a very short word (the man at the bell had a pocket watch in hand), he was not to mention his denomination or say what church he was from. He was just another man among men, sharing what was on his heart.

In terms of sheer magnitude and speed of spreading, the prayer revival in New York was the most spectacular, but it was hardly the first. In a number of other cities, businessmen's prayer meetings were already under way by the time Jeremiah had started his; in fact, it was only later, when people began to compare notes, that they realized how many had spontaneously begun that summer and fall of 1857, and earlier. Clearly this new "awakening," as it began to be called, was a sovereign act of God.

Today the word *revival* has become so cheapened from overuse as to be almost worthless. In the true meaning of the word, revival was a nationwide, earthshaking, awe-inspiring event—a direct intervention of God Himself, reaching down and changing the lives of men and societies.

This country had experienced such revivals. The first was the Great Awakening, which began in the mid-1730s. By the time it subsided, it had swept the Atlantic seaboard and converted the majority of the people in the Colonies. Without that spiritual preparation, America could never have survived the struggle for independence.

The next awakening came at the dawn of the 19th century, just as the French Enlightenment was gaining a foothold in America's centers of learning. This time the lightning struck the frontier and the Eastern academic establishment simultaneously. Summer revival camp meetings grew and grew, until one at Cane Ridge, Kentucky, in 1801 saw approximately a tenth of the state get converted.

Back on the campus of Yale College, President Timothy Dwight was combating the Enlightenment's basic tenet that the Bible was a collection of myths and fantasies. With careful, Scripture-based logic, he appealed to his young students' moral rudders. A few gave their lives to Christ, then a few more, and they began to share their faith with their friends. At the revival's peak, half the college had been converted, and it spread to campuses throughout the East.

That revival, which came to be known as the Second Great Awakening, never really died away. A fresh wave began in 1824, in Oneida County, New York, under the "new measures" evangelism of Charles Finney. It, too, subsided but never died, as we have seen from the occurrences at Lane Seminary under the leadership of Theodore Dwight Weld.

Now it was beginning to happen again on a truly national scale. The necessary spiritual spadework had been done. For years many had been faithfully praying (and undergirding their prayers with personal repentance) for just such a revival. And God was once again keeping the promise He made in 2 Chronicles 7:14. His people, the ones called by His name, *were* praying and seeking His face and turning from their wicked ways. And He was hearing their prayers and was pouring out His Spirit upon all flesh.

Commencing in 1857, the editors of Boston's *Watchman and Reflector* determined to focus their entire publication on a campaign to promote spiritual awakening "throughout New England."[9] Their news columns were soon filled with enthusiastic reports of special efforts to precipitate revivals in Massachusetts, Rhode Island, Brooklyn, and in half a dozen New York City churches.

By April 2, they were jubilant. "We believe that the people of God may now believingly address themselves to the work of promoting revivals everywhere!"[10]

In Newark, Baptist pastor Henry Clay Fish cried, "What can save our cities but a powerful revival of religion? What one thing does this whole country so loudly call for, as the descent of the Holy Ghost upon the churches?"[11]

Nor were the Congregational ministers far behind. Heman Humphrey, converted under Timothy Dwight at Yale and now president of Amherst College, became a prominent "new measures" revivalist. Mark Hopkins, president of Williams College, was working for revival on his campus, as was Leonard Bacon at Yale, which once again became a center of revival, with half the student body converted.[12] (Though much of Boston was awakening spiritually, the revival passed over Harvard, entrenched as it was in Unitarianism.)

Perhaps the best-known of the New England revivalists was Edward Norris Kirk, minister of the Mt. Vernon Church in Boston, which became the major soul-winning institution in the city, producing in 1851 the first Young Men's Christian Association. The revival introduced the strongly evangelical YMCA movement in many cities, showing young men of different denominations that it was possible to set doctrinal differences aside and join forces for a common goal. In 1858, that goal became citywide evangelism campaigns.

Revival *was* in the air, but years before this mass outpouring of God's Spirit, fires had been kindled. In 1854 the churches in the industrial cities of Nashua, New Hampshire, and Lawrence, Massachusetts, were reporting scores of conversions after several weeks of nightly meetings. The whole town of Campton, New Hampshire, had undergone a powerful awakening the year before, which prompted one participant to declare, "We could no longer hesitate to say, 'The Pentecost has fully come.'"[13]

In 1857 the clergy of Boston invited Charles Grandison Finney, the most famous 19th-century revivalist, to conduct a six-week campaign at Park Street Church. He accepted with a smile, for some of these men or their fathers had once bitterly opposed his "new measures." Now he applied these new measures for the men of Boston, while in the vestry his wife was holding similar meetings for the ladies. Once more, God honored Finney's obedience by pouring out His Spirit; Finney stayed, and the Park Street Church became a spiritual powerhouse, lighting up much of Boston.

But not all. Boston's best-known minister, Unitarian theologian Theodore Parker, now attacked the prayer revival with all the contempt he could muster. He proudly declared that he and his fellow Unitarians were above such lamentable doings: "As well might we expect to produce fire by friction of ice blocks, as to expect a revival among Unitarians."[14]

As the revival came to full bloom in 1858, so did Parker's loathing of it. The revival that was really needed, he proclaimed, was a revival of the Christian churches; "no institutions in America are more corrupt than the churches. No thirty thousand men and women are so bigoted and narrow as the thirty thousand ministers."

Finney did what the Bible told him to do under such circumstances. He went to his adversary's home to see if some reconciliation might not be achieved; they were, after all, both men of the cloth, presumably praying to the same God. But when a servant announced Finney, Parker refused to see him.

Throughout the length and breadth of the land, it soon became apparent that the Holy Spirit was doing an altogether extraordinary work. And as if to confirm that it *was* the sovereign hand of God, a ship arrived in New York Harbor whose captain and entire crew of 29 men had been converted in the middle of the Atlantic Ocean, "without any obvious special instrumentality!"[15] Soon after that, five other ships sailed in, all of whose captains had been brought to Christ on the open sea.

As for their crews, the very dregs of New York's inhabitants were the seamen temporarily ashore in the Battery district at the bottom of Manhattan. Gambling, boozing, brawling, and carousing with "ladies of questionable virtue," they kept the police of the Water Street precinct fully occupied. But then revival broke out in the Baptist Mariner's Church on Cherry Street. Among those whose lives were transformed were crewmen from the USS *Congress,* whose chaplain reported that subsequently other members of the crew were "strangely affected while on a cruise to the eastern Mediterranean." Similarly, the crew of the USS *North Carolina* had become "so pious and serious" that they conducted meetings aboard the vessel.

In the meantime, the beneficent contagion spread ashore, infecting both the Methodist Seamen's Chapel and the Presbyterian Mariners' Church, which reported 230 seamen "won to the faith."[16] Sometimes men at sea would, in fact, become so convicted that the first thing they wanted to do when they were granted shore liberty after a 30-day ocean crossing was to seek out a place of worship!

But the Holy Spirit had only begun to move.

"Stand Up, Stand Up for Jesus"

*T*he man stood at the open window, looking down at the busy noonday street far below. On the desk behind him was an open bank ledger, with a series of entries indicating that in the past two weeks he had lost $63,258. Next to it was a demand note from his broker for $13,412, which he did not have. The sum of his assets was in his pockets: $14.63.

The town house on 57th Street would have to go, and the cottage in the country. The servants, the horses, the clubs, his wife's jewelry . . . They would have to rent rooms somewhere while he tried to find a job. The boys would be affected, too; they would have to drop out of Columbia. But how could he face his friends? How could he face life? It was all so utterly hopeless. He ran his finger along the sill of the open window. . . .

In the noon prayer meetings that were flourishing in downtown New York that fall of 1857, there were more than a few finely tailored suits, their presence occasioned by what had suddenly happened to the economy. That summer, all of northern America had been caught up in a paroxysm of greed. Entrepreneurs had speculated in railroads stretching ever westward, often where there was no urgent need. And staying one step ahead of them, bogus land developers were reaping fortunes. Everyone knew that nothing appreciated so fast as land bought where the railroad would soon be going. So if you had inside information on where the *next* Chicago was likely to rise. . . .

In the growing certainty that Kansas would soon come in as a free state, land speculation reached a fever pitch. On the barren plains vast mythical metropolises were laid out, and their lots sold back East at ever higher prices, until some of the pieces cost almost as much as real urban landscape. So vast and numerous were these blueprint cities, they covered as much territory as all the real cities in the Northern and Middle states combined.[1]

With fortunes being made and doubled almost overnight, even the most conservative financiers began to lose their perspective. Some of the newer banks began to speculate themselves—despite clear signals that the long-booming, go-ahead economy was slowing down.

The bubble burst in August with the shocking failure of a large and trusted Ohio bank. Suddenly people everywhere began to wonder if their own banks were safe. They decided to get their life savings out, only to discover that the banks had insufficient funds. The ensuing nationwide panic precipitated such a run on the banks that the entire system collapsed. The stock market crashed, factories closed, unemployment soared. In New York City, 30,000 men were out of work, and ugly mobs roamed the streets shouting "Bread or work!"[2]

The crash cut across all levels of society. Only the very rich, whose vast holdings in land, real estate, and other hard assets insulated them, came through relatively unscathed. As did the South. Cotton continued to be in great demand, and the slaveholders took the crash as a sign of the superiority of their system.

Strangely, there was nothing intrinsically wrong with the economy when the crash happened. While it was no longer booming, it was still growing. And in less than six months it would regain a full head of steam; banks were, in fact, reopening by December. What had caused it? The financial experts were at a loss to say, other than that once it had begun, the crash fed on itself. Some clergy speculated that God had grown vexed that so many were worshiping Mammon.

Whatever the cause, all agreed on the effect, which no one described better than Heman Humphrey: "Then suddenly came the crash, as if thunders from a clear sky had simultaneously broken over the whole land. Like a yawning earthquake, it shook down the palaces of the rich no less than the humble dwellings of the poor, and swallowed up their substance. Thus men went to bed dreaming all night of their vast, hoarded treasures, and woke up in the morning hopeless bankrupts."[3]

Some Wall Street financiers, horrified at having become instant paupers, could not face the prospect and took their lives.[4] Others found themselves in dire need of a Savior—when they had thought they would never again need anything.

One or two historians have attempted to put the revival down as nothing more than an emotional, panic response to the crash. But that perspective ignores the seeds of revival sprouting everywhere long before the crash. There *were* clergy who were quick to claim, as did James W. Alexander, pastor of the Old School Presbyterian Church in New York, that God had allowed "the ploughshare of His judgments to furrow the ground for the precious seed of salvation."[5] But the authors prefer the assessment of historian Perry Miller: "And then, just when there seemed no alternative to despair, when 'there was weeping in secret places over the general decline, and many prayers were offered for the return of the Spirit,' the miracle was wrought."[6]

During early January 1858, Presbyterians reported unusual awakenings in Memphis, Cleveland, and Nashville. Baptists announced that revival had come to their churches throughout New England, New York, Pennsylvania, and the western states. The Methodists had similarly experienced revival in cities from Yonkers, New York, to Jacksonville, Illinois.

Before long, all denominations and all the states in the Union were heard from. Philadelphia, Albany, Boston, Cincinnati, Chicago—all reported outbreaks of prayer meetings. There were numerous revivals in schools, the most spectacular being in Cleveland, where all but two boys experienced conversion.[7]

In Chicago, a shoe salesman who had moved there from Boston was astonished when the merchant he was calling on looked at his watch and said he had to go to a prayer meeting. Already converted several years earlier at Mt. Vernon Church in Boston, the shoe salesman went with him and was deeply moved. Soon the salesman wrote home to his mother: "I go to meeting every night. Oh, how I enjoy it! It seems as if God were here Himself. O Mother, pray for me! Pray that this work may go on till every knee is bowed!"[8] Soon Dwight L. Moody would turn in his shoe sample kit and go into full-time evangelism.

The phenomenon was hardly confined to large cities; in towns and villages the same thing was happening. In New England, congregations were spontaneously instituting days of fasting and prayer for the "descent of the Spirit." This caused the editors of the *Watchman and Reflector* to rejoice; surely a deluge of divine grace was imminent!

They were right. In January 1858, the Spirit of God suddenly seemed to be everywhere. Word had it that in some New England towns it was hard to find a person who was *un*converted. At one of Finney's meetings in Boston, a traveling businessman stood up and said, "I'm from Omaha, in Nebraska. On my journey east, I have found a continuous prayer meeting . . . about two thousand miles in extent."[9]

Across the country, the "new measures" were finally convincing the rock-ribbed, die-hard old guard; indeed, it was ironic that many of the last pockets of resistance holding out against the Holy Spirit were in exactly the sort of rural and frontier churches where the previous great revival had begun. But nothing could constrain the Spirit of God. Like a mighty river He flowed around any obstacles in His path.

In February, the rising tide became a tidal wave. In the Green Street Methodist Church in Philadelphia, so many wanted to worship that the two brothers serving as ministers had to preach simultaneously, the one to the packed crowd in the sanctuary upstairs, the other to those gathered downstairs in the meeting hall. In the first three months of '58, the *Mother's Journal* of New York reported 25,000 new conversions in that city. In two months that figure had doubled.[10] Nationwide, the number of conversions peaked at 50,000 *a week,* and for the next two years would continue at a rate of 10,000 a week.[11]

Several things differentiated this third great wave of revival from what had happened before. First, it was *quiet*. Gone were the lung-bursting, shouted sermons of the great frontier camp meetings. Gone were the loud praying and pounding on benches. As Finney observed, businessmen were for the most part educated and conservative in their ways. "Inquirers needed more opportunity to think than they had [in the previous awakening] when there was so much noise."[12]

Secondly, it was a laypeople's revival. This time God had not selected specific lightning rods like George Whitefield and David Brainerd or the Methodist circuit riders. This time the work of the revival was carried on independently of the ministers. Clergy were not excluded, but neither were they put in charge—which was a good thing, said Finney:

> There was such a general confidence in the prevalence of prayer, that the people very extensively seemed to prefer meetings for prayer to meetings for

preaching. The general impression seemed to be, "We have had instruction until we are hardened; it is time for us to pray." The answers to prayer were constant, and so striking as to arrest the attention of the people generally throughout the land. It was evident that in answer to prayer the windows of heaven were opened, and the Spirit of God poured out like a flood.[13]

Evangelist and author Phoebe Palmer, spark plug of the holiness movement and founder of the famed Five Points Mission in downtown New York, could not agree more. In 1857, in a widely read tract entitled "A Laity for the Times," she had urged church members to take the lead in the crusade for personal evangelism. Now, in early 1858, after consulting with Harriet Beecher Stowe, she followed the tract with a solid and well-received book that established women's religious rights on the authority of the Holy Spirit.

And now God used Jeremiah Lanphier one more time. He was given a comparatively small assignment—with enormous repercussions.

In late February, he was led by the Holy Spirit to call on James Gordon Bennett, editor of the powerful New York *Herald*. He told Bennett of the quiet spiritual revolution under way in their great city, assuring him that it was truly nondenominational and might be something Bennett would want to cover.

Bennett was skeptical. Anything as big as Lanphier was describing he would surely have heard about by now. Still, he did send a man down to Fulton Street, just to see what was going on. When he read the man's file copy, he realized just how big a story he was sitting on. "The Prayer Revival," he headlined it, because it was independent of every human agency except prayer.[14] And though he remained cynical, he put his top men on it and played it up.

Bennett's archrival was Horace Greeley, editor of the New York *Tribune*. Not to be outdone, Greeley sent his own ace reporters to get the story and made it the focus of his editorials. What he wrote was entirely uncynical—because some of his best men were coming back converted. More and more stories appeared, until the climax came in April, with an entire issue of the weekly edition devoted exclusively to the revival.

This revival was a huge event, the publishers discovered, involving countless thousands of people, and the more astonishing because it had begun so quietly. Past attempts at revival had been characterized by great drum-beating fanfares—the pastor's or evangelist's advance team would be scouring the hedges and byroads for weeks, to be sure the tent was at least half full. There would be handbills and advertisements in the papers; other churches would be strongly encouraged to invite their congregations to attend.

But there was nothing "got up" about these prayer meetings; they just happened. Consequently they got more coverage in the secular press than any religious event in memory. Today the New York *Times* and the Washington *Post* have more influence than any other dailies in the country. A century ago that honor belonged to the *Herald* and the *Tribune*. So when they gave front-page attention to what was happening in New York, it was news everywhere.

And to the surprise of editors across the country, it turned out the same thing was quietly happening in their own cities. Reporters from the Philadelphia *Press* went to a midday meeting at Jayne's Hall, "and to our amazement found it densely crowded. . . . There were certainly not less than three thousand persons who entered the hall during the hour, and our reason for announcing it as an epoch is the fact that it was . . . the largest meeting convened for the simple purpose of prayer to God, that has ever been assembled in this country."[15]

Leadership of the Jayne's Hall meetings soon became the responsibility of a young Episcopal minister, Dudley Tyng. Though Mr. Tyng was a decidedly Low Church (i.e., evangelical) Episcopalian, he never allowed emotional excesses or extravagance in his meetings. Following the rules of the Fulton Street Meetings, they were models of decorum. Visitors and observers from the press were constantly struck by their orderliness— and by their quiet power. As in New York, the meetings in Philadelphia and elsewhere continued to receive positive coverage because so many reporters (and editors) were being converted.

Nevertheless, the High Church Episcopalian leadership mounted a campaign against Tyng, accusing him of fanaticism and wild enthusiasm. This did not deter him, nor did it rally opposition to his meetings. Now averaging 3,000 attendees a day, they came to be known as the largest prayer meetings in the world. But even Jayne's Hall was soon too small for all in Philadelphia who wanted to pray. The Handel and Haydn Hall and the American Mechanics' Auditorium were also opened, bringing the daily attendees to more than 5,000.[16]

On Sunday, March 30, 1858, Dudley Tyng, just turned 33, preached to over 5,000 men crammed into Jayne's Hall on Exodus 10:11, "Ye that are men . . . serve the LORD." It was a powerful challenge; more than 1,000 men confessed Christ that morning.[17]*

Now all the big halls in Philadelphia were not sufficient to contain the prayer supplicants. Thirty-five firehouses opened their doors, with the incidental result that 1,500 firemen got converted. These were burly, rough-hewn men, and traditionally, on their way back to the station after fighting a blaze, they would fill the night sky with bawdy songs. No longer—now they came home marching in order and singing revival hymns.[18]

A few days after his "Ye that are men" sermon, Dudley Tyng got his arm caught and mangled in a piece of farm machinery. An amputation was necessary, and he did not recover. As he lay dying in the hospital, he asked his friend George Duffield to be sure to tell the men at Jayne's Hall to "stand up for Jesus." The grieving Duffield wrote the hymn that soon became the standard for the prayer revival everywhere:

> Stand up, stand up for Jesus,
> ye soldiers of the Cross;
> lift high His royal banner,
> it must not suffer loss:
> From victory unto victory
> His army shall He lead,
> till every foe is vanquished,
> and Christ is Lord indeed.[19]

Other hymns became favorites as well—"He Leadeth Me," which also came out of the Philadelphia revival, and "Jesus Loves Me," written in 1858. "Just As I Am," written earlier by the invalid Englishwoman Charlotte Elliott, came into its own during the revival, as did the Irish immigrant Joseph Scriven's, "What a Friend We Have in Jesus." Until 1858, the blind poet Fanny Crosby, who taught English at the Institution for the Blind in New York City, had published only secular work. Converted in the revival, she became America's most prolific hymn writer. Among her best-known

---

* They stayed confessed. Henry Clay Fish reported that 40 new churches sprang up in Philadelphia in 1857–58.

are "To God Be the Glory," and one she wrote to go with a melody by Phoebe Palmer's daughter, "Blessed Assurance."[20]

As it became apparent that the revival was occurring across the country, businessmen started wiring colleagues in other cities, updating them on what was happening in their prayer meetings. The telegraph companies helped by keeping their offices open after business hours and letting the men send their messages free of charge.[21]

Indeed, so wide and deep was the phenomenon that in his last book, *The Life of the Mind in America,** esteemed Harvard historian Perry Miller designated the 1857–58 Revival as "the event of the century."[22]

In all, how many men had stood up for Jesus? According to the late J. Edwin Orr, definitive historian of that revival, a conservative estimate drawn from the 1857–59 records of all the mainline denominations would put the total at just over a million souls.[23] That figure is even more impressive when one remembers that at the beginning of 1857 America's population was around 28 million, about a tenth what it is today.[24] Had there been a Gallup organization to poll Americans as to how many had *already* believed Christ to be their Lord and Savior prior to the revival, probably more than half of them would have said yes. In light of that, the increase during the revival was truly phenomenal.

Also phenomenal was the impact of the Holy Spirit on New England. Practically every village and town in Rhode Island was hit. Vermont and Maine were similarly struck, and in Massachusetts not a single community went untouched.

Near "Hell's Corner," New Hampshire, resided 20 isolated families renowned for their profanity, gambling, and all-around wickedness. Five of the men proposed to mock the revival by holding a "prayer meeting" of their own, and they invited a deacon from a nearby church to lead it. Suspecting what they were up to, the deacon nonetheless decided to go, but he invited a friend to accompany him. Later reporting what had happened, the two of them insisted that the Spirit of God must have gone before them. Four of the five hardened men were converted in the first meeting, and the holdout was converted in the second. Then they invited their friends, who couldn't believe what had happened to them. Soon there were 100 people coming to the Hell's Corner revival![25]

* published posthumously in 1965

And what of the South? Antislavery activists were convinced that revival was next to impossible there. Wrote William Hosmer, editor of the *Northern Christian Advocate*: Given that the mission of the church was "to establish the Kingdom of God on earth by the banishment of unrighteousness and the introduction of universal holiness . . . wherever slavery is tolerated in the church, [there is] a religion without holiness, Gospel progress without Gospel morals." Christianity even became a curse, "sanctioning and perpetuating that which it was designed to remove."[26]

Some modern historians have, in fact, claimed that the Holy Spirit skipped the South, citing as the last word on the subject Finney's assessment in his memoirs: "Slavery seemed to shut [the revival] out from the South. The people there were in such a state of irritation, of vexation and committal to their peculiar institution which had come to be assailed on every side, that the Spirit of God seemed to be grieved away from them. There seemed to be no place found for Him in the hearts of the Southern people at that time."[27]

But even Finney, who knew the ways of the Holy Spirit as well as any man of his era, had his blind spots. To the authors it did not make sense that if God was spiritually preparing His people in the North for the coming ordeal, He would not do the same for His people in the South, black and white.

And of course, He did. But it took patient, methodical Edwin Orr to uncover the truth. He found that in Beaufort, South Carolina, a black Baptist pastor named J. M. C. Breaker reported that by the end of 1857, he had broken his record for annual baptism of new members—565! That brought his membership up to 3,511—which made his church probably the largest in North America. It should be noted that 108 of his parishioners were white.[28]

Methodist Bishop Warren C. Candler reminded those attempting to downplay the impact of the prayer revival on the South that the region was primarily rural, not urban.* It was all the more remarkable, therefore, that this revival, which was predominantly urban in nature, should actually achieve higher church gains per capita in the South than anywhere else

---

* Of the nine American cities with more than 100,000 people, only one, New Orleans, was in the South.

in the country! In 1858 the increase in Methodist church membership more than trebled from the year before.[29]

Episcopal records bore Candler out. In Kentucky, they reported a 22 percent increase in church membership in 1858 alone.[30] And by the spring of that year, Tennessee had experienced revival in 40 towns. In Mississippi, the Presbyterians reported that 600 converts had been added to the churches of Natchez—a tenth of the town's total population.[31]

The crowning Southern story occurred in the heart of proslavery feeling—Charleston, South Carolina. Hearing what was going on elsewhere in the country, the Reverend John L. Girardeau had begun nightly prayer meetings in his church, to seek an outpouring of the Holy Spirit. As night after night he led his flock in prayer, gradually his church had filled to capacity. Still, nothing out of the ordinary happened, and eventually the officers of the church appealed to him: Prayer was fine, but now he should start preaching as well.

Dr. Girardeau refused. It was his view that "the Father had given to Jesus, as the King and Head of the Church, the gift of the Holy Spirit, and that Jesus in His sovereign administration of the affairs of His Church, bestowed the Holy Spirit on whomsoever He pleased, and in whatever measure He pleased." So he kept to prayer alone, and his prayer was addressed directly to Jesus, asking Him to send "the Holy Spirit in mighty receiving power."

The night his prayer was answered, no one was more surprised than the pastor himself. As his biography would later recount:

> One evening, while leading the people in prayer, he received a sensation as if a bolt of electricity had struck his head and diffused itself through his whole body. For a little while he stood speechless under the strange physical feeling. Then he said: "The Holy Spirit has come; we will begin preaching tomorrow evening." He closed the service with a hymn, dismissed the congregation, and came down from the pulpit; but no one left the house. The whole congregation had quietly resumed its seat.
>
> Instantly he realized the situation. The Holy Spirit had not only come to him—He had also taken possession of the hearts of the people. Immediately he began exhorting them to accept the Gospel. They began to sob softly, like the falling of rain; then, with deeper emotion to weep bitterly, or to

436

rejoice loudly, according to their circumstances. It was midnight before he could dismiss his congregation.

The meetings went on night and day for eight weeks, often numbering 1,500 to 2,000 in attendance. Large numbers of young men were converted and joined his church or others in the city. When contemplating the meaning of this outpouring of the Spirit, Dr. Girardeau, with remarkable premonition, would refer to it as "the Lord's mercy in gathering His elect for the great war that was soon to sweep so many of them into eternity."[32]

The only place untouched by the revival was Southern California. In Northern California, the vigilance committees had done such a thorough job of running thieves and murderers out of the mining camps that these ne'er-do-wells had all wound up down around Los Angeles. The men of the American Home Mission Society reported that as a mission field it was hopeless. There had been 47 murders the previous year without a single arrest.[33]

A year after the revival had begun, the leaders of the Fulton Street Meetings* conducted an anniversary service in which ministers testified to the good fruit of the tree. Methodist Nathan Bangs said he had "laid aside the polemic armor." The revival caused men to "for a moment forget their denominational peculiarities; it tears down their sectarian prejudices, and makes them all feel as one."[34]

For once, they were all just Christians, standing at the foot of the Cross and gazing up at the One who had given His life that they might be one.

Best of all, social reform—what Finney had always held was the key fruit of any true revival†—had occurred everywhere. Men and women were again learning to *care* for one another. Phoebe Palmer, one of the prominent voices of the revival, warned new converts against selfishly seeking "ecstatic enjoyment." Holiness made one a servant—at times a suffering servant—of one's fellowman. And the crusading Episcopal Bishop of western New York, Frederic Dan Huntington, concurred: "Christ comes, not to make righteous individuals, but to build a righteous kingdom,

---

* which would continue for a hundred years

† As Finney put it: You needed a new understanding of who your neighbor was, and what it meant to love him as much as you habitually loved yourself.

whereof each individual is a member, so that no one can say to another, 'I have no need of thee.'"[35]

Finally, the revival had made it abundantly clear that the entire slavery question must be viewed from a spiritual perspective. It was not just a social evil; it was sin. And it had to go, even if it took a holy crusade. . . .

Give men a righteous cause to believe in, and they will, if necessary, die for it. Northern resolve had yet to coalesce to that degree. But it was growing.

This heightened awareness of the spiritual anathema of slavery further widened the breach in the ranks of the antislavery movement. The radical abolitionists, led by Garrison, were already jealous of Christian leaders like Weld, the Grimké sisters, and the Tappan brothers, whose more compassionate tone drew far more adherents to the cause. When Harriet Beecher Stowe wrote her book, Garrison had only lukewarm praise for it, acknowledging that the attacks of Southern editors, always *his* chief measure of success, were now directed more toward her than himself.

Now, as the influence of the 1857–58 Revival began to eclipse all else, he and other radicals openly attacked the Christians. They had already condemned the Bible for containing passages that Southern theologians could cite as evidence of God's tolerance of slavery; now they went further. In a Garrisonian convention in Boston, Wendell Phillips denounced both Jesus Christ and George Washington as traitors to humanity—the former for giving us the New Testament with its offending verses, the latter for giving us a Constitution that condoned slavery. Parker Pilsbury went so far as to declare himself "bold enough to deny the creation of credulity and priestcraft named the Deity."[36]

Such statements served only to further alienate the radicals; as Georges Fisch observed, these extremists had placed themselves "outside the great religious current that was carrying the nation on."[37] The leadership of the antislavery movement was now clearly with the evangelicals.

Some people even hoped that the immense goodwill and charity generated by the revival might be enough to dissipate the dark storm of God's gathering judgment. They pointed to the lesson of Nineveh, in Biblical times one of the great city-states in the known world. The prophet Jonah arrived with the message that God would destroy their city in 40 days. Incredibly, they all repented, and God changed His mind and spared them.

There was, of course, one great difference between Nineveh and mid–19th-century America. The citizens of the former had enough respect for the wrath of God to listen to this reluctant prophet cast up on their shores from the belly of a whale. As they listened, the finger of the Holy Spirit touched their hearts, and they turned from their wicked ways.

During the 1857–58 Revival millions listened and turned. But millions more did not, many of them convinced that they had already heard God on the subject of slavery, and that He approved of it. And so, concerning the resolution of the slavery issue, nothing had really changed, and the point of no return was passed.

But God had another purpose for the revival, which Dr. Girardeau had glimpsed: Before the War for Independence, He had spiritually prepared the entire nation to go through the refining fire that was coming.

He was doing the same thing again.

41

A House Divided

Surrounding the tall, pensive figure in the Statehouse library were twelve of his most trusted friends and advisors. For the past eight months these twelve had toiled cheerfully and earnestly throughout the state to bring Abraham Lincoln to this place at this time for this purpose.

The place was Springfield, Illinois, the time was the middle of June 1858, and the purpose was the Republican State convention, which would pick a slate of candidates for the legislature's election in the fall. Senator Douglas's current six-year term was about to expire, and the newly elected legislators would decide whether to send him back to Washington for another six years. Or send someone else.

No party's Senatorial candidate had ever been decided on this early before, but the Illinois Republicans were leaving nothing to chance. They wanted everyone to know that Abe Lincoln was their man, and they wanted him nominated by acclamation. Nor was this merely for the citizens of Illinois; it was to make a point to certain self-styled kingmakers of the four-year-old Republican party.

Back East, Horace Greeley and other influential Republicans had been so impressed with Senator Douglas's impassioned and effective leadership of the Congressional fight against the Lecompton constitution, that they began making overtures to him to come over to the Republican party. At the very least, they definitely wanted him returned to the Senate and would have preferred that he run unopposed. But the Illinois Republicans did not appreciate Eastern nabobs meddling in their affairs, and the best way to make that clear was to send an unequivocal message of unanimous support behind their own candidate.

Knowing that he would be nominated, Lincoln had gone to work on his acceptance speech. Writing it without assistance, as he always did, he put more effort into it than any address he had ever delivered. For it would define not only his candidacy but the principles of the new party he would be representing. The Republican party had formed in resistance to the spread of slavery into the Territories; now he was prepared to take the party one step farther.

From studying slavery's (and America's) past, Lincoln felt he could see where it was going, and if unchecked, what it would mean for the future of the country. America's foundation stones were the truths embodied in the Declaration of Independence—so obvious that the Founding Fathers deemed them "self-evident." All men were created equal. All men were endowed by their Creator with certain inalienable rights: to life, liberty, and the pursuit of happiness. There was nothing in the Declaration that said these truths pertained only to men of a certain color.

But that was exactly what others were claiming now. And Lincoln had come to the conclusion that *right now*—during this fall's elections and the Presidential election two years hence—America was passing through the most pivotal epoch in her fourscore years of existence.

He and the Republican party (for after this speech their goals would be the same) would not attack slavery in the states where it already existed. But the party *would* mightily resist the current trend of the administration and the Supreme Court to make slavery legal in states and territories where it had always been denied. And the party *would* state that it expected slavery to die out in the United States of America, as it already had everywhere else in Christendom. It might take a generation or two, possibly longer, but eventually it would be gone. And its demise would be achieved not by "bloody bullets but peaceful ballots."[1] That was Lincoln's objective, and in a few hours, it would be the Republican party's as well.

But before he delivered the speech, he wanted the honest reaction of these twelve. Some men were born orators; Lincoln had no illusions about being one of them. He spoke straight from the heart and straight to the point, eschewing 50-cent words in favor of the common, garden variety that would not obscure what he wished to convey. If his speech was remembered, it would be for its depth, not its delivery.

He read them his opening statement, which addressed popular sovereignty. "We are now far into the fifth year since a policy was initiated with the avowed object and confident promise of putting an end to slavery agitation. Under the operation of that policy, that agitation not only has not ceased, but has constantly augmented." He paused. "In my opinion, it will not cease until a crisis shall have been reached and passed."

The twelve were still, waiting for what he would say next. He looked at each, then quoted what another had said in the midst of His twelve. "*A house divided against itself cannot stand.* I believe this government cannot endure permanently, half slave and half free."

They were dismayed. It was one thing to privately believe that, another to put it irretrievably on record. For there would be reporters present; whatever he said would soon be known at all points of the compass.

"I do not expect the Union to be dissolved," he went on. "I do not expect the house to fall. But I *do* expect it will cease to be divided. It will become all one thing, or all the other. Either the opponents of slavery will arrest the further spread of it, and place it where the public mind shall rest in the belief that it is in the course of ultimate extinction; or its advocates will push it forward until it shall become alike lawful in all the states, old as well as new, North as well as South."[2]

The rest of the speech was devoted to attacking the policies of Judge Douglas (as he preferred to call him), the Dred Scott decision, and the vagaries of the Buchanan administration. When he finished, he asked his friends what they thought. According to his former law partner, Billy Herndon, all were alarmed at the "house divided" phrase. "Too radical and too far in advance of the public sentiment" was how Herndon summarized their reaction in his subsequent biography of Lincoln.[3] But the negative spell was broken when Herndon, with remarkable prescience, declared: "Lincoln, deliver that speech as read, and it will make you President!"[4]

Whether or not Herndon actually spoke those stirring words, there was the ring of authenticity in what he recorded as Lincoln's response. Lincoln was grateful for their input, but in no way a slave to it. He did not care if the "house divided" concept was ahead of its time. "The proposition is indisputably true," he told them, "and has been for more than six thousand years; and I will deliver it as written. . . . I would rather be defeated with this expression *in* the speech, held up and discussed before the people, than to be victorious without it."[5]

If ever there was an example of standing by one's principles, that was it. But now, seeing his friends somewhat chastened, he smiled and softened his tone. "The time has come when these sentiments should be uttered. And if it is decreed that I should go down because of this speech, then let me go down linked to the truth—let me die in advocacy of what is just and right."[6]

When Lincoln entered the hall, he was greeted with tumultuous enthusiasm; they were already solidly behind him. During his speech he was frequently interrupted with applause and wild cheering. When he finished, the approval was deafening. But the next day, as the sober light of dawn greeted the delegates, they remembered what he had said about a house divided being unable to stand.

Lincoln had crossed the Rubicon, and he had taken them with him.

Back East, Stephen A. Douglas was bringing his battle against the Lecompton constitution to a hard-fought, successful conclusion. Daily he was being lionized in Greeley's New York *Tribune* (which had some 15,000 subscribers in Illinois), with the editor calling him the greatest antislavery hero then on the horizon.

So when the acceptance speech of the Illinois Republicans' Senatorial candidate appeared in the newspapers, Douglas's handlers and new Republican friends assured him that he had nothing to worry about. Wasn't he the man of the hour? An 11-year veteran of the Senate, had he not bested the best debaters on both sides of the aisle? Was he not a true giant eclipsing everyone else on the national stage? At or near the top of everyone's list of Presidential candidates for 1860? And who was Lincoln? A nothing. A candidate that most conservatives considered "visionary"—"impractical"—even "revolutionary."[7] A suspender-snapping, cracker-barrel lawyer in ill-fitting clothes who looked more like a scarecrow than a man. No one had ever heard of him; Douglas would crush him like an ant!

But Douglas was not so sure. He had seen Lincoln in action; in Springfield he'd had a front-row view. And he had seen the mesmerizing effect that this too tall, too thin, too awkward bumpkin with a voice that cracked and was pitched too high could have on a crowd. And unlike most of his previous opponents, this man could *think*—deeply and carefully. "I shall have my hands full," he cautioned his handlers. "He is the strong man of his party—full of wit, facts, dates—and he is the best stump speaker in the West. He is as honest as he is shrewd, and if I beat him, my victory will be hardly won."[8]

But face him he must. And he must defeat him—so convincingly that Lincoln could never rise to fight him again. His advisors assured him that Seward would be the Republicans' standard-bearer in 1860. But he knew Seward, and he knew Lincoln. On the strength of the latter's "House Divided" speech, Douglas suspected it would be Lincoln he would have to face two years hence. All the more reason to put him down now, *knock him out!*

Stephen A. Douglas began to study his opponent carefully, assessing his moves, learning his responses, finding his weaknesses.

He would have preferred to fight a one-front war, but that luxury came rarely to Douglas. Now, in addition to Lincoln, he had the Directorate to worry about. James "Buck" Buchanan, a weak President to begin with, was no longer his own man. He was under the control of a group of four proslavery men who were, in effect, directing administration policy—Cabinet members Howell Cobb, Jacob Thompson, and Jere Black, plus Mississippi Senator John Slidell. When an acquaintance asked Cobb on one occasion why he looked so troubled, the Secretary of the Treasury replied with a smile, "Oh, it's nothing, only Buck is opposing the administration."[9]

In his break with Buchanan, Douglas had made no secret of how much he despised the Directorate. Consequently they were determined to bring him down no matter what it cost, even if it meant entering a "National" (i.e., pro-administration) Democratic candidate against him in Illinois. When the Douglas camp attempted a reconciliation, Buchanan was receptive. But the Directorate coldly refused, setting up nine pro-administration newspapers in Illinois and replacing every pro-Douglas patronage appointment from postmaster on down with a man of their own. It was war, sneaky but total.

Lincoln had his own two-front war to fight. Abolitionists and old Whigs alike wanted to know how the new Republican party, to which Lincoln would have them give their allegiance, reconciled excluding slavery from the Territories, while tolerating it in the Southern states?

After some thought, he gave them a prairie parable that any frontiersman could readily grasp.

For instance, out in the street, or in the field, or on the prairie I find a rattlesnake. I take the snake and kill it. Everybody would applaud the act and say I did right. But suppose the snake was in a bed where children were sleeping. Would I do right to strike him there? I might hurt the children; or I might not kill, but only arouse and exasperate the snake, and he might bite the children. Thus, by meddling with him here, I would do more hurt than good.

Slavery is like this. We dare not strike at it, where it is. The manner in which our Constitution is framed constrains us from making war upon it, where it already exists. The question that we now have to deal with is: Shall we be acting right to take the snake and carry it to a bed, where there are children? The Republican party insists on keeping it out of the bed.[10]

After defeating the Lecompton constitution in Congress, Douglas's arrival back in his home state took on the trappings of a Roman general's triumphal return. Thousands lined the streets to hail their conquering hero. Right away, he began speaking in Chicago and Springfield, rebutting the points Lincoln was making in those same cities.

On his part, Lincoln noted that he and Judge Douglas were frequently crossing paths, and he wondered if they might both save their supporters a substantial sum by appearing in the same place at the same time on the same platform. He wrote Douglas a letter, suggesting a series of debates in different parts of Illinois.

Douglas's handlers did not like the idea. The only person to benefit from such an arrangement would be Lincoln; Douglas was already far outdrawing him. In fact, outside of Springfield, and except to ardent Republicans, Lincoln was still the unknown man. The Senator would, of course, thrash him, but what was the advantage of giving him so much more exposure than he would ever gain otherwise?

Once again Douglas disagreed with his advisors. First of all, if he did not accept the challenge, it would look as if he were afraid to face Lincoln—and nothing could be farther from the truth. Secondly, Lincoln was a persuasive man; left to his own devices, there was no telling how much damage he might do. No, the best thing was to face him squarely and beat him at his own game. Besides, Douglas had never ducked a fight, and was never happier than when carrying the battle to a foe.

So the schedule was set and the rules drawn. There would be seven debates, two in the north (Republican country), two in the south (Douglas country), and three in the middle (up for grabs). The first would be in Ottawa, in the middle of the state, on August 21; the last, in the southwest at Alton on October 15. Each debate would last three hours. The leadoff speaker would have an hour, his opponent would have an hour and a half, and the first speaker would have the final half hour. Since the opening speaker would also have the last word, for fairness they would alternate, and since Lincoln was the challenger, he would lead off one less time than Douglas.

Interest ran high. The whole nation got ready to watch what promised to be the best verbal duel since Hayne and Webster. Not only did it concern the most momentous issue ever to face the Republic, it would be a classic pitched battle: the Democratic champion—the last hope of anyone who still believed in moderation—versus the Black Republicans' new challenger. People wanted to read every word.

And to make sure they could, the biggest papers sent their best reporters to cover the debates in their entirety. Joseph Medill, editor and publisher of the mighty Chicago *Press & Tribune* and friend of Lincoln, went further. He dispatched Robert Hitt, the first shorthand reporter in Chicago, to record Lincoln's every word.* Not to be outdone, the rival Chicago *Times* sent its own shorthand reporter to catch Douglas's immortal prose. And both papers would make their coverage available to editors in other cities. Now, for the first time, a series of debates would be read word for word by the entire country.

* Throughout history shorthand has been a useful tool, preserving Cicero's orations, Martin Luther's sermons, and Shakespeare's plays.

42

A Matter of Principle

*S*urrounded by fields of corn slowly ripening in the golden haze of late summer, Ottawa was a tree-shaded, sleepy little town of 6,000 on the Illinois River, about 75 miles west-southwest of Chicago. On August 21, 1858, the weather was neither too hot nor too humid—"pleasant" was how the reporters described it. There were a lot of them there, for the oratorical fight of the century was going to take place in Ottawa that afternoon.

Throughout the morning, special trains decked with bunting and banners had been arriving from Chicago and La Salle, along with special boats. The roads to town were choked with dust from an unbroken succession of carriages, buckboards, and buggies, each with a plump food basket under its seat. By one o'clock, the town's population had swollen to upward of 20,000—an enormous, unheard-of crowd, considering the thin population of mid–19th-century Illinois.[1]

The townspeople were equal to the challenge. They had scythed their lawns, whitewashed their fences, tacked up large flags and bunting to their porches. Across Main Street hung canvas banners with mottoes like "Abe the Giant-Killer" and "Edgar County for the Tall Sucker."[2] Companies of militia in their parade-dress uniforms marched and countermarched. Children shouted, horses neighed, dogs barked, drums banged, fifes trilled, and all of Ottawa, jam-packed with humanity, throbbed with excitement.

Shortly before one o'clock, a great cheer arose from the Democrats. Their man was coming in on the La Salle road! And talk about arriving in high style! The Senator and his regal, strikingly beautiful new wife were traveling in a four-horse carriage! A cavalcade of horsemen galloped out of town, banners flying, to escort him in.

As the carriage came into view, a band struck up, and the cheering became deafening. The carriage came to a halt, the door opened, and Douglas alighted, waving to his ecstatic fans and pausing to bask in their tumultuous adulation. Even the sun seemed to be shining a little brighter on him. Attired in an impeccably tailored, dazzling white linen suit, black patent-leather shoes, and a broad-brimmed fedora (what his Republican detractors referred to as his "plantation outfit"), he was magnificent.

Tradition has it that Lincoln, on the other hand, came into town unheralded and unannounced. But tradition is not always reliable. Not to be outdone, the Republicans greeted their man at the train station and placed him in a carriage adorned with evergreens for the ride to the mayor's house. As the appointed hour approached, rival processions formed and carried their candidates to the public square.

Here the crowd was dense, and for the first time in political gatherings, women were present in significant numbers. The closer the processions got to the platform, the more tightly packed the crowd became; it took them half an hour to cover the final hundred yards and get the speakers and their committees up on the platform. No sooner were they seated than a section of the wooden awning overhead, erected to shelter them from the relentless sun but now covered with men and boys, collapsed on the Democratic committee (fortunately without causing serious injury).

From the cheers that went up as each of the principals was introduced, the number of backers was about even. The cheering shook the buildings; each side was convinced that their man, and only their man, was the one destined to save the nation.

The Senator spoke first. "Everyone knows Douglas," scribbled the New York *Evening Post*'s man, "a short, thickset, burly man with a large round head, heavy hair, dark complexion, and fierce bulldog look."[3] Of the two, he had by far the better speaking voice—deep and rolling, pleasing to the ear—except that it was more suited to the confines of the Senate Chamber. Out in the open, in front of this vast crowd, it did not carry. Only the closest third were able to get most of what he said. The middle third were frustrated, cupping their hands to their ears, and the outer third had to be content with the visual spectacle.

Too bad, for Douglas launched into a vicious personal attack. He accused Lincoln of conspiring to subvert both the Democratic and the Whig parties in order to create "an Abolition party, under the name and disguise of a Republican party."[4] Then, like a prosecuting attorney confronting a defendant, he challenged Lincoln to tell the assemblage exactly where he stood on the original Republican platform erected at the party's founding convention in Springfield four years before. Republicans claimed Lincoln's endorsement everywhere, and reading from an apparent draft of that platform, Douglas now enumerated it resolution by resolution, demanding to know if Lincoln still favored the unconditional repeal of the Fugitive Slave Act? Did he still oppose the admission of any more slave states to the Union? Did he still support the abolition of slavery in the District of Columbia? Was he still pledged to end the interstate slave trade? Did he still oppose the acquisition of additional territory unless slavery was explicitly prohibited in it?[5]

By the rules of the debate, Lincoln could not immediately reply. He could only sit and wait until it was his turn, but he looked shocked and stunned. Turning from the seated defendant, Douglas now addressed the "jury," charging Lincoln with plotting to "abolitionize the Old Whig party all over the State, pretending that he was as good a Whig as ever."[6]

Now Douglas appeared to praise Lincoln, while making snide innuendoes that implied the prairie lawyer was a heavy drinker, fond of watching horse races and fistfights. He reminded his audience that during Lincoln's brief appearance on the national political stage, he had taken the side of the common enemy (Mexico) against his own country and had been driven out of politics as a result. He had returned in 1854, just in time to help form the abolitionist platform of the Black Republicans.

But Douglas saved his biggest gun for Lincoln's "House Divided" speech, calling it nothing less than a declaration of war against the slaveholding South. Talk about disunion! The Founding Fathers had made this Government divided into free states and slave states, and left each state to do as it pleased on the subject of slavery.[7] The country had endured half slave and half free for 70 years; why should it not continue to exist with the diversity of institutions befitting a land so vast and varied?[8]

As for Lincoln's extolling the equality of man, Douglas made it clear that "I am opposed to Negro citizenship in any and every form. [Cheers.] I believe this government was made on the white basis. [Cries of affirmation.] I believe it was made by white men, for the benefit of white men and their posterity forever, and I am in favor of confining citizenship to white men . . . instead of conferring it upon Negroes, Indians, and other inferior races. [More affirmation.]

"I do not question Mr. Lincoln's conscientious belief that the Negro was made his equal, and hence his brother [laughter], but for my own part, I do not regard the Negro as my equal, and positively deny that he is my brother. . . . He belongs to an inferior race, and must always occupy an inferior position."[9]

He concluded by reminding the audience that the key to the status of the Negro, slave or free, rested solely with the citizens of the individual states—in other words, popular sovereignty, which was the true democratic spirit.

He sat down to a thunderous ovation. When it subsided, Lincoln arose and received a prolonged ovation of his own.

In style and appearance Abraham Lincoln offered a total contrast. "Built on the Kentucky type, he is very tall, slender, angular, awkward even, in gait and attitude," wrote the reporter from New York. "His face is sharp, large-featured, and unprepossessing. His eyes are deep set under heavy brows, his forehead high and retreating, and his hair is dark and heavy." Then, as if realizing the negative portrait he had just painted, he went on, "But stir him up, and the fire of his genius plays on every feature. His eye glows and sparkles, every lineament now so well-formed, grows brilliant and expressive, and you have before you a man of rare power and of strong magnetic influence."

The reporter's personal preference now became apparent. "He takes the people every time, and there is no getting away from his sturdy good sense, his unaffected sincerity, and the unceasing play of his good humor, which accompanies his close logic and smoothes the way to conviction."[10]

But this afternoon Lincoln did not seem at all smooth or sure of himself; if anything, he seemed disconcerted by the ferocity of Douglas's personal attack. He was clearly uncomfortable with the debate format, which required one to extemporize on the spot and swiftly rearrange one's arguments to ward off an opponent's unexpected thrust. He did respond with vigor, insisting that the Republican party was not an abolitionist party. Then he stated, as he had many times before, that "I have no purpose, either directly or indirectly, to interfere with the institution of slavery where it exists. I believe I have no lawful right to do so, and I have no inclination to do so. I have no purpose to introduce political and social equality between the white and the black races."*

But, Lincoln went on, the natural right of the Negro to life, liberty, and the pursuit of happiness must be respected. "In the right to eat bread without the leave of anyone else, which his own hands earns, he *is* my equal, and the equal of Judge Douglas, and the equal of every living man!"[11]

Regarding the Republican platform, instead of rebutting Douglas's specific charges, he merely pointed out that he had not been present at the founding convention. He then proceeded to read at great length from his Peoria speech of four years before, where he had gone on record as saying that even given all the power on earth, he would not know how to bring an end to slavery. Rushing through his speech, he sat down long before his allotted time had expired.[12]

Both sides claimed victory. Both sides' newspapers offered irrefutable evidence that their candidate had won the first round.

Yet had there been a supposedly impartial panel of pundits and commentators (as is our mixed blessing today, after any televised political event), they would have agreed that Lincoln seemed badly shaken, possibly even cornered. Not only had he never rebutted Douglas's charges, he had never seemed to regain his balance.

Lincoln himself felt he had done so poorly that he called a conference of his advisors. Publicly they had insisted that he had won; now privately they urged him to become more aggressive. "Don't act on the defensive at all," advised Joseph Medill, and then, wincing at the disaster of Lincoln reading interminably from his old Peoria speech, he added, "Don't refer to your past speeches or positions. . . . Hold Doug up as a traitor and conspirator, a proslavery bamboozling demagogue."[13] If that seemed a bit extreme to Lincoln, an event was about to unfold that would prove it less so.

Of the multitude of Lincoln biographers, one was a professional journalist who was able to interview principals and witnesses present at many of the key episodes described. This was Ida Tarbell, top feature writer for *McClure's Magazine,* whose investigative series on Standard Oil in 1904 would expose the unfair business practices used to form a great industrial

---

* Lincoln was speaking in the context of the 1850s; what sounds segregationist to modern ears was actually several generations ahead of its time.

monopoly. In book form, it became a bestseller and earned her a place alongside Upton Sinclair and Lincoln Steffens in the front rank of the journalists whom Teddy Roosevelt dubbed "muckrakers." Her fearless reporting style and nose for hidden corruption made her a favorite of American readers, and in 1900 her biography of Lincoln would eclipse all others to that time.

One can imagine Ida Tarbell's delight with what journalist Robert Hitt uncovered after the Ottawa debate. Because Hitt was there primarily to capture Lincoln's words, when Douglas began enumerating the planks of the original Republican platform, he took down just the first line of each resolution, intending to get a copy of the whole document from the Senator after the debate. When he missed Douglas, he was not unduly concerned; he would send a cub reporter to find a copy of the Republican platform when he got back to Chicago.

But when the young assistant returned with the copy, and Hitt started filling in the blanks, he found that nothing matched. Whatever document Douglas had read, it differed widely from and was far more radical than the actual platform. Had Douglas pulled a fast one? Hitt raised the question with Joseph Medill, who decided to find out. Medill committed his entire editorial staff to finding out whence Douglas's document had come.

They did. It had originated at a Kane County meeting of extreme abolitionists who had nothing to do with the Republican party, and none of whom Lincoln had ever known.

In our present-day climate of negative political advertising and unscrupulous politicians willing to condone any "dirty trick" their aides might devise, such a tactic would scarcely raise an eyebrow. But in 1858 it was front-page news, and Medill cranked out extra editions to let the city—and the country—read all about it.

Condemning editorials began to appear in other papers. Said the Louisville *Journal*: "The particularity of Douglas's charge precludes the idea that he was simply and innocently mistaken."[14] Douglas had flat out lied. He had knowingly cheated and had gotten caught at it. As Tarbell put it, "Lovers of fair play were disgusted, and those of Douglas's own party who would have applauded a trick too clever to be discovered, could not forgive him for one which had been found out."[15]

Horace Greeley was enraged, perhaps the more so in view of the fact that a few scant months before he and the New York *Tribune* had been so totally behind Douglas. Greeley had already been enough impressed with Lincoln's "House Divided" speech to run it in his paper, accompanied by an editorial of cordial praise, and he stopped urging Illinois Republicans to vote for Douglas. But now that Douglas had shown his true colors, Greeley—and the *Tribune*—became his implacable foe.

Freeport loomed. Lincoln shook off his despair and focused on his preparation. As Medill had urged, he *would* take the battle to his opponent. But he would do it with truth, not attack or innuendo. The strongest card in Douglas's hand was popular sovereignty. But it contained a fatal flaw: It had apparently been ruled null and void by the Supreme Court's Dred Scott decision, which Douglas had also supported. So which was it to be? How could the people of a Territory decide to refuse entrance to slavery, if the Supreme Court said a man could take his property anywhere?

It was a loaded question, and Lincoln knew it. If Douglas declared that the Court's decision was indeed supreme, then he would lose the Illinois election. But if he said it wasn't, as Lincoln anticipated he would, he might win Illinois, but he would lose whatever Southern support he might still have after opposing the Lecompton constitution. Lincoln planned to open the Freeport debate by posing four questions for Douglas to answer; this would be the second.

When he showed the questions to his advisors, they all begged him to skip the second, which could cost *him* the election. Even as they rode on the train to Freeport, Medill pleaded with him to leave it out. But Lincoln refused. To him, it was a matter of principle.

Just south of the Wisconsin line, Freeport was the northernmost town in which the debates would occur, and therefore the most ardently Republican. The three railroads offered excursion rates and even special trains, so that by the time the principals arrived, there were some 15,000 waiting to hear them. Once again a brass band was playing, and the town was bedecked with bunting and banners. But the day was cool and overcast, with an occasional fine drizzle.

When Lincoln stepped to the podium, he was a different man than he had been in Ottawa. Here he was confident, assured, and determined. He opened by answering Douglas's charges the previous week. He had never asked for the repeal of the Fugitive Slave Act, for he believed the South was entitled to the law. He was not pledged to the abolition of slavery in the District of Columbia or the prohibition of the domestic slave trade, though he would not be unhappy to see either of them disappear. He *was* "impliedly if not expressly pledged" to prohibit slavery in all Federal Territories. As to acquiring additional territory, he "would or would not oppose such an acquisition," depending on whether it "would or would not aggravate the slavery question among ourselves."[16]

Then he went over on the attack, and now he put his four questions to the Senator. The second was the one with the stinger in the tail: Could "the people of a United States Territory, in any lawful way . . . exclude slavery from its limits prior to the formation of a State constitution?"

As for Douglas's attempt the week before to sandbag him with a phony Republican platform, Lincoln showed remarkable restraint. Referring to the matter only once in passing, he wryly observed that it was "most extraordinary" that Douglas "should so far forget all the suggestions of justice to an adversary, or of prudence to himself, as to venture upon the assertion . . . which the slightest investigation would have shown him to be wholly false." And with that, he determined to let bygones be bygones— however, when he would quote from documents in subsequent debates, he could not resist noting with a smile that, of course, he could not be absolutely certain of their authenticity.

Douglas was as shaken as Lincoln had been the week before. But he was a skilled debater, expert at repositioning himself as the situation required. And Lincoln's second question required some fast footwork.

Douglas could see the pitfall as clearly as Lincoln had. If he did not back his popular sovereignty to the hilt right now, he would lose his Senate seat. But if he denied the validity of the Dred Scott decision, he might lose the South—and with it, the Presidency in 1860. As he glanced at his tall opponent at the podium, he fervently hoped Lincoln would use all of his allotted hour, for he needed every minute to formulate his response.

When he stood and delivered it, it was brilliant—the best possible ma- neuver out of an impossible situation. Through the passage of "unfriendly legislation," Douglas declared, a people could keep slavery out of any Ter- ritory, because "slavery cannot exist a day or an hour anywhere, unless it is supported by local police regulations." Consequently, "the people of a Territory can, by lawful means, exclude slavery from their limits prior to the formation of a State constitution."[17]

He now amplified, so there could be no misunderstanding: "No matter what the decision of the Supreme Court, the right of the people to make a slave Territory or a free Territory is perfect and complete."[18]

As Douglas approached the end of his hour and a half, he sensed he was making no headway with this audience, and started calling them Black Republicans. They stood it for a while, but as he kept it up, each time he used the phrase, they would chant "white, white." Then, as he had when heckled in Chicago, he lost his temper at them. "I have seen your mobs before, and I defy your wrath!"[19]

When Lincoln stood to deliver his closing remarks, he repeated Douglas's response to his second question, wanting to be certain that everyone understood exactly what the judge had gone on record as saying: that by means of unfriendly legislation, any community could effectively ban slavery.

Douglas's interpretation became known as the "Freeport Doctrine," and eventually it would indeed have the political ramifications that both contestants anticipated.

Once again, each side's papers claimed impressive victories. But this time, had there been an objective panel of pundits to pass judgment, they would have given the round to Lincoln. He had scored deeply, forcing Douglas to scramble and resort to personal attacks, not only on Lincoln but on the audience.

But most of all, Lincoln had forced Douglas to declare his Freeport Doctrine, that slavery *could* be kept out of the Territories, if the people there didn't want it.

43

"A Slip, but Not a Fall"

*T*he old caboose they were jouncing along in that afternoon was hardly as comfortable as the parlor car at the front of this freight train, but the Illinois Republicans did not have much of a war chest for this campaign. They had to catch their rides where they could, and they were lucky to get this one. Besides, as one wag pointed out, both cars reached the station at the same time.

The two double-decker bunks were taken by party workers, trying without much luck to catch a little shut-eye. Four men were playing cards around a table, while the rest were in wooden chairs, either looking out the window or pulled up in a circle around Lincoln, chatting and whittling, their shavings blending with the sawdust on the floor.

Unaccountably the train slowed and came to a stop. Everyone looked out to see why, but in the gathering dusk no one could make out anything. Then a trainman climbed aboard to tell them they'd been shunted onto a siding to make way for a special—one with a private car for Senator Douglas.*

Hearing a whistle in the distance, everyone crowded to the window on the side where she would pass. She never even slowed, and the caboose shook as she thundered by. And sure enough, there at the end of the express was Douglas's car, its lights ablaze. Then it was gone. In the heavy silence that followed, Lincoln rallied his friends. "The gentleman in that car," he said with a chuckle, "evidently smelt no royalty in our carriage!"[1]

While he and Douglas would not meet again for two and a half weeks

---

* The Democratic machine had far deeper pockets. One prominent Democrat was young George McClellan, a West Pointer who had resigned his commission the year before to run the Illinois Central Railroad. When Douglas was traveling on *his* line, he got a special train.

after Freeport, there was no rest for the weary. Each continued to travel the length and breadth of the state, delivering one stump speech after another. They each were alone on the platform, but it was as if the other one was right there; they were still debating.

Douglas persisted in trying to tack the false Republican resolutions on Lincoln, and the latter was forced to keep reiterating his position on slavery. Lincoln bore it with good humor as long as he could, but finally, probably in Clinton on September 2, he was reported to have confided in exasperation: "You can fool all of the people some of the time, and some of the people all of the time, but you cannot fool all of the people all of the time."[2]

The pace was wearing them both down. But though Douglas was four years younger, it seemed to be taking a greater toll on him. At Havana, where Lincoln appeared the day after Douglas, he learned that the Senator had been so frustrated that he had challenged Lincoln to settle the whole thing in the ring. The rail-splitter smiled. "I am informed that my distinguished friend yesterday became a little excited—nervous, perhaps— and he said something about fighting, as though referring to a pugilistic encounter between him and myself. Did anybody in the audience hear him use such language?" (Cries of "Yes.")

"I am informed further, that somebody in *his* audience, rather more excited and nervous than himself, took off his coat and offered to take the job off Judge Douglas's hands, and fight Lincoln himself. Did anybody here witness that war-like proceeding?" (Widespread laughter and cries of "Yes!")

Chuckling himself, Lincoln said he would decline for two reasons. First, such a fight would prove only which of them was the stronger, and whichever way it went, it would not change the rightness or wrongness of their respective positions.

"My second reason for not having a personal encounter with the Judge is, that I don't believe he wants it himself. He and I are about the best friends in the world, and when we get together, he would no more think of fighting me than fighting his wife!"

There was much laughter, and when it subsided, Lincoln concluded, "Therefore, ladies and gentlemen, when the Judge talked about fighting, he was not giving vent to any ill feeling of his own, but merely trying to excite—well, *enthusiasm* against me on the part of his audience. And as

I find he was tolerably successful, we will call it quits."[3] (Laughter and much applause.)

For the debate down in Jonesboro, in the southern tip of the state, the turnout was disappointing; though it doubled the town's population, there were fewer than 2,000 in attendance. Still, they were nearly all Douglas men, and so Douglas, hoping to goad Lincoln into an angry outburst, repeated again his racist charges. But Lincoln refused to be baited, assailing Douglas's Freeport Doctrine by observing that slavery certainly had enough vigor to install itself in a Territory where it might not be wanted.

Three days later in mid-State Charleston, the crowd was friendlier to Lincoln and much bigger, over 10,000. He was greeted by an open wagon with 32 beautiful maidens in it, all dressed in white, representing the 32 states. Behind them came another maiden, also dressed in white, representing Kansas. "She's single now," quipped one reporter, "but she won't be single long!"[4]

A number of those who lived there remembered Abe's father, and a huge banner across Main Street showed the Lincoln family arriving in a pioneer wagon hauled by three teams of oxen. A Democratic banner was entitled Negro Equality and showed a white man, a black woman, and a mulatto child in the background. The Republicans considered it too offensive and tore it down, but Lincoln patiently restated his position on the respective races as soon as he started speaking. He then went into a long and convoluted exposure of a long and convoluted plot of Douglas's to extend slavery into Kansas.

As it happened, it was Senator Lyman Trumbull's theory, not Lincoln's, and when it was Douglas's turn to speak, he denounced the theory as patently false, and was amazed that Lincoln would spend so much time on it. He then told the audience that Lincoln had voted against sending food and supplies to the American boys when they were at war with the Mexicans.

When Lincoln closed the debate, he turned suddenly to Douglas's group of supporters and dragged one of them onto the platform—O. B. Ficklin, who had served with Lincoln in Congress in 1848. Lincoln forced him to admit that Douglas's accusation was untrue.

He then defended Trumbull and tried to insist that his conspiracy theory *was* true. But he had gotten badly "off-message," as modern pundits might say, and they would have agreed afterward that it was Lincoln's worst showing so far.

By the time they reached Galesburg on October 7, however, it was obvious that Lincoln had made a splendid recovery. He was in high spirits and strong voice, and now it was Douglas who seemed weary. The afternoon was gray and damp, and a hard, cold wind was tearing the banners and bunting to shreds. Nonetheless, some 20,000 people had gathered to listen. And they stayed, shivering and chilled to the bone. But as the great poet-biographer Carl Sandburg observed, these were rawboned Illinois farmers; they could stand the cold if there was something worth listening to.[5]

Had it been a nicer day, Galesburg would have been the most picturesque setting of all. Not only was the little town distinguished by the presence of Knox College, on whose campus the debate took place, but the well-trimmed lawns and stately elms gave it the appearance of a New England town, and the pastor of the white-spired Congregational Church was none other than Henry Ward Beecher's brother, Edward.

One of the prominently displayed banners caused Lincoln to chuckle. In the Senate back in April, James Hammond of South Carolina had made a speech that proclaimed that cotton was king of the economic world, greater even than the Bank of England. He said that whether one was in the North or the South, there would always be a ruling class sustained by a menial class. In the South the menials were slaves; in the North they were the small-fisted farmers, the grease mechanics, the mudsills of society. Now in Galesburg flew a bold banner proclaiming:[6]

SMALL-FISTED FARMERS, MUDSILLS OF SOCIETY,
GREASE MECHANICS FOR A. LINCOLN.

Douglas went first, and he kept his remarks on a high plain. He portrayed the truly national mission of the Democrats and contrasted it with what he called the bigoted sectionalism of the Republicans. Lincoln, when it was his turn, harkened back to Henry Clay. Douglas kept referring to slavery as if it were a matter of personal choice: If a man wanted to keep another man in bondage, that was his choice. Said Lincoln:

> I do think that Judge Douglas and whoever like him teaches that the Negro has no share, humble though it may be, in the Declaration of Indepen-

dence . . . is blowing out the moral lights around us, when he contends that whoever wants slaves has a right to hold them; that he is penetrating, so far as lies in his power, the human soul, and eradicating the light of reason and the love of liberty, when he is in every way possible preparing the public mind, by his vast influence, for making the institution of slavery perpetual and national.[7]

Douglas had said that freedom of choice was the cornerstone of American democracy. Now Lincoln was saying that there was a higher law: A man's freedom of choice ceased the moment that choice affected another man's freedom. In 1858 the pro-choice argument laid America open to charges of the worst sort of hypocrisy.

Both speakers requited themselves well, reaching new levels of eloquence, but in the end the pundits would have given the nod to Lincoln. His advisors had certainly revised their opinion of their man. Before the debates began, there was not one among them who, if he were honest, would have thought much of Lincoln's chances.

But he had surprised them. (He may have even surprised himself.) One evening in Medill's office in Chicago, Medill and Hitt and some of the other *Tribune* men were asking themselves if Lincoln might even be *great,* when as if by reply, a letter arrived from a prominent Eastern statesman. "Who is this man who is replying to Douglas in your State? Do you realize that no greater speeches have been made on public questions in the history of our country? That his knowledge of the subject is profound, his logic unanswerable, his style inimitable?"[8]

In Quincy, the next-to-last debate, 12,000 people gathered. Here the German-born journalist Carl Schurz described both candidates as the campaign wound to a close. Lincoln wore a black dress coat with too-short sleeves, a battered stovepipe hat, and black trousers that ended well before they met his shoes. His neck extended from a soft white collar encircled by a black string tie. In his left hand he carried a scarred black satchel and an umbrella, with a gray wool shawl folded over his arm, which left his right hand free for handshaking. When they were introduced, he treated Schurz like an old friend, telling quaint stories to illustrate his points, so that the journalist soon felt like they *were* old friends.

As the debate began, Lincoln spoke first and so persuasively that Schurz could not imagine how he could possibly be answered. But then Douglas spoke, and while Schurz found his baritone hoarse and rough, his tone angry, dictatorial, even insolent, and his language offensive, he also noted that "his sentences were well put together, his points strongly accentuated, his argumentation seemingly clear and plausible."

Lincoln spoke last, and he was in rare form. His speech was frequently punctuated by laughter, and "the meeting again and again broke out in bursts of delight by which even many of his opponents were carried away, while the scowl of Douglas's face grew darker and darker."[9]

But the tall prairie lawyer could also be serious, and never more so than when he said, "Judge Douglas says that whoever wants slaves, they have a right to have them. He is perfectly logical, if there is nothing wrong in the institution; but if you admit that it is wrong, he cannot possibly say that anybody has a right to do wrong."[10]

With this simple, brilliant stroke, Lincoln had laid bare the fundamental flaw in popular sovereignty. Taken to its extreme, the doctrine claimed, in effect, that people could do anything they wanted to, without regard to others. Yet the very essence of moral self-government required that the people maintain constant vigilance to preserve and protect the God-given, inalienable rights of *all* the people.

The Declaration of Independence defined these rights and embodied this vision. Since it had been inspired by Biblical principles, only a vital, vibrant Christian faith in the hearts of the people, renewed each generation, could sustain its vision. It must be kept alive. For without it, there would be nothing to check or control evil passions, and eventually the people would cease to want to do the right thing. They would become a mob, and a mob always elected a Caesar.[11]

Schurz felt that Lincoln carried the day, but of course Lincoln had gone last. With refreshing candor, Schurz also admitted that he considered Douglas an unscrupulous demagogue.[12] (One suspects that the pundit panel would have called this debate a draw.)

The final debate was at Alton, where abolitionist editor Elijah Lovejoy had been murdered by an angry mob 21 years before. It was Douglas's finest hour in the debates. Speaking of his beloved popular sovereignty, he proclaimed, "I will never violate or abandon that doctrine, if I have to stand alone. I . . . have stood immovably for that principle, fighting for it when assailed by Northern mobs, or threatened by Southern hostility. I have defended it against the North and the South, and I will defend it against whoever assails it, and I will follow it wherever its logical conclusion leads me."[13]

Lincoln matched the Senator's eloquence, summing up by saying that all the debates, all the speechifying, boiled down to one thing: whether slavery was right or wrong. Douglas refused to treat it as wrong; he himself could never treat it as right.

> That is the issue which will continue in this country when these poor tongues of Judge Douglas and myself shall be silent. It is the eternal struggle between these two principles—right and wrong—throughout the world. . . . The one is the common right of humanity, and the other is the divine right of kings. It is the same principle in whatever shape it develops itself. It is the same spirit that says, "You toil and work and earn bread, and I'll eat it."[14]

The final debate—and the contest—was over. Both sides felt they had won. Douglas was now certain he would be returned to the Senate, and Lincoln thought he probably would be, too. But he would not have changed a word.

In an editorial, the New York *Evening Post,* whose reporter had been at every debate, gave the contest to Lincoln. "No man of this generation has grown more rapidly before the country than Lincoln in this canvass."[15]

As historian Harry Jaffa noted,

> Americans could not, Lincoln held, accept slavery as a matter of moral indifference, without coming to accept their own freedom as a matter of moral indifference. What they owed to Negroes, they owed to themselves. And what they owed to themselves, they owed to Negroes—*because* they owed it to themselves. "As I would not be a slave," said Lincoln, "so I would not be a master."[16]

Slavery, declared Lincoln, was totally inconsistent with republican government; the Spirit of '76 and the spirit of popular sovereignty could not be more incompatible. To imagine that the forces of history were working against slavery, and that we should just let history take its course, was the worst kind of folly. To quote Jaffa:

> The only rock upon which man's political salvation might be built, was man's moral sense, the determination of some men to be free, and the awareness

that no man can rightfully achieve freedom for himself or, in the presence of a just God, long retain his freedom, if he would deny to any other man, of whatever race or nation, the right to perfect freedom.[17]

If requests for copies of their speeches were any indication, Lincoln won in a landslide: Everyone wanted his; no one wanted Douglas's. And it was the Republicans, not the Democrats, who printed up full-text copies of what both men had said and made them available to any thinking man or woman who asked for them.

There were quite a few more of those around now. Said George Beatty of Ottawa, "I tell you, that debate set people thinking on these important questions in a way they hadn't dreamed of. I heard any number of men say, 'This thing is an awfully serious question, and I have about concluded Lincoln has got it right.'"

Then George quoted his father. "Douglas's speeches of 'squatter sovereignty' please you younger men, but I tell you that with us older men, it's a great question that faces us. We've either got to keep slavery back, or it's going to spread all over the country."[18]

In the end, the election did go to Douglas. Lincoln actually won the popular vote, 125,121 to 121,090 (with 5,071 going to Buchanan's candidate), but the Democrats retained control of the legislature and voted 54 to 46 to return Douglas to the Senate.

Nevertheless, Abraham Lincoln had now become established in the public mind as the chief spokesman of the antislavery cause—"the leader in the army of freedom," in the words of the Senate sage John Crittenden.

Lincoln was back in his law office when word of the outcome reached him. Though it was late in the afternoon and already getting dark, he turned up the lamp and stayed long enough to pen a letter to a friend. "I am glad I made the late race. It gave me a hearing on the great and durable question of the age, which I could have had in no other way. And though I now sink from view, and shall be forgotten, I believe I have made some marks which will tell of the cause of civil liberty long after I have gone."[19]

He folded the sheet of stationery and slipped it into an envelope for the post in the morning. Outside, it was dark as he made his way home. The footing was tricky, and at one point he slipped. But he quickly caught himself and murmured, "A slip, but not a fall." Then he said it again, and one can imagine him smiling—"Yes, a slip, but not a fall!"[20]

After the rest of the fall elections, conventional wisdom had to be drastically revised. Republican gains had surprised everyone, and if the trend continued, by 1860 Illinois would be in the Republican camp. By the end of October, Indiana, Ohio, and even Pennsylvania were already there. In November, all of New England joined them. And finally, so did New York. It began to look as if the Republicans could actually win in 1860, even without the South. The only thing that could stop them was the Democratic party, with its North and South factions reunited behind a common champion. But as the Southern fire-eaters began to gnaw on the bone of Douglas's Freeport Doctrine, that seemed less and less likely.

All that remained was for the Republicans to pick the right candidate.

When Seward, speaking in Rochester, New York, in September, had referred to the likelihood of disunion and the possibility of civil war as the "irrepressible conflict," moderates on both sides shuddered. But no one was shocked now. Southern extremists, whose ranks were swelling, guaranteed secession if the Republicans, who were pledged to contain slavery, managed to put a man in the White House in 1860. Northern extremists, whose ranks were also swelling, longed for an excuse to *do* something about slavery. Moderates, whose ranks were dwindling, were in despair.

Then, just when it seemed the situation could not deteriorate any further, from the twisted mind of a crazed fanatic came the terrible, swift blow that would render the looming conflict truly irrepressible.

44

SWORD OF VENGEANCE

*T*he creaking wheels made the only sound in the moonless, misty night, as the white-bearded figure driving the wagon turned to check his troop. Behind him marched 21 men in a double column, each with a rifle and a brace of pistols. There was no talking in the ranks. They were young but well trained; the importance of absolute silence had been drilled into them. From his raiding days, John Brown knew the value of surprise.

It began to drizzle; he shivered and drew the long coat closer about him. And smiled; the rain would keep people indoors on this night and their dogs under cover. A barking dog could set off other dogs.

It had all come down to this—all the schemes, the skirmishes in Kansas, the raids into Missouri, the escape to Canada with the slaves they had freed. Missouri had put a price on him for that—$3,000, with President Buchanan personally adding $200 more to the sum.[1] All the recruiting, all the open meetings at which he spoke and the secret meetings at which he conspired—and now at last, on this Sunday night of October 16, 1859, the Provisional Army of the United States, as he had named it, was on the march.

A few months before, he had spoken at a meeting in Concord, Massachusetts. Out in Kansas his hair had turned white, and he had let his beard grow so long that people said he really did look like an Old Testament prophet. And these Massachusetts people had been more ready to hear than ever before. The climate in America was grim.

Half the nation had rejected the Supreme Court's Dred Scott decision, and in a few weeks the New York weekly *Tribune* would bluntly portray the "inexorably widening" gulf between the North and the South. "Is it not clear that the 'irrepressible conflict' affirmed by Mr. Seward is . . . a sober and present reality? Is it not plain that we are already, in effect, two nations, held together by the ties of tradition and interest, but at heart as hostile as the Romans and Carthaginians of old?"[2]

The meeting had been a fund-raiser, ostensibly for further operations in Kansas, and one could imagine Brown reminding his Concord listeners of their local heritage, of what a few brave men, perhaps including their fathers or grandfathers, had accomplished there fourscore and four years before. Those precious few had stood their ground in Concord and defied the mightiest military power on earth. They had acted in advance of a formal declaration of war, but their courage and their willingness to die for the cause of freedom had quickened the hearts and stiffened the backbones of thousands of patriots. And perhaps their act of selfless valor had hastened the conflict that all knew had to come.

Once again the cause of freedom was in peril. Four million souls in bondage, said Brown, were crying out for release. Once again it was time to take up musket and ball and shout to the oppressor: Enough! Your iniquity shall continue no longer!

The men of Concord had cheered that night. And some, with tears in their eyes, had come forward to shake his hand. But none had joined him. Not one. Brown's abolitionist friends, who had arranged his speaking tour throughout New England, had nevertheless assured him that he had done well. At the end of the tour they had given him $5,000—more money than he had ever had in his life. But they had not given themselves.

So Brown had decided that like Gideon, he would make do with the handful that God had given to him. It would be enough. God's sword of vengeance would be as terrible and swift as at Pottawatomie, two years before. There, he had claimed his actions were "decreed by Almighty God and ordained from Eternity."[3] But the action he had set in motion this night would eclipse all that had gone before.

The wagon went over a rock in the road, and the load under the canvas behind him shifted. Fifty Sharps rifles were there and nearly 500 pikes. Brown had always been impressed with the killing power of the Bowie knife; now, putting the abolitionist funds to the use for which they were intended, he'd had a Connecticut blacksmith make him a thousand such blades affixed to the end of long poles. He called them pikes, and when anyone asked, "What are they for, Captain Brown?" he would explain they were for the defense of Free-Soilers who in Kansas were called "Jayhawkers." Sometimes the questioners would look at him oddly, but they never pressed him. Brown was a guerrilla fighter, and there were some things you didn't ask such men.

The pikes were obviously not intended for Kansas; a "Beecher's Bible" was the weapon of choice out there. The pikes were for men who had no experience with firearms, but who were ready to fight for their freedom, and if necessary, die for it. Like Brown.

The same could not be said for the abolitionist leaders he had recently left. Those cultured, eloquent men in their brocaded silk vests and paneled drawing rooms wrote books and poems, sermons and editorials so great that their names were known throughout the country and even the world—Thoreau and Emerson, Whittier and Beecher, Alcott and Hoare. But they were men of words; he was a man of deeds.

It was ironic, their friendship; Brown envied their ease with words and their ability to stir men's hearts. Had they not stirred his? Yet they seemed to envy the fact that he was actually *doing* what they kept encouraging everyone else to do—but never did themselves.

Some had come close—the ones he called his Secret Six. They liked that title and began to call each other that. They had become his committee of conspirators. The most prominent was Theodore Parker, whose sponsorship did much to authenticate Brown in the eyes of New England's intelligentsia. But Parker, who had long suffered from consumption, had gone to Rome to seek relief.

Also among the six was Parker's protégé, Thomas Wentworth Higginson. A Harvard-trained Unitarian minister like his mentor, he was a hard-core disunionist anxious to organize a private army, to be ready when the time came. "Half the people I meet are within an inch of Disunion, and I wish to keep them there, so that when the fight comes . . . they will be ready to act themselves and drive their politicians."[4] He soon went even farther, declaring that blind superstitious loyalty to the national Government was declining. Men were ready for revolution, and he, for one, did not shrink from the prospect of a little blood being spilled for a good cause.

Brown assured his conspirators that bloodletting would be held to the absolute minimum essential for self-defense. The slave families who joined him would, of course, be expected to defend themselves, as would his men when the white slaveholders attacked them. But he did remind them that Paul had adjured the Hebrew believers that without the shedding of blood, there was no remission of sins. Brown's interpretation of that Scripture, however, was somewhat different than the Apostle's.* To Brown, since the sins were the slaveholders', the sacrificial blood would be theirs also—and he would be the priest who would shed it.

Among the Secret Six was another Harvard man, the esteemed founder and director of the Perkins Institute for the Blind, Samuel Gridley Howe. He, at least, had come out to Kansas to offer what help he could. And there was Gerrit Smith, the young millionaire philanthropist whose father had been John Jacob Astor's partner, and who had been the Liberty party's candidate for President in 1852. Smith, who had once told an appreciative audience that Brown was the nearest approach to a perfect Christian,[5] clearly enjoyed dabbling in something so daring. While Brown had little confidence in the durability of Smith's commitment, his money was always welcome.

Rounding out the six was the well-to-do journalist Franklin Benjamin Sanborn, a graduate of Philips Exeter Academy and Harvard, who acted as Brown's agent in New England, and George Luther Stearns, a prosperous manufacturer of linseed oil.

It had become increasingly clear to Brown that the time had come for his masterstroke, the one great act for which he had been born and which it had always been his destiny to achieve.

His visit to Senator Sumner's home in Boston had further distilled his resolve. He had been shown the bloodstained coat that Sumner had been wearing two years before, on that fateful day when he had been bludgeoned to the floor of the Senate Chamber. The coat had been carefully preserved, and as Brown examined it, he did so with reverential silence, as if he had been handed the relic of a saint.[6†]

God, he felt, had shown him what he must do: He would strike into Virginia, taking the armory at Harpers Ferry, just across the border at

---

* Paul was, of course, likening Moses' cleansing the temple with the shed blood of a sacrificial lamb to the cleansing of a Christian's soul by the shed blood of the Lamb, without which there could be no remission of sins.

† Recalling the visit, Sumner said Captain Brown's "lips compressed, and his eyes shone like polished steel."

the confluence of the Potomac and the Shenandoah. And this audacious thrust would be the trigger for the long-awaited servile insurrection.

There was evidence of widespread unrest among the slaves, and an uprising did seem imminent. In December 1856, Robert Bunch, the British consul in Charleston, South Carolina, wrote to his superiors in London's Foreign Office that a secret plan for a slave revolt had been uncovered involving slaves in Kentucky, Tennessee, Louisiana, and Georgia, with its headquarters in Nashville. Apparently, many Negroes had been executed and several whites had been arrested. His report was subsequently confirmed by the British consul in Richmond, who added that while the conspiracy seemed to be vague and disjointed, it did involve states from Delaware all the way to Texas. The implication of several whites indicated that the plot may have originated in the North. He, too, had heard that many Negroes had been executed, and that one white man had been flogged to death.[7]

Why had the newspapers not played up the story? Obviously, Southern editors did not want word of a potential uprising to spread, let alone to furnish Northern critics with fresh ammunition. But word would have reached the most prominent abolitionists nonetheless, via escaped slaves or in private correspondence from friends in England. And they would have assured Brown that the slaves *were* ready to rise, that in fact, his raid might well provide the spark that would set the whole South ablaze.

The Secret Six were not the only ones to know of Brown's scheme. A year before, a British mercenary whom Brown had hired to drill his recruits and teach them the ways of war, grew angry at never having been paid. He defected and betrayed the mission to several Republican leaders. Seward, foremost among them, was furious at having been told. As his party's likely Presidential candidate in 1860, he of all men should have been able to claim no foreknowledge of such an act. Senators Sumner and Wilson of Massachusetts, Hale of New Hampshire, and Governors Chase of Ohio and Fletcher of Vermont had also been informed.

Seward and Wilson privately remonstrated with Howe and the others for ever having gotten involved in such a harebrained scheme and advised them to get back from Brown the weapons they had given him. Five of the six panicked and decided that the raid must be postponed for at least a year. Only Higginson stood in favor of it; to postpone it for a year, he said, was to postpone it forever. The others overruled him, and Brown returned to Kansas.

But in his absence, Kansas had quieted down. The new Governor had clamped down on all freelance vigilante activity, and the Free-Soil moderates had undeniably gained the upper hand. With Kansas now certain to come into the Union as a free state, Captain Brown's services were no longer required. As one farmer challenged him: "We are settlers—you are not. You can strike a blow and leave; the retaliatory blow falls on us. . . . No Southern immigrants are coming, and your agitation only keeps out our Northern friends."[8] Clearly the Jayhawkers regarded Brown as unbalanced, afflicted with what 19th-century physicians termed *monomania*: He was entirely rational on any subject but the one with which he was obsessed.

Finding himself no longer welcome in Kansas, where he had next hoped to start the war that would free the slaves, he led 16 men on a raid into Missouri. In its wake he left a man murdered, a number of homes looted, and 11 slaves freed, whom he took to Detroit and put on a boat across the river to Canada. He also left the Free-Soil citizens of Kansas expressing outrage and condemning what he had done. The Lawrence *Herald of Freedom* deplored the fact that someone purporting to be a Free-State man should be guilty of the same mindless villainy as the Border Ruffians.[9]

When he returned to Massachusetts, however, in radical abolitionist circles he was more of a hero than ever. Wherever he spoke, he was greeted with prolonged cheering. (That this should be the welcome accorded a ruthless serial killer of innocent civilians was an indication of how little choice there was between the Northern radicals and their Southern counterparts.)

After a year had passed without the Republican leadership exposing his planned action into Virginia, Brown took their silence as approval. The raid was back on.[10]* But as he began to lay out his detailed plan for the assault on the Harpers Ferry armory, with its well-stocked arsenal and its rifle works, some of the Secret Six began to get distinctly queasy. What had once been a thrilling vicarious adventure—imagine, helping to

---

* Not all those informed were Republicans (and presumably sympathetic). In August someone sent an anonymous letter to John Floyd, Buchanan's proslavery Secretary of War, warning him that John Brown was planning to invade Virginia at Harpers Ferry in the next few weeks. Though he did save the letter, Floyd dismissed it as a hoax.

plan a war!—suddenly took on the aspect of deadly earnest reality, with potentially horrendous consequences. Except for Higginson, they pleaded with Brown not to tell them any details, so that afterward they could deny having had any precise knowledge of his intent. But it was a little late for that; Captain Brown had sent each of them detailed progress reports.

Frederick Douglass, the escaped slave and prominent abolitionist spokesman, was another outsider who knew of the assault Brown planned on Harpers Ferry; in fact, they had argued about it. Douglass had been impressed with Brown, but he condemned the proposed raid on strategic grounds: Surrounded by mountains and rivers, the Ferry was a perfect trap. Once they got in there, there was no way to get out. A superior force could get there all too quickly by rail and turnpike and seal off the escape routes. They were sure to be killed or captured.[11] But Brown was adamant. He needed the rifles and ammunition stored in that arsenal for his campaign. Besides, its very centrality would make it all the easier for supporters from Pennsylvania, Maryland, and western Virginia to rally to him. In those surrounding hills, he told Douglass, were many men who hated slavery and were a different breed than the dissolute planters of the tidewater. By this point he had convinced himself that the moment word went out of what he had done, local antislavery men and any slaves in the area would hurry to join him. At least as many would come to his aid as were likely to oppose him, and he would brook no suggestion to the contrary.

Recently he had slipped into Harpers Ferry to reconnoiter the town (cropping his beard close so as not to draw attention) and work out the phases and timing of his attack. No escape plan had been formulated, for none would be needed; it was inconceivable that his plan could fail. The moment the slaves thereabouts learned what was afoot, they would rise; his abolitionist friends had convinced him of that.

In their writings they had described the black man as highly intelligent (if not educated) and high-minded, with a heart yearning for freedom, who was ready to throw off his shackles at a moment's notice.[12]* And if anyone doubted this, they had only to look at Frederick Douglass; a higher-

---

* It was another case of groupthink. The radical abolitionists wanted so badly to believe this utopian myth, that by repeating it to each other often enough, they convinced themselves that it was, in fact, true.

minded, more freedom-loving man—black or white—would be hard to find. It never occurred to Brown that few, if any, of the abolitionist writers had any firsthand knowledge of the nature and character of the average field hand, let alone of the years and generations of unremitting oppression under which he had lived.

No, Brown had no doubt that as soon as the slaves heard that a deliverer had finally arrived, they would flock to him, and soon his movement would gain a momentum of its own. More would come, until the band of men that was sure to pursue them would be no match for them. They would be a mighty army of freemen, and they would head south, following the Appalachian Mountains, until there were so many that they would form their own impregnable state, for which Brown had already drawn up the constitution. Slaves from all over the South would hurry to join them. Slavery would be finished.

So there would be no escape plan; only a plan of attack.

Brown had not informed his followers of all this, however. They had assumed this would be another hit-and-run raid, with a quick exit north, running more slaves to Canada. They were waiting for him at a rented farmhouse five miles from Harpers Ferry. When he arrived and told them of his full plan, there had been "dissension" in the ranks—with the majority siding against him, including his three sons. No record exists of who said what to whom, but from Charles Tidd, who was present, we do know that "it nearly broke up the camp."[13]

No attempt had been made to alert the slaves or sympathetic whites that they were coming. No plan had been made to spread the word through the local countryside, once they got there. Nor had they given any thought to what they would do in the event they were outnumbered. But the biggest shock came when he told them that after the raid they would be going *south*, not north.

When everyone objected, according to Tidd, Captain Brown then threatened to resign and turn the command of the Provisional Army of the United States over to someone else. Then John Henry Kagi, the schoolteacher and best educated among them, said that only Brown could lead them, and the rest had fallen into line.

Now they were behind him, marching to glory—13 white men, 4 free blacks, 1 escaped slave, and Brown's 3 sons—though several were convinced that they were going to their doom.[14]

As the road began to descend to the river, Brown drew up the horse and raised his right hand. The column behind him stopped, then gathered round the wagon. He pointed to the lights of the town below and silently waved his hand forward.

Two men detached themselves to cut the telegraph wires, while the rest ran forward without a word onto the covered, 900-foot wagon-and-railroad bridge. Seizing the surprised night watchman, they left two men as guards and hurried on to the second bridge, similarly securing it. On they rushed to the rifle works half a mile up the Shenandoah. Maintaining silence, they took the watchman by surprise here, too. The telegraph wires at this end of town were also cut, and a three-man guard was posted at the rifle works.

Brown was pleased. The first phase of the attack had been completed; all Federal property, including several million dollars' worth of arms and munitions, was now in their hands.[15] And it was still two hours before midnight.

For the second phase, he sent a detachment of six men into Virginia, to the home of the most prominent slaveholder in the immediate vicinity, Colonel Lewis W. Washington, great-grandnephew of the first President of the United States. That gentleman was taken into custody and was forced to yield his most precious possession: the sword purportedly given to General Washington by Frederick the Great. Four of his slaves were also awakened, informed that they were now free, and told that their former master was now their prisoner. Thoroughly bewildered, the slaves were escorted with the colonel back to the armory.

The plan of attack called for the men to make one more stop on the way: John Allstadt, his son, and six of their slaves were similarly roused from their sleep and marched back to the armory. When the detachment returned, John Brown admired the sword of George Washington and put it on. One of the hostages asked him what he was trying to do. "Free the slaves," he responded. On what authority? "By the authority of God Almighty!"[16]

He ordered that pikes be distributed to the freed slaves, and that they be put in charge of the hostages. The entire operation had taken less than three hours.

All that remained now was to let the country know that they were there, and what they had accomplished. Then their reinforcements would start to come. The instrument for this third phase would be the midnight mail express from Wheeling to Baltimore, due to arrive at the Harpers Ferry station at one o'clock.

It showed up right on schedule. As the train was leaving the town, it appeared to the engineer that there was some sort of obstruction on the track ahead at the bridge. He stopped the train and went forward to investigate. Suddenly fired upon by the sentries there, he ran back to the cab, threw the big drivers into reverse, and backed the train into the station.

The station's baggagemaster, a free black named Shepherd Hayward, now went forward down the track to locate the watchman and find out what was going on. "Halt!" shouted an unseen sentry inside the bridge. But the baggagemaster had no idea what the word meant. All he knew was that it was not the voice of his friend. As he hurried forward to see what had happened, a shot rang out, and he took a bullet in his stomach. For 12 hours he lay in torment, begging for water, until at last he died.[17]

The first blood drawn by the sword of vengeance that had come to free all blacks was the blood of a black man who was already free.

The town began to wake up. What was that shooting? And what was the Midnight Special still doing in the station?

At five in the morning, as the sky began to lighten, Brown released the train, knowing that it would spread the word far and wide, as soon as it reached the next station and an open telegraph key. He counted on the conductor to convey his invitation to all men, black and white, who were prepared to strike a blow for freedom to come join him. He posted his son Owen at the schoolhouse to meet and arm the slaves that would be coming from Maryland. The slaves from Virginia were to report to his son Oliver at the Shenandoah bridge and then go to the men on guard at the rifle works under Kagi, where they would be given arms. Everything had gone according to plan. All they had to do now was wait.

As Brown anticipated, the train did stop at the first station. But the conductor's version of what was transpiring at Harpers Ferry did not exactly coincide with John Brown's—or anyone else's. And presumably, as each telegrapher picked up the news and passed it farther, they added their own sense of alarm to the message. In any event, the following is what the nation was told, early on that Monday morning:

NEGRO INSURRECTION AT HARPERS FERRY, VIRGINIA [STOP] SEI-
ZURE OF THE UNITED STATES ARSENAL BY THE INSURRECTION-
ISTS [STOP] EXTENSIVE NEGRO CONSPIRACY IN VIRGINIA AND
MARYLAND [STOP] BRIDGE TO HARPERS FERRY FROM MARY-
LAND FORTIFIED AND DEFENDED BY CANNON [STOP] SEVEN
HUNDRED AND FIFTY BLACK AND WHITE ABOLITIONISTS HOLD
ARSENAL AND GUN WORKS [STOP] THE NAME OF THE LEADER
IS OSAWATOMIE BROWN [STOP] BROWN EXPECTS REINFORCE-
MENTS OF FIFTEEN HUNDRED MEN [STOP] ALMOST ALL LEAD-
ING CITIZENS OF HARPERS FERRY ARE HELD AS HOSTAGES[18]

When the conductor's telegram was received in Baltimore, it was at first treated with incredulity. But soon the Governor was alerted, and also the commander of the Maryland Militia. President Buchanan and Governor Wise of Virginia were informed that apparently a full-scale slave revolt, with whites assisting, was under way.[19]

The sky, still overcast, was growing brighter. And now the shooting and commotion at the arsenal and the train station were beginning to attract the town's attention. One citizen came too close and was fatally shot. At seven o'clock, the first of the armory's employees, sleepily entering the yard to work, were taken prisoner.

After that, everyone in town knew what was going on, and riders had alerted the countryside. Farmers from the surrounding area gathered up their shotguns or squirrel rifles and headed for the Ferry—not to join Brown, but to do something about this band of Northern invaders.

By 11 o'clock, farmers and townsmen had begun exchanging fire with the raiders. In the brick firehouse that was serving as their headquarters, John Brown wondered where his reinforcements were. The train had left six hours earlier. By this time the entire countryside should have been apprised. So where were they?

He called up to the lookout in the cupola, but there was no sign of slaves or abolitionists approaching from any direction. There *was* a company of volunteers though, heading for the Shenandoah bridge, and behind them another company was moving into covering position in the mountains.

And now a third company of uniformed militia was approaching the covered bridge.

Brown was disconcerted. He had not anticipated that raw farmers could move so quickly and efficiently, nor had he realized that the men who lived in Virginia's Blue Ridge Mountains were among the best shots in the country. His situation was deteriorating rapidly—and there was still no sign of reinforcements.

Finally, one of Brown's lieutenants pleaded with him to make a run for it, while they still could. But Brown did not seem to hear him.

"Where are they?" he muttered. "Why haven't they come?" Things were no longer going at all according to plan, and for the first time he seemed confused.

By noon, the militia company, the Jefferson Guards from Charlestown,* the nearest town of any size, had taken the covered bridge. In addition, the volunteer company now commanded the Shenandoah bridge. The sentries, hopelessly outnumbered, had fallen back and joined Brown and the others in the firehouse, whose heavy oak door they had barricaded. The heights behind them were now completely occupied, sealing off the last escape route. They were trapped.

As the afternoon wore on, the local men, frustrated at the seeming impregnability of the raiders' position, brought out their jugs. Gradually the whole scene seemed to take on the almost festive air of a turkey shoot. A party stormed the rifle works, killing Kagi, mortally wounding a second raider, and seizing a third.

For a long time Brown had seemed dazed, incapable of making a decision. Now he came to his senses, and realizing the situation was hopeless, decided to play the one card he had left: his hostages. He would release them in exchange for his party's freedom, with the promise that they would not be pursued. He sent a man out to ask for a truce, so that he could begin negotiations, but the man was taken prisoner, then killed by a vengeful mob.

An hour later, Brown tried again. This time he sent two men, including his son Watson, under a white flag. No sooner did they appear than they were fired upon. Both men were hit, but Watson, shot through with several slugs, managed to drag himself back inside the firehouse.

* now Charles Town, West Virginia

At four o'clock a train pulled into the station, and several hundred volunteers jumped out. All through the night more men arrived, and more jugs came out. Inside the firehouse the remaining defenders spent a cold, hungry night. It was also sleepless because of the drunken carousing going on outside.

By this time Oliver Brown had also been hit, and he was lying next to his dying brother Watson. At one point he called to his father who was sitting on the wagon peering out through a loophole he had made in the heavy door. Oliver, in agony from his wound and aware that he did not have long to live, pleaded with his father to put him out of his misery.

Brown was disgusted. "If you must die," he snarled, "die like a man!"

After a while, Oliver fell silent. His father called to him. Receiving no answer, he said, "I guess he is dead."[20]

In Washington, the news from Harpers Ferry, a scant 60 miles away, had thrown the city into an uproar. Every policeman was put on duty patrolling the streets, and Buchanan dispatched some 90 Marines, practically the entire garrison protecting the capital, to the scene. To take charge of the situation and assume overall command, he sent the most competent field officer available, Lieutenant Colonel Robert E. Lee of the Second Cavalry, and as his aide, a young cavalry officer who had combat experience fighting Indians on the western frontier, Lieutenant James Ewell Brown Stuart, known to his friends by his initials, "Jeb."

It was so late when they arrived that Lee decided not to do anything until dawn. As the sky began to brighten over the Ferry for the raid's second day, the occupants of the firehouse looked out to see some 2,000 men gathered with rifles or muskets. In the foreground a company of uniformed Marines were taking their bayonets from their belts and affixing them to the barrels of their muskets. Obviously they were preparing for some close-in work, most likely a charge.

Inside the firehouse only Brown and four others remained unwounded. The end would be coming soon. But Brown still hoped to negotiate their way out of the debacle. There were U.S. Army officers out there now; surely they would see the value of trading hostages for freedom.

The senior officer present, Robert E. Lee, offered the honor of the final charge to the colonel of the local militia. The latter hastily declined, saying "Your men are paid for this kind of work. Mine have wives and children."[21]

Lee told Lieutenant Israel Green of the Marines to pick 12 of his best men for an assault team, and to caution the men not to fire until they were inside. Only at close range could they be certain of not hitting hostages. Several Marines carried a heavy ladder to smash through the doors. Lee then instructed Lieutenant Stuart to go forward with a note containing the terms of surrender. They were unconditional: If the insurrectionists laid down their arms and came out, they would not be harmed. They would be taken into protective custody by the Marines and delivered to the proper authorities.

The terms should be attractive to the raiders, reasoned Lee, for if they were to fall into the hands of the mob, they would be the object of cruel sport followed by a mass lynching—something that Lee was determined was not going to happen under his command. He told Stuart that if the raiders rejected the terms or made any attempt to parley, he was to get out of the way and signal the attack.

Stuart took the note, saluted, and started walking slowly and erect toward the firehouse. Watching the back of the young West Pointer, Lee nodded approvingly at his immense personal courage.

The door opened a crack, and Stuart was surprised to see staring out at him the bearded face of old Osawatomie Brown, whom he had once held under detention out in Kansas. They had heard a rumor from one of the reporters on the scene that Brown was in charge, but he had discounted it as just another rumor. He handed Brown the note.

The latter glanced at it, then passed it back. "You read it!" he hissed. Stuart began, but before he could finish, Brown interrupted him and let him know that he, not the young officer facing him, would be the one to dictate terms. They held a number of hostages, Brown informed him (at which point the hostages started crying out, with Lewis Washington identifying himself), whom he was prepared to release unharmed, if they were guaranteed safe passage over the bridge and—

Stuart just shook his head, and Brown snarled, "We soldiers are not afraid of death. I would as leave die by a bullet as on the gallows."[22]

With a sigh, Stuart leaped aside, took off his cap, and used it to wave the Marines forward. That was the signal: With a yell, they charged behind their lieutenant, who had his sword in his hand. "Sell your lives dear!" cried Brown as the Marines ran toward them. The men with the heavy ladder used it as a battering ram, and though the oak planks were stout, in a short while they gave way. Lieutenant Green was the first through and went for Brown, who fired at him, but the shot went wild.

Now other Marines poured in through the opening, and both sides opened fire at point-blank range. Two Marine privates fell, mortally wounded, as Lieutenant Green thrust at Brown's chest. But his light dress sword was meant for the parade ground, not close combat; its point hit leather, and the blade bent double and snapped. Using its hilt as a club, the lieutenant rained down blows on the man who had just tried to kill him, till Brown sank to his knees, senseless.

It was over.

45

The Making of a Legend

*N*ews of the raid electrified the nation. Still believing the initial reports that hundreds of men were involved, the South was terrified. Amid rumors of similar raids in other states, slave patrols were doubled, militias were called out, and travelers who weren't from the South moved at their peril. Virginia and Maryland were especially alarmed, expecting at any moment a force of Yankee invaders bent on rescuing Brown. All the South blamed the North—and particularly the Republicans—for fomenting a full-scale servile insurrection.

Conservative Northerners denounced the raid as the act of a deranged madman. Edward Everett announced himself disgusted and alarmed, referring to Brown's "blood guilt."[1] Richard Henry Dana exclaimed that Brown was demonstrably insane. Even John Greenleaf Whittier, poet laureate of the antislavery movement, deplored such violence. And Abraham Lincoln, increasingly the spokesman for moderate Republicans, commented that the plot was ridiculous from its very inception, "an attempt by white men to get up a revolt among slaves, in which the slaves refused to participate—so absurd that the slaves, with all their ignorance, saw plainly enough it could not succeed."[2]

Republican leaders quickly distanced themselves from Brown and his supporters, who now went into a panic, especially when a carpetbag full of Brown's papers and correspondence was discovered at the farmhouse, revealing the complicity of the Secret Six. Theodore Parker stayed in Rome for his health. Terror-stricken Samuel Gridley Howe persuaded George Stearns to accompany him in fleeing for Canada. Benjamin Sanborn, learning that he might be arrested and extradited to Virginia, decided to visit Quebec himself. Gerrit Smith suffered a nervous collapse and had himself committed to an insane asylum in Utica.

Even Frederick Douglass, after seeing to the concealment of his own papers, decided to pay England a visit—by way of Canada. As he frankly admitted, "I have always been more distinguished for running than fighting and, tried by the Harpers Ferry-Insurrection test, I am most miserably deficient in courage."[3]

Only Thomas Higginson stood his ground, working with a few others to provide for Brown's defense.

Brown was held in the jail at Charlestown, where he was soon visited and interrogated by Virginia's Governor, Henry Wise.* The public was beginning to wonder if Brown wasn't simply insane, but Wise found him quite the contrary, describing him as "cool, collected, and indomitable."[4] Brown told Wise that if he could have conquered Virginia, the other states "would nearly conquer themselves, there being such a large number of slaves in them."[5]

But now that the blow had been struck and had failed, Brown seemed determined to wrest victory from defeat. They were going to execute him? Very well, he would die a martyr. He now set his iron will at playing that part as well and as nobly as any saint who had ever faced the stake or the block or the colosseum's ramping lions. More than once, according to his son Owen, he had told his men, "We have only one life to live, and one to die; and if we lose our lives, it will perhaps do more for the cause than our lives would be worth in any other way."[6]

Now he would prove it.

Henry Wise was enjoying his turn at center stage and was anxious to extend it. Fate seemed to have dealt him a role to play, too—that of the concerned, high-minded statesman—and he played it to the hilt. It was not long before he imagined himself as the Democrat's candidate next year, the one who just might be able to bring the party's warring factions together. To enhance his role, Wise, instead of treating the raid as the work of a few fanatics, deployed many of the Old Dominion's militias while putting the rest on full alert.

Former Virginia Congressman James Seddon condemned Wise's ac-

---

* The reader will remember Wise as one of John Quincy Adams' most bitter adversaries over the gag rule.

tions, writing that the foolish Governor, mad for the Presidential nomination, "has conjured a devil neither he nor perhaps anyone else can lay, and arraying the aroused pride and animosities of both sections against each other, has brought on a *real* crisis of imminent peril to both."[7]

Wise decided that John Brown should be tried separately, and that the trial should be held as quickly as possible, to put the potentially inflammable proceedings to rest. But it should not be done in unseemly haste. Brown must receive as fair a trial as the Old Dominion could provide. Wise was impressed with the captive, finding him "a broken-winged hawk, lying on his back, with a fearless eye, and his talons set for further fight, if need be."[8] He took seriously the rumors of a rescue or escape attempt that were beginning to surface.

The next character in this unfolding drama was the presiding judge, Richard Parker, who imbued his role with dignity and decorum, strictly preserving order in his court. He appointed lawyers to defend Brown, and soon others arrived from the North to assist.

The lawyers quickly came to the conclusion that the only chance of saving their client from the scaffold was to enter a plea of insanity. In 1859 it was a recognized defense with legal precedent. Brown's monomania was self-evident. All they needed to do was enter testimony of acceptable witnesses who were prepared to testify that Brown was mad, and apparently there were more than a few. Plus, there was the long history of insanity in his family. There was the mother and the grandmother and an aunt, too, apparently, and three of his first cousins were at that moment under restraint.[9]

But Brown would not hear of it. If he was declared insane and put away in an asylum somewhere, his act would be written off as the aberrant behavior of a madman. The public, both North and South, would so badly *want* to believe that. If he was mad, then everyone could breathe a sigh of relief, and he would soon be forgotten.

But if he was sane . . . then no one could forget him. Then others would be inspired by his example. Other men would find the courage to do what must be done. Women would have the conviction to wave them on their way. And long after his body lay moldering in its grave, his truth would go marching on.

So Brown rejected the insanity defense. He now focused his monomania on playing out the martyr role to the utmost of his considerable ability.

He maintained resolute dignity and stature, never losing his temper, never giving in to self-pity or behaving in an unmanly fashion. And it appeared that he would be able to stay in character to the very end.

In the calm, steady light of his example, Northern opinion began to shift. At first the Northern press, even the antislavery papers, had been outraged at his arrogant disregard for the fundamental laws of decent society. Clearly the man was criminally insane.

But now some papers were modifying their original perspective on Harpers Ferry. Horace Greeley's *Tribune* said that Brown and his men "dared and died for what they felt to be right, though in a manner which seems to us fatally wrong."[10]

The rehabilitation of John Brown's public image had begun.

The trial began on October 25. When his lawyers, over their client's objection, made a motion to enter a plea of insanity, Brown, not fully recovered and present in the courtroom on a cot, rose up and said, "I reject, so far as I am capable, any attempt to interfere in my behalf on that score."[11] The motion was dismissed, and the trial continued.

Judge Parker kept it moving at an efficient pace, though never at the expense of fairness to the defendant. Observers North and South commented on the smoothness and evenhandedness of the proceedings, and Brown himself said that everything was being done well, and he was indeed receiving a fair trial.

A week later, the jury had found him guilty. Before pronouncing sentence on November 2, Judge Parker asked the prisoner if he had anything to say. At last John Brown had his day in court. He had carefully prepared his remarks, knowing that they would be widely reprinted and would help carry him to his place in history. Rising to his feet with difficulty, he pointed to the court's Bible, used for swearing in witnesses, and declared that it "teaches me that all things whatsoever that men should do to me, I should do even so to them. . . . I believe that to have interfered as I have done, as I have always freely admitted that I have done, in behalf of [God's] despised poor, I did no wrong, but right."

Stating that "I feel no consciousness of guilt,"[12] he then claimed that he had never intended to foment a servile insurrection but only to carry off slaves to Canada, and that he had never tried to induce men to join him but merely accepted volunteers. None of these statements were true, though they would soon be accepted as truth by millions of Northerners—and would continue to be accepted, despite all evidence and testimony to the contrary. As Robert Penn Warren would observe, "It was all so thin that it should not have deceived a child, but it deceived a generation."[13]

Frederick Douglass was not deceived. In his memoirs, he recalled their private meeting in which Brown had denounced slavery "in look and language fierce and bitter," stating that slaveholders had "forfeited the right to live." He had contemplated "the creating of an armed force, which should act in the very heart of the South." He was "not averse to the shedding of blood" and felt that carrying arms, prepared to "fight for their freedom," would give black men a new sense of their manhood.[14]

Brown had one more point to make. Looking at the judge and the courtroom, but seeing beyond them all the countless thousands who would soon be reading his words, he said, "Now, if it is deemed necessary that I should forfeit my life for the furtherance of the ends of justice, and mingle my blood further with the blood of my children and with the blood of the millions in this slave country whose rights are disregarded by wicked, cruel, and unjust enactments, I say, let it be done."[15]

He sat down, and shorthand reporters raced to the nearest telegraph office. The beatification of John Brown was about to be taken to a new level.

Pressure now came at Governor Wise from all directions, pulling him in all directions. Numerous letters arrived, begging on humanitarian grounds that the Governor spare Brown's life. The mayor of New York City commended Wise's fairness and said that his firmness was highly applauded in his city. Then he added, "Now, my friend, dare you do a bold thing, and temper justice with mercy?"[16]

Sincere evangelical Christians joined the letter-writing campaign. The antislavery activist Amos A. Lawrence, repenting of the support he had once given Brown, nonetheless advised the Governor not to execute him but to put him away, as his mind had clearly become "disordered by hardship and illness." There was another reason not to put him to death: "From his blood would spring an army of martyrs, all eager to die for the cause of human liberty."[17] Conversely there were some evangelical abolitionists for whom Brown's death would better serve their purposes than having his sentence commuted. Henry Ward Beecher, alarmed that so many of his great flock were praying for Brown's life to be spared, admonished them *not* to pray for his release: "Let Virginia make him a martyr. . . . His soul was noble; his work miserable. But cord and gibbet would redeem all that, and round up Brown's failure with heroic success."[18]

One cannot help speculating on what might have happened, had Wise opted to show mercy on the grounds of insanity. And there was fresh evidence to that effect: Brown's brother Jeremiah had now certified in writing that in talking with him two years before, "I had no doubt that he had become insane upon the subject of slavery, and gave him to understand this was my opinion of him."[19] Moreover, Brown's lawyers had collected no less than 19 such affidavits from Brown's neighbors and relatives, including his uncle and a brother-in-law.[20]

Wise may have actually been considering such a course; he did see Brown one more time. But his second interview only confirmed the impression formed of the first. "Did I believe him insane," he informed a visitor shortly before the execution, "if I could entertain a rational doubt of his perfect sanity, I should stay the execution, even at this hour. . . . But I have no such belief, no such doubt."[21]

With his state clamoring for retribution, the Governor needed a man to hang. Besides, in a few months the Democratic party would be picking their candidate for the Presidency. They might look with more favor on the man who firmly but fairly brought the whole matter to a quick, final resolution. There would be no eleventh-hour Governor's pardon for John Brown.

The date of the execution was set for December 2. Visitors to the condemned man's jail cell were deeply impressed with Brown's quiet courage and serenity; women wept at his noble dignity. On his last Sunday, he wrote his sisters that he experienced perfect consolation and peace. He credited that in part to the belief that his death would aid "the crushed millions who have no comforter."[22]

When he learned of a planned last-minute, jailhouse rescue, Brown rejected it. "I am worth now infinitely more to die than to live."[23] Besides, harm and possibly death might come to the sheriff and his deputies, and these men had been kindly and humane in their treatment of him. The Old Man's decision was final; nothing, not even his friends, was going to keep John Brown from his destiny.

Now the radical abolitionist writers and editors were in full cry, some even likening him to Jesus standing before Pilate. And Brown, reading what was now being written about him, became all the more determined to fulfill the role being assigned to him. Henry David Thoreau exclaimed that Brown was "the bravest and humanest man in all the country. . . . I rejoice that I live in this age, that I was his contemporary," and he compared his hero's inevitable execution to the crucifixion of Christ.[24]*

Theodore Parker weighed in with this final judgment: "There have been few spirits more pure and devoted than John Brown's, and none that gave up their breath in a nobler cause. Let the American State hang his body, and the American Church damn his soul. . . . The road to heaven is as short from the gallows as from a throne."[25]

But Ralph Waldo Emerson outdid them all. Speaking at Boston's Tremont Temple on November 8, he referred to Brown as that "saint whose fate yet hangs in suspense, but whose martyrdom, if it shall be perfected, will make the gallows as glorious as the Cross."[26] Louisa May Alcott picked up on that, calling the gallows "a stepping-stone to heaven."[27]

Not surprisingly, the South was dumbfounded at the North's extravagant eulogizing of a demented mass murderer. In their eyes John Brown was nothing more than a criminal, and those who had financed and encouraged him, and then gone into hiding, were even worse. The fact that Northern women could weep for such a man and that responsible Northern newspapers could call for other men to follow Brown's example was proof beyond question of the North's implacable hatred of the South. As a Richmond newspaper put it, Brown's hapless "invasion" had "advanced the cause of Disunion more than any other event that has happened since the formation of our government."[28]

The fury of the Southern response only elicited greater fury in reply. No one in the North suggested that their neighbors stop to think how they might feel if an armed body of Southerners had invaded their state, occupied a Federal armory, and invited all who were unhappy with the existing Government to join them in overthrowing it.

The South felt they had already had a bellyful of the North's moral superiority; now these Northern hypocrites were condoning murder, kidnapping, and the attempted overthrow of the Government, all because the lunatic leading the raid was against slavery. The situation was hopeless. The North would not rest until the South was conquered, and they could

---

* He also called him an "angel of light"—which may have been more discerning than he knew.

impose their will and their way of life on them. What was the point of staying in the Union long enough to let them achieve their goals?

As Dwight L. Dumond put it, after Harpers Ferry, "Republicans were all John Browns to the Southerners, and slaveholders were all Simon Legrees to the Northerners."[29]

Out in Kansas, one voice of reason could still be heard. Abraham Lincoln was speaking to a Free-Soil audience when he was informed of John Brown's sentence. "We cannot object," he cautioned his listeners, "even though he agreed with us in thinking slavery wrong." He shook his head. "That cannot excuse violence, bloodshed, and treason."[30] Lincoln was saying, in effect, what Jesus had taught 18 centuries before: The end *never* justified the means.

December 2 dawned bright and warm. When Brown was brought out of jail, six companies of Virginia infantry stood ready to escort him. In front of the jailhouse a wagon waited with a large pine box in it containing a heavy oak casket. The jailer got up in the wagon and sat on the box, and bade Brown, who was wearing bedroom slippers and an ill-fitting dark suit, to join him. Brown gave the jailer a scrap of paper, on which he had written what he hoped would be recorded as his last words: "I, John Brown, am now quite certain that the crimes of this guilty land will never be purged away, but with blood."[31]

The driver slapped his reins and clucked to his team, and the wagon started. The soldiers fell in, forming two columns, one on either side. Brown said nothing. Less then seven weeks before, he had been in another wagon, leading two other columns to their destiny—which turned out to be this destiny.

In a field outside of Charlestown, some 1,500 soldiers from different troops had assembled, including a detachment of cadets from the Virginia Military Institute. Accompanying them was their professor of artillery tactics and natural philosophy, Thomas J. Jackson.

As a precaution, civilian onlookers and reporters were kept at a great distance; after Harpers Ferry, one never knew what the abolitionists might attempt. One of the civilians looking on was Virginia's leading secessionist,

Edmund Ruffin. Another was a young Shakespearean actor and passionate advocate of slavery, John Wilkes Booth.

At noon John Brown walked erect to the scaffold and was the first up the steps. When the others joined him, he shook hands with the sheriff and his jailer and bade them farewell. Then he stood straight, as a white linen hood was lowered over his head. The noose was placed around his neck, and the jailer asked him to step onto the trapdoor. "You must lead me," replied Brown quietly. "I cannot see." All was ready—but then began a wait of eight interminable minutes, while late-arriving troops were marched and countermarched into their assigned places.

"Are you tired?" asked the jailer softly.

"No, not tired," came the reply. "But don't keep me waiting longer than necessary."[32]

The last column finally came to attention. With a hatchet the sheriff cut the rope holding the trapdoor.

At that moment throughout the North, funeral bells were tolling. In some places cannon were being fired at one-minute intervals. And countless prayers were being said.

Something had happened in America, from which there could be no return. In his epic poem *John Brown's Body*, Stephen Vincent Benet portrayed a Connecticut farmer looking up from the New York *Tribune*'s account of the trial and saying to his wife, "I didn't say I thought he was wrong. I said they had the right to hang the man. But they'll hang slavery with him."[33]

John Brown became a legend. Within a year and a half, companies of young volunteers in Union blue would parade down main streets and off to war singing—

> John Brown's body lies a-moldering in the grave,
> John Brown's body lies a-moldering in the grave,
> John Brown's body lies a-moldering in the grave,
> His soul goes marching on.

46

PARANOIA

*D*own the track could be seen the glowing headlamp of an approaching engine with the white flag of Virginia flying from her stack. She blew her whistle, and the crowd on the platform took an involuntary step backward. A brass band struck up, and Governor Wise, standing on a baggage cart where all could see him, led the massive throng that had assembled at the Richmond station in a great cheer. With a blast of steam the train shuddered to a halt, and mothers, wives, and sweethearts strained for a glimpse of their loved ones among the young men descending from the coaches. The greeting grew deafening.

"Let Virginia call home her sons!" the Governor had earlier proclaimed, and 160 of the Old Dominion's best and brightest, studying to become doctors in the medical schools of Philadelphia, had dutifully boarded the next train home. This train.

They would not be going back. Instead, they would continue their studies in the medical schools of Virginia. But now, as they swung off the train to a heroes' welcome by the ladies of Richmond, it was as if they were fresh young officers on their way to a war that was about to begin.*

Their recall was only the latest of Henry Wise's ill-considered and inflammatory acts in the wake of the Harpers Ferry raid. Moderate men, who still valued reason and a calm approach to the mounting crisis, were anxious to see Harpers Ferry forgotten. But immoderate men, North and South, who preferred to play to emotions, were just as anxious that it remain on the front burner of the national cookstove. Wise, who alone believed he

---

*Within two years, nearly all would be just that, putting their new skills to work in surgeons' tents.

had a middling chance of being nominated for the Presidency, was in the latter camp.

Emotions over John Brown were running high and headed higher. Emerson had declared him a new saint on the calendar, and his literary colleagues were outdoing one another to confirm the canonization. In Longfellow's diary, the entry on the day of Brown's execution made an extraordinary claim for December 2, 1859, calling it "the date of a new revolution, quite as much needed as the old one."[1] Young William Dean Howells, future editor of the *Atlantic Monthly*, wrote to his father: "Brown has become an idea, a thousand times purer and better and loftier than the Republican idea."[2]

Thoreau concurred. "I meet him at every turn. He is more alive than he ever was."[3]

A martyr legend was fast growing around Brown, and even antislavery moderates were caught up in the enthusiasm. Opined the Springfield *Republican*, "We can conceive of no event that could so deepen the moral hostility of the people of the free States to slavery as this execution. This is not because the acts of Brown are generally approved, for they are not. It is because the nature and spirit of the man are to be seen to be great and noble." His death was due "to his own folly, to be sure, but that will not prevent his being considered a martyr to his hatred of oppression, and all who sympathize with him in that sentiment will find their hatred growing stronger."[4]

In the South, a legend of the opposite sort was growing around John Brown. No one believed that only six men had supported Brown in his raid. The general feeling was that the entire Republican leadership had been aware of what was being planned, if not actively involved. The Richmond Whig carried an advertisement by a man offering to put up $100 if 99 other men would join him in doing the same, to offer a $10,000 reward for the delivery of the corpse of Joshua Giddings, or half as much for his head.[5*]

Conservative voices in the North were condemning Brown's raid; conservative voices in the South were condemning Wise's hysteria-inciting response. But neither side was listening to these voices. The South was

---

* When Giddings learned that his head might fetch $5,000, he allowed as how he would take advantage of the offer himself; they could have it, as soon as he was done with it.

shocked at the North's venerating a murderous madman; the North was shocked at the South's shock. Everyone was shouting; no one was listening. Paranoia had met counterparanoia.

Throughout the South, men and women began to regard Yankees as people who hated them, who were willing to see them assassinated in their beds by their slaves, and who were ready to support armed invasions of Southern soil. And increasingly the new Republican party became the focus of their reciprocal hatred, despite the fact that its leaders continued to vehemently denounce the raid and deny having anything to do with it.

Southerners did not believe them. As Jefferson Davis said, the raid on Harpers Ferry was instigated "by extensive combinations among the non-slaveholding States." It was an act of war against the State of Virginia, and after all, hadn't the Republican party been "organized on the basis of making war" against slavery, which meant against the South?[6]

Noting the vast number of Southerners inclined to agree with the Senator from Mississippi, Horace Greeley was quick to recognize Davis's emerging prominence:

> Mr. Davis is unquestionably the foremost man of the South today. Every Northern Senator will admit that from the Southern side of the floor the most formidable to meet in debate is the tall, thin, polished, intellectual-looking Mississippian with the unimpassioned demeanor, the habitual courtesy, and the occasional unintentional arrogance which reveals his consciousness of the great commanding power.[7]

Davis's conviction was equally shared by the ladies of the South. Major Edmund Kirby Smith* was serving on the western frontier when he received a letter from his mother in St. Augustine, in which she spoke for countless others: "The whole country is in a state of fearful agitation. Disunion! Disunion is the cry with our Southern friends, and is boldly spoken by the fireside, in public, in all places it is the absorbing subject. The aggression of the North and the insults to which we are subjected in their papers . . ."

She could see what lay over the horizon. "Disunion must follow. Southern men and Southern women will not sit down with folded hands, if the

---

* not to be confused with Captain Ephraim Kirby Smith, who was killed in the Mexican War

masses elect a Black Republican President. . . . These are fearful times. What will be the end, I know not. . . ."

But she knew where her son belonged. "I feel confident that your sword will be offered to the land of your birth—was not the stampede of the Southern students from the Northern colleges a beautiful thing? How I honor those youths!—I have the blood of a soldier of the Revolution in my veins, and it warms up as I think how the noble fabric of this building has been desecrated."[8]

If Mrs. Smith was typical of the ladies of St. Augustine, it was small wonder that Florida was in the front rank of States now prepared to secede.*

Harpers Ferry was also responsible for significant changes in the Senate and other legislative bodies. Texans, for instance, would no longer be spoken for in the Senate by unionist Sam Houston; from now on they would be represented by a disunionist, Louis Wigfall. And Robert Toombs of Georgia came over from the House; previously a staunch unionist, John Brown's raid and the Northern reaction to it had convinced him that secession was a necessity. In the South Carolina Senate, another staunch unionist, E. J. Moses, announced that while he had never expected his feelings to change, he was now ready for secession. He believed that peace, safety, and honor could no longer be found in a yoke with the North.[9]

And in Richmond, another South Carolinian, Christopher Memminger, on a mission to persuade the Virginia legislature to join other Southern states in a convention to discuss means of protecting their rights and property, was warmly received. South Carolina would abide by the will of her sisters, he assured them. "If our pace be too fast for some, we are content to walk slower; our earnest desire is that all may keep together."[10]

There were still a few men of good intent in the South, still attempting to find a way out of the slavery quagmire. But finally, the Richmond *Examiner* cried *enough*. "It is an hallucination to say that we are ever going to get rid of slavery, or that it will ever be desirable to do so. It is a thing that we cannot do without; that is righteous, profitable, and permanent, and that belongs to Southern society as inherently, intrinsically, and durably as the white race itself."[11]

---

* Honoring his mother's wishes, Kirby Smith would offer his sword to the Confederacy, becoming one of her most brilliant and resourceful generals.

Senator A. G. Brown of Mississippi went even further, expressing his desire to see Cuba, Mexico, and Central America come under the slavery umbrella. "I would spread the blessing of slavery . . . to the uttermost ends of the earth." But Mississippi's other Senator, Jefferson Davis, increasingly the spokesman for all the Deep South, was more thoughtful and reserved, as he offered his estimation of the Southern mindset: "There is not probably an intelligent mind among our citizens who doubts either the moral or the legal right of the institution of African slavery."[12]

In the South the level of paranoia had risen to the point where it was now regarded as an act of treason to speak openly against slavery. Declared the Atlanta *Confederacy*: "We regard every man in our midst as an enemy to the institutions of the South, who does not boldly declare that he believes African slavery to be a social, moral, and political blessing."[13]

Rumors abounded of abolitionist agents fomenting insurrection or burning crops. The restrictions on slaves became much harsher on many plantations, and manumission of any kind became illegal throughout the South. In county after county, free blacks were given the choice of either leaving or voluntarily returning to slavery. Vigilance patrols were doubled. Traveling salesmen from the North were tarred and feathered and run out of town on a rail—just for being from the North.

In Charleston, the British Consul reported that a veritable Reign of Terror was now in place in the Lower South. A 60-year-old minister had been given 70 lashes for speaking mildly against slavery, and more than one person had been lynched for having been overheard to utter the wrong sentiments.[14]

Only the disunionists were ecstatic. "Never before, since the Declaration of Independence," exclaimed the Sumter (South Carolina) *Watchman*, "has the South been more united in sentiment and feeling."[15]

In the Louisiana legislature, a resolution was offered (and narrowly rejected) that should a Black Republican be elected in 1860, Louisiana would consider that grounds for dissolving the Union. Florida did pass a similar resolution, and Mississippi called for a Southern convention for the purpose of discussing collective defensive action. Alabama declared that in the event of a Black Republican entering the White House, she would call a convention of her own, to discuss secession. The Governor of South Carolina declared that with the Harpers Ferry incident, the North had crossed the Rubicon, and that it was hopeless to look for protection from the Democratic party. He began exchanging letters with the Governors of Mississippi and Alabama concerning their next move.

As Congress reconvened in December, the new bitterness in Washington presented a daunting challenge to the capital's hostesses. Planning a formal dinner party was a bit like negotiating a no-man's-land filled with unexploded and highly sensitive shells. Guest lists and seating diagrams were revised again and again, as friends of many years' standing were suddenly no longer speaking.

At least the guests came to dinner unarmed; the same could not be said of their daytime activities. Civility and gentlemanly comportment, so long a hallmark of Capitol Hill, had died a sad and poignant death. . . . In the heat of passion, men with hardened hearts cast aspersions at colleagues, which they knew to be untrue. Gestures of reconciliation were coldly shaken off. As 1859 drew to a close, there was undeclared war in the House and Senate.

"We seem to be drifting into destruction before our eyes, in utter helplessness," reported Caleb Cushing on New Year's Day to former President Pierce, whom he had served as Attorney General. "The Administration is utterly depopularized; the President is embarrassed with insoluble questions; Congress is paralyzed by party spirit; and everybody seems to despair of any help coming from man, though many are looking vaguely for they know not what interpositions from Providence."[16]

Paralyzed was putting it mildly: The new Congress had been in session a month and was still unable to elect a Speaker. The Republicans with 109 members wanted John Sherman of Ohio. The 101 Democrats did not, and the 27 Know-Nothings and Whigs could not decide with whom to side. The balloting went on for days, with the atmosphere growing increasingly acidulous. Nothing was getting done, not even the legislation for badly needed internal improvements or making land available in the Territories. The fight over the Speakership had, in fact, paralyzed the entire governmental process. Ill will became hatred, and once unleashed, hatred could not be recalled.

When Thaddeus Stevens of Pennsylvania accused the men of the South of trying to intimidate the men from the free states, Martin Crawford of Georgia strode up to him and with his face inches away called him a hypocrite for pretending to respect Southern rights yet continually planning war. Instantly other men were on their feet behind their respective champions, and only the grace of God prevented a showdown.

The next day Morris of Illinois exclaimed, "A few more such scenes as we had on this floor yesterday, and we will hear the crack of the revolver and see the gleam of the brandished blade."[17] He was not exaggerating; nearly all members were now coming to the House armed. According to the precursor of the Congressional Record, when one member's pistol accidentally discharged in his desk, in a flash 30 or 40 other members had drawn their pistols.[18]

Scarcely had that dust settled than Kellogg of Illinois understood Logan of Illinois to call him a "spaniel coward." The two rushed at each other and were parted with difficulty. Once again a serious episode was avoided only by the narrowest of margins.

Civil war was now being spoken of openly, in terms not of *if*, but *when*. "Try to stir up insurrection in our midst, or to force us back into the Union once we decide to secede," exclaimed Bonham of South Carolina, "and we shall welcome you Yankees to bloody graves!"[19]

Things were not much better in the Senate. "We will sunder the Union," declaimed freshman Senator James Chesnut, just arrived from South Carolina, "pull it to pieces, column, base, and tower, before we shall submit to be crushed by a government which is our own as well as yours!"[20]

With the entry of Iowa and Minnesota into the Union, the 18 free states now outnumbered the slave states by 3. Moreover, the early results of the 1860 census indicated that the free states held some 20 million people, while the slave states held 7 million whites and 4 million blacks.* But of the upper house's 22 standing committees, 16 were chaired by Southern Senators and the remaining 6 by Northern Democrats known to be sympathetic to the South. In other words, in the Senate the South still held the power.[21]

The deterioration of conduct in the Senate matched that of the House. There were bursts of hand-clapping, foot-stomping, jeering laughter, and the worst sort of barracks language. Haskin of New York nearly set off

---

* or 2.4 million "persons," according to the arcane formula for allotting Representatives to Congress

a brawl when he likened McRae of Mississippi to a circus rider. Reuben Davis declared that he was for hanging Seward and anyone else who shared his "murderous sentiments." Grimes of Iowa sadly wrote to his wife, "The Capitol resounds with the cry of dissolution, and the cry is echoed throughout the city."[22] Members of both houses and visitors to their galleries were all "packing" concealed weapons. Said Senator Hammond, "The only persons who do not have a revolver and a knife are those who have two revolvers."[23]

Many expected gunplay at any moment. Wise had 10,000 Virginia militia ready to move on Washington the moment a shot was fired, and Governor Gist of South Carolina privately notified his state's Congressmen that, should they "decide to make the issue of force in Washington," they were to wire him and he "would have a regiment in or near Washington in the shortest possible time."[24]

Finally, on February 1, after two months of wrangling and 44 ballots, the House chose its Speaker—William Pennington of New Jersey.*

Things *did* quiet down then—but only for a season, and a short one at that. In April, Pryor of Virginia responded in fury to the language of Lovejoy of Illinois, and Crawford backed Pryor, declaring that not a dozen overseers in Georgia would resort to such language as Lovejoy had used.

Owen Lovejoy, whose brother Elijah had been murdered by an anti-abolitionist mob in 1837, was shaken. As he later confided in a letter to Thaddeus Stevens, "I never said a word to anybody, but quietly cocked my revolver in my pocket and took my position in the midst of the mob, and as coolly as I write to you now, I had made up my mind to sell out my blood at the highest possible price."[25]

It was little short of a miracle that there was no shooting incident to trigger a melee, shock the world, and start the war.

Both parties prepared to select their candidates for the crucial election coming in the fall. On February 29, William H. Seward delivered the address with which he intended to put his leadership of the Republi-

---

* perhaps the most incompetent man ever to occupy that seat

can party beyond the reach of any other aspirant. He spoke to his fellow Senators—and to many Representatives who had come over from the House to hear. But he was also speaking to Republicans throughout the North; copies of the speech had already been distributed to the editors of the major Republican papers.

It was an epic of moderation, designed to remove the stigma of being labeled too radical. Upon returning from a trip to Europe, Seward was alarmed to find himself lumped with the radical abolitionists who were presumably behind John Brown's raid. Realizing that no extremist would ever carry the party's nomination, he made no mention of the two concepts for which he had become famous (or infamous, depending on who was referring to him), that men owed allegiance to a "higher law" than the Constitution, and that proslavery and antislavery were headed for an "irrepressible conflict" that none could avoid. And as for John Brown, Seward went on record that Brown had been guilty of sedition and treason and deserved to be hanged.

He closed on a conciliatory note: If his party won, they would protect freedom of speech and the press, favor speedy improvement of the public domain under a homestead law, encourage mining and manufacturing (presumably through higher tariffs), and promote internal commerce and a transcontinental railroad. But since keeping the Territories free was his party's primary aim, it would approach other matters with care, for "already it feels the necessity of being cautious in its care of the national health and life."[26] (Let those who would brand him radical read that!)

The speech was well received and did what Seward had hoped, confirming him in the majority of Republican minds as the party's best choice for its candidate in the national convention, now less than three months away. The New York *Times* declared that it should remove any unfounded prejudice about Seward from the public mind, and on the day after the speech, the New York *Tribune* boasted that it had already printed 250,000 copies of it and would have a million more out by the end of the month.[27]

But two days previous, in New York City, another Republican hopeful (one whom the *Tribune* put down on its second rank of possible candidates) also gave a speech that was widely reprinted. Abraham Lincoln had never spoken in an eastern metropolis; now at the invitation of Henry Ward Beecher he was to give an address in the largest city of them all. At the last minute the venue was shifted from Beecher's Plymouth

Church in Brooklyn to the large new hall of the Cooper Union, built by philanthropist Peter Cooper,* where free courses were given in science, engineering, and art.

It was a bitterly cold night, made even colder by a strong wind that was adding new snow to the several inches that had already fallen. In other words, it was a night to stay in by the fire with shawl and slippers, a mug of something hot, and a good book. And yet on this night some 1,500 people, scarves wrapped tightly around their necks, their breath steaming in the cold air, trudged to Cooper Union to hear this prairie lawyer whom Horace Greeley was so keen on.

Bryant of the *Herald* was there and would introduce him. Greeley was also there, and G. P. Putnam, the publisher, Abram S. Hewitt, the manufacturer, former Governor King, and Peter Cooper himself. Indeed, noted the *Tribune,* not since the days of Clay and Webster had anyone spoken to such a large and impressive assemblage of the city's best people.

Lincoln had prepared his speech as carefully as he had prepared for his debates with Judge Douglas. His friends were concerned for him, that this sophisticated audience would be so bemused by his country mannerisms that they would fail to appreciate the depth of his message. Would they find him too tall and awkward? Would they see only the poor cut of his suit? His suits never fit well—and this one was brand-new. Well, good fit or poor, this night would decide whether Lincoln belonged in the same ring with Seward.

Lincoln was ready. But he was also nervous; once again, his voice started off too high and shrill, and it took a few moments before he could get it down and under control. He started off by reminding his audience (and the thousands of readers who were certain to read the reprint) through precept and example that the Founding Fathers had viewed slavery as an evil that for that period had to be tolerated, but that also had to be contained. It was time for the country to readopt that perspective.

The Southern people, he remarked after he had warmed to his subject, were as just and reasonable as any.

The question recurs: what will satisfy them? Simply this: We must not only let them alone, but we must, somehow, convince them that we do let them

* It was Peter Cooper who had built the "Tom Thumb" and founded the B&O Railroad.

498

alone. This is no easy task. [laughter] We have been trying to convince them from the very beginning of our organization, but with no success. . . . What will convince them? This, and this only: cease to call slavery *wrong*, and join them in calling it *right*. And this must be done thoroughly—done in *acts* as well as in *words*. Silence will not be tolerated—we must place ourselves avowedly with them.

That, of course, was impossible, if one believed that slavery was wrong. But Southerners believed that slavery was right. And therefore, their position was entirely understandable. "If slavery is right, all words, acts, laws, and constitutions against it, are themselves wrong, and should be silenced and swept away. If it is right, we cannot justly object to its nationality—its universality; if it is wrong, they cannot justly insist upon its extension— its enlargement."

And that was the crux of it. Economics, tariffs, foreign trading partners, internal improvements—none of these things were pertinent. The issue, first, last, and always, was slavery.

"All they ask, we could readily grant," Lincoln went on, "if we thought slavery was right; all we ask, they could as readily grant, if they thought it wrong. Their thinking it right, and our thinking it wrong is the precise fact upon which depends the whole controversy."

And yet, Lincoln went on, they had to be tolerant, even as their forefathers had been. "Wrong as we think slavery is, we can yet afford to leave it alone where it is, because that much is due to the necessity arising from its actual presence in the nation; but can we, while our votes will prevent it, allow it to spread to the National Territories, and to overrun us here in the Free States? If our sense of duty forbids this, then let us stand by our duty fearlessly and effectively."

In closing, he said that when it came to principle, there could be no equivocation. "Let us be diverted by none of those sophistical contrivances . . . such as groping for some middle ground between the right and the wrong . . . such as Union appeals beseeching true Union men to yield to Disunionists, reversing the divine rule, and calling, not the sinners, but the righteous to repentance. . . . Neither let us be slandered from our duty by false accusations against us, nor frightened from it by menaces of destruction to the Government nor of dungeons to ourselves. *Let us have faith that right makes might, and in that faith, let us, to the end, dare to do our duty as we understand it.*"[28]

The audience, which had grown progressively more enthusiastic, now erupted in cheers, applause, and foot-stamping, with men waving their hats and women their handkerchiefs. Wrote one urbane observer, "His manner was, to a New York audience, a very strange one, but it was captivating. He held the vast meeting spellbound. . . . I think I never saw an audience more thoroughly carried away by an orator."[29]

Noah Brooks, the *Tribune* reporter, agreed. Exclaiming that Lincoln was the greatest man since Saint Paul, he rushed away to his office to write that "no man ever before made such an impression on his first appeal to a New York audience."[30]

Four New York papers, including the *Herald* and the *Tribune*, reprinted the speech the following day, and subsequently the *Tribune* revised its projection for the coming Republican convention: Seward was still the front-runner, but there was now someone behind, fast closing the gap.

47

A Tale of Two Cities

*M*agnolia blossoms, tall palmettos gently waving in a soft breeze, shimmering, sunbaked waterfront in contrast with the cool green shade of tree-lined streets, elegant white-columned facades highlighted with wrought-iron railings—old Charleston is still redolent with the grace and charm of a bygone era. Little has changed in a century and a half—as little had changed in the century before 1860. There was not a more beautiful city, North or South, nor one more rightfully proud of its heritage.

At the close of the Democratic party's previous nominating convention in Cincinnati in 1856, they had picked Charleston as their next site. It was almost an afterthought, a conciliating gesture to the Southern wing of the party. But in the interim, so much had happened to exacerbate the differences between the two wings of the party that the choice of Charleston, the center of the secessionist movement, now seemed exceedingly unfortunate to the Douglas men who comprised the bulk of the Northern wing. The fire-eaters, led by Messrs. Yancey, Rhett, and Ruffin, would have the advantage of a packed gallery behind them, and in the evening the city's hostesses could not be more sympathetic to their cause. Southern hospitality was legendary, and nowhere more so than in Charleston. But that hospitality most pointedly did not include the Douglas men, who began arriving for the convention on Wednesday, April 18.*

Still, they came confident and optimistic. The radical Southerners might not like him, but their man was the only one who could hold the

---

*Douglas was not with them. In those days it was deemed unseemly for a candidate to appear at the convention that might nominate him.

party together. And as long as the party remained intact, they had enough strength to beat the Republicans come November. It was that simple, that logical, and it was sure to win.

There was only one flaw in their reasoning: The radical wing did not *want* to hold the party together. They preferred a Southern candidate, even if it meant losing to the Republicans. In fact, such a loss would actually serve their purpose better, for many Southern States had already vowed to leave the Union in the event of a Republican victory. And that was the real goal of the fire-eaters: secession. The founding of a new Confederate nation.

Normally, the first order of business at a national convention was to elect their candidate. But the radicals knew that a majority of the convention's 303 delegates were already committed to Douglas. True, he needed a two-thirds majority, but he would probably get that on the second ballot, after different states' favorite sons dropped out. It was impossible to be lukewarm about Douglas; you either loved him or loathed him.

Coming down on the train, Maurat Halstead, editor of the Cincinnati *Commercial,* had been stunned to find that virtually every Southerner he met, from Georgia, South Carolina, and Mississippi, despised Douglas, and that was not too strong a word. The Northern Democrats, a shaken Halstead realized, had profoundly underestimated Southern resistance to the Little Giant. The Southern delegates did not trust him and would not be satisfied with any candidate who was not from the South.[1]

Nevertheless, by the fire-eaters' reckoning there were still too many Douglas-lovers at the convention to risk going straight to the balloting. So they called for a change in the customary order of events: The matter of the platform would have to be settled *before* the convention voted for its candidate.

It was a crucial shift. Two months before in the Senate, Jefferson Davis had proposed the adoption of a national slave code, which would guarantee the protection of slaveholders' "property" wherever they were, or into whatever Territory they might choose to take "it." Such a code would also prohibit the people of any Territory from outlawing slavery, until such time as they were actually being admitted to statehood. The slave code had been rejected by the Senate, but the fire-eaters were now determined to have such a plank in the Democratic party platform; in fact, only with its eventual national acceptance would they be interested in remaining in the Union.

But because such a code obviously did away with the Freeport Doctrine, Douglas had made a pledge to his Northern supporters: He would not accept the nomination if the party's platform contained such a plank.

At this point in the proceedings, had calmer heads prevailed, they might have simply agreed to accept the party platform of four years before, which contained no mention of popular sovereignty or a slave code.

But in Charleston that April, calm heads were in short supply. For seven days they debated popular sovereignty and the slave code, with neither side backing down.

Finally the one they called the Prince of the Fire-eaters, William L. Yancey,* took the floor. The Southerners, he informed his Northern colleagues, had come to Charleston to secure their Constitutional rights with a slave code. If they lost, and a popular sovereignty platform prevailed, they would be bankrupt. The Northern Democrats were treating slavery as an inherited evil, when they should be supporting their Southern brethren by boldly pronouncing it a positive good!

That speech may have inwardly turned more than a few Northern Democrats into Republicans. That evening, in an atmosphere that could not be more chilly, George Pugh of Ohio rose to reply. He, too, soon gave in to his emotions. How long, he demanded, must the Democratic party be dragged at the chariot wheel of 300,000 slave masters? Such a fearless, outspoken challenge had never been issued at a convention. It was as if the Little Giant were there himself, locked in mortal verbal combat. The split that many feared—and a few zealously anticipated—was now occurring before their eyes.

Pugh closed by confronting the Southern demand that the long-suffering Northern Democrats not only avow slavery to be right, but endorse its extension as desirable. "Gentlemen of the South," he cried, "you mistake us! *You mistake us! We will not do it!*"[2]

He sat down, and the convention adjourned in an uproar. All but a few dreaded what the morning would bring.

When the platform deliberations resumed the following morning, it soon became apparent to the Southern radicals that, while they might

---

* whose father was an antislavery Presbyterian minister

keep a popular sovereignty plank *out* of the platform, they would never be able to get a slave code plank *into* it. L. P. Walker, leader of the Alabama delegation, rose and gained the chair's attention. He had an announcement to make. As he walked to the front of the hall, a hush fell over the assembly. Some were smiling, their eyes bright at the prospect of what was about to happen; others seemed on the verge of tears.

Walker informed them all that at the Alabama State convention, which had sent them here, they had been instructed that if they could not obtain a slave code resolution, they were to withdraw from the convention. At that, the entire Alabama delegation rose and began to file out. No sooner had they left their seats, than the chairman of the Mississippi delegation was on his feet. He and his associates, he announced, would also be leaving.

Cries of "Mr. Chairman! The delegation from the honorable State of . . ." echoed through the hall, as the delegations from Louisiana, and South Carolina, and Florida, and Texas, and Arkansas followed Alabama and Mississippi out of the convention.

Up in the gallery, the ladies of Charleston rose and applauded the gallant men of the South who were departing. But down on the floor, there was widespread dejection. A few Northerners still hoped that somehow they could pull something workable together before they adjourned. After all, only 49 delegates had walked out; there were still 254 at the convention. But many others felt with foreboding that they had just witnessed an enactment of what would soon be the fate of America.

That night the streets of Charleston were thronged with excited men. No one could sleep. Yancey, Rhett, and the other radicals were jubilant. They had achieved what they had come to do. At 11 o'clock, Yancey addressed a large crowd that had assembled at the steps of the old courthouse. "Perhaps even now," he cried, "the pen of the historian is nibbed to write the story of a new revolution!"[3] A roar of approval rose from the crowd.

Robert Glass, delegate from Virginia and editor of the Lynchburg *Republican,* summed up the radicals' action: "The seceding states came to the convention with a deliberate purpose to break up the convention if they failed to get, as they knew they would fail to get, their extreme ultimatum, and their ultimate design is to break up the Union by breaking up the Democratic party."

The correspondent from the Cincinnati *Enquirer* concurred: "The secessionist movement* is universally regarded as a concerted plan for the dissolution of the Union."[4]

When the vote finally came, Douglas, with 145 delegates, had well over half the remaining delegates, and was more than 100 ahead of his nearest challenger. But half was not two-thirds. That day 11 more ballots were taken, and 44 more the next, but the highest the Douglas men could get was 152. With the convention hopelessly deadlocked, they agreed to adjourn and meet again in two weeks' time in Baltimore.

The most poignant scene of the convention occurred two days after the Southern delegations had walked out. Those first to arrive in the hall discovered that on each chair vacated by a Southern delegate, the ladies of Charleston had carefully laid a bouquet of fresh-cut flowers. It was a wonderfully romantic gesture—and none of the ladies could foresee the ominous, tragic overtones of that act of laying fresh-cut flowers on the places of their recently departed heroes.

The Republican convention took place a month later in Chicago, and the contrast of the two cities told a tale. Already booming a generation before, Chicago was now bursting at the seams—hog butcher and meat-packer to the world, and now iron maker, too; its blast furnaces were running 24 hours a day, as a succession of steam-driven lake freighters brought iron ore from upper Michigan. Hammers seemed to be banging 24 hours a day, too, as construction struggled to keep up with the demands of a burgeoning business population.

If stately Charleston with its serene and courtly ways seemed to be looking back with fondness to the 18th century, go-ahead Chicago seemed to be looking forward with impatience to the 20th century. In a curious way, Chicago seemed to reflect—and encourage—the Republicans convening there. As historian Bruce Catton put it: "The party was new, and the city was new, and each was growing too fast, and was too enthusiastic about its own growth to worry very much about restraint or dignified behavior."[5]

And now, with the Democratic party in shambles, the Republicans were even less restrained, aware that whomever they nominated would

---

* He meant the delegations that had left the convention.

almost certainly become the next President of the United States. Euphoria overflowed the gigantic hall known as "the Wigwam," built especially for this occasion and capable of holding (barely) the 10,000 people who crammed inside of it.

Seward was the odds-on favorite to win the nomination. Back in his hometown of Auburn, New York, his friends had wheeled a cannon onto his front lawn, to be fired the moment word came of his victory. According to the party's pundits, the only possible challengers were Edward Bates of Missouri or Ohio's Senator, Salmon Chase. Wrote Charles A. Dana to a friend, "It is either Bates or Seward. I can't see any third chance. The Northwest won't have Chase. With Seward, we are dead, beaten. He can't carry Indiana, Illinois, Pennsylvania, or New Jersey. With Bates we can carry Missouri certainly; Maryland and Tennessee probably. He may be elected. No one else can. That is the beginning, middle, and end of the story."[6]

But Bates was considered to be anti-immigrant, and many young Republicans found him too stodgy for their taste—what they called "a wet blanket."*

No one mentioned Lincoln except the Lincoln men. But ever since Cooper Union, Lincoln had been doing quite a bit of traveling and speaking, especially in New England. Wherever he spoke, the subject was always slavery. He wanted people to know exactly where he stood on the South's "peculiar system": He preferred the North's, "which lets a man quit when he wants to."

But slavery was going to be a phenomenally difficult problem to solve. It now involved at least $2 *billion* worth of human "property"—which was why it aroused such a strong protective instinct among slaveholders. But it had to be solved, and soon: America could not go on much longer, with one-sixth of her population in bondage. Southerners kept saying that if they were just left alone, they would eventually solve it. But they *had* been left alone, and *were* being left alone, and they had done nothing. And since slavery touched the vital future of the nation and America's standing in the world, the North simply had to discuss it. "If slavery is right, it ought to be extended; if not, it ought to be restricted—there is no middle ground."[7] Not for Lincoln, and not for the moderate wing of the Republican party.

---

* a telling pejorative for anyone who had ever experienced a sodden bedroll

Lincoln told his loyal lieutenants in Chicago two things: Make no enemies, and let us try to be everyone's *second* choice for candidate. It was good advice; though he was not considered among the likely candidates, as the convention began nobody had anything but warm feelings for him.

As for the more thoughtful delegates who had read Seward's Senate speech and Lincoln's Cooper Union address side by side in the weekly Tribune, the "prairie statesman," as Seward had derogatorily referred to him, had the keener mind and the stronger intellect. Even those who had not done their homework had that sense about the two men, as well.*

The Lincoln men, led by his floor managers Judge David Davis and Leonard Swett, were working hard. Knowing the importance of the gallery, they had managed to get 1,000 good, strong-lunged Lincoln men up there in the best seats, before the Seward men even showed up at the Wigwam. Like everyone else, they were passing among the delegations, cajoling and making deals, trying to line up and hold firm as many delegates as possible before the first ballot.

At noon on Wednesday, May 16, Governor Morgan gaveled the convention to order, and by Thursday evening they were ready to start balloting. Had they started then, historian Catton believed, Seward would have won. But the tally sheets were not quite ready. It would take only a few more minutes—would the delegates wait for them? But at that point the delegates were in no mood to wait for anything, and so the meeting was adjourned for the night. They would start the balloting in the morning.

That gave Davis and Swett 12 more hours. It just might be enough. "I authorize no bargains," Lincoln had wired them, "and will be bound by none." But to those who would be up all night trying to shift delegates, that was unwelcome input. "Lincoln ain't here," growled Davis, "and don't know what we have to meet, so we will go ahead as if we hadn't heard from him, and he must ratify it."[8]

In the morning the tally sheets were ready for the first ballot, and so were Davis and Swett—barely. The Republicans required only a simple majority, which meant that the first person to gain 233 of the 465 votes would be the Republican nominee—and in all likelihood the next President.

To no one's surprise, the first ballot, which was only expected to show

---

* Voter intuition seemed to be perpetually underestimated by political pundits in the middle of the nineteenth century (as currently).

general trends, showed Seward out in front, *way* out in front with 173 votes. To everyone's surprise, the man who came in second was not Bates. Nor Chase. It was Lincoln! True, he trailed Seward by more than 70 votes, but he was ahead of Cameron, Chase, and Bates (who was a sorry fifth).

They soon called the roll of state delegations for the second ballot, and as they did, Seward picked up 12 votes, to 184. But now, with the favorite sons dropping out and the convention roaring enthusiasm, incredibly, Lincoln gained most of the freed-up votes! Apparently he, rather than Seward, was everyone's second choice. He now trailed the New Yorker by only 4 votes.

The roll call for the third ballot had barely reached the fourth state when the chairman of the Massachusetts delegation jumped up, out of order, and shouted that four of their votes had switched to Lincoln.

Pandemonium broke out! State after state followed suit, and when the roll was done, Lincoln had amassed 231 votes. He now needed only 2 more votes for the nomination. The Wigwam grew so quiet that one could distinctly hear the reporters rapidly tapping their telegraph keys.

Sitting next to one of the key delegates from Ohio was Joseph Medill, publisher of the Chicago *Tribune* and an old friend of Lincoln's. According to Carl Sandburg, in the ensuing silence he whispered to the delegate, "If you can throw the Ohio delegation for Lincoln, Chase can have anything he wants." When the delegate wondered if Medill knew whereof he spoke, the publisher replied, "I *know,* and you know I wouldn't promise, if I didn't know!"[9]

The delegate whispered with his group, then all at once jumped up on his chair and spread his arms to gain the chairman's attention. "Mr. President! I rise to change four votes from Mr. Chase to Mr. Lincoln!"*

Ida Tarbell quoted a man who had been there and described what had happened. "After an instant's silence, as deep as death, which seemed to be required to enable the assembly to take in the full force of the announcement, the wildest and mightiest yell (for it can be called by no other name) burst forth from ten thousand voices which we ever heard from mortal throats."[10] On the roof a cannon went off, and the delegates forthwith made it unanimous. The rail-splitter was going to the White House!

Now it came time to deal with the platform. Youth, with all its enterprise

---

* Mr. Chase became Mr. Lincoln's Secretary of the Treasury.

and energy, was the keynote of the Republican convention in Chicago. Youth had caught the new vision for a free America, youth had toiled to bring it to pass, and now youth would be served.

But sometimes youth could (and can) be extraordinarily callous and insensitive. Joshua Giddings of Ohio, who had been fighting slavery before many of those present had been born, who had stood staunchly by John Quincy Adams during his battle against the gag rule and kept a vigil at JQA's deathbed, had noticed that none of the resolutions in the Republican platform reaffirmed the truths of the Declaration of Independence. They had been included in the party's platform four years before; were they not even more appropriate now? But when he moved to have "Life, liberty, and the pursuit of happiness" worked into the preamble, conservative members decided the sentiment was inappropriate. The words had become stinging barbs to slaveholders, and there was no point in unnecessarily riling them. The convention voted him down.

Deeply wounded, the old warrior got to his feet and started to leave the hall. As friends gathered round him, trying to persuade him not to go, George William Curtis, a popular columnist and future political editor of *Harper's Weekly*, rose and gained the chairman's attention. The tall gentleman from New York had an arresting presence and voice, and the convention quieted as he moved to amend the platform to include the Declaration's words.

Annoyed, the chairman refused to accept the motion and attempted to move on to more important business. But Frank Blair, the Free-Soil Congressman and editor from Missouri, seconded Curtis's motion and insisted on a vote. Before the vote was cast, Curtis stood up and said, "I rise simply to ask gentlemen to think well before, upon the free prairies of the West, in the summer of 1860, they dare to wince and quail before the assertion of the men of Philadelphia in 1776."[11]

A thunderous cheer shook the Wigwam to its foundations, and the motion carried by acclaim. According to one observer, "Ten thousand voices swelled into a roar so deafening that for several minutes every effort to restore order was in vain."[12] Giddings, his white-haired head erect, tears gleaming in his eyes, returned to his seat.

48

STORM WARNINGS

*T*he schism in the Democratic party proved irreparable. The Baltimore conference was no more harmonious than the one in Charleston. Once again the dissenters walked out before the balloting could begin. The remaining delegates went overwhelmingly for Douglas, who was awaiting the outcome in Washington. But when friends came to him to celebrate, instead of finding him jubilant, they found him subdued.

"Can the seceders," he asked them, "fail to perceive that their efforts to divide and defeat the Democratic party, if successful, must lead directly to the secession of the Southern States? I trust that they will . . . return to the organization and platform of the party before it is too late to save the country."[1]

But they did not return. Instead, they held their own convention and nominated John C. Breckinridge of Kentucky, the current Vice President, as their candidate.

There was yet another convention in Baltimore, the Constitutional Union party, which met on May 9 and nominated John Bell and Edward Everett. It was a party primarily of old Whigs and old-line moderates whose sole aim was to save the Union.

So there would be four candidates running for President in the summer and fall of 1860. But only one would break with tradition and do personal campaigning—Douglas, the one with the greatest fear for the immediate fate of the Union.

For all his political acumen, Abraham Lincoln—and *all* the Republican leaders—seemed to be completely blind where the true sentiments of the South were concerned. Perhaps the Republicans in the House and Senate had heard their Southern counterparts threaten secession once too often. No one took it seriously; they all reassured one another that the alarms had as much merit as those of the little boy who cried wolf.

The Northern press certainly agreed with the Republican perception. The New York *Tribune* asserted that the stale Southern threats would appall nobody but fools, and that the diabolical mask did not frighten men who knew at what toy shop it was bought.[2]

Seward, campaigning for the Republican ticket, told a Minneapolis audience that the Southern menaces to the Union were absurd—nobody was afraid. And at La Crosse, he maintained that the very homogeneity of the American people should put to rest any vague apprehension of national dismemberment. Similarly, Bates of Missouri, who should have known the Southern mind better than most Republicans, dismissed what he called the idle fears of nervous people. According to him, only a few conceited egotists were talking of a Southern confederacy; the Southern people as a whole could never be guilty of such wicked folly as rending the country in half.[3]

Lincoln, apparently, bought into the consensus of his advisors. On August 15, he wrote to a friend that he had received many assurances that "in no probable event will there ever be any very formidable effort to break up the Union."[4]

One can hardly blame Lincoln for not wanting to believe that his election was going to be the cause of wholesale secession and civil war. But supposing, on a deeper level, he *did* sense what might be in the offing?

He had already gone on record: Slavery was wrong. It *must* be circumscribed and contained. Eventually it must also become extinct, and the sooner, the better. He had stated that so often, in fact, that when people would ask him to repeat his positions, he would refuse to do so, referring them instead to his widely reprinted speeches. "Those who will not read and heed what I have already publicly said, would not read and heed a repetition of it."[5]

After all that, was he going to modify his position now, because of the likelihood of the South seceding if he were to be elected? Absolutely not.

It was a matter of principle. And if the majority of the American people elected him because they believed in that principle, then so be it. To go out of his way to ameliorate the South now would not change the heart of anyone bent on disunion; it would only create division in the party and give Douglas an opportunity to pick up votes.

Would he break with tradition, as Senator Douglas had, and leave Springfield to go out on the campaign trail himself?

No. Two years before, in Illinois, hardly anyone knew who he was or what he stood for. Then, he had *had* to let people know, and so he campaigned as tirelessly as his far better-known opponent. But now, the people knew who he was. Anyone who could read had seen his speeches in countless papers and in millions of tracts. Besides, he wanted the people to vote the issue, not the man. And the issue was slavery. That was what had brought him back into politics, and on that issue would he rise or fall.

Ironically, it was that issue that brought Stephen A. Douglas out onto the hustings, to campaign as hard as he ever had in his life. For years, the Senator's supporters had referred to him as a statesman. And now, in a battle that he knew he would lose and in the last year of his life (which he did not know), he became a statesman in the eyes of all who knew him—including Lincoln.*

Douglas's great power lay in the impact of his personal charisma, and he knew it. The more people who came out to hear him, the more people on whom he would leave a lasting impression. There was something else driving him now: Perhaps because of the harrowing experience of being rejected by the Southern wing of his own party, he knew, far better than Lincoln, just how serious was the threat of wholesale secession. And if there was one thing Douglas cared about more than popular sovereignty, it was the fate of the Union itself. For once, he was not campaigning because he believed that he was the best man to lead the country. Rather, he believed that he was the only candidate with the ability to attract voters in sufficient quantities from all sections to hold the nation together. From South Carolina to Texas, Southern leaders had made it abundantly clear that if the Republicans came to power, the slave States would leave the Union. The Republicans did not believe them. Douglas did.

The sanctity of the Union now became a message of greater importance to him, especially when speaking in the South. In Norfolk, Virginia, on August 25, he stood on the front steps of City Hall and spoke to a crowd of some 7,000 men and women who had come to hear him. He told them

---

* The feeling was mutual. In speaking to a group of Washington Republicans, some of whom were lamenting that they had not chosen Seward, Douglas told them they had made no mistake: "Gentlemen, you have nominated a very able and honest man."

in no uncertain terms that while he coveted their votes, he wanted only the votes of those who wished the Union preserved by faithful execution of every line in the Constitution.

After his speech, he agreed to answer two of the questions that had been submitted on slips of paper by the audience. The first asked: If Lincoln were elected, would the Southern states be justified in seceding? And the second was like unto it: If the South did secede, would he advise resistance to her withdrawal?

"I answer emphatically," proclaimed the Senator, projecting his voice to the utmost so that as many as possible could hear his response, "that it is the duty of the President of the United States and all others in authority under him, to enforce the laws of the United States as passed by Congress and as the courts expound them."

Douglas went on. "And I, as in duty bound by my oath of fidelity to the Constitution, am to do all in my power to aid the Government of the United States in maintaining the supremacy of the laws against all resistance to them, come from whatever quarter it would."

He paused, then proceeded slowly, making it unmistakably clear where he stood. "In other words, I think the President of the United States, whoever he may be, should treat all attempts to break up the Union by resistance to its laws, as Old Hickory treated the Nullifiers in 1832."[6]

That quote was carried verbatim in newspapers throughout the South, kicking up an anti-Douglas storm among the fire-eaters (and undoubtedly, fervent prayers of thanks from old-line unionists who dared not speak openly in the current climate).

From his glorious battle against the Buchanan administration's attempt to gain approval of the Lecompton constitution, we have seen how Douglas loved nothing better than a bare-knuckled brawl against superior odds, when he knew his cause was just. At such times there was nothing little about the little giant; his heart and his courage were as big as all outdoors.

Four days later, speaking in Raleigh, North Carolina, he came on even stronger. Like Andrew Jackson, "I would hang every man higher than Haman who would attempt to resist by force the execution of any provision of the Constitution which our fathers made and bequeathed to us." In Baltimore, he declared: "I am for burying Southern disunionists and Northern abolitionists in the same grave." And in New York, he told an immense open-air picnic gathering: "I wish to God we had an Old Hickory now alive, in order that he might hang Northern and Southern traitors on the same gallows!"[7]

The national election was scheduled for the first Tuesday in November, but in those days individual states could hold their internal state contests in advance of that date, if they so chose. Indiana and Pennsylvania, two states in which the Democrats were confident of doing well if not winning, chose to hold their state elections a month earlier.

Douglas was campaigning out in Cedar Rapids, Iowa, when word reached him that the Republicans had swept Pennsylvania and Indiana. He turned immediately to his traveling secretary, James Sheridan, and said, "Mr. Lincoln is the next President." Then without a moment's hesitation he added, "We must try to save the Union. I will go South."[8]

Sheridan was stunned. There was still a chance, albeit remote, that the Senator might yet win. If Lincoln could not win a clear majority in the electoral college, the election would have to be decided in the House of Representatives. Douglas was still in the running, but it would depend on his expending all his remaining time and energies in the Northern States where his support was the strongest. Instead, for the sake of the Union, he chose to sacrifice his last chance at the Presidency.

Douglas knew that while he could not raise much support in the Deep South, he just might be able to give encouragement to those in the Border States who could keep their states from seceding. He spoke twice and sometimes three times a day, wearing himself out, destroying his health. He would be hoarse, exhausted, barely able to speak. But once he stepped up to the podium, a power seemed to come over him, and he would be strong and unforgettable till he finished.

Only God knows what difference Stephen A. Douglas's last, supreme effort on behalf of the Union made in the eventual outcome. But he surely had an impact; in Memphis, Tennessee, he was greeted with a tremendous ovation—and several death threats, which only encouraged him further. In Nashville, he drew the greatest crowd in 20 years (in sharp contrast to the chilly reception accorded Yancey there that same night). In both Chattanooga and Jackson, he was warmly received. One Jackson planter, Harrod Anderson, went home exclaiming that hearing Douglas that night was the most notable event of his life, and that the Senator was the greatest statesman of the age. He reported that Douglas had utterly demolished both the Southern secessionists and the Northern abolitionists, and concluded by saying that Douglas could excite more enthusiasm among the masses than any man alive.[9]

Even in the Deep South, Douglas found that he had a surprising number of friends, including some in high places. Alexander Stephens was one. Stephens, who himself had been mentioned in the conventions as a possible Presidential candidate, was a confirmed unionist. A Southern friend, pleased with the departure of the Charleston delegates, asked him, "What do you think of matters now?" Stephens acidly replied, "Why, that men will be cutting one another's throats in a little while. In less than twelve months we shall be in a war, and that the bloodiest in history."[10]

A few weeks later, interviewed by a correspondent from the New York *Herald,* Stephens spoke as if he could see the horror unfolding. If Lincoln were elected, he said sadly, South Carolina would secede at once. She would be immediately followed by the Gulf States. And after some hesitation by the border region, war would begin.[11]

So Stephens had invited Douglas to come down to Georgia, hoping that somehow his compatriots might be awakened to the certain nightmare into which they were rushing headlong. Introducing Douglas in Atlanta with warm praise, he said that the Senator had shown greater moral courage than any other statesman living in defending his convictions of right against prejudice and fanaticism at home, and that he had always stood by the South in her perils, and was the most powerful friend the South ever had.[12]

Few things were more frightening than to be caught in a mob gone out of control. If you were lucky, you would not get trampled or squeezed to death. If you were unlucky, you might get so swept up in the emotion of the moment that you might do something you would regret for the rest of your life. A mob acted as if possessed—and was capable of action as insane as a herd of pigs plunging off a cliff to their death.

In the long, hot summer of 1860, men were being lynched by Southern mobs. Some had expressed antislavery views; others were hanged by mistake, simply because they looked like they *might* be from the North. One such incident occurred in New Orleans and was described by George

Cable. All at once a mob was roaring down Royal Street in pursuit of a pale stranger. "Hang him! Hang him!" cried the running mob. In the nick of time the man was rescued. It turned out he was a traveling vendor of campaign medals, and New Orleans was a good prospect; half the people in town were wearing beribboned Breckinridge emblems. But in packing up his wares the poor salesman had not noticed that he had failed to remove a Lincoln/Hamlin badge. The oversight had nearly cost him his life. As the mob dispersed, an onlooker observed: "Didn't I tell you? Bound to have war. It's already begun."[13]

In a sense, it had. Southern postmasters began stopping all Northern newspapers, except for the very few known to be sympathetic to the South. And in the Federal Government, Southern officials in a position to do so were shipping vast quantities of arms and munitions to Southern armories, where they would be readily available to Southern militias, in the event of hostilities breaking out.

The climate was now so dangerous in the South that Northern firms called their salesmen home. On the other hand, Henry Foote of Mississippi, a deeply committed unionist who had always opposed the Southern extremists and had even once exchanged blows with Jefferson Davis, came North. Shocked at the complacency he found in New York, in a letter to the *Herald* he tried to warn the nation of the impending catastrophe.

Four hundred miles south, the Richmond *Enquirer* was taking the opposite tack. Reminding its readers of the Patriots' motto on the eve of the War for Independence, it proclaimed that "resistance to wrong and injury—to tyranny, whether of one man or eighteen million—is the cherished birthright of every citizen of the Federal Union."[14]

And farther south, in Charleston, the *Mercury* issued its call for secession, in the event of a Lincoln victory:

> The *under*ground railroad will become the *over*ground railroad. . . . Secret conspiracy [fomenting servile insurrection] and its attendant horrors, with rumors of horrors, will hover over every portion of the South. . . . Timid men will sell out and leave the South. Confusion, distrust, and pressure must reign. Before Messrs. Lincoln and Hamlin can be installed in Washington . . . the Southern States can dissolve peaceably (we know what we say) their Union with the North. Mr. Lincoln and his abolition cohorts will have no South to reign over. Their game would be blocked.[15]

A few halfhearted attempts were made to form a fusion ticket to stop the Republicans, but nothing came of it. Breckinridge could not accept popular sovereignty; Douglas could not accept a slave code, and neither had much use for the "Old Gentlemen's Club," as they referred to the Constitutional Unionist party.

Perhaps the most colorful aspect of the campaign was the appearance of the "Wide Awakes"—clubs of young Republicans pledged to get the vote out. The first Wide Awake club had formed in Hartford in March, as 50 young men donned caps and bright capes and marched at night, each carrying a symbolic fence rail topped by a tin lamp. The idea caught on, and soon there were Wide Awake clubs in all the major Northern cities.

On October 3, all the Wide Awakes who could get to New York for a torchlight parade were invited to do so. Fully 90,000 showed up and stepped off smartly down Broadway, as tens of thousands of onlookers cheered, and fireworks were set off from roofs along the parade route. "Broadway was one river of fire," a reporter exclaimed, "as though Vesuvius had poured forth a torrent of molten lava."[16]

The Wide Awakes were marching four abreast like soldiers, but instead of singing a martial tune, they were keeping time to a campaign ditty, set to the tune of "The old gray mare, she ain't what she used to be." The new words were simple and fun, and the familiar melody had such a hook that it replayed unbidden in the mind for days: "Ain't you glad you joined the Republicans?"

On election eve, no less than 400,000 Wide Awakes marched through the streets of Northern cities,[17] while in the South, at least as many recently activated militiamen were out on village greens, practicing formation maneuvers.

The bands played on, the shining youth of North and South marched, and the dark cloud that had once been no bigger than a man's hand on the distant horizon now loomed huge and cold and roiling, shot through with jagged streaks of lightning. In a short while, it would blot out the sun.

Epilogue

On November 6, 1860, America went to the polls. Though no one was certain of the outcome, everyone was certain that this election was the most pivotal in the nation's history. Lincoln—and therefore the Republicans, for he was their leader now, as much as Calhoun had been the South's—had made his position clear. If elected, he would take no action against slavery, where it was already established.

He had said that repeatedly, but the South was not hearing him. What they were hearing was that war had been declared on slavery—on *them*—and it was only a matter of time before the burgeoning Northern majority would impose its will on them.

The states of the Deep South had said repeatedly that if a Black Republican was elected President, they would secede. But the North was not hearing them. They could not believe that the Southern states would leave the Union without provocation, and they were determined not to give them any.

Lincoln believed that the majority of the Southern people did not want to leave even if he was elected, and he was right. But in the South, the majority was no longer directing policy.

Alexander Stephens of Georgia, wisest of the Southern leaders, spoke for the majority of his countrymen (though he and they were unaware of it). From their days in Congress together, he and Lincoln had developed a cordial friendship, based on mutual respect. He believed that Lincoln would be a President of integrity and would do nothing to precipitate secession. Personally, he intended to vote for Douglas, and he hoped all Southern unionists would do the same. (The great surprise of the election would be the vast number who would do just that, revealing far more support for the Union in the South than the secessionists were willing to admit.)

Election Day dawned in Springfield, Illinois, to the report of cannon, which awakened its citizens perhaps a little earlier than many intended. Some exuberant Lincoln supporters had brought a couple of old field-pieces into town, and though the polls would be open all day, they wanted to make sure that Republicans would rise and shine and do their civic duty. The town didn't mind; in fact, all of Springfield was in a celebratory mood: One way or another, a son of Illinois was going to the White House today.

In all likelihood, it would be Honest Abe, who was presently ensconced in the Governor's room in the State House, directly across the street from the courthouse where most of Springfield would vote. Lincoln was in good spirits, telling stories to a roomful of friends who had gathered to keep him company during the long wait till the polls closed. Visitors kept dropping in to pay their respects, and with each he would listen attentively and give them cause to go away smiling.

Among the handful of reporters in their midst, the New York *Tribune*'s man was amazed at Lincoln's "winning manner, his ready good humor, and his unaffected kindness and gentleness toward all who approach him. His affability appears to have no limit as to persons. All share it." And next to it, "his most marked characteristic is the steady earnestness with which he considers and reviews all subjects that are brought before him. . . . There is something beyond all art in the frank and honest sunshine of his countenance."[1]

Around three in the afternoon, when the steps of the courthouse were nearly vacant, someone suggested it might be a good time for Lincoln to vote. He nodded, went downstairs, and started across the street. Just then, an old man with him said that on second thought, he would prefer to remain back at the window of the Governor's room. To the *Tribune* reporter's astonishment, "Mr. Lincoln went back with him, put him in a favorable position for seeing all that was to pass, and started out again."[2]

As soon as Lincoln was sighted, a shout went up, a crowd quickly gathered, and wild cheering commenced, even from Douglas supporters. Lincoln voted (modestly removing his name from the top of the Republican ticket, as was then the custom), and returned across the street.

That evening, after the polls had closed, he went to the telegraph office, where operators were receiving the early returns. They indicated that a Republican sweep of the North was in the making, and Lincoln's supporters were ebullient. The candidate himself remained quiet and unperturbed, awaiting word of New York; if he took the Empire State, victory was his.

The rapid-fire telegraph keys never stopped clicking. Pennsylvania was secure. And Ohio. And Indiana. Still no word from New York. A little after midnight Lincoln and his party adjourned to a nearby hall, where some ladies of Springfield had prepared a late supper for them. As Lincoln entered, they chorused, "How do you do, Mr. President?"

Lincoln smiled and was just sitting down, when a messenger burst in waving a telegram from Simeon Draper, a reliable New York source: the Empire State was safe.

Cries of "You're elected now!" and "It's all over!" filled the hall. Someone started up the campaign song, and everyone picked it up, glad indeed that they had "joined the Republicans, down in Illinois."[3]

As Election Day drew to a close, down in Mobile where Stephen A. Douglas awaited the returns, there was no singing, no wild cheering or cannon fire. Douglas and his secretary, James Sheridan, had gone to the offices of the *Register,* which had an excellent telegraph line. As the results started coming in, Douglas was not surprised. Four weeks earlier he had told Anson Burlingame that Lincoln would be elected, and he even rejoiced that there would now be *four* good Illinois men serving in the capital—"McDougall returned Senator from California, Baker from Oregon, and Douglas and Old Abe, all at Washington together!"[4]

When the outcome was no longer in doubt, they walked back to their hotel through the deserted streets. Sheridan later recalled that Douglas was "more hopeless than I had ever seen him before."[5]

It would be several days before the tallies were complete. Though Douglas would gain only 12 electors, when the final popular vote was in, he would come within half a million votes of winning. Lincoln had not received a single ballot in nearly one-third of the states, which meant that had Breckinridge not been in the running, Douglas would have won.

But it was not the election results that were depressing Douglas this night. He could see what was now certain to come. The Union he loved so much was about to be torn asunder, and there was nothing anyone could do to stop it. Though his heart was breaking, he determined to serve her to the end.*

Election Day in Georgia found the editorial staff of the previously moderate Atlanta *Confederacy* jubilant. Their proclamation, which had been read throughout the South, would now come to pass: "Let the consequences be what they may—whether the Potomac is crimsoned with gore, and Pennsylvania Avenue is paved ten fathoms deep with mangled bodies, or whether the last vestige of liberty is swept from the face of the American continent, the South will never submit to such humiliation and degradation as the inauguration of Abraham Lincoln."[6]

Not all Georgians were ready to start piling bodies. Alexander Stephens tried to persuade the Georgia legislature not to break the Constitution. But though they loved "Little Ellick," as they called him, they did not hear him.

Lincoln did, however, and when he wrote Stephens and asked for a copy of his remarks, the latter replied that, alas, he had only a reporter's notes. Then he added, "The country is certainly in great peril, and no man ever had heavier responsibilities than you have at this present momentous crisis."

Lincoln wrote back a confidential note, marked "for your eye only." In it he assured his friend that during the next four years the South would be in no more danger from the Government than she was in the days of George Washington. "I suppose though," he sadly concluded, "this does not meet the case. You think slavery is *right* and ought to be extended; while we think it is *wrong* and ought to be restricted. That, I suppose, is the rub. It certainly is the only substantial difference between us."[7]

Stephens replied that neither Lincoln's election, nor fears of the new administration's immediate action, had caused the rift between them. But now the institutions of nearly half the states had been put under "the ban of public opinion and national condemnation." It was enough "to arouse a spirit not only of general indignation but of revolt on the part of the proscribed." He hoped that his friend in Illinois would be able to find some way of alleviating men's minds, for "conciliation and harmony,

---

* His own end would come in less than seven months—but not before he would carry out one more vital task for the Union, at the personal request of President Lincoln.

in my judgement, can never be established by force. Nor can the Union under the Constitution be maintained by force."[8]

Thus ended this brief, poignant exchange between the two wisest and most moderate leaders on either side of the Mason-Dixon line. If these sad friends who loved the Union could not find a way out of the impasse. . . .

The results of Election Day in Charleston, South Carolina, were also celebrated with wild cheering and cannon fire, but there was a cold-steel edge to it. When the band of the famed Palmetto Regiment struck up a tune, it was no campaign ditty. It was the battle hymn of the French Revolution, the *Marseillaise.*

We will close with one more Election Day episode, from Carl Sandburg's superb biography of Lincoln.[9] Earlier that evening Lincoln, emotionally drained, had gone home to catch a few moments of rest. As he stretched out on a haircloth sofa in the parlor, in a mirror across the room he saw himself—but there were two images. One was normal; the other was much paler, almost sepulchral.

In the excitement of the election that night, he forgot about it. But it happened again later, and it haunted him. He told his wife Mary about it, and she worried, too. A few evenings later, when he tried lying down on the sofa again, the double-image in the mirror returned for the last time. Again he mentioned it to his wife, and now Mary Todd Lincoln expressed an ominous interpretation of the strange vision: her husband would serve two terms as President, but he would not survive the second.

Authors' Note

At the close of *Uncle Tom's Cabin*, Harriet Beecher Stowe made an impassioned appeal: If the reader was moved by what he or she had read and wanted to help eradicate the stain of slavery, they should do so by all means available to them, starting with prayer. As we have seen, millions responded to her call.

The Great Prayer Revival of 1857–58 was a partial answer to those prayers, as a merciful God extended to the nation one last opportunity to hear His voice and turn and seek His face. Many did. But not enough. And so, what might have been a solution became instead a preparation.

As 1860 drew to a close, men and women of spiritual vision could see armies of angels and archangels gathering for the coming struggle for the soul of America. They could hear the sound of distant trumpets that would never call retreat.

Now, as we move deeper into the twenty-first century, men and women of vision are again seeing signs and wonders, indicating that God's judgment, so long deferred, is close at hand. In the ten years since the first edition of this book was published, the moral standards of our society have deteriorated precipitously. The litany is all too familiar—soaring illegitimacy, divorce, gambling addictions, and drug abuse. The blight of Internet pornography has invaded every strata of society. And the monstrous slaughter of the innocent unborn continues unabated.

But perhaps the most fearsome aspect of what is becoming of us, is that we are growing inured to the decay. Scandal and corruption in public (let alone private) life now occur so frequently that our response is often to shrug and ask: Is there really anything that can be done?

It is too late now for a human solution. But with God, nothing is impossible. We believe that the only hope for America is a full-scale, national revival. There are, even now, indications such a revival may be in the offing—pockets of genuine, sustained spiritual awakening occur periodically in various cities. But at best we have a case of "revival measles."

In order for revival to spread from coast to coast and border to border, more than a remnant of us will have to take God's promise in 2 Chronicles 7:14 to heart—to repent, seek His face, and turn from our wicked ways.

We must do so at once. As Mrs. Stowe concluded, "O Church of Christ [and we would include *anyone* who believes in the existence of God], read the signs of the times! A day of grace is yet held out to us . . . for not surer is the eternal law by which the millstone sinks in the ocean than the stronger law by which injustice and cruelty shall bring on nations the wrath of Almighty God."

The wrath she foresaw was the terrible, tragic ordeal of the Civil War. Heaven only knows what cataclysmic disaster awaits us if we do not, as a nation, turn back to Him. One thing is certain: We can hear the sound of distant trumpets.

NOTES

Chapter 1: The Opening Gun

1. William Lee Miller, *Arguing About Slavery* (New York: Alfred A. Knopf, 1996), 40.

2. Thomas Jefferson, *Writings of Thomas Jefferson*, ed. Andrew A. Lipscomb, vol. 15 (Washington, D.C.: Thomas Jefferson Memorial Association, 1903), 249.

3. Miller, *Arguing About Slavery,* 117.

4. Leonard Falkner, *The President Who Wouldn't Retire* (New York: Coward-McCann, 1967), 122.

5. Ibid., 123.

6. Ibid.

7. Miller, *Arguing About Slavery,* 134, 39.

8. Ibid., 144.

9. Falkner, *President Who Wouldn't Retire,* 133–35.

10. Ibid.

11. Ibid., 136.

12. Ibid.

13. Carl Degler, in *Perspectives and Irony in American Slavery*, ed. Harry P. Owens (Jackson, Miss.: University Press of Mississippi, 1976), 7.

14. Miller, *Arguing About Slavery*, 21.

15. Samuel Flagg Bemis, *John Quincy Adams and the Union* (New York: Alfred A. Knopf, 1956), 29.

16. Falkner, *President Who Wouldn't Retire,* 154.

17. Ibid., 159.

18. Leonard L. Richards, *The Life and Times of Congressman John Quincy Adams* (New York: Oxford University Press, 1986), 128; Falkner, *President Who Wouldn't Retire,* 160.

19. Bennett Champ Clark, *John Quincy Adams: "Old Man Eloquent"* (Boston: Little, Brown & Co. 1932), 369.

20. Ibid., 162.

Chapter 2: The Last Puritan

1. Miller, *Arguing About Slavery*, 297.

2. Falkner, *President Who Wouldn't Retire,* 31.

3. Miller, *Arguing About Slavery*, 156.

4. Ibid., 162.

5. Ibid., 187–88.

6. Ibid., 189.

7. Richards, *Life and Times*, 7.

8. Falkner, *President Who Wouldn't Retire,* 24.

9. Ibid., 29.

10. Miller, *Arguing About Slavery*, 235.

11. Falkner, *President Who Wouldn't Retire,* 162.

12. Richards, *Life and Times*, 130.

13. Falkner, *President Who Wouldn't Retire*, 163–64.
14. Miller, *Arguing About Slavery*, 266–67.
15. Falkner, *President Who Wouldn't Retire*, 42–43.
16. Miller, *Arguing About Slavery*, 193.
17. Falkner, *President Who Wouldn't Retire*, 164.
18. Ibid., 166.

Chapter 3: The Impossible Dilemma

1. Gilbert H. Barnes, in *The Abolitionists*, ed. Richard O. Curry (Hinsdale, Ill.: Dryden Press, 1973; reprint Storrs, Conn.: UConn Co-op), 13.
2. Miller, *Arguing About Slavery*, 10.
3. Louis Filler, *The Crusade against Slavery: 1830–1860* (New York: Harper & Brothers, 1960), 57.
4. Ibid., 56.
5. *Encyclopaedia Britannica*, 1970, s.v. "Garrison."
6. Gilbert Hobbs Barnes, *The Antislavery Impulse, 1830–1844* (Gloucester: Peter Smith, 1957), 43.
7. Louis Ruchames, *The Abolitionists: A Collection of Their Writings* (New York: G. P. Putnam's Sons, 1963), 31.

Chapter 4: The Watchmaker

1. Barnes, *Antislavery Impulse*, 10.
2. Ibid., 11.
3. Ibid.
4. Ibid., 5.
5. Ibid., 7.
6. Ibid.
7. Ibid., 8.
8. Ibid.
9. Ibid., 9.
10. Donald Scott, in *Antislavery Reconsidered*, ed. Lewis Perry and Michael Fellman (Baton Rouge: Louisiana State University Press, 1979), 62.
11. Ibid.
12. Barnes, *Antislavery Impulse*, 12.
13. Bertram Wyatt-Brown, *Lewis Tappan and the Evangelical War against Slavery*

(Cleveland: Case Western Reserve University Press, 1969), 99.
14. Barnes, *Antislavery Impulse*, 15.
15. Ibid., 18.
16. Ibid., 15.
17. Wyatt-Brown, *Tappan*, 101.
18. John R. McKivigan, *The War against Proslavery Religion* (Ithaca, N.Y.: Cornell University Press, 1984), 20.
19. Ibid., 21–22.
20. Barnes, *Antislavery Impulse*, 16.
21. Ibid., 21.
22. Milton Rugoff, *The Beechers: An American Family in the Nineteenth Century* (New York: Harper & Row, 1981), 78.

Chapter 5: A New Gideon's Army

1. Gilbert H. Barnes and Dwight L. Dumond, eds., *Letters of Theodore Dwight Weld, Angelina Grimké Weld, and Sarah Grimké, 1822–1844*, vol. 1 (New York: Appleton-Century Co.: 1934), 14.
2. Ibid., vol. 2, 580.
3. Robert H. Abzug, *Passionate Liberator: Theodore Dwight Weld and the Dilemma of Reform* (New York: Oxford University Press, 1980), x.
4. Ibid., 80.
5. Ibid., 85.
6. Scott, in Perry and Fellman, *Antislavery Reconsidered*, 65.
7. Barnes, *Antislavery Impulse*, 44–45.
8. Ibid., 45.
9. Scott, in Perry and Fellman, *Antislavery Reconsidered*, 73.
10. Dwight L. Dumond, *Antislavery Origins of the Civil War in the United States* (Ann Arbor: University of Michigan Press, 1959), 29.
11. Barnes, *Antislavery Impulse*, 66.
12. Ibid., 64.
13. Ibid., 66.
14. Scott, in Perry and Fellman, *Antislavery Reconsidered*, 69.
15. Abzug, *Passionate Liberator*, 91.
16. Barnes, *Antislavery Impulse*, 66–67.
17. Abzug, *Passionate Liberator*, 92.
18. Barnes, *Antislavery Impulse*, 69–70.

19. Ibid., 68.

20. Ibid., 69.

Chapter 6: Fire-Starter

1. Barnes, *Antislavery Impulse*, 81.

2. Ibid., 79.

3. Ibid.

4. Ibid., 82.

5. Ibid., 80.

6. Ibid.

7. Miller, *Arguing About Slavery*, 109.

8. Barnes, *Antislavery Impulse*, 80.

9. Ibid., 81; Miller, *Arguing About Slavery*, 109–10.

10. Barnes, *Antislavery Impulse*, 81.

11. Ibid., 82.

12. Ibid., 86.

13. Ibid., 236.

14. Scott, in Perry and Fellman, *Antislavery Reconsidered*, 70.

15. Wyatt-Brown, *Tappan*, 129.

16. Ibid., 129–30.

17. McKivigan, *War against Proslavery Religion*, 22.

18. Lorman Ratner, *Powder Keg: Northern Opposition to the Antislavery Movement, 1831–1840* (New York: Basic Books, 1968), 92.

19. Ibid., 97.

20. Ibid., 104.

21. Ibid., 107.

22. Ibid., 114.

23. Ibid., 94.

24. Barnes, *Antislavery Impulse*, 86.

Chapter 7: The Flood

1. Joseph Clark Robert, *The Road from Monticello* (Durham, N.C.: Duke University Press, 1941), 6.

2. Barnes, in Curry, *The Abolitionists*, 14.

3. Barnes, *Antislavery Impulse*, 95–96.

4. Ibid., 96.

5. Ibid., 93.

6. Ibid.

7. Wyatt-Brown, *Tappan*, 189.

8. Barnes, *Antislavery Impulse*, 102.

9. Wyatt-Brown, *Tappan*, 152–56.

10. Ratner, *Powder Keg*, 4.

11. Ibid., 70.

12. Ibid., 72.

13. Wyatt-Brown, *Tappan*, 163.

14. Barnes, *Antislavery Impulse*, 105.

15. Ibid.

16. Miller, *Arguing About Slavery*, 303.

17. Ibid., 303–4.

18. Ibid., 110–11.

19. Barnes, *Antislavery Impulse*, 142–44.

20. Miller, *Arguing About Slavery*, 309.

21. Edward Beecher, *Narrative of Riots at Alton* (Alton, Ill.: George Holton, 1838), 89–91.

Chapter 8: Desk 203

1. John Quincy Adams, *Memoirs of John Quincy Adams*, vol. 9, ed. Charles Francis Adams (Philadelphia: J. B. Lippincott, 1876), 417ff.

2. Miller, *Arguing About Slavery*, 344.

3. Barnes, *Antislavery Impulse*, 165.

4. Miller, *Arguing About Slavery*, 354.

5. Falkner, *President Who Wouldn't Retire*, 197.

6. Ibid., 198.

7. Ibid., 200.

8. Barnes, *Antislavery Impulse*, 166.

9. Falkner, *President Who Wouldn't Retire*, 200.

10. Barnes, *Antislavery Impulse*, 127.

11. Adams, *Memoirs*, vol. 9, 365.

Chapter 9: Sounding Forth the Trumpet

1. Falkner, *President Who Wouldn't Retire*, 224.

2. Ibid., 226.

3. Ibid., 235.

4. Ibid., 236.

5. Ibid.

6. Miller, *Arguing About Slavery*, 371.

7. Ibid., 372.

8. Barnes, *Antislavery Impulse*, 179.

9. Miller, *Arguing About Slavery*, 406.

10. Barnes, *Antislavery Impulse*, 183.

11. Miller, *Arguing About Slavery*, 408.

12. Falkner, *President Who Wouldn't Retire*, 249.

13. Ibid., 250.

14. Miller, *Arguing About Slavery*, 433.

15. Barnes, *Antislavery Impulse*, 111.

16. Falkner, *President Who Wouldn't Retire*, 252.

17. Ibid., 253.

18. Ibid., 254–55.

19. Miller, *Arguing About Slavery*, 445.

20. Falkner, *President Who Wouldn't Retire*, 260–61.

21. Ibid., 259.

22. Miller, *Arguing About Slavery*, 444.

23. Falkner, *President Who Wouldn't Retire*, 262.

24. Miller, *Arguing About Slavery*, 446.

25. Ibid., 453.

26. Falkner, *President Who Wouldn't Retire*, 268.

27. Ibid., 269–70.

28. Ibid., 270.

29. Miller, *Arguing About Slavery*, 462–63.

30. Barnes, *Antislavery Impulse*, 272.

31. Miller, *Arguing About Slavery*, 463.

32. Ibid., 485.

Chapter 10: The Eagle Has Departed

1. John Edward Weems, *To Conquer a Peace: The War between the United States and Mexico* (College Station, Tex.: Texas University Press, 1974), 37.

2. Allan Nevins, ed., *Polk: The Diary of a President, 1845–1849* (New York: Longmans, Green & Co., 1952), xiv.

3. This quote and the following three quotes are from Robert V. Remini, *Andrew Jackson and the Course of American Democracy, 1833–1845*, vol. 3 (New York: Harper & Row, 1984), 492.

4. Ibid., 503.

5. Ibid., 508.

6. Ibid., 509.

7. Ibid., 512.

8. Ibid., 513.

9. Ibid., 517.

10. Ibid., 519.

11. Ibid., 521.

12. Ibid., 524.

13. Ibid., 447.

Chapter 11: Proceed without Delay

1. Weems, *To Conquer a Peace*, 13.

2. John S. D. Eisenhower, *So Far from God: The U.S. War with Mexico, 1846–48* (New York: Random House, 1989), 15.

3. T. R. Fehrenbach, *Lone Star: A History of Texas and the Texans* (New York: Macmillan, 1968), 264.

4. William Jay, *A Review of the Course and Consequences of the Mexican War* (Boston: Benjamin Mussey & Co., 1849), 87–88.

5. Justin Smith, *The War with Mexico*, vol. 1 (New York: Macmillan, 1919), 68.

6. Ibid., 84.

7. Ibid., 92.

8. Ibid., 94.

9. Ibid., 92.

10. Remini, *Andrew Jackson*, 496.

11. Fehrenbach, *Lone Star*, 264.

12. Weems, *To Conquer a Peace*, 26.

13. Ibid., 49–51.

14. Smith, *War with Mexico*, 136.

15. Odie B. Faulk and Joseph A. Stout, *The Mexican War: Changing Interpretations* (Chicago: Sage Books, 1973), 1.

16. Ibid., 206.

17. Smith, *War with Mexico*, 106.

18. Joseph Shattan, "One-Term Wonder," *The American Spectator*, October 1996, 34.

Chapter 12: "Hostilities Have Begun!"

1. Weems, *To Conquer a Peace*, 67.

2. Ibid., 68.

3. Ibid., 70.

4. Ibid., 70–71.

5. Ibid., 96.

6. Ibid., 94.

7. Eisenhower, *So Far from God*, 45.

8. Smith, *War with Mexico*, 107.

9. Ibid., 120–21.

10. Ibid., 121.

11. Eisenhower, *So Far from God*, 49.

12. Smith, *War with Mexico*, 149.

13. Ibid., 155.

14. Eisenhower, *So Far from God*, 66.

Chapter 13: Flying Artillery

1. David Nevin, *The Mexican War* (Alexandria, Va.: Time-Life Books, 1978), 64.
2. Weems, *To Conquer a Peace*, 128.
3. Ibid., 132.
4. Ibid., 133.
5. Bernard De Voto, *The Year of Decision: 1846* (Boston: Houghton Mifflin, 1942), 194.
6. Eisenhower, *So Far from God*, 80.
7. Ibid., 81.
8. Weems, *To Conquer a Peace*, 144.

Chapter 14: "A New Spirit Abroad in the Land"

1. Nevin, *Mexican War*, 31.
2. Smith, *War with Mexico*, 191.
3. Glenn W. Price, *Origins of the War with Mexico* (Austin: University of Texas Press, 1967), 89.
4. Ibid., 95.
5. Weems, *To Conquer a Peace*, 152.
6. Ibid., 148.
7. John Wingate Thornton, *The Pulpit of the American Revolution* (Boston: D. Lothrop & Co., 1876), 311.
8. Albert K. Weinberg, *Manifest Destiny: A Study of Nationalist Expansionism in American History* (Baltimore: Johns Hopkins University Press, 1935), 123–24.
9. Ibid., 107.
10. Ibid., 120.
11. Frederick Merk, *Manifest Destiny and Mission in North America: A Reinterpretation* (New York: Alfred A. Knopf, 1963), 31–32.
12. Weinberg, *Manifest Destiny*, 143.
13. Ibid.
14. Falkner, *President Who Wouldn't Retire*, 294–96.
15. Merk, *Destiny and Mission*, 31.
16. Ibid., 25.
17. Ibid., 54.
18. Weems, *To Conquer a Peace*, 164.
19. Merk, *Destiny and Mission*, 28.
20. Eisenhower, *So Far from God*, 196.
21. Weinberg, *Manifest Destiny*, 115.
22. Merk, *Destiny and Mission*, 32.
23. Ibid., 53.

Chapter 15: Idyll in Paradise

1. Weems, *To Conquer a Peace*, 269.
2. Ibid., 178.
3. Eisenhower, *So Far from God*, 58.
4. Price, *Origins of the War*, 87.
5. Nevin, *Mexican War*, 101.
6. Weems, *To Conquer a Peace*, 267.
7. Eisenhower, *So Far from God*, 231.

Chapter 16: "A Little More Grape, Mr. Bragg"

1. Eisenhower, *So Far from God*, 89.
2. Ibid., 91.
3. Ibid., 94.
4. Nevin, *Mexican War*, 57.
5. Ibid., 65.
6. Ibid., 67.
7. Ibid.
8. Ibid., 23.
9. Eisenhower, *So Far from God*, 138.
10. Ibid., 146.
11. Weems, *To Conquer a Peace*, 233–34.
12. Charles Dudley Warner, *My Summer in a Garden* (1870).
13. Weems, *To Conquer a Peace*, 298.
14. Eisenhower, *So Far from God*, 188.
15. Nevin, *Mexican War*, 87.

Chapter 17: Six Thousand Miles

1. E. Alexander Powell, *The Road to Glory* (New York: Charles Scribner's Sons, 1915), 246–47.
2. Ibid., 254–55.
3. Ibid., 256.
4. Weems, *To Conquer a Peace*, 257.
5. Isaac George, *Heroes and Incidents of the Mexican War* (Greensburg, Pa.: Review Publishing Co., 1903), 82.
6. Weems, *To Conquer a Peace*, 375.
7. Eisenhower, *So Far from God*, 250.
8. Powell, *Road to Glory*, 242.

Chapter 18: Vera Cruz

1. Nevin, *Mexican War*, 129.
2. Eisenhower, *So Far from God*, 264.
3. Nevin, *Mexican War*, 139.

4. Ibid.

5. Weems, *To Conquer a Peace*, 185.

6. Nevin, *Mexican War*, 140.

7. Weems, *To Conquer a Peace*, 338.

Chapter 19: Mr. Wilmot's Proviso

1. Weems, *To Conquer a Peace*, 346.

2. Ibid.

3. De Voto, *Year of Decision*, 295.

4. Ibid., 298.

5. Ibid.

6. Nevin, *Mexican War*, 170.

7. Eisenhower, *So Far from God*, 288.

8. De Voto, *Year of Decision*, 299.

9. Weems, *To Conquer a Peace*, 347.

10. Ibid., 346.

11. Allan Nevins, *Ordeal of the Union*, vol. 1 (New York: Charles Scribner's Sons, 1947), 9.

12. Weems, *To Conquer a Peace*, 346–47.

13. Nevins, *Ordeal*, vol. 1, 9.

14. Ibid., 10.

15. Nevin, *Mexican War*, 169–70.

16. Price, *Origins of the War*, 91.

17. Abraham Lincoln, speech in the House of Representatives, January 12, 1848, in *The Collected Works of Abraham Lincoln*, vol. 1, ed. Roy P. Basler (New Brunswick, N.J.: Rutgers University Press, 1953), 431–42.

18. Weems, *To Conquer a Peace*, 352.

19. Ibid., 353.

Chapter 20: "My Duty Is to Sacrifice Myself"

1. Weems, *To Conquer a Peace*, 355.

2. Nevin, *Mexican War*, 142.

3. Weems, *To Conquer a Peace*, 364.

4. Eisenhower, *So Far from God*, 298.

5. Weems, *To Conquer a Peace*, 385.

6. Ibid., 390–91.

Chapter 21: To the Halls of Montezuma

1. Weems, *To Conquer a Peace*, 399.

2. Ibid., 408–9.

3. Ibid., 414.

4. Nevin, *Mexican War*, 203.

5. John G. Waugh, *The Class of 1846* (New York: Warner Books, 1994), 91.

6. Ibid., 120.

7. Nevin, *Mexican War*, 215.

8. Ibid., 217.

9. Weems, *To Conquer a Peace*, 428.

10. Nevin, *Mexican War*, 215.

11. Walter Prescott Webb, *The Texas Rangers* (Austin: University of Texas Press, 1987), 122–24.

Chapter 22: Transitions

1. Weems, *To Conquer a Peace*, 444.

2. Falkner, *President Who Wouldn't Retire*, 306.

3. Nevins, *Ordeal*, vol. 1, 14.

4. Ibid., 20.

5. Ibid., 21.

6. A. A. Livermore, *A Discourse Preached on the Occasion of the Death of John Quincy Adams* (Keene, N.H.: J.W. Prentiss & Co., 1848), 10–16.

7. Paul I. Wellman, *The House Divides* (Garden City, N.Y.: Doubleday & Co., 1966), 306.

8. Price, *Origins of the War*, 89.

9. Nevins, *Ordeal*, vol. 1, 30.

10. Ibid., 189.

11. Ibid., 198.

12. Ibid., 200.

13. Ibid., 206.

14. Ibid., 211.

15. Ibid., 212–13.

16. Ibid., 214.

Chapter 23: Gold in California!

1. Page Smith, *The Nation Comes of Age* (New York: McGraw-Hill, 1981), 455.

2. Ibid.

3. Ray Allen Billington, *The Far Western Frontier: 1830–1860* (New York: Harper & Brothers, 1956), 222.

4. Ralph K. Andrist, "Gold!" *American Heritage*, December 1962, 9.

5. Malcolm J. Rohrbough, *Days of Gold* (Berkeley: University of California Press, 1997), 21, 28.

6. Smith, *Nation Comes of Age*, 456.

7. Ibid., 457.
8. Wellman, *House Divides*, 313.
9. Rohrbough, *Days of Gold*, 52.
10. Ibid., 173.
11. Ibid., 50.
12. Ibid., 51.
13. Ibid., 40.
14. Ibid.
15. Ibid., 192.
16. Ibid., 220–29.
17. Ibid., 165.
18. Ibid., 128.
19. Ibid., 194.
20. Ibid., 206.
21. Smith, *Nation Comes of Age*, 474.

Chapter 24: The Go-Ahead Age

1. Smith, *Nation*, 269-70.
2. *Encyclopaedia Britannica*, 1970.
3. Smith, *Nation Comes of Age*, 813.
4. Ibid., 814.
5. Ibid., 814–15.
6. Ibid., 815–16.
7. Ibid., 906.
8. Ibid., 511.
9. Nevins, *Ordeal*, vol. 1, 86.
10. Smith, *Nation Comes of Age*, 738.
11. Nevins, *Ordeal*, vol. 1, 131.
12. Ibid., 127.
13. Smith, *Nation Comes of Age*, 699.
14. Nevins, *Ordeal*, vol. 1, 35.
15. Ibid.
16. Smith, *Nation Comes of Age*, 749.
17. Nevins, *Ordeal*, vol. 1, 36.
18. Smith, *Nation Comes of Age*, 765.
19. Ibid., 278.

Chapter 25: The Wages of Fear

1. Eugene D. Genovese, *Roll, Jordan, Roll* (New York: Random House, 1974), 456.
2. Kenneth M. Stampp, in *American Negro Slavery*, ed. Allen Weinstein and Frank Otto Gatell (New York: Oxford University Press, 1968), 58.
3. Genovese, *Roll, Jordan, Roll*, 15.
4. Stampp, in Weinstein and Gatell, *American Negro Slavery*, 59.
5. Frederick Law Olmsted, *The Cotton Kingdom* (New York: Alfred A. Knopf, 1953), 440–41.
6. Ibid., 440.
7. Genovese, *Roll, Jordan, Roll*, 17.
8. Ibid., 21.
9. Ibid., 94–95.
10. Ibid., 95.
11. Ibid., 41.
12. Ibid., 55.
13. Ibid., 60.
14. Elizabeth Keckley, in *Steal Away: Slaves Tell Their Own Stories*, ed. Abraham Chapman (London: Ernest Benn Ltd., 1973), 106–14.
15. *Encyclopaedia Britannica*, 1970.
16. This quote and the preceding quote are from John Hope Franklin, in Weinstein and Gatell, *American Negro Slavery*, 162.
17. Genovese, *Roll, Jordan, Roll*, 204.
18. Ibid., 207.
19. Donald G. Mathews, *Religion in the Old South* (Chicago: University of Chicago Press, 1977), 219.
20. Genovese, *Roll, Jordan, Roll*, 190.

Chapter 26: The Peculiar Institution

1. Genovese, *Roll, Jordan, Roll*, 354.
2. Nevins, *Ordeal*, vol. 1, 422–23.
3. Ibid., 423.
4. Genovese, *Roll, Jordan, Roll*, 64–65.
5. Ibid., 307.
6. Ibid., 66.
7. Stampp, in Weinstein and Gatell, *American Negro Slavery*, 55–56.
8. Nevins, *Ordeal*, vol. 1, 451.
9. Ibid., 455–56.
10. Olmsted, *Cotton Kingdom*, 239–40.
11. Ibid., xxxviii.
12. Ibid., 240.
13. Mary Chesnut, *Mary Chesnut's Civil War*, ed. C. Vann Woodward (New Haven: Yale University Press, 1981), 29.
14. Degler, in Owens, *Perspectives and Irony*, 10.
15. Nevins, *Ordeal*, vol. 1, 416.
16. Olmsted, *Cotton Kingdom*, 19.
17. Ibid., 21–22.
18. Nevins, *Ordeal*, vol. 1, 488.
19. Ibid., 492–93.

20. Olmsted, *Cotton Kingdom*, 516.

21. C. G. Parsons, *Inside View of Slavery* (New York: Argosy-Atiquarian Ltd., 1969), 164–66.

22. Olmsted, *Cotton Kingdom*, 370.

Chapter 27: "A Great Good!"

1. Mathews, *Religion in the Old South*, 68.

2. Ibid., 69.

3. Peter Marshall and David Manuel, *From Sea to Shining Sea* (Grand Rapids: Fleming H. Revell, 1986), 378–79.

4. Charles Sellers Jr., in Weinstein and Gatell, *American Negro Slavery*, 174.

5. Miller, *Arguing About Slavery*, 116.

6. Ibid., 115.

7. Sellers, in Weinstein and Gatell, *American Negro Slavery*, 176.

8. John Hope Franklin, in Weinstein and Gatell, *American Negro Slavery*, 164.

9. Sellers, in Weinstein and Gatell, *American Negro Slavery*, 180.

10. Ibid., 176.

11. Ibid., 175.

12. Ibid.

13. Ibid., 190.

14. Franklin, in Weinstein and Gatell, *American Negro Slavery*, 164–65.

15. Ibid., 165.

16. Ibid., 165–66.

17. Ibid., 167.

Chapter 28: The Next Best Thing

1. Anne C. Loveland, *Southern Evangelicals and the Social Order: 1800–1860* (Baton Rouge: Louisiana State University Press, 1980), 188.

2. Mathews, *Religion in the Old South*, 75.

3. Loveland, *Southern Evangelicals*, 192.

4. Ibid., 191.

5. Ibid., 192.

6. Ibid.

7. Ibid., 195.

8. Ibid., 195–96.

9. Franklin, in Weinstein and Gatell, *American Negro Slavery*, 166.

10. Bertram Wyatt-Brown, *Yankee Saints and Southern Sinners* (Baton Rouge: Louisiana State University Press, 1985), 160–61.

11. Blake Touchstone, *Planters and Slave Religion in the Deep South* (Ann Arbor, Mich.: Universal Microfilms International, 1973), 39–40.

12. Ibid., 61–62.

13. Ibid., 64.

14. Ibid., 65–66.

15. Ibid., 36.

16. Wyatt-Brown, *Yankee Saints*, 162.

17. Touchstone, *Planters and Slave Religion*, 104–5.

18. Ibid., 80–81.

19. Ibid., 81.

20. Ibid., 96.

21. Ibid., 92.

22. Mathews, *Religion in the Old South*, 179.

23. Wyatt-Brown, *Yankee Saints*, 165.

24. Touchstone, *Planters and Slave Religion*, 85.

25. Kenneth S. Greenberg, *Masters and Statesmen: The Political Culture of American Slavery* (Baltimore: Johns Hopkins University Press, 1985), 94.

26. Ibid., 99.

27. William Scarborough, in Owens, *Perspectives and Irony*, 110.

28. Nevins, *Ordeal*, vol. 1, 496.

29. Ibid., 496–97.

30. Chapman, *Steal Away*, xv.

31. Sellers, in Weinstein and Gatell, *American Negro Slavery*, 178.

32. Franklin, in Weinstein and Gatell, *American Negro Slavery*, 166.

33. Kenneth Stampp, *America in 1857* (New York: Oxford University Press, 1990), 113.

34. Sellers, in Weinstein and Gatell, *American Negro Slavery*, 189.

35. Mathews, *Religion in the Old South*, 182.

36. Sellers, in Weinstein and Gatell, *American Negro Slavery*, 189.

37. Mathews, *Religion in the Old South*, 69.

38. Loveland, *Southern Evangelicals*, 189.

39. Sellers, in Weinstein and Gatell, *American Negro Slavery*, 182.

40. Ibid.

41. Ibid., 191.

42. Ibid., 183.

43. Ibid.

44. Ibid., 179.

45. Ibid., 181.

46. John B. Boles, ed., *Masters and Slaves in the House of the Lord* (Lexington: University of Kentucky Press, 1988), 101.

47. Sellers, in Weinstein and Gatell, *American Negro Slavery*, 187–88.

48. Touchstone, *Planters and Slave Religion*, 75.

49. Ibid., 53.

50. Sellers, in Weinstein and Gatell, *American Negro Slavery*, 172.

51. Ibid., 194.

Chapter 29: The Grand Old Guard

1. Don E. Fehrenbacher, *The South and Three Sectional Crises* (Baton Rouge: Louisiana State University Press, 1980), 40.

2. Ibid.

3. Ibid., 26–27.

4. Nevins, *Ordeal*, vol. 1, 252.

5. Edwin C. Rozwenc, *The Compromise of 1850* (Boston: D. C. Heath and Co., 1957), 3.

6. Wellman, *House Divides*, 323.

7. Rozwenc, *Compromise of 1850*, 2.

8. Ibid., 3.

9. Ibid., 7.

10. Ibid., 2.

11. Ibid., 7.

12. Ibid., 5–6.

13. Peter Harvey, *Reminiscences and Anecdotes of Daniel Webster* (Boston: Little, Brown & Co., 1890), 215.

14. Ibid., 218.

15. Holman Hamilton, *Prologue to Conflict: The Crisis and Compromise of 1850* (Lexington: University of Kentucky Press, 1964), 53.

16. Rozwenc, *Compromise of 1850*, 7.

17. Hamilton, *Prologue to Conflict*, 54.

18. Harvey, *Reminiscences and Anecdotes*, 218.

19. Joseph M. Rogers, *The True Henry Clay* (Philadelphia: J. B. Lippincott, 1904), 342.

20. Hamilton, *Prologue to Conflict*, 59.

21. Harvey, *Reminiscences and Anecdotes*, 219.

22. Nevins, *Ordeal*, vol. 1, 281.

23. Philip Hone, *Diary*, ed. Bayard Tuckerman (New York: Dodd, Mead and Co., 1889), 375.

Chapter 30: "Peace in Our Time"

1. Walker Lewis, *Speak for Yourself, Daniel: A Life of Webster in His Own Words* (Boston: Houghton Mifflin, 1969), xviii-xix.

2. Ibid., xix.

3. Ibid., 401–9.

4. Harvey, *Reminiscences and Anecdotes*, 221–22.

5. Smith, *Nation*, 1069.

6. Nevins, *Ordeal*, vol. 1, 289.

7. Ibid., 295.

8. Hamilton, *Prologue to Conflict*, 78.

9. Rozwenc, *Compromise of 1850*, 10.

10. Hamilton, *Prologue to Conflict*, 79.

11. Nevins, *Ordeal*, vol. 1, 290.

12. Ibid., 296–97.

13. Ibid., 300; Rozwenc, *Compromise of 1850*, 11.

14. Nevins, *Ordeal*, vol. 1, 300.

15. Ibid., 301–2.

16. Hamilton, *Prologue to Conflict*, 152.

17. Nevins, *Ordeal*, vol. 1, 331.

18. Ibid.

19. Rozwenc, *Compromise of 1850*, 74.

20. Nevins, *Ordeal*, vol. 1, 334.

21. Rozwenc, *Compromise of 1850*, 75.

22. Smith, *Nation Comes of Age*, 1082.

23. Nevins, *Ordeal*, vol. 1, 345.

24. Ibid., 343.

25. Ibid., 346.

26. Ibid., 345.

27. Fehrenbacher, *The South*, 44.

Chapter 31: Reactions

1. Gilbert Haven, *National Sermons* (Boston: Lee & Shepard, 1869), 23–24.

2. Ibid., 31.

3. Nevins, *Ordeal*, vol. 1, 353.

4. Ibid.

5. Ibid., 383.

6. Ibid., 353.

7. Ibid., 349.

8. Hamilton, *Prologue to Conflict*, 166.

9. Nevins, *Ordeal*, vol. 1, 391.

10. Ibid., 392.

11. Ibid., 356.

12. Ibid., 379.

13. Ibid., 385–86.

14. Smith, *Nation Comes of Age*, 1074.

15. Nevins, *Ordeal*, vol. 1, 380.

16. William C. Davis, *Brother against Brother: The War Begins* (Alexandria, Va.: Time-Life Books, 1983), 46.

17. Nevins, *Ordeal*, vol. 1, 387.

18. Smith, *Nation Comes of Age*, 1076.

19. Ibid.

20. Arna Bontemps, *Great Slave Narratives* (Boston: Beacon Press, 1969), 286–315.

21. Smith, *Nation Comes of Age*, 1077.

22. Ibid.

Chapter 32: Freedom Road

1. Levi Coffin, *Reminiscences* (Cincinnati: Western Tract Society, 1876), 255–56.

2. Ann Petry, *Harriet Tubman: Conductor on the Underground Railroad* (Lakeville, Conn.: Gray Castle Press, 1991), 69.

3. Wilbur H. Siebert, *The Underground Railroad* (New York: Macmillan, 1898), 187.

4. Ibid., 188.

5. Ibid., 185.

6. Nell Irvin Painter, *Sojourner Truth* (New York: W. W. Norton & Co., 1996), 30–31.

7. Ibid., 125.

8. Ibid., 160.

9. Coffin, *Reminiscences*, 13.

10. Ibid., 20.

11. Ibid., 76.

12. Ibid., 128.

13. Ibid., 109.

14. Ibid., 312–16.

15. Ibid., 147–49.

16. Ibid., 120.

17. Ibid., 520–22.

Chapter 33: The Little Lady

1. Smith, *Nation Comes of Age*, 1086.

2. Glyndon Van Deusen, *The Life of Henry Clay* (Boston: Little, Brown & Co., 1937), 424.

3. B. F. Tefft, *Webster and His Master-pieces* (Auburn, N.Y.: Miller, Orton & Mulligan, 1854), 458.

4. Smith, *Nation Comes of Age*, 1086.

5. Ibid., 1088.

6. Rugoff, *The Beechers*, 319.

7. Ibid., 320.

8. Smith, *Nation Comes of Age*, 1089.

9. Charles H. Foster, *The Rungless Ladder: Harriet Beecher Stowe and New England Puritanism* (Durham, N.C.: Duke University Press, 1954), 58.

10. Rugoff, *The Beechers*, 326.

11. Foster, *Rungless Ladder*, 27.

12. Ibid., 59.

13. Nevins, *Ordeal*, vol. 1, 408.

14. Harriet Beecher Stowe, *Uncle Tom's Cabin* (New York: Coward-McCann, 1929), 443, 446.

Chapter 34: Kansas-Nebraska

1. Wellman, *House Divides*, 338.

2. Nevins, *Ordeal*, vol. 2, 182–83.

3. Wellman, *House Divides*, 339.

4. Ibid., 340.

5. Nevins, *Ordeal*, vol. 2, 115.

6. Ibid., 116–17.

7. Ibid., 108.

8. Wellman, *House Divides*, 340.

9. Nevins, *Ordeal*, vol. 2, 122ff.

10. Ibid., 135.

11. Ibid., 123.

12. Carl Schurz, *Reminiscences of Carl Schurz*, vol. 2 (New York: The McClure Co., 1908), 31.

13. Nevins, *Ordeal*, vol. 2, 144.

14. Ibid., 113.

15. Smith, *Nation Comes of Age*, 1092.

16. Nevins, *Ordeal*, vol. 2, 156.

17. Smith, *Nation Comes of Age*, 1092–93.

18. Davis, *Brother against Brother*, 47.

19. Ibid.

20. Nevins, *Ordeal*, vol. 2, 301.

21. Bruce Catton and William Catton, *Two Roads to Sumter* (New York: McGraw-Hill, 1963), 93.

22. Nevins, *Ordeal*, vol. 2, 158.

23. Smith, *Nation Comes of Age*, 1095.

Chapter 35: Rail-Splitter

1. Nathaniel Wright Stephenson, *Lincoln* (Indianapolis: Bobbs-Merrill, 1922), 24.

2. Ibid., 67.

3. Ibid., 67–68.

4. Ibid., 68.

5. Nevins, *Ordeal*, vol. 2, 336–37.

6. Abraham Lincoln, *The Collected Works of Abraham Lincoln*, vol. 2, ed. Roy P. Basler (New Brunswick, N.J.: Rutgers University Press, 1953), 255.

7. This quote and preceding quotes are from Lincoln, *Collected Works*, vol. 2, 271–75.

8. Catton and Catton, *Two Roads to Sumter*, 106–11; Lincoln, *Collected Works*, vol. 2, 276.

9. Lincoln, *Collected Works*, vol. 2, 266.

Chapter 36: Bleeding Kansas

1. Wellman, *House Divides*, 356.

2. Nevins, *Ordeal*, vol. 2, 431.

3. Davis, *Brother against Brother*, 74.

4. Nevins, *Ordeal*, vol. 2, 433.

5. Smith, *Nation Comes of Age*, 1100; Davis, *Brother against Brother*, 74.

6. Davis, *Brother against Brother*, 75.

7. Nevins, *Ordeal*, vol. 2, 417.

8. Smith, *Nation Comes of Age*, 1101.

9. Nevins, *Ordeal*, vol. 2, 427.

10. Ibid.

11. Wellman, *House Divides*, 352.

12. Catton and Catton, *Two Roads to Sumter*, 121.

13. Smith, *Nation Comes of Age*, 1118.

14. Ibid.

15. Nevins, *Ordeal*, vol. 2, 443.

16. Ibid., 447.

17. Wellman, *House Divides*, 353.

18. Stampp, *America in 1857*, 18.

19. Nevins, *Ordeal*, vol. 2, 449.

Chapter 37: Captain Brown

1. Richard O. Boyer, *The Legend of John Brown* (New York: Alfred A. Knopf, 1973), 314.

2. Smith, *Nation Comes of Age*, 730.

3. Ibid., 1156.

4. Davis, *Brother against Brother*, 71.

5. Wellman, *House Divides*, 358.

6. Davis, *Brother against Brother*, 77.

7. Ibid.

8. Ibid., 70.

9. Allan Nevins, *The Emergence of Lincoln*, vol. 2 (New York: Charles Scribner's Sons, 1950), 9.

10. Carl Sandburg, *Abraham Lincoln: The Prairie Years and The War Years* (New York: Harcourt Brace Jovanovich, 1954), 136.

Chapter 38: 1857

1. Allan Nevins, *The Emergence of Lincoln*, vol. 1 (New York: Charles Scribner's Sons, 1950), 63.

2. Wellman, *House Divides*, 368.

3. Ibid., 369.

4. Smith, *Nation Comes of Age*, 1124.

5. Ibid.

6. Stampp, *America in 1857*, 65.

7. Smith, *Nation Comes of Age*, 1126–27.

8. Davis, *Brother against Brother*, 80.

9. Smith, *Nation Comes of Age*, 1129.

10. Stampp, *America in 1857*, 104.

11. Davis, *Brother against Brother*, 80.

12. Nevins, *Emergence*, vol. 1, 96.

13. Ibid., 253.

14. Stampp, *America in 1857*, 302.

15. Nevins, *Emergence*, vol. 1, 277.

16. Ibid., 280.

17. Stampp, *America in 1857*, viii.

Chapter 39: Revival!

1. Frank Granville Beardsley, *A History of American Revivals* (New York: American Tract Society, 1912), 219.

2. Samuel Prime, "The Prayer That Awakened New York City," in *The Power of Prayer* (London: Sampson Law, Son & Co., 1860).

Reprinted in *The Forerunner* (Spring 1983), 21.

3. J. Edwin Orr, *The Event of the Century: The 1857–1858 Awakening*, ed. Richard Owen Roberts (Wheaton: International Awakening Press, 1989), 53–54.

4. Prime, "Prayer That Awakened New York," 22.

5. Beardsley, *American Revivals*, 222.

6. William C. Conant, *Narratives of Remarkable Conversions and Revival Incidents of the Great Awakening of 1857–1858* (New York: Derby & Jackson, 1858), 383–84.

7. Conant, *Narratives*, 387.

8. Orr, *Event of the Century*, 282–83.

9. Timothy L. Smith, *Revivalism and Social Reform in Mid-Nineteenth Century America* (New York: Abingdon Press, 1957), 48–49.

10. Ibid., 49.

11. Ibid.

12. Orr, *Event of the Century*, 181–82.

13. Smith, *Revivalism*, 51.

14. Orr, *Event of the Century*, 246.

15. Conant, *Narratives*, 444.

16. Orr, *Event of the Century*, 44.

Chapter 40: "Stand Up, Stand Up for Jesus"

1. Wellman, *House Divides*, 387.

2. Ibid.

3. Orr, *Event of the Century*, 15.

4. Ibid., 17.

5. Smith, *Revivalism*, 64.

6. Perry Miller, *The Life of the Mind in America* (New York: Harcourt, Brace & World, 1965), 88.

7. Smith, *Revivalism*, 64.

8. Grover C. Loud, *Evangelized America* (New York: Dial Press, 1928), 222.

9. Beardsley, *American Revivals*, 227.

10. Orr, *Event of the Century*, 73–74.

11. Ibid., 77.

12. Smith, *Revivalism*, 60.

13. Charles Grandison Finney, *An Autobiography* (Westwood, N.J.: Fleming H. Revell, 1908), 444.

14. Orr, *Event of the Century*, 280.

15. Conant, *Narratives*, 367.

16. Orr, *Event of the Century*, 84.

17. Cliff Barrows, *Crusader Hymns and Hymn Stories* (Minneapolis: Billy Graham Evangelistic Association, 1966), 19–20.

18. Ibid., 310.

19. Ibid., 20; Orr, *Event of the Century*, 293.

20. Orr, *Event of the Century*, 292–95.

21. William G. McLoughlin Jr., *Modern Revivalism* (New York: Ronald Press, 1959), 163.

22. Miller, *Mind in America*, 88.

23. Orr, *Event of the Century*, 326–27.

24. *Encyclopaedia Britannica*, 1970. Census of 1850: 23.2 million; census of 1860: 32.4 million.

25. Orr, *Event of the Century*, 115–16.

26. Smith, *Revivalism*, 206.

27. Orr, *Event of the Century*, 155.

28. Ibid., 42.

29. Ibid., 156.

30. Ibid., 164.

31. Ibid., 171.

32. Benjamin Rice Lacey, *Revivals in the Midst of the Years* (Richmond: John Knox Press, 1943), 112–14.

33. Orr, *Event of the Century*, 151.

34. Miller, *Mind in America*, 91.

35. Smith, *Revivalism*, 159.

36. Ibid., 180.

37. Ibid.

Chapter 41: A House Divided

1. Lincoln, *Collected Works*, vol. 2, 454.

2. Ibid., 461–62.

3. Smith, *Nation Comes of Age*, 1134.

4. Nevins, *Emergence*, vol. 1, 360.

5. Smith, *Nation Comes of Age*, 1134–35.

6. Nevins, *Emergence*, vol. 1, 360.

7. Ida M. Tarbell, *The Life of Abraham Lincoln*, vol. 1 (New York: Macmillan, 1923), 309.

8. Davis, *Brother against Brother*, 105.

9. Nevins, *Emergence*, vol. 1, 240.

10. Abraham Lincoln, *The Collected Works of Abraham Lincoln*, vol. 4, ed. Roy P. Basler (New Brunswick, N.J.: Rutgers University Press, 1953), 5.

Chapter 42: A Matter of Principle

1. Smith, *Nation Comes of Age*, 1137.
2. Tarbell, *Abraham Lincoln*, vol. 1, 314.
3. Nevins, *Emergence*, vol. 1, 377.
4. David Herbert Donald, *Lincoln* (New York: Simon & Schuster, 1995), 216.
5. Ibid.
6. Lincoln, *Collected Works*, vol. 3, 3.
7. Paul L. Angle, *The Lincoln-Douglas Debates* (Chicago: Chicago Historical Society, 1958), 1.
8. Nevins, *Emergence*, vol. 1, 379.
9. Lincoln, *Collected Works*, vol. 3, 9–10.
10. Nevins, *Emergence*, vol. 1, 377.
11. Lincoln, *Collected Works*, vol. 3, 16.
12. Donald, *Lincoln*, 216–17.
13. Ibid.
14. Tarbell, *Abraham Lincoln*, vol. 1, 315.
15. Ibid.
16. This quote and the following ones are from Lincoln, *Collected Works*, vol. 3, 38–44.
17. Ibid., 51.
18. Ibid., 52.
19. Ibid., 63.

Chapter 43: "A Slip, but Not a Fall"

1. Tarbell, *Abraham Lincoln*, vol. 1, 311.
2. Nevins, *Emergence*, vol. 1, 382, 384.
3. Lincoln, *Collected Works*, vol. 2, 541–43.
4. Tarbell, *Abraham Lincoln*, vol. 1, 313.
5. Carl Sandburg, *The Prairie Years*, vol. 2 (New York: Harcourt, Brace & Co., 1926), 149.
6. Nevins, *Emergence*, vol. 1, 387.
7. Lincoln, *Collected Works*, vol. 3, 234.
8. Tarbell, *Abraham Lincoln*, vol. 1, 322.
9. Schurz, *Reminiscences*, 90–96.
10. Lincoln, *Collected Works*, vol. 3, 226.
11. Harry V. Jaffa, *Crisis of the House Divided* (Garden City, N.Y.: Doubleday & Co., 1959), 224–25.
12. Schurz, *Reminiscences*, 33.
13. Lincoln, *Collected Works*, vol. 3, 296.
14. Ibid., 315.
15. Ibid., vol. 1, 322.
16. Harry Jaffa, "In Defense of Political Philosophy," *National Review*, January 22, 1982, 40–43.
17. Jaffa, *Crisis of the House Divided*, 409.
18. Tarbell, *Abraham Lincoln*, vol. 1, 321.
19. Ibid., 323.
20. Sandburg, *Prairie Years*, vol. 2, 168–69.

Chapter 44: Sword of Vengeance

1. Smith, *Nation Comes of Age*, 1155–56.
2. Nevins, *Emergence*, vol. 2, 32–33.
3. C. Vann Woodward, in *America in Crisis*, ed. Daniel Aaron (Hamden, Conn.: Archon Books, 1971), 112.
4. Nevins, *Emergence*, vol. 2, 22.
5. Ibid., 26.
6. Davis, *Brother against Brother*, 84.
7. Nevins, *Emergence*, vol. 2, 85–86.
8. Ibid., 25.
9. Ibid.
10. Truman Nelson, *The Old Man: John Brown at Harpers Ferry* (New York: Holt, Rinehart & Winston, 1973), 2–4.
11. Nevins, *Emergence*, vol. 2, 74–75.
12. Ibid., 21.
13. Ibid., 75.
14. Davis, *Brother against Brother*, 87.
15. Nevins, *Emergence*, vol. 2, 79.
16. Wellman, *House Divides*, 419.
17. Stephen Vincent Benet, *John Brown's Body* (New York: Farrar & Rinehart, 1941), 33.
18. Nelson, *The Old Man*, 9–10.
19. Nevins, *Emergence*, vol. 2, 80.
20. Davis, *Brother against Brother*, 88.
21. Benet, *John Brown's Body*, 40.
22. Harold Holzer, "Raid on Harpers Ferry," *American History Illustrated*, March 1984, 12.

Chapter 45: The Making of a Legend

1. Wellman, *House Divides*, 427.
2. Holzer, "Raid on Harpers Ferry," 12.
3. Nevins, *Emergence*, vol. 2, 94–95.
4. Ibid., 84.
5. Ibid., 87.
6. Ibid., 84.

7. Ibid., 103.
8. Holzer, "Raid on Harpers Ferry," 16.
9. Woodward, in Aaron, *America in Crisis*, 114.
10. Nevins, *Emergence*, vol. 2, 86.
11. Holzer, "Raid on Harpers Ferry," 15.
12. Benet, *John Brown's Body*, 55.
13. Woodward, in Aaron, *America in Crisis*, 119.
14. Nevins, *Emergence*, vol. 2, 90.
15. Ibid., 89.
16. Ibid., 91.
17. Ibid.
18. Ibid.
19. Ibid.
20. Woodward, in Aaron, *America in Crisis*, 114.
21. Nevins, *Emergence*, vol. 2, 93.
22. Ibid., 96.
23. Benet, *John Brown's Body*, 56.
24. Woodward, in Aaron, *America in Crisis*, 119.
25. Louis Ruchames, *John Brown: The Making of a Revolutionary* (New York: Grosset & Dunlap, 1969), 21.
26. Ibid., 20.
27. Woodward, in Aaron, *America in Crisis*, 119–20.
28. Holzer, "Raid on Harpers Ferry," 13.
29. Woodward, in Aaron, *America in Crisis*, 122–23.
30. Wellman, *House Divides*, 427.
31. Benet, *John Brown's Body*, 57.
32. Nevins, *Emergence*, vol. 2, 97.
33. Benet, *John Brown's Body*, 50.

Chapter 46: Paranoia

1. Nevins, *Emergence*, vol. 2, 98.
2. Ibid., 99.
3. Ibid., 115.
4. Ibid., 100.
5. Ibid., 102.
6. Ibid., 105.
7. Catton and Catton, *Two Roads to Sumter*, 166.
8. Nevins, *Emergence*, vol. 2, 130.
9. Ibid.
10. Ibid., 126.

11. Ibid., 156.
12. Ibid.
13. Ibid., 108.
14. Woodward, in Aaron, *America in Crisis*, 126–27.
15. Nevins, *Emergence*, vol. 2, 110.
16. Ibid., 130.
17. Ibid., 118.
18. *Newsweek*, January 8, 1996, 72.
19. Nevins, *Emergence*, vol. 2, 118.
20. Ibid., 125.
21. Ibid., 119.
22. Ibid., 121.
23. Ibid.
24. Ibid., 122.
25. Ibid., 124.
26. Ibid., 182.
27. Ibid., 183.
28. Lincoln, *Collected Works*, vol. 3, 547–50.
29. Tarbell, *Abraham Lincoln*, vol. 1, 327.
30. Nevins, *Emergence*, vol. 2, 187.

Chapter 47: A Tale of Two Cities

1. Bruce Catton, *The Coming Fury* (Garden City, N.Y.: Doubleday & Co., 1961), 7–9.
2. Nevins, *Emergence*, vol. 2, 217.
3. Ibid., 221.
4. Ibid., 227.
5. Catton, *Coming Fury*, 49.
6. Nevins, *Emergence*, vol. 2, 238.
7. Ibid., 243.
8. Catton, *Coming Fury*, 61.
9. Sandburg, *Prairie Years*, vol. 2, 345.
10. Tarbell, *Abraham Lincoln*, vol. 1, 356.
11. Nevins, *Emergence*, vol. 2, 254.
12. Miller, *Arguing About Slavery*, 501.

Chapter 48: Storm Warnings

1. Nevins, *Emergence*, vol. 2, 271.
2. Ibid., 306.
3. Ibid.
4. Ibid., 298.
5. Tarbell, *Abraham Lincoln*, vol. 1, 377.
6. Nevins, *Emergence*, vol. 2, 294.
7. Ibid.
8. Ibid., 295.
9. Ibid., 296.

10. Catton, *Coming Fury*, 46.

11. Nevins, *Emergence*, vol. 2, 289.

12. Ibid., 296.

13. Ibid., 287.

14. Ibid.

15. Smith, *Nation Comes of Age*, 1169–70.

16. Davis, *Brother against Brother*, 114.

17. Ibid.

Epilogue

1. Philip Van Doren Stern, *Prologue to Sumter* (Bloomington: Indiana University Press, 1961), 135–38.

2. Ibid., 138.

3. Nevins, *Emergence*, vol. 2, 315.

4. Stern, *Prologue to Sumter*, 315–16.

5. Ibid.

6. Ibid.

7. Lincoln, *Collected Works*, vol. 4, 160.

8. Catton, *Coming Fury*, 114.

9. Sandburg, *Prairie Years*, vol. 2, 423–24.

BIBLIOGRAPHY

Aaron, Daniel, ed. *America in Crisis*. Hamden, Conn.: Archon Books, 1971.

Abzug, Robert H. *Passionate Liberator: Theodore Dwight Weld and the Dilemma of Reform*. New York: Oxford University Press, 1980.

Adams Family Correspondence. Vol. 2. Edited by L. H. Butterfield. Cambridge: Harvard University Press, 1963.

Adams, John Quincy. *The Diary of John Quincy Adams 1794–1845*. New York: Frederick Ungar Publishing Co., 1969.

_____. *Letters to His Constituents*. Boston: Isaac Knapp, 1837.

_____. *Memoirs of John Quincy Adams*. Vols. 8–12. Edited by Charles Francis Adams. Philadelphia: J. B. Lippincott, 1876.

_____. *Speech upon the Right of the People to Petition*. New York: Arno Press, 1969.

_____. *The Writings of John Quincy Adams*. Vols. 5–6. Edited by Chauncey Ford Worthington. New York: Macmillan, 1915, 1916.

Andrist, Ralph K. "Gold!" *American Heritage*. December 1962.

Angle, Paul M. *The Lincoln-Douglas Debates*. Chicago: Chicago Historical Society, 1958.

Barnes, Gilbert Hobbs. *The Antislavery Impulse, 1830–1844*. Gloucester: Peter Smith, 1957.

Barnes, Gilbert H., and Dwight L. Dumond, eds. *Letters of Theodore Dwight Weld, Angelina Grimké Weld, and Sarah Grimké, 1822–1844*. 2 Vols. New York: D. Appleton-Century Co., 1934.

Barrows, Cliff. *Crusader Hymns and Hymn Stories*. Minneapolis: Billy Graham Evangelistic Association, 1966.

Beardsley, Frank Granville. *A History of American Revivals*. New York: American Tract Society, 1912.

Beecher, Edward. *Narrative of Riots at Alton*. Alton, Ill.: George Holton, 1838.

Bemis, Samuel Flagg. *John Quincy Adams and the Union*. New York: Alfred A. Knopf, 1956.

Benet, Stephen Vincent. *John Brown's Body*. New York: Farrar & Rinehart, 1941.

Bidwell, John. *Echoes of the Past about California*. Edited by Milo Milton Quaife. Chicago: The Lakeside Press. R. R. Donnelley & Sons Co., 1928.

Billington, Ray Allen. *The Far Western Frontier: 1830–1860*. New York: Harper & Brothers, 1956.

Boles, John B., ed. *Masters and Slaves in the*

House of the Lord. Lexington: University of Kentucky Press, 1988.

Bontemps, Arna. *Great Slave Narratives.* Boston: Beacon Press, 1969.

Bowen, Catherine Drinker. *Miracle at Philadelphia.* Boston: Little, Brown & Co., 1966.

Boyer, Richard O. *The Legend of John Brown.* New York: Alfred A. Knopf, 1973.

Bushnell, Horace. *The Northern Iron.* Sermon preached at North Church, Hartford, Connecticut, on April 14, 1854. Hartford: Edwin Hunt and Son, 1854.

Candler, Warren A. *Great Revivals and the Great Republic.* Nashville: Publishing House of the M. E. Church, South, 1904.

Carwardine, Richard J. *Evangelicals and Politics in Antebellum America.* New Haven: Yale University Press, 1993.

Catton, Bruce. *The Coming Fury.* Garden City, N.Y.: Doubleday & Co., 1961.

Catton, Bruce, and William Catton. *Two Roads to Sumter.* New York: McGraw-Hill, 1963.

Chapman, Abraham, ed. *Steal Away: Slaves Tell Their Own Stories.* London: Ernest Benn Ltd., 1973.

Chesnut, Mary. *Mary Chesnut's Civil War.* Edited by C. Vann Woodward. New Haven: Yale University Press, 1981.

Chittenden, L. E. *Personal Reminiscences: 1840–1890.* New York: Richmond, Croscup & Co., 1893.

Clark, Bennett Champ. *John Quincy Adams: "Old Man Eloquent."* Boston: Little, Brown & Co., 1932.

Clark, Thomas D. *Frontier America.* New York: Charles Scribner's Sons, 1959.

Coffin, Levi. *Reminiscences.* Cincinnati: Western Tract Society, 1876.

Conant, William C. *Narratives of Remarkable Conversions and Revival Incidents of the Great Awakening of 1857–1858.* New York: Derby & Jackson, 1858.

Connor, Seymour V., and Odie B. Faulk. *North America Divided: The Mexican War 1846–1848.* New York: Oxford University Press, 1971.

Cousins, Norman. *In God We Trust.* New York: Harper & Brothers, 1958.

Curry, Richard O., ed. *The Abolitionists.* Hinsdale, Ill.: Dryden Press, 1973.

Davis, Burke. *Old Hickory: A Life of Andrew Jackson.* New York: Dial Press, 1977.

Davis, William C. *Brother against Brother: The War Begins.* Alexandria, Va.: Time-Life Books, 1983.

Degler, Carl. N. *The Other South.* New York: Harper & Row, 1974.

De Voto, Bernard. *The Year of Decision: 1846.* Boston: Houghton Mifflin, 1942.

Donald, David Herbert. *Lincoln.* New York: Simon & Schuster, 1995.

Dumond, Dwight L. *Antislavery: The Crusade for Freedom in America.* Ann Arbor: University of Michigan Press, 1961.

_____. *Antislavery Origins of the Civil War in the United States.* Ann Arbor: University of Michigan Press, 1959.

Eisenhower, John S. D. *So Far from God: The U.S. War with Mexico, 1846–48.* New York: Random House, 1989.

Everett, Edward. *A Eulogy on the Life and Character of John Quincy Adams.* Boston: Dutton and Wentworth, 1848.

Falkner, Leonard. *The President Who Wouldn't Retire.* New York: Coward-McCann, 1967.

Faulk, Odie B., and Joseph A. Stout. *The Mexican War: Changing Interpretations.* Chicago: Sage Books, 1973.

Faust, Drew Gilpin. *A Sacred Circle.* Baltimore: Johns Hopkins University Press, 1877.

Fehrenbach, T. R. *Lone Star: A History of Texas and the Texans.* New York: Macmillan, 1968.

Fehrenbacher, Don E. *The South and Three Sectional Crises.* Baton Rouge: Louisiana State University Press, 1980.

_____. *Prelude to Greatness: Lincoln in the 1850's.* Stanford, Calif.: Stanford University Press, 1962.

Filler, Louis. *The Crusade against Slavery: 1830–1860.* New York: Harper & Brothers, 1960.

Findlay, James F., Jr. *Dwight L. Moody: American Evangelist 1837–1899.* Chicago: University of Chicago Press, 1969.

Finkelman, Paul, ed. *His Soul Goes Marching On.* Charlottesville: University of Virginia Press, 1995.

Finney, Charles Grandison. *An Autobiography.* Westwood, N.J.: Fleming H. Revell, 1908.

Foster, Charles H. *The Rungless Ladder: Harriet Beecher Stowe and New England Puritanism.* Durham, N.C.: Duke University Press, 1954.

Freehling, William W. *The Road to Disunion.* New York: Oxford University Press, 1940.

Fuller, John Douglas Potts. *The Movement for the Acquisition of All Mexico.* Baltimore: Johns Hopkins University Press, 1936.

Genovese, Eugene D. *Roll, Jordan, Roll.* New York: Random House, 1974.

George, Isaac. *Heroes and Incidents of the Mexican War.* Greensburg, Pa.: Review Publishing Co., 1903.

Greenberg, Kenneth S. *Masters and Statesmen: The Political Culture of American Slavery.* Baltimore: Johns Hopkins University Press, 1985.

Hamilton, Holman. *Prologue to Conflict: The Crisis and Compromise of 1850.* Lexington: University of Kentucky Press, 1964.

Hamilton, Virginia. *Anthony Burns: The Defeat and Triumph of a Fugitive Slave.* New York: Alfred A. Knopf, 1988.

Harvey, Peter. *Reminiscences and Anecdotes of Daniel Webster.* Boston: Little, Brown & Co., 1890.

Haven, Gilbert. *National Sermons.* Boston: Lee & Shepard, 1869.

Holzer, Harold. "Raid on Harpers Ferry." *American History Illustrated,* March 1984.

Hone, Philip. *Diary.* Edited by Bayard Tuckerman. New York: Dodd, Mead and Co., 1889.

Hooper, Manny. *The Great Awakening of 1858.* Unpublished essay. New Haven: Yale University Divinity School, 1992.

Jaffa, Harry V. *Crisis of the House Divided.* Garden City, N.Y.: Doubleday & Co., 1959.

_____. "In Defense of Political Philosophy." *National Review,* January 22, 1982.

Jay, William. *A Review of the Course and Consequences of the Mexican War.* Boston: Benjamin Mussey & Co., 1849.

Jefferson, Thomas. *Writings of Thomas Jefferson.* Vol. 15. Edited by Andrew A. Lipscomb. Washington, D.C.: Thomas Jefferson Memorial Association, 1903.

Lacey, Benjamin Rice. *Revivals in the Midst of the Years.* Richmond: John Knox Press, 1943.

Lamon, Ward Hill. *Recollections of Abraham Lincoln.* Chicago: A. C. McClurg & Co., 1895.

Lewis, Lloyd. *Captain Sam Grant.* Boston: Little, Brown & Co., 1950.

Lewis, Walker. *Speak for Yourself, Daniel: A Life of Webster in His Own Words.* Boston: Houghton Mifflin, 1969.

Lincoln, Abraham. *The Collected Works of Abraham Lincoln.* 4 Vols. Edited by Roy P. Basler. New Brunswick, N.J.: Rutgers University Press, 1953.

Livermore, A. A. *A Discourse Preached on the Occasion of the Death of John Quincy Adams.* Keene, N.H.: J. W. Prentiss & Co., 1848.

Loud, Grover C. *Evangelized America.* New York: Dial Press, 1928.

Loveland, Anne C. *Southern Evangelicals and the Social Order: 1800–1860.* Baton Rouge: Louisiana State University Press, 1980.

Marshall, Peter, and David Manuel. *From Sea to Shining Sea.* Grand Rapids: Fleming H. Revell, 1986.

_____. *The Light and the Glory.* Grand Rapids: Fleming H. Revell, 1977.

Martinez, Orlando. *The Great Landgrab: The Mexican-American War 1846–1848.* London: Quartet Books, 1975.

Mathews, Donald G. *Agitation for Freedom: The Abolitionist Movement.* New York: John Wiley & Sons, 1972.

_____. *Religion in the Old South.* Chicago: University of Chicago Press, 1977.

McKivigan, John R. *The War against Proslavery Religion.* Ithaca, N.Y.: Cornell University Press, 1984.

McLoughlin, William G., Jr. *Modern Revivalism.* New York: Ronald Press, 1959.

Merk, Frederick. *Manifest Destiny and Mission in North America: A Reinterpretation.* New York: Alfred A. Knopf, 1963.

Miller, Perry. *The Life of the Mind in America.* New York: Harcourt, Brace & World, 1965.

Miller, William Lee. *Arguing About Slavery.* New York: Alfred A. Knopf, 1996.

Morrison, Samuel Eliot, Frederick Merk, and Frank Freidel. *Dissent in Three American Wars.* Cambridge: Harvard University Press, 1970.

Nelson, Truman. *The Old Man: John Brown at Harpers Ferry.* New York: Holt, Rinehart & Winston, 1973.

Nevin, David. *The Mexican War.* Alexandria, Va.: Time-Life Books, 1978.

Nevins, Allan. *The Emergence of Lincoln,* 2 Vols. New York: Charles Scribner's Sons, 1950.

———. *Frémont: Pathfinder of the West.* New York: Longmans, Green and Co. 1955.

_____. *Ordeal of the Union.* 2 Vols. New York: Charles Scribner's Sons, 1947.

New York Pulpit in the Revival of 1858. New York: Sheldon, Blakeman & Co., 1858.

Nichols, Charles H. *Many Thousands Gone.* Leiden, the Netherlands: E. J. Brill, 1963.

Oates, Stephen B. *The Approaching Fury.* New York: HarperCollins, 1997.

_____. *With Malice toward None.* New York: New American Library, 1977.

Olmsted, Frederick Law. *The Cotton Kingdom.* New York: Alfred A. Knopf, 1953.

Orr, J. Edwin. *The Event of the Century: The 1857–1858 Awakening.* Edited by Richard Owen Roberts. Wheaton: International Awakening Press, 1989.

Owens, Harry P., ed. *Perspectives and Irony in American Slavery.* Jackson: University Press of Mississippi, 1976.

Painter, Nell Irvin. *Sojourner Truth.* New York: W. W. Norton & Co., 1996.

Parker, Theodore. *Discourse Occasioned by the Death of John Quincy Adams.* Boston: Bela March, 1848.

Parsons, C. G. *Inside View of Slavery.* New York: Argosy-Atiquarian Ltd., 1969.

Perry, Lewis, and Michael Fellman. *Antislavery Reconsidered.* Baton Rouge: Louisiana State University Press, 1979.

Petry, Ann. *Harriet Tubman: Conductor on the Underground Railroad.* Lakeville, Conn.: Gray Castle Press, 1991.

Polk, James Knox. *Polk: The Diary of a President, 1845–1849.* Edited by Allan Nevins. New York: Longmans, Green and Co., 1952.

Powell, E. Alexander. *The Road to Glory.* New York: Charles Scribner's Sons, 1915.

Price, Glenn W. *Origins of the War with Mexico.* Austin: University of Texas Press, 1967.

Prime, Samuel. "The Prayer That Awakened New York City," in *The Power of Prayer.* London: Sampson Law, Son & Co., 1860. Reprinted in *The Forerunner,* Spring 1983.

The Pro-Slavery Argument. New York: Negro Universities Press, 1968.

Raboteau, Albert J. *Slave Religion.* New York: Oxford University Press, 1978.

Ratner, Lorman. *Powder Keg: Northern Opposition to the Antislavery Movement, 1831–1840.* New York: Basic Books, 1968.

Redpath, James. *Echoes of Harpers Ferry.* Boston: Thayer and Eldridge, 1860.

_____. *The Roving Editor: Or, Talks with Slaves in the Southern States.* New York: Negro Universities Press, 1968.

Remini, Robert V. *Andrew Jackson and the Course of American Democracy, 1833–1845.* Vol. 3. New York: Harper & Row, 1984.

Richards, Leonard L. *The Life and Times of Congressman John Quincy Adams.* New York: Oxford University Press, 1986.

Robert, Joseph Clark. *The Road from Monticello.* Durham, N.C.: Duke University Press, 1941.

Rogers, Joseph M. *The True Henry Clay*. Philadelphia: J. B. Lippincott, 1904.

Rohrbough, Malcolm J. *Days of Gold*. Berkeley: University of California Press, 1997.

Rozwenc, Edwin C. *The Compromise of 1850*. Boston: D. C. Heath and Co., 1957.

Ruchames, Louis. *The Abolitionists: A Collection of Their Writings*. New York: G. P. Putnam's Sons, 1963.

_____. *John Brown: The Making of a Revolutionary*. New York: Grosset & Dunlap, 1969.

Rugoff, Milton. *The Beechers: An American Family in the Nineteenth Century*. New York: Harper & Row, 1981.

Sandburg, Carl. *Abraham Lincoln: The Prairie Years and the War Years*. New York: Harcourt Brace Jovanovich, 1954.

_____. *The Prairie Years*. Vol. 2. New York: Harcourt, Brace & Co., 1926.

Schurz, Carl. *Reminiscences of Carl Schurz*. Vol. 2. New York: The McClure Co., 1908.

Siebert, Wilbur H. *The Underground Railroad*. New York: Macmillan, 1898.

Smith, George Winston, and Charles Judah. *Chronicles of the Gringos: The U.S. Army in the Mexican War, 1846–1848*. Albuquerque: University of New Mexico Press, 1968.

Smith, Justin. *The War with Mexico*. 2 Vols. New York: Macmillan, 1919.

Smith, Page. *The Nation Comes of Age*. New York: McGraw-Hill, 1981.

_____. *The Shaping of America*. Vol. 3. New York: McGraw-Hill, 1980.

Smith, Robert Benjamin. "Two Bloody Days at Buena Vista." *Military History*, February 1997.

Smith, Timothy L. *Revivalism and Social Reform in Mid-Nineteenth Century America*. New York: Abingdon Press, 1957.

Stampp, Kenneth M. *America in 1857: A Nation at the Brink*. New York: Oxford University Press, 1990.

_____. *The Imperiled Union: Essays on the Background of the Civil War*. New York: Oxford University Press, 1980.

Steele, John. *In Camp and Cabin*. Edited by Milo Milton Quaife. Chicago: The Lakeside Press. R. R. Donnelley & Sons Co., 1928.

Stephenson, Nathaniel Wright. *Lincoln*. Indianapolis: Bobbs-Merrill, 1922.

Stern, Philip Van Doren. *Prologue to Sumter*. Bloomington: Indiana University Press, 1961.

Stowe, Harriet Beecher. *A Key to Uncle Tom's Cabin*. Port Washington, N.Y.: Kennikat Press, 1968.

_____. *Uncle Tom's Cabin*. New York: Coward-McCann, 1929.

Sydnor, Charles S. *The Development of Southern Sectionalism*. Baton Rouge: Louisiana State University Press, 1948.

Tarbell, Ida M. *The Life of Abraham Lincoln*. 2 Vols. New York: Macmillan, 1923.

Tefft, B. F. *Webster and His Master-pieces*. Auburn, N.Y.: Miller, Orton & Mulligan, 1854.

Thomas, Benjamin P. *Theodore Weld: Crusader for Freedom*. New Brunswick, N.J.: Rutgers University Press, 1950.

Thornton, John Wingate. *The Pulpit of the American Revolution*. Boston: D. Lothrop & Co., 1876.

Touchstone, Blake. *Planters and Slave Religion in the Deep South*. Ann Arbor, Mich.: Universal Microfilms International, 1973.

Van Deusen, Glyndon. *The Life of Henry Clay*. Boston: Little, Brown & Co., 1937.

Waugh, John G. *The Class of 1846*. New York: Warner Books, 1994.

Webb, Walter Prescott. *The Texas Rangers*. Austin: University of Texas Press, 1987.

Weems, John Edward. *To Conquer a Peace: The War between the United States and Mexico*. College Station, Tex.: Texas University Press, 1974.

Weinberg, Albert K. *Manifest Destiny: A Study of Nationalist Expansionism in American History*. Baltimore: Johns Hopkins University Press, 1935.

Weinstein, Allen, and Frank Otto Gatell, eds. *American Negro Slavery*. New York: Oxford University Press, 1968.

Wellman, Paul I. *The House Divides*. Garden City, N.Y.: Doubleday & Co., 1966.

Wiltse, Charles M. *John C. Calhoun: Sectionalist, 1840–1850*. New York: Russell & Russell, 1968.

Wyatt-Brown, Bertram. *Lewis Tappan and the Evangelical War against Slavery*. Cleveland: Case Western Reserve University Press, 1969.

_____. *Yankee Saints and Southern Sinners*. Baton Rouge: Louisiana State University Press, 1985.

INDEX

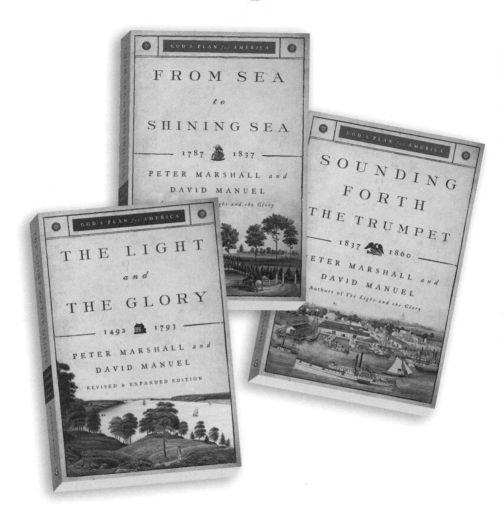

Beautiful repackages of the
God's Plan for America series

Revell

a division of Baker Publishing Group
www.RevellBooks.com